THIRD EDITION

THE CHANGING FAMILY

Mark Hutter
Rowan University

Allyn and Bacon
Boston • London • Toronto • Sydney • Tokyo • Singapore

TO LORRAINE,
DANIEL, and ELIZABETH

Series Editor: Sarah L. Kelbaugh
Editor-in-Chief, Social Sciences: Karen Hanson
Editorial Assistant: Jennifer Muroff
Marketing Manager: Karon Bowers
Editorial-Production Administrator: Rob Lawson
Editorial-Production Service: Walsh & Associates, Inc.
Composition Buyer: Linda Cox
Manufacturing Buyer: Suzanne Lareau
Cover Administrator: Suzanne Harbison

Copyright © 1998 by Allyn & Bacon
A Viacom Company
Needham Heights, MA 02194

Internet: www.abacon.com
America Online: keyword: College Online

Library of Congress Cataloging-in-Publication Data

Hutter, Mark
    The changing family / Mark Hutter. — 3rd ed.
      p.   cm.
    Includes bibliographical references and index.
    ISBN 0-02-359252-4
    1. Family—Cross-cultural studies.   2. Marriage—Cross-cultural
studies.   3. Intergenerational relations—Cross-cultural studies.
    4. Family—United States.   I. Title.
    HQ515.H87 1997
    306.85′0973—dc21   97–1292
                                              CIP

Photo Credits are on page 576, which constitutes a continuation of the copyright page.

Printed in the United States of America
10 9 8 7 6 5 4 3 2   02 01 00 99 98

CONTENTS

BOXES

THE HISTORICAL FAMILY

PREFACE

In the preface to the second edition, I wrote that this book reflects the increased concern of the American public and of social scientists to study family change from both a historical and a cross-cultural perspective. In the more than a decade and a half since the publication of the first edition, our interest in our historical and cultural roots continues unabated. In addition, in this constantly changing world, the continued impact of worldwide revolutionary events has had a dramatic effect on all our lives. This has heightened our desire to gain a better understanding of other cultures.

The interest in the global nature of the family during this period of dramatic change has been matched by an impressive upsurge of significant information about the family from social history and cross-cultural scholarship. To keep up with this trend, instructors, not only in the area of the family but also throughout the sociology curriculum, are offering comparative courses that devote more time to historical and cross-cultural materials.

In addition, family diversity has become the anchoring theme of sociological attention to the study of the family. It is no longer legitimate for sociology of the family courses to focus narrowly on the contemporary middle-class family. The approach now favored includes comparative materials from other cultures as well as from our own historical past integrated within the context of the diversity of the family experience in the United States.

The earlier editions of this textbook were in the vanguard of this comparative emphasis. They reflected, systematized, and further enhanced these developments with new insights and a wealth of new information on the dynamics of family change and the making of the contemporary family. *The Changing Family* uses a wide variety of cultural and historical examples, examines selected societies, and reveals both general trends and unique variations. The reader will find the diversity of family dynamics in our society illuminated by these comparisons.

The topical coverage maintains this comparative view. For example, the great changes in family structure due to industrialization and urbanization are revealed through issues from Western and non-Western societies. The sociological perspective is similarly developed as the book explores macroscopic and microscopic concerns equally, building a balanced picture of the changing family. The text comparatively highlights changes in personal value systems, interpersonal relationships, gender-role relationships, marriage, and the structure of the family.

This new edition is characterized by increased attention to topical coverage and recent sociological analyses of the family in the United States. The historical and theoretical materials found in Part I have been rewritten and reorganized and are now presented more concisely and clearly. Part II reflects the increased attention given to the diversity of the family in the United States. The chapter on urban family dynamics has been extensively reworked and now integrates a comparison of families in the cities of the United States and in Nigeria. The chapter on immigrant and ethnic family dynamics demonstrates the important influence of ethnicity on family life. The analysis of poverty and its impact on families is examined globally as well as in the United States context. A new analysis of homelessness has been added.

The examination of contemporary family themes in our society has been expanded. There is added emphasis on current social issues that helps the reader relate sociological theory to his or her world. This includes discussions on the feminization of poverty, teenage mothers, singlehood, the dual career family, abortion, grandparents and the four-generation family, family violence, and divorce and remarriage. An up-to-date analysis of heterosexuality, homosexuality, and the effect of AIDS on each is integrated in the chapter on gender and sexuality. The implications of critical social policies on these family concerns are discussed and given added attention.

The exploration of societal and cultural similarities, using current examples, continues to illuminate comparative family dynamics. Topics covered include the Islamic revolutionary movements and their impact on women's rights and divorce; the political changes in South Africa and their impact on family life now that the policies of apartheid have been discredited and removed; arranged marriages and the dowry system in India; and information on work, gender roles, and policy implications in Sweden and Israel has been updated. Evolving gender role relationships and family dynamics in the aftermath of the collapse of the Soviet Union is discussed in the context of the political, economic, and social turmoil in the new Russia. I remain fascinated by industrialization and urbanization and its impact on courtship and mate-selection processes in Japan. The examination of the one-child policy in China is now incorporated in the chapter on fertility and parenthood.

A distinctive feature of this text is the use of news articles. New materials have been selected to illustrate concepts and theories in everyday language. Case studies and excerpts from popular nonfiction also serve a useful pedagogical purpose and add to the relevance of the text. These materials reveal the impact of change on a personal level and add a human dimension to the analysis. They are now grouped into three major categories that reflect cultural, historical, and contemporary family emphases.

Another outstanding feature of *The Changing Family* is its richness in providing historical and comparative illustrations that go beyond those found in most family texts. These materials are interwoven throughout the text. Instructors have welcomed this emphasis in the previous editions. Those instructors who do not emphasize families in other societies will be able to elaborate on the diversity of the American family in their class lectures with the full knowledge that the comparative perspective presented in this textbook will complement and enhance their own presentation.

ACKNOWLEDGMENTS

In the years that have passed since the publication of the first edition of this book, I am increasingly aware of the lifelong intellectual debt that I owe the late Alfred McClung Lee and Murray A. Straus. My point of view also has been influenced by Peter L. Berger and by too many who have passed away including Sidney Aronson, Reuben Hill, and Gregory P. Stone. The insights and knowledge of these scholars and of other members of the departments of sociology at Brooklyn College and at the University of Minnesota are reflected throughout this book.

Colleagues and friends continue to enlighten me about sociology and how it should be taught. The faculty members, past and present, of the Sociology Department at Rowan University are most esteemed. I am blessed with a large number of significant others that stem from other academic affiliations and professional involvements. Those professional associations that command special mention include the Society for the Study of Symbolic Interaction, Alpha Kappa Delta, and the International Sociology Honors Society. Involvements in National Endowment of the Humanities seminars and institutes have sharpened my interdisciplinary perspective.

I am most grateful to the many students at Rowan University (formerly Rowan College of New Jersey and Glassboro State College); the University of California, Davis; the University of Denver; and Temple University who have fired my sociological imagination. Rowan University has provided numerous grants that have been invaluable in my research and writing.

I would like to thank my editors at Allyn & Bacon, Sarah Kelbaugh and Karen Hanson. I would also like to thank the production staff, especially Rob Lawson, who is personable as well as able. Lastly, I would like to acknowledge the reviewers of *The Changing Family, Third Edition*: Russell Craig, Ashland University; Sally Bould, University of Delaware; Allan Lee Bramson, Wayne County Community College; and Kristi Hoffman, Virginia Polytechnic Institute. I owe them a debt of thanks.

Finally, like a broken record but one that is not broken, I repeat my most special gratitude to my wife Lorraine, and our children, Daniel and Elizabeth, for sharing our family life with my work on *The Changing Family*. I sincerely hope that they continue to feel that the sacrifice has been justified. My parents and my parents-in-law have taught me to value and understand the diversity of family experiences, and by so doing, have enriched my life.

I

UNDERSTANDING
THE CHANGING FAMILY

1

A GLOBAL VIEW
ON AMERICAN FAMILIES

INTRODUCTION

Change seems to be the most permanent feature in the world today. Dramatic and revolutionary changes that affect all humanity are occurring in the contemporary world in attitudes and behaviors regarding politics, economics, and social life. Fundamental ideas and values pertaining to religion, morality, and ethics are being questioned, examined, and—in some cases—reevaluated. Massive modifications and breakdowns of societal structures and cultural values are associated with social and individual crises in which customary experience and meaning are no longer taken for granted. The conventional assumptions regarding gender-role relationships, marriage, and the family are being challenged.

Politically, we have seen the final dissolution of the colonial empires of Western European societies, some of which began over 500 years ago. In the last fifty years, new nations have arisen and begun to establish viable governmental systems; to integrate and consolidate diverse and, in some cases, antithetical cultural and social groups; and to make themselves felt as important political entities on the world scene. At the same time, countries that were born during the early part of the twentieth century (most notably the Union of Soviet Socialist Republics and Yugoslavia) that had incorporated diverse cultural and social groups have recently dissolved as a consequence of political, economic, and social failure. In addition, the advanced industrially developed nations of the Western world have been undergoing major political changes with resultant national identity crises and reexaminations in the light of world economic and political realignments.

Economically, the forces of industrialization and urbanization are making themselves felt in both the developed and the undeveloped nations of the world. The ramifications of these forces affect all humanity and transcend political, cultural, and national boundaries. Further, the dynamic interrelationship of energy sources is becoming so obvious that many express surprise at the myopia of those in the recent past who failed to recognize this fundamental fact of world life. The rapidity of the economic changes that are sweeping the contemporary world is almost beyond comprehension. Today, we are all affected by a global economy.

Social and individual changes have been as radical as those that have been occurring in the political and economic spheres. In developing societies, there is a transitory quality to all patterns of social life. The following quote from *The New York Times*—datelined Teheran, Iran, January 16, 1975—illustrates this point:

> Haji Mahmud Barzegar, a seller of songbirds, scowled at the new cars that streamed unceasingly along the avenue past his neglected shop. "The people do not buy nightingales these days," he intoned glumly. "They are too busy doing other things." (Pace, 1975)

This observation was made nearly a quarter of a century ago and prior to the revolutionary events that have occurred in Iran. It underscores my emphasis on the rapidity of the processes of change.

Cross-culturally, the family is undergoing massive changes. The opening statement of William J. Goode's seminal work, *World Revolution and Family Patterns*, states:

> For the first time in world history a common set of influences—the social forces of industrialization and urbanization—is affecting every known society. Even traditional family systems in such widely separate and diverse societies as Papua, Manus, China, and Yugoslavia are reported to be changing as a result of these forces. (Goode, 1963:1)

Goode prophetically declared that the worldwide changes spell doom for the old social orders and the traditional family systems. The social revolutions in Iran and China, Yugoslavia and the Union of Soviet Socialist Republics, Somalia and Rwanda, Haiti and Afghanistan, in recent years, reflect the continued instability and nonpermanence of much of the changes.

These revolutionary changes have not been restricted to non-Western societies; equally radical events have occurred in the family of Western industrial societies, particularly in the United States. In recent years, the nature of marriage, family, and kinship systems in American society has been the subject of intensive scrutiny and analysis. Questions have centered on the conventional assumptions about the necessity of maintaining kinship relations and the role of the nuclear family, the inherent nature of male–female gender–role relationships, the marital relationship, and the importance and desirability of parenthood. A new, more permissive sexual morality—in part precipitated by the activities of the women's movement and some segments of the youth counterculture—is reflected in the reexamination of previously held attitudes opposed to premarital and extramarital sexual relations, out-of-wedlock pregnancies, and abortions. In fact, the very necessity, desirability, and relevancy of marriage and the family have been challenged.

Concomitantly, there has been a dramatic change in behavioral practices relating to family structure. A married couple with one or more children was the norm in American society as recently as 1960; married couples comprised three-quarters of all households, and more than half of these couples had one or more dependent children. By 1990, a little more than half (55 percent) of American households consisted of married couples. Further, the number of married couples with children declined from almost 50 percent of all families in 1970 to only 37 percent in 1990 (Ahlburg and De

Vita, 1992). Concomitantly there has been a rise in the share of people either living alone or with other (unrelated) individuals. This increase primarily affects the aging of the population and the growing number of elderly who live alone. It also reflects the increased number of young adults who either live alone or share housing while attending college or starting their careers (De Vita, 1996).

The transformation of the family in the United States has been influenced by changing marriage and divorce patterns, the movement of women into the labor force, the stagnation of men's wages, and the aging of the baby-boom generation (De Vita, 1996). The American family of the 1950s and 1960s characterized by the male being the sole wage earner and the married couple having two or more children has been replaced by today's family with one or two children and with both parents working outside the home.

Marriage rates have fluctuated over the last sixty years, reflecting many factors: the number of young adults who reach marriageable age, changing attitudes toward marriage, economic cycles, and war involvements (De Vita, 1996). Marriage rates were at their highest in 1946, right after World War II, and their lowest in 1958 when an economic recession and a relatively small population of young adults reached marriageable age. Marriage rates remained low in the 1960s and began to rise in the 1970s and 1980s, as members of the large baby-boom generation entered their prime marriage years—their twenties and early thirties. The 1990s has seen a slight decline in marriage rates, reflecting in part demographic trends with the much smaller post-baby-boom generation replacing the larger baby-boom cohort. However, young adults are now delaying entrance into marriage, and the median age at first marriage is now at an all-time high (De Vita, 1996). For women, it was 24.5 years of age in 1994; for men, 26.7. Factors for the delay in marriage include economic conditions where the stagnation of men's incomes makes the prospects of marriage less affordable. For women, expanding educational and employment opportunities are contributing factors to the rising age of marriage.

While the United States still has a marriage rate higher than in any other industrialized country, Table 1-1 shows that the divorce rate is nearly twice as high as those in other industrialized countries (De Vita, 1996). There has been a doubling of both the number of divorces and the divorce rate since the 1960s. In the late 1980s, it was predicted that if trends continued that at least half of all marriages will end in divorce. Sociologists Teresa Martin and Larry Bumpass (1989) estimated that as many as two-thirds of all couples getting married today may divorce. Most recent demographic evidence indicates a leveling of the divorce rate since the late 1980s. This has led to new estimates on projections of divorce. The new estimates lower the percent of all marriages ending in divorce from 50 percent to 40 percent. Explanations for this most recent plateau attribute it to the presumed greater maturity of young people who are marrying later and to the aging of the baby-boom generation who have now passed through the stage of life when the odds of divorce are less. Most who divorce, however, remarry. Nearly half of all marriages in 1990 were remarriages for one or both partners. The high levels of divorce and remarriage may reflect a significant change in the attitude toward marriage. "Americans may be placing a high value on forming *successful* marriages and may be less tolerant of marital problems than were earlier generations" (De Vita, 1996: 32).

TABLE 1-1 Marriage and Divorce Rates for Selected Countries, 1960–1992

Country	Marriages per 1,000 population ages 15–64				
	1960	**1970**	**1980**	**1990**	**1992**
United States	14	17	16	15	14
Canada	12	14	12	10	NA
France	11	12	10	8	7
Germany*	14	12	9	9	8
Italy	12	11	9	8	8
Japan	15	14	10	8	NA
Sweden	10	8	7	7	6
United Kingdom	12	14	12	10	NA

	Divorces per 1,000 married women				
	1960	**1970**	**1980**	**1990**	**1992**
United States	9	15	23	21	21
Canada	2	6	10	11	11
France	3	3	6	8	NA
Germany*	4	5	6	8	7
Italy	NA	1	1	2	2
Japan	4	4	5	5	NA
Sweden	5	7	11	12	12
United Kingdom	2	5	12	13	12

Source: U.S. Bureau of the Census, *U.S. Statistical Abstract, 1991*, table 1439; and *1995*, table 1366. Census data adapted by Carol J. De Vita, 1996. *Population Bulletin*, 50(4), "The United States at Mid-Decade."
Note: NA is not available.
*Data for 1960 to 1990 refer to West Germany

The number of families in which both partners work in the paid labor force has increased at a steady rate. In the fifty-year span from 1940 to 1990 the proportion of single-income families fell from nearly 70 percent to about 20 percent. Dual-worker families are now the dominant family form among workers in the labor forces (Ahlburg and De Vita, 1992).

The population of the United States is aging. At the beginning of the twentieth century only 4 percent of the population (3 million people) was over the age of 65; in 1990, 31.7 million people, representing 12.7 percent of the population, was in this age group. This group is expected to increase to nearly a quarter of the population by the year 2050. The future will contain increasing numbers of people over the age of 65 and a significantly increasing rise in the number of people over the age 85. This has major implications for the elderly, for families, and for societies. The prospects, then, are of an aging population taking care of a very old population, with all the consequent emotional and financial strains. As the four-generation family becomes a commonplace reality, the problems of the elderly and the sandwich generation—adult parents with elder parents—will also become commonplace.

Occurring simultaneously with the changes in traditional family structures is the development of alternative family patterns. Current data indicate that more and more people are remaining single or postponing entry into first marriage. In addition to the increase in those choosing to live alone, there is a startling increase in the number of couples who choose to live together without marriage. According to a 1991 Census Bureau report, the number of unmarried heterosexual couples living together was slightly over half a million in 1970; ten years later, the figure was placed at more than 1.5 million people, triple the earlier figure. By 1990 that figure nearly doubled to 2,856,000 households (U.S. Bureau of the Census, 1991). Cohabiting couples include college students, young working adults, middle-age people, and the elderly. The cohabiting group with the highest percentage increase contains people between the ages of 25 and 34. In addition, the number of same-sex persons living together is growing.

Cohabitation has, for many, become an American way of life that comments not only on premarital or nonmarital relationships; it has implications for marital relationships as well. For those who eventually marry, the full implications of cohabitation as a facilitator for, or a hindrance to, marital adjustment and happiness is still unknown. However, there is some evidence that couples who live together prior to marriage are likely to have less successful marriages (Whyte, 1992).

Singlehood is accepted by many. In 1950 there were less than 5 million (4.7 million) one-person households; by 1970, twenty years later, the number more than doubled to 10.7 million households. Twenty years later (1990), the figure more than doubled again to 23 million households (U.S. Bureau of the Census, 1991).

In 1960, 75 percent of young women aged 20 to 24 were married; by 1990 two-thirds of them were not married. Older single women are faced with fewer marriage eligibles because, in large part, our culture discourages women from marrying younger men. In 1990, for every 100 unmarried women between the ages of 40 to 45, there were only 83 unmarried men of the same age (U.S. Bureau of the Census, 1991). Media discussion of the "marriage squeeze" raises questions on whether singlehood is a voluntary permanent option or a state caused principally by the relatively low number of eligible men for "career" women. However, the greater participation of women in the labor force would seem to indicate that women who are economically secure may view marriage as an option. Regardless, singlehood involves a different series of life commitments than marriage and family.

For those who do marry, many voluntarily choose not to have children. The number of married couples who will remain childless and not simply delay the birth of children is difficult to determine. However, a Roper survey (1990) has found that an overwhelming majority of American women stated that children were not a necessary ingredient for a full and happy marriage. Arthur G. Neal and his associates (1989) reports that about 29 percent of both married and unmarried women born in the 1950s will remain childless. I would suspect that if current trends continue, an even greater percentage of women born in the 1960s and afterward might remain childless. Charles Westoff, director of Princeton University's Office of Population Research makes a similar point. He believes that if current trends continue, as many as 25 to 30 percent of women might remain childless (Iaconetti, 1988).

Changes in the behavior of women have especially affected family life. Between 1970 and 1990, the number of single-parent families headed by women in the United States doubled. Much of this increase was caused by the rising divorce rate, but another major factor was the rising illegitimacy rate, despite the legalization of abortion in 1973. Also, as mentioned there has been a rapid surge in married women's labor-force participation in the last fifty years. Only 14 percent of wives were gainfully employed in 1940; by 1980, a majority of them (51 percent) were employed. The group most impacted by this development have been children. These include the increased number of children living in households where both parents are employed for the good part of the day to those in which a single-parent household is the norm.

Women have also been affected by changes in family life. The number of single-parent families headed by women has been steadily growing. Much of this increase was caused by the rising divorce rate, but another factor was the rising illegitimacy rate, especially among poor teenage females. These trends have led to the feminization of poverty; the increasing incidence of women often accompanied by their children in poverty circumstances. Nearly half (48 percent) of all single-mother families lived in poverty. African American single-mother families faced with the additional burden of racial discrimination have been particularly impacted by poverty (Taylor, Chatters, Tucker, and Lewis, 1990).

A significant number of working wives have children, especially young children. Beverly Burris (1991) reports that in 1950 only about 12 percent of women with children under the age of 6 were in the labor force. By 1991, two-thirds of such women were so involved. The estimate is that about 80 percent of married women under the age of 35 hold outside-the-home jobs. Among the women who have one or more children under the age of 6, more than half (58 percent) are employed. And of these, about two-thirds are employed full-time (Ahlburg and De Vita, 1992). Because mothers are generally the primary caretakers, women have had to juggle their career aspirations and family responsibilities. This has led to the demand for increased day care facilities and to talk of a "mommy track" career ladder depending on the ages of children and the husband's career patterns.

Intertwined with the demographic factors are economic changes that have vastly impacted on the family. The earnings of men have fallen by about 20 percent since 1970. This is a startling reversal to the post–World War II period when men's salaries were rising. Particularly hard hit have been minority men—African American and Hispanic. This decline in wage earnings is in part attributable to the decline in manufacturing jobs, the proliferation of part-time and temporary jobs, and the increased globalization of the economic marketplace. Often out of economic necessity, if for no other reason, the result has been the movement of women into the paid labor force. Still, the number and proportion of families living in poverty has grown in the last twenty years (Ahlburg and De Vita, 1992).

Remarriage continues to be a popular option for divorced people. Not surprisingly, this is particularly true for men who usually derive greater benefits out of marriage than women. When there are children involved, the resultant blended family is composed of biological as well as stepparents. The 1990 census listed 2.3 million blended family households. These included more than five times as many stepfather households than stepmother households (2.15 million versus 338,000). One hundred and fifty thousand households contained children from previous marriages of both spouses (Coleman and Ganong, 1990). As Andrew Cherlin (1981) has observed, blended family members have a particularly difficult time in adjusting to each other given the fact that developed norms are often not spelled out to govern the emerging relationships among parents, stepparents, children, stepchildren, siblings, and stepsiblings.

The emergence of gay and lesbian families as an open and increasingly recognized family form is still hotly contested. In a major feature of a special issue of *Newsweek*, Jean Seligmann (1990) cites a 1988 count of 1.6 million same-sex couples living together. Yet, for the most part, homosexuals are denied significant legal and economic benefits of marriage. They are denied health-care and pension benefits, rights of inheritance and community property, and "marriage" benefits in filing joint income tax returns. In recent years gays and lesbians have taken their cause to courts and local governments seeking recognition as a "nontraditional" family form. "Domestic partnership" legislation has been passed in a number of municipalities that would qualify gay and lesbian couples for health insurance, hospital visiting rights, mourning rights, and pension benefits. The passage of such legislation will continue to contribute to the broadening of the traditional definition of marital and family relationships. Yet, at the same time, counter legislation has been proposed that would severely limit the legal rights of gay and lesbian individuals and couples. However, the noted demographer Paul Glick (1990) believes that in the near future the Census Bureau will expand its definition of the family, which is now limited to people related by blood, marriage, and adoption, to include gay and lesbian relationships.

Reactions to changes in family behavior have crystallized over the issue of legalized abortion. In 1973, the Supreme Court of the United States allowed a woman to have a legal abortion if she so desires. Although it seems evident that the legalization of abortions has had relatively little impact on the national birthrate (one demographer states that two-thirds of all legalized abortions would have been performed illegally), the law reflects the striking changes occurring in America regarding not only this issue but also many related ones concerning sexual, marital, and familial attitudes.

Another apparent change in the family has been the increase in family violence. Reports of wife, child, and elderly abuse and incest have led many to wonder how prevalent is such violence. Sociologists concede that domestic violence is difficult to measure because so much of it goes unreported. Researchers estimate that so many millions of people are assaulted every year by family members that the home may well be the most dangerous place in which to be.

Attitudes toward homosexuality have coalesced divergent opinions not only on homosexuality but also on heterosexuality. In 1986, the Supreme Court ruled that states can ban sodomy between homosexuals, even if it is practiced by consenting adults in the privacy of a home. This has led many to speculate that the court's decision also has ramifications for the legality of various sexual practices for heterosexuals as well, regardless of marital status. The vehement pro and con reactions by the public, politi-

BOX 1-1 The Contemporary American Family

Sharp Changes Forecast for U.S. Households

Sheryl Stolberg
LOS ANGELES TIMES

WASHINGTON — The American household of 2010 will look vastly different from today's, with fewer children and a sharp rise in middle-aged people living alone, according to a forecast to be issued by the U.S. Census Bureau today.

The report, which marks the first time in a decade that government demographers have attempted to draw a picture of the household of the future, projects that in 15 years, nearly three in five American families will have no children under 18 living at home. That figure is slightly more than half now.

The shift will not occur because fewer people are having children but because there are fewer people of child-bearing age now that the baby-boom generation is beginning to turn 50 and the subsequent baby bust generation is growing up.

With the kids out of the house, many baby-boom parents who divorced will find themselves living alone. There are 6.1 million 45- to 64-year-olds living alone today. That number will rise to 10.5 million in 15 years, when the baby boomers constitute the entire age group, the Census Bureau predicts.

"This is a natural result of the aging of the entire American population and really the middle-aging of the baby boom," said Peter Francese, president of American Demographics magazine, which recently issued a similar forecast.

With respect to marriage and family status, the report predicts a gradual continuation of trends that many find troubling. There will be fewer people getting married and more single-parent households.

Currently about three quarters of families with children include two married parents. That will drop to 71.8 percent by 2010, Census officials predict. During the same period, the percentage of people who have never married will rise from 21.8 percent to 22.5 percent.

These marriage and family figures are "not incredibly dramatic," said Gregory Spencer, chief of the Census Bureau's population projections branch, which wrote the report. Nonetheless, family advocates are gloomy about the numbers.

"If you look at all the positive indicators for family life — first-time marriage, children born to married mothers — all those positive indicators are moving in a downward trend," said Glenn Stanton, a social research analyst for Focus on the Family, a conservative public policy group based in Washington.

Demographers said that the change which will have the biggest social and economic impact will be the absence of children in many households. Francese said that he foresees a boon for the travel and recreation industries as the baby boomers have more time — and money — to spend on leisure.

Philadelphia Inquirer, 3 May 1996.
Reprinted with permission by the
Philadelphia Inquirer, 1996.

cians, and media on this controversial decision highlight the increased importance and attention public debate has taken on sexual, marital, and family matters.

The controversy surrounding sexuality, marriage, and the family has entered the world of politics and public policy in a show of greater visibility than ever before. Laws regarding illegitimacy and regulations regarding welfare support for single-parent households containing mothers and children are being written, argued, rewritten, and reargued. Passions are ignited over the issue of abortion. Legislation regarding not only the circumstances of legally allowable abortion but also the more fundamental level of the legality of abortion under any circumstances is constantly being tested in the courts. The same holds true for both public and private issues on the rights for homosexual activity and on the legal rights of homosexuals themselves. Politics has also intruded on the government's responsibilities to provide public support for child-care facilities, and arguments and counterarguments continuously ensue on issues of economic discrimination and women's "proper" role in the economy against their "natural" role in the family. Similarly, increased attention is being given to parallel concerns regarding men's roles vis-à-vis commitment to occupational careers and the family.

As a result of all these changes, debates, and controversies, there has been great discussion and national debate about the future of the family. A widespread view declares that the family is a dying institution and expresses much concern about the consequent implications for the "American way of life." A counter view holds that the "family" itself is not dying, but rather that one form of the family is declining and being replaced by a new type of family that will be supportive of individuals of both sexes and of all ages. This new family will usher in emancipatory and egalitarian transformations in social relations that include, but are not limited to, marital and family relations.

The aim of this book is to aid in the understanding of the causes, conditions, and consequences of these changes for the individual, the family, and the society. It seeks to answer questions on the contemporary status of the family. I believe that it is futile to examine the family without attending to the almost continuous and radical changes occurring not only in the United States but also throughout the world. Thus, my entire analysis of the family must be grounded in change, and it particularly must be linked with the universal concomitant changes in modernization, industrialization, and urbanization.

THE WHYS OF COMPARATIVE ANALYSIS

Americans have been notorious for their lack of understanding and ignorance of other cultures. This is compounded by their gullible ethnocentric belief in the superiority of all things American and not only has made them unaware of how others live and think but also has given them a distorted picture of their own way of life. In the light of today's startling changes in personal value systems and interpersonal relationships, I would argue that by using a comparative perspective we gain both a better understanding of other people and a better understanding of ourselves.

The basic aim, then, in the comparative analysis of the family is to further the understanding of the family in our own society and in other societies. The sociologist William F. Kenkel (1977:6-8) outlines four major objectives of cross-cultural comparative analysis:

1. *Appreciation of intercultural family variability and uniformity.* An examination of other societies' family systems provides knowledge about the diversity of family institutions and helps develop our own insights into the meanings a practice has for the people involved. For example, by studying polygyny (the marriage of one male to two or more females)—a practice that has had worldwide popularity as a preferred marriage form—we see its importance to the people who practice it in their everyday life, and thus it is taken out of the realm of an ethnocentric "playboy" fantasy.

2. *Increasing objectivity.* Kenkel argues that comparative analysis develops our objectivity by placing a familiar phenomenon in an unfamiliar setting. For example, most people are able to make more objective analytical statements about the status of other people's relationships with their parents than they are about their relationships with their parents. Likewise, a greater degree of objectivity can be gained in the comparative study of family systems than in the study of the family systems of our own society. We gain much objectivity and emotional detachment through comparative analysis, and thus the task of self-examination becomes easier.

3. *Increased sensitivity toward the American family.* The diverse and idiosyncratic features of contemporary American society come into greater focus when we compare them with other societies. For example, we can gain a better understanding of the dating and courtship patterns of Americans by comparing these patterns with the different customs and practices surrounding mate selection in other societies.

4. *Formulation and hypotheses.* Comparative analysis gives us a different perspective and increases our perception and analytical ability to examine the family. Through the process of comparative analysis, the observer begins to be able to develop hypotheses concerning the family in its relationship with other institutions in society and also in the relationship that family members have with each other. For example, the study of the family life of the Hutterites or the Amish may provide us with insights into the development of hypotheses concerning the relationship between religion and the family. Kenkel concludes that whether hypotheses developed through comparative analysis "prove to be original, or commonplace, testable or untestable, is not nearly so important as the fact that scientific curiosity about the family has been stimulated and an attempt has been made to channel it" (Kenkel, 1977:8).

John Sirjamaki succinctly summarizes the major rationale for the use of the comparative method in the sociology of the family:

> Used in family studies, the comparative method makes possible a cultural and historical analysis of family organization and institutions in societies. It permits cross-cultural generalizations about families which reveal their universal character in world societies and their particular character in individual societies in the same or different regions or periods. It provides a means to interpret historical changes in families, and to relate these to other social and cultural changes in societies. These functions of comparative analysis are of enormous importance; they make the comparative method indispensable to the scientific understanding of the family. (Sirjamaki, 1964:34)

Systematic comparative analysis of the family is vital; many of the assertions about the family must be examined and investigated with data from cross-cultural societal settings. This is of crucial importance in testing generalizable assertions about family processes and structures. The main reason, then, for the comparative analysis of the family is to see which assertions are universal and which are unique, and, if the latter, what accounts for their uniqueness. This is of crucial significance if we wish to answer questions about family processes and structures and their relationships to other societal institutions.

The changes in the family that are so apparent in the United States are not limited to the United States. In their demographic analysis of changes in the American family in the last few decades, the demographers Dennis A. Ahlburg and Carol J. De Vita (1992) point out that our changing family patterns reflect broad social, economic, and demographic changes that are occurring in most industrialized societies. Our

A contemporary family having breakfast before separating for the workday.

BOX 1-2 The Global Family

Report: Families Have It Tough Everywhere

Fawn Vrazo

More marriages falling apart. More homes headed by women. More out-of-wedlock births.

While the problems may seem uniquely American, a new report says these symptoms of family breakups are occurring around the world, in countries both rich and poor.

The report released today by the Population Council in New York, which analyzes population trends and funds research on contraceptives, said the Western family model long idealized as the gold standard—mother at home, father working at an outside job, and both parents raising their own children—is now clearly a myth.

Increasingly, the report said, mothers are raising children alone and also working outside the home; fathers are absent because they have left to form new families, have migrated for work or have died; children are at a greater risk of being poor and often are left to fend for themselves without adult supervision.

That is true whether one is talking about North America, Europe, South America or southern Africa, said the researchers, who relied on a mix of data from fertility, family, demographic and health surveys done between the 1970s and early 1990s.

While the report found positive trends—delayed childbirth, smaller families and a decrease in the number of orphans—the overall picture is a threatening one for the world's children, said Population Council president Margaret Catley-Carlson.

"We're above all concerned about conditions in which the children will be raised," she said.

Most striking was the report's findings on women's overburdened lives. It indicated that mothers everywhere are doing the "second shift" described by American professor Arlie Hochschild in her landmark 1989 book of the same name—taking outside jobs but still assuming nearly full responsibility for child care and household jobs.

In such developed countries as the United States, Canada, France and Sweden, the report said, more women are entering the labor force while more men are leaving it. And in most countries, it said, women are required to meet their families' needs by both working in the home and earning outside wages.

The upshot, the report said, was that women are working "much longer hours than men in general."

That was the case whether the country was the United States, where one study showed that women worked roughly 20 percent longer than employed men, or Kenya, where a 1991 census reported that women of reproductive age worked 18 hours more per week than men.

With mothers working and fathers working or absent, children "are roaming around on their own," said Cynthia Lloyd, the Population Council's social science director. In Mexico City, said researcher Ann Leonard, it had been assumed that grandparents were minding children whose parents worked—"but in fact children were literally tied to beds; they were safer that way."

The report, described as the first research project using all available data to track family trends worldwide, also found that:

• Divorce rates are rising or are substantial everywhere, resulting in more households headed by single women. Though the United States still has the highest divorce rate—at 55 divorces for every 100 marriages—divorce doubled between 1970 and 1990 in Canada, France, Greece, the Netherlands, the United Kingdom and West Germany. Between 40 and 60 percent of women in their 40s in the Dominican Republic, Ghana and Indonesia reported that their first marriages had dissolved. So did at least 25 percent of women in most other countries.

(continued)

• A substantial number of children in both rich and poor countries are being born to unmarried women. The rates are rising in developed areas, including Northern Europe, where more than one-third of all births are to unmarried mothers; in America, where 28 percent are; and in Western Europe, where more than 16 percent are. More than 20 percent of unmarried women in Kenya and Liberia have children, and 43 percent of unmarried women in Botswana have children before they are 20.

• Birth rates are dropping. In most developed countries in North America and Europe, fertility has fallen to rates just adequate to replace the population. In Germany, Italy, Spain, and much of Eastern Europe and the former Soviet Union, it is at below the rate of replacement. But rates have also dropped markedly in less-developed countries, including Argentina, Chile, China, Indonesia and Sri Lanka, where women are having fewer than three children.

While declining birth rates might be considered a good trend, said Population Council associate and researcher Judith Bruce, it has been offset by the increased cost of raising children even as there are fewer of them to contribute financially to poor households.

Worldwide, Bruce said, "parents understand they will have to make investments in their children; children do not make an investment in them."

Leonard said parents in poor countries are especially pressed to pay for education and social services for their children because governments are cutting back social spending to repay international loans.

The Population Council report was critical of fathers worldwide. They work far fewer hours than women on child care, it said, and also spend greater proportions of their income on themselves. Among several other surveys, the report cited a study of 14 typical poor villages in South India, where men retained up to 26 percent of their income for personal spending, while women had none.

But in general the report described both fathers and mothers as victims of large social and economic trends. Men "are raised with the myth that they can't take care of children," Leonard said. "Men believe it, and women reinforce it."

Yet the mother-nurturer, father-breadwinner model no longer works in a world where most mothers—whether heading households alone or living with men—must earn outside wages in order to meet their families' financial needs, the researchers said.

The Population Council's report is titled "Families in Focus," a name researchers said was unintentionally similar to that of the conservative Christian media conglomerate Focus on the Family. Nonetheless, the report took a swipe at conservative politicians and religious leaders who have linked family breakup to a decline in religion and morals, and the movement of mothers out of the home and into the paid workforce.

"One of our main goals is to promote a family-centered research and policy process that can provide an empirical counterpoint to the deafening rhetoric on 'family values,'" it said.

"We at least need to ask the question, 'What are the minimum that children are owed and what do they deserve?'" said Bruce, the council's program director for gender, family and development.

Encouraging women to return to the home is not the answer to improving children's lives, she said, "because in very few cases is there a family wage that one person will earn that will take care of one dependent adult and children."

The work-home burden has to be shared more equitably between women and men, Bruce said. "We have to expand the concept of fatherhood so that even when men have declining economic prospects, they understand they have family responsibilities they can fulfill that are valued. So that means socializing boys so they have two roles when they grow up."

Philadelphia Inquirer, 30 May 1995.
Reprinted with permission by the
Philadelphia Inquirer, 1995.

low marriage and fertility rates and high divorce rates and nonmarital birth are also evident in many other industrialized societies. They argue that since these societies have their own social and political traditions, we can learn through our understanding of how these societies have responded to these changes how to better understand our own family dynamics.

Most recently, the Population Council, an international nonprofit group that studies reproductive health, reports that the structure of family life is undergoing profound changes internationally. Judith Bruce, an author of the study, *Families in Focus*, states:

> The idea that the family is a stable and cohesive unit in which father serves as economic provider and mother serves as emotional care giver is a myth. The reality is that trends like unwed motherhood, rising divorce rates, smaller households and the feminization of poverty are not unique to America, but are occurring worldwide. (cited in Lewin, 1995)

The implications for generating new ideas for social policy and particularly on the role governments should play in supporting families comes out of this finding that families are changing in similar ways cross-culturally.

The sociologist Brigitte Berger (1971) stated that the marked rapid economic, political, and social changes characteristic of the contemporary world have forced social scientists to understand these changes, not only for pragmatic and political reasons but also because comparative sociology contributes to the development of sociological theory even for those who are not primarily interested in the problems of social change. It is my firm belief that the wisdom of her remarks, written a quarter of a century ago, is of particular relevance to the sociology of the family today.

AIMS OF THIS BOOK

This book does not claim to present an encyclopedic account of comparative family forms. My selections and illustrations are designed to aid in the understanding of present-day family structures and processes in a world of change. Further, they are used to highlight such changes and to indicate the similarities and diversities of families and individuals in the United States and other societies.

This book is not intended to be exhaustive; it does not contain an account of every society in the world today. I have been selective in my choice of the societies I discuss, preferring to deal with a few in depth rather than to provide a comprehensive cross-cultural account. My aim in this approach is to establish some general themes, to identify the nature of family change, and to provide the means for a better understanding of future changes.

Another aim of this selective approach is to bring to life in the mind of the reader the family systems I discuss. For many, the image of a different society is so abstract and "foreign" that they cannot relate to it. I discuss different family systems so that the reader will have a fuller and deeper understanding of them and will be able to use them comparatively in the analysis of American society. Thus, by attempting to examine other family systems in comparison to our own, I hope to shed light on the worldwide changes that are affecting all family systems.

It is not my intention to overburden the reader with a seemingly endless presentation of family and kinship classification terms. Rather, I will sketch out the variations in kinship systems to highlight how family relationships have implications not only for the individual but also for the preservation and continuation of societal patterns. I must also caution the reader to keep in mind that some of this discussion may not be of immediate apparent usefulness; however, the material introduced here will be elaborated on in the following chapters. With this cautionary note, let us proceed.

THE FAMILY IN CROSS-CULTURAL PERSPECTIVE: A BRIEF SKETCH

Throughout history, the family has been the social institution that has stood at the very center of society. For most individuals, the family is the most important group to which they belong; it provides intimate and enduring interaction, acts as a mediator between themselves and the larger society from birth until death, and transmits the traditional ways of a culture to each new generation. The family fulfills human needs as few other institutions can. It is the primary socializing agent as well as a continuous force in shaping the course of our lives. It is through the family that men and women satisfy most of their sexual, emotional, and affiliational needs. Children, inevitably raised in their families, provide a tangible link with future generations. For the society, the family provides the necessary link between it and the individual; the family motivates the individual to serve the needs of the society and its members. It is through the family that the society determines the everyday interactional patterns of the individual. In many societies, it is the family that provides the bonds of mutuality that define their members' occupations, religious lives, political roles, and economic positions (Keniston, 1965).

It is true that every society may develop its own variations on these universal themes. Yet, as the French anthropologist Claude Levi-Strauss (1971) has so astutely observed, one central feature emerges in all structural variations of the family: The family links individuals into an intermeshed network of social relationships. It regulates and defines social relationships through contractual marital relationships. The incest taboo may be seen as functioning to assure patterned forms of marital exchange between families instead of within families. The division of labor between husband and wife serves to enhance their dependency on one another, just as the marriage of man to woman serves the development of reciprocal ties between family groups. The continued accumulation of reciprocal obligations linking man to woman, family to family, and kinship groups to the wider social system is seen as the very basis for the social structure of a given society.

We can get a better appreciation of this perspective by examining the cross-cultural variations of the family. By paying particular attention to how the family interrelates the individual to the societal matrix through kinship structures, the importance of the orientation becomes clear. Further, if we keep in mind that there is now occurring what Goode (1963) has called a "world revolution in family patterns," we can more readily understand why it is so vitally necessary to understand the role of the family in the world today.

Family, the first and most important term in our study, is so familiar that it does not seem to warrant clarification. However, when we take a closer look at family systems in other societies as well as the diversity of forms in our society, we come to realize that the familiar can be rather complex; there is no universal family form, but many forms and variations. However, each form and structure of the family serves important functions for a given society and its members. The student, while noting these variations, should pay close attention to the purposes these forms serve rather than simply memorizing and cataloging them.

George Murdock suggested that "The family is a social group characterized by common residence, economic cooperation, and reproduction; it includes adults of both sexes, at least two of whom maintain a socially approved sexual relationship, and one or more children, own or adopted, of the sexually cohabiting pair" (Murdock, 1949:2-3). This definition has been questioned in that there are families that contain neither cohabiting adults nor adults who work and live together.

Exceptions to Murdock's definition have led sociologists to modify the definition and to stress the predominant characteristics of the family arrangement. These definitions usually refer to the fact that the family finds its origin in marriage, which is an institutionally sanctioned union between a man and a woman that assumes some permanence and conformity to societal norms. A primary function of the family is the reproduction of legitimate offspring, their care and socialization into the traditions and norms of the society, and the acquisition of a set of socially sanctioned statuses and roles acquired through marriage and procreation.

The definition lays down guidelines that emphasize the social arrangements relating to marriage and the family and deemphasize the human biological aspects of the family. For humans, unlike animals, social determinants set limits, constraints, and meanings on biological determinants. Marriage and the family should not be confused with biological mating and resultant offspring.

> The mating phenomenon is shared with other animals, whereas marriage is strictly human. Mating, even on the human level, may be quite impersonal, random, and temporary. Marriage, on the other hand, is a social institution, and it assumes some permanence and conformity to societal norms. Marriage is society's way of controlling sex and fixing responsibility for adult sexual matings. In this connection it is worth noting that all societies, both past and present, prescribe marriage for the majority of their members. Marriage, in other words, is a universal social institution, and, although extramarital sexual contacts frequently are permitted, it is the marriage arrangement that is most strongly sanctioned for most men and women during most of their life spans. (Christensen, 1964:4)

Thus, although the family is based on biological processes, these processes are channeled by a society to conform to its traditions, rules, and attitudes.

Stephens (1963), in his influential examination of the family in cross-cultural perspective, developed definitions of marriage and the family that place proper emphasis on social and cultural characteristics as opposed to biological characteristics. Stephens defines marriage as "(a) socially legitimate sexual union, begun with (b) a public announcement, undertaken with (c) some idea of permanence, and assumed with a more or less explicit (d) marriage contract, which spells out reciprocal rights and obligations between spouses, and between the spouses and their future children" (1963:7). The definition of the family builds on the one for marriage: "The family is a social arrangement based on marriage and the marriage contract, including recognition of the rights and duties of parenthood, common residence for husband, wife and children, and reciprocal economic obligations between husband and wife" (Stephens, 1963:8).

Such definitions of the family as developed by Murdock and then elaborated by Stephens have raised a number of issues. Critics recognize that these definitions seek to incorporate cross-cultural documented evidence that there is a wide variety of marriage and family forms. But, they argue, the underlying premises of these definitions have an implicit family value orientation that emphasizes a cooperative and consensus model of the family. This is a model that focuses on the family as a cohesive unity with shared values, orientations, and interests of its family members. Critics claim that it does not place sufficient attention on the fact that family members may have different and often conflicting interests, values, and orientations. These family member differences may stem from power differentials that exist between wife and husband and child(ren) and parent(s). This relates to the amount of relative power that given family members have to achieve their individual desires over and against the wishes of other family members.

In essence, then, some sociologists point out how these definitions ignore *power* as a defining characteristic of the family. Families are in fact small groups composed of members that differ in gender, age, and size who differ in their access to economic and other resources (cf. Jones, Tepperman, and Wilson, 1995). This can often lead to inequalities among family members. The emphasis on the family as the site for a variety of activities including production, reproduction, socialization, and sex often reifies and implies a false exclusivity. Feminists sociologists (for example, Mitchell, 1984, and Thorne, 1992) feel that such definitions fail to give proper attention to the diversity of these activities and that these activities must be viewed in their various manifestations both within and outside the family.

Such definitions also imply an emphasis on the family over the individuals that compose it. They do not give the same attention to individuality and freedom and equality as they do to nurturance and sharing of responsibility (Thorne, 1992). They also tend to imply love and cooperation as opposed to conflict and competition as normal family dynamics.

A further argument, especially heard within recent years in the United States and other Western societies, is that these definitions, by talking about the "family" rather than "families," do not, in fact, give sufficient recognition to the multiple types of family forms that characterize Western contemporary societies. The definitions thus lead to a conceptualization of the family that deemphasizes its diversity. Further, by using the singular term "family," the implicit definition seems to set the "traditional" family of husband, wife, and children living in a single household with husband/father as principal if not exclusive wage earner, and wife/mother as principal if not exclusive caretaker of children and household. Such definitions leave out consensual unions, same-sex unions, dual income families, single-parent arrangements, and multigenerational arrangements as normative family entities. The result is that such variations are often labelled as abhorrent or deviant from the traditional form.

I will have much more to say about these matters throughout this book. For now, and by reason of an explanation, let's state that the title of this book, *The Changing Family*, while reflecting the conventional terminology, does so more for stylistic reasons than for ideological ones. As should be apparent, my concern is with the tremendous diversity of family forms and processes both cross-culturally and within American society and does not reflect a belief in the superiority of one form or process over another.

Forms of Marriage and the Family

Sexual interaction and children occur biologically, but they are socially defined. The family can also be analyzed from several vantage points, depending on its structural characteristics.

1. The family can be classified according to the form of marriage allowed by a given society:

Monogamy:	One man to one woman
Polygamy:	A plurality of spouses for one man or one woman
Polygyny:	One man to two or more women
Polyandry:	One woman to two or more men
Group marriage:	Two or more men to two or more women

Monogamy is the only form of marriage that is universally accepted by all societies; it is the predominant form even in those societies that accept other forms of marriage. In those societies that do permit other marriage forms, economic conditions usually prevent an individual from having more than one spouse. George Murdock, in his comprehensive surveys of marital and family forms, found that monogamy was the preferred and exclusive form of marriage for only 43 (18 percent) of the 238 societies in his 1949 sample and 135 (24 percent) of the 554 societies in his 1957 world ethnographic sample.

Murdock (1949, 1957) observed that polygyny existed in 193 (81 percent) of the societies he sampled in 1949 and 415 (75 percent) of the societies in the expanded 1957 sample. For men in polygynous-allowing societies, the privilege of having multiple spouses is restricted to a small minority, usually members of the higher social strata. William N. Stephens (1963) states that polygyny serves as a status distinction, a mark of prestige, by virtue of the economic and political advantages of having several wives; that is, when women have economic and political value, there is greater demand for polygyny than monogamy. Polygyny is also often associated with societies in which ideologies of male power and authority—patriarchy—predominate.

Another reason that most persons in polygynous societies remain monogamous relates to the biological factor relating to sex ratios. The sex ratio is the number of men per 100 women in the society, with the denominator of the fraction usually not stated. If, for example, there are 110 men to every 100 women in a give society, the sex ratio is 110. Likewise, if there are 97 men to every 100 women, the resultant sex ratio is 97. The biological fact of life is that the sex ratio for each of the world's societies is 100; that is, 100 men to every 100 women. This equal proximation of males and females places great demographic pressure on the society for monogamous marriage. When the society allows for polygyny, and a given male has two or three wives, one or two men do not have any. The result is that, while polygyny is preferred and valued in the vast majority of societies, monogamy is more widely practiced.

Polyandry, which is relatively rare (only one percent—two and four societies respectively in Murdock's two samples), tends to be prevalent where there is a limited amount of land, conditions are hard, and wives are not economic assets. Where it occurs, the society is characterized by severe economic conditions, female infanticide, and a marked lack of jealousy among the cohusbands, who frequently are related. In the polyandrous marital system, there is a patriarchal (male dominant) organization in which one male agrees to share his wife in common with other men in exchange for the men's work services. Group marriage has not been a permanent characteristic of societal family patterns. Frequently, a polyandrous-allowing community takes on this form. It occasionally occurs during periods of societal turmoil and transition or in short-time-span experimental forms, as in the case of the Oneida community in New York from the 1840s to the 1880s and the briefer but well-publicized hippie communal groups of the late 1960s and early 1970s.

The family can be classified according to one point of reference. The family that one is born into and from which the individual receives his or her initial and most basic socialization is called the *family of orientation*. The *family of procreation* refers to the family established by the individual through marriage and childbearing. The salience of these different family forms leads us to our next categorization.

2. The family can be categorized in terms of the family formed:

Nuclear Family:	Husband, wife, and children
Conjugal Family	A form of nuclear family in which the emphasis is on the marital bond
Extended Family:	Persons related by common descent
Consanguineal Family	A form of extended family in which the emphasis is on blood relatives

In the structure of kinship, priority can be given to either marital relationships or generational relationships. The nuclear family is composed of a husband and wife and their children; the extended family is composed of combined nuclear families through the parent–child relationship. This results in family units of three or more generations—at least grandparents, parents, and children.

Although the nuclear family is a recognizable unit in most societies, there is great variation in its autonomy. When it is relatively autonomous from extended family ties and the marital bond is of primary importance, it is referred to as a *conjugal* family. In contrast, when there is an emphasis on blood ties between generations or between siblings, the extended family is referred to as a *consanguineal* family. The nuclear family has less autonomy when it is part of a functioning consanguineal family system. In such circumstances, it is inappropriate to refer to the nuclear family as a conjugal family.

Thinking of the conjugal family and the consanguineal family as two systems of extremes, or polar types, contrasting patterns can be delineated. Conjugal families, consisting of only two generations, are more transitory and fragile than consanguineal families; they are more fragile and transitory in that they are susceptible to such potentially disruptive events as death, illness, divorce, and separation. For example, the death of a parent can mean fundamental reworking of the remaining parent's role relationships with children as well as dealing with economic readjustments.

In contrast, consanguineal families are in a sense immortal; they encompass all blood relations from at least three generations. The continued existence of the consanguineal family is relatively less dependent on any one person or nuclear family. For example, the death of a parent can be compensated for by the presence and involvement of other kin stepping in to fill the various facets of the parental role. Similarly, financial and economic difficulties can best be handled through the multiple resources of the consanguineal family system. Consanguineal families are better able to acquire property and material wealth and tend to transmit it intact to future generations. Conjugal families tend to split such wealth and property at each generation.

The conjugal family, with its focus on the marital relationship, emphasizes the importance of individualism with freedom of mate choice, romantic love, separate residence, and strong husband-and-wife relationships and parent–child involvements. In the consanguineal system, the family is more likely to arrange the marriage of offspring, the residence of the husband and wife will be with either of their extended families, and children will be socialized by extended kin as well as by the parents.

The conjugal family gives greater emphasis and larger autonomy to the individual and also relieves that person of most formal commitments, obligations, and duties to other family members. While this gives the individual greater independence from familial involvements, it may have deleterious effects on those extended kin who may be economically disadvantaged or physically or mentally handicapped. For example, in our society the conjugal family does not have a good "track record" in providing for the psychological, social, and economic needs of aged family members.

The other classifications of the family are based on the dominance and authority of family members, on the manner in which descent is reckoned, and on the residence of the nuclear family.

3. Authority:

Patriarchal	Authority held by the male (eldest male, usually the father)
Matriarchal	Authority held by the female (eldest female, usually the mother)
Egalitarian	Husband and wife share equally

4. Descent

Patrilineal	Names, property, obligations, and duties descend through father's line
Matrilineal	Names, property, obligations, and duties descend through mother's line
Bilineal	Names, property, obligations, and duties descend through both lines

5. Residence

Patrilocal	Newly married couple resides with husband's consanguineal family
Matrilocal	Newly married couple resides with wife's consanguineal family
Neolocal	Newly married couple sets up own household

Patriarchy, by far, is the most common authority arrangement. Older men have the right to make those decisions that affect the overall operation of the family and the community at large. Its prevalence is attributed to the males' size and strength and, perhaps most important, to the fact that men are not encumbered by pregnancy and the burdens of infant and child care.

Patriarchy does not mean only the subservience of women to men. It also means the submission and obedience of the young, both boys and girls, to the old. Where authority is based on age and kinship, children have little freedom and can take little initiative in determining their future. This includes the freedom of choosing marriage partners.

Bernard Farber (1964) points out that individuals' rights and obligations are specified through lineage membership. The reckoning of descent determines inheritance, authority, economic privilege, ceremonial and ritual rights of participation, choice of marital partners, and warfare and conflict alliances and opponents.

The most common form of descent, patrilineage, focuses on the man's lineage only. Men reckon their kinship obligations and duties through their father's relatives. They have minimal formal involvements with their mother's kinship groups. Women marry into their husband's family and their male children belong to their spouse's family.

Matrilineage is *not* the mirror image of patrilineal descent. Even though lineage is traced through the female line, authority and responsibility for the maintenance of the line is held by men (especially the mother's brother). The marital relationship has little significance. The biological father-ties to children are solely through affectional bonds. The maternal uncle serves as the predominant authority figure and is in fact the child's social father.

A second variation, pointed out by Farber (1964), that contrasts matrilineage from patrilineage is the role of the woman vis-à-vis the man. The man in a matrilineal society retains supervisory obligation over his own lineage; however, the woman in a patrilineal system does not have these same rights. She does not take part in any of the decisions of her own lineage after she marries. The rationale is to enhance her incorporation into her husband's lineage group. Thus, the woman in a patrilineal society does not have authoritative influence, nor does she have it in a matrilineal society.

Children in a patrilineage are the property of the father's lineage. They thus serve as the replacement population for that lineage. The wife's lineage has no rights to these children. In contrast, in matrilineal societies the wife's lineage in the person of her brother controls her children. Further, although the husband has the right of sexual access to his wife, he does not have the right to raise his children; he must raise his sister's children.

In societies characterized by consanguineal family relationships, on marriage, which is usually arranged by the respective extended-family systems, the couple usually resides in the residence of one of their families. The residential pattern is patrilocal when the couple resides within the husband's family home or matrilocal when the couple resides within the wife's family home. In either case, the married couple and their children are subservient to the larger extended-family system. The emphasis is on the consanguineal organization and its continuation, as opposed to the autonomy of the nuclear family.

Farber (1964) sees marital rules of residence along with lineage as instrumental in delineating kinship continuity. Marital residence is important in that children can be supervised and socialized by the given lineage group. In the patrilocal situation, the wife comes as a stranger to live with her husband and his family. As a result, she is at a distinct disadvantage in maintaining control over her children, who are thus raised in the social traditions and the norms and values of her husband's family. The children have minimal contact and involvement with their mother's lineage. The reverse holds true in the matrilocal situation.

There are also rules of residence governing where children and youths are to reside. In some societies, children are separated from their families as they mature. These societies are characterized by marked differentiation of age groups. During their earlier years, boys reside with their parents, but as they get older they are separated from their parents and are reared in villages populated solely with their age cohorts. Such age-differentiated societies are characterized by rigid rules, obligations, and duties that govern generational relationships, with the younger generations subsumed under the authority of the older ones.

In summary, according to Murdock (1949), the majority of the world's societies have been characterized by an emphasis on the consanguineal family form and have extended kinship structures organized in blood-related clans or tribes. These extended kinship organizations have served as the major structural units in most societies of the world. Through kinship lineages and authority and residence patterns, inheritance as well as economic and status patterns are determined. These controlled marital and sexual partnerships and relationships determine child-rearing patterns.

This prefatory examination outlines the major cross-cultural variations and normative patterns governing family systems. It suggests why the family is of vital importance to the society and to the individual. It should be apparent that changes in the family either precipitated by internal factors or influenced by external processes of social change will have serious ramifications for a given society and its people. Social scientists have increasingly observed that there is now a worldwide trend toward variants of the conjugal family. These families are characterized by egalitarian patterns of authority, bilineal descent, and neolocal residence.

The sources of these changes stem from the major social, economic, religious, political, and familial upheavals that began making themselves felt on a universal scale in the nineteenth century. My study begins with the examination of social change and the family systems existing in Western societies a century ago. Integral to this discussion is the analysis of sociological thought that not only sought to understand these changes but also became influential in directing that change in the nineteenth as well as in the twentieth century.

CONCLUSION

This book is divided into five main parts. In Part I, Chapters 1 to 3, I examine the main issues in the sociology of the family with particular attention to the global diversity of the family. These issues influence both the discipline and the very phenomenon they seek to study: the family. A historical account of the development of comparative family analysis is presented and related to the historical developments of Western societies. In addition, I look at the major theoretical orientations used by sociologists to study social change, modernization, and the family.

Part II focuses on the family in relation to the community. I apply the theoretical orientation presented in the first three chapters to my later discussions. Chapter 4 is concerned with the family in cities and suburbs with particular emphasis on the family in England and the United States. The concluding section of this chapter examines urban family dynamics in a non-Western context—Lagos, Nigeria. Chapter 5 focuses on the experience of immigrant families and their transition to ethnic American families. The diversity of immigration and ethnic experiences is highlighted through the analysis of Eastern and Southern European Americans, Japanese Americans, and Mexican Americans. Chapter 6 examines how poverty and resultant social policies impact on American families. The analysis is enhanced through a comparison of poverty conditions in the United States with those in Latin America.

Part III, Chapters 7 to 11, takes an in-depth look at gender roles, courtship, and marital relationships in changing societies. These chapters focus on topics of current interest. Chapter 7 compares biological, religious, and sociological viewpoints to explain male–female differences. The discussion of sexuality and the family includes a discussion of homosexuality; AIDS and its impact on human sexuality concludes my discussion. The next two chapters examine gender–role relationships in the context of dating, cohabitation, courtship, and mate–selection patterns. These are followed by two chapters that are concerned with gender–role relationships, intimacy, work, and marriage and the family. Chapters 10 and 11 can be seen as conceptually linked, with Chapter 10 providing a global view and Chapter 11 focusing on the United States. Preliterate societies, the Republic of South Africa, Russia (the former Soviet Union), Sweden, and Israel provide the global illustrations. Chapter 11 deals with the same issues but places particular stress on Western and American marriage and family patterns. It builds on previous chapters and takes a historical approach to a better understanding of contemporary American marital relationships.

Part IV is comprised of three chapters that deal with different aspects of generational relationships and the changing family. While the previous part of this book dealt largely with marital relationships, this part of the book deals with parent–child and family–elders relationships. Chapter 12 examines changing fertility patterns, issues regarding abortion, and medical innovations in fertility technology and their respective influences on family dynamics; the global views are of India and China and their population-planning programs. I then shift gears and examine what may be the most crucial stage of the family life cycle—the transition to parenthood. American social-class variations are discussed and analyzed, and changing roles of mothers and fathers also come under scrutiny. Chapters 13 and 14 are centered around the theme of generational relationships as expressed through age-differentiation and age-stratification processes. First, in Chapter 13, I study childhood and adolescence, then, in Chapter 14, I examine the elderly. The discussion of the relationship of the individual to the family and, in turn, to the community serves as an additional anchoring theme. Contrasts and comparisons between historical preliterate societies and industrial societies in the West are made. Historical changes in the West are also analyzed to help our understanding of contemporary American patterns.

Part V is concerned with families in crisis and change. The emphasis in Chapter 15 is on two of the most dramatic manifestations of family violence—wife battering and child abuse. In handling the topic of family violence, the emphasis is on how the structure of the contemporary Western conjugal family system plays a role in the manifestation of violence. Further, patriarchal ideology is seen as a contributing factor in explaining other forms of family violence including rape. The concluding Chapter 16 deals with divorce, single parenthood, teenage motherhood, and remarriage. To understand how divorce can impact differently on individuals and marital and family relations, a global view is called for. This chapter examines divorce in Japan and then shifts attention to Islamic attitude and behavior toward divorce. Contemporary changes in Iran are analyzed. This is followed by a detailed investigation of changing divorce patterns in the United States. Such issues as no-fault divorce, changing adjudication decisions on child custody, and the effects of divorce on children are discussed and analyzed. Single-parent households, the problems they face, and the solutions to these problems next gain my attention; teenage mothers are examined as a case in point. The chapter closes with a detailed study of remarriage after divorce.

This book is about families in change. I hope that the global approach taken makes a contribution to the understanding of family change worldwide while it enhances our ability to understand the complexity and diversity of family changes occurring in the United States.

2

SOCIOLOGY AND THE RISE
OF THE MODERN FAMILY

European societies during the nineteenth century underwent massive changes. The old social order anchored in kinship, the village, the community, religion, and old regimes was attacked and fell to the twin forces of industrialism and revolutionary democracy. The sweeping changes had particular effect on the family. There was a dramatic increase in such conditions as poverty, child labor, desertions, prostitution, illegitimacy, and abuse of women. These conditions were particularly evident in the newly emerging industrial cities. The vivid writings of a novelist such as Charles Dickens in *Oliver Twist* and *Hard Times* provide startling portraits of a harsh new way of life.

The Industrial Revolution dramatically changed the nature of economic and social life. The factory system developed, and with its development there was a transformation from home industries in rural areas to factories in towns and cities of Europe and America. Rural people were lured by the novelty of city life and the prospects of greater economic opportunity. The domestic economy of the preindustrial family disappeared. The rural- and village-based family system no longer served as a productive unit. The domestic economy had enabled the family to combine economic activities with the supervision and training of its children; the development of the factory system led to a major change in the division of labor in family roles.

Patriarchal authority was weakened with urbanization. Previously, in rural and village families, fathers reigned supreme; they were knowledgeable in economic skills and were able to train their children. The great diversity of city life rendered this socialization function relatively useless. The rapid change in industrial technology and the innumerable forms of work necessitated a more formal institutional setting—the school—to help raise the children. Partially in response to the changing family situation, the British passed legislation to aid children. Separated from parental supervision, working children were highly exploited. Laws came into existence to regulate the amount of time children were allowed to work and their working conditions. The law also required that children attend school. These legal changes reflected the change in the family situation in the urban setting; families were no longer available or able to watch constantly over their children.

The separation of work from the home had important implications for family members. Increasingly, the man became the sole provider for the family and the women and children developed a life comprised solely of concerns centered around the family, the home, and the school. Their contacts with the outside world diminished, and they were removed from community involvements. The family's withdrawal from the community was tinged by its hostile attitude toward the surrounding city. The city was depicted as a sprawling and planless development bereft of meaningful community and neighborhood relationships. The tremendous movement of a large population into the industrial centers provided little opportunity for the family to form deep or lasting ties with neighbors. Instead, the family viewed their neighbors with suspicion and weariness. Exaggerated beliefs developed on the prevalence of urban poverty, crime, and disorganization.

This discussion deals with the different approaches taken by social scientists in their analysis of the family in the wake of the Industrial Revolution. Throughout the nineteenth and the early twentieth centuries, they voiced concern about the excesses of industrial urban society and the calamitous changes in the family system. Social Darwinists and Marxists tried to make sense of these changes through utilization of evolutionary theories. Radicals, conservatives, and social reformers called for fundamental changes in the society and in the family and its new way of life. However, by mid-twentieth century, the dominant perspective in sociology, structural functionalism, proclaimed that the family was alive, well, and functioning in modern industrial society.

EVOLUTIONARY THEORY AND THE ORIGIN OF THE FAMILY: SETTING THE STAGE

Sociological interest in the study of social change and the family was very strong in the mid-nineteenth century in Western Europe. There are a number of important factors to help account for this involvement. First, the fabric of Western European and American society was undergoing major changes. Societies were rapidly industrializing and urbanizing. The old social class systems were being reworked and a new class structure was developing. Family relationships were also undergoing radical changes. The individual's rights, duties, and obligations to the family and, in turn, to the larger community were being questioned and challenged.

Second, Western colonial expansionism and imperialism were developed fully. Unknown and hitherto unsuspected cultural systems with strange and diverse ways of life were discovered and analyzed. Family systems were found to have differences almost beyond imagination.

Third, an intellectual revolution was occurring. The controversy surrounding evolutionary theory was sweeping Western Europe and America. Prior to the nineteenth century, Western thought generally held to a biblical belief in the origins of the family stemming from God's creation of the world, including Adam and Eve. Although there was a recognition of relatively minor familial changes over time, the biblical family form and its underlying patriarchal ideological precepts were seen as continuing intact into the nineteenth century. Western thought clung to uniformity throughout the world in terms of family structures, processes, and underlying familial beliefs and values. These governed the behavior of men, women, and children in families. It led to ramifications on the nature and place of the human species and affected the traditional institutions of the church, the state, and the family. Coinciding with the doctrine of evolutionism was the development of individualism and democracy.

Developing out of this social and intellectual ferment was the application of evolutionary thought to the analysis and understanding of the social origins of the human species. This discussion is concerned with the resultant theories of social change and their applicability to the study of family change.

EVOLUTIONARY THEORY: THE SOCIAL DARWINISTS AND THE MARXISTS

The theory of evolutionary change developed by Charles Darwin in his *Origin of the Species* in 1859 was the culmination of an intellectual revolution begun much earlier that promoted the idea of progressive development. Progressive development believed that the human species evolved from stages of savagery to civilization. As the theory of evolution became the dominant form in explaining biological principles, social scientists of the nineteenth century developed the belief that there was a link between biological and cultural evolution. The basic argument was that since biological evolution proceeded by a series of stages (from the simple to the complex), the same process would hold for cultures. Thus, the Social Darwinists shared in the basic assumption of unilinear evolution (the idea that all civilizations pass through the same stages of development in the same order). They then sought to apply the ideas of progressive development to social forms and institutions—a primary concern being the development of explanatory schemas on the evolution of marriage and family systems.

Social Darwinism was characterized by nineteenth-century evolutionary theories and was associated with, among others, the names of Herbert Spencer (*The Principles of Sociology*, 1897), J.J. Bachofen (*Das Mutterecht* [The Mother Right], 1861/1948), Henry Sumner Maine (*Ancient Law*, 1861/1960), and Lewis Henry Morgan (*Ancient Society*, 1877/1963). Social Darwinists seemingly dealt with such nonimmediate concerns as the origins and historical development of the family, yet their theories had social and political implications. Social Darwinism provided "scientific" legitimation for Western colonization and exploitation of "primitive" peoples through the erroneous belief that Western culture represented "civilization" and non-Western cultures particularly among nonliterate, low-technology societies represented a primeval state of savagery or barbarity. And through its advocacy of evolutionary progress, Social Darwinism provided laissez-faire guidelines that supported neglect of the poorer classes of American and Western European societies.

The Social Darwinists differed concerning specific lines of development. Some [cf. Bachofen (1861/1948)] argued that there was a historical stage of matriarchy in which women ruled the society, whereas most others [cf. Maine (1861/1960)] argued that a matriarchal stage of social evolution never existed. This controversy had implications for the roles of men and women in nineteenth-century family systems. The prevalent view was for a patriarchal evolutionary theory of male supremacy and dominance over females. Thus Social Darwinists gave implicit support to the Victorian notions of male supremacy and female dependency.

In summary, the evolutionary theory of the Social Darwinists ostensibly dealt with such nonimmediate concerns as the origins and historical development of the family, but underlying their theorizing were implications for the roles of men and women in contemporary nineteenth-century family systems. Indeed, their twentieth-century evolutionary theory counterparts continue to put forth these same arguments—over a century later. The initiative for this rebirth of interest in the evolutionary reconstruction of family forms has been the development of arguments and counterarguments stemming from the concern of the women's movement with origins of patriarchy and male sexual dominance.

An important rebuttal to Social Darwinism that in part developed out of evolutionary theory was made by the nineteenth-century founders of communist thought, Karl Marx (1818-1883) and Friedrich Engels (1820-1895). They made gender–role relationships a central and dominating concern of evolutionary theory. Engels ([1884]1972) in *The Origins of the Family, Private Property, and the State* used it to address his primary concern—the social condition of the poor and working classes and the exploitation of men, women, and children (Figure 2-1).

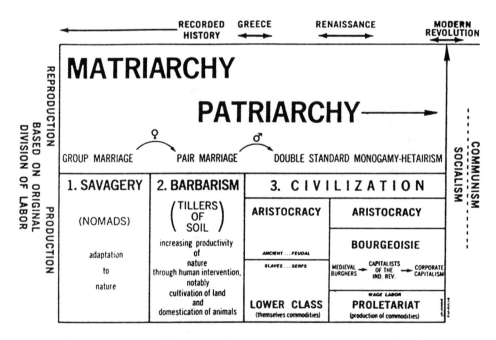

FIGURE 2-1   **Shulamith Firestone's schematic presentation of Engel's inter-development of matriarchy to patriarchy and the division of labor on a time scale.**

(*Source:* Shulamith Firestone. 1970. *The Dialectic of Sex: The Case for Feminist Action.* New York, William Morrow, p. 5. Copyright © 1970 by Shulamith Firestone. Reprinted by permission of William Morrow & Company.)

Concern for gender role egalitarianism, as opposed to patriarchy and male sexual dominance, achieved its fullest evolutionary theory expression in this work. Engels' evolutionary theory saw economic factors as the primary determinants of social change and linked particular technological forms with particular family forms. Echoing Lewis Henry Morgan, Engels depicted the stage of savagery as one with no economic inequalities and no private ownership of property. The family form was group marriage based on matriarchy. During the stage of barbarism, men gained economic control over the means of production. In civilization, the last stage, women became subjugated to the male-dominated economic system and monogamy. This stage, in Engels' view, rather than representing the apex of marital and familial forms, represented the victory of private property over common ownership and group marriage. Engels speculated that the coming of socialist revolution would usher in a new evolutionary stage marked by gender equality and by common ownership of property.

Engels' main achievement was in defining the family as an economic unit. This has become a major focus in much of the subsequent historical research on the family and is of great theoretical importance in the sociology of the family. But, insofar as Engels' Marxist view constituted a branch of evolutionary thought, it was subject to many of the same objections (see below) raised against other evolutionary theories.

By the end of the nineteenth century, the popularity of Social Darwinism was rapidly declining. Contributing to this decline were the methodological weaknesses of the approach (data obtained by nontrained, impressionistic, and biased travelers and missionaries) and growing rejection of both its explicit value assumptions on the superiority of Western family forms and its belief in unilinear evolutionary development of the family. This belief was replaced by multilinear evolutionary theory (Lenski and Lenski, 1982) that recognizes that there are many evolutionary tracks that societies can follow. It rejects the unilinear evolutionary view that all cultures advance toward a model represented by Western culture as ultimately ethnocentric and often racist.

Social Darwinism also made the fatal error of equating contemporary nonliterate cultures with the hypothetical primeval savage society. They failed to understand that *all* contemporary peoples have had a prolonged and evolved past. The failure of many of them to have a written record of the past led the Social Darwinists to assume erroneously that they had none. Further, they did not understand than many nonliterate societies deemphasize changes in the past to stress their continuity with it. This is especially true in cultures that glorify traditions and reify their sameness with their ancestors. Social Darwinists made ethnocentric and subjective pronouncements. They viewed their own society's art, religion, morals, and values according to their notions of what was good and correct, explaining such "barbaric" practices as polygamy and sexual promiscuity based on their own national and individual norms. They biased their analysis with their own moral feelings on such customs and practices.

Another factor in the decline of evolutionary theory was that it was involved with an irrelevant set of questions. For instance, what difference does it make which society represents the apex of civilization and which the nadir if it does not aid in understanding contemporary marriage and family systems? This is especially the case in a world undergoing revolutionary changes and one in which formally isolated cultures are becoming more and more involved with Western civilization as a result of colonization. Social scientists felt that attempts to theorize about the historical evolutionary process were not as important as examining the influences cultures had on each other. Societies did not evolve in isolation but continually interacted and influenced each other.

One final factor in the decline of evolutionary theory was the shift in focus of the sociology of the family. This shift was in part precipitated by the sweeping changes in American and European societies during the nineteenth century. There was a dramatic increase of awareness to such conditions as poverty, child labor, desertions, prostitution, illegitimacy, and abuse of women and children. Social scientists were appalled by the excesses of industrial urban society and the calamitous changes in the family system. The precipitating factor seen in this change in the family was the sweeping changes in American and European societies during the nineteenth century brought about by the Industrial Revolution.

NINETEENTH-CENTURY CRITICS OF THE INDUSTRIAL REVOLUTION

Social scientists began to see the decline in the importance of kinship and community involvements and the changes in the makeup of the nuclear family as more important areas of investigation than the study of the evolutionary transformations of the family. Their research and theories focused on the causal connections relating family change to the larger industrial and urban developments occurring in the last two centuries. Much attention was given to theoretical analyses of the effects these changes have had on the individual; on women, men, and children; on the family; on kinship structures; and on the larger community and the society.

An examination of radical and conservative perspectives on these changes would be most instructive. The radicals, as typified in the writings of Marx and Engels, saw the necessity for the overthrow of the new capitalist-based industrial system to establish equality between the sexes. The conservatives, Frederic Le Play (1806-1882) being the most important to family study, called for the reestablishment of the old social order. Many of the family issues raised by these ideologically opposed camps are relevant to the analysis of the contemporary family system. It is highly important to see how these theorists examined the pressures on the family created by the social changes that were transforming Western European and American societies.

If we remove the evolutionary trappings from the works of Marx and Engels we are left with an outstanding critique of mid-nineteenth-century family life. Indeed, this insightful analysis has been most influential in the understanding of later twentieth-century family dynamics. Marx and Engels examined changes in the nuclear family that were instituted with the rise of industrial and monopolistic capitalism. The new economic system separated work from the home. In the domestic economy of preindustrial Europe, work and family activities were integrated in the household. Husband, wife, and children were all involved in economic production. With the change in the economic order, small landholdings and businesses were lost, and the men became wage earners in factories. As men became dependent on their bosses, the more fortunate women and children became dependent on their husbands and fathers.

The poorest and most unfortunate women and children worked as marginal laborers in the mills, factories, and mines under exploitative conditions for wages that were barely subsistent.

The new economic system was particularly harsh on women. Those who had husbands to provide for them were domestically confined to household tasks and childcare chores. Women's lack of economic independence led to an increased division of labor between men and women and to the subservience of women to men. In the domestic economy of preindustrial society, women had a public role; in the capitalistic industrial society, women had a private role. In Engels' view "The emancipation of women and their equality with men are impossible and must remain so as long as women are excluded from socially productive work and restricted to housework, which is private" (1884/1972:152).

The privatization of the family becomes the key conceptualization in the Marxian analysis of the family. The withdrawal of the family from economic and community activities led to the development of inequality. This inequality was based on the sexual differentiation of labor and the different family roles for men and women. As we will see throughout this book, the study of privatization in the family becomes for us, too, a key conceptualization in the analysis of social change and the family.

Frederic Le Play (1855), a leading exponent of political conservatism, was profoundly influenced by the effects of the industrial and democratic revolutions on Western society. A devout Catholic, he was appalled by the loss of power and prestige of the family, church, and local community. He strongly reacted against what he saw as the atomizing effects of such forces as technology, industrialization, and the division of labor. He cared less to develop grand evolutionary theories than to react against the growing decline of the extended family and the instability of the nuclear family.

His magnum opus, *Les Ouvriers Europeens (The European Workers)* was published in 1855 and is a comprehensive comparative analysis of more than 300 working-class families who are representative of those who labor in characteristic industries and are from typical localities all over Europe and parts of Asia. *The European Workers* places great stress on the familial form and seeks to demonstrate that the major outlines of any society are set by its underlying type of family. The family types that are characterized by a high degree of stability, commitment to tradition, and security of the individual are delineated. Also dealt with are family systems undergoing disorganization. In the analysis of French families, secularism and individualism are seen as destroying the bases of tradition and community and rupturing the relations between tradition and the family.

Three dominant types of families are recognized by Le Play: (1) the patriarchal, or extended, family; (2) the unstable, or nuclear, family; and (3) the stem family, a compromise between the two. The patriarchal family is authoritarian and based on tradition and lineage. The father has extensive authority over all his unmarried sons and daughters and is the sole owner of the family property.

The unstable family is seen to prevail among working populations who live under the factory system of the West. This family type is seen to be inherently disorganized and is the prime cause of social disorganization. It is strongly individualistic, mobile, and secular. "Where individualism becomes dominant in social relations men rapidly move towards barbarism" (Le Play cited in Zimmerman and Frampton, 1966:14). The unstable family shows little attachment to family lineage. It has no roots in property and is an unstable structure from generation to generation. It is associated with the pauperization or poverty of working-class populations under the new manufacturing regime in the West.

The stem family is seen as the happy compromise between the two other types. It is free of the authoritarianism of the patriarchal family, but it is still rooted in traditionalism. It is stable in structure and committed to perpetuating the family lineage. The stem family is seen to arise partly from traditional influences of patriarchal life, but it finally forms itself under the influence of individually owned property. Le Play sees it as combining the best features of the patriarchal system with the individualism of the unstable family form.

Each family type, then, is seen to be related to other types of institutions in the community. Le Play's central concern is the ties uniting the family with other parts of the community—religion, government, education, and economy. His analysis of the family is intertwined with the analysis of the community in which the family finds itself. It is this insightful perspective that has made Le Play's work stand out in the history of family analysis. His conservative orientation should not obscure the importance of his empirical findings on the economic basis of family and community life.

The family issues raised by Marx, Engels, and Le Play still are the central core of contemporary analysis of social change and the family. Both the radical perspective and the conservative perspective are highly critical of the emerging family form of the nineteenth century. Marx and Engels refer to it as the monogamous family characterized by the privatization of family life; Le Play refers to it as the unstable family.

Robert A. Nisbet (1966) has provided us with a highly useful comparison of Le Play and Marx. Both were aghast at the bourgeoisie democracy of the nineteenth century. Rather than providing for liberty and prosperity, it was seen as leading to disabling competition and strife. Both sought social orders that would remove the excesses of bourgeoisie democracy and the evils of industrialism. Yet the differences stemming from their opposing ideologies lead to different assessments and conclusions.

> Both Le Play and Marx were sensitive to the institutional component in history. . . . For Marx the key institution is social class. For Le Play it is kinship: the structure of society varies with the type of family that underlies it. Marx detested private property, Le Play declared it the indispensable basis of social order and freedom. Marx treated religion as something superfluous to an understanding of human behavior and, in its effects, an opiate. For Le Play religion is as essential to man's mental and moral life as the family is to his social organization. For Marx, the whole rural scheme of things is tantamount to idiocy as far as its impact on human thought is concerned. Le Play, for all his conscious acceptance of industry, plainly prefers rural society, seeing in it the haven of security that urban life, by its very nature, must destroy. Marx was socialist; Le Play put socialism, along with mass democracy, secularism, and egalitarianism, among the major evils of his time—all of them unmistakable signs of social degeneration. (Nisbet, 1966:67)

It is the tension between the radical perspective and the conservative perspective that echoes throughout the contemporary analysis of the family in change and takes different forms depending on different substantive issues. But, taken together, these perspectives can be seen as critical perspectives questioning the nature and makeup of contemporary family systems and their relationships with the individuals that compose them and the communities that surround them.

THE IDEAL TYPE: COMMUNITY AND THE FAMILY

European sociology, which rejected the theoretical assumptions of Social Darwinism by the turn of the twentieth century, developed the ideal type as an alternative procedure to account for and explain historical changes in Western societies—from agriculture-based economies to industrialization-based ones.

The ideal type is a conceptual construct used in the analysis of social phenomena. The techniques for its use were developed by the German sociologist Max Weber (1949). The ideal type is constructed from observation of the characteristics of the social phenomena under investigation, but it is not intended to correspond exactly to any single case; rather, it designates the hypothetical characteristics of a "pure" or "ideal" case. The ideal type, then, does not imply evaluation or approval of the phenomena being studied. The ideal type characterizes a social phenomenon by emphasizing its essential characteristics. It is an analytically constructed model.

The ideal type does not conform to reality, being an abstraction that hypothesizes certain qualities or characteristics of the social phenomena under study. For example, an ideal type is constructed on the characteristics of cities. No cities would actually conform in an absolute sense to this ideal type, but the construct is useful in that it provides a focus point, a frame of reference, for the study of a given city. Or take the illustration of "the American family." No particular American family can match all the characteristics of a hypothetical construct of the American family, but such a construction can be useful in examining given families in comparison with this construct and in comparison with each other.

Social scientists have found ideal types highly useful as analytical tools. These types make possible a conceptualization of social phenomena and facilitate cross-cultural and historical comparison among them. They aid in locating factors of social change in societies and enable the comparative investigation of institutions, such as the family, over time and space. Yet they have severe limitations. In this chapter, some ideal types of communities will be examined in terms of relevancy in the study of urbanization processes and the family.

The dominant sociological view was that the perceived chaotic world of the city was countered by the family turning to itself. What Marx described as the privatization of the family reflects this development. A strong emotional transformation characterizes the nineteenth century. The emotional bonds that individuals held for the community, the village, and the extended family were transformed into the development of an exclusive emotional attachment to family members. With the work world seen as hostile and precarious, the family took on an image as a place of refuge. The home was seen as a place that provided security and safety from a cruel, harsh, and unpredictable industrial urban society.

This antiurban state of mind was echoed in the works of nineteenth century social scientists. The revulsion toward the city and the bemoaning of the loss of an idealized past naturally led sociologists to develop contrasting models of city life versus rural life. The city became identified with social disorganization, alienation, and the loss of community and meaningful relationships. In comparison, the small village and rural community were romanticized for their orderliness, noncompetitiveness, and meaningfulness of personal relationships.

As Robert A. Nisbet (1966) points out, both radicals and conservatives viewed the past with nostalgia and the urban present with distaste. Although the radicals eventually embraced the city, seeing in it the hope for the revolutionary future, they too were aghast at the social conditions existing in the emerging industrial cities of the nineteenth century. Friedrich Engels, a romantic radical, was appalled by the urban prospect:

> We know well enough that [the] isolation of the individual . . . is everywhere the fundamental principle of modern society. But nowhere is this selfish egotism as blatantly evident as in the frantic bustle of the great city. (Engels cited in Nisbet, 1966:29)

One is struck with the similarity of Engels' view with that of the conservative Alexis de Tocqueville (1805-1859), who wrote the following after a visit to Manchester, England:

> From this foul drain the greatest stream of human industry flows out to fertilize the whole world. From this filthy sewer pure gold flows. Here humanity attains the most complete development and its most brutish, here civilization works its miracles and civilized man is turned almost into a savage. (Cited in Nisbet, 1966:29)

Keeping in mind this antiurban bias, let us now look at some of the famous and influential typologies that were developed during this period.

Henry Sumner Maine's (1862/1960) distinction of "status to contract" society was one of the earliest of such typologies. Maine postulated that *status* societies are characterized by group relations that are anchored in tradition. Tradition, in turn, determines the rights and obligations of individuals. The individual's status was fixed by his or her family and kinship system, which served as the foundation of social organization. The movement to *contract* relations was fostered by urbanization, with kinship bonds becoming less strong. With the ascendancy of the state, civil law replaced traditional customs in enforcing and regulating social obedience and social control. Maine argued that with the increased power of the state, the influence of the family over the individual would decline and women's social status, which was extremely low in status in communities, would rise and familism would decline. The essence of Maine's argument was that the powers, privileges, and duties that were once vested in the family had shifted to the national state. Concomitantly, people's social relationships, which were based on their *status*, shifted to individually agreed *contracts*.

Maine's work had a great influence on his nineteenth-century contemporaries. Ferdinand Tönnies (1855-1936), whose *Gemeinschaft und Gesellschaft* (*Community and Society*, 1887/1963) has been an inspirational source for students of community analysis to the present day. *Gemeinschaft* and *Gesellschaft* are ideal types and refer to the nature of social relationships, basic social groups, and institutions.

Gemeinschaft (community) relationships are intimate, traditional, enduring, and based on informal relations determined by *who* the individual is in the community as opposed to *what* he or she has done—in sociological parlance, ascriptive status rather than achieved status. The culture of the community is homogeneous and the moral custodians are the family and the church. For Tönnies, there are three central aspects of *Gemeinschaft*: kinship, neighborhood, and friendship. These institutions serve as the foundation for social life and activities.

Gesellschaft (society association) refers to the large-scale, contractual, impersonal relationships that Tönnies saw emerging in industrializing and urbanizing Europe in the late nineteenth century. *Gesellschaft* includes business-oriented relations based on rational calculations geared to instrumental ends. Personal relationships are subordinate. In the *Gesellschaft*, family groups and institutions no longer serve as the basis of social life; rather, such societies are organized around work relationships and bureaucratic institutions.

Tönnies was antagonistic to the growth of individualism. He believed that acute individualism led to egotistic, self-willed individuals who sought friends only as means and ends to self-interested gains. He decried the involvement of women in the labor force and feared the loss of their involvement in the family. Likewise, he saw the destructive effects of child labor on the family. Basically a conservative, Tönnies cites Karl Marx in documenting the ill effects of child labor. Taken together, these changes are seen as destroying the fabric of traditional society and the solidarity of its people. Old values and attitudes are no longer internalized by the young, and the intertwining rights and obligations that bound the traditional community together are weakened and gradually dissolve. The family itself becomes subordinated to personal interests. "The family becomes an accidental form for the satisfaction of natural needs, neighborhood and friendship are supplanted by special interest groups and conventional society life" (Tönnies, 1887/1963:168).

In summary, Tönnies' depiction of the *Gesellschaft* is strikingly similar to that of Karl Marx. But unlike Marx, who sought future revolutionary changes, Tönnies yearned for the return of the romantic past described in his ideal typification of the *Gemeinschaft*. In Table 2-1, a schematic representation of Tönnies' societal types are delineated.

Emile Durkheim (1855-1917) also distinguished the nature of social relationships with these two contrasting types of social orders. Durkheim's doctoral dissertation, *The Division of Labor in Society*, was published in 1893. He compared societies based on *mechanical solidarity* with societies based on *organic solidarity* in regard to social integration. Mechanical solidarity describes the form of social cohesion that exists in small-scale societies that have a minimal division of labor. The type of relationships that link members of such small, stable communities are characterized as being overlapping

TABLE 2-1   Summary of the Contrasts between *Gemeinschaft* and *Gesellschaft*

Social Characteristic	Societal Types	
	Gemeinschaft	**Gesellschaft**
Dominant social relationships	Fellowship Kinship Neighborliness	Exchange Rational calculations
Central institutions	Family law Extended kin group	State Capitalistic economy
The individual in the social order	Self	Person
Characteristic form of wealth	Land	Money
Type of law	Family law	Law of contract
Ordering of institutions	Family life Rural village life Town life	City life Rational life Cosmopolitan life
Type of social control	Concord Folkways and mores Religion	Convention Legislation Public Opinion

Source: Don Martindale. 1960. *The Nature and Types of Sociological Theory*, 2nd ed. Cambridge, MA: Houghton Mifflin, p. 84. Copyright © 1960 by Don Martindale. Copyright © 1981 by Harper & Row, Publishers, Inc. Reprinted by permission.

and interrelated; they are cohesive because of shared bonds and habits. Social unity, Durkheim said, is mechanical and automatic in that the parts of the society are interchangeable. Close friendship and kinship groups are typical of mechanical solidarity in that they are secured by personal, stable, and emotional attachments.

In contrast, societies based on organic solidarity, which Durkheim believed was emerging in Europe, were founded on increased specialization and the division of labor. Organic solidarity-type relationships are impersonal, transient, fragmented, and rational. The source of societal unity is the interdependence of specialized and highly individualized members and the complementary diversity of their positions and life experiences. In relationships marked by organic solidarity one does not relate as a whole individual, but one relates to those qualities that are relevant to the particular function one is performing in relation to others. Durkheim associated the shift in these two types of solidarities, from mechanical to organic, as resulting from the increased size and density of population, the ease and rapidity of communication, and especially with the increased division of labor. All of these factors are seen to be linked with the rise of industrialization and the growth of cities.

Durkheim mirrors the conservatism of Maine and Tönnies. In *The Division of Labor in Society* as well as in his other works—notably *Suicide* (1897/1951)—Durkheim argues that the cohesive and stabilizing forces of European society are disintegrating. The destructive forces of industrialization, secularization, and revolution account for the alienation, anomie, and isolation of modern urban life. Indeed, in his *The Elemen-*

tary Forms of Religious Life (1915/1912), Durkheim viewed collective consciousness as arising out of the individual's participation in the communal life. The origins of man's conceptualization of the universe and the categories of knowledge, he said, stem from this communal perspective. It is no wonder, then, that Durkheim reflects the concern of his contemporaries, both sociologists and lay people, about the problems inherent in the modern industrial urban society.

In conclusion, the ideal type was developed to contrast the emerging industrial city with the preindustrial rural and village community. This typological approach was tinged with an antiurban bias that distorted both the analyses of these sociologists and the many subsequent analyses of the city. Further, since typologies were too broadly based and too vague, rather than aid in the analysis of urban family-life patterns, they led to obfuscation and distortion. Finally, the typologies failed to deal with the wide range of variations within cities as well as with cross-cultural and historical variations. In the next chapter, my discussion will continue on this theme on the relationship of the family to the city. But now I will pick up on my account of the impact of industrialization on the family by examining American sociology in the late nineteenth and early twentieth centuries.

AMERICAN FAMILY SOCIOLOGY: LATE NINETEENTH AND EARLY TWENTIETH CENTURIES

Toward the end of the nineteenth and through the early twentieth centuries, sociology in the United States shifted its emphasis away from the study of social evolution to the study of social problems and the advocacy of social reform. The paramount concern was the study of the family in the context of the abuses of rapid industrialization and urbanization. The emphasis switched from the development of theories of family systems to the more urgent concerns of individual families and their members—illegitimacy, prostitution, child abuse, and other resultant abuses, were seen as arising from nongovernmental supervision of industrial and urban institutions. This underlying assumption about the causes of social problems was held by the social reform movement's major advocate, the Chicago School of Sociology, and is reflected in the following quotation from its publication the *American Journal of Sociology* (founded in 1894): "We understand both the family and the effects of urban and industrial developments; what we must do is solve the resulting problems and strengthen the family" (cited in Adams, 1975:5).

The Chicago School and Social Disorganization

The University of Chicago's intellectual activities can be best understood within the historical context of Chicago during the first half of the twentieth century. Chicago epitomizes the phenomenal population growth of American cities: In 1860, its population was 112,000; by the turn of the century (1900), its population was over 1.5 million, and it proceeded to grow at a rate of over 500,000 for each of the next three decades, culminating in a population of over 3.5 million by 1930. As Maurice Stein (1964) has stated, these statistics can give but a suggestion as to what it means in human terms to live in a city whose population swells at such a rapid rate. The unprecedented demands for the development of municipal services—street and transportation systems, sanitary water supplies, garbage disposal and sewage systems, fire and police protection, schools, libraries, parks, playgrounds, and so on—must have been overwhelming. Further complicating the situation was the fact that the new urban population was comprised predominantly of an influx of European immigrants (who had little familiarity with American customs and language) and migrants from rural America, groups unfamiliar with and unaccustomed to city life and each other.

It is not surprising, given the momentous and unplanned changes taking place in American cities during this period, that social scientists emphasized the negative and opposed the positive qualities of urban life. They focused on social disorganization and its consequences—alienation, anomie, social isolation, juvenile delinquency, crime, mental illness, suicide, child abuse, separation, and divorce—as inherent characteristics of urban life. "Small wonder that the Chicago sociologists focused on the absence of established institutional patterns in so many regions of the city, stressing that the neighborhoods grew and changed so rapidly that sometimes the only constant feature appeared to be mobility . . . and why 'disorganization' accompanied 'mobility' " (Stein, 1964:16).

The Chicago School of Sociology was composed of such important sociologists as Robert E. Park, Ernest W. Burgess, Louis Wirth, E. Franklin Frazier, W.I. Thomas, and Florian Znaniecki. They contributed much to the development of family sociology and urban sociology. The Chicago School developed a distinct contrast between urban and rural life. They saw traditional patterns of life being broken down by debilitating urban forces, resulting in social disorganization within the family. An underlying theme was the loss of family functions as a result of urbanization and industrialization. As we shall see, this position was developed and expanded so that it became a major cornerstone in much of structural-functionalist analysis of the family and particularly in the writings of Talcott Parsons.

Louis Wirth's essay, "Urbanism as a Way of Life" (1938), was one of the most, if not the most, influential statements on urbanism and on the family that came out of the Chicago School. Wirth's position was that size, density, and heterogeneity were the key elements determining city life. The consequences of these three variables are the relative absence of personal relationships; the depersonalization and segmentation of human relations, characterized by anonymity, superficiality, and transitoriness; and the breakdown of social structures and increased mobility, instability, and insecurity. Wirth summarizes his view of the influence of the city on the people who live there in the following statement: "The distinctive features of the urban mode of life have often been described sociologically as consisting of the substitution of secondary for primary contacts, the weakening of the bonds of kinship, and the declining social significance of the family, the disappearance of the neighborhood, and the undermining of the traditional basis of social solidarity" (Wirth, 1938: 21-22).

The work of Wirth, like that of his European predecessors who developed typologies on the urban-rural dichotomization of society, shared a common orientation—a negative view of the impact of the city and urban life on the family. I will examine the consequences of these biases in the analysis of the poor and ethnic working-class family systems in later chapters. Now I want to switch my attention to the other theme developed by the Chicago School, which concerns the loss of family functions as a result of urbanized and industrialized society. It is reflected in the works of Ogburn, Burgess, and Parsons. William F. Ogburn sees this loss negatively; Ernest Burgess is more positively disposed. Finally, Talcott Parsons synthesizes these positions and persuasively develops a more positive, or functional, view that still dominates American sociology and proves to be a pivotal anchoring position of modernization theory and the cross-cultural analysis of the family.

Ogburn's Culture Lag Theory and Family Change

William F. Ogburn's work has had an important impact on American sociology—the sociology of the family in particular—from the publication in 1922 of *Social Change*, to 1955 when his last major work, *Technology and the Changing Family*, was published with the collaboration of Meyer F. Nimkoff. Ogburn's primary concern was with the processes of social change. His contribution to sociology lies in the distinction he made between *material* culture (technology, factories, machines, transportation, and so forth) and *adaptive* culture (values, ideas, attitudes, customs, and so forth). He

"Flappers" of the 1920s fixing a flat tire. The automobile was a prime example of technical innovation that fostered change in gender roles and family dynamics.

argued that the real sources of progressive change were found in material innovations, with customs, beliefs, and philosophies adapting themselves to the material substructure. The fact that the adaptive culture follows the material culture led Ogburn to postulate the hypothesis of *culture lag*—changes in the material culture occur and cause changes in the adaptive culture that result in continuous social maladjustment between the two types of cultures.

The particular interest of this for students of the family lies in Ogburn's ideas about the processes of social change and the impact of technology, innovations, and ideologies on family systems. Applying this theory to the family, it is seen that the family system changes as a result of technological changes; the family, then, is an example of adaptive culture. Ogburn and Nimkoff (1955) present the argument that inventions and discoveries of modern technological society have led to the decline of the family's economic, educational, recreational, religious, and protective functions. This was in disaccord with the satisfactory adjustment of the family during the earlier history of America, which was dominated by an agricultural economy. The negative changes in the American family system that reflect the debilitating effects of cultural lag are:

1. Increasing divorce rate
2. Wider diffusion of birth control and decline in family size
3. Decline in authority of husbands and fathers
4. Increase in sexual intercourse apart from marriage
5. Increase in number of wives working for pay
6. Increasing individualism and freedom of family members
7. Increasing transfer of protective functions from family to state
8. Decline of religious behavior in marriage and family

The major theoretical criticism of Ogburn's works lies in his oversimplification of the notions of material and adaptive cultures, his overemphasis on resistances to changes in the area of adaptive culture, and his underemphasis on the resistances in the area of material culture. Sociologists of the family have particularly criticized his work because it views the family as a passive recipient adapting to changes in the materialistic culture, which is viewed as the active causal agent. They believe that the family may itself be a causal faction in the rate and growth of materialistic culture. The strength of Ogburn's work lies in his exhaustive descriptions of the changed relations of the family and other institutional structures, which he documented for more than three decades: the increased participation of government, economic enterprises, education, and so on, in the once private domain of the family (Leslie, 1979).

Burgess' Family from Institution to Companionship

At the same time that the Chicago School was making its influence felt in American sociology, another approach was developing that focused on the examination of the internal relationships of family members. This new orientation centered on the organization of roles in family life; for example: What is the role of the father or mother in the family structure? Two major conceptual frameworks developed during this period—symbolic interactionism and structural functionalism. Symbolic interactionism dominated much of early twentieth-century sociology, with structural functionalism serving a similar role in the period after World War II.

Symbolic interactionism, as applied to the study of the family, is a social-psychological perspective that emphasizes the various forms of family interactional patterns: courtship, the honeymoon period, child-rearing practices, divorce and separation, the role of the elderly, and so on. Charles Horton Cooley, George Herbert Mead, W.I. Thomas, and especially Ernest W. Burgess (who spoke of the family as "a unity of interacting personalities") developed this perspective. Symbolic interactionism made important methodological contributions to the study of the family, including the social survey, interview and questionnaire schedules, and participant observation.

The focus of symbolic interactionism is on the study of the family as a small-scale social phenomenon. It became almost completely devoted to the study of the American middle-class family structure. Symbolic interactionists were not as involved with the impact of larger societal institutions and processes on the family. Ernest W. Burgess (1886-1965), however, does pick up on the work of his colleague, William F. Ogburn, to explain the shifting of traditional functions of the family to outside agencies. Industrialization and urbanization are seen as primarily responsible for this shift. Burgess observes that the economic, educational, recreational, health protection, and religious functions of the family were being transformed to other institutions. The family was left with the functions of achieving the happiness and the personal growth of its members. The family now rested on "mutual affection, the sympathetic understanding, and comradeship of its members" (Burgess and Locke, 1945:vii).

This shift in family functions led to Burgess' famous classification of family types as moving from "institution to companionship." According to this conceptualization, the institutional family is one in which the unity is determined entirely by traditional rules and regulations, specified duties and obligations, and other historical social pressures impinging on family members. The extended patriarchal type of family most closely approximates the institutional family. It is authoritarian and autocratic; it demands the complete subordination of each family member and his or her spouse and children to the authority of the husband or eldest male (the patriarch). The emphasis is on compliance with duty and the following of tradition. Marriages are arranged with an emphasis on prudence, economic and social status, and the subordination of the married couple to the extended family group.

The companionate or democratic family is the recently emerging family type. It has moved away from an institutional character towards a "unity which develops out of mutual affection and intimate association of husband and wife and parents and children" (Burgess and Locke, 1945:27). This type of family includes affection as a basis for its existence, equal status and authority between the spouses, egalitarian decision making, and the sharing of common interests and activities, coexisting with divisions of labor and individuality of interests. According to Burgess, the institutional family is sustained by external community pressures and involvements; the companionate family, on the other hand, is sustained by the emotional attachments among its members.

Talcott Parsons and the Isolated Nuclear Family

Beginning in the late 1930s and accelerating after World War II, many of the views of the Chicago School of Sociology either merged with or influenced newer perspectives. By the 1950s, the dominant school was structural-functionalism, under the intellectual leadership of Talcott Parsons (1902-1980), who was one of the most predominant and influential sociologists of the twentieth century. According to Parsons, the isolation of the nuclear family "is the most distinctive feature of the American kinship and underlies most of its peculiar functional and dynamic problems" (1943:28). The typical American household consists of a husband, wife, and children economically independent of their extended family and frequently located at considerable geographical distance from it.

Parsons views American society as having been greatly changed by industrialization and urbanization. In particular, he believes it has become highly "differentiated," with the family system's previous educational, religious, political, and economic functions being taken over by other institutions in the society. By differentiation, Parsons means that functions performed earlier by one institution in the society are now distributed among several institutions. Thus, schools, churches, peer groups, political parties, voluntary associations, and occupational groups have assumed functions once reserved for the family. Rather than view industrialization and urbanization negatively, Parsons sees the family as becoming a more specialized group. It concentrates its functions on the socialization of children and providing emotional support and affection for family members.

Parsons further suggests that the isolated nuclear family may be ideally suited to meet the demands of occupational and geographical mobility that is inherent in industrial urban society. Unencumbered by obligatory extended kinship bonds, the nuclear family is best able to move where the jobs are and better able to take advantage of occupational opportunities. In contrast, the traditional extended-family system bond of extensive, obligatory economic and residential rights and duties is seen to be dysfunctional for industrial society.

Arguing against the social disorganization thesis on the breakdown of the contemporary family, Parsons (1955) finds support for the importance of the nuclear family in the high rates of marriage and remarriage after divorce, the increase in the birthrate after World War II, and the increase in the building of single-family homes (particularly in suburbia) during this time period. All these trends provide evidence of the continuing visibility, *not* social disorganization, of the family and *increased* vitality of the nuclear family bond. Thus, a specialized family system functionally meets the affectional and personality needs of its members. Further, it may be admirably fitted to a family system that is a relatively isolated and self-sustaining economic unit of mother, father, and children, living without other relatives in the home and without close obligations and ties to relatives who live nearby.

In summary, Parsons emphasizes the importance of the nuclear family—in the absence of extended kinship ties—in that it meets two major societal needs: the socialization of children and the satisfaction of the affectional and emotional demands of husbands, wives, and their children. Further, the isolated nuclear family, which is not handicapped by conflicting obligations to extended relatives, can best take advantage of occupational opportunities and is best able to cope with the demands of modern industrial urban life.

In Chapter 4, I critically examine Parsons' ideas on the isolated nuclear family in the city, conducting my investigation within the context of research that questions the Chicago School assumption that the city is antithetical to family life in general, and to extended kinship ties in particular. This research also argues against Parsons' position that the isolated nuclear family may be uniquely suited to meet the needs of an industrial urban society. We discuss the accumulated research that postulates the existence of viable kinship ties among many urban dwellers and examines the research on kinship family ties in the context of both geographical and social mobility. But, before I return to the urban family issues generated by Parsons' schema, I first must pick up on a dominant theme in this first part of the book, and that is the nature of cross-cultural social change and the family. My discussion in the next chapter centers on an examination of modernization theory with particular emphasis on the work of William J. Goode, who extends Parsons' concept of the isolated nuclear family to a belief that, cross-culturally, families are moving to various forms of the "conjugal" family.

CONCLUSION

This chapter was concerned with the historical development of sociological interest in the study of social change and the family that was precipitated by the Industrial Revolution of the nineteenth century. I began with an analysis of the evolutionary theories of Social Darwinism and Marxism. These theories sought to make sense of the changes in the family that were occurring through an employment of a social variation of Darwinian evolutionary thought. While ultimately rejected because of severe theoretical and methodological limitations, these theories were and to a certain extent still are influential in justifying gender role stratification and cross-cultural family diversity.

Toward the end of that century and into the early twentieth century, the sociology of the family was dominated by the issues of social reform, which was an outgrowth of what was viewed as the excesses of industrial and urban society and the calamitous changes in the family system. I highlighted my discussion by comparing the conservative perspective of Frederic Le Play with the radical perspective of Marx and Engels. I indicated that these two schools developed alternative and opposing viewpoints and solutions to their common perception of the evils of the emerging family form—Le Play's unstable family and Marx's and Engels' privatized family. Both schools were highly critical of the emerging family form, its treatment of family members, and its relationship to the surrounding community.

A particular concern of sociologists was the impact of the emerging urban industrial city on the family. The ideal type was an analytical technique that was developed to contrast the different forms of social and family life that existed in rural areas compared to urban areas. I sought to demonstrate that there was an ideological bias underlying these typologies that was both antiurban and anti-urban family. I implied and will later develop this viewpoint that these biases distorted the analysis of both the city and the family as it was developing in urban industrial societies.

In the last topic of this chapter, I noted that American sociologists turned to the study of internal family dynamics, paying little attention to the broader issues of social change during the first fifty years of the twentieth century. Yet a significant segment of American sociology continued to wrestle with the themes and issues raised by conservatives and radicals in the nineteenth century. The theories of William F. Ogburn and Ernest W. Burgess (with Harvey J. Locke) were discussed for their contemporary significance.

Another notable exception was the Chicago School, which focused on urban structures and dynamics. I discussed the ideal typologies of urban-rural families of nineteenth-century theorists and the position of the Chicago School sociologist Louis Wirth, emphasizing the social disorganization of families in the city. The structural functionalist Talcott Parsons reworked these themes in his conceptualization of the isolated nuclear family and its functionality to urban industrial society.

However, until the end of World War II, American sociology was characterized by almost no interest in large-scale comparative analysis. The interests and concerns of the Chicago School and the symbolic interactionists were picked up and developed by the dominating perspective of the postwar era, that of structural functionalism. An offshoot of structural functionalism, "modernization theory," attempted to reestablish the importance of cross-cultural and historical analyses of social change and the family. The most significant contribution of this theory was the work of William J. Goode and his thesis of the worldwide movement of the family from the consanguineal form to the conjugal one. In the following chapter, I devote attention to a critique of structural functionalism and modernization theory and the analysis of comparative family systems. I return to themes on the family in the community and in the city in Part II.

3

WORLD PATTERNS
AND THE CHANGING FAMILY

Since the mid-nineteenth century, there has been a vacillation of interest in cross-cultural family research. It reached a peak during the second half of the nineteenth century, dropped during the first half of the twentieth century, and returned to comparative study since World War II. The rebirth of interest in comparative studies has two prime sources. The first is an intellectual rebellion against the limitation of the rigorous empirical methods emphasized during the early twentieth century. The development of this methodology, frequently statistical in nature, was used to investigate small-scale social phenomena and paid little attention to social change and its consequences for the family. American sociologists limited their analysis to their own society, ignored other societies and cultures, and left comparative analysis to the other social sciences, particularly anthropology.

The second factor that stimulated comparative analysis was the revived interest in social change. The postwar period was marked by rapid dissolution of the colonial empires of the Western industrial societies and the concomitant transformation of what Westerners called "underdeveloped and backward" societies. In addition, Western societies were also undergoing processes of social change. What was becoming particularly clear was that "scientific" sociological study of the family was not able to come to grips with the dominant social issues and problems of contemporary times.

The sociology of the family was dominated by two conceptual frameworks, symbolic interactionism and structural functionalism. *Symbolic interactionism* has not been involved with the study of social change; it has, by and large, focused on internal family dynamics as opposed to the family in relation to other institutions in a given society. On the other hand, *structural functionalism*—and particularly its offshoot, modernization theory—have been involved in this endeavor, as well as in cross-cultural and historical analyses of social change and the family. However, as I will demonstrate, their frame of reference is inadequate to study family change.

As I discussed in my presentation of the ideas of Talcott Parsons, structural functionalism is concerned with the family's changing functions in light of industrialization and urbanization. It views every society as a system made up of subsystems, often called "institutions." The major ones are the family, religion, economy, politics, and education. These institutions are intertwined so that change in one institution, such as the economy, invariably affects other institutions, such as the family and education. Change results as the society seeks to restore its equilibrium in the light of institutional changes. Structural functionalism has an implicit evolutionary theme integrated into its concern with functional changes.

In this chapter, I investigate some of the factors that help to account for the current interest in cross-cultural study of the family. I look at the dominant perspective, modernization theory, and at its strengths and weaknesses. Modernization theory combines the conceptual orientation from both Social Darwinism and structural functionalism to elaborate the theoretical relationship between societal development and family change. I then present a theoretical critique of modernization theory and provide a comprehensive analysis and assessment of that perspective's strengths, weaknesses, and limitations. I highlight theoretical developments that have extended, modified, and changed the way we think of the family and modernization in nonindustrial and industrial societies and in capitalist and socialist ones as well. Through this analysis, I seek to demonstrate the complexity of family change in a rapidly changing and increasingly industrial and urban world.

MODERNIZATION THEORY AND FAMILY CHANGE

The structural-functionalist perspective tends to see society as an organism that strains toward maintaining itself in some form of balance—an equilibrium model. The concern is with the functional connections among the various parts of a system, whether the society or the family. For example, it views the family as a social system. Its constituent parts, husband-father, wife-mother, and children, are bound together by interaction and interdependence. It is concerned with whether any given part is either functional or dysfunctional to the family; that is, whether it adds or detracts from the system's operation. Stability and order are implicitly viewed as being natural and normal. Conflict and disorder are seen as being deviant phenomena and evidence that the system is not working properly.

The inherent problem of structural functionalism is in its handling of social change, which stems from its emphasis on consensus and cooperation, its failure to acknowledge the possibility of conflicting interests of constituent elements in a social system, and its reification of the status quo. The structural-functionalist perspective does not lend itself readily to explain or describe the phenomenon of social change. When the system, whether it is a society or the family, is reified and seen as being in a state of equilibrium, it can only emphasize slow, orderly change. Conflict and rapid social change are regarded as pathological trends and the only source of change is by outside agents. Structural functionalism, although in the forefront of cross-cultural family study, has not been able to handle satisfactorily the problem of social change because of its emphasis on studying societies in the historical present and then making cross-cultural historical comparisons, much in the same manner as the Social Darwinists.

Modernization theories were developed from a combination of conceptualizations derived from evolutionary theory and structural functionalism. Modernization theory is concerned with the changes that societies and individuals experience as a result of industrialization, urbanization, and the development of the nation-state. Modernization theories have been widely used in sociology since World War II. However, the basic conceptual problems of both evolutionary theory and structural functionalism in their handling of social change have also led to similar problems in the development of adequate conceptual tools by the proponents of modernization theory.

The concept of modernization and the theories stemming from it have been the dominating perspective in the analysis of global social change and the family. *Modernization* is usually used as a term in reference to processes of change in societies that are characterized by advanced industrial technology. Science and technology are seen to guide societies from traditional, preindustrial social institutions to complex, internally differentiated ones.

Modernization is often linked with a wide range of changes in the political, economic, social, and individual spheres. For example, there is a movement from tribal or village authority to political parties and civil service bureaucracies; from illiteracy to education that would increase economically productive skills; from traditionalistic religions to secularized belief systems; and from ascriptive hierarchical systems to greater social and geographical mobility resulting in a more achievement-based stratification system. Likewise the extended family kinship ties are seen to lose their pervasiveness and nuclear families gain in importance (Smelser, 1973).

The impact of modernization on the family is explained through reference to a

A scene from the movie *Fiddler on the Roof.* Tevye, embraced by his daughter, shakes hands with his future son-in-law after his agreement that she can marry the man she loves rather than be forced to marry another in an arranged marriage.

key concept of structural functionalism—structural differentiation. Smelser (1973) explains structural differentiation as the manner in which, after industrialization, family functions lose some of their former importance in matters of training and economic production, and schools and economic organizations begin to fill these functions. As the family ceases to be an economic unit of production, family members may leave the household to seek employment in the outside labor market. With the decline of the family's function in the economic sphere, the family (particularly in the figure of the father) loses its economic-training function, which further leads to a decline in general paternal authority. The family's activities become more concentrated on emotional gratification and socialization, with the mother developing more intense emotional relationships with children because of the absence of the father in the job market. Echoing Talcott Parsons, Smelser concludes that "modernization tends to foster the rise of a family unit that is formed on emotional attraction and built on a limited sexual-emotional basis . . . [that is] isolated and specialized" (1973:752).

Modernization theorists have attempted to make the development of Western European and American technological society the model for the comparative analysis of developing countries. Daniel Lerner in his influential study, *The Passing of Traditional Society: Modernizing the Middle East*, argued that "the same model reappears in virtually all modernizing societies on all continents of the world, regardless of variations in race, color, creed . . ." (1958:46). This belief that most nations would eventually imitate Western societies by industrializing has been called diffusion theory. The sociologist who brought this viewpoint into the analysis of the family in worldwide social change was William J. Goode (1963). Let us now turn to an examination of his ideas.

William J. Goode's *World Revolution and Family Patterns*

The dominant theme emphasized by sociologists who studied the family both in the nineteenth and the twentieth centuries was that industrialization and urbanization radically transformed the family from an extended, authoritarian, stable rural form into a nuclear, more egalitarian, and relatively isolated and unstable one. Goode picked up on this by extending the analysis to a worldwide historical survey of family systems.

The major work coming out of modernization theory, which centers on the family in change, is William J. Goode's *World Revolution and Family Patterns* (1963). This work has had a profound impact on the comparative study of social change and the family. Goode's major contribution is the comprehensive and systematic gathering and analyses of cross-cultural and historical data to attack the notion that industrial and economic development was the principal reason that the family is changing. Goode concluded that changes in industrialization and the family are parallel processes, both being influenced by changing social and personal ideologies—the ideologies of economic progress, the conjugal family, and egalitarianism. Finally, Goode proposes that in the "world revolution" toward industrialization and urbanization, there is a convergence of diverse types of extended family forms to some type of conjugal family system.

Goode's conceptualization of modernization processes and the classification of societies and family systems sees societies moving from traditional systems to modern systems and the family moving from extended kinship family systems to the conjugal family form. Goode takes issue with theories that view change in family patterns as a simple function of industrialization. Rather, he sees modernization represented by ideological value changes as being partially independent of industrialization as well as having important impacts on both the family system and industrialization itself.

Following a structural-functionalist framework, Goode is critical of the position that the conjugal family emerges only after a society is exposed to industrialization. This position ignores the theoretical "fit" (empirical harmony) between the conjugal family and the modern industrial system. For example, the independence of the conjugal family from extended kinship ties permits the family to move where the jobs are. The increased emotional component of the conjugal family relationship provides a source of psychological strength in the face of pressures from the industrial order and the absence of extended kin relations. This seeming "fit" is not seen as obscuring either the importance of ideological factors or the fact that the family itself may be an independent factor influencing the industrialization process.

Goode believes that the ideology of economic progress and technological development, as well as the ideology of the conjugal family, occurred in non-Western societies prior to industrialization and family changes. The significance of the ideology of economic progress lies in its stress on societal industrial growth and change and its relegation of the issue of tradition and custom to a lower level of importance. The ideology of the conjugal family asserts the worth of the individual over lineage, and personal welfare over family continuity. A third ideology is that of egalitarianism between the sexes. The emphasis is on the uniqueness of each individual within the family, with lesser importance given to sex status and seniority. This ideology reduces the sex status and age inequalities of families and also undermines the traditional subordination of the young to the old.

All three modernization ideologies aim directly or indirectly at ending the dominance of the extended family system over the conjugal family and, in particular, over the young and women. Further, all three ideologies minimize the traditions of societies and assert the equality of the individual over class, caste, or sex barriers.

Goode's theoretical position centers around two major functional fits. The first is that between the desire of the individual to maximize his or her need for equality and individualism and the type of family system that can best satisfy those needs. The second functional fit is between the type of family system that can best serve the needs of an industrial and technological social order.

Goode argues that the ideology of the conjugal family system, which emphasizes the relationship of husband and wife and their children and deemphasizes the obligatory relationship with extended kinship systems, is best able to maximize the values of individualism and egalitarianism. The extended family system tends to subordinate the individual to the family group—family continuity is more important than individual welfare and desires—whereas the ideology of the conjugal family asserts the equality of individuals over sex, kinship, caste, and class barriers.

The ideology of the conjugal family proclaims the right of the individual to choose his or her own spouse, place to live, and even which kin obligations to accept, as against the acceptance of others' decisions. It asserts the worth of the individual as against the inherited elements of wealth or ethnic group. The *individual* is to be evaluated not his lineage. (Goode, 1963:19)

The second functional fit is between the family system and industrialization. Goode states that the ideology of the conjugal family and industrialization fit each other through the sharing of common ideas and values intrinsic within both systems. In addition, he argues that these shared ideas and values are necessary for the development of both types of systems. The conjugal family system is closely tied with the ideology of economic progress and technological development, which stresses industrial expansion and the freedom of economic activity that is demanded in a rapidly changing industrializing economy.

Goode assembles a massive amount of comparative data, both historical and cross-cultural (the West, Arabic Islam, sub-Saharan Africa, India, China, and Japan) to test these hypotheses. The conclusion reached is that *all* family systems are moving toward some form of conjugal family system. The trends and changes that are occurring take on the following characteristics.

1. *Free choice in mate selection.* In extended-family systems, marriages are arranged by family elders, frequently without the couple meeting prior to the actual marriage. This is to minimize the development of potentially conflicting emotional and obligatory ties between spouses and to maintain control over the future generational development of the extended kinship system. Marriages today, Goode concludes, are being based on love; dowry and bride-price are disappearing.

2. *Emphasis on individual welfare as opposed to family continuity.* The authority of parents over children and husbands over wives is diminishing, and greater sexual equality is becoming manifest in changes in legal systems regarding such matters as divorce and inheritance. Further evidence is the weakening of sex, kinship, class, and caste barriers and the assertion of the equality of individuals in various substantive legal actions.

3. *Greater emphasis on the conjugal role relationship.* Husbands and wives are moving more and more in the direction of setting up their own independent households (neolocal residences) as opposed to living within the confines of either the husband's family's residence (patrilocality) or the wife's family's residence (matrilocality), thus diminishing the everyday interaction control of either extended family system. Another development that tends to support the independence of the conjugal system is the development of bilineal descent systems (tracing lineage equally through both family lines) in contrast to a unilineage descent system (either patrilineal or matrilineal). Goode shows that the development of a bilineal descent system results in the loss of power for both unilineage systems and changes the nature of extended kinship ties to one based on affection and choice rather than on obligation. Thus, neolocality and bilineality aid in the development of relative freedom of the conjugal-family system from the extended-family system and prevent the continuation or the development of powerful unilineage systems that dominate the husband-wife marital relationship.

In summarizing Goode's work, we see that the basis of his argument revolves around the legitimacy of extended-family systems in terms of their domination over the individual and the belief that the conjugal-family system maximizes the ideology of equality and individuality. This desire for egalitarianism results in a power conflict between the individual and the traditional extended-family systems. Further, the ideology of the conjugal family links up with the ideology of economic progress associated with industrial and economic development. The ideology of economic progress runs counter to the ideology of traditionalism, which emphasizes the continuity of historical traditional patterns. Both ideologies operate to foster change in the society and affect one another. At the end of his seminal work (1963), Goode gives his own evaluation of the changes that are occurring. Although he is aware of the dysfunctions these changes may have—particularly to the elders of extended kinship systems—Goode welcomes them.

> I welcome the great changes now taking place, and not because it might be a more efficient instrument of industrialization, for that is irrelevant in my personal schema. Rather, I see in it and in the industrial system that accompanies it the hope of greater freedom: from the domination of elders, from caste and racial restriction, from class rigidities. Freedom is for something as well: the unleashing of personal potentials, the right to love, to equality within the family, to the establishment of a new marriage when the old has failed. I see the world revolution in family patterns as part of a still more important revolution that is sweeping the world in our time, the aspiration on the part of billions of people to have the right for the first time to choose for themselves—an aspiration that has toppled governments both old and new, and created new societies and social movements. (Goode, 1963:380)

Goode's great work stimulated a large amount of empirical studies in social change and the family. Soon after the publication of his monograph, a series of comparative studies, both cross-cultural and historical, presented evidence contrary to his hypothesis that there was a worldwide trend toward the conjugal-family system. In recent years, new developments in the analysis of modernization processes and in the sociological study of the family have pinpointed limitations in modernization theory and begun to show how these limitations can lead to distortions in the comparative analysis of social change and the family.

MODERNIZATION THEORY AND THE FAMILY: ASSESSMENTS AND DEVELOPMENTS

There has been widespread dissatisfaction with many of the underlying assumptions of modernization theory and how it relates to the family. Here I will group these criticisms into three major categories. The first questions modernization theory's reliance on an evolutionary model grounded in the notion of progress. Critics believe that it erroneously supports the idea that progress is a more valued phenomenon than traditional stability and that modern societies—that is, Western industrial societies—are superior to traditional nonindustrial societies. The second questions the belief that modern social systems, with their emphasis on the autonomy of the nuclear family and on the individual, are without problems. Critics argue that modernization theory fails to see the negative effects of such autonomy both for the family and for the individual. The third questions the "liberating" effects of modernization and its perceived benevolent impact on less developed societies and the families within these societies. The focus of my attention is how these criticisms will heighten our understanding of changes in the family as a consequence of modernization.

Tradition, Traditionalism, and Modernity

Modernization theory has been criticized for its simplified conceptualization of traditional and modern societies as polar opposites and viewing them as static entities. Wilbert E. Moore (1964) has stated that the three-stage model—tradition, transition, and modernity has inherent problems. By focusing on societies in transition, the theory implies a static traditional stage with a social structure persisting in equilibrium without change, as well as a modern society that is also static and unchanging. Moore argues that "change is an intrinsic characteristic of all societies and the historic paths to the present inevitably and significantly affect the continuing paths to the future" (1964:884).

Other scholars emphasize the continuity and reconstruction of tradition as a society modernizes. The general argument made is the need to look at developing, modernizing, and modern societies in terms of processes of change. The concern should not be on whether these societies are moving to a similar form of society and culture as the West. Rather the focus should be on how these societies adapt their cultural identities and traditions to modernization processes. By so doing it will be found that: (1) tradition is not a static and unchanging entity with no changes occurring in the given traditional society, and (2) it is wrong to assume that tradition and modernity are conflicting alternative polarities.

The problem of modernization theory is its erroneous belief that *all* industrial societies are based on the Western archetype. It led to the conclusion that human beings who did not share Western ideologies and value systems were antithetical to modernization and their traditional societies were opposed to modernization. Myron Weiner (1966) suggests that the problem of conceptualization of traditional societies as static entities opposed to modernization and the development of industrial and economic systems stems from a confusion between the concepts *traditionalism* and *tradition*.

> Tradition refers to the beliefs and practices handed down from the past; as we reinterpret our past, our traditions change. In contrast, traditionalism glorifies past beliefs and practices as immutable. Traditionalists see tradition as static; they urge that men do things only as they have been done before. This distinction between tradition and traditionalism calls attention to a fundamental

BOX 3-1   The Historical Family

Industrialization and the Family in China and Japan

Both China and Japan were affected by Western industrial technology and Western ideology regarding the individual, the family, and the society in the late nineteenth century. These two societies illustrate the importance of family patterns in facilitating or hindering industrial social change. In Japan a feudal system prevailed. The prevailing pattern of inheritance was one in which the eldest inherited all. There was a narrow pattern of social mobility within the merchant class. No matter how successful a merchant family was they could not move up to the nobility class, although they could achieve high status (and wealth) within the merchant class. These factors allowed for the accumulation of family capital. There was a feudalistic loyalty of individuals to their extended families and, in turn, there was a feudalistic loyalty of extended family to the state imperial system. All these factors assured the rapid industrialization of the society.

In contrast, in China a familistic system prevailed. In China the prevailing pattern was equal inheritance. This handicapped the accumulation of family capital. The Chinese, unlike the Japanese, accorded a low social rank to the merchant status. Thus, when wealth was gained, individuals sought to achieve prestige and power by becoming members of the gentry and moving out of the merchant class This too prevented the steady accumulation of financial and technical expertise. Finally, the relationship of the family to the state was familistic not feudalistic. That is, an individual owed loyalty to both the extended family and the state, personified in the emperor. However, in the case of conflict between the two, the individual's first loyalty was to the family.

These different family systems played an important part in the industrial achievement of Japan and the lack of such achievement in China.

The family system in China was a hindrance to rapid industrialization, whereas the family system in Japan aided in the industrialization of that country. It is important to note that the Japanese experience does *not* reflect an adaptation to Western ideologies and value systems. Rather, industrialization adapted to Japanese ideology and value system that adapted to industrialization. The sociologist Myron Weiner makes the following comparison between China and Japan: "While the Japanese sought to reinterpret their past so as to make it congruent with their efforts to modernize, many Chinese leaders were hostile to innovations that violated previous practices" (Weiner, 1966:7). In Japan, *tradition* was subject to reinterpretation and modification and thus constituted no barrier to industrialization; in China, *traditionalism* was hostile to innovation and was opposed to the development of modernization.

Modernization theory does not systematically develop the idea that tradition and modernity may not be conflicting and polar opposites. Critics of modernization theory (Bendix, 1967; Gusfield, 1967; Moore, 1964) have reached the conclusion that tradition and modernity can be inseparable; modernity can be incorporated into the traditional order, and the traditional culture can permeate and have an impact on the individual, social, economic, and political spheres of modernization.

Bendix, 1967; Goode, 1963;
Gusfield, 1967; Moore, 1964.

A young Chinese family enjoys a quiet moment of leisure time together.

issue in development: How do people see their past? Are the values and practices of the past to be preserved or adapted? . . . When people are attached to the past in such a way that they will not adopt new practices that modify past behavior, we are confronted with an ideology of traditionalism. Traditionalism, by virtue of its hostility to innovation, is clearly antithetical to the development of modernization; traditions, which are constantly subject to reinterpretation and modification, constitute no such barrier. (Weiner, 1966:7)

I illustrate this difference between traditionalism and tradition in my discussion on the differences between nineteenth-century China and Japan in the box insert, "Industrialization and the Family in China and Japan."

Modernization Theory, the Individual, and the Family

Of particular relevance to us is the fact that modernization theory has not given sufficient attention to the negative impact of economic, structural, and political processes on the everyday lives of the people living in countries that are undergoing radical change. Modernization theorists have examined the different orientations between individuals living under traditional circumstances and their modern counterparts.

Probably the most influential sociologist to develop such a comparative schema is Alex Inkeles (1983).

Inkeles, in a study of 6,000 people in Argentina, Chile, India, Israel, Nigeria, and East Pakistan (Bangladesh), found a set of personal qualities that distinguished modern individuals from those who were more traditional. The modern individuals were characterized by (1) an openness to new experiences, (2) independence from traditional authority figures such as parents and religious leaders, (3) beliefs in the effectiveness of science and modern medicine, (4) ambitions for themselves and for their children's upward mobility and success, (5) strong interest in community activities and in local, national, and international affairs, (6) being time oriented and able to keep appointments. Those with a traditional orientation were very reluctant to try something new, were dependent on authority figures, were superstitious and fatalistic, lacked interest in the community, and were not concerned with politics either at the local, national, or international levels. Inkeles concluded that formal education and factory work were key organizational structures in changing an individual's orientation and developing a sense of modernity.

Rose Coser (1991) in her book, *In Defense of Modernity*, provides an interesting illustration in modernity's support. She compares similar incidents in Pakistan and in the United States in which an individual accidentally fell into a well. In Pakistan, eleven family members independently went to the well to find and extricate the fallen member. Each was asphyxiated by the toxic gas fumes found in the well and perished. Coser comments that the members of the family had little relatedness to the larger community and were dependent upon the resources of each other, which in this case proved disastrous. In the American comparison, when a 4-year-old fell into a well, the 8-year-old brother threw life preservers into the well, called a telephone operator for help, and ran to neighbors for assistance. Coser notes that this individual was more aware of the world outside the family than his Pakistani counterparts. She concludes:

> Closely knit groups, even though they give individuals a feeling of security and a sense of belonging, have less survival value, at least in the modern world, than those that permit or encourage their members to actively pursue relations with individuals or groups on the outside and to orient themselves toward other institutions for their needs. This is because such rigid conformity does not permit readaption to changing circumstances and conflicting demands, which is what the modern world is all about. (Coser, 1991:26)

The negative impact of modernization processes on individuals and families is deemphasized by modernization theorists. Critics, however, point out the difficulties in adjustment, especially in the cases in which a modern culture directly confronted and superimposed its system on a non-Western nonmodern culture. Szymon Chodak (1973) observes that in Africa, a new semi-developmental buffer culture that was marginal to both the European colonial culture and the traditional African culture developed. This culture promoted duality in norms, patterns of behavior, attitudes, and structural affiliations. Colin Turnbull (1962), an anthropologist who studied the impact of modernization, in his book, *The Lonely African*, describes his experiences with one individual who led a dual existence in two cultural worlds:

> In Accra I stayed in the town household of a Kwahu family, their home residence being between Accra and Kumasi, in the depths of the countryside. In his country home the family head was a chief—*Kwame*, or "He who was born on Saturday." In his Accra house the chief became Harold, a prosperous merchant and a politician. His town house was large and rambling, on two floors. He occupied the upper floor with his wife by Christian marriage and their small children. It was a magnificent apartment, with every possible luxury—including a well stocked cocktail cabinet, for the one tradition that dies the hardest is the tradition of hospitality. In this apartment lived a happy, settled, thoroughly westernized family. But downstairs lived his other family, the family of Kwame as opposed to that of Harold—all his nephews and other appendages of his extended Kwame family which, as Kwame, he felt obliged to support, even in Accra.
>
> It was like going from one world to another, and I lived a completely double life with ease and pleasure in that household. Upstairs we drank whiskey, danced the cha-cha and the mambo, ate bacon and eggs for breakfast, and drank tea at teatime. From upstairs, we sallied forth for evenings at the various smart night clubs (evening dress compulsory) or to elegant private dinner parties. But downstairs I ate fufu (a kind of unsweetened dough made from maniac flour, from which one tears pieces to dip in a sauce) with my fingers, drank palm wine, danced Abalabi, and learned what real family life is like. (Turnbull, 1962:322)

But Chodak sees the acculturative process as a process of alienation. He reports that Colin Turnbull calls these individuals alienated, whereas Franz Fanon (1968) in his book, *The Wretched of the Earth*, sees them as men and women with a black skin and a white mask. Chodak views the acculturated alienated individual as being transformed into a "superior inferior" (Chodak, 1973:265). Although such alienated individuals acquire the habits of the European colonizers and are told that they are superior to nonacculturated individuals, they are at the same time treated as inferiors by Europeans. Chodak provides a powerful illustration of this situation in the writings of an African, Robert Mueme Mbate, who, as he searches for his identity, asks: "Who am I?"

> I am not a Mkamba, yet I am Mkamba, I was born of Kamba parents. In my veins there flows Kamba blood. . . . I know a number of Kamba customs, but what I know is so little that I am ashamed. . . . Can I claim to be a European? A black European? Now wait a minute! In my veins, there flows Kamba blood. My skin is black like a Mkamba's. . . . And when I eat European food my stomach rebels. It wants most of all the Kamba dish—isye, maize with beans and green vegetables. . . .
>
> I speak the English language. I write in English. I even dress like English

people. In my best clothes, I look like an Englishman. I struggle hard to learn the manners of the English people. . . . I fall short of European customs and culture. When they say, "Don't be silly," I feel I have been insulted. Yet it's not so. When a daughter kisses her father, my blood says, "Oh no!" It is odd to me. . . .

When I was a young boy, I was "Kambanized." I learned how to make bows and arrows, the Kamba traditional weapons . . . I don't know how to dance the traditional Kamba dances. I went to school too early to learn them. At school I learned English and Scottish dances. Yet I don't know why the English and Scottish dances are danced. . . .

What then, am I? A conglomeration of indigenous and borrowed ideas and ideals. As such, I must find my footing in the whole nation, and indeed in the whole human race. I am not a Mkamba, yet a Mkamba, in whose veins Kamba blood flows. (Mbate cited in Chodak, 1973:266)

This theme is continued and expanded in Berger, Berger, and Kellner's work, *The Homeless Mind: Modernization* and *Consciousness* (1973). Here, the argument is made that the process of modernization and the institutions that accompany it have had a negative impact on human consciousness of reality. The modernization process, which was supposed to free individuals, is seen instead as increasing feelings of helplessness, frustration, and alienation that beset individuals with threats of meaninglessness. Berger and his associates examine the processes of modernization in the Third World and its effect on traditional ways of life, kinship patterns, and "social constructions of reality" and find them being changed.

Modernization is seen to have helped lead the individual away from the domination of the extended family, clan, and tribe and has given the individual the opportunity to pursue previously unheard of choices and options. Both geographical mobility (the movement from the small rural community to the larger urban community) and social and occupational mobility have freed the individual from these previously dominating institutions.

As is readily apparent, this position parallels that of William J. Goode, who welcomed these changes in that they provided men and women the potential for greater individual freedom and the "unleashing of personal potentials, the right to love, to equality within the family, to the establishment of a new marriage when the old had failed . . . the right for the first time *to choose* for themselves . . ." (Goode, 1963:380). However, Berger and his associates (1973) go beyond Goode and see that modernization has, in fact, not led to freedom and the maximization of individual potentialities but, instead, has led to a condition of "homelessness" and to feelings of helplessness, frustration, and alienation.

They observe that modernization is often experienced in terms of cultural contact and imposition. Often, even when modern technology is encountered, most people in the Third World are related to it in terms of low-skill labor without experiencing the ideologies of modernity. "What frequently happens in such cases is that there are very destructive effects on traditional patterns of life *without* any significant modernization of consciousness in terms of positively identifiable themes" (Berger et al., 1973:121).

They illustrate this very persuasively by looking at how mining in South Africa has had the immediate consequences of weakening village life and its traditional cultural patterns. Men are separated from their families and their traditional way of life and are placed in an industrial life-world that is amorphous and composed of uprooted individuals.

> In such a situation the structures of modernity . . . must necessarily appear to the individual as an alien, powerful and, in the main, coercive force that completely uproots his life and the lives of those he most cares about. In such a situation, there is little if any direct identification with modernity. (Berger et al., 1973:122)

The development of an identification with modernization can only begin to occur when individuals begin to settle into a new life and if and when they are joined by their families. Berger and his associates also observe that initially only a small number of individuals adapt to modernization. These people—who are labeled modern types—are seen to have been marginal to the life of the traditional community. Colin Turnbull's "the lonely African" is a good case in point.

Berger, Berger, and Kellner (1973) extend their analysis to the industrialized world and particularly the United States. They argue that in the advanced industrial nations modernization is seen to lead to a variety of discontentments stemming from the technologized economy, the bureaucratization of major institutions, and the "pluralization of social worlds," resulting in a condition that they label as "homelessness."

The key term here is the "pluralization of social worlds." By this they mean that modern life is segmented (pluralized) to a high degree. The pluralization of life-worlds is distinguished by the dichotomy of private (home) and public (work) spheres. Further, these different spheres or sectors of everyday life that an individual experiences are not related and may represent vastly different worlds of meaning and experience. In contrast, according to these authors, traditional society is characterized by a life-world that is relatively unified, with a high degree of integration existing among the various groups in which the individual participates. Thus, individuals do not experience the sense of segmentation of modern life and do not have the feeling that a particular social situation took them out of their common life-world, whether they are involved with their family, religious groups, or work groups.

These authors conclude that technology's primary consequence has been in the separation of work from private life. This condition has also had an impact on the individual's "levels of consciousness." Technological production, they say, is characterized by anonymous impersonal social relations. Individuals interact with each other in terms of the functions they perform in their structured work tasks. There is no need to be aware of each other's uniqueness as individuals. The consequence of this is that "the individual now becomes capable of experiencing himself in a double way; as a unique individual rich in concrete qualities and as an anonymous functionary" (Berger et al., 1973:34). The implication of this dichotomization of self is that it is only in their private lives that individuals can express elements of their subjective identity, which is denied them in their work situation. However, people are unable to find ample satisfaction in their private lives because their private lives tend to be composed of weak institutions, a prime illustration being the family.

The family is said to be weak because people often marry people of different backgrounds, children sever their ties with their parents when they reach their adulthood, neighborhood ties are fragmentary and viewed with suspicion, and, as a consequence, dissatisfied family members seek satisfactions elsewhere.

> . . . the individual attempts to construct a "home world" which will serve as the meaningful center of his life in society. Such an enterprise is hazardous and precarious. Marriages between people of different backgrounds involve complicated negotiations between the meanings of discrepant worlds. Children habitually and disturbingly emigrate from the world of their parents. Alternate and often repulsive worlds impinge upon private life in the form of neighbors and other unwelcome intruders, and indeed it is also possible that the individual, dissatisfied for whatever reason with the organization of his private life, may himself seek out plurality in other private contacts. This quest for more satisfactory private meanings may range from extramarital affairs to experiments with exotic religious sects. (Berger et al., 1973:66-67)

In summary, these authors put forth the argument that marriage—which was seen as providing a meaningful world for its participants—is, in fact, unable to overcome the homelessness resulting from the pluralization of life-worlds in modern society. This conclusion is diametrically opposite to that reached by William J. Goode. Where Goode welcomes the changes and is optimistic about the actualization of individualism and egalitarianism, Berger and his associates are quite pessimistic. In their delineation of the public and private life, they hit at a key variable in explaining much of the tensions surrounding the contemporary American family system.

In essence, I am in agreement with this latter position. The dichotomization of public and private spheres of activities is a main characteristic of contemporary Western family systems. It is this dichotomization that provides the key to the analysis of social change and the family. Much of cross-cultural and historical analysis of family change has ignored this characteristic. Influenced by modernization theory, scholars have overemphasized the need to investigate structural changes in the family. These theorists have built up the case that the distinctive feature of modern society is the predominance of the nuclear family and the prevalence of the large patriarchal extended kin group of traditional societies from the historical past of Western Europe and America.

Interestingly, William J. Goode (1963) debunks the myth that the "classical family of Western nostalgia" was the large extended family living happily in the large rambling house on the farm. But, in his emphasis on the close "fit" between industrialization and the conjugal family and on the retarding effects of the extended family with industrialization, his argument takes a different twist; it centers on changes in the structural nature of the family and limits the analysis of changes to the family's involvement in the community. His argument, then, becomes one aspect of the theme that industrialization means the end of the viable extended family and the development of the conjugal family, which has severed meaningful involvements with other kin.

Family historians have taken issue with the conclusion that the history of the Western family is a movement from the consanguineal system to the conjugal one. And, in their historical analysis of the Western family form, they reach strikingly similar conclusions to cross-cultural comparative sociologists such as Peter L. Berger and to the conclusions of Karl Marx and Friedrich Engels on the privatization of the family. In the next chapter, I turn my attention to these developments and examine these research findings and conclusions. This is part of my larger discussion of the family in the community context. I conclude this chapter with an examination of development theory that provides an alternative perspective in the analysis of the impact of modernization processes on the family. Further, this perspective places a strong emphasis on the disabling effects of global inequality and poverty on the family.

DEVELOPMENT THEORY: AN ALTERNATIVE PERSPECTIVE

The third criticism of modernization theory questions the "liberating" effects of modernization and its perceived benevolent impact on less developed societies and the families within these societies. Modernization theory assumed that economic development was a path that all nations would follow. Further, they believed that the cultures of the less developed nations would increasingly come to resemble those of the modernized world.

Modernization theory, while it recognized to some extent that cultural values of non-Western societies might impact on the pace of industrialization argued that it would not affect its inevitability. Modernization theory made the basic assumption that *the* model for development is that which occurred in Western Europe and the United States after the Industrial Revolution. Diffusion theory and the convergence hypothesis, offshoots of modernization theory, predicted that cultural differences would diminish as less developed countries industrialized. As societies modernize, they will come to resemble one another more and more over time (individual characteristics will converge) and their cultural uniqueness will give way as they begin to act and think more like one another and more like the more developed societies. As we saw earlier, this position was reflected Goode's *World Revolution and Family Patterns*, in which it is seen that families worldwide would eventuate into a close approximation of the Western conjugal family form.

This prediction by diffusion theory is called the convergence hypothesis. The hypothesis is that unique cultural traditions would diminish when less developed countries achieve a certain level of industrial production, education, and urbanization. Then, these countries' economies would experience a similar sustained economic growth to the industrialized West. This would allow these countries to compete in world markets with the advanced industrial economies. This change would first occur in urban areas and then proceed to the more economically backward rural areas. Accompanying that economic development would be a shift to "modern" attitudes and beliefs and a change in the family and kinship system.

Dependency theory takes strong exception to these predictions articulated by modernization theory's hypotheses. Further, and more importantly, proponents of dependency theory have changed the focus of the analysis of the impact of industrialization and globalized economy. Rather than focus on whether there is a convergence to Western models of modernity and family structure, they have focused on the impact of the globalization of the economy on the poor, not only in Third World societies but in industrial ones as well. Let us now turn our attention to this viewpoint.

In opposition to modernization theory are the more radical "dependency/underdevelopment" approaches also known as development theory or world system theory. These viewpoints were first put forth by scholars studying Latin America including Andre Gunder Frank (1966/1995) and also by Immanuel Wallerstein (1974) who extended the analysis historically and internationally. Frank argued that Western nations became modernized by exploiting other nations and that their continued exploitation prevents less-developed nations from becoming fully modernized.

Economic underdevelopment, according to this view, is not so much an original condition shared by all societies but rather it is created from the outside by more advanced societies. Frank observes that "the now developed countries were never *under*developed, though they may have been *un*developed" (Frank, 1966/1995). It was through colonization of other countries that Western nations became developed and non-Western countries became underdeveloped.

Essentially, dependency theory saw that more developed societies have put Third World countries in a state of economic dependency. These less developed countries are handicapped in their economic development because their economies are controlled by multinational corporations and the international banking community, which are located in and controlled by the more economically developed societies. Thus, while they provide the raw resources and the cheap labor required by economically developed countries, the less developed countries remain economically weak and exploitable.

In essence, dependency theory argues that the development of modern industrial countries is enhanced by, and in turn impedes, the development of the less developed countries. Dependency theory would argue that the major barrier to economic development is not the tradition or traditionalism of less developed countries but their economic domination. For broad-based industrialization and urbanization to occur, economic profits must stay in the countries where they are earned, so they can be invested and consumed there. As things now stand, these societies that export raw materials remain poor. This is so because the demand for such materials has remained virtually stable in that industrial societies have had negligible population growth. Also the dependency of the less developed countries usually prevents them from forming economic coalitions to enhance the economic worth of their products. Therefore, rather than being in economic cooperation with each other, they are often in direct competition.

A final point, and one that is crucial for my analysis, is that dependency theory observes that a dual economic system develops in these less developed countries that make up the Third World. One economy is modern and profitable; the one that involves the export of raw materials. However, the export economy does not provide either incentives nor resources for modernizing the rest of the society. Unfortunately, the other economy is the one in which most of the population finds itself. And it is in this economy that poverty is so prevalent. I will investigate the relationship of poverty to the family in more detail in a later chapter. For now, the following remarks will suffice.

Dependency theory is of particular relevance in its analysis of global inequality on those who are most economically vulnerable—women, children, the elderly, and families living in poverty. Modernization theory attributes Third World poverty to environmental deficiencies and overpopulation, detrimental traditional customs and values, political unrest, and inadequate technology. Dependency theory, on the other hand, argues that poverty occurs in less developed countries because of their subservient economic position.

Poverty in the less developed economic societies tends to be more severe and extensive than in the more advanced economic societies. Lack of adequate food, shelter, and health care characterizes much of the everyday life situation of much of the world's poor. It has been estimated that about 20 percent of the population—at least 800 million people—in the less developed countries feel the brunt of the devastating effects of poverty with some 15 million people, many of them children, dying of starvation every year (Macionis, 1993).

Women are particularly impacted by global poverty. Lynne Brydon and Sylvia Chant (1989) in their analysis of women in the Third World are critical of modernization theory and to a lesser extent of dependency theory for taking essentially "top-down" views of development (1989). In particular, they fault both in their failure to examine the place for women as societies undergo change. The failure stems from a lack of realization that women are not analyzed as a social group in their own right. They state that "those who suggest that women's status improves with economic development, frequently fail to take into account the widespread structures of patriarchy which keeps women in subordinate positions" (1989: 7).

Patriarchy is the ideology of masculine supremacy that emphasizes the dominance of males over females in virtually all spheres of life, including politics, economics, education, religion, and the family. Its worldwide pervasiveness is particularly acute in the Third World. In Third World countries women have relatively little political power. Economically, when women are not solely relegated to household work, they are often found in lower echelon jobs where they work longer hours for less pay than men. Land, the principal source of wealth in most Third World countries, continues to be controlled by men. Education is often seen as a male prerogative, and lacking education, women have fewer economic options. Women's role in religion often is of secondary or of little importance. And, as we shall see in much greater detail throughout this book, modernization, rather than significantly increasing women's independence, often results in and perpetuates their dependency and subordination.

CONCLUSION

In this chapter, I examined the post-World War II nature of interest in comparative family sociology. I began with an examination of the basic premises of structural functionalism, the theoretical perspective most influential in the comparative analysis of social change and the family. I argued that an inherent problem of structural functionalism is its basic assumption that social change is an "abnormal" phenomenon and detrimental to the functioning of the social system. This approach tends to reify the given social system, whether it is of the society or the family, and thus overlooks the inequalities that may exist within it.

Given the limitations of structural functionalism, it is somewhat surprising that it has been so dominant in American sociology. It has been incorporated with evolutionary theory into modernization theory. A main component of modernization theory is the construct of structural differentiation. This construct has been open to criticism for its tendency to view society as a mechanistic equilibrating system. In addition, modernization theory's use of Social Darwinist evolutionary theory has led to the biased viewpoint that Western industrial societies are superior to non-Western nonindustrial societies and to the deemphasis of the problems of non-Western and Western societies.

The most significant and important representation of modernization theory in the comparative analysis of social change and the family is William J. Goode's *World Revolution and Family Patterns* (1963). Goode's study is of pivotal importance in that it is the culminating work on both the strengths of modernization theory and its weaknesses in the analysis of family systems.

Goode's major contribution to the comparative analysis of the family is the comprehensive and systematic analysis of cross-cultural and historical data on the family. Goode attacks the hypotheses that see the family as a dependent variable changing as a result of industrial processes. Goode emphasized the interaction of family and industrial processes of change, which are both influenced by ideological changes and, in turn, are influenced by them. Finally, Goode proposed that in the "world revolution" toward industrialization and urbanization, there is a convergence of diverse types of extended-family forms with some type of conjugal-family system.

I argued that Goode's theory suffers from the limitations of modernization theory. Modernization theory has a conservative bias developed out of the use of an equilibrium model that tends to deemphasize conflict and social change. The framework was seen to suffer from a simplified conceptualization of traditional and modern societies, seeing them primarily as static entities. Traditional societies were viewed as being antithetical with modernization processes. This is a gross distortion; it has been countered with a new emphasis on how non-Western societies may incorporate their own social and cultural heritages with modernization processes.

Further, the biases and inadequacies of modernization theory were seen to be derived from its implicit reification of the societal order or system and a deemphasis of the individual. Or, when it does focus on the individual, it tends to have too much of a positive viewpoint that sees no tension between individual needs and aspirations in a period in which the society is undergoing major social change. I looked at the works of critics of modernization theory who were concerned with the manner in which modernization processes affect the way individuals see themselves and their roles in life. These viewpoints examine society and the individual in terms of processes of change as opposed to being static entities. Accordingly society is seen as composed of "active" human beings who are conscious of their world and who take an active part in constructing their social reality and social world.

Finally, developmental theory can be viewed as an alternative perspective that is particularly relevant for the analysis of the family in a world undergoing global change. It sees that the development of modern industrial societies is enhanced by and in turn has impeded the development of less developed societies. Further, dependency theory focuses on the impact of worldwide industrialization and globalized economic processes on those who are most economically vulnerable—women, children, and families living in poverty.

Essentially, in conclusion, in evaluating the perspectives put forward in the opening chapters of this book, we become cognizant of a twentieth-century replay of the ideological positions and arguments put forth by the Social Darwinists, the conservatives, and the radicals. In my earlier discussions of nineteenth-century theories of social change and the family, I examined the moral valuations inherent in these orientations. Modernization theory through its utilization of structural functionalism can be seen as the twentieth-century counterpart of Social Darwinism echoing the position of conservatives like Frederic Le Play. Likewise, developmental theory can be seen as a twentieth-century counterpart that shares many of the assumptions put forth by nineteenth-century radicals such as Marx and Engels.

In Part II, I investigate changes in the family's relationship with the larger community and with political and economic processes of social change. As we shall see, although the historical evidence seems to indicate that the nuclear family has been prevalent in the West for the last 300 years, there has been a fundamental change in the family's involvement with the world of work and with the community. In non-Western societies where forms of consanguineal family life have predominated, change is also occurring but not necessarily in ways forecast by modernization theory.

In Chapter 4, I focus on Western communities, with particular attention to the diversity of American families and changing kinship relationships. To provide a comparative perspective, I examine the family in sub-Saharan African cities. This is followed in Chapter 5 by an examination of ethnic-family group variations within the community setting. Chapter 6 is devoted to the impact of modernization processes and structures on poverty families, and it examines social policy implications for families living in economically deprived communities. The global view is that of Third World squatter settlements and of poverty conditions in Latin America.

II

FAMILIES AND COMMUNITIES

4

URBAN AND SUBURBAN FAMILY LIFE

Chapter Outline

Social History, the Community, and Family Change

The City, the Suburbs, and the Rise of the Private Family

The City and Urban Kinship Patterns

The Rediscovery of the Urban Family

Urban Kinship Networks and the African American Family

Urbanism and Suburbanism as Ways of Life

Urban Villagers and Closed Communities

The Suburban Family

The Dispersal of Kin and Kin-Work

Kinship Interaction in Nigerian Cities

Conclusion

Sociologists studying historical changes and cross-cultural variations in family institutions have employed various methods of comparative analysis. Social scientists of the nineteenth century used the evolutionary-progress conception of Charles Darwin. This approach was largely discarded by the turn of the twentieth century for numerous reasons: ethnocentric value judgments, biased and distorted methodological techniques, and erroneous theoretical assumptions headed the list. A contemporary offshoot of Social Darwinist evolutionism is modernization theory.

Another major approach favored by social scientists was the comparison of rural agricultural communities with urban industrial communities by using typologies, or ideal types, of communities. As I demonstrated, this approach was a direct outgrowth of the antiurban bias of sociologists of the nineteenth and early twentieth centuries. Their ideological biases were coupled with a strong distaste for emerging urban family forms. Ultimately, their values distorted their analysis of the phenomenon that they sought to investigate—the family in the city.

I begin the chapter with an extensive examination of the research by family historians who have taken issue with the conclusion that the history of the Western family was a movement from the consanguineal system to the conjugal one. Throughout this chapter the underlying theme is the diversity of the family especially as affected by social class. The reader should pay particular attention to differences in kinship involvement patterns that are articulated among different urban and suburban family groups.

SOCIAL HISTORY, THE COMMUNITY, AND FAMILY CHANGE

For the last twenty-five years, social historians have been gathering evidence that seriously questions the assumptions that the emergence of the nuclear family in the Western world is a post-Industrial Revolution phenomenon. Research on the historical European and American family system has convinced most social scientists that modernization theory, which postulates the historical existence of the large extended patriarchal family and its transformation into the nuclear family, is wrong. Now social scientists are reaching relative agreement that the nuclear family has predominated in Western societies for the last 300 years.

Most interestingly, their historical investigation of the size and composition of the family has led them to a research focus on the relationship of the family to the larger community. Family historians emphasize changes in Western society, a society that has seen the development of private life and the private sphere. The great public institutions of the society, including work and the community, are seen as being separated from the private sphere of social life, particularly the most important one—the family.

It is observed that this development is in striking contrast to the family's historical position in the nonindustrial and early industrial past. Historically, the family has served as the very foundation of social life and the center of the institutional order. There was no segregation between the family and the totality of the institutions in the society. It is precisely this change in the texture of private family life and the family's involvement in work and the community that is seen as the outstanding feature of the contemporary family. It is this change, rather than the transformation from the consanguineal extended-family system to the nuclear conjugal-family system, that is the distinguishable characteristic of the modern family.

I now briefly discuss the research findings that questioned the hypothesis that the Western trend was from the consanguineal to the conjugal family. Particular attention is given to the emerging position that believes that the general concern over structural and size changes was misspent. This position asserts that the new research concern should be with the examination of the familial texture of the nuclear family and its relationship to social, economic, and political changes in Western societies during the last 300 years.

I begin my analysis by looking at the important contributions of Peter Laslett and the Cambridge Group for the Study of Population and Social Structure. Their concern has been in examining household size and composition and internal family relationships. They have employed a technique of data analysis that has been given the name *family reconstitution*. Essentially, this technique uses demographic data culled from records of births, deaths, marriages, wills, and land transfers to establish lineages and relationships. The aim is to reconstruct family and household patterns of ordinary people who have directly passed down little information of their way of life. Although data on the wealthy and wellborn have been more readily available, family reconstitution is one way of retrieving information on people whose everyday life has heretofore been hidden from history.

Peter Laslett in *The World We Have Lost: England Before the Industrial Revolution* (1965) contrasts the small-scale, primarily rural and familial society of seventeenth-century England with the large-scale, industrial and urban English society of contemporary times. Laslett utilizes the family reconstitution technique in examining the household size of preindustrial England. Parish registers provided him with data on household size in rural English villages. His findings indicate that, although many English households contained servants, there was a general absence of extended kin; this data led him to conclude that the nuclear family was predominant in preindustrial England and to question the thesis that emphasizes the connection between industrialization and the small nuclear family.

Based on this conclusion, Laslett and the Cambridge Group used the family reconstitution technique and examined historical census data from a number of societies. Laslett posited a series of questions and dictated the methodological format based on census lists to provide comparative evidence on changes in household size and organization. Papers from the resultant volume, *Household and Family in Past Time* (1972), are concerned with the size and structure of domestic groupings over the last three centuries in England, France, Serbia, Japan, and the United States.

According to Laslett, research findings reveal that, except for Japan and possibly Serbia, household size has not varied to a great extent in the last 300 years. The extended-family system is found not to be particularly prevalent. Households contain nuclear families, with the poor serving as servants of the rich. Laslett reaches the conclusion that these findings support his earlier one that the small nuclear family was an essential part of these societies long before industrialization.

Studies of colonial American family life have provided additional evidence of the prevalence of the nuclear family in Western history. Philip J. Greven, Jr.'s (1970) analysis of colonial Andover, Massachusetts, documents that newly married couples were expected to set up their own households. Greven examined four generations of settlers in Andover, using family reconstitution techniques. His findings reveal the

Settlement of the Pilgrims at Plymouth. All members of the family participated in the building of the "little commonwealth."

control parents had over children through their control and ownership of the farming land. Although patriarchal control was reinforced through inheritance patterns and the availability of land, Greven documents how children prevailed and how the nuclear family predominated family life.

John Demos (1970) found the family reconstitution technique instrumental in his study of Plymouth Colony, the settlement founded by the Pilgrims in the seventeenth century. Demos examined official records of the colony and the content of wills and physical artifacts—which included houses, furniture, tools, utensils, clothing, and the like—to reconstruct family patterns. He sought to relate demographic and psychological approaches to demonstrate that the extended-family system was by and large absent in the colonial era.

Demos analyzed the structure of the household and the relations between households and the larger community. He found that households were composed of nuclear families, and the basic structure of the family and the roles and responsibilities of family members were essentially the same as the American pattern of the 1960s: Husbands were the dominating individuals in the family; women were given considerable authority in their own sphere of concern; and children were expected to take on adult responsibilities and activities by the age of 6 or 7—much earlier than in contemporary society.

The distinguishing feature of life in Plymouth Colony was the prevalence of nonkin-related members of households. The presence of these individuals in the household is explained by a different conceptualization of the role of the family in relation to the community than the one we have today. Demos uses a structural-functionalist perspective and develops the point that the range of functions performed by the family contrast strikingly with contemporary patterns. He sees the family being charged with social responsibilities that have subsequently been taken over by institutions specifically designed for this purpose.

> The Old Colony family was, first of all, a "business"—an absolutely central agency of economic production and exchange. Each household was more or less self-sufficient; and its various members were inextricably united in the work of providing for their fundamental material wants. Work, indeed, was a wholly natural extension of family life and merged imperceptibly with all of its other activities.
>
> The family was also a "school." "Parents and masters" were charged by law to attend to the education of all the children in their immediate care—"at least to be able duely to read the Scriptures," Most people had little chance for any other sort of education, though "common schools" were just beginning to appear by the end of the Old Colony period.
>
> The family was a "vocational institute." However deficient it may have been in transmitting the formal knowledge and skills associated with literacy, it clearly served to prepare its young for effective, independent performance in the larger economic system. For the great majority of persons—the majority of whom became farmers—the process was instinctive and almost unconscious. But it applied with equal force (and greater visibility) to the various

trades and crafts of the time. The ordinary setting for an apprenticeship was, of course, a domestic one.

The family was a "church." To say this is not to slight the central importance of churches in the usual sense. Here, indeed, the family's role was partial and subsidiary. Nonetheless, the obligation of "family worship" seems to have been widely assumed. Daily prayers and personal meditation formed an indispensable adjunct to the more formal devotions of a whole community.

The family was a "house of correction." Idle and even criminal persons were "sentenced" by the Court to live as servants in the families of more reputable citizens. The household seemed a natural setting both for imposing discipline and for encouraging some degree of character reformation.

The family was a "welfare institution"; in fact, it provided several different kinds of welfare service. It was occasionally a "hospital"—at least insofar as certain men thought to have special medical knowledge would receive sick persons into their homes for day-to-day care and treatment. It was an "orphanage"—in that children whose parents had died were straightaway transferred into another household (often that of a relative). It was an "old people's home"—since the aged and infirm, no longer able to care for themselves, were usually incorporated into the households of their grown children. And it was a "poorhouse" too—for analogous, and obvious, reasons. (Demos, 1970:183-184)

According to Demos, the family in America has increasingly contracted and withdrawn from social responsibilities. The central theme is the gradual surrender to other institutions of functions that once lay very much within the realm of family responsibility. The result was that the family became more isolated and detached from the community as a whole. Replacing the declining social functions, it now took on more important psychological functions for its members. The inseparable and indistinguishable facets of social life—family and community, private life and public life—were cleaved.

Thus, although Demos differs from Goode in his stress on the historical prevalence of the nuclear family in the West, he shares Goode's viewpoint (and that of other modernization theorists) on the predominant characteristics of the contemporary family. These characteristics include the decline in the functions of the family and the severing of the family's ties with the community, which has led to the development of the private family. This family form has turned inward; the home is seen as a private retreat. The emotional intensity of the ties between family members has heightened as the ties with the community have lessened.

The study of ordinary families through the use of family reconstitution techniques has provided social science with fascinating information on the historical Western family. Taken together, these historical studies have led to the questioning of the thesis of the emergence of the nuclear family tied to industrialization processes. The extended-family historians generated much controversy in social science. It stems in part from their overemphasis on structural changes in the size and composition of the family and their neglect of the emotional arrangement of the family. And, when they do look at the emotional texture of the family, they do so from an inadequate base: census data and household size. Critics (see, for example, Berkner, 1975; Henretta, 1971; and Rothman, 1971) question how we can infer emotional qualities of family life from the analysis of birth, death, and marriage records, or from household size and composition, or from the physical layout of the household.

A prime example of this criticism was developed by Christopher Lasch (1975a,b,c). In his caustic reviews of Peter Laslett and the Cambridge Group, he states his belief that their fifteen years of laborious investigations into the structure of the household have only established the unimportance of the question to which they have devoted much of their attention. He criticizes the "empty" findings of those who seek answers by looking at census data and exclude from analysis the emotional nature of the family. The position taken is that sociologists cannot describe the family solely in terms of size or structure alone; they must take into account the emotional dynamics of family life. Further, changes in the emotional character of the family must be seen in relation to the changes in the economic, social, and political activities occurring in given societies.

In summary, family historians have established the fact that the nuclear family has been prevalent for the last 300 years. These findings have convinced sociologists that it was wrong to identify the distinctive feature of the modern family as its structural isolation from the larger extended-kinship structure. The new position that has emerged believes that the modernization of the family can best be understood in terms of changes in nuclear-family values and orientations and in the changing involvement of the family with work and the community.

Tamara K. Hareven (1971), picking up on John Demos' findings on the family's relationship to the community, has observed that the modernization of the family can be better estimated in terms of household membership. Modernization involves the gradual withdrawal of nonkin-related individuals from the household. As we have seen, extended kin were never present in significant numbers in the household. Family historians have provided the evidence on the relative nonimportance of extended kin in everyday household activities. They have also revealed the importance of nonkin-related individuals in the household. The involvement of the latter in the household reflect the different conceptualizations of the ideology of the nuclear family over the last 300 years. It is the implications of this fact that should have been studied but were not.

Unfortunately, too often family historians got caught up in asking structural questions on the size and composition of families within households in their attempt to investigate the thesis on the transformation of the Western family from extended to nuclear. They further confused the issue by failing to distinguish between *household* composition and *family* composition. They did not give proper attention to the fact that members of the same family may not live in the same household, nor are households restricted to only family members. The absence of extended kin in the household led them to dismiss the thesis of structural changes in the family, but they ignored the involvement of nuclear families with extended kin outside the household. Nuclear families were intertwined with a network of relatives, all residing in the same community. Further, although extended kin did not reside in the household, this did not mean that the nuclear family was not involved with them or that they had no influence on them.

Although the majority of households studied historically were composed of nuclear families, they did not conform to the characteristics of the conjugal family described in modernization studies by sociologists such as William J. Goode. The historical Western European and American nuclear family was not a conjugal family. It was not intimate and did not encourage domesticity or privacy. It was neither detached from the community nor highly mobile, either socially or geographically. The overemphasis on family-structure variables, that is, from extended family to nuclear family, obfuscated the variations in orientations and values of the historical nuclear family.

Why did this transformation take place? Why did the personal life in the eighteenth and nineteenth centuries move toward privatization and domesticity? Why is the significance in the change of the historical family seen not so much in terms of size and composition of the household but in the detachment of the nuclear family from the outside world? Why did the family develop an ideology that saw it as the center for emotional support and gratification? What were the implications of these changes for the family, for the husband, for the wife, and for the children? How successful has the family been in becoming a private institution? I have only briefly sketched out some of the answers so far. The answers to these historical questions on the Western family will be examined in greater detail in this and ensuing chapters.

THE CITY, THE SUBURBS, AND THE RISE OF THE PRIVATE FAMILY

To help answer some of the questions just posed let me now return to a theme that I introduced in the first part of this book. Family sociologists have emphasized that changes in Western society resulted in the gradual separation of the public institution of work and community from the private sphere of the family. Middle-class family life in America since the nineteenth century has been distinguished by this removal from the community setting. This fact can be best examined through an analysis of the development of the American suburbs as a reaction against the perceived deterioration of family life in the city. In my discussion I follow the model developed by Kenneth T. Jackson (1985) in his important work, *Crabgrass Frontier: The Suburbanization of the United States*.

Between 1820 and 1920, there was a major social and cultural revolution transforming American life. The small town agrarian society was rapidly giving way to the emergence of a vast industrial urban society. Further, this new society was being populated by two major waves of immigrants that differed remarkably from the predominant England-derived population and from each other. The first wave of immigrants began arriving in the 1830s, and for the next fifty years, in addition to those who came from England, many came from Ireland, Germany, and Scandinavia. This wave was soon followed by a second wave of equal duration coming from Eastern and Southern Europe and comprised in main part of Poles, Italians, Greeks, Slavs, and Jews.

Many of these immigrants, especially the Irish from the first wave and almost all the others from the second wave, moved to the job-rich urban centers and by so doing, dramatically transformed not only these cities but the country itself. For the descendants of the original English immigrants, especially, those in the emerging

American middle class and those even more affluent, the city became the symbol of the new America. And, that symbol often was fraught with danger of the unknown paths that the future of city life would take.

As these changes began in the second third of the nineteenth century, the growing industrial cities of the United States began to be perceived by many as a place to be feared. The city was depicted as the site of sinfulness and greed. The antidote was seen in the family and the virtues of domestic life. This was a reaction to the new roles taken by men and women in adapting to industrial life.

The growth of manufacturing meant that men left the home for outside work sites. For the more affluent families, wives did not work in the paid labor force. The residence soon became their sole responsibility. As a consequence, the husband and wife relationship assumed the "traditional" division of labor that we for so long took as a given. The men's sphere was tied to paid work, and the women's sphere was tied to the home and children. Furthermore, this sphere came to be regarded as morally superior. It was during this period that the "cult of domesticity" developed, anchored by what Barbara Welter (1966) has called the "Cult of True Womanhood." Four cardinal virtues—piety, purity, submissiveness, and domesticity—were tied to the idealization of feminine roles of mother, daughter, sister, and wife.

During this period women's magazines and religious pronouncements began extolling the virtues of domesticity, privacy, and isolation. Ministers such as the Reverend William G. Eliot preached to a female audience in 1853: "The foundation of our free institutions is in our love, as a people, for our homes. The strength of our country is found in the declaration that all men are free and equal, but in the quiet influence of the fireside, the bonds which unite together in the family circle. The corner-stone of our republic is the hearth-stone" (cited in Jackson, 1985:48).

The song "Home, Sweet Home," came to be the most widely sung lyric of the period (Jackson, 1985). The song, written in 1823, gives an account of the wishfulness of a wanderer yearning for his childhood home—a theme quite appropriate to a society undergoing major changes. Christopher Lasch (1977a) refers to the home as a sought "Haven in a Heartless World." It is here that the privatization of the family could occur, and it is here that the home could serve as a refuge and a private retreat. The home would serve as the center for the development of a new form of emotional intensity between husband and wife and parents and children. The home was also seen as the ideal site for women to pursue their god-given destiny as wives, mothers, and homemakers.

Further, the ideal site for the private home was seen as being the suburb, not the city. Kenneth T. Jackson provides an historical overview of the development of the private family ideology and the suburbanization of the United States. He documents how "the suburban ideal of a detached dwelling in a semirural setting was related to an emerging distinction between 'Gemeinschaft,' the primary face-to-face relationships of home and family, and 'Gesellschaft': the impersonal and sometimes hostile outside society" (Jackson, 1985: 46).

The nineteenth century ideology of female domesticity was wedded to the ideology that glorified the sanctity of the home. The ideal setting for both was the middle-class suburb. The city was reviled as the setting for infamy and anonymity; the suburb, with its green spaces and clean air, was the setting that women could provide the proper wholesome and moral atmosphere to raise children (Palen, 1995).

In an era when activities were divided between men's and women's spheres, the city was Gomorrah—a world of men, factories, crowding, and vice. The suburban home by contrast, was sacred space in which, under the wife's tutelage, men would be encouraged to become more civilized and children would be raised in health and virtue. (Palen, 1995:153)

I will be devoting considerably more attention to the development and articulation of the "dual spheres" ideology and its implications for male and female gender and family roles throughout this book. For now, however, let us make note of the fact that the privatized home located in the privatized middle-class suburb became the American ideal. But what of those who remained in the city? Let us turn our attention now to the nature of family and kinship relationships in the city.

THE CITY AND URBAN KINSHIP PATTERNS

Was city life as destructive to family life as those who chose to leave the city for the suburbs thought? How had urban industrial society altered kinship solidarity? Earlier, I observed that Peter Laslett and others concerned with household structure thought that they found the answer in its composition of kin and nonkin. But, as I pointed out, household composition does not tell us about the nature of relations with kin. The concentration on the household restricted the definition of the functions of the family and overlooked functions of extended-family members who resided outside the household. This misguided emphasis, in turn, inadvertently reinforced the myth of the "isolated nuclear family" in modern urban society.

The contention put forward by sociologists such as Talcott Parsons and William Goode was that the family had to change to meet the needs of the industrial system, which required a mobile labor force that was detached from rigid rules and economically irrational demands of extended kin. The isolated nuclear (conjugal) family was viewed as the functionally ideal institution to meet the labor demands of modern industry.

Historical studies have convincingly refuted the claim that industrialization destroyed the three-generation family and the assumption concerning Goode's notion of the "fit" between the nuclear family and the industrial family. One of the earliest of these studies was done by Neil Smelser in 1959. In that work, Smelser investigated the recruitment of workers into the textile mills during the early stages of the Industrial Revolution. He found that textile mills recruited entire family groups who served as work units. Fathers not only contracted for their children but also collected their wages and disciplined them within the factory. A reciprocal relationship developed between the family and the factory: The entire family was dependent on the factory as the employer at the same time that the employer depended on the recruitment of family groups to maintain a continuous labor supply. Smelser, however, concluded that the family worked together only during the early stages of the Industrial Revolution. He believed that by 1830, industrial specialization that included the development of new machinery led to the dissolution of the family as a work unit.

In a later study, Michael Anderson (1971) discovered that among textile workers in mid-nineteenth-century Preston—an industrial city in Lancashire, England—recruitment of family units into the textile industry still occurred. Especially intriguing is Anderson's finding that there was a higher incidence of three-generation families (involving older, often widowed parents) in Preston than in the surrounding rural countryside. He argued that these people were important economic assets, assisting in such matters as child care, that allowed the mother to do industrial work. Anderson stressed the survival of vital kinship ties and the continuity of kinship roles in migration and adaptation to industrial life, seeing these ties as viable because of the reciprocal services performed by the three-generational family members.

Tamara Hareven's research on workers at the Amoskeag mill in Manchester, New Hampshire, during the opening years of the twentieth century extends the period that reciprocal extended nuclear-family ties predominated. She states that extended nuclear-family ties were not only important at the onset of industrialization, but also were very useful in the subsequent adaptation of migrants to the industrial setting. In Amoskeag, the largest textile mill in the world at the time, kinship provided an important element in the recruitment of workers from Canada and in the organization of mill work itself. The French-Canadian immigrants initially carried over kinship ties and traditional practices of kin assistance in Manchester and subsequently adapted them and continued to provide aid and assistance to each other during periods of need. Hareven concludes that geographical migration did not sever kinship links:

> Geographic distance did not disrupt basic modes of kin cooperation, but rather revised and diversified priorities and modes of interaction. Under certain conditions, migration strengthened kinship ties and imposed new functions upon them, as changing conditions dictated. Kin affiliation in the new setting not only facilitated migration to and settlement in Manchester but also served as reminders and reinforcers of obligations to premigration communities. (1978:160)

In another study by Hareven (1975) of the industrial town of Manchester, New Hampshire, from the end of the nineteenth century through the first quarter of the twentieth, she found that kin served as conveyers of individuals from preindustrial to industrial settings. They did not "hold down individuals" nor did they delay their mobility. Her research reveals that the kinship patterns of immigrant groups may be representative of a modern adaptation to new conditions. Kin relationships changed and were modified so that they could function within the industrial system, but such relationships were quite different from what they had been in their rural origins. Her findings led her to conclude that the ideal typology of city life and family life, with its either/or assumptions, might be a simplification of the historical process.

Studies of long-distance overseas migration during the mass-immigration period in America that extended from 1880 to 1920 also reveal that relatives on both sides of the Atlantic maintained ties and transmitted aid and assistance. We examine these immigrant family groups in the following chapter. But, for now, let us turn our attention to the post-World War II research that has documented the persistence of kinship interaction and mutual support in contemporary American society outside the confines of the nuclear family. In the remainder of this chapter, I examine research that questions the assumption that the city is antithetical to family life. This theme is also continued in the other chapters in this part of the book.

The Rediscovery of the Urban Family

Since 1950, a mass of empirical data has accumulated that questions the basic assumptions of theorists such as Louis Wirth and Talcott Parsons on the isolation of the nuclear family in the city. These studies have shown that viable relationships exist among relatives and that they constitute a family's most important social contacts; they also demonstrate that relationships with kin are a major source of recreational and leisure activities and that there is a considerable interchange of mutual aid among related families. The studies directly contradict the prevalent notions about the social isolation of the urban nuclear family and the underlying theme of social disorganization as a characteristic of urban life that leads to the disintegration of families and the alienation and anomie of individual city dwellers.

These studies of urban family relations in New Haven (Sussman, 1953), East Lansing (Smith, Form, and Stone, 1954; Stone, 1954), Detroit (Axelrod, 1956), Los Angeles (Greer, 1956), San Francisco (Bell and Boat, 1957), Philadelphia (Blumberg and Bell, 1959), Cleveland (Sussman, 1959), and Buffalo (Litwak, 1959-1960, 1960a,b) all provided evidence of the significant role played by extended kin in contemporary American families. Sussman and Burchinal (1962) summarized this relevant research and concluded that the urban nuclear family must be seen within the context of an interrelated kinship structure that provides services and aid in a reciprocal-exchange system.

They find that the major forms of help and service include the following: help during illness, financial aid, child care, personal and business advice, and valuable gifts. Social activities were found to be the principal functions of the interrelated family network. The major forms being interfamily visits; joint participation activities; and participation in ceremonial activities, such as weddings and funerals, which are significant demonstrations of family unity. These findings led Sussman to answer the posed question on whether "the isolated nuclear family . . . fact or fiction? is mostly fiction" (1959:340).

Sussman (1953, 1959), Litwak (1960a,b), and Sussman and Burchinal (1962) provide a theoretical explanation accounting for the existence of viable kinship relations in urban centers when the early theorists hypothesized that they did not exist. Whereas Parsons (1943) suggests that the isolated nuclear family is ideally suited to the demands of occupational and geographical mobility, which are an inherent part of urban industrial society, these researchers suggest that it may not be the most functional family type. They hypothesize that the *modified extended family* (a term coined by Litwak) may be more functional than the isolated nuclear one (see Figure 4-1).

Litwak (1959-1960, 1960a,b) found that an extended-family kinship structure existed in a modern urban center—Buffalo, New York. This extended-family structure differed from the classical extended family in that there was no authoritarian leader,

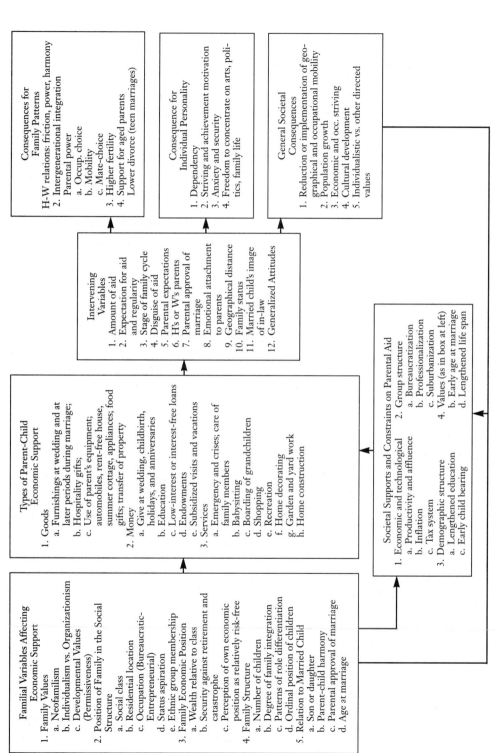

FIGURE 4-1 Functional analysis of parental aid to married children.

(*Source:* Marvin B. Sussman and Lee Burchinal. 1962. "Kin family network: Unheralded structure in current conceptualizations of family functioning." *Marriage and Family Living* 24:233. Copyright 1962 by the National Council on Family Relations, 1910 West County Road B, Suite 147, St. Paul, Minnesota 55113. Reprinted by permission.)

and it was not dependent on geographic mobility or occupational similarity to assure its viability. This modified extended-family structure consisted of a series of nuclear families joined together on an egalitarian basis for mutual aid. It differed from the isolated nuclear family in that considerable mutual aid is assumed to exist among these family members, and thus the family does not face the world as an isolated unit.

The question naturally arises as to how these later findings reporting on the viability of extended-kinship relationships can be reconciled with the earlier sociological accounts reporting the existence of isolated nuclear families and the absence of viable kinship network (cf. Hutter, 1970). William Key (1961) suggested that the hypothesis on the disintegration of the extended family was focused on the experiences of immigrant groups coming to the city during the period of urbanization in Western society before these immigrants had the opportunity to establish families. In addition, this period of industrialization was characterized by rapid change and great geographical mobility from rural areas to newly urbanized ones. The events that occurred in many American cities, such as Chicago, during the first thirty years of the twentieth century dramatically illustrate this point.

It is my contention that the earlier theorists, particularly Wirth and Parsons, did not look at the effects of the Americanization experience on generational relationships in the extended family when they examined the relationship between industrialization and kinship solidarity. That is, when they looked at that relationship, they did not control for the "transformation of identity" of family members as a result of their different socialization experiences—the older generation's European experiences with the younger generation's American experiences.

This belief is shared by Peter L. Berger (1963), who notes that kinship ties are weakened by social mobility when social mobility has consequences in terms of the reinterpretation of our lives. Berger argues that individuals reinterpret their relationship to the people and events that used to be closest to them because their self-image changes as they move up the occupational and ethnic assimilation ladder. "Even Mama, who used to be the orb around which the universe revolved, has become a silly old Italian woman one must pacify occasionally with the fraudulent display of an old self that no longer exists" (Berger, 1963:60).

During this first half of the twentieth century stage of industrialization and urbanization, then, social mobility was accompanied by differential socialization experiences that accounted for the "transformation of identity" of the younger family members and the resultant weakening of kinship ties. This period of rapid social change—great geographical mobility from rural areas to newly urbanized ones and, in the United States, a great influx of Europeans emigrating from their homelands—caused great social and cultural mobility and separation among intergenerational families. Once the descendants of these immigrants went through the Americanization process and emerged as ethnic Americans, their social-class differences based on cultural diversity became moderate and shrank.

Litwak (1960b) maintains that among white Americanized groups, especially those of the middle class, upward mobility does not involve radical shifts in socialization and, therefore, does not constitute a real barrier to extended family communication. Here, then, is one key intervening variable between social mobility and kinship solidarity—transformation of identity caused by differential socialization experiences.

It is because differential socialization experiences shrank among these studied groups that helps to account for the appearance of the modified extended family.

A further limiting aspect of the isolated family ideal type was its failure to take into consideration differences in class and ethnicity. The working-class extended family still served as a basic economic unit. It had a strong influence on the work and occupational careers of its individual members. Working-class and ethnic families banded together in their attempt to overcome their poor economic circumstances. The middle-class family with its values of privacy and individualism best approximates the ideal type of the isolated urban family, but the working class developed its own "modern" and urban family value system to allow its members to cope with the vicissitudes of urban industrial life. As we shall next see, the African American family also developed an urban adaptation form that took shape from historical experiences as well as from city involvements. It too differed radically from the isolated nuclear family model. Thus, within the same historical period there was a myriad of urban adaptation processes.

Urban Kinship Networks and the African American Family

The first part of the twentieth century witnessed a "great migration" of African Americans from rural areas of the South to the industrial cities of the North. Beginning during the First World War, when Eastern and Southern European white immigration was halted, approximately 500,000 rural southern African Americans moved to northern cities in the years 1916 to 1919. This was followed by nearly one million more in the 1920s. The depression of the 1930s temporarily put a halt to the migration. But, with the mechanization of the cotton picker in the early 1940s and another labor shortage precipitated by the Second World War, the great black migration resumed in even greater numbers. In a twenty-year period, more than five million African Americans joined their compatriots to the big cities of the North. Nicholas Lemann in his gripping account of this migration observes that this "one of the largest and most rapid mass internal movements of people in history—perhaps *the* greatest not caused by the immediate threat of execution or starvation" (1991:6). These migrants not only transformed their way of life, but in the process transformed American society (cf Grossman, 1989; Lemann, 1991).

Like their white immigrant counterparts (whom I shall discuss in the next chapter), African Americans found themselves in urban ghettos. But, to an even greater extent than these Southern and Eastern Europeans, their residential patterns and economic experiences were defined by societal imposed patterns of segregation and discriminatory employment practices. They were gouged for higher rents and were forced to live in segregated housing. Often they were barred from jobs by employers and denied admission into unions that controlled access to other jobs. When they got jobs, they were paid lower wages than whites. Yet, a majority of these migrants helped establish the black middle class, working class, and lower working classes in northern cities. For them and for those who found themselves ravaged by poverty it was the strengths of the African American family and its strong kinship support structures that helped them prevail. In this discussion, let us look at the African American family in these urban centers with particular focus on kinship networks.

The strength of the African American kinship system stems from its western African origins as well as from the extraordinary historical experience it has had in the United States. Niara Sudarkasa (1988), in a much cited article, provides an overview of African family and African American family structure as it developed in the political and economic context of American history. The cultural and historical importance placed on the extended consanguineal kinship relationship over the importance of the marital or conjugal relationship is seen to distinguish the African American family from the American family of European origin.

Sudarkasa observes that the most important properties in African societies—land, titles, and entitlement—were transmitted through lineages. Spouses did not inherit through each other. Women played a distinctive role in the articulation of family dynamics. Western African women were important economically; they were farmers, traders, and craft makers (cf. section on Kinship interaction in Nigerian cities, and Chapter 7). Decision making centered in the consanguineal family group. Polygyny also played a role distinguishing this nuclear unit from the monogamous Western model. The stability of the African family system was rooted in the extended family, not in the nuclear family. The socialization of young was seen as an involvement shared by the entire extended family and not by separated nuclear units. Overall, the emphasis was on the collectivity and not on the nuclear family.

Sudarkasa then sees how the African family dynamic was transposed under slavery. Citing Herbert Gutman's (1976) major analysis, *The Black Family in Slavery and Freedom: 1750-1925*, she observes that in addition to a fairly stable nuclear family pattern there is evidence that a strong extended-kinship structure existed. This system was integrated with a strong sense of community and interdependence. Sudarkasa argues that the extended family networks that were formed during this period and were carried to future generations have their source in the institutional heritage of African culture. But, "the specific forms they took reflected the influence of European-derived institutions as well as the political and economic circumstances in which the enslaved population found itself" (Sudarkasa, 1988:35).

In reviews of the evidence, scholars have observed that historically from slavery, Reconstruction, the Great Depression, and the Great Migration from the 1940s through the 1960s, a major source of strength in African-American families is the extended kin networks composed of grandparents, uncles, aunts, cousins, and adult siblings (Taylor, Chatters, and Tucker, 1991). Extended living arrangements in all socioeconomic statuses were found to be twice as common in African American families than in white families (Farley and Allen (1987). These kin provided economic as well as emotional supports. They have been pivotal, despite a history of racial oppression and material deprivation, in the remarkable resilience and adaptive capacity of the African American family to survive relatively intact despite severe urban conditions (Billingley, 1968).

In a later work, *Climbing Jacob's Ladder: The Enduring Legacy of African-American Families*, Billingsley (1992) reviews the literature and finds that the values of kinship and mutual assistance is a characteristic feature of family relations that encompasses all family income levels as well as both single-parent and two-parent types in both city and suburb. A fundamental characteristic of the African American family is love of children and emphasis on family cooperation. However, he points out that beyond such family values is the need for a caring society to provide opportunity structures. "The family, church, school, and workplace in dynamic interaction can become an ecosystem which surrounds, protects, and enhances the emotional, intellectual, physical, social and economic well-being of all our children" (Billingsley, 1992:333).

Unfortunately, for many Americans, including African Americans, the larger "caring society" has been absent, with devastating consequences in the last three decades. Despite its strengths, the support networks of African Americans has not been able to overcome significant changes in the structure and stability of families living under poverty conditions. These changes include declining rates of marriage, higher rates of divorce, a reduction in fertility rates, an increase in female-headed families, higher percentages of births to unmarried mothers, higher percentages of children living in single-parent households, and a larger percentage of children living in poverty (Farley and Allen, 1987). These demographic trends have impacted all Americans. However, they have particularly affected African American families. This story will be picked up in the chapter devoted to examining the family in poverty.

URBANISM AND SUBURBANISM AS WAYS OF LIFE

The preceeding discussions reveal that within the same historical period there was a myriad of urban adaptation processes. Herbert Gans (1962b) has represented the first and most important statement on these developments. Gans takes issue with the dominant sociological conceptualizations concerning cities and urban life held by the Chicago School, as well as with the definitive summary statement in Louis Wirth's "Urbanism as a Way of Life." Gans makes the following points: (1) Wirth's urbanites do not represent a picture of urban men and women but rather depict the depersonalized and atomized members of mass society—they are representative of society, not of the city; (2) residents of the outer city tend to exhibit lifestyles more characteristic of suburbia than of the inner city; and (3) Wirth's description of the urban way of life fits best the transient areas of the inner city—here, too, it is best to view the inner city as providing diverse ways of life rather than a single way.

While it is of some interest to note here that Wirth himself, in his classic article, referred to the city as a "mosaic of social worlds" with *different ways of life* including ethnic quarters such as "the ghetto" (a self-reference to his own work on the Jewish community of Chicago), he does not make reference to such ways of life in his definition of the city. Gans, on the other hand, builds on urban differences and postulates that there are at least five urban ways of life that characterize the downtown areas and vary depending on the basis of social class and the stages in the family life cycle. Gans uses the following classifications:

1. Cosmopolites
2. The unmarried or childless
3. Ethnic villages
4. The deprived
5. The trapped and downwardly mobile

The cosmopolites place a high value on the cultural facilities located in the center of the city and tend to be composed of artistically inclined persons, such as writers, artists, intellectuals, and professionals. A large proportion of inner-city dwellers are unmarried or, if married, childless. This group is composed of the affluent and the powerful members of the city. The less affluent cosmopolites may move to suburban areas to raise their children while attempting to maintain kinship and primary-group relationships and resist the encroachment of other ethnic or racial groups.

The deprived population find themselves in the city out of no choice of their own. This group is composed of the very poor, the emotionally disturbed or otherwise handicapped, broken families, and—in significant number—the nonwhite poor who are forced to live in dilapidated housing and blighted neighborhoods because of discrimination and an economic housing marketplace that relegated them to the worst areas of the city.

The fifth and final group is composed of trapped people who stay behind in the city as a result of downward mobility, who cannot afford to move out of a neighborhood when it changes, and who cannot economically compete for good housing. Aged persons living on fixed incomes and families that do not have a stable economic income fall into this category.

Gans goes on to describe a sixth urban way of life that is characteristic of individuals and families who live in the outer regions of the city or in the suburbs. He describes the relationship between neighbors as *quasi primary*: "Whatever the intensity or frequency of these relationships, the interaction is more intimate than a secondary contact, but more guarded than a primary one" (Gans, 1962b:634).

In the course of this book I will focus in turn on each of these urban groupings. It should be apparent that family relationships in the city will vary depending on which social class group the family belongs. The cosmopolites, professionals who are single or cohabitating, and those who are married but childless live in the city by choice. The city does not have the social disorganization character described by earlier theorists. Those living in the outer areas of the city or in suburbia, with their middle-class way of life, tend to live in single-family dwellings; more of them are married, they have higher incomes, and they hold more white-collar positions than their inner-city counterparts.

The poor and those trapped in the poverty areas of the city have no choice in where to live. For them, at least at first appearance, the city seems to be associated with all the characteristics of social disorganization vividly depicted earlier. Their family system also seems to take on all the negative characteristics of the family described by the social disorganization and alienation theories of urban life. But as we shall see in the next chapter, their family life structures and processes are much more complicated than supposed. Now let us turn our attention to the one remaining category described by Gans that I have refrained from discussing—ethnic villages.

Urban Villagers and Closed Communities

Among the city resident groups described by Gans, the ethnic working-class villages are the most highly integrated and tend to resemble small-town homogeneous communities more than they resemble Wirth's depiction of urbanism. Far from being depersonalized, isolated, and socially disorganized, ethnic, or urban, villagers (the terms are interchangeable) put an emphasis "on kinship and the primary group, the lack of anonymity and secondary-group contacts, the weakness of formal organization, and the suspicion of anything and anyone outside their neighborhood" (Gans, 1962b:630).

John Mogey (1964), in his essay "Family and Community in Urban-Industrial Societies," draws on the descriptive writings about urban villages in England, France, and the United States and develops a theoretical dichotomy between *open communities* and *closed communities*. The closed community is the urban village, characterized as one in which scenes of intense interfamilial cooperation exist; that is cohesive, homogeneous in cultural values; and closed against outsiders. The open community, on the other hand, is similar to Gans's depiction of the urban way of life of the cosmopolites, the unmarried, and the married without children. In these communities, people have voluntary attachments to a variety of associations and secondary groups. Families who live in these communities interact with individuals from other areas as well as from their own.

An open community has an in-and-out migration of population, whereas the closed community is characterized by relatively little mobility. The closed community or urban village has families who are acquainted with each other and have extensive ties with neighbors; in the open community, each family lives in relative anonymity and few personal relationships exist among members of the community.

Mogey states that the conjugal family is not prevalent in the closed community. No isolated nuclear family structure exists, since it requires an open community structure, with secondary-group relationships predominating over primary ones. Family mobility is also seen as leading to the abandonment of segregated family-role patterns.

Young and Willmott (1957/1963), in their classic study of the working-class community of Bethnel Green in east London, report that the extensive family ties, far from having disappeared, were still very much prevalent. They provide an interesting illustration of the extensiveness of family relations in Bethnel Green—the report by one of their children who was attending a local school. The child came back from school one day and reported the following.

> The teacher asked us to draw pictures of our family. I did one of you and Mummy and Mickey and me, but isn't it funny, the others were putting in their Nannas and aunties, and uncles and all such sorts of people like that. (Young and Willmott, 1957/1963:14)

A similar observation is made by Gans (1962a). He reports that the Italian Americans residing in the working-class community on the West End of Boston have a family system that shares some of the characteristics of the modified extended family and the classical extended family. Although each of the households is nuclear—composed of husband, wife, and children—there are extended family ties.

> But although households are nuclear or expanded, the family itself is still closer to the extended type. It is not an economic unity, however, for there are few opportunities for people to work together in commercial or manufacturing activities. The extended family actually functions best as a social circle, in

which relatives who share the same interests and who are otherwise compatible enjoy each other's company. Members of the family circle also offer advice
and other help on everyday problems. There are some limits to this aid, however, especially if the individual being helped does not reciprocate. (Gans,
1962a:46)

Mogey describes the impact of the closed community on mantel roles as one characterized by husbands and wives each performing a separate set of tasks. The wife is in
charge of household tasks and child raising, the husband is primarily responsible for
being the breadwinner. Leisure-time activities are similarly segregated. In times of
emergency, aid for either the husband or wife is provided by same-sex relatives. Within families with segregation-role patterns, mother-daughter relations tend to be
stronger than father-son relations. This is particularly true when the husband has
moved his residence at the time of marriage to the street of the wife's mother. Both
Gans (1962a) as well as Young and Willmott (1957/1963) report that a particularly
strong relationship exists between married daughter and mother:

> Marriage divides the sexes into their distinctive roles, and so strengthens the
> relationship between the daughter and the mother who has been through it
> before. The old proverb applies:
>
> > My son's a man till he gets him a wife, My daughter's a daughter all
> > her life.
>
> The daughter continues to live near her mother. She is a member of her
> extended family. She receives advice and support from her in the great per-
> sonal crisis and on the small domestic occasions. They share so much and
> give such help to each other because, in their women's world, they have the
> same functions of caring for home and bringing up children. (Young and
> Willmott, 1957/1963:61)

Of particular importance to the Italian Americans of Boston are the peer-group
relations with friends and kin of the same generation. Social gatherings of married adults
do not revolve around occupational roles as they do among the middle class, but rather
among the same-age kin and longstanding friends. Social gatherings tend to occur regularly—for example, once a week to play cards—and usually with the same people.
These activities as well as major family events, such as christenings, graduations, and
weddings, are all sex segregated—men staying in one group, the women in another.
    The working-class families are an adult-oriented family system. Children do not
have center stage as they do among families of the middle class and upper-middle
class. Gans reports that in the West End of Boston, the child is expected to develop
and behave in ways satisfying to adults. Little girls are expected to assist their mothers
with household tasks by the age of 7 or 8; little boys are treated in a similar way as
their fathers are, free to go and come as they please but staying out of trouble. Thus,
the children tend to develop a world for themselves that is relatively separate from
their parents and in which the parents take little part:

. . . parent-child relationships are segregated almost as much as male-female ones. The child will report on his peer group activities at home, but they are of relatively little interest to parents in an adult-centered family. If the child performs well at school or at play, parents will praise him for it. But they are unlikely to attend his performance in a school program or a baseball game in person. This is his life, not theirs. (Gans, 1962a:56-57)

Of considerable interest are the studies that report the effects of social and geographical mobility—from the inner city's ethnic villages to the outer city and the suburbs—on the family's way of life. Now, I would like to turn my attention to a more detailed look at the family life of working-class and middle-class residents in this geographical area.

The Suburban Family

Young and Willmott (1957/1963) contrasted the working-class urban village of Bethnel Green in east London with the upwardly aspiring working-class suburban community of Greenleigh, located outside London. They found that the migrants from Bethnel Green did not leave because of weaker kinship attachments. Rather, they left for two main reasons: first was the attraction of a house with its modern conveniences as opposed to the antiquated, crowded flats that pervade Bethnel Green; second was that Greenleigh was generally thought to be "better for the kiddies." These migrants left their extended kin in Bethnel Green with regret. However, these people were not deserting family so much as acting for it, on behalf of their children rather than the older generation.

The effect of moving to Greenleigh was a significant drop in the frequency of visiting relatives in Bethnel Green, despite the close proximity of the two areas. Life in Greenleigh became much different than life in east London. In day-to-day affairs, the neighbors rarely took the place of kin. Even when neighbors were willing to assist, people were apparently reluctant to depend on or confide in them. For the transplanted Bethnel Greeners, their neighbors were no longer relatives with whom they could share the intimacies of daily life. This had a particularly strong impact on wives, who were no longer in daily contact with their mothers and sisters; their new neighbors were strangers and were treated with reserve. The neighbors did not make up for kin. The effect on the family was that the home and the family of marriage became the focus of a couple's life far more completely than in Bethnel Green.

Young and Willmott (1957/1963) conjecture that, since Greenleigh was a newly developed community populated by upwardly aspiring working-class couples, they neither shared longtime residence with their neighbors nor had kin ties to serve as bridges between themselves and the community. Young and Willmott believed that it would not have mattered quite so much in their neighborhood relationships if the migrant couples from Bethnel Green had moved into an established community. Such a community would have already been crisscrossed with ties of kinship and friendship; thus, one friend made would have been an introduction to several more.

A parallel study of working-class suburban life in Los Angeles by Bennett Berger

(1960) reached a similar conclusion to that of Young and Willmott. In Berger's *Working Class Suburb*, male workers and their families were forced to move to an outlying suburb when their automobile factory relocated. Separated from extended kin and their extensive involvement with them, these families had great difficulty in readjustment. They found that their new neighbors, even though they were much like themselves, did not provide the same support and social relationships as did their now-distant kin.

The impact on working-class wives relegated to spend all their daytime hours in their new "bedroom" suburbs had a particularly rough time in adjusting. The effect of the move of working-class couples from inner-city communities in Minneapolis-St. Paul to a suburban community outside the Twin Cities is a case in point (Tallman, 1969; Tallman and Morgner, 1976). This research was concerned with what effect social and geographical mobility had on couples who had lived in urban villages and who were intimately tied to networks of social relationships composed of childhood friends and relatives. It found that despite the considerable amount of neighborhood contacts established by these couples after they moved to the suburban community, the wives experienced a considerable amount of dissatisfaction and personal unhappiness and feelings of anomie and personal disintegration.

The wives believed that this resulted from the loss of contacts with their relatives and longstanding childhood friends in the city and the failure of the couple to reorganize their conjugal relationship. The emotional and psychological supports that the wife received from her relationships with her relatives and friends were severed by the move to the suburbs and this required fundamental changes in the husband-wife relationship to make up for this loss. The working-class wife who was very dependent on extranuclear family, primary-group relations was not able to make adequate adaptations to the suburban move.

> The disruption of friendship and kinship ties may not only be personally disintegrating for the wife but may also demand fundamental changes in role allocations within the family. Suburban wives may be more dependent upon their husbands for a variety of services previously provided by members of tightknit networks. In addition, the ecology of the suburbs makes it necessary for the women to interact with strangers and to represent the family in community relations. Such a reorganization can increase the strain within the nuclear family and take on the social-psychological dimensions of a crisis in which new and untried roles and role expectations are required to meet the changing situation. (Tallman, 1969:67)

Tallman's work suggests, then, that the movement from working-class urban villages of the inner city to outer city and suburban open communities necessitates fundamental reorganization of conjugal and community roles of working-class couples to the middle-class type that emphasizes the importance of the conjugal-role relationship. To support this contention, research indicates that the anomie and alienation characteristic of working-class couples does not exist to the same extent with middle-class families in suburban communities.

The study of middle-class families who voluntarily moved to the suburbs is a different story. Earlier in this chapter I examined how suburbia was developed as the antidote to the perceived deterioration of urban life and the haven in a heartless world for the privatized family. Studies of the middle-class suburbs of the post-war era report first on the motives for movement to them and second, the family life experienced there.

The study by Wendell Bell (1958) of 100 middle-class couples residing in two adjacent Chicago suburbs provides a vivid contrast to the working-class couples' experiences. Bell tested the hypothesis that the move to the suburbs expressed an attempt to find a location in which to conduct family life that is more suitable than that offered by inner cities; that is familism—spending the time, money, and energy of the nuclear conjugal family—was chosen as an important element of the couples' way of life.

Bell devoted his concern to probing the reasons that the couples moved to the suburbs. He found three themes shared by the overwhelming majority of new suburbanites. The first had to do with better conditions for their children, a finding similar to Young and Willmott's (1957/1962) Greenleigh couples. A second was "enjoying life more." This classification was composed of such responses as being able to have friendlier neighbors, greater participation in the community, and easier living at a slower pace than in the city. A third major theme was classified as "the-people-like-ourselves" motive. These couples wanted to live in a neighborhood where people were the same age and had the same marital, financial, educational, occupational, and ethnic status as themselves.

It is important to note that the latter two themes, "enjoying life more" and "the people like ourselves," were not given by the working-class couples of Young and Willmott's study of Greenleigh. The different social-class compositions of these two suburban populations account for these differences; only one-third of Bell's couples were identified as blue collar, whereas all of Young and Willmott's couples fell into that category. It is particularly relevant in Bell's finding that only 14 percent gave as the reason for their moving to the suburbs more space inside the home; this was the major factor for the Greenleighers. Finally, the fact that the Greenleighers all had moved from the closed community of Bethnel Green, as opposed to Bell's couples who moved from transitional inner-city neighborhoods or from the outer city, may account for the differences in their attitudes toward the suburban community and their neighbors.

A most important variation in these two groups of people is the overwhelming familistic orientation of the Chicago suburban couples. This familism, as it enters into the suburban move, largely emphasizes the conjugal-family system. This is indicated by the fact that only a small percentage of the respondents moved to be closer to relatives. In fact, in vivid contrast to the working-class couples described by Young and Willmott (1957/1963) and by Tallman (1969), several of the middle-class couples moved to get away from their relatives, a condition they considered desirable. In conclusion, Bell's (1958) findings support his hypothesis that the suburbanite couples have chosen familism as an important element in their lifestyles and, in addition, have a desire for community participation and involvement in neighborhood affairs. Both factors are absent as motivators for the blue-collar families of Greenleigh and the

Twin Cities and may be the crucial reasons for the instability and unhappiness of the transplanted urban villagers.

In contrast to the adult-centered life of the urban villagers and the transplanted couples in the outer city and suburbs is the child-centered orientation of their middle-class counterparts. Wendell Bell has indicated the importance of familism and the involvement of parents with their children, as opposed to their extended family; a similar finding has been made by John Seeley and his collaborators (Seeley, Sim, and Loosley, 1956) in their study of an upper-middle-class, outer-city suburban community in Toronto. Seeley reports that the focus in these families is on the children; close, continuous attention is given to them. Tied with this is the extensive involvement of the couple with each other, a condition that is not present to the same degree in working-class couples of the city and suburbs. The Crestwood Heights suburban couple of Toronto is characterized by intense interaction and exchange by all family members—the family is viewed as a refuge from the trials and tribulations of the outside world. The dominant theme is home-centeredness; family members are expected to ask for and achieve psychic gratifications from each other.

Willmott and Young (1960) report a similar pattern in a predominantly middle-class suburban community (Woodford) in England. The young middle-class couples see little of their relatives and do not depend to any great extent on the extended family for regular help or companionship. Instead, they create social networks with people of their own age in the community. However, Willmott and Young believe that although they have a larger circle of friends outside the family than do the urban villagers of Bethnel Green, their social relationships are not as closely knit nor are their loyalties as strong. The "friendliness" does not have the same characteristics in the two districts. In Bethnel Green, people are seen to take each other for granted based on long-term friendship ties; in Woodford, relations are not so easygoing. This results in sociability becoming a sort of how-to-win-friends-and-influence-people contest, with a great amount of superficiality and noncommitment—and with people leaving out some part of their inner self in the process. This corroborates Gans's (1962b) observation that the common element in the ways of life of the outer city and suburban family is quasi-primary relationships that are more intense and occur with greater frequency than secondary contacts, but that are more guarded and less intimate than primary relationships.

Gans's own work, *The Levittowners* (1967c) provides us with the classic study of suburban family life. Levittown, now Willingboro, New Jersey, located about 25 miles from Philadelphia, was one of three vast postwar suburban developments built through the application of mass-production techniques for the white lower-middle class by Levitt and Sons. Restrictive covenants against selling to African Americans were based on the notion that community harmony could best be achieved if racial, although not religious, homogeneity could be achieved by people who shared similar regional, class, and white ethnic backgrounds.

The majority of Levittown wives developed social ties with neighbors and did not feel the sense of aloneness and isolation as reported by their working-class counterparts. These people shared similar attitudes toward family togetherness—particularly on the attention given to raising and involvement with their children. While some reported missing relatives left in the city, most compensated through the use of the phone and on regularly scheduled family gatherings.

Gist and Fava (1974) have concluded that the vast literature on suburban family relationships makes similar observations. Finally, as with the research on suburban couples in America, Willmott and Young find that the area for intense emotional relationships for their English suburbanites lies not in contacts with friends, neighbors, or relatives, but within the nuclear family. The conjugal role organization of these families is home-centered; couples share in many household tasks, including the raising of the children.

The Dispersal of Kin and Kin-Work

A parallel theme regarding the relationship of family and community centers on the changing nature of kinship relationships among extended family members. I have been observing that the privatization of the family was the result of the gradual separation of the public institutions of work and community from the private sphere of the family. Middle-class family life since the nineteenth century has been distinguished by this removal from the community setting. The American suburb fostered this privatization process.

Many sociologists see the privatization of the middle-class family as antithetical to women's independence. More specifically, the spatial segregation of residence from home and the development of the single-family house led to the increased dependence of women on income-earning husbands. In addition, and most significantly, the house became the setting that required the full involvement of women. As Ruth Schwartz Cowan (1983) and Susan Strasser (1982) have demonstrated, women's domestic labor paradoxically increased with the development of mechanized techniques, for example, vacuum cleaners and sewing, washing, and dishwashing machines that were designed supposedly for efficiency's sake but in fact have set new housekeeping standards.

In addition, suburbia, with its low density housing community and minimal public transportation services, further increased women's household and domestic involvements. The automobile fostered the end of home delivery services for all kinds of goods and services, thus requiring that families own an automobile to perform these services. These new tasks including driving spouses to commuter stations, picking up and delivering children to school and after-school activities, and taking sick family members to doctors, who no longer made house calls. The automobile became "mom's taxi."

All of these factors impacted on the nature of community involvements and also led to the relative separation of the nuclear family from extended kinship ties. However, kinship ties, rather than being permanently broken and destroyed, have emerged in a new form. In this section I will first examine how the middle class has responded to the dispersal of kin and then on how the working classes have utilized a women's "kin-work" to maintain such relationships.

Claude Fischer, a sociologist at the University of California, Berkeley, has conducted an important research study (1982a,b) that provides information regarding kinship involvements in today's automobile society. Fischer investigated kinship patterns of almost 1,000 adults living in northern California. He was concerned with the geographical distribution of relatives deemed active and important in those individuals' lives; the respondents' social characteristics associated with their various patterns of spatial distribution; the nature of the interaction patterns that they had with kin who lived outside the household; and what factor distance had in shaping the interaction patterns.

Fischer described the social networks of "modern" California kinship as being geographically dispersed. Individuals were not necessarily isolated from kin, but dispersed kin were infrequently used as helpers. The type of specified aid included borrowing money, considering opinions for decisions, talking about personal matters, and joining in social activities. Those relations that were most viable with ongoing exchanges were most likely to be with parents, siblings, and children. Extended-kinship ties were not actively utilized. This dispersal of kin was greater for educated and urban individuals than for their less educated and rural opposites, and these educated individuals were least dependent on kin.

Fischer reasons that educated people lived further away from relatives as a consequence of a number of interrelated processes. These people may be participating in a continental job market that demands that they be highly mobile. (For example, college and university teachers often find that jobs in their areas of specialization are not regionally located but may be found throughout the country.) The likelihood of their living near kin is further diminished by the fact that these kin may also be well educated, so that even if they remain geographically stable, their kin may be mobile. A third possibility is that the value system of the educated may place relatively little value on maintaining kinship ties (a "modernity" ideology). Finally, they may be better able to keep in touch with and call on their kin than the less educated. In such circumstances, there may also be greater reliance on the telephone and mail to keep contact with kin.

Urban residents were also likely to have fewer kin living in close geographical proximity. Fischer believes that migrants to large cities, particularly in the West, may be transplanted easterners who have moved large distances. Another explanation is that people who reside in metropolitan areas are likely to have alternative opportunities for social affiliations—business associates, activities, and social worlds that would permit them to disregard nearby kin. Finally, urban residents, like their well-educated counterparts, may exhibit a "modernity" ideology that places less emphasis on kinship.

Overall, Fischer believes that modern American patterns of kinship may be limited to involvements and commitments with parents and siblings (family of orientation) and with children (family of procreation) than with other relatives. The ties with parents, siblings, and children may thus survive distance and competing social involvements with nonkin, whereas other kin ties may not survive. The result is a family form that is neither the isolated nuclear family nor the extended family. Fischer states that "modern extended kin networks are distinctive in being spatially elongated, in losing out to nonkin relations in certain regards, and perhaps in being more functionally specialized" (1982a:366).

Fischer concludes his work by asking how his findings might be explained. He outlines three fruitful areas for speculation: industrialization, culture, and technology. He does not feel that contemporary geographical dispersion patterns are a result of industrial or factory work; rather, they may have been generated more by office work and white-collar occupations. He reasons that during the rise and establishment of the industrial order, work and extended kinship may have been intertwined as scholars such as Michael Anderson and Tamara Hareven have argued. But during the period of growth in white-collar and professional work, there may have been little necessity to connect work and extended kinship. "Such jobs—in law, medicine, corporate management, academia, specialized accounting, etc.—have national job markets, tend to be insulated from nepotism and cronyism more than is factory work (although not as much as we think), tend to be filled through 'weak tie' networks . . . and have as entry requirements educational credentials which can often be most advantageously gotten by leaving home" (Fischer, 1982a:362).

The second area of speculation may be in terms of ideological changes regarding kinship structures and involvements. The emerging view may be toward tolerance, or even preference, for spatial dispersion of kin. The well-educated and the urban respondents conform to this belief in their expression of opinion that living close to relatives or seeing them frequently is not very important to them. But Fischer believes that this cultural value alone is insufficient explanation and, rather, it is more likely that it was stimulated by structural changes in the society.

Some of these structural changes that Fischer deems to have facilitated the geographical dispersal of kin may be the advent of rapid mass communication and transportation; that is, the telegraph and telephone, and trains, planes, automobiles, and so forth may be as important to dispersion as is industrialization, since these means of communication/transportation make possible dispersion without isolation.

Fischer cites an interesting study of rural France by Eugen Weber (1976), entitled *Peasants into Frenchmen*, to indicate how transportation changes can impact on kinship ties. Weber, in his chapter "Roads, Roads, and Still More Roads," discusses how previously isolated back-country regions were opened up by roads, rail lines, bicycle paths, and the like. These conduits to the outside world removed the necessity for the rural French people to remain in the village for either a day or a lifetime. It, of course, also removed the mandatory requirement for the individual to participate in extended-kinship networks.

Fischer concludes by bemoaning the lack of attention given to this topic by historians and sociologists and the potential significance that mass communication and transportation may have to understanding contemporary family-kinship patterns.

> It may be that, in our effort to understand the nature of "modern" as opposed to "traditional" social and personal life, of which spatially dispersed kinship networks are but one element, we have been too mesmerized by the dramatic sight of the "satanic mills," gargantuan dynamos, and seemingly endless assembly lines to give due notice also to the car keys in our pockets and the telephones on our nightstands. These mundane symbols represent dramatic changes in the material "givens" of social life, changes that alter the context within which people negotiate and manage their personal relations, including their kin ties. (Fischer, 1982a:369)

The historical changing role of the telephone in our lives serves as a lead-in to my next point. And that is that technology, while permitting the geographical dispersal of kin, can also serve to help maintain kinship ties. One technological advance that ran counter to the prevailing "more work for mother" pattern described earlier was the residential telephone. Fischer (1992), in a fascinating account, examines how the telephone was used by women to foster gender-linked social relationships and involvements. At the turn of the twentieth century the telephone was seen by the industry to be of great aid in the business world. By extension, telephone companies saw it as a tool that would help manage the housewife's household activities by ordering goods and services. It was not viewed in the way that it began to be used and continues to be used—for purposes of sociability, especially by women.

Fischer locates three sources that account for the fact that most people see the domestic phone as being in the women's domain. The first source was women's "structural position," that is, her increasing isolation from daily adult contacts as a consequence of her extensive involvement within the house. The second was "normative gender rules" where the expectation was that women would serve as the social managers.

> Both men and women commonly expect the latter to issue and respond to social invitations; to organize the preparations for group dinners, outings, church affairs, and so forth, and more generally, to manage the family's social networks—keeping in touch with relatives (including the husbands' kin), exchanging courtesies and token gifts with neighbors and the like. (Fischer, 1992:138)

The third source is "personality differences." Fischer contends that in our society women's greater comfort with the phone than men's is a reflection of their greater sociability. In summary, by the mid-1990s the use of the telephone for social contacts is not only taken for granted but is also used as the basis for calculating long-distance telephone rates, "calling circles of family and friends," by at least one major telephone company. "Circles" in particular are used by women to aid in "kin-work."

Micaela di Leonardo (1992) develops the concept of "kin-work" to refer to all the forms of work that include the "conception, maintenance, and ritual celebration of cross-household kin ties, the organization of holiday gatherings; the creation and maintenance of quasi-kin relations; decisions to neglect or to intensify particular ties; the mental work of reflection about all these activities; and the creation and communication of altering images of family and kin. . . ." (di Leonardo, 1992: 248). She distinguished kin-work from two other types of women's work so familiar to us all that we rarely think about them. The first is housework and child care; the second is work in the labor market. Essentially, di Leonardo develops this third category to distinguish between those forms of work that are tied to the paid labor market and those forms of work that are geared to the nurturance of children and the maintenance of family life. Kin-work is seen to fuse both the labor perspective and the domestic network categories of female work. The concern is with the interrelationships between women's kinship and economic lives.

Kin-work, like housework and child care, is largely an exclusive female work activity. Often women are more knowledgeable not only about their own family relations but of their husbands' as well. Citing cross-cultural evidence as well as research from the United States, di Leonardo asserts that kin-work should be seen as gendered-based rather than class-based. She attributes this to the ideology of separate spheres that often resulted in men's work activities with nonkin and women's involvements including the responsibility for the maintenance of kinship ties to fall within the provence of women just as child rearing and housework did.

KINSHIP INTERACTION IN NIGERIAN CITIES

I conclude this chapter with an examination of the relationship between kinship interaction and city life by looking at a non-Western society—Nigeria in sub-Saharan Africa. I do so to shed comparative light on urban ways of life. My main concern is to look at the profound effect urbanization has had on the family and to compare the adjustments, modifications, and new emerging patterns of the people in Lagos, Nigeria, with those that have occurred in Western industrial cities, particularly in the United States. In addition, I will be able to explore the validity of the isolated nuclear family theories of Louis Wirth and Talcott Parsons and that of William J. Goode's conjugal family thesis.

Nigeria, a very large nation on the western coast of Africa, is typical of the phenomenal urban growth pattern occurring in Africa. In particular, the urban centers of Nigeria are growing at a rapid rate. In 1950, the urban population was 2.4 million and, in 1980, it rose 480 percent to 16.4 million people. The United Nations estimates that the total number of urban dwellers in 2010 will be more than 94.1 million.

In Nigerian cities, as elsewhere in sub-Saharan Africa, the spectacular rise in the urban population is the result of a desire for paid employment, which for those fortunate enough to obtain jobs is many times higher than in rural areas. Cities are also the center for such important social services as schools, health facilities, potable water, and entertainment. For those migrants who do not benefit fully from city life, the hope is that their children will have opportunities not available to them in the countryside. As Thomas J. Goliber of the Population Reference Bureau points out: "Despite the squalor of huge garbage piles, abandoned automobiles, open sewers, shanty housing, air pollution, noise, and physical danger, urban centers still offer a glimmer of hope for a better life" (1985:28). The family system is an integral factor in obtaining this objective.

In the study of family and kinship ties in urban areas, a landmark research monograph was written by Peter Marris (1961), *Family and Social Change in an African City: A Study of Rehousing in Lagos*. Marris' aim was to replicate Michael Young and Peter Willmott's (1957) study of working-class families of Bethnel Green in east London, England, and the effect of the move to a suburban housing development, Greenleigh, located outside of London. As you recall from my discussion earlier in this chapter, Young and Willmott found that Bethnel Green working-class families were characterized by widespread cohesive kin groups embedded in a closed community with a strong sense of homogeneity and togetherness. The immediate effect of the move to Greenleigh was the loss of this sense of community, restrictions in contact with neighbors and friends, and a withdrawal of the husband and wife into their household's home-centeredness.

Lagos, Nigeria, the African city studied by Marris, is a city with a strong Yoruba traditional history that is being subjected to the demands of modernization and industrialization. The Yoruba have a tradition of nonindustrial urban residence while working in adjacent rural areas. Men are urban-based farmers and women are traders and retailers. Marris was fortunate in finding a parallel situation to that which occurred in east London; the central district of Lagos, which was inhabited by extended-family systems, was undergoing a slum-clearance disruption. Marris was concerned with comparing the family life in the central area before people were forced to move with the life of those living in the newly established rehousing estate. He was also interested in people's assessments of life in the central district before they moved. Finally, he wished to compare his findings with those of Young and Willmott's London study.

Marris describes the traditional Yoruba family as residing in a family compound based on a lineage that traced its descent from the same male ancestor. The characteristic pattern of residence consisted of a group of sons and grandsons—with their wives, children, and descendants—of the man who established the compound. Although they resided in the same compound, the members of it did not form a single economic unit; rather, each married man with his wives and unmarried children and any other kin for whom he was responsible (for example, a widowed mother or unmarried brother) formed a separate household. Each household would become an independent economic unit centered around the farmland the man owned.

In cases where the man had more than one wife, each wife and her respective children would form a subsidiary household within the larger one, with the mother as the focal point of the children's ties, loyalties, and affections. This, then, was the smallest family unit in the Yoruba pattern of kinship—the mother and her children. The mother and her children formed part of the husband's household; the husband's household, in turn, was incorporated with several that resided within the same compound under the dominance of a single senior male; and these lineages, in turn, were part of a larger and more comprehensive lineage residing in separate dwellings. Ultimately, the whole lineage became part of still larger social groupings, with members recognizing the bonds of distant kinship with each other (Marris, 1961:12-13).

The traditional Yoruba extended family was composed of individuals with strong obligations to give economic assistance to kin while maintaining their social ties within the customary residential unit of a compound based on lineage. The extended family recognized the authority of a single head, usually the senior male member, and concomitantly the status of each family member was defined by his seniority. Finally, family relationships emphasized the importance and predominance of the family group over the individual.

The large family compound described by Marris was becoming more and more scarce with fewer houses in Lagos under common family ownership or entirely occupied by an extended family. The separate household has replaced the compound as the predominant unit of residence. However, the vast majority of the residents of the central district of Lagos still have strong family ties with their kin. And despite the predictions of such sociologists as Louis Wirth and Talcott Parsons, "the households are not isolated; their connections branch out into the neighborhood, and their lives are still centered on the affairs of their family group" (Marris, 1961:27). Friendship and kinship networks are maintained by daily meetings, which serve as communicative interchanges to pass on family news and to discuss family problems. Assistance patterns continue, with regular sums of money given for the support of kinfolk; the feeling is that the needs of relatives assume first obligatory priority. Individuals, rather than being primarily responsible and having first loyalties to themselves or to their conjugal nuclear families, see their prime responsibility to their extended family. Marris observed that the extended family also serves as the basis for some of the voluntary associations individuals join to further their economic interests.

Of the families studied by Marris, two-thirds of them were Muslim, one-third Christian. Of the 126 marriages studied, 118 had a customary marriage solemnized by the consent of the bride's family, the bridegroom usually providing an agreed on monetary sum and ritual gifts. Although traditionally these marriages are arranged between the kinsfolk of the couple, 8 of 16 men sampled chose their wives themselves. Of the remaining 8 marriages, 7 were performed in church and one was a civil ceremony. The significance of this is that to be married in church places one under the rights and penalties derived from English custom rather than Nigerian custom.

Two-thirds of the householders in central Lagos were Muslim and half had more than one wife. Polygyny was also found in the Christian households but to a lesser degree. Polygyny is correlated with wealth and social status, and most important, more children are beneficial for the extended family system (Marris, 1961:47-49). There are also practical and moral advantages associated with polygyny. The Yoruba consider it wrong to have sexual relationships with pregnant women and women who are breast feeding.

In the polygynous household, the senior wife enjoys a privileged position and has authority over the junior wives, especially in allocating heavy housework. The junior wives, in turn, can benefit from this arrangement since the household can provide aid to them in times of need, for example, sickness. However, Marris observes that most women in Lagos do not prefer polygyny and that polygyny is particularly vulnerable to the precarious economic circumstances of the husband.

The disappearance of the extended-family traditional compound has led to the weakening of the extended-kinship control of the husband's family over the wife. This, combined with the fact that most marriages are no longer arranged by the couple's kinfolk, has led to greater freedom of the wife from the husband's lineage and at the same time has lessened the extended family's support, especially if some misfortune befalls the husband. Marris believes that the weakening of the traditional sanctions has also made divorce more prevalent than previously. This has led women to secure an independent income to replace the dependency on their husband's extended family—nine out of ten wives work in some kind of trade.

The greater independence of the wife has had an effect on the raising of children. In the traditional family compound, children were raised by all members of the lineage. Although kinfolk still care for each other's sons and daughters, the breakdown of the compounds has led to a lessening of this everyday contact. Grandparents still have grandchildren residing with them to help with the household chores, since failure of the parents to respond to such a request is a serious breach of familial respect. Although there is an increase in the number of women who set up economically independent households from their husbands and the extended family of their husbands, and although there is an increase in the divorce rate, children who live with only one parent may still see the other parent very often. The pattern emerging is one in which, despite the breakdown of extended-family solidarity, there are various accommodations made to maintain intimate and continuous relationships of children with their larger families.

Marris sees an evolution of the family resulting from the new urban patterns. There has been a gradual weakening of the extended-family system and an increase in the independence of wives from family control and the control of their husbands. New patterns of marriage and kinship are beginning to be formed with the outcome still in doubt. However, from Marris' description we can see that a variation of a modified extended family form similar to that described by Litwak in American cities was forming. Families related through kinship met to reassert common interests and fulfil mutual obligations such as caring for children. However, these larger kinship groups were not able to assert authority over relationships between husbands and wives. Marris observes that the reconciliation of ties of marriage and kinship seems a crucial issue in the evolution of Lagos family life (1961:65).

In contrast to family life in Lagos, a study of the rehousing estate outside the city highlights and accentuates the social dynamics of family processes and the dissolution of extended family ties. Here, families saw less of their relatives and the characteristic qualities of these relationships also change. Although in central Lagos the communal family compound was gradually disappearing, there remained strong vestiges of the extended family. In the rehousing development, extended-family ties are disappearing; individuals find it more difficult to visit their relatives and to fulfill their familial obligations:

> We used to see them almost every day when we were in Lagos, sometimes two or three times. But they don't come because of the transport, and they think this place is far.
>
> The slum clearance has scattered us. Apart from those of the same father and mother, I don't see my family again. All other family is scattered . . . some of them have gone to the bush of their villages. I've not been able to see some of my family for two years, and I don't even know where they are.
>
> I don't see my sister at all unless I force myself there. If you don't go to see them they don't come. Sometimes I visit them four times before they come—they don't like this side. They have to change bus six times.
>
> When I was in Lagos they were with me. We lived in the same street. Old wife's family, new wife's family, we see each other every day. In Lagos you see everybody nearly every day. Do you see any of my family visiting me here?
>
> On Saturday I made 5s gain, and I ran to see my mother. I've not seen her since Saturday, and God knows when I shall see her again. She wept when I was to leave, because she didn't want to leave me, and she is afraid to come here. When I was in Lagos there was not a day I don't see her. (Marris, 1961:110-111)

Marris asserts that for some of the young married couples moving to the rehousing estate was a welcome occurrence as they became more independent from extended kin. Three main reasons were delineated: (1) They were able to free themselves from the controls of their elders; (2) they were free from the quarrels between wives and mothers, which divided their loyalties; and (3) they were free from the continual demands of extended kin for monetary aid. [The reader will be aware of the motivational similarities of these people with those of middle-class Americans who moved from the city to outer city and suburban areas in the United States (Bell, 1958).] The Nigerians who welcomed this change tended to be Christian rather than Muslim, Ibo rather than Yoruba. Marris suggests that their occupations—many were civil servants—provided with governmental security and prospective old-age pensions allowed them to be less dependent on their extended kin and thus helped them to repudiate the traditional kinship obligations.

However, the more traditionally oriented Yoruba who were forced to migrate to the rehousing development found their family life in turmoil—a similar reaction of the transplanted working-class Bethnel Greeners who were forced to move to Greenleigh. The increased costs of living in the rehousing estate led to the withdrawal of financial aid to their kinfolk and a decrease in their visits to them. The slum clearance scattered the family group. It may have pleased a few non-Yorubas, but for the Yorubas to be out of reach of their relatives was distressing. It was particularly disruptive for the elderly who had lived on family property and had been cared for by relatives and now found themselves isolated from them:

> "There's plenty of breeze and it's quiet here," said an old woman, who had been moved from her uncle's house. "But this seems to be a sort of hidden place—some of my family have never been able to find me here. And if you think of going to see them, you have to think of transport. . . . There's a proverb says there's no good in a fine house when there's no happiness. It's by the grace of God that you find me still alive. I've tasted nothing since morning, and I'm not fasting yet. The money I'd have spent on food has all gone on light. I handed over six and threepence this morning." (Marris, 1961:112-113)

In the end, the isolation of the estate led to an impoverished social life and disruption of the family, and it did not increase the self-sufficiency of the husband and wife. The greater expenses of suburban life led many husbands to send their wives to their families and distribute their children among relatives who could care for them. Further, the increased emotional dependence and intimacy necessary to cope with the loss of supportive extended-kinship relations did not develop, leading to additional feelings of dependency. [Again, the reader is alerted to a similar phenomenon occurring among blue-collar suburban wives in the United States who developed feelings of alienation and anomie as a result of the severing of their ties with their extended kin (Berger, 1960; Tallman, 1969; Tallman and Morgner, 1970).]

Marris ends his discussion with the plea that future city planners take into account the social and psychological needs of the populace. Drastic dislocations mean disruptions not only in economic activities but also in social lives; although good housing is a necessity, it must be provided without causing major disruptions in people's lives.

Despite the extreme dislocations of families resulting from the slum clearance of central Lagos, the overall picture of family life in the towns of western Africa continues to show the vitality of the extended-family system. These family systems continue to exist because they serve useful purposes for their members. Joan Aldous (1968) reported that extended-family and kinship ties are important in meeting economic, religious, legal, and recreational needs because of the absence of such services by the central government. As long as substitute institutions do not develop to satisfy the demands of the populace, the vitality of the extended family and kinship ties will play an important role in the urbanization of African cities. The continued viability of the extended-family system runs counter to the theoretical positions of such sociologists as Louis Wirth and Talcott Parsons, who suggested that the extended family would disappear in the urban milieu.

In a special issue of the *Journal of Comparative Family Studies*, two researchers shed additional light on more recent developments in the nature of kinship interactions in urban Nigeria. Let us examine each in turn.

In the paper by E. Adewaide Oke (1986), a sociologist at the University of Ibadan in Nigeria, the argument put forth is that although industrialization and urbanization affect the structure and functions of the extended family, the extended-kin group remains a dynamic and viable force. It maintains its importance by being highly flexible and adaptive in terms of the relationships between family and kinship structures and political and economic needs. Strains on the traditional extended family include the peer group, various religious sects, social clubs, unionism, politics, and ideology. These groups often demand loyalty to them as opposed to continued loyalty to the family. Yet the family continues to play an important role in the lives of its urban members. Frequently, the family sponsors the training of and securing of accommodations and work for the migrant family member. It also provides financial and moral help and mutual support among family members whenever needed.

The family member is able to balance potentially conflicting loyalties by being highly pragmatic. Kinship interaction is manipulated and varies with both situational and individual needs. The degree of interaction or involvement is influenced by the extent that the family member views the Nigerian kin system and interacting with other family members as necessary and important for sustaining the solidarity or continuity of the unit. Oke outlines five interaction strategies that are utilized by family members. The first, avoidance, is a common practice among upwardly mobile individuals who wish to minimize kinship responsibilities. For these individuals, it is only when there is a need to assert political power or when economic aid is required that efforts are made to coordinate family and professional responsibilities. One informant, who studied at an overseas university, married a foreign woman, and is now head of a unit in the civil service epitomizes this pattern:

> I have not disclosed my residential address to any of them (kin group), except my immediate brothers/sisters. If you do, they keep on coming every day. If I spend all my salary, on them, I'd still be in debt and they'll still complain—I

have never been home (his village home) since my homecoming or my arrival.
—And you know what, they are trying to get me a wife, despite the fact that I
went home with my wife. (Quoted in Oke, 1986:191)

The second strategy is selective interaction. The urban Nigerians who exhibit this
pattern interact only with those members of the kin group who are also living in the
city and who share a similar social status. They participate with these family members
in joint activities and provide mutual assistance. They avoid associating with kin who
are considered liabilities or potential embarrassments.

Inconsistency/flexibility is the third interaction pattern. This pattern is demonstrated by individuals who use the kin system to achieve social mobility and, once that
is achieved, they minimize their family relations. Oke tells of a man, Mr. Bayo, who
received a doctoral degree from an overseas university and upon his return became a
university lecturer. He did not interact with his family or identify with his native village. He avoided participating in monthly family meetings, although he continued to
pay his monthly dues. However, when he decided to run for political office, he became
an active family member, socializing with members of his kin group both in the city
and at home in the village. On losing the election, he reverted back to his noncontact
patterns. Now, once again, he is thinking of running for political office and he has
started to participate actively with his kin.

The fourth pattern is close interaction. Here, the individual is strongly committed to the extended family. The extended-family-oriented member often travels long distances to maintain contact with the family and social mobility does not diminish his
commitment to the family. Often, however, such commitment often causes conflicts
with his two lives—his professional one and his extended family one. The case study of
a personnel manager, Mr. Taiwo, who works for a large firm and lives in a respected
section of the city, is provided. He met his educated wife at an overseas university. Yet,:

Mr. Taiwo participates actively in all small activities by his kin group in the
city and attends every family meeting in his village, a distance of several hundred kilometers. His residence is now filled with relatives from his village.
Some are attending school; some are working. Seemingly, he is able to maintain these numerous relatives in a peaceful environment. But upon closer
notice, it is evident that he is unable to keep the peace. His home is often
noisy, quarreling and untidy. Moreover, the situation is causing some problems between Mr. Taiwo and his wife. With Mr. Taiwo, the family (extended)
comes first; and he has decided to meet all its demands. (Oke, 1986:193)

Oke believes that often these types of marriages end in divorce. The scenario follows this pattern. The urban wife often encourages her son not to respect the patriarchal family's authority. In turn, the husband's kin group instigates and initiates the
push for divorce and remarriage, often to an uneducated woman from the patrilocal
village. This woman would not question the extended kin's authority. Oke observes
that men who fall into the close interaction pattern are usually not as successful as professionals or businessmen. The desire to sustain family supremacy prevents this.

Those who are successful come from kin groups that have wealth or power to support them and their number is minimal.

The fifth pattern is relatively complex and refers to the extension of kinship ties to nonmembers (fictive kin). These fictive kin are usually people who are of the same social-class background or professional group. Kinship terminology is indiscriminately used by these people to refer to each other as "uncle," "aunt," "niece/nephew," and even "brother/sister" regardless of actual consanguineous relationship. The fictive kin perform many of the actual kin functions and are seen as a threat to the future of the extended family. They also do not make what may be thought of as unreasonable demands on the individual, nor are they burdensome. In summary, Oke emphasizes the flexibility and adaptability of traditional African family structure to explain its continued persistence in the industrial urban setting of contemporary Nigeria. Further, "Reconsideration of the adaptability, versatility and utility of the extended family will contribute to knowledge of social interaction, particularly the interrelations between the individual and the kinship group" (Oke, 1986:194).

The second study that has relevance for us here is a comparison of three Nigerian ethnic groups—the Yoruba, the Igbo, and the Ibibio—to the processes of industrialization. The author, Sheilah Clarke Ekong (1986), a member of the department of sociology and anthropology at the University of Ife in Nigeria, argues that the historical development of kinship in Nigeria has necessitated the development of alternative approaches to industrialization than those found in the Western model. The result has been alternative patterns to the Western one regarding urbanization and the transition to nuclear families.

Ekong is of the opinion that industrialization occurred differently among these three Nigerian ethnic groups. She refers to the variations as examples of differential "ethnic industrialization." According to this concept, industrialization is achieved through the utilization of the indigenous skills and customs, including those pertinent to the family and kinship, of the respective ethnic group. The Yoruba, the Igbo, and the Ibibio ethnic groups are examined in regard to their kinship patterns, the resources available to them, and their traditional occupations. These are seen as determining factors in their orientation to industry.

The Yoruba, as I noted earlier, have a tradition of nonindustrial urban residence while working in adjacent rural areas. Men are urban-based farmers and women are traders and retailers. The Yoruba are the most industrialized, and their industrial development has been predominantly urban-based. The Yoruba have experienced little disorganization in the transition to urban industrialization, despite the fact that the emigration of young men in particular has altered the character of not only the traditional rural areas but also the urban areas. The most pervasive reinforcing factor in maintaining kinship solidarity and meeting family obligations is the corporate descent group. Joint ownership and interest in both rural and urban land and residential housing is transmitted between generations. This ensures that landed property remains in the family.

Yoruba industrialization is primarily confined to small-scale family companies such as service-repair industries, motor dealerships, and long-distance urban transportation systems. These family industries have provided the impetus for the expansion of an entrepreneurial class among the Yoruba. It has allowed them to take advantage of urban land holdings and to manage and dispose of them to the benefit of the economic corporate group—the family. Ekong states that "adapting commercial ventures to preexisting kinship structures maintains continuity in kinship patterns. The Yoruba kinship system, therefore, has not hampered the processes of industrialization because no change is necessary in the orientation toward kinship and its consequent obligations" (Ekong, 1986:200).

The Igbo are less industrialized than the Yoruba. They traditionally have been a rural people with agriculture as the basis of their economy. Their philosophy encourages individual effort within a communal context and individual achievement with the necessity to maintain kinship obligation. They have not adapted their kinship pattern to industrialization or urbanization. In the urban areas where they have settled, they have developed a reputation of being excessively clannish or tribalistic. Their industrialization tends to utilize their indigenous skills and materials in the making of tools, iron, and brass work. These manufactured products are attributed to and demonstrate the expressive bond between kinsmen in passing down "family craft skills."

The third ethnic group studied, the Ibibio, have a very elaborate kinship structure and network that has remained virtually stable over the years. The Ibibio have a transitional economy based on subsistence farming and a philosophy that is inconsistent with productivity. The Nigerian state that they reside in has quite limited industrial development, and they have continued their primary occupation of farming in government-run plantations. Ekong believes that "although eventually the Ibibio may follow a path toward greater industrialization, the strength of their kin ties and primary group relationships, a philosophy that does not emphasize productivity, and an erroneous understanding of industrialized societies make industrialization at this time difficult and limited" (1986:203).

In assessing Nigeria's industrialization process, Ekong believes that the concept of ethnic industrialization is useful in understanding how various ethnic groups direct their economic activities to certain types of industry in accord with their own social, cultural, and historical development. She argues for the Nigerian development of national agriculture and industry based on the use of local products and structured to be consistent with the cycle of indigenous farming and consistent with established kinship systems. Further, she observes that the disorganization that is seen to accompany industrialization has been minimal in Nigeria because the kinship structure accommodates to the processes of industrialization and urbanization.

In summary, in this section, I examined illustrative cases of family and kinship ties in Lagos, Nigeria, a city in West Africa, and its relationship to urban family systems. My discussion sought to test the basic hypothesis of the urban sociologists who see family life in the city as gradually diminishing in importance, particularly causing the dissolution of the extended-family system and the substitution of the isolated nuclear-family type. Writing in 1963, William J. Goode shared this position: "If the new African nations follow the paths of many other emerging nations, the next decade will witness an accentuated move away from tribal family patterns, and toward a conjugal system" (1963:201-202). My research review indicates that the extended family system remains viable.

In examining the evidence, I found that in the African city of Lagos, Nigeria, the fundamental family pattern took on the pattern of the extended family. This runs contrary to the position of such social scientists as Louis Wirth and Talcott Parsons, who believed that the extended family form would be relatively nonexistent in cities, whether industrialized or not. Finally, my two concluding research studies provided further indication that the flexibility and adaptability of traditional African family structure explains its continued persistence in urban centers in Nigeria. This research also revealed that ethnic variations must be accounted for in explaining the diversity of kinship structures and processes as well as the extent and nature of industrialization in these cities. It is vital to understand the cultural context of the populace under study to predict in what manner urbanism as a way of life will evolve.

CONCLUSION

I opened this chapter with an extensive examination of the recent research by family historians, who have taken issue with the conclusion that the history of the Western family was a movement from the consanguineal system to the conjugal one. Family historians have emphasized that changes in Western society resulted in the development of distinct public and private spheres. The result has been the gradual separation of the public institutions of work and the community from the private sphere of the family.

During the early stages of the Industrial Revolution and through much of the nineteenth century, there was some intertwining of work, the family, and kinship relations. However, what was undergoing major change was the texture of nuclear family life. I emphasized the position that the modernization of the family can best be understood in terms of changes in nuclear family values and orientations. Thus, although the historical evidence seems to indicate that the nuclear family has been prevalent in the West for the last 300 years, there has been a fundamental change in the family's involvement with the world of work and the community. This change drew my attention.

I then compared and contrasted the different ways of family life of urban and suburban families. My particular focus was on working-class families of the urban villages (closed communities) and the middle-class families of the outer city and suburbs (open communities). In addition, I looked at the impact of the movement to open communities by both middle-class and working-class couples. I were concerned with the variations in these two classes in regard to their relationships with their communities and extended kin and the internal family relations of husband, wife, and children. I concluded the comparison by examining the latest changes in family life and involvement with kin of well-educated urban families living in a prime example of modern technological society, northern California.

In light of the previous discussions of the ideal typologies of urban-rural families and the position of Wirth, Parsons, and Goode on the relative isolation of the nuclear family system in urban industrial societies, we saw that the issue is much more complicated than it was made out to be by these earlier theoretical schools of thought. Urban villagers have a family life that is a combination of traditional extended-kinship ties and modified extended-kinship ties, whereas the middle-class family system tends to have way of life that is a combination of relative nuclear-family isolation (with emphasis on the conjugal-role relationship) and modified extended family form (which allows the conjugal family to take advantage of the extended family for mutual aid without giving up structural independence).

I speculate that in today's automobile society comprised of well-educated urban families, there may be a greater reliance on nonkin involvements, with kinship ties restricted to members of the families of orientation and of procreation. However, kinship ties can still be viable. This remains true to a large degree among the working classes. Even among the more affluent, kinship relationships remain as an important component in their lives. Further, it is women through kin-work who have the primary responsibility in maintaining and assuring that such relationships remain a part of family life. The diversity of family experiences is related to social class factors. Further, as in the case of African American families, there often is an interactive effect of cultural and historical factors with social class factors that helps explain differences in kinship and social network involvements in community settings.

I concluded the chapter by looking at family and kinship ties in Lagos, Nigeria. In this non-Western society variations in the articulation of kinship relationships in the urban setting demonstrate how sociological theory must take a broader global approach to be better able to understand the nature of families in communities. By using this comparative approach, we are best able to grasp the complexity of relationships in family systems undergoing processes of change in contemporary communities of the world. Rather than being "isolated," kinship involvements still remain an everyday part of so many urban family members' lives.

In the following chapter, the analysis of divergent family forms is extended historically. The concern is on cultural diversity within the United States. The changing nature of American families is examined by looking at the processes of assimilation and pluralism of immigrant family groups. In Chapter 6, attention is turned to poverty family systems that are located in industrial and nonindustrial settings in the United States and Latin America.

5

FROM IMMIGRANT FAMILY
TO ETHNIC AMERICAN FAMILY

In previous chapters, and notably in Chapter 4, I observed that most sociological research on the family has historically held to the belief that industrialization and urbanization have transformed the family in Western society. This position was taken to the extreme by sociologists who argued that industrialization and urbanization disrupted the traditional family patterns to the extent that extended-family ties had virtually disappeared and the isolated nuclear family emerged in its place. This position particularly categorized sociologists of the Chicago School, such as Robert Park and Louis Wirth, who were guided by an orientation that argued that industrial development and urban life brought about social disorganization and caused the disintegration of the family unit.

The functionalists such as Talcott Parsons and William J. Goode—while disagreeing with the notion of social breakdown and the declining social significance of the family—argued that the *isolated nuclear family* (Parson's term) and the *conjugal family* (Goode's term) "fit" the functional requirements of industrial urban society. In my discussion of working-class families in urban centers I observed that more recent sociological studies have refuted the claim that industrialization destroyed the extended family and the assumption concerning the "fit" between the nuclear family and industrial urban society. In examining the working class, I saw how urban villagers have a family life that is a combination of traditional extended-kinship ties and modified extended-kinship ties. In the middle-class family system, there tends to be a family system that is a combination of relative nuclear-family isolation, with emphasis on the conjugal role relationship, and the modified extended-family form, which allows the conjugal family to take advantage of the extended family for mutual aid without giving up its interpersonal and structural independence.

In this chapter, I extend the analysis on the effects of modern industrial urban society on family systems by focusing on ethnic families in America. I begin with an historical overview of the "new" immigration in the late nineteenth and early twentieth centuries of Eastern and Southern Europeans and their family experiences in urban America. By so doing, we see how these ethnic families adapted to the United States and how their current ethnic-family patterns emerged. To highlight my discussion of the "new" immigrant family, I look at Jewish Americans and Italian Americans. To round out my presentation, I also study two other prominent American ethnic groups, Japanese Americans and Mexican Americans. Of particular interest is the continued importance of extended kinship involvements as these immigrant families moved to ethnic-American family status.

IMMIGRATION: THE MELTING POT AND CULTURAL PLURALISM

The period of time from 1880 to 1924, when immigration laws placed severe limitations on movement into the United States, witnessed a massive exodus of people from Southern and Eastern Europe. This "new" immigration was from countries like Austria-Hungary, Greece, Italy, Poland, Rumania, Russia, and Serbia (now a part of Yugoslavia). Immigrants from these countries were joined by others from China and Japan, Mexico, French Canada, and the West Indies. In contrast, the peoples of the "old" immigration, those who arrived between 1820 (when federal statistics of origin were first recorded) and 1880, were made up almost entirely of northwest Europeans who came from countries such as England, Ireland, Scotland, France, Germany, Norway, and Sweden.

Immigration in the three decades before the Civil War totaled five million. Between 1860 and 1890 that number doubled, and between 1890 and the beginning of World War I in 1914 it tripled. The peak years of immigration were in the early twentieth century, with over a million people entering annually in 1905, 1906, 1907, 1910, 1913, and 1914. The main explanation for this massive movement of people to the United States was that the countries of origin of the "new" immigrants were experiencing population explosions and dislocations. By the latter part of the nineteenth century, the pressures of overpopulation, combined with the prospects of economic opportunity in the United States and the availability of rapid transportation systems that included railroads and steamships, set the wheels of world migration moving. Maldwyn Allen Jones, whose study, *American Immigration* (1960), has been a standard work on the subject, comments on the shared motives of the culturally diversified immigrants for coming to America.

> The motives for immigration . . . have been always a mixture of yearning-for riches, for land, for change, for tranquillity, for freedom, and for something not definable in words. . . . The experiences of different immigrant groups . . . reveal a fundamental uniformity. Whenever they came, the fact that they had been uprooted from their old surroundings meant that they faced the necessity of coming to terms with an unfamiliar environment and a new status. The story of American immigration is one of millions of enterprising, courageous folk, most of them humble, nearly all of them unknown by name to history. Coming from a great variety of backgrounds, they nonetheless resembled one another in their willingness to look beyond the horizon and in their readiness to pull up stakes in order to seek a new life. (Jones, 1960:4-5)

There was a great deal of variation in immigrant family migration arrangements. Some immigrant groups from Scandinavian societies and Germany came as nuclear families responding to America's need to settle and farm the vast lands of midwestern America. For these groups, settlement often meant the almost complete reconstitution of Old World rural village life and family patterns to rural America (Hareven and Modell, 1980). One extreme example of this practice was the Hutterites, a German religious group that lived in Russia and migrated to the United States in the late nineteenth century. They settled in isolated rural agricultural sections in order to maintain their distinctive family patterns, which included early marriage, exceptionally high fertility, and near-universal remarriage after widowhood. The Hutterite community was a highly cooperative economy ruled by a family patriarch that operated through kinship affiliations created by the high fertility and strict laws of intermarriage. This isolated group could and has maintained itself until today because of its ability to find marriage partners within the group.

As agricultural opportunities in rural America declined and the demand for skilled and especially unskilled urban workers grew, young unattached males became the mainstay of the migration population. The ethnic historian Thomas J. Archdeacon (1983) reports that in the decades between 1840 and 1899, males constituted 58 to 61 percent of the arrivals. By contrast, single males constituted 70 percent of the newcomers between 1900 and 1909 and 66 percent of those between 1910 and 1914 (Table 5-1). Data on immigration and emigration compiled annually by the U.S. Commissioner of Immigration reveal that the proportion of males to females did not take place evenly

TABLE 5-1   Family Characteristics of Major Immigrant Groups, 1909–1914

Group	Estimated Percent of Departures of Males Arrivals Within Period	Number of Males per 1,000 Females	Percentage Under Age 14	Percentage Married Males Ages 14–44	Estimated Percent of Departures of Female Arrivals	Number of Married Males per 1,000 Married Females
Czechs	5	1,329	19	36	10	1,453
English	6	1,358	16	35	13	1,157
Finnish	7	1,812	8	25	15	1,882
Germans	7	1,318	18	35	16	1,312
Greeks	16	11,696	4	29	12	8,643
Hebrews	2	1,172	25	36	3	1,258
Hungarians (Magyars)	22	1,406	16	63	38	1,968
Italians, South	17	3,200	12	46	15	3,181
Poles	13	1,876	10	38	16	2,695
Slovaks	19	1,622	12	55	27	2,659

Source: U.S. Bureau of Immigration and Naturalization, 1910–1914. *Annual Reports, 1910–1014.* Washington, DC. *Note:* Median annual observation except for estimated departure rate.

across the immigrant nationalities. Jews displayed the best balance with an almost fifty-fifty split; southern Italians, on the other hand, had more than three times as many males as females. The sex ratio among the Greeks was the most extreme, indicating that for every Greek female there were eleven Greek men. Commenting on these statistics, Tamara Hareven and John Modell (1980) observe that this obviously set limits on the possibility of Greek family life during this time period.

The ultimate success of an immigrant group depended in large part on its ability to reestablish a normal pattern of family life in America. This initially proved quite difficult. Common themes in the popular literature of that time were stories of wives forgotten in the old country and of families torn asunder by the clash of the old ways of life with the new. The editorial columns of the immigrant press frequently reported on the life struggles of its readers. Many newspapers had "advice" columns with the editors serving as lay clergy, social workers, friends, and relatives to those who had nowhere else to turn. The "Bintel Brief" ("Bundle of Letters") of *The Jewish Daily Forward* has become the most famous of these advice columns. Through it, readers wrote

---

BOX 5-1   The Historical Family

A Bintel Brief

Isaac Metzker (Ed.)

1906

Worthy Mr. Editor,

I was married six years ago in Russia. My husband had not yet been called up for the military service, and I married him because he was an only son and I knew he would not be taken as a soldier. But that year all originally exempted men were taken in our village. He had no desire to serve Czar Nickolai and since I didn't want that either, I sold everything I could and sent him to London. From there he went to America.

At first he wrote to me that it was hard for him to find work, so he couldn't send me anything to live on. I suffered terribly. I couldn't go to work because I was pregnant. And the harder my struggles became, the sadder were the letters from my husband. I suffered from hunger and cold, but what could I do when he was worse off than I?

Then his letters became fewer. Weeks and months passed without a word.

In time I went to the rabbi of our town and begged him to have pity on a deserted wife. I asked him to write to a New York rabbi to find out what had happened to my husband. All kinds of thoughts ran through my mind, because in a

big city like New York anything can happen. I imagined perhaps he was sick, maybe even dead.

A month later an answer came to the rabbi. They had found out where my husband was but didn't want to talk with him until I could come to America.

My relatives from several towns collected enough money for my passage and I came to New York, to the rabbi. They tricked my husband into coming there too. Till the day I die I'll never forget the expression on my husband's face when he unexpectedly saw me and the baby.

I was speechless. The rabbi questioned him for me, sternly, like a judge, and asked him where he worked and how much he earned. My husband answered that he was a carpenter and made twelve dollars a week.

"Do you have a wife, or are you single?" the rabbi asked. My husband trembled as he answered, "I have committed a crime," and he began to wipe his eyes with a handkerchief. And soon a detective appeared in the rabbi's house and arrested my husband, and the next day the story appeared in the Jewish newspapers. Then some good women who had pity on me helped me. They found a job for me, took me to lectures and theaters. I began to read books I had never realized existed.

In time I adjusted to life here. I am not lonely, and life for me and my child is quite good. I want to add here, too, that my husband's wife came to me, fell at my feet and cried, but my own problems are enough for me.

But in time my conscience began to bother me. I began to think of my husband, suffering behind bars in his dark cell. In dreams I see his present wife, who certainly loves him, and her little boy living in dire need without their breadwinner. I now feel differently about the whole thing and I have sympathy for my husband. I am even prepared, when he gets out of jail, to wish him luck with his new life partner, but he will probably be embittered toward me. I have terrible pangs of conscience and I don't know what I can do. I hope you will print my letter, and answer me.

Cordially,

Z.B.

ANSWER:

In the answer to this letter, the woman is comforted and praised for her decency, her sympathy for her husband and his second wife. Also it is noted that when the husband is released he will surely have no complaints against her, since he is the guilty one in the circumstances, not she.

1910

Worthy Editor,

My husband, _____ [here the name was given], deserted me and our three small children, leaving us in desperate need. I was left without a bit of bread for the children, with debts in the grocery store and the butcher's, and last month's rent unpaid.

I am not complaining so much about his abandoning me as about the grief and suffering of our little children, who beg for food, which I cannot give them. I am young and healthy. I am able and willing to work in order to support my children, but unfortunately I am tied down because my baby is only six months old. I looked for an institution which would take care of my baby, but my friends advise against it.

The local Jewish Welfare Agencies are allowing me and my children to die of hunger, and this is because my "faithful" husband brought me over from Canada just four months ago and therefore I do not yet deserve to eat our bread.

It breaks my heart but I have come to the conclusion that in order to save my innocent children from hunger and cold I have to give them away.

I will sell my beautiful children to people who will give them a home. I will sell them, not for money, but for bread, for a secure home where they will have enough food and warm clothing for the winter.

I, the unhappy young mother, am willing to sign a contract, with my heart's blood, stating that the children belong to the good people who will treat them tenderly. Those who are willing and able to give my children a good home can apply to me.

Respectfully,

Mrs. P.*
Chicago

ANSWER:

What kind of society are we living in that forces a mother to such desperate straits that there is no other way out than to sell her three children for a piece of bread? Isn't this enough to kindle a hellish fire of hatred in every human heart for such a system?

The first to be damned is the heartless father, but who knows what's wrong with him? Perhaps he, too, is unhappy. We hope, though, that this letter will reach him and he will return to aid them.

We also ask our friends and readers to take an interest in this unfortunate woman and to help her so that she herself can be a mother to her children.

*The full name and address are given.

Isaac Metzker (ed.). 1971. Excerpts from *A Bintel Brief*. Translation copyright © 1971 by Isaac Metzker. New York: Ballantine Books, pp. 50–52, 104–105. Reprinted by permission of *Doubleday Publishing*, a division of Bantam, Doubleday, Dell Publishing Group.

of their marital and family problems, the impact of poverty on their lives, religious conflicts in terms of attitudes and behavior, and other life concerns. The two letters reprinted from *A Bintel Brief*, edited by Isaac Metzker (1971), are illustrative.

URBAN COMMUNITIES AND IMMIGRANT-FAMILY SYSTEMS

Immigrants from Southern and Eastern Europe concentrated in the industrial cities of the Northeast and the Midwest because it was in these urban areas where job opportunities were plentiful and chances of success were greatest. By 1920, almost 60 percent of the population of cities of more than 100,000 inhabitants were first- or second-generation ethnic Americans (Seller, 1977). The immigrants settled in ethnic enclaves that people referred to as "Little Italys," "Polonias," "Little Syrias," and "Jewtowns." Each enclave reflected its distinctive ethnic flavor with its own church, stores, newspapers, clothing, and gestural and language conventions. The Chicago newspaper journalist Mike Royko, reminiscing on his own Slavic community background, recalls that you could always tell where you were "by the odors of the food stores and the open kitchen windows, the sound of the foreign or familiar language, and by whether a stranger hit you in the head with a rock" (cited in Seller, 1977:112).

Yancey, Ericksen, and Juliani (1976) explain that the establishment of immigrant "ghettos" reflects a stage in the development of American cities because there was a great need for occupational concentration as a result of the expansion of the industrial economy. Low-paid industrial immigrant workers were forced by economic pressures to live close to their places of work. The particular choice of residence and occupation was strongly influenced by the presence of friends and relatives in a

A series of photographs documenting the assimilation of an immigrant family: (left) The Gustozzo (Justave) family at Ellis Island in 1905; (middle) the Justave family in Scranton, Pennsylvania in 1927; and (right) again in 1954.

process that has been called chain migration. *Chain migration* refers to the connections made between individuals in countries of origin and destination in the process of international migration and to the process in which choices of residence and occupation were influenced by friends and relatives.

Networks of friends and relatives established in America maintained their European kinship and friendship ties and transmitted assistance across the Atlantic. Relatives acted as recruitment, migration, and housing resources, helping each other to shift from the often rural European work background to urban industrial work. A number of social historians (Anderson, 1971; Hareven, 1975; Yans-McLaughlin, 1971) have observed that nineteenth-century, as well as twentieth-century, migrants chose their residential and occupational destinations in large part because of the presence of kin-group members in the new area.

Chain migration can be seen as facilitating transition and settlement. It assured a continuity in kin contacts and made mutual assistance in cases of personal and family crises an important factor in the adjustment to the new American environment. Workers often migrated into the new industrial urban centers, keeping intact or reforming much of their kinship ties and family traditions. As previously mentioned, a prevalent practice was for unmarried sons and daughters of working age, or young childless married couples, to migrate first. After establishing themselves by finding jobs and housing, they would send for other family members. Through their contacts at work or in the community, they would assist their newly arrived relatives or friends with obtaining jobs and housing. In a classic work, *Old World Traits Transplanted*, the authors (Park and Miller, 1925) present a map of the borough of Manhattan in New York City in the mid-1920s (Figure 5-1). It depicts the distinct ethnic villages created in this city by *paesani* (countrymen) from different parts of Italy.

The fact that so many individuals came to America alone accounts for the fact that turn-of-the-century urban households of immigrants often included people other than the nuclear family. These people were not kinship-related but were strangers, boarders, and lodgers who for various reasons came to America alone and for a period of time lived with fellow immigrants. This practice of taking in boarders and lodgers proved extremely valuable in allowing new migrants and immigrants to adapt to urban living (Hareven, 1982).

The family can be seen as being an important intermediary in recruitment of workers to the new industrial society. Family patterns and values often carried over to the urban setting and provided the individual with a feeling of continuity between the rural background and the new industrial city. Immigrants tended to migrate in groups; often entire rural communities reconstituted themselves in ethnic enclaves. They helped recruit other family members and countrymen into the industrial workforce. Migration to industrial communities, then, did not break up traditional kinship ties; rather, the family used these ties to facilitate its own transition into industrial life. Tamara Hareven (1982), after examining the historical evidence, concludes that it is grossly incorrect to assume that industrialization broke up traditional kinship ties and destroyed the interdependence of the family and the community.

What is of particular interest to us here is that these findings on the viability of kinship involvements of urban immigrants in the early twentieth century provide additional and earlier historical support to the post-World War II studies by Litwak,

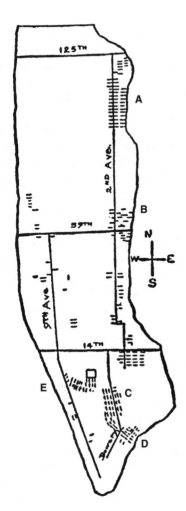

A. "Little Italy" colony from
     Piedmont
     Emilia
     Lombardy
     Venetice

B. 69th Street colony from
     Sicily, including the
     Cinisis group

C. Bowery colony from
     Sicily
     Naples
     Basilicata
     Calabria
     Abruzzi
     Apuglia
     Genoa

D. Chatham Square colony from
     Sicily
     Basilicata

E. Washington Square colony from
     Genoa
     Lombardy
     Tuscany
     Piedmont
     Venice
     Emilia

FIGURE 5-1   **Location of Italian ethnic villages in New York City, with sources of emigration from Italy.**

(Source *Old World Traits Transplanted* by Robert E. Park and Herbert A. Miller, 1925.)

Sussman, and others (who questioned the sociological assumption by the Chicago School that the city is antithetical to family life) and to the assumptions by functionalists such as Talcott Parsons and William Goode (who postulated that the isolated nuclear family or conjugal family best "fit" the needs of urban industrial society).

Poverty and Immigrant Families

My discussion until now has not focused on the severe problems that confronted the immigrant families in America. I do not want to mislead the reader in thinking that all went smoothly for immigrant families; that was far from the case. The huge influx of immigrants to the American cities gave new meaning and visibility to urban poverty.

Ghetto housing was appalling; ill-conceived and inadequate buildings were cheaply and quickly built to meet immediate needs, which soon outgrew them. People lived in overcrowded, dirty, unsanitary, poorly ventilated, and badly heated apartment buildings that were still expensive because of the demand. Boarders and lodgers were numerous and helped provide some of the needed money to pay the rent. It was not uncommon for beds to be occupied around the clock, with day-shift workers using them at night and night-shift workers using them during the day.

The horrible living conditions were dramatically exposed in the muckraking works of novelists such as Upton Sinclair, whose famous novel *The Jungle* exposed the grinding poverty of the Slavic communities in Chicago located within the stench of the blood and entrails of cattle being slaughtered in the neighborhood stockyards, and in the journalistic accounts of newsmen such as Lincoln Steffens, whose book *The Shame of the Cities* refers to the ghetto slums as literally looking like hell. The journalist Jacob Riis, himself an immigrant from Denmark, wrote and photographed the urban poverty of New York's ghetto life in his epic work, *How the Other Half Lives*. His graphic descriptions of the barren and filthy firetraps of New York's tenements startled the nation. The following passage from his book is typical of what life was like in one of these buildings:

> —Cherry Street. Be a little careful please. The hall is dark and you might stumble over the children. . . . Not that it would hurt them; kicks and cuffs are their daily diet. They have little else. Here where the hall turns and dives into utter darkness is a step, and another, another. A flight of stairs. You can feel your way, if you cannot see it. Close? Yes! What would you have? All the fresh air that ever enters these stairs comes from the hall-door that is forever slamming, and from the windows of dark bedrooms that in turn receive from the stairs their sole supply of the elements God meant to be free, but man deals out with such niggardly hand. . . . The sinks are in the hallway, that all the tenants may have access—and all be poisoned alike by their summer stenches. . . . Hear the pumps squeak! It is the lullaby of tenement house babies. In summer, when a thousand thirsty throats pant for a cooling drink in this block, it is worked in vain. But the saloon, whose open door you passed in the hall, is always there. The smell of it has followed you up. Here is a door. Listen! That short hacking cough, that tiny, helpless wail—what do they mean? They mean . . . a sadly familiar story—before the day is at an end. The child is dying with measles. With half a chance it might have lived; but it had none. That dark bedroom killed it. (Riis, 1890/1957:33-34)

In the late nineteenth and early twentieth centuries, as a result of the public outcry generated by the exposures by social-minded individuals such as Sinclair, Steffens, and Riis, and tragedies such as the Triangle Shirtwaist Factory fire (which claimed the lives of 146 people), reforms were directed to change the living and working environments of immigrants. These movements included tenement-house reforms, workmen's compensation, abolition of child labor, and protection of women and children in industry.

However, the pervasive poverty in rapidly growing industrial cities led many to the erroneous conclusion that it was an immigrant phenomenon. This led to the development of a wide number of social programs aimed directly in changing the immigrant families themselves. Social reformers created both private and public welfare agencies to help alleviate the problems of the sick, the poor, and the delinquent or criminal. Immigrant families and especially their children became the major targets for discipline and reformation and programs were designed to intervene in the affairs of immigrant families. The concern was to Americanize them into what they saw as the great American melting pot, where the cultural variations of the given immigrant group would be altered to the standard American way of life.

The settlement house, a private social-welfare agency, is a typical example of how some of these practices became articulated. The term *settlement* meant giving the immigrant newcomers the wherewithal to survive in a modern industrial city. Located right in the heart of the immigrant communities, it sought to help the immigrant families cope with poverty and improve their living standards. Settlement-house workers tried to teach English, American social customs, and—when necessary—the rudiments of household management, health care, and sanitation. They encouraged family-member involvement in work and household roles that often conformed to their own middle-class standards of family morality. When successful, as in the case of Jane Addams of Chicago's Hull House, they integrated their work without undermining the immigrants' native culture. Unfortunately, much too frequently, workers saw as their primary task the eradication of "non-American" cultural points of view and family traditions regarding marital roles and parent-child relationships.

Education and Immigrant Families

Education was seen as the key institution to eradicate immigrant cultures and achieve Americanization. For example, in the years before World War I, Henry Ford required all of his foreign workers to attend English school. For a five-year period, 1915 to 1920, the Federal Bureau of Education subsidized a Division of Immigrant Education, which encouraged school districts throughout the nation to establish special Americanization programs. The response was favorable, and many state governments provided funds for the education of immigrants. During this period and continuing afterward, numerous public school systems instituted night classes in which foreign students could learn English and gain knowledge of American government to acquire citizenship (Archdeacon, 1983).

For the Americanization of immigrant children, the school system became the primary vehicle to help accomplish this task. Education meant more than simply teaching proper English and the three "Rs" of reading, 'riting, and 'rithmetic; it also meant socializing children to American ways of life, habits of cleanliness, good housekeeping, nutrition, and social graces. Children were also graded on their level of acculturation to American values, as measured by behavior in school. State legislation was passed, making compulsory attendance laws more stringent to help insure that children were adequately exposed to the assimilative influences of the schools. Settlement house workers also played a role here by assisting in the supervision of school attendance and observance of child-labor laws.

To illustrate how conflict or cooperation could arise between an immigrant-family culture and an Americanizing institution such as the school system, let us briefly examine the experience of the Italian immigrant family and the Jewish immigrant family with the school system in the early twentieth century. Such an analysis can also emphasize the point that immigrant-family cultures were not alike and that immigrant groups often experienced different occupational and educational opportunities in America. A comparison of the profoundly different experiences of Italian and Jewish children in schools will document this. Different cultural and economic factors played a decisive role in their respective educational success and failure in the first half of the twentieth century.

The children of immigrant Jews from Eastern Europe were very successful in American schools. There are several possible explanations for this. First, while they did experience considerable discrimination, the Jews were not treated as a separate caste group as blacks were; they were able to pursue, for the most part, whatever economic activities they chose. Second, they came to America with exceptionally strong backgrounds in skilled trades and entrepreneurial activity (67.1 percent in skilled occupations for the eleven years between 1899 and 1910, compared to 20.4 percent for northern Italians and less for southern Italians) and established traditions of literacy (Hogan, 1983). Third, soon after they arrived in America, they were able to establish themselves in the skilled trades and manufacturing in a rapidly expanding economy. Fourth, they were able to take advantage of the educational opportunities offered them in urban centers. Finally, on graduation from high school and college, there were job opportunities in chosen occupations. David Hogan (1983), in commenting on Jewish educational success, observes that it was not merely the product of a Jewish commitment to education: "Jewish traditions of literacy and scholastic application resulted in classroom achievement because the structural conditions—the opportunities, the educational facilities, and a record of economic success—sponsored expectations that academic success would result in occupational success" (1983:44-45).

In contrast, Italian students were viewed by school personnel as more difficult to discipline and more irresponsible than their Jewish counterparts when they both were newly arrived immigrants during the turn of the century. Truancy was not uncommon; many of the children were not in school because they were working. There was an appreciably higher number of Italian children in the workforce than any other ethnic group. Attendance in secondary school or college was rare. In general, Italian children were viewed as difficult to discipline, slow to learn academic skills, and more concerned with outside jobs than with the classroom (Berrol, 1975).

The explanation that is frequently offered for this behavior pattern stems from the significance attached to work by the students' parents and the disdain placed by them on the value of education. Richard Gambino (1974), in his *Blood of My Blood*, states that the *contadino*, the Italian peasant, viewed being educated in terms of proper behavior with the elders and did not refer to formal schooling. According to Leonard Covello (1967) in his comprehensive study *The Social Background of the Italo-American School Child*, there were many aspects of southern Italian cultural patterns and structural factors that contributed to the Italian child's resistance to American education. In southern Italy and Sicily, schooling had very little relationship to material success and this view carried over to America. And, indeed, as Stephen Steinberg (1981) observes, this attitude toward education also reflected conditions of Italian life in this country. Their chances of reaching college were slim, and the likelihood of occupational and status achievement was not dependent on their school performance. Steinberg notes the parallel view in the poor black men of Eliot Liebow's (1966) *Tally's Corner*, who also adjusted their aspirations and strategies to what they believed they could realistically hope to achieve.

Covello refers to the importance of family ties and the associated belief that education was an indoctrination process into an alien culture that would destroy family unity and break down accepted social patterns, creating a generation gulf. This belief was interlocked with the one that saw the parents as the prime socializing agents for future occupational involvement. Finally, the expectation was that children from the age of 12 had responsibility to contribute to the economic needs of the household. (The late nineteenth-century American middle-class invention of adolescence as a stage in the life cycle was not shared by the poorer Italians.) Little benefit was seen for staying in school beyond the age of 12 for girls in particular, and somewhat less so for boys. This attitude put them in direct conflict with compulsory education laws.

The totality of this belief system and the consequent behavior of the Italian student was reinforced by teachers in the school system. In contrast to the Jewish student, who was usually placed in the higher-ranked academic curriculum track, the Italian student was tracked in either lower-ranked academic programs or nonacademic programs that included general, vocational, and commercial tracks. The result was that school officials had low expectations regarding the Italian student and, while they may not have explicitly prevented Italian students from achieving success in school, they did relatively nothing to encourage it (Berrol, 1975). The result was that a self-fulfilling prophecy began to operate, making it easier for Jewish children to succeed in school and more difficult for Italian students. It was only after World War II, when the occupational structure and opportunities began to change, that we saw an appreciable change in the educational achievement rate of Italian youngsters.

THE NEW ETHNICITY AND ETHNIC FAMILIES

In the late 1960s and 1970s, there was great attention in the popular media, as well as by social scientists, on the increased ethnic consciousness among numerous urban Catholic working-class groups. They were categorized as "white ethnics" and their vocal advocacy of their ethnic identity became labeled as the "new ethnicity." Some saw this ethnic revival as a backlash to the increased militancy of blacks and Hispanics and to the antiwar movement of the affluent children of white liberals, politicians, and intellectuals. Michael Novak, a Slovak American, interpreted the ethnic revival not as part of the assimilation process but as evidence of "unmeltable ethnics." He sees two basic elements in the "new ethnicity"—a sensitivity to ethnic pluralism that is combined with a respect for the cultural differences among ethnic groups and a self-conscious involvement and examination of our own cultural heritage.

The prediction of Robert E. Park and the Chicago School in the 1920s was on the inevitable Americanization and assimilation of immigrant groups and their cultures into American society. Therefore, how can we understand the resurgence of ethnicity in the 1960s that continues to the present time? The important essay, "Emergent Ethnicity: A Review and Reformulation" by William L. Yancey, Eugene P. Ericksen, and Richard N. Juliani (1976), argues that ethnic-group behavior and identity are contingent in significant ways on a number of interrelated societal conditions that include occupation, residence, and institutional affiliation that were tied to the changing technology of industrial production and transportation of late nineteenth-century and early twentieth-century American cities.

> ... [E]thnicity, defined in terms of frequent patterns of association and identification with common origins ... is crystallized under conditions which reinforce the maintenance of kinship and friendship networks. These are common occupational positions, residential stability and concentration, and dependence on common institutions and services. These conditions are directly dependent on the ecological structure of cities, which is in turn directly affected by the processes of industrialization. (Yancey, Ericksen, and Juliani, 1976:392)

Prior to the fifty-year dramatic growth period—1876 to 1925—of the industrial urban centers of the United States, the "old" immigrants had a geographically dispersed residential pattern. The "new" immigrants were bunched together because of concentrated large-scale urban employment and the need for low-cost housing near the place of employment. When immigrants arrived, they were drawn to the urban areas of economic expansion, and the migration chain—the subsequent arrival of relatives and friends—continued the concentrated settlement pattern.

What distinguishes the work of Yancey, Ericksen, and Juliani (1976) from the earlier work of the Chicago School is their ability to integrate an economic causal model with one that allows for the utilization of cultural and symbolic factors. The Chicago School saw the gradual disappearance of the culture of the old immigrant group as the Americanization process proceeded. Their urban theoretical model was essentially one that viewed social disorganization as an urban way of life and placed too great an emphasis on spatial patternings based on an economically determined urban ecology. It did not give sufficient attention to the nature of social-interactional patterns that were developing in the city. Overwhelmed by a secondary-group orientation toward city life, it did not see the emergent primariness of urban communities. It also did not see that urban social relations, like any other set of human interactions, are in a continual state of change, transition, or process.

What the Chicago School did not foresee was the emergence of new ethnic cultures with institutional, structural, and community supports for the subsequent generations of these immigrant groups. The thesis developed by Yancey and his associates is that the ethnic communities and the cultures that make up what is popularly called the "new ethnicity" become elaborated and developed out of the American urban experience and not the largely rural European background of the original immigrant generation; that is, rather than emphasize the transplanted cultural heritage as the principal antecedent and defining characteristic of ethnic groups, Yancey, Ericksen, and Juliani suggest that the development and persistence of ethnicity is dependent on structural conditions characterizing American cities and positions of groups in American social structure. The expression of ethnicity is more the expression of structural conditions in American society than the influence of the cultural heritage of ethnic groups. They therefore conclude that examination of ethnic experience should use the urban American-ethnic community, rather than the place of origin, as the principal criterion of ethnic group membership.... Ethnicity may have relatively little to do with Europe, Asia or Africa, but much more to do with the exigencies of survival and the structure of opportunity in this country. In short, the so-called "foreign heritage" of ethnic groups is taking shape in this country. (Yancey, Ericksen, and Juliani, 1976:400)

It is my view that the above quotation overstates their case. It would be more correct to see the expression of ethnicity as a consequence of the interaction of American structural conditions and the influence of the cultural heritage of ethnic groups. Yet these authors are on target in observing that ethnicity was elaborated and reinforced through systemic isolation of ethnic groups that historically occurred in the United States in residential segregation and occupational stratification. These factors allowed for the emergence of ethnic-group consciousness. This is particularly true of working-class ethnic groups. The next section of this chapter discusses a phenomenon called symbolic ethnicity, intermarriage, and ethnic-family patterns of the educated and more affluent middle and upper classes who may not live in homogeneous urban villages.

SYMBOLIC ETHNICITY, INTERMARRIAGE, AND ETHNIC-FAMILY GROUPS

In their important article, Yancey, Ericksen, and Juliani (1976) observe that communication and participation in ethnic organizations on a cosmopolitan level can reinforce ethnic identity even among residentially dispersed groups. This "situational" ethnicity may be characterized by such things as "church and synagogue attendance, marching in a Saint Patrick's or Columbus Day parade, voting for a political candidate of a similar ethnicity, or supporting a political cause associated with the country of origin, such as the emigration of Russian Jews to Israel or the reunification of Ireland" (Yancey, Ericksen, and Juliani, 1976:399).

Herbert Gans' article (1982/1979), "Symbolic Ethnicity: The Future of Ethnic Groups and Cultures in America," observes the same phenomenon but reaches a different conclusion. His essay can be seen as tying together a number of loose sociological ends and, to a large extent, bringing back the basic assimilationist view of Park and the Chicago School, but with greater sensitivity to symbolic as well as territorial communities and their meaning to the descendants of the early twentieth-century immigration groups.

Gans, in this piece and in his earlier major work *The Urban Villagers* (1962a), emphasizes the importance of controlling for social class in the examination of ethnicity in the community context. *The Urban Villagers* sees a working-class culture as compared to an "Italian-American" culture per se as being an important determinant of individual behavior and social organization. Likewise, in the "Symbolic Ethnicity" article he raises this theme. He sees the rise of the "new ethnicity" primarily as a working-class phenomenon that uses ethnicity and ethnic organization on behalf of mobilizing working-class interests. His discussion of symbolic ethnicity is largely in terms of third- and fourth-generation upwardly mobile ethnics, with American Jewry being the case in point. It is defined largely in nostalgic cultural terms with a situational manifestation of ethnic identification.

> Symbolic ethnicity . . . is characterized by a nostalgic allegiance to the culture of the immigrant generation, or that of the old country; love for and a pride in a tradition that can be felt without having to be incorporated in everyday behavior. The feeling can be directed at a generalized tradition, or at specific ones: a desire for the cohesive extended immigrant family, or for the obedience of children to parental authority, or the unambiguous orthodoxy of immigrant religion, or the old-fashioned despotic benevolence of the machine politician. People may even sincerely desire to "return" to these imagined pasts, which are conveniently cleansed of the complexities that accompanied them in the real past, but while they may soon realize that they cannot go back, they do not surrender the wish. Or else they displace that wish on churches, schools, and the mass media, asking them to recreate a tradition, or rather, to create a symbolic tradition, even while their familial, occupational, religious and political lives are pragmatic responses to the imperatives of their roles and positions in local and national hierarchical social structures. (Gans, 1982/1979:501)

Gans concludes that, in the long run, acculturation and assimilation as secular trends will culminate in the eventual absorption of the given ethnic group into the larger culture and general population. These ethnics, while they retain some form of their religious heritage, will find their secular heritage to be only a dim memory and will have only the minutest traces of their national origins.

In recent years, there is again a questioning of the nature and future of (white) ethnicity in the United States. One empirical measure of this is the increased incidence and prevalence of interethnic and interfaith marriage. Norval D. Glenn (1982), in a study of patterns and recent trends in interfaith marriage in the United States, estimates that about 15 to 20 percent of today's marriages are between spouses with different religious preferences, such as Protestant, Catholic, and Jewish. This is a substantial increase in the intermarriage rate since 1957. The apparent change in the willingness of people to marry persons of a different religion and to change their own religion to that of their spouse led Glenn to speculate that "marriage in the United States has become very largely a secular institution, with religious institutions exerting only weak influences on marital choice" (1982:564).

Paradoxically, this increase in the intermarriage rate has been occurring at the same time that sociological arguments on behalf of the melting pot ideal have been eroded and where has been growing acceptance of the ideology of cultural pluralism. Cultural pluralism is the belief that ethnic groups have neither acculturated or integrated into the broader society and that they may have different cultural value systems and different networks of social and organization relations. However, as least as far as white ethnic groups are concerned, and citing rising intermarriage rates as indicative, the pendulum has swung again to those who see assimilation and acculturation in the future of these ethnic groups.

Richard D. Alba (1990) in a review of the literature of inter-religious and inter-ethnic marriages among whites reports a major increase in the last few decades. Surveying the 1980 census, he found that three of every four marriages involved partners of different ethnic backgrounds. Using the rapid rise in intermarriage rates as providing the ultimate yardstick, sociologists influenced by the work of Alba (cf. 1976, 1981, 1986) foresee the "twilight of ethnicity." They reach the obvious conclusion that the rise in intermarriage was a direct reflection of the trend toward increasing assimilation.

The high interfaith marriage rate has been a cause of much debate among religious leaders of the major American religious groups. For example, 4 percent of Jews married outside their faith in 1957, by the end of the 1970s that rate nearly tripled to 12 percent for Jews (Glenn, 1982). Astonishingly, by 1990, the National Jewish Population Survey reported that more than half (52 percent) of Jews married outside their faith (Kosmin, 1991). In these interfaith marriages, 72 percent of children were being raised in a non-Judaic religion or in no religion at all. Further, 90 percent of these children are marrying outside the Jewish faith.

Anticipating these trends, members of twenty-eight major Jewish groups—including the rabbinical associations for the Orthodox, Conservative, Reformed, and Reconstructionist branches of Judaism, along with such secular Jewish groups like B'nai B'rith International, Hadassah, and the American Jewish Committee—met in 1983 at a conference entitled the "National Conference on Jewish Population Growth" (Brozan, 1983). At the conference, they reported that with a current birthrate of 1.6 children per couple, American Jews had a lower birthrate than the population at large, for which the birthrate was 2.2. This—combined with a number of accelerating trends that include increasing intermarriage, delayed marriage and childbirth, and rising divorce rates—led them to forecast that by the year 2000, the Jewish population in this country, now 5.5 million, may shrink by 25 percent.

The theme of the conference was to develop a list of programs that would encourage the growth of Jewish families. These programs included establishment of Jewish day-care services with scholarship aid; provisions for mortgage assistance, in which organizations would subsidize mortgages on homes for large families; development of family-centered activities programs; and the establishment of Jewish dating services. Two years earlier, in 1981, the synagogue branch of Reform Judaism started a vigorous program to invite conversions by non-Jewish partners in interfaith marriages and by those Americans who express no religious preference (Briggs, 1981). The emphasis placed by Reform Judaism on conversion was largely in response to the above-mentioned factors and particularly to the alarm felt to the rising intermarriage rate between Jews and non-Jews. Surveys have shown that one-third of the nation's Jews marry outside their faith and that their non-Jewish spouses have often faced difficulties in being accepted into a synagogue. The program planned by the Union of American Hebrew Congregations, an organization of 735 Reform synagogues, was to develop a more hospitable climate for non-Jewish marriage partners and children of interfaith marriages in the synagogue and to provide information for those who seek religious identity and involvement.

The relationship between intermarriage and religious and ethnic identity has been a topic of concern for many sociologists. Eleanore Parelman Judd (1990) examines this interrelationship by examining the differences between two competing sets of sociological theory. One set of theories, led by the influential work of Milton Gordon

(1964), sees intermarriage as one of several stages toward assimilation. Goldscheider and Zuckerman (1985) developed a counter theory that views intermarriage as neither equivalent to assimilation nor automatically leading to communal dissolution. Judd favors the later theory and also questions whether intermarriage is an indication of assimilation and acculturation.

She believes that the ultimate test of assimilation is not in intermarriage, but rather, how intermarried couples raise their children. The basis for her conclusion is research on Jewish-Christian married couples whose children were enrolled in a Jewish religious school that provided parents with information to explain and carry out Jewish activities at home. She reaches the conclusion that intermarriage does not necessarily lead to assimilation, but that assimilation can lead to intermarriage. Her belief is anchored in the view that communal as well as religious factors must be understood in examining the relationship between intermarriage and assimilation.

Miriam G. Vosburgh and Richard N. Juliani (1990) also addressed themselves to the question of whether marriage serves as a stimulus to further assimilation. To answer this question they felt that it is necessary not only to assess the cultural differences that the intermarried couple bring with them to the marriage but what actually happens to personal identity, cultural values, and patterns of behavior during the course of such marriages. They examined differences in the family-related values and behavior patterns of Irish and Italian Catholics to measure the extent to which cultural compatibility and similarity already exist. These value and behavior patterns include number of children desired (Italians want fewer); opinions on divorce laws and divorce rates (Italians less opposed to making divorce easier to obtain); opinions on children's independence (Irish stress independence values more than Italians).

Vosburgh and Juliani see as quite problematic what ethnic identities will be selected and which ethnic traits will be passed on to the children produced by those families. They believe that the problem with the "twilight of ethnicity" position is its failure to examine the emergent quality of marriage as it unfolds. They conclude that the historical evidence continues to point to the fact that the ethnic character of these two groups still remains distinctive compared to each other as well as to the national culture. They end with the warning that the increase in the intermarriage rate "may not signify greater integration, but possibly greater disruption within an already troubled institution" (Vosburgh and Juliani, 1990:284).

In conclusion, the family served as the center of social interaction and socialization. Just as the family played an essential role in organizing social life in the Old World setting, it did the same in the new world. However, the family is but one of the many institutions (including the school, church, mass media, and occupational settings) that has an effect on individuals. Present ethnic-family patterns can be seen as a result of interaction of cultural tradition with continuous American experience contingencies. The result is that ethnic families are not the equivalent of immigrant families; they have undergone significant changes through the generations. Ethnic-family variations are a consequence of cultural background, recency of migration, residency and geographical locale, socioeconomic status, educational achievement, upward mobility, and political and religious ties. The nature of the response of the given ethnic group and the nature of its adaptation reflect the interaction of these factors. Ethnic families have been affected by social change and have, in turn, affected it. In sum, contemporary ethnic groups have been actively involved in delineating their particular family patterns; they have not been the passive recipients of a one-way Americanization process.

THE JAPANESE AMERICAN FAMILY

The year 1853 is a milestone in Japanese and American relations because, in that year, Commodore Perry sailed into Tokyo Bay and ended more than 200 years of self-imposed governmental isolation of Japan in which foreign visitors were prohibited and Japanese were not allowed to leave their country. Beginning in 1868, the Japanese began emigrating, first as laborers and eventually as permanent settlers to the United States. They shared the same motives for movement to America as other immigrant groups: better jobs, better lives, and an escape from harsh living conditions in Japan. Movement was slow at first; U.S. Census records indicate that only 55 came to the United States in 1870, and 2,039 in 1890. The period after that witnessed a much greater number of immigrants—reaching 24,326 in 1900, 72,157 in 1910, and 110,010 in 1920 (Parrillo, 1985).

During the period beginning in 1890, a significant number of the immigrants were young single men—like their Italian, Slav, and Greek counterparts—who came with the hope to earn sufficient money to return to their homeland and buy land or a small business. They settled in the Pacific states and, meeting discrimination in more economically remunerative occupations, they found jobs in domestic service, farm labor, and contract gardening.

The fact that single men initially sought to return to Japan is reflected in the great imbalance in the ratio of the males and females who came to America. In 1900, out of the total Japanese population of 24,326 there were only 985 females. Although an unknown number of Japanese males returned to Japan, a larger number stayed and make a permanent home in America. This change is reflected in the sex ratio during succeeding decades with the arrival of additional females. In 1910, the number of females was 9,087, and by 1920 there were 22,193 out of the total population of 110,010 (Gee, 1978).

The increase in the number of women came about from either the single young males returning to Japan for brides or the already married males sending for their wives and children. Another method was the "picture-bride" practice that grew out of the traditional Japanese practice of arranged marriage. Through agreed-on "go-betweens," pictures were exchanged between potential spouses and their families. Apart from the fact that the couple neither met during the course of the negotiations nor were present at the actual marriage ceremony, the marriage was socially and legally recognized in Japan. A Japanese woman on her way to meet her unseen husband in an unknown America conveys her thoughts in the following passage:

> On the way from Kobe to Yokohama, gazing upon the rising majestic Mount Fuji in a cloudless sky aboard the ship, I made a resolve. For a woman who was going to a strange society and relying upon an unknown husband whom

she had married through photographs, my heart had to be as beautiful as Mount Fuji. I resolved that the heart of a Japanese woman had to be sublime, like that soaring majestic figure eternally constant through wind and rain, heat, and cold. I never forgot that resolve on the ship, enabling me to overcome sadness and suffering. (Cited in Gee, 1978:56-57)

This practice was denounced as "immoral" by American immigration exclusionists and was terminated after 1921 (Gee, 1978). Yet, as Kikumura and Kitano (1981) emphasize, the picture-bride and other practices bringing the Japanese women to America were crucial in shaping the Japanese immigrant experience and moving it toward a more "normal" family life. For, by having a family, the Japanese were able to make a stronger commitment to remaining in and adapting to their new country. This is especially the case for a people who believe that "no matter what possessions a man may have, he is not a success unless he is married and has a family . . . to fail in this is to fail in life" (cited in Gee, 1978:55).

The Japanese were industrious and knowledgeable in cultivation. Despite discrimination, they acquired farms of their own. Often this was on marginal land, and abandoned, and only coaxed into productivity with prodigious labor. Both the husband and wife worked long hours in fields or shops. One woman who was a picture-bride recounts her experience and provides a vivid picture of the laborious nature of agricultural work:

> At the beginning I worked with my husband picking potatoes or onions and putting them in sacks. Working with rough-and-tumble men, I became weary to the bones; waking up in the mornings I could not bend over the wash basin.
>
> Sunlight came out about 4:00 A.M. during the summer in the Yakima Valley (Washington). I arose at 4:30. After cooking breakfast, I went out to the fields. There was no electric stove or gas like now. I took over one hour to cook, burning kindling wood.
>
> As soon as I came home, I first put on the fire, took off my hat, and then I washed my hands. After cooking both breakfast and lunch, I went to the fields. (Cited in Gee, 1978:58)

Similarly, urban work also proved very difficult, as indicated in this account of a woman who operated a laundry with her husband. After working the entire day, she reports:

> . . . I started at 5:00 P.M. to prepare supper for five or six persons, and then I began my evening work. The difficult ironing remained. Women's blouses in those days were made from silk or lace, with collars and long sleeves and lots of frills.
>
> I could only finish two in one hour, ironing them with great care. Hence, I worked usually until 12 to 1 A.M. But it was not just me—all women who worked in the laundry business probably did the same thing. (Gee, 1978:58)

The economic competitiveness of the Japanese, particularly in agriculture, led to discriminatory legislation by the California state government. In 1913, the California Alien Land Act was enacted to prevent the Japanese and other Asian immigrants from owning or leasing land. Under the United States Naturalization Act of 1790, then still in effect, citizenship was available to any white alien who was not a slave. This act was modified in 1868, after the Civil War, to extend citizenship to persons of African descent. The foreign-born who were neither white nor black therefore could not become citizens. However, since Japanese children who were born in America were automatically U.S. citizens, this law was somewhat circumvented by the Japanese holding land in their children's names. In reaction, California in 1920 passed a law prohibiting first-generation immigrants (*Issei*) from being guardians of their native-born children's property. The Supreme Court upheld this law in 1923, and similar legislation was swiftly passed in New Mexico, Arizona, Louisiana, Montana, Idaho, and Oregon (Parrillo, 1985).

Patterns of discrimination against the Japanese continued with the *Nisei*, or the second generation, who were American-born children of the *Issei*. While the *Nisei* had a distinct advantage over their parents—American citizenship—this did not help them when Japan declared war against the United States in 1941. On February 19, 1942—two months after the attack on Pearl Harbor—110,000 Japanese, many of them second- and third-generation Americans, were removed from their homes and placed in concentration camps (euphemistically called relocation centers). There were a number of factors that led to the forced expulsion of Japanese Americans from the West Coast. Part of it is explained in terms of the war hysteria of the time, but probably a more perfidious and accurate assessment was that it was the logical culmination of the history of American discriminatory practices against the Japanese and a convenient way for white businessmen and farmers to end the competition of Japanese enterprises.

The effect on family life in the internment camps was profound. Family life was disrupted; old people and children were disoriented; and farms, shops, household property, and skills were lost. The authority of the parents was undermined. Husbands-fathers could no longer act as primary providers and wives-mothers could not function in their household roles. Children ate in mess halls, and dormitory living was prevalent. The atmosphere was one of boredom and stagnation. The consequence was that gambling became prevalent, and often family quarrels escalated into violence (Kitano, 1980).

In spite of these early discriminatory and prejudicial historical experiences, by the 1970s Japanese Americans were considered one of America's most "successful" minorities. Kikumura and Kitano (1981) attribute this to (1) the economic mobility of the family; (2) the compatibility of American and Japanese values, particularly the emphasis on politeness, diligence, long-term goals, respect for authority and parental wishes, keeping up appearances, social sensitivity, and suppression of desires and emotional feelings; and (3) the wartime evacuation that broke up the ghettos and the subsequent scattering of many of the young into parts of the country that did not have a Japanese population. The last factor "exposed them to American ways, dissolved old institutions and structures, and reordered the family structure by putting more power into the hands of the *Nisei*" (Kikumura and Kitano, 1981:45).

Contemporary Japanese American Family Patterns

In the 1980s, there was considerable discussion by scholars on the contemporary Japanese American family. At the end of that decade, the belief articulated was that ethnic identity was losing its importance; at the beginning of that decade researchers saw its continued viability. Let's examine that debate, by examining the changes in thought of Harry H.L. Kitano, a leading authority on the Japanese American family. He observes (1988) that the use of generational designations—*Issei, Nisei, Sansei*—beyond the third generation to the fourth, or *Yonsei*, and subsequent generations may be unnecessary. In the past, each generational designation connotated a common historical experience and similar exposures and lifestyles. However, the increased heterogeneity of the fourth generation as a consequence of increased mobility, acculturation, and involvement in a more open and racially accepting America makes that designation inappropriate, according to Kitano.

However, in an essay written seven years earlier, Kikumura and Kitano (1981) do speak to the continued vitality of ethnic identity. Commenting on the contemporary Japanese American family, they see it as containing features of Japanese and American cultures. The process of acculturation still contains salient features regarding family solidarity and the retention of certain Japanese values. Using 1970 census data, they found that 86 percent of the families included both husband and wife, which was the same rate for the country as a whole. The percentage of children under 6 (27 percent) was also at the national norm. The size of the nuclear family was slightly above the national average (3.7 to 3.5 persons) as was the extended family (16 to 12 persons). This similar pattern to that of Americans as a whole reflects a high degree of acculturation.

In the 1980s, the stability of the Japanese American family was higher than the national average. Less than 2 percent of the men and women were separated, and only 3 percent of the men and 5 percent of the women were divorced. Nearly 56 percent of the men were married as compared to 61 percent of the women. The majority of Japanese Americans lived in family households; 50 percent of these households contained children below the age of 18 and nine out of ten children were living in households with both parents present (Fernandez, 1992; Takagi, 1994).

Income figures from U.S. census data reveals that the median family income of Japanese Americans was higher than the national average. These demographic and economic figures have provided evidence for the belief that this ethnic group has become a "model minority" and has "made it" in America (Takagi, 1994).

The rise in the intermarriage rate is one dramatic change that is occurring in family patterns. Antimiscegenation laws prohibiting Japanese from marrying Caucasians were in effect in many states until they were declared unconstitutional in the late 1960s. In part, this kept the intermarriage rate down through the 1950s. However, since then the rate has risen quite rapidly. For example, Kitano reports that in 1972, 49 percent of Japanese American marriages were to non-Japanese. Similarly high figures were obtained in data surveys from San Francisco, Fresno, and Honolulu. Kitano sees that "these changes in marital patterns reflect increased opportunity for social contact, a weakening of the traditional Japanese family, acculturation, upward social mobility, and changing attitudes toward the Japanese" (1980:570). He predicted that the trend toward more interethnic marriages will continue.

Similarly, Darryl Montero (1981) reported similar trends in his study of changing patterns of assimilation over three generations of Japanese Americans. Montero studied data derived from a sample of 2,304 *Nisei* and 802 *Sansei* and earlier collected data on the *Issei*. He examined four basic indicators of assimilation: visiting patterns with relatives, ethnicity of two closest friends, ethnicity of favorite organization, and ethnicity of spouse. These indicators were used to answer the broader question of whether socioeconomic mobility led to cultural, structural, and marital assimilation.

He found that with socioeconomic success measured in terms of education and occupation, there was greater assimilation among those who made it than those who did not. Economic success also was seen to encourage movement from "Little Tokyos" and "Japantowns" into the surrounding suburbs with the consequent splintering of community ties. Further, for those who lived in non-Japanese communities, they formed friendships and professional acquaintances among Caucasians that had important implications for racial intermarriage.

Montero examines the view that Japanese ethnic identity may be breaking apart in favor of an Asian American ethnic identity. He sees some evidence for this in studies that report on Japanese Americans marrying members of other Asian groups. Also, there is some collective political movement of Asian Americans, there are changes occurring in their historical attitudes to each other, and there is a greater number of Asians in metropolitan areas. However, Montero's data on the intermarriage patterns of the *Nisei* and *Sansei* do not confirm this Asian identity viewpoint. The overwhelming number of these second- and third-generation Japanese Americans who intermarry marry Caucasians. Ninety-two percent of the intermarried *Nisei* married Caucasians; the comparable figures for intermarried *Sansei* are 78 percent marrying Caucasians, 19 percent marrying other Asians, and 3 percent marrying other ethnic groups.

The more salient finding for Montero is that 40 percent of the *Sansei* intermarried, compared to only 10 percent of the older-generation *Nisei*. He observes that the remarkable strides in socioeconomic advancement by the *Nisei* and *Sansei* are accompanied by an accelerated role of assimilation that may contribute to the demise of some of the traditional Japanese values that accounted for that success in the first place. This, in turn, may foster a leveling off of future socioeconomic achievement. Montero ends his paper by wondering about what the consequences of future high intermarriage rates may mean for Japanese American family patterns in particular and what similarly high intermarriage patterns may mean to other ethnic groups as well.

> Given the dramatically increasing trend of outmarriage among the *Sansei*, with its concomitant erosion of ethnic ties and affiliation, we are justified in wondering whether a Japanese-American ethnic community can be maintained into the next generation—the *Yonsei*. If it cannot, the survival of other distinct ethnic groups may be similarly uncertain as their members advance socioeconomically. (Montero, 1981:837-838)

Kitano (1988) picks up on these themes and argues that the data on intermarriage is the most dramatic change in the Japanese American family. "The increase in out-group marriage rates is the result of the breakup of the ghetto, loss of family control over marital choices, changes in the law, and more liberal attitudes toward interracial unions on the behalf of both the ethnic and majority communities" (Kitano, 1988:274). Further, the issue of "ethnic identity" remains salient. Using Gans' conceptualization of "symbolic ethnicity," Kitano (1988:273) observes that it manifests itself in "such diverse activities as attending ethnic festivals, eating ethnic foods, and seeing a Japanese movie, but it would not necessarily include studying and learning about Japan, its culture and language, or becoming deeply involved in ethnic-group activities and giving high priority to ethnic-group concerns."

The issue of symbolic ethnicity becomes particularly important in the context of intermarriage. Takagi (1994), citing the statistical evidence, concludes that if current trends continue, more than 50 percent of married-couple households will contain non-Japanese as either wives or husbands. He asks whether such households constitute a Japanese American family.

In a study of the consequences of intermarriage on ethnic identity of "mixed-heritage" Japanese Americans in Hawaii and "mixed-heritage" Hispanics in the Southwest, Stephen and Stephen (1989) provides some interesting findings. Nearly three-quarters of the part-Japanese and almost 45 percent of the part-Hispanics had multiple ethnic identities. The questions that these two populations of college students responded to included the ethnic identity of their friends, what ethnic designation they would use when filling out an employment questionnaire, how they designate themselves and family members, and with which ethnic group do they identify themselves most closely.

The authors reached two tentative conclusions. The first is that groups that strongly socialize children into the culture of the group are more likely to preserve their ethnic identity. The second is that ethnic identity depends on the geographical location where the intermarriage occurs, the status of the ethnic groups, as well as the prevalent socialization practices. The mixed-heritage Japanese Americans located in Hawaii, a multicultural state, had more biological and cultural ties with more groups than their part-Hispanic counterparts. The mixed-heritage Hispanics were located in New Mexico, a bicultural state with a low intermarriage rate. Stephen and Stephen (1989) believe that New Mexico "lacks a rich and commonly used vocabulary for designating mixed-heritage identity" and "this absence of ready labels for mixed-heritage status may make it more difficult for the individual and others to identify the respondent as mixed-heritage" (1989:515).

In summary, the greater ethnic-racial tolerance for Japanese Americans may result in their increased assimilation into American society. Intermarriage, in this regard, will heighten that occurrence especially for the children of such intermarriages who will more likely identify themselves as multiethnic. Hispanics, and I would speculate African Americans, who usually receive a less accepting response when they intermarry, will have offspring who more likely will identify themselves with a single ethnic group.

THE MEXICAN AMERICAN FAMILY

Mexican Americans have a unique place in American immigration history. They can be considered in terms of being a native American group as well as an immigrant group. Their historical immigration patterns have shown great variation. Within the last sixty years there has been a major change from being a major ethnic group with the largest rural population to one that is strongly urbanized, with 88 percent being city dwellers (Baca Zinn, 1994). In 1988, 12.1 million people of Mexican origin or descent inhabited the United States. This figure represented 62 percent of the total Hispanic population. This was five times the estimated number of 2.3 million Puerto Ricans. About 87 percent lived in the southwestern states, with the vast majority in California and Texas. An increasing number have migrated to urban areas throughout the United States; for example, Los Angeles has more than a million Mexican American residents. As Carlos E. Cortes (1980:697) has observed: "The shifts from regional to national minority, from farm to city, and from field to factory have set in motion a series of other changes whose consequences are still unfolding." Here I focus attention on the impact of these changes on family life.

Initially, Mexican Americans were created through conquest and annexation rather than through immigration. The Mexicans were here when what is now Texas, New Mexico, Arizona, California, and parts of Colorado, Nevada, Utah, and Wyoming were acquired by the United States through the war of separation of Texas from Mexico, the United States–Mexican War, and the Gadsden Purchase during the period between 1845 and 1854. This annexed regional minority experienced a diminishing influence in the economy of the southwestern states throughout the nineteenth century. Queen and his associates (Queen, Habenstein, and Quadagno, 1985) make the point that as slavery is a key element in understanding the black American experience, so too is the labor utilization of Mexican Americans and Mexicans in understanding the Mexican American experience. This historical experience has influenced their contemporary social position and, to a lesser extent, their family patterns.

In Texas, first cattle ranching, then land ownership, and then cotton farming determined economic superiority and the Mexican Americans became a subjugated, exploitable minority group. What land they owned was obtained both legally and illegally during this time. Anglo-dominated agricultural production became large-scale and labor intensive. Mexican Americans were relegated to serve as cheap labor and to compete economically with job-starved Mexican nationals who were willing to work for even lower wages. The immigration policy allowed for the crossing back and forth over the border of Mexican migrants and this further undermined the economic position of Mexican Americans.

In New Mexico, their situation was somewhat better. When they were in the demographic majority through the 1860s, they dominated the economy and controlled the territorial legislature. However, with the expansion of the railroads, the depletion of grazing lands, the development of industrial mining, and the consequent movement into New Mexico of Anglos or Anglo-Americans (white persons of non-Hispanic descent), the balance of power gradually shifted. Still, by the turn of the century, they retained some economic and political power. However, many Mexican Americans were forced to become part of the unskilled labor force.

In southern and central California, powerful rancheros dominated the economy at the time of annexation. However, the Gold Rush of 1849 brought more and more Anglos into both the northern and the southern parts of the state. Prejudice reinforced by legislative actions biased against Mexican Americans resulted in the loss of most of the old Mexican land grants. By 1900, their political and economic power plummeted throughout the Southwest, with only New Mexico being the notable exception.

The dominant Anglos gained economic and political control of the Southwest, and their ethnic stereotypes prevailed. Mexican Americans became characterized as an inferior people whose religion, language, and culture were seen as antithetical to the "American" way of life. The resultant consequences of being relegated to manual labor, poverty, and subjugation only served to reinforce the stereotype of Mexican Americans as ignorant, shiftless people.

The United States shares a 2,000-mile boundary with Mexico. Two rivers, most notably the Rio Grande, and open land separate the two countries. Mexican immigration into the United States during the second half of the nineteenth century was relatively modest compared to what it is in the twentieth century. The total number of native-born and foreign-born Mexican people in the United States was estimated at being between 381,000 and 562,000 in 1900 (Cortes, 1980).

Social, political, and economic factors in both countries led to a substantial rise in the number of immigrants from Mexico to the United States in the first three decades of the twentieth century. Political upheavals, social unrest, and poverty in Mexico, combined with the growth of the American Southwest, accounted for the movement of more than 500,000 legal immigrants in the 1920s alone. Dinnerstein and Reamers (1975) observe that Mexican laborers provided more than 60 percent of the common labor force in the railroad track gangs, the mines of Arizona and New Mexico, the fruit and truck gardens of Texas and California, and the packing plants on the West Coast. They also dominated the sugar beet farming industry that extended from Colorado to Montana, Michigan, and Ohio. The use of these laborers coincided with the rapid growth of the Southwest and with the changes in the immigration laws that severely restricted the immigration of Chinese and Japanese laborers at the beginning of the century and European immigration in the mid-1920s.

Mexican immigration began to decline in 1928 and remained low through the Depression and the coming of World War II. Indeed, during the 1930s, many Mexicans either returned home voluntarily or were pressured to do so by communities where there were high rates of unemployment. During the war, labor shortages encouraged American industry to welcome Mexican workers. The number of Mexicans with permanent visas continued to grow in the 1940s, expanded rapidly in the 1950s, and exceeded 30,000 in every year from 1960 to the end of the 1970s (Cortes, 1980). In addition, countless numbers of Mexicans have entered the United States illegally throughout the twentieth century. The estimated number of illegal aliens is between 3.5 to 6 million (Parrillo, 1985). Warren and Passel (1987) estimated that a little over 2 million illegal aliens lived in the United States and that more than half of them (55 percent) came from Mexico. Nearly 60 percent of the Mexican-born undocumented population were young men with the vast majority being in the 15 to 44 age group.

The proportion of Mexican Americans born in the United States and those born in Mexico has radically changed in the last twenty-five years. For example, in 1960 Mexican-born immigrants were a rarity in California, nearly nine out of ten Mexican Americans were born in the United States. By 1990 the ratios were reversed because of the massive immigration to California (Baca Zinn, 1994). Baca Zinn comments that "the concentration of immigrants was so high that it formed a virtually new population with family characteristics that differ from those of the native-born Mexican or 'Chicano' brethren" (1994:65).

Contemporary Mexican American Family Patterns

Especially in light of the recent new wave of immigration, we recognize that there is no such thing as the Mexican American family, and that there are social-class variations and historical-experience variations in relation to when these people settled in the United States. Yet a distinct set of values centering on the family and not on the individual has been an overriding cultural feature. The *familia* is the center of Mexican American culture and is seen as the single most important social unit (Queen et al., 1985). Traditionally, it has been an extended family containing not only parents and children but also grandparents, uncles, aunts, and cousins. Migration patterns usually require the relocation of both the nuclear family and the consanguineal one.

Familism, incorporated in a theme of family honor and unity, is seen not only to persist in today's ethnic enclaves, or *barrios*. *Barrios* are the equivalent of the urban villages that characterized the urbanization patterns of such "new" immigration groups as the Italians, Poles, and Eastern European Jews in the Northeast and Midwest. Baca Zinn (1994), in reviewing recent research, reports that the familism of Mexican Americans can also be seen as having important roots that developed as a response to

A happy gathering of four generations of a Mexican American family.

socioeconomic depravation conditions of United States society. An example of the persistence and adaptation of traditional cultural family values can be seen in the changes that have affected *compadrazqo* (godparentage), a special form of ritual kinship that promotes continuing close relationships among extended families.

The *compadrazqo* is designed to generate social and interpersonal cohesion and, at the same time, to reduce the potential extrafamilial conflict that might arise in a highly family-centered society. Mutual patterns of obligations are expected to develop between *compadres* (people or groups). In the event of trouble or difficulty, *compadres* are expected to offer help and advice. Cortes (1980) has observed that the practices of the traditional family and the *compadrazqo* have been declining in the face of the pressures of the more militant young Mexican Americans (Chicanos). Similarly, these practices are in decline throughout Latin America and in many Mediterranean nations; however, they still maintain a viable force in the *barrios*, even where the dynamics of urban life strain traditional practices. Cortes explains: "Although these traditional structures and practices have eroded among all immigrant groups, it is likely that they have survived more widely among Mexican-Americans because of their historical isolation, residential segregation, continuing immigration, geographical proximity to Mexico, and deep commitment to these social institutions" (1980:714).

Ruth Horowitz's (1983) monograph *Honor and the American Dream* is an excellent study of an inner-city Chicano community in Chicago. (She refers to all people of Mexican ancestry in the United States as Chicanos and therefore her use of this term differs from the political implications noted previously.) She finds support for Cortes' belief that *compadres* serve, in part, to maintain cultural continuity. In addition, the naming of friends as *compadres* not only strengthens the relationships with each other, but also "the mutual obligations further strengthen the relationship of the entire expanded family unit both as a symbol of their cohesiveness and because they need each other" (Horowitz, 1983:56). Horowitz observes that the exchange of economic and personal services is frequently needed since these families rarely turn to outside agencies such as public welfare or public employment. This help is regarded as a failure of a family's solidarity and social worth. In addition, *compadres* and relatives provide emotional and social support.

> Having a large, close family that can be augmented by *compadres* who can and will readily help in time of need is very highly valued. Being seen as a cohesive family transcends economic success. In such a family on 32nd Street and in other Chicano communities, members lend each other money, locate a car mechanic, and help out in innumerable other situations. "We can hardly keep track of all the money that goes around between us anymore. We just assume it's about equal," a young couple declared while discussing the state of their finances and their family's aid. (Horowitz, 1983:57)

Horowitz goes on to observe that the strong network of intergenerational ties among the families fosters the continuation of traditional gender-role relationships in the family. Horowitz sees the articulation of gender-family role relationships in terms of male domination, virginity, motherhood, and respect. Manhood is defined in terms of independence, personal strength, situational control, and dominance over wives and daughters. Great importance is given to a daughter's identity as a virgin. Tension is seen in the more assimilated young woman's attempt for autonomy over parental control regarding dating and freedom to do things unsupervised, and the parents' desire to assure that such activities are not perceived as the activities of nonvirgins. Motherhood is the culturally acceptable identity; the role of independent career woman is not. Women's identities are anchored in their familial roles as wives, sisters, and mothers. Respect, another symbol of family life, refers to systems of chivalry and etiquette that formalize social interaction both in the family and in the community. Formal rules delineate ways of acting; for example, swearing in front of females is strictly forbidden, older people must be greeted with courtesy, and insolence or rudeness is not tolerated within the home.

Horowitz believes that these symbols of family life, taken together, provide order and stability for everyday social interactions in the context of an urban community that is highly industrialized and educated. Yet the changing nature of urban life results in many circumstances that prove problematic for the traditional culture. Horowitz focuses on the ambiguity and conflict that are found in the expectations concerning gender-role behavior and child-parent relationships particularly faced by youths. "Youths are caught between the traditional model of social relationships and the urban Chicago reality: the streets, the school, the media, and the job scene. With the freedom they take or are given, the youths are faced with many dilemmas as they venture beyond the confines of the communal and familial order" (Horowitz, 1983:76).

Similarly, Lea Ybarra (1982) has investigated changes in Mexican American family life in Fresno, California. Her study of 100 married couples found that marital-role relations ranged from a patriarchal pattern to a completely egalitarian one. However, the most prevalent pattern was one in which the husband and wife shared in decisions. The factor that appeared to have the strongest impact on whether household chores and child care would be shared between spouses was whether the wife was employed outside the home. These families demonstrated a more egalitarian family pattern relative to decision making, sharing of household tasks, and caring of children. Further, in her investigation of other studies of Mexican American families in different regions of the United States, Ybarra found that egalitarianism was the predominant conjugal-role relationship. Similarly, Staples and Mirande (1980) found that "virtually every systematic study of conjugal roles in the Chicano family has found egalitarianism to be the predominant pattern across socioeconomic groups, educational levels, urban-rural residence, and region of the country." Such findings led Ybarra to question previously accepted assumptions on the nature of Mexican American family life that more often than not viewed it negatively, especially compared to "mainstream" American family life.

Ybarra touches on an important critique that has been made of the biases inherent in many of these studies. Staples and Mirande (1980) have observed that much of the research has a pejorative view of the Mexican American family. This research, based on psychoanalytical assumptions, examines *machismo* (masculine patriarchal authority) as the key variable in explaining the dynamics of both family life and culture, seeing machismo as a compensation for powerlessness resulting from feelings of inadequacy, inferiority, and rejection of authority. However, beginning with the influential studies by Miguel Montiel (1970, 1972), "the social science myth of the Mexican American family" has been exposed.

This myth developed a pathological view of Mexican American culture in terms of three characteristics: fatalism; patriarchy; and familism, or strong orientation to kin. *Machismo* was not equated with honor, respect, and dignity; it was defined in terms of power, control, and violence (Staples and Mirande, 1980). Murillo (1971) has redefined *machismo* in positive terms: "An important part of the [father's] concept of *machismo* . . . is that [of] using his authority within the family in a just and fair manner." Similarly, the family is depicted in terms of its warmth and nurturance and providing emotional security and a sense of belonging to family members. This pattern continues through generations and "the mother continues to be close and warm, serving and nurturing even when her children are grown, married, and having children of their own" (Murillo, 1971:104).

The next chapter addresses the concern on families living under poverty conditions. In closing this presentation on Mexican American families let us, in anticipation of that later discussion, examine the impact of poverty on this ethnic group. In an important anthology, *In the Barrios: Latinos and the Underclass Debate*, Joan Moore and Raquel Pinderhughes (1993) bring together a collection of articles about the nature of poverty among Latinos in different communities. Of particular interest to us here are the studies that examine the Mexican American poverty experience.

One common theme addressed by these authors (Rodriguez, Gonzales, Valdez, and Velez-Ibanez) is the impact of economic "restructuring" on these families. Economic restructuring refers to the changes in the global economy that has resulted in a shift from a manufacturing to a service economy in the United States. It has led to deindustrialization, loss and relocation of jobs, and a decline in the number of middle-level jobs. This has had devasting impact on the economy of so-called "rustbelt" cities in the northern and midwestern sections of the United States. But, it also has had an impact on many regions, both urban and rural, in the "sunbelt" as well. A second concern is that of immigration, which has had major significance for poor Latino communities. For Mexican Americans the large numbers of Mexicans migrating to the United States has impacted on the community, economic as well as family life.

Moore and Vigel (1993) examine four separate *barrios* in Los Angeles, "the Chicano 'capital' of the United States" (1993:27). They report three major changes within the past decade. They include economic restructuring combined with immigration that has changed, for the worse, the economic opportunities for Mexican Americans. The second is that these communities are increasingly becoming "Mexicanized." The third major dimension of change is the reconfiguration of community-based organizations in the light of governmental policies that have contracted the welfare state in the 1980s.

What this means in regard to the family is that the recent Mexican immigrants bring with them many traditional family extended networks. In addition, Mexican American families are moving towards more egalitarian, dual leadership arrangements, while some are becoming single-parent households. The overall result is that the addition of new immigrants has helped enliven and regenerate Mexican culture within a broad configuration of family styles and patterns (Moore and Vigel, 1993).

In addition, despite the era of welfare state contraction, the community has developed its political voice and has become more adept in airing its grievances. While street problems exist and youth male gangs are quite visible, the process of "choloziation" (social, familial, and economic marginalization) has been resisted by the traditions of family solidarity exhibited both by Mexican American and newly arrived Mexican families. Together they seek to regenerate community social controls (Moore and Vigel, 1993).

Velez-Ibanez (1993) studied Mexican American poor in a number of southwestern borderland communities with a focus on Tucson, Arizona. He emphasizes the need to examine the individual who is poor within the context of localized kin groups made up of a number of related households involved in extended social and economic exchange relations. He argues that poor persons "should be understood as *individually poor* but not part of a cluster that is necessarily impoverished" (Velez-Ibanez, 1993:209).

Phillip B. Gonzales (1993) provides a historical examination of poverty, restructuring effects, and integrative ties in Mexican American neighborhoods located in Albuquerque, New Mexico. Here again we see the emphasis that is placed on the structures of integrative ties and the impact of economic restructuring on them. The historical importance of residential stability and the importance of strong ties of ethnic culture and family relations in combatting economic and social problems is delineated. He observes how economic changes can erode the structures of these legacies. "Assaulting traditional neighborhoods are increasing poverty among families, drug and alcohol problems, crime, gentrification, changing development patterns resulting in the loss of primary jobs to fringe areas, and other threats to a historic stability" (Gonzales, 1993:170). Yet, they are better able to resist these threats than other communities where residents lack a strong sense of neighborhood identity, familiarity, and belonging.

In summary, this overview of the Mexican American family has sought to demonstrate that the understanding of this ethnic group has been distorted by both social and intellectual biases. Ruth Horowitz has observed that the understanding of Mexican American family structure and dynamics must be viewed in the context of community involvement. The economic hardships often faced by Mexican Americans, whether in the urban *barrios* or in agricultural regions where they make up a large percentage of the migrant labor force, plays a crucial role in the articulation of patterns of adaptation and survival of the family. In recent years, the Chicano movement has resulted in an attempt to overcome economic discrimination and subordination while maintaining familial cultural values. As Ruth Horowitz observes of the Mexican American family system (which, in principle, also holds true for the other groups that make up America's ethnic heritage):

> Some aspects of culture, such as the expanded family network, will survive, even if their content alters slightly by ecological or class changes. Not only do Mexican Americans have a low divorce rate compared with other ethnic groups, regardless of the length of United States residency and location, but the expanded family network remains the valued and predominant family form. Some traditions may persist much longer than any class-based theory

would hypothesize, while other symbols, values, and norms may change as community members achieve greater economic stability and begin to spread through the city and into the suburbs. The United States as a melting pot may not only be unachievable but undesirable. Why should everyone be the same? (Horowitz, 1983:235)

CONCLUSION

This chapter examined ethnic-family variations within the community setting. I utilized a social-historical context with a focus on immigration patterns and the sociological response and analysis of those patterns. My discussion began with an historical overview of the "new" immigration of the late nineteenth and early twentieth centuries. The setting was New York City and Chicago, and the particular concern was on family dynamics of Italian and Jewish immigrants. The social-disorganization biases of the Chicago School of sociology distorted and underemphasized the integrative effects of the family and community institutions in the assimilation patterns of these immigrant groups.

I followed the emerging patterns of these two Southern and Eastern European peoples as they moved from immigrant-family status to ethnic-family status. We saw that both Italian Americans and Jewish Americans have undergone significant cultural changes as they experienced America in the twentieth century. The resultant ethnic-family variations were seen as a consequence of cultural background; recency of migration; residency and geographical locale; socioeconomic status; educational achievement; upward mobility; and political, social, and religious factors. I emphasized how ethnic families not only have been affected by social change but also have affected it. The result is that for these two groups of ethnic Americans, the resultant family patterns have been a consequence of their active participation in the Americanization process—acting on it as well as being affected by it.

Similarly, when focus was shifted to the Japanese American and the Mexican American experiences, further evidence of the active role that these ethnic groups have had in determining their family structure and cultural dynamics. The changing assimilation patterns of these two ethnic groups were discussed within the specific social-historical contexts of their respective experiences in the United States. Prejudices and biases—along with social, political, cultural, and economic discrimination patterns and processes by local, state, and federal government agencies—were seen to have affected these ethnic groups. Their adaptation to both formal and informal discriminatory policies and practices was discussed and analyzed.

In the following chapter, I continue the study of the diversity of the American family experience within the community context by examining families living under poverty conditions. In addition, I broaden the understanding of the impact of poverty on family dynamics by opening with a cross-cultural examination of poverty and family systems in Latin America.

6

POVERTY FAMILY EXPERIENCES

Chapter Outline
Squatter Settlements and Poverty Families
Oscar Lewis and the Culture of Poverty
Critique of the Culture of Poverty
The Culture of Poverty and the Moynihan Report
White Families in Poverty
African American Families in Poverty
Homeless Families in America
Conclusion

In the preceding chapters of Part II, I discussed sociological theories on the nature of city life. These theories often placed stress on the social-disorganizational qualities of city life and its negative implications for the family. They have influenced sociologists in their descriptive analysis of the city. In particular, the dichotomization of rural and urban life through the use of various ideal-type conceptual constructs has led many sociologists to stress the positive qualities of rural life and to develop nostalgic views of the rural-family system. Conversely, the model of urban life has been essentially negative, focusing on the social disorganization of the city and its consequences—alienation, anomie, social isolation, family isolation, juvenile delinquency, crime, child abuse, separation, and divorce.

In the examination of the family in American cities (and the working-class families of Bethnel Green, London), in African cities, and in immigrant families and their ethnic descendants, we see that the previously held position was an oversimplification of reality. In particular, studies of working-class urban villagers—both in the United States and in England—who resided in closed communities are seen to have an urban way of life far different than the one theorized. These studies emphasized the importance of neighborhood ties and relationships with relatives, friends, and neighbors in the tightly knit community. These communities were relatively homogeneous and, as far as possible, excluded outsiders from involvement in the community.

The validity of the social-disorganization model to the study of immigrant and later ethnic-family systems was challenged in the previous chapter. I sought to demonstrate that often these family groups are characterized by social organization and viable family structures. Despite the oversimplifications and distortions of the social disorganization model, it has continued to be used in the analysis of the poverty classes. In addition, both in anthropology and in sociology, a viewpoint has been developed that stems from this position and stresses the development of a *culture of poverty* by those individuals and families who live in poverty conditions. This culture is seen to exhibit all the negative qualities associated with social disorganization. This viewpoint argues that there exists a culture among the poor that transcends given societies and exists in the slums, ghettos, and squatter settlements of the United States, Latin America, Africa, and Asia. The people and families who exhibit this culture of poverty are seen to tend to share similar attitudinal and behavioral patterns relating to the family, work, and the given society. In this chapter, I investigate the poverty family in light of the social policy implications of this contemporary social-disorganization model—the culture of poverty. My focus is on the poor of the United States and the global view is of Latin America.

SQUATTER SETTLEMENTS AND POVERTY FAMILIES

Almost a quarter of a century ago, the geographer Brian J.L. Berry (1973) pointed out that it was in the Third World societies of Latin America, Africa, and Asia where the major thrust of urban growth was occurring. While the industrializing societies of the world had increased in urban population from 198 million to approximately 546 million in the previous fifty years, the urban population of Third World societies had increased from 69 million to 464 million. Although the Third World accounted for only 25 percent of the world's urban population in 1920, it accounted for 51 percent in 1980.

The urban sociologist J. John Palen (1992) points out that unlike Europe and North America that saw the process of large-scale urbanization occurring in over a hundred-year period, the process of urban growth in the less developed countries (LDCs) of the Third World is occurring more rapidly and in even greater population numbers in a much smaller span of time. In 1950 there were only two cities in the Third World with populations of over 5 million; today there are twenty-six cities in LDCs with as large or larger population, and by the end of the century forty-six of the sixty cities in the world with populations over 5 million will be found in LDCs.

Palen further observes that as the world's population increases by 90 million persons each year, 90 percent of this population growth is accountable in the less developed countries. For example, Mexico City, which reached a population of 1 million in 1930, may well become the most populated city in the world with a population of 26 million by the year 2000. Similarly, other Third World cities such as Sao Paolo (24 million), Bombay and Calcutta (16-17 million), and Seoul and Jakarta (14 million) will also have experienced such startling increases in population. In essence then, "the so-called population explosion is in actuality an urban population explosion" (Palen, 1992:361). And, that urban population explosion is largely found in the Third World.

It is important that I emphasize a major variation in the urban growth patterns of Third World societies and industrial societies. The rapid urbanization of the industrial societies of Western Europe and North America occurred at the time when these societies had the highest level of economic development. In contrast, the contemporary accelerated growth occurring in the Third World is taking place in the countries with the lowest level of economic development. This urban growth is also occurring in countries with the lowest life expectancy at birth, nutrition, energy consumption, and education. In addition, Third World urbanization, although it involves greater numbers of people than it did for the industrial societies, is characterized by less industrialization. One consequence of this is that many of the population are unemployed or finding marginal employment in the cities.

A further striking variation in the Third World urbanization patterns is the development of peripheral settlements, squatter settlements, around a city; they serve in transforming rural societies into urban societies and account for a substantial percentage of the urban population. The squatter settlements are shantytowns that have sprung up around large cites, largely because of the inability of the governments in those cities to provide adequate housing for the overwhelming influx of migrants. The residents are migrants from rural areas who have banded together and have established squatter settlements by constructing their own houses on land, both publicly and privately owned, usually against the armed opposition of the government. Often

A woman washing clothes in a *favella* (squatter settlement) of Rio de Janeiro.

these settlements, as in Latin America, disregard urban planning and building regulations; nevertheless, they provide "uniquely satisfactory opportunities for low income settlers" in that they are built according to the needs of the inhabitants in terms of social and economic urban changes (Turner, 1970:10).

While they do try to meet the needs of their inhabitants, squatter settlements throughout the world—whether they are known as *barriadas* (Mexico), *favellas* (Brazil), *bustees* (India), *kampongs* (Southeast Asia), *bidonvilles* "tin-can towns" (Africa), *poblaciones* (Chile), or the most appropriately named *villas miseria* (Argentina)—are cites of crushing poverty and public health crisis. Yet, as Palen (1992) points out, squatter settlements everywhere function to provide housing and community to those who have the least resources and who have no alternative choices.

It has long been observed (Turner, 1969, 1970) that squatter settlements vary greatly in terms of permanency and security of tenure settlement and in the financial and social resources of its inhabitants. A correlation exists between the conditions of the settlement with the wealth and income levels of a given society's population. The *bustee* settlements of Old Delhi, India, are among the poorest, whereas the *cuevas barriada* of Lima, Peru, has residents whose income approaches that of the average working-class level. Twenty-five years ago, settlements such as those in Peru were seen to be transitory phenomena that would eventually evolve into working-class suburban areas. Their state at that time was merely at, or a little above, the poverty level. William Mangin (1960) presented a vivid picture of the *barriadas* around Lima and noted that "Construction activity usually involving family, neighbors, and friends is a constant feature of 'barriada' life and, although water and sewage usually remain critical problems, a livable situation is reached with respect to them (1960:911-917).

The people who inhabit the *barriada* are portrayed in the following manner:

> The early stereotype held by most middle- and upper-class Peruvians of the barriada dwellers as illiterate, nonproductive, lawless, recent communistic Indian migrants is still held by many—but is giving way among young architects, politicians, academics, and anthropologists to an equally false picture. Perhaps as an antidote to the first, it paints them as happy, contented, literate, productive, adjusted, politically conservative—forever patriotic citizens. They are, in fact, about like the vast majority of Peruvians, moderately to desperately poor, cynical and trusting of politicians, bishops, outside agitators, and their own local leaders. They are alternately hopeful and despairing about the future of their children and themselves. They love and resent their children and their parents. They are, in short, human beings. (Mangin, 1968:56)

By 1986, it was reported that of Lima, Peru's 4 million residents, an estimated one-third lived in these shantytowns now called *pueblos jovenes*, young towns (Bissinger, 1986). Villa El Salvador, one of the largest of these shantytowns with a population of 300,000, had become a separate political district with its own mayor for fifteen years of its illegal founding. While massive poverty still prevails, improvements were everywhere. While streets remain unpaved, sandy strips between rows of brick houses in various states of completion, electricity, and drinkable water have become available.

BOX 6-1   The Global Family

Death without Weeping

Nancy Scheper-Hughes

Alto do Cruziero, a hillside shantytown, is adjacent to Bom Jesus de Mata, a factiously named town in northeast Brazil. The land in this part of Brazil is solely devoted to the production of sugar-cane for the global marketplace and the forests and gardens have long been surrendered to "600,000 square miles of suffering" (de Castro cited in Scheper-Hughes, 1992:31). The inhabitants of "the Alto" are rural peoples who are the descendants of African slaves, Indians, and Portuguese settlers. Faced with the declining sugar-cane economy they have become stigmatized squatters. They are forced to subsist on a diet so inadequate that one can make comparative reference to the similar caloric intake of inmates at the World War II concentration camps of Buchenwald and Belsen.

The central focus is on the everyday violence experienced by the women and children of this hillside *favela* (shantytown) and more specifically on "mother love and child death" (1992:15). The high infant mortality rate is an everyday reality; 25 percent of babies succumbed to inadequate diets. What strikes one is the reaction of mothers to apathetic and dying infants. Rather than mourn, the mothers have adopted behavioral patterns that hasten the death of children who are identified by their mothers as unlikely to survive. Patterns of nurturing are followed for those infants thought of as "thrivers" and "keepers." Babies who are labelled as "already wanting to die" and stigmatized as "doomed" are allowed to die of "mortal neglect." *Mortal neglect* is Scheper-Hughes' term for a fatalistic withholding of not only emotional commitment but also of a systematic withholding of nourishment and maternal care.

The behavior of the mothers of the Alto can be understood in terms of a broader analysis of mother love and infant bonding. Mother love is a social and cultural conceptualization and not a universal biological instinct. What seems like the seeming callousness of mothers is in fact a not irrational response to the misery experienced by these women. Scheper-Hughes attacks the stereotyping of a "universal maternal script" that stigmatizes impoverished women who abandon their infants rather than place the blame on those who set the "political agendas and goals" for these people (Scheper-Hughes, 1992:341).

> Mother love is anything *other* than natural and instead represents a matrix of images, meanings, sentiments, and practices that are everywhere socially and culturally produced. In place of a poetics of motherhood, I refer to the pragmatics of motherhood, for, to paraphrase Marx, these shantytown women create their own culture, but they do not create it just as they please or under circumstances chosen by themselves. (Scheper-Hughes, 1992:341-342).

In essence, the behavior of these mothers can be seen as just as natural as those of mothers who under different political circumstances and situations nurture and protect their children. Politically based political distress causes mothers to emotionally protect themselves by refraining from forming attachments to their infants until they are assured that these infants will survive. Emotional detachment takes many forms including not registering children's deaths at the civil registry office and not attending their children's funerals.

The acceptance of infant death is supported by a Catholic ideology that traditionally encouraged the poor to think of infant death as a blessing, to be treated almost with joy, since the baby was a "little angel" not having had time to sin. Such a "little angel's" salvation is thus assured and the "angel" will go to heaven to be with Mary and "Baby Jesus." An alternative "poetics" of mothering develops "that requires calling on all the resources and strengths necessary to help one's own sickly, disabled, or weak infant or young baby to let go, that is, to die quickly and well. Although in dying the infant ceases to exist in normal space and time, she passes into eternity where she exists entombed in an eternal moment

(continued)

of transcendent love . . ." (Scheper-Hughes, 1992: 364).

The underlying point of Scheper-Hughes' account is that it is the political and social environment that creates the situation in which women's learning how to be mothers includes knowing when to let go of a child who shows that he wants to die. Women know that they cannot develop emotional attachment to all infants because so many of them die. To do so would cause emotional turmoil and grieving that would be devastating. A cultural climate is produced that enables the women of the Alto to minimize the individuality of each infant and become stoic in the face of such high rates of infant mortality. And yet, women know the horrors of their lives. Scheper-Hughes provides one account that summarizes the plight of these women. Black Irene's husband was murdered and then her oldest son, Nego De, was murdered by an assassination death squad.

> "I am three times cursed. My husband was murdered before my own eyes. And I cannot protect my son. The police made me pick over the mutilated bodies in the morgue to find my De. And now I am forced to go on living. I only wish I had the luxury to hang myself. My husband could die. My son could die. But I *cannot die.* . . . Don't pity the young men and the infants who have died here on the Alto do Cruziero. Don't waste any tears on them. Pity us. . . . Weep for the mothers who are condemned to live." (Scheper-Hughes, 1992:408)

Scheper-Hughes, 1992

The community established medical centers, schools, nurseries, and a sports complex. Communal kitchens to feed the needy were established. The progress was so great that Villa El Salvador was nominated for the Nobel Peace Prize in 1986.

Life in the squatter settlements has been portrayed in two predominant conceptualizations. The first and more prevalent emphasizes the chaotic and socially disorganized aspects of the settlement; marital breakdowns, anomie, alienation, poverty, and misery are the lot of the migrant population. The second position takes an opposite stance; it argues that the settlement is able to maintain community organization and family continuity and that the residents have the general ability to adjust to the somewhat overwhelming demands of the potentially debilitating consequences of urban poverty.

As I have discussed, the social-disorganization approach stems from the intellectual tradition in the social sciences that has developed an ideal-type dichotomization of rural and urban life. The ideal typification of rural life stresses the group solidarity and the primacy of personal relationships anchored by familial and kinship bonds. The typification of urban life, on the other hand, sees the development of secondary relationships based on a pragmatic philosophy of looking out for oneself, the absence of viable family and neighborhood relationships, which ultimately lead to social and personal disorganization; the breakdown of personal integration; and crime, delinquency, and individual isolation.

A third approach may be most appropriate. Such an approach recognizes the strength of families and individuals to adapt to social misfortunes and economic poverty. This often takes innovative and creative forms. However, the life of quiet desperation—a life without rest or relaxation—is often the everyday reality of people living under poverty. The account of the experience of Nancy Scheper-Hughes in Brazil provides us with a realistic picture of the plight of the Third World poor. She was a Peace Corps volunteer who came to Alto do Cruziero, a hillside shantytown adjacent to the factiously named town of Bom Jesus de Mata in northeast Brazil in the 1960s and returned as an anthropologist on and off for the next twenty-five years.

OSCAR LEWIS AND THE CULTURE OF POVERTY

Oscar Lewis' studies of the poor in Mexico, Puerto Rico, and New York have appeared in a series of anthropological monographs that have stimulated a vast amount of interest in both academic and public circles. His biographical analysis and sympathetic portrayal of different families are organized around a conceptual framework that he called the culture of poverty.

In *La Vida: A Puerto Rican Family in the Culture of Poverty—San Juan and New York*, Lewis presents a benumbing and almost overwhelming portrayal of three generations of a Puerto Rican family in the slums of San Juan and New York. He portrays through a family biographical framework (much of which is told in the tape-recorded words of the subjects themselves), "the life histories of the individuals . . . reveal[ing] a picture of family disruption, violence, brutality, cheapness of life, lack of love, lack of education, lack of medical facilities—in short, a picture of incredible deprivation, the effects of which cannot be wiped out in a single generation" (Lewis, 1966: xiv). Lewis believes that the study of specific families can best help us understand the relationship between societal institutions and the individual. Through intensive analysis of family systems, the interrelationship between culture and personality becomes meaningful with "whole-family studies bridg[ing] the gap between the conceptual extremes of culture at one pole and the individual at the other" (Lewis, 1966: xx).

The culture of poverty is seen to flourish in societies that have the following characteristics: high rate of unemployment and underemployment, low wages for manual labor, stress on the importance of accumulated wealth and property, and an interpretation that attributes the lack of the accumulation of wealth by the poverty people residing in these societies as a result of their personal inadequacies and inferiorities. In these societies, a virtually autonomous subculture exists among the poor, one that is self-perpetuating and self-defeating. Oscar Lewis sees the culture of poverty developing from families adapting to societal conditions. These adaptations represent an effort to cope with the feelings of hopelessness and despair that arise from their realization that achieving success in terms of the prevailing values and goals is improbable. This hopelessness and despair, this sense of resignation and fatalism involves an inability to put off the satisfaction of immediate desires to plan for the future. A self-perpetuating cycle develops: Low educational motivation leads to inadequate job preparation that, in turn, perpetuates unemployment, poverty, and despair.

Oscar Lewis's (1966) study identifies over seventy traits that characterize the culture of poverty. They are grouped by him into four major categories: the relationship between the subculture and the larger society; the nature of the ghetto, slum, or squatter settlement community; the nature of the family; and the attitudes, values, and character structure of the individual.

1. *The relationship between the subculture and the larger society.* Lewis believes that one of the most crucial characteristics of the culture of poverty is the disengagement and nonintegration of the poor in the major institutions of the larger society. Poverty, segregation and discrimination, fear, suspicion, and apathy are all factors accounting for this lack of effective participation, especially in the larger economic system. Low wages, chronic unemployment, and underemployment lead to low incomes, little savings, the use of the services of exploitative money lenders, the payment of high prices for used furniture and secondhand clothing, and the overpayment for smaller quantities of food staples. There is a low level of literacy and education among the poor that further aggravates the situation.

Although exposed to middle-class values, poor people, on the whole, do not live by them. For example, although many will claim that marriage by law, by the church, or by both is ideal, few will marry. For those with few job prospects, no property, and with little expectation for improvement in the future, a consensual marriage or free union makes good sense and avoids the legal expenses and difficulties involved in marriage and divorce. Women will often turn down marital offers because they feel that it will unnecessarily tie them down to men who are immature, difficult, and generally unreliable. As with the men, the women feel that a consensual union gives them greater freedom and flexibility. By not giving the fathers of their children legal status as husbands, the women have a stronger claim on the children and also maintain exclusive rights to their own property.

2. *The nature of the ghetto, slum, or squatter settlement community.* Poor housing conditions, crowding, and gregariousness characterize the slum community. More important, however, is the minimum of organization beyond the nuclear and extended family. Oscar Lewis (1966) observes that most preliterate people have achieved a higher level of sociocultural organization than the urban slum dweller.

3. *The nature of the family.* The family in the culture of poverty is characterized by the absence of the middle-class trait that cherishes childhood as a specially prolonged and protected stage in the life cycle. In the culture of poverty there is, for example, an early initiation into sex. Free unions or consensual marriages are common, and there is a relatively high incidence of the abandonment of wives and children by men. With the instability of consensual marriage, the family tends to be mother-centered and tied more closely with the mother's extended family of orientation. The female-centered household is given to authoritarianism. Although there is lip service given to family solidarity, it is rarely achieved because of intense sibling rivalry for the limited supply of goods and maternal affection.

4. *The attitudes, values, and character structure of the individual.* Individuals who grow up in the culture of poverty have strong feelings of fatalism, helplessness, dependence, and inferiority. Oscar Lewis (1966) points out that these characteristics are common among black Americans who have the additional disadvantage of racial discrimination; they are also prominent in slum dwellers in Mexico City and San Juan who are not segregated or subject to discrimination as distinct ethnic or racial groups. He lists other traits including a high incidence of weak ego structure; confusion of sexual identification, which reflects maternal deprivation; a strong present-time orientation, with relatively little disposition to delay gratification or plan for the future; and a high tolerance for psychological pathology of all kinds. Finally, there is a widespread belief in male superiority and, among men, a strong preoccupation with *machismo* (masculinity).

CRITIQUE OF THE CULTURE OF POVERTY

The urban anthropologist William Mangin (1970), reviewing the literature on squatter settlements in Peru, Turkey, Athens, Hong Kong, and Brazil, reports that they are characterized by an absence of the culture of poverty. He further points out that: "In terms of cultural views of the world, ideal family and kinship patterns, aspirations, values, and even body movements and language habits, the poor of a country have more in common with the rest of their country (or culture) than they have with the poor of another country (or culture)" (Mangin, 1970: xvii).

Mangin criticizes the view of the cyclical nature of the culture of poverty—the passing down of the patterns from one generation to the next. Mangin believes that it is necessary to emphasize the fact that peasant communities are part of the larger society, and that decisions made by the more powerful elements of the society relating to the peasant community are more important in maintaining their economic depression than are any questionable social and personality attributes of the poor.

Oscar Lewis' culture of poverty position is similar to the social-disorganization view that sees the impact of urbanization in terms of depersonalization and anomie with the poverty community almost totally devoid of community and associational life. However, as Charles A. Valentine (1968) has pointed out in his much-cited critique of the culture of poverty, Lewis himself contradicts this position in his description of La Esmeralda:

> The setting for the story of the Ries family is La Esmeralda, an old and colorful slum in San Juan, built on a steep embankment between the city's ancient fort walls and the sea. Squeezed into an area not more than five city blocks long and a few hundred yards wide are 900 houses inhabited by 3,600 people. . . .
>
> Seen from the walls above, the slum looks almost prosperous. This is because all the houses have roofs of new green tar paper. . . .
>
> Even though La Esmeralda is only ten minutes away from the heart of San Juan, it is physically and socially marginal to the city. The wall above it stands as a kind of symbol separating it from the city. La Esmeralda forms a *little community of its own* [italics added] with a cemetery, a church, a small dispensary and maternity clinic, and one elementary school. There are many small stores, bars and taverns. . . .
>
> To the people of Greater San Juan, La Esmeralda has a bad reputation . . . today the residents of La Esmeralda think of it as a relatively elegant healthful place, with its beautiful view of the sea, its paved streets, its new roofs, the absence of mosquitoes, the low rentals and its nearness to their places of work.

. . . the general mood of the people of La Esmeralda is one of gaiety and exuberance. They seem outgoing, friendly and expressive, with relatively little distrust of outsiders. They live amid constant noise from radios, juke boxes, and television sets, and spend a great deal of time in the stores and bars, where they drink and play dominoes. (Lewis, 1966: xxxii-xxxiii)

Valentine (1968) argues that the essence of the culture of poverty position is the comparison of the lifeways of groups who live by a distinctive poverty culture consisting largely of negative qualities, lacks, and absences—group disintegration, personal disintegration, and lack of purposeful action—in contrast to that of the more affluent segments of the population, who exhibit positive qualities.

Valentine poses an alternative interpretation by suggesting that the destructive nature of the social life of these poverty-level people is determined by the structure of the society as a whole, as well as by forces beyond the control of poor people; that is, the variations in lifestyles of the poor are not shaped by a distinct culture. Rather, they are influenced by the actual conditions of life under poverty that is inconsistent with the fulfillment of the cultural design.

More specifically, consensual unions and female-centered or mother-centered households may be regarded as flexible adaptations to the uncertainty and fluctuations of economic circumstances. Thus, alternative family structures are developed as necessities to cope with poverty conditions and should be seen as positive contributions to the health and well-being of family members. For children, socialization occurs in a wider network of relatives, adults, and peers rather than being concentrated in the nuclear family. Valentine asserts that this may contribute to healthy early maturity, including development of numerous supportive relationships and sources of emotional security.

In a similar vein, Hyman Rodman (1965) states that it would be more appropriate to interpret the behavior of poverty families (he uses the term, lower-class families) as *solutions to problems* they face—owing to life under poverty conditions—than as *problems*. In an insightful illustration, Rodman points out that the characteristics attributed to the poor—promiscuous sexual relationships, *illegitimate children, desertion* by husbands and fathers, unmarried mothers—use middle-class-biased terminology and distortions that tend to emphasize a social-disorganization model of family behavior. Rodman emphasizes that these italicized concepts are not utilized by the poor and that it is misleading to describe their behavior in this manner. Since such words as *promiscuity, illegitimacy,* and *desertion* have middle-class meanings and judgmental implications, Rodman believes that it is necessary to analyze and describe the family patterns of the poor by paying more attention to the language and description that the poor employ in analyzing their own behavior. By doing this, social scientists can avoid "the major middle-class conception of lower-class families—viewing certain patterns as problems, when in reality they can easily be viewed as solutions" (Rodman, 1965:225).

Rodman (1963) introduced a concept, "value stretch," which is helpful to further understand this argument. By value stretch, he means that values are stretched to adjust to conditions of poverty and depravation. He utilized this concept later in his analysis (1971) of lower-class family behavior and attitudes in Coconut Village, a small rural village in northeastern Trinidad. Rodman focuses on the impact that poverty has on cultural and family organization.

Rodman finds three types of marital or quasi-marital relationships—*friending, living*, and *married*—in Trinidad. The three types vary in the degree of acceptance of marital responsibility, especially on the part of the man. *Friending* involves the least responsibility and occurs most frequently. The marital pair do not live together in the same household. In this form of relationship, the woman is supposed to make herself sexually available and the man is supposed to provide support for the woman and any children they may have. Rodman reports that most *friending* relationships eventually dissolve, but a substantial number evolve into a *living* relationship. During *living*, the couple live together but are not legally married. The *living* relationship is seen to combine the advantages of common residence characteristic of legal marriage, without its legal responsibility but with the limited responsibility of *friending*. The *married* relationship, to all extent and purposes, is similar to a *living* relationship, but there is a church wedding and legal ties between the man and woman. The *married* relationship occurs less frequently than the *living* among the lower class and is seen to reflect the reluctance to take on responsibility.

Rodman believes that the reluctance to take on the responsibility of marriage is closely related to the generally cautious attitude of both sexes in placing trust and confidence in the other, as well as to a shared feeling that any marital relationship is a temporary one. These attitudes reflect the relation of family life to the structure of the larger society, particularly to its economy. The lower-class families of Coconut Village suffer from economic deprivation. The land is poor and the meager crops that are produced are difficult to market because of inadequate transportation systems. Consequently, wage earning is necessary to supplement and, in most cases, to provide a more reliable income base for the family. Unfortunately, wage earnings are unreliable. The lower-class man involved in wage labor finds much unemployment, underemployment, poorly paid employment, and unskilled employment.

Since the man's role as wage earner and income provider is central to the family relationship, his status within the family is determined by his economic success. If the man is responsible for the financial support of his wife and children and his economic circumstances are precarious, it becomes more understandable why men are reluctant to take on the additional responsibilities of marriage. The consequences for the man when he is unable satisfactorily to complete his duties as a wage earner are the loss of status, esteem, income power, and position in the community and in the family. It is this economic factor that explains the greater frequency of *friending* relationships than *living* relationships than marriages. These variations provide the individual with different patterns to permit some semblance of family life in the face of economic uncertainties in Coconut Village.

These three forms of marital and quasi-marital relationships are seen by Rodman as being functional for the lower-class family since they provide solutions to social, economic, and legal problems. In response to the culture of poverty argument, Rodman suggests that members of the lower class stretch the values of the society to fit their circumstances—they do not develop a distinct culture of poverty. They do not abandon the values of legal marriage and legitimate children but stretch these values to allow for other marital systems (for example, *friending* and *living*, which allow for the existence of nonlegal unions and illegitimate children). By not rejecting the general value system of the society (its culture), the poor are able to add additional value choices to their cultural base, which helps them to adjust to their deprived circumstances.

THE CULTURE OF POVERTY AND THE MOYNIHAN REPORT

The Moynihan report, *The Negro Family: The Case for National Action*, is a document prepared in 1965 by the Office of Planning and Research of the U.S. Department of Labor under the supervision of the Assistant Secretary of Labor, Daniel Patrick Moynihan. The report is an illustration of the use of the culture of poverty position and has had important social-policy implications since its publication more than thirty years ago. The report is loaded with such terms as *tangle of pathology*, *broken families*, *illegitimacy*, and *social disorganization* to describe the family structure of African Americans living in poverty. These terms are commonly associated with the culture of poverty orientation, which was described previously. The implications of the report are that it is necessary to change the culture of poor African American families if the government expects them to improve their economic position. The focus of social-policy legislation that follows from this position is concerned with psychiatric treatment, social-welfare reforms, dissemination of information relating to birth control and family planning, and other individual-oriented programs. Alternative policy would see the need to create jobs, to train individuals to fill these jobs, and to institute reform designed to reduce the large economic distribution inequalities in the United States. Although the report was published in 1965 and has been severely criticized for its biases and distortions, it still reflects a viewpoint that is held by many laypersons, social scientists, and legislators in the United States. This is especially important in that such a position has led to the wastage of public monies and has diverted maximum effort away from the task at hand—the ending of poverty and its concomitant evils in the United States.

The dominant thesis of the Moynihan report is stated dramatically:

> At the heart of the deterioration of the fabric of Negro society is the deterioration of the Negro family.
> It is the fundamental source of the weakness of the Negro community at the present time.
> The white family has achieved a high degree of stability and is maintaining that stability. . . .
> *By contrast, the family structure of lower-class Negroes is highly unstable, and in many urban centers is approaching complete breakdown.* [Printed in boldface.] (U.S. Department of Labor, 1965:5)

Although the Moynihan report discusses discrimination and unemployment and sees them as being contributory causes of the difficulties of poverty in black family systems, the report places its primary emphasis on the demographic data culled from census and governmental reports on households—*dissolved* marriages, *broken* families, *illegitimacy*, welfare rates, Aid to Families with Dependent Children figures, and delinquency and crime rates. From these sources, Moynihan develops a social-disorganization thesis with a lower-class subculture that is characterized by matriarchy, emasculated males, educational failure, delinquency, crime, and drug addiction.

Rainwater and Yancey (1967) note that the report is neither a scholarly article prepared for a professional journal nor a simple governmental position paper. It is a hybrid, presenting certain social science information to advocate a social-policy position that follows the guidelines of the culture of poverty argument and postulates the existence of a self-perpetuating cycle of poverty anchored by the family system. The policy implications follow directly from this position:

> The fundamental problem . . . is that of family structure . . . the Negro family in the urban ghettos is crumbling . . . for vast numbers of the unskilled, poorly educated, city working class the fabric of conventional social relationships has all but disintegrated. . . . So long as this situation persists, the cycle of poverty and disadvantage will continue to repeat itself.
>
> . . . a national effort towards the problems of Negro Americans must be directed towards the question of family structure. The object should be to strengthen the Negro family so as to enable it to raise and support its members as do other families. After that, how this group of Americans chooses to run its affairs, take advantage of its opportunities or fail to do so, is none of the nation's business. (U.S. Department of Labor, 1965: Preface, 47-48)

The controversy surrounding the report lies in its support of the culture of poverty position in its stress on the cultural deprivations of the black family that have impeded it from taking advantage of the opportunities the United States offers. Further, although briefly stating that the socioeconomic system played a role in the deterioration of the Negro community, the Moynihan report emphasizes the dysfunctional characteristics of an African American matriarchal family structure.

It is vital to consider the basis of the culture of poverty criticism of the African American matriarchal family structure and its alleged consequences. At the onset, a conceptual clarification must be made. The term *matriarchy* refers to a family authority system controlled by females, whereas a female-headed household refers to a household where no male head is present. It does not necessarily follow that a census-defined female-headed household is a matriarchy. Thus, it is a gross oversimplification simply to equate the two, which is what Moynihan does without any further basis of information; that is, Moynihan does not justify his use of social statistics as indicators of cultural patterns. Although census figures give us a demographic picture of statistical shape, they tell us nothing directly about either the structure or process in a cultural system or about the variety of cultural designs underlying it.

Robert Staples (1971) argues that regardless of the role of African American women in the family, it is necessary to stress that the female role evolved out of the struggle for African American survival. The position is similar to that of Rodman

(1965, 1971), who views the behavioral adaptations of poverty people as solutions to the problems of economic deprivation. Andrew Billingsley (1969) has shown that many families in the black inner-city ghettos have demonstrated an impressive capacity to adapt to the social, cultural, and economic deprivations fostered in them by the larger society and have developed strong family relationships. Finally, Rainwater (1966) contradicts the notion that female-centered households are dysfunctional; in research of poverty families, Rainwater finds an *adaptive* urban matricentric family form (among others) that successfully copes with the problems of poverty. Carol B. Stack offers additional support to this position.

Carol B. Stack's *All Our Kin* (1974) is an anthropological study of a poor black community, which she called The Flats, that is located in a midwestern city called Jackson Harbor. She examines how families cope with poverty by adapting domestic networks to link people who are not necessarily related. Stack emphasizes that a census-defined, female-headed, single-parent household does not indicate separatedness or isolation. A cooperative support network exists that is composed of both relatives and fictive kin, who are treated as kin by family members and are given such kinship terms as sister, aunt, and uncle. These people unite for mutual aid and to meet daily needs.

> Black families living in The Flats need a steady source of cooperative support to survive. They share with one another because of the urgency of their needs. Alliances between individuals are created around the clock as kin and friends exchange and give and obligate one another. They trade food stamps, rent money, a TV, hats, dice, a car, a nickel here, a cigarette there, food, milk, grits, and children.
>
> . . . Without the help of kin, fluctuations in the meager flow of available goods could easily destroy a family's ability to survive. . . . Kin and close friends who fall into similar economic crises know that they may share the food, dwelling, and even the few scarce luxuries of those individuals in their kin network. Despite the relatively high cost of rent and food in urban black communities, the collective power within kin-based exchange networks keeps people from going hungry. (Stack, 1974:32-33)

Stack stresses that social scientists who employ such culture of poverty terms as *pathology* and *social disorganization* fail to understand the adaptive forms of familial and quasi-familial relationships and structures that have developed in these economically deprived communities. Further, they are not aware how resilient urban black families are to the socioeconomic conditions of poverty, the inexorable unemployment, and the limited access to scarce economic opportunities of single-parent mothers and their children who receive welfare under such programs as Aid to Families with Dependent Children (AFDC). Stack points out that these structural adaptations do not lock people into a cycle of poverty or prevent them from marrying or removing themselves from the networks. But her study does indicate that the very success of these cooperative networks force women to think twice about marriage:

Forms of social control both within the kin network and in the larger society work against successful marriages in The Flats. In fact, couples rarely chance marriage unless a man has a job; often the job is temporary, low paying, insecure, and the worker gets laid off whenever he is not needed. Women come to realize that welfare benefits and ties within kin networks provide greater security for social mobility. A woman may be immediately cut off the welfare roles when a husband returns home from prison, the army, or if she gets married. Thus, the society's welfare system collaborates in weakening the position of the black male. (Stack, 1974:113)

In summary, Stack's work graphically reveals how viable family structures develop to handle chronic poverty and governmental programs that reinforce welfare dependency and unemployment. Unfortunately, in the years since Stack's research, poverty has significantly increased among African Americans. As we shall see later in this chapter, this poverty has undermined these extended family network support systems and has had a particularly negative impact on female-headed households. However, without them the plight of the African American poor would be in even worse condition.

In discussing coping with poverty I would remind the reader of the existence of extended kinship networks reported earlier in this book for other ethnic groups including white ethnics and Mexican Americans who are experiencing economic uncertainties. Similar systems are also found among Native Americans (American Indians) located both in urban and nonurban settings (Metcalf, 1979; Red Horse, 1980; Red Horse, Lewis, Feit, and Deeker, 1978). However, for Native Americans living under poverty conditions in urban areas, urbanization patterns and Americanization processes have been very harmful to the family and familial support networks. Dorothy Miller (1979) studied Native Americans living in Oakland, California. She identifies four individual types that represent different "modes of adaptation" to urban life:

Traditional, in which the person clings to Indian values and behaviors; Transitional, where the individual adapts to white means and ends and leaves traditional values and behaviors behind; Bicultural, in which the person is able to hold onto Indian values and means and is also able to adapt to white ends without considering them primary value structure; and Marginal, whose individuals are anomic in both worlds, with ends and means neither Indian nor white. (Miller, 1979:479)

Each of these different modes of adaptation has a corresponding family classification reflecting its adherence to traditional cultural values and the degree of acceptance of Anglo-American values and lifestyles. Miller believes that the family type that has had the greatest difficulty in making the social and psychological adjustments to urban life was the "marginal" family. This form of family suffers in the city, and because it has lost its Indian language and culture, it is maladapted to that form of life as well. The family group that has the best pattern of adjustment is the "bicultural." It retains its native language and many practices and beliefs while making it in the city. The other two family groups, the "traditional" and the "transitional" are seen to be undergoing transformation into the bicultural type as they adapt to the conditions of the city of Oakland.

As for the Moynihan report overall, most social scientists conclude that it was more of a polemical document with social-policy implications than a scientific one. Gans (1967a) believes that the focus on family problems leads to a clamor for pseudopsychiatric programs as well as to a wave of social and psychiatric solutions that are intended to change the alleged dysfunctional black female-headed family to an alleged functional white middle-class type of family. Gans feels that too much attention is devoted to the disabilities and that insufficient attention is given to the causes. He advocates that instead of psychiatric solutions the following types of programs should be instituted: the establishment of jobs, the development of income maintenance programs, the building of housing outside ghetto areas, and the desegregation of existing housing.

His position is an illustration of the situational approach. This orientation argues that although the behavior of poverty families is different than the middle-class pattern, both groups have a similar culture. The behavior is viewed as an adaptation to poverty conditions. This is a direct rebuke of the culture of poverty position. In a different paper, Gans (1967b) views the poor as an economically and politically deprived group whose attitudes and behavior are seen as adaptations, just as the behavior and attitudes of the affluent are adaptations to their social situation.

Similarly, Elliot Liebow (1967), in his ethnographic study *Tally's Corner—A Study of Negro Street Corner Men*, stresses the point that although each generation may provide role models for each succeeding one, of greater importance is that the similarities between generations "do not result from 'cultural transmission' but from the fact that the son goes out and independently experiences the same failures, in the same areas, and for much the same reasons as his father" (Liebow, 1967:223). Liebow, in his study of lower-class black men in Washington, DC, found no evidence indicating deviation from white middle-class norms nor did he find that family role deviancy is perpetuated intergenerationally. Liebow concludes that there is a direct relationship between socioeconomic discrimination and family instability.

William Ryan (1971) argues that the culture of poverty position and such manifestations of it as the Moynihan report blame the victim for being poor; the reform is still to be of the lower classes, the poor, with some saying that they should reform themselves and others saying that the rich and more affluent classes should help. As Charles A. Valentine (1968) has argued, few say that the more powerful, the influential controlling classes of the culture, should change or that the total social structure needs changing. Instead, they place the burden for reform on the poor and are primarily concerned with doing away with a culture and not with poverty.

My position is that the culture of poverty perspective that focuses on family structure is too narrow. It does not matter whether we evaluate family structure as pathological (a problem) or as a positive functional adjustment (a solution); the real issue is the causes and consequences of racial, economic, political, and social inequality. The following statement by Leonard Reissman (1972), although concerned with the

African American poverty family, can be generalized to all families who live under the wretched conditions of poverty:

> It must certainly be the case that, if blacks did not suffer from inequalities and were economically secure, then the type of family they have would not bother anyone; at the most, the nature of the concern would be of an entirely different order than it is now. By the same reasoning, I must assume that the efforts to change the matriarchy, and thus to cure the pathology, are not likely to make much difference in the conditions of blacks if the causes and consequences of their inequality are left untouched. Rather, I am convinced that if the causes and consequences of inequality are removed, then the structure of the Negro family will become much less important as an issue for reformers. (Reissman, 1972:94)

WHITE FAMILIES IN POVERTY

I believe that it would be instructive to discuss the characteristics of poor *white* families living in poverty. All too frequently, sociology textbooks focus solely on poor black families in America and disregard the plight of their white counterparts. In addition, discussions of the American white family in these textbooks virtually ignore the existence of poor white families and tend implicitly to juxtapose in the reader's mind poverty and social minorities.

Robert Coles (1968) describes the situation of poor white families in Appalachia and notes that their adaptation to poverty is similar to the adaptation made by persons living in the racial ghettos of urban American and the squatter settlements of the Third World. He sees the behavior of the poor as reasonable responses to poverty conditions and not the symptoms of a dysfunctional cultural system. The following statement summarizes Coles' position:

> Appalachia is full of ironies, but nothing is more ironic than the fact that America's oldest ethnic group, its white Anglo-Saxon Protestants, live there in poverty as desperate as that experienced by any other impoverished people. It took courage and enterprise to settle the region—and now the region's people are called inert, apathetic, and unresourceful. The region has experienced the severest kind of unemployment as a result of technological change, and yet side by side one sees an almost primitive economy. If ever there was a section of America that needed planned capital investment, federally sustained—as indeed this country has done in other regions of the world with its money—then indeed Appalachia is that region.
>
> In my experience the people of Appalachia do not fit the usual sociological and anthropological descriptions applied to them. By that I mean that their apparent inertia and apathy are reasonable responses to a lack of opportunity and a lack of employment. Given jobs, real jobs, jobs that are not substitutes for work, Appalachian men and women work well and hard. They

also can be open, friendly, and generous—even to an outsider like me. What they do not want is a kind of patronizing and condescending sympathy. They are proud and stubborn people who want from this country a share of its wealth. Given that, I don't think we would have any "psychological problems" with the region's citizens. (Coles, 1968:27)

In another study of the nonethnic white poor of Appalachia, Rhonda K. Halperin (1990) provides a comparative example to Carol B. Stack's analysis of kinship and exchange analysis of poor African Americans in their community. Halperin studies a rural community in Kentucky. Here the people did things "the Kentucky way." They earned their living through many kinds of paid and unpaid work. Most importantly, they shared their resources within extended family networks incorporated within a complex, family-oriented economy. Kinship involvements serve as a sense of identity as well as promoting economic well-being for its family members.

In what Halperin (1990) calls "multiple livelihood strategies," she depicts how families integrate involvement in three economic sectors: agrarian, marketplace, and wage labor. The illustrated family members' activities include housepainting and indoor house renovations; the selling of odds and ends, obtained in garage sales and auctions, at a local marketplace; the processing of homegrown beans and cucumbers to be used during the winter; and the temporary shift work provided by a nearby factory. The schedules of the family members' work must be coordinated with each other and with kin who provide supportive services such as baby-sitting and sharing with each other surplus farm produce.

Halperin believes that the strategies employed by these families can be understood as a form of resistance to capitalism and of dependency upon the state. She compares their rural agrarian economy to that of a subsistence economy of a peasant society, the ultimate aim being the provisioning and maintenance of family networks. In summary, Halperin sees as the goal of the familial economy ". . . to make ends meet economically and psychologically and to keep the kin network intact through everyday economic activities, many of which have been going on for decades . . ." (1990: 144).

The impact of modern urban life on these people can be conjectured from a now classic participant observation field study of poor white families by Joseph T. Howell (1973), *Hard Living on Clay Street*, about a blue-collar suburb of Washington, DC where southern migrants moved to Washington from farms in North Carolina and the mountains of West Virginia. The men had service-oriented jobs: painters, plasterers, plumbers, repairmen, auto mechanics, truck drivers, and so on. Stereotypically, they were called rednecks, lower class, irresponsible, and white trash.

Howell (1973:263–352) distinguishes between two opposing lifestyles, which represent two ends of a continuum of family life on Clay Street—hard living and settled living—by delineating seven general areas of attitudes and behavior:

1. *Heavy drinking.* Heavy drinking occurred quite frequently in hard-living families and occurred only occasionally, if at all, among settled families.

2. *Marital stability.* Hard-living families were married more than once, with their current marriages being precarious. Settled families had long-term stable marriages.

3. *Toughness.* Profanity, talk of violence, and general attitudes of "toughness" were commonplace among both hard-living husbands and wives, whereas the settled-living families had a moderate approach to life.

4. *Political alienation.* Clay Street's hard-living families rarely voted or held strong political beliefs. This was based on their view that government was unresponsive, corrupt, and irrelevant to their needs. In contrast, despite their feelings of frustration, the settled-living families voted as political conservatives and felt that it was worthwhile to fight for and preserve the society.

5. *Rootlessness.* The hard-living families were more mobile; they rented their houses, moved frequently, and had a general attitude that they had no roots in the community or elsewhere. The settled families owned their homes, lived in the same home for a period of time, and felt ties to the community.

6. *Present-time orientation.* Hard-living families were preoccupied with surviving from day to day and gave little thought to the future. The settled families of Clay Street, by virtue of the fact that they could save a little money, expressed greater concern about the community and their family's future.

7. *Individualism.* Hard-living families valued independence and self-reliance, calling themselves loners. They had little involvement with or use for clubs or organizations, and they liked to work alone. The settled families, on the other hand, participated in community life and in groups and rarely had the same feelings of individualism.

Howell believes that the degree of marital stability was a key indication of involvement in either of the two lifestyles. Howell quotes a local police officer to illustrate this:

> Well, there are basically two types of folks in this community: middle class and what you might call lower class. The middle-class folks, the working people, they never cause no trouble—law abiding, upright, quiet. Now the lower class, they are different. We're all the time getting calls when husbands and wives get into fights, husband leaves, wife leaves, that sort of thing. (Howell, 1973:274)

The hard-living families of Clay Street were characterized by family instability. Howell reports that practically every hard-living family member had been married more than once, with many having common-law consensual marriages. A striking characteristic of the Clay Street marriages was the changing nature of the marriage relationship: Many marriages were on shaky ground and apparently stable couples would suddenly break up, their marriage dissolved. The causes of marital dissolution varied—adulterous affairs, drinking, and unemployment were the most frequently cited causes. The couples viewed divorce as an eventual consequence of marriage; remarriage was also seen as an integral part of the hard life. Howell quotes a frequent philosophical attitude regarding marriage: "Divorce is simply part of life, that's just the way things are" (Howell, 1973:290). Their ambivalence toward marriage is illustrated by a quote from a male resident of Clay Street:

> Well it's too bad. Sure, I want my marriage to work out. But it didn't. And it doesn't for most folks around here. The way I see it, it's inherited. My grandaddy, he had it. He was married several times. My dad and mom, hell, they had it. And my children, they are going to have it, too. Divorces, separations, broken marriages. Hell, that's just the way life is. It just runs in the family. It's inherited. (Howell, 1973:292)

The frequency of divorces and other forms of marital instability had ramifications not only for the couple but also for their involvement with each of their extended families. Howell reports that the residents of Clay Street rarely saw their relatives, including such close ones as sisters and brothers. Many did not know whether these relatives were alive or not. The absence of ties with relatives is partially explained by the fact that the husbands and wives were themselves from broken homes. Further, the ones who moved from the South or from the Appalachian Mountains to Clay Street described themselves as black sheep compared to the rest of their families. The general pattern, according to Howell, was for the families to scatter, with some remaining on the farm; some settling in the Washington, DC, area; some going to industrial northern cities or moving out West; or some just disappearing. The result was that although many of the hard-living families of Clay Street had nostalgia for their rural homes, there was no "home" for them to return to and there were very few close relatives who stayed there. The result was a feeling of rootlessness.

Most husbands and wives fought, and both tried to maintain an image of toughness and independence. These attitudes reflect the difficult marital experiences of the couple. One hard-living wife experienced an early marriage, divorce, the birth of six children and the death of two of the children, poverty, poor health, and her current husband's alcoholism and violence. She explains her attitudes this way: "Take me . . . If I wasn't a fighter I'd never of made it, not to say that I've made it now" (Howell, 1973:303). Yet underneath that tough image, Howell reports that most hard-living families of Clay Street were compassionate and sensitive and demonstrated compassion and affection for each other and their children.

Howell concludes that simplistic social-psychological and social and cultural causal theories do not provide an adequate explanation of these families. He argues that providing social-psychological reasons for a particular individual's behavior—coming from a broken home, alcoholism prevalent, and so on—obscures the structural and cultural forces that influence an individual's and a family's behavior patterns. Howell also condemns sweeping societal generalities to explain the behavior of the poor. He rejects simplistic structural arguments and culture of poverty theories that see the main reason for "reckless" and "unstable" behavior as a result of self-perpetuating family instability. In his concluding cautionary statement he argues a point that is important for all of us to keep in mind in our own personal analysis and depiction of poverty families:

BOX 6-2   The Contemporary American Family

Statistics on Marriage and Out-of-Wedlock Births Represent a Series of Disasters

William Raspberry

Some statistics contain their own dissertations, providing enough ammunition to support virtually any theory that comes to mind.

Try this: "In 1975, nearly 77 percent of black women in their late 20s had been married at some time in their lives. By 1990, the corresponding figure was 45 percent—a drop of over 30 points in 15 years."

What *can't* you make of numbers like those? Or these: The percentage of at-least-once-married black women in their early 30s declined from 87 percent in 1975 to 61 percent in 1990—26 percentage points.

The statistics (from Nicholas Eberstadt, writing in the January/February issue of Society magazine) can be used as grist for virtually any social-policy mill: welfare reform, gender equity, criminal justice, job creation, profound—and not necessarily negative—changes in America's economics and culture.

For me, the numbers represent a disaster—no, a series of disasters.

To get one matter out of the way: The statistics on black women merely foreshadow a trend involving white women as well. As is so often the case, if you want to see how black problems would look wearing a white face, just wait a generation.

But as to the problem now at hand, why do I insist on seeing it in terms of disaster? To begin with, I doubt that the majority of these never-married women are single entirely by choice. I can't give you statistics, but I can tell you from personal experience that an enormous number of eligible black women are single because they can't find comparably eligible black men.

And where are the men? In a depressing number of cases they are unemployed, undereducated, in the clutches of the criminal justice system, involved in criminal activity, or dead—of violence or of disease, notably AIDS. Moreover, one need only look at the makeup of college en-

Nonmarriage doesn't mean just the absence of men from families; it means the transformation of men, and of boys.

rollments to see that the proportion of men that might reasonably be considered "eligible" for professional women continues to shrink.

It is possible to argue, of course, that nonmarriage, however socially awkward it may be for a time, is simply the result of a trend that has seen women become less economically dependent on men. Women no longer have to marry their financial security. (And women who have no financial security don't help themselves by marrying financially insecure men.) The role of the husband as protector and breadwinner has been on the decline for a long time, and we shouldn't be surprised to see the decline in marriage rates and stability.

All true, though not necessarily benign. Besides, we are not talking only about free-choosing adults. As Eberstadt notes: "High rates of nonmarriage, of course, can no longer be interpreted as signifying high rates of childlessness. Paralleling the breakup of two-parent families is the rise of families that never formed. Over the past four decades, our country has experienced a veritable explosion of out-of-wedlock births."

In 1960, for example, only about one birth in 20 was to an unmarried mother. By 1992, it was three in 10, and climbing. That's for *all* births, not just black births.

"As these large fractions should indicate," Eberstadt says, "out-of-wedlock birth is not only, or even predominantly, a black phenomenon. . . . In 1992, 37 percent of the country's illegitimate births were black; 63 percent were *not*." Moreover, black teenagers accounted for fewer than *one-eighth* of the out-of-wedlock births of 1992.

We've learned to stop calling these children "illegitimate," but terminology is the least of their problems. They are extremely likely to be

(continued)

poor—significantly poorer even than the children of divorce. The are more likely to spend some time as welfare dependents, with all the negative implications that involves. They (especially the boys) are far more likely than their two-parent counterparts to become involved in crime.

And even that isn't the end of the disasters. Nonmarriage doesn't mean just the *absence* of men from families; it means the *transformation* of men, and of boys. When men become unnecessary to their families, they are stripped of the socially acceptable purpose for their in-built aggressiveness. They don't stop being aggressive; they merely turn it to antisocial activity. Barbara Defoe Whitehead has written that if you control for family makeup, you eliminate the relationship between race and crime and even of low income and crime.

One more thing: Children of never-married parents are more likely to become unwed parents themselves, continuing the disaster yet another generation.

I look at Eberstadt's statistics and ask myself: How can we start to make marriage a big deal again?

Syndicated columnist William Raspberry won the 1994 Pulitzer Prize for commentary.

Philadelphia Inquirer, 29 March 1996. Reprinted with permission by the Philadelphia Inquirer, 1996.

June [a Clay Streeter] put it better than anyone else: "You can call us what you want to, but folks around here, hell, we're just plain folks. We got problems like everybody else. Maybe the difference is we don't try to shove 'em all into some closet. That's 'cause we ain't too proud to admit we're just folks." Above all else, the people on Clay Street were "just folks," and their humanity expressed itself in every aspect of their lives. (Howell, 1973:359-360)

AFRICAN AMERICAN FAMILIES IN POVERTY

In the more than thirty years since the publication of the Moynihan Report, the African American family has made great strides. Today, there are over 30 million African Americans. A larger percentage of African Americans are more educated, earn higher salaries, have more prestigious jobs, and are more politically active. Four times as many African American families, over one million, are affluent compared to their counterparts of thirty years ago. O'Hare and others (O'Hare, Pollard, Mann, and Kent, 1991) attribute this rise to a realization of the opportunities in education and employment of the 1960s civil rights movement. They identify these people as well-educated (about a third are college graduates), homeowners, (more than three-quarters own their own home), in the prime earning years (66 percent are age 35 to 55), married (nearly eight out of ten), and live in the suburbs.

Charles Willie (1988) describes these affluent African American families as having spouses with college or graduate degrees and at least one partner having a professional job. They also tend to have husbands who are the dominating person in the household. He further observes that there is a sense of community responsibility held by these families. "All achievement by members in black middle-class families is for the purpose of group advancement as well as individual enhancement (Willie, 1988:183). The white family, in contrast, tends to overemphasize individual autonomy and freedom without sufficient attention to family solidarity.

Yet, there is growing class diversity within the African American community and between African Americans and whites. African American families' median income is about 56 percent as much as white families' income. This is even less than the 61 percent ratio of 1969 (Staples, 1994). This figure is even more startling if we take into consideration the fact that more African American families (two-thirds) have multiple income earners than white families (one-half). Employment and salary figures for African American males is much less than white males. The unemployment rate is twice that of whites, and more are in lower income jobs. This fact has serious ramifications for their marital status. Robert Staples, a leading scholar on the African American family observes: "Men who cannot find work not only have trouble maintaining a stable marital and family life but often cannot find a woman willing to marry them in the first place" (1994:254).

About 50 percent of African American families have both parents present. This compares to 56 percent in 1980 and 68 percent in 1970. For white families, in comparison, more than three-quarters (83 percent) are headed by married couples, although this figure has also slipped in the past two decades (O'Hare et al., 1991). In the early 1980s over 80 percent of adult African American males worked and supported their households. Ten years later, only about 70 percent work and contribute the majority of the family household income. Approximately 26 percent of African American families have incomes below $10,000 compared to only 8 percent of white families. Similarly 42 percent were in the $25,000 or more income bracket; 69 percent of whites were in this category.

Andrew Billingsley (1992) has observed that there has been a dramatic change in the status of working-class nonpoor families. In 1969 they composed nearly half (42 percent) of all African American families. Their number then started to decline so that by 1990 they represented less than a third (31 percent) of all African American families. At the same time, the poverty rate has increased. It now is roughly three times that of whites with more than 30 percent living in poverty. In the past fifteen years, there is a pattern of declining rates in marriage, later age of first marriage, higher divorce rates, increase in female-headed households, and higher proportion of children living in female-headed families. While there is an increase in these family characteristics among whites as well, they are not nearly as dramatic. The fatherless home has become a reality, for the majority—62 percent—of families with children are now headed by one parent. In 1965, the Moynihan Report put this figure at 25 percent. These family characteristics are particularly prominent in the poorer segments of the African American population.

As I have indicated, these prevailing African American family variations have been interpreted, in part, as adaptations to the special circumstances in which African Americans find themselves and, in part, to certain differential values attributable to these circumstantial variations. In this section, I examine and try to shed light on the contemporary state of affairs of African American families living under poverty conditions.

To try to explain the growing class diversity within the African American community, social scientists have developed a number of views and diverging opinions that have led to considerable debate. In his 1978 book *The Declining Significance of Race,* William J. Wilson argued that racial distinction is not as important a factor in determining the economic opportunities of blacks as is their social class. Wilson does not claim that racism has completely vanished, but rather he contends that economic and class differences have become more important now than race for determining access to positions of power and privilege and for entering middle-class and upper-status groups. Through affirmative-action programs, qualified blacks (his term) meeting the educational criteria are able to take advantage of new opportunities for better paying white-collar jobs found in the expanding government and private corporate sectors. Unfortunately, blacks in the underclass continue to be subordinated; relegated to low-paying service, unskilled labor, and farm jobs; and trapped in poverty.

Wilson feels that present trends offer little hope unless there is recognition of the dependency nature of welfare and until there is recognition of the need to provide skills and education to the urban poor. If this is not done, society cannot effectively attack the problem of inequality. Wilson believes that the Moynihan report mistook a social-class problem for a problem of black culture. The problem for Wilson, then, is no longer race but the existence of an extremely poorly equipped and disadvantaged underclass that makes up about one-third of the black population and a sizable number of whites, Hispano-Americans, and Native Americans as well. The causes are broad changes in the American economy that has seen the rapid decline in factory jobs and an emergence of service jobs that are either very low skill, low pay or very high skill, high pay.

In another work, Wilson, with his associate Kathryn Neckerman (1986), demonstrates that high unemployment is a major factor in explaining the low number of marriages among young African American men and the explosive growth of families headed by women. Expanding on this theme, *The Truly Disadvantaged* (1987) documents the relationship between male joblessness and high divorce rates, low remarriage rates, and the high ratio of out-of-wedlock births. Wilson critically examines public policy approaches to the ghetto underclass and calls for comprehensive public policy attention to the connection between the poverty status of female-headed families and black male prospects for stable employment. Other sociologists do not agree with Wilson. One of his most vocal opponents is Charles V. Willie, whose *Caste and Class Controversy* (1979) and *A New Look in Black Families* (1981) maintain that economics is but one facet of the larger society and should therefore not be considered in isolation. Willie argues that white racism permeates society, affecting all social institutions and controlling entry to all desirable positions in education, employment, housing, and social status. Willie points out that while they have moved up on many social indicators of social position, including education, blacks have not caught up in income. Further, Willie asserts that blacks, while gaining middle-class status, often become psychologically chained in a white world that permits only token entry and retains actual power, control, and wealth.

Willie, in his influential book *A New Look at Black Families* (Third edition, 1988), puts forth the opinion that economic factors in themselves can provide only partial explanations for black poverty. He continues to argue that racism still permeates American society, affects all social institutions, and controls entry to all desirable positions in education, employment, housing, and social status.

Wilson's thesis on male joblessness as being the main factor on why there is a such a significant increase in female-headed families has been given a thorough analysis by Andrew Cherlin (1981, 1991) (see also Staples, 1981). Cherlin found that from the late nineteenth almost through the first half of the twentieth century, blacks tended to marry at a younger age than whites. However, single-parent black families began to occur on a much larger scale within the last sixty years; this trend accelerated in the 1970s and continues to the present. Further, other differences between black and white families grew larger as well. Cherlin concludes that today's female-headed, lower-class black family represents a relatively recent type of family structure.

What accounts for these differences? Why has there been such a divergent typical family pattern of blacks and whites in the past thirty years? In 1981, Cherlin rejected answers that seek explanations in terms of the presumed still-felt long-lasting effects of slavery on black family life; rather, bolstered by the statistical evidence that the contemporary divergence goes no further back than the depression of the 1930s and has accelerated since 1960, he argued that the causes lie in part in the contemporary diverse economic experiences of blacks and whites in today's urban society. This view parallels Wilson's. However, ten years later, Cherlin (1991: 70) alters his opinion stating: "I now think that was an overstatement that paid too little attention to the historical roots of the recent changes." Let us look at Cherlin's ideas a little more closely to understand why he changed his mind.

Cherlin (1991) reports that whereas whites used to wait longer to marry than blacks, ever since 1950 blacks have been marrying at a later age than whites, having a higher divorce rate than whites at all class levels, and taking longer to remarry or never marrying. "Black women, in sum, are less likely to marry, stay married, and remarry" (1991:95).

Childbearing data reflect further differences. Over the course of their lives, black women have the same number of children as white women. But, there is a significant difference when they have children and under what circumstances. In the 1980s black women had children, on the average, three years earlier in their lives than white women. In the last three decades, while whites were postponing marriage and childbearing, blacks were postponing marriage even more but having children at an earlier age. "These developments have led to what is perhaps is the most striking difference between the current family patterns of blacks and whites: a far higher proportion of black children are born to young, unmarried mothers than is the case for white children" (Cherlin, 1991:96).

Cherlin also makes the interesting point that while the commonly held opinion is that there has been a major rise in the last thirty years of unmarried black teenagers and unmarried black women ages 20 to 24 having children, that is not the case. What makes it seem so is the fact that there has been a significant decline in the 1960s and 1970s in the number of *married* black women having children and the marriages of young black women. While there has been a similar trend in white women, it has not been as pronounced.

A number of factors are cited by Cherlin to explain why there has been this decline of marriage among blacks. These include economic factors—"some combination of the increasing earnings of black women; the continued employment problem of black men; the higher rate of out-marriage among black men; the toll of violence, imprisonment, and drugs; and perhaps the expansion of welfare in the late 1960s and early 1970s" (Cherlin, 1991:107). But, and this is most important, economic trends alone cannot fully explain this decline. The history of blacks in America and their culture are seen as major contributing factors to explain why black family patterns differ from white family patterns.

Cherlin believes that historically the extended-kin support network has been a predominant characteristic of the black family. Its origins, he speculates, may have derived from slavery and before that to Africa, where lineage systems where all important and marital status was seen as an auxiliary process of support. The strong ties among extended kin is seen to continue through slavery. Cherlin now believes that this longstanding cultural pattern of extended kinship ties, childbirth outside of marriage, female employment, and having children raised by other relatives has once again become prominent. He agues that in the last sixty years, two major developments have accentuated the importance of this cultural pattern. The first is a society-wide shift in values that has resulted in the weakening of the family; the second is the economic restructuring of America from a production-based to a service-based economy.

The first factor, one that we have repeatedly discussed, is the movement toward a value system that places more emphasis on individual freedom and self-fulfillment than on obligations to others, including one's marital partner. The second factor, as Wilson described, has resulted in the loss of semi- and low-skilled factory jobs and their replacement by more highly skilled jobs requiring much more education. Cherlin argues that the response of blacks to these cultural and economic changes was a reemphasis on extended kinship networks and a deemphasis on marriage. The support system characterized by cooperation and sharing among a wide number of relatives became the operative family system, especially among poor blacks.

This support network composed of both kin and nonkin neighbors in poverty communities was a rational adaptive response to economic deprivation that prevented poor men and women from marrying and living together. Cherlin refers to the research of Carol B. Stack (1974), who found that most residents in a low-income black neighborhood participated in a complex social network that exchanged mutual support. Cherlin believes that the functionality of such networks, and particularly networks composed of kin, may have contributed to a situation where marriage is of less central importance to the lives of these poor families than it is to the population at large.

This view takes the position that for many blacks, ties to a network of kin may be the more important family bond over the long run. Often, the extended-kin networks characteristic of many low-income blacks provide a dependable, stable, and functioning family environment. While household compositions may change, the network tends to remain intact. Cherlin (1991) notes that such households are often defined as containing "single-parent families." This concept is not designed to identify this network support structure of kin and others who reside in different households and share and exchange goods, services, and emotional support. Use of the term "single-parent families" can give the mistaken impression that most single parents and their children belong to unstable families without any social supports.

Yet Cherlin cautions that we should not overestimate the strengths of these kinds of family structures. For they, themselves, are not immune to problems; they tend to foster group loyalty that may mitigate against the goals of individuals. For instance, they may make it difficult for one individual to accumulate sufficient capital to advance his or her own standard of living because of obligations to share gains with others in the network. The combined resources of the support network, then, may not eliminate the economic hardships of the single-female parent and her children. Evidence indicates that financial difficulties are typically severe for single mothers as compared to single fathers.

In summary, the statistical evidence and academic research studies all point to the fact that there is a sharp divergence in recent decades between blacks and whites in the typical patterns of marriage. This divergence is centralized in the black underclass. And, as Cherlin points out, this is a relatively recent phenomenon that is characterized by a family structure composed of a strong network of kin, but fragile ties between fathers and mothers. The consequence of this development may be ominous, for "(a)lthough the family networks among low-income blacks ease the burdens of poverty, they may also make it difficult for individuals to rise out of poverty" (Cherlin, 1991:117)

In the concluding chapter of this book, I shall return to this topic by focusing on the social policy implications of the various theories put forth on why and how poverty effects families and what steps can be taken to remedy the situation. Also, in a later chapter I shall discuss the feminization of poverty and childization of poverty with particular focus on the consequences of inequality in divorce laws. But for now, let us turn to a concluding discussion of another manifestation of poverty—the experiences of homeless families.

HOMELESS FAMILIES IN AMERICA

Andrew Cherlin's (1991) warning that the kinship network may not be able to ease the burdens of poverty unfortunately is evident in the cases of homelessness, particularly among African Americans. Sosin (1986) identifies three factors that distinguish the homeless from the poor in general: extreme poverty, fewer years of schooling, and less family support. In this section I will look at homeless families in America, but first let's put this matter in comparative perspective.

I began this chapter by looking at squatter settlements in Third World countries. I observed that rapid population growth combined with social and cultural changes often resulted in large segments of the population being destitute and forced to live on the street or in makeshift temporary housing. I do not want to give the reader the false impression that homelessness is a phenomenon only existing in less developed countries. It is evident in industrial countries as well. For example, two reports in *Statesman and Society* in 1993 found that in Great Britain 400,000 people representing 175,000 families were declared homeless and given government housing. An additional one million people have found temporary accommodations in the homes of relatives or friends (Platt, 1993; Stearn, 1993).

In the 1980s increasing numbers of homeless besieged America's urban centers. The estimates of the number of homeless ranged from the United States Department of Housing and Urban Development's figure of 350,000 to the U.S. Department of Health and Human Services' figure at 2 million. Advocates of the homeless put the figure much higher into the double digits—10 to 20 million. The variations in these estimates is attributable to the difficulty in getting accurate assessments of people who

Homeless begging for spare change in San Francisco, California.

are highly transient and often unwilling to be counted. Censuses and sample surveys are inadequate in that the data they collect are based on tabulating people who have relatively permanent residences (Rossi, 1989, 1994).

Who are these homeless people? The evidence that has been collected indicates that they vary greatly from the "old" homeless who populated the nation's Skid Rows of the 1950s and 1960s and were almost all white males with an average age of around fifty years old. The new homeless are much younger—around thirty years of age—25 percent are women, and, proportionately, blacks and Hispanics constitute an increasing number of them (Rossi, 1994). The Ford Foundation (1989) estimates that about 44 percent of homeless people are from racial and ethnic minority groups.

What accounts for the vast number of Americans who are homeless? Frequently cited factors include those who are mentally ill but never diagnosed and the deinstitutionalization of those who were classified as mentally ill; unemployment; cutbacks in public assistance and the consequent falling through the alleged "safety net"; and the decline in affordable housing, especially in urban areas. The growing shortage of affordable housing occurs as rents increase above what the increasing number of poor people can afford to pay. The decline in affordable housing also results from redevelopment in which poorer housing stock is converted through extensive renovation to much more expensive apartments or condominiums, or demolished to give way to such luxury housing or to other uses such as office buildings or shopping malls. This process of "gentrification," while beneficial to the "revitalization" of cities, often leaves the dispossessed without housing.

David Snow and Leon Anderson (1993) provide overwhelming evidence that to understand the plight of the homeless in contemporary America it would be misguided to employ a pathological and medicalized view of them. In their field research of homeless people in Austin, Texas, they found that the vast majority of homeless men and women were highly adaptive, resourceful, and pragmatic as they cope with their situations. They argue that to focus on disabilities is a distorted characterization of the homeless. Their differences are a consequence of the dismal situation in which they find themselves rather than from character frailties. "Confronted with minimal resources, often stigmatized by the broader society, frequently harassed by community members and by law enforcement officials, and repeatedly frustrated in their attempts to claim the most modest part of the American dream, they nonetheless continue to struggle to survive materially, to develop friendships, however tenuous, with their street peers, and to carve out a sense of meaning and personal identity" (Snow and Anderson, 1993:316).

In an earlier study, Snow and his associates (Snow, Baker, Anderson, and Martin, 1986) make the point that the emphasis on the personal sources of homelessness is another example of blaming the victim. It also deflects attention away from its economic sources, leads to faulty generalizations, and channels social policies that are doomed to fail.

> It is demeaning and unfair to the majority of the homeless to focus so much attention on the presumed relationship between mental illness, deinstitutionalization, and homelessness. To do so not only wrongfully identifies the major

problems confronting the bulk of the homeless, it also deflects attention from the more pervasive structural causes of homelessness, such as unemployment, inadequate income for unskilled and semi-skilled workers, and the decline in the availability of low-cost housing. (Snow et al., 1986:422)

Peter Rossi (1994) observes that the primary reason for the upsurge in homelessness is related to the structural changes occurring in the economy as it moves from a manufacturing base with large numbers of low-skill manual jobs to a service base requiring higher educational attainment and greater occupational skills. He observes that while the low-level job prospects of both men and women were adversely affected directly by this economic restructuring, women were also affected indirectly by the decline in the supply of economically stable men who earned enough to provide for a family. The deteriorating value of AFDC payments and the crisis in affordable housing are contributing factors. The most significant change in the demographic composition of the new homeless was the appearance of homeless families (Rossi, 1994). These families are identified as being single-parent, mostly young mothers in their twenties, with very young children.

Rossi (1994) also observes that the processes that produce family homelessness operate selectively along ethnic lines. He explains that extreme poverty and single-parent families are more prevalent among minority families. Shelter and welfare systems, in turn, are geared to these single-parent families and particularly toward African American and Puerto Rican families located in urban areas. Finally, minorities are also the ones disproportionately affected by difficult housing situations at the local level. A final key factor is the failure of the social network of friends and relatives to provide the support needed to keep these families from experiencing homelessness. Rossi states: "They [homeless families] may not be complete isolates, but there are certainly few among their friends and kin on whom they can count for support" (1994:364). The population at risk of becoming homeless, the "precariously housed," are forced to rely on the benefice of a fragile support network of relatives or acquaintances for their shelter, which is also vulnerable to economic uncertainties and downturns.

Shinn and Weitzman (1994), based on their early study (Shinn, Knickman, and Weitzman, 1991) of homeless families in New York City, found that those who request shelter are not isolates. Rather, they had mothers and grandmothers living, other close relatives, and close friends whom they saw on a regular basis. The homeless families were unable to stay with relatives and friends—in large part because they had already "worn out their welcome" by staying with them previously. The researchers, agreeing with Rossi, believe "that the kin of homeless families may themselves be too poor to offer much assistance. . . . Also, the parents of homeless families were more likely than the parents of housed public assistance families to have been on public assistance themselves" (Shinn and Weitzman, 1994:441).

Let us zero in on this last point, the relationship of kinship (including quasi-kin) networks and homeless families. It will be instructive to do this by comparing Latino poor families and African American poor families. Susan Gonzales Baker (1994), in examining the research literature, finds that Latinos (predominantly Mexican Americans), in light of their high poverty rate, are underrepresented among the homeless. She attributes this underrepresentation to variations in patterns of familial support and network ties.

Baker (1994) observes that close-knit family based social networks are important to both Latinos and African Americans. Both are sources for not only emotional support but also for the exchange of guidance, useful information, personal services, and material assistance. However, they functioned in different ways in dealing with social services under different conditions. Latino family networks do not provide enabling information assistance on social services regarding shelters for families who are faced with homelessness. However, they do provide alternative residential arrangements including living with parents; nonrelated adults sharing living quarters; multiple families doubling up; and in the case of older immigrants, living with their adult children. The data sources are Mexican Americans living in the Southwest and West. Puerto Ricans living in New York City do not as readily avail these family-residential assistance options. Instead, they use social services and shelters and are found to be demographically represented among the homeless.

For African Americans, social service usage was encouraged by family networks who also provided enabling information and assistance. Baker (1994) believes that a primary motive in doing so was the inability of the network to provide the necessary support and constrained housing and economic opportunities. The Southwestern and Western Latinos, on the other hand, may find such social services not as geographically readily available and may not face the same racial discrimination in housing as African Americans.

Baker concludes that the explanation for the "Latino paradox"—their underrepresentation among the homeless—may be explained by an interaction between culture and economic necessity.

> Latino social support seems to be more likely to include diverse housing arrangements within the interpersonal network as a strategy for avoiding life on the streets in the face of persistent poverty. Thus it appears likely that the Latino paradox can be explained in large measure by the particular way in which Latino populations have adapted to their constrained opportunity structure by sharing housing as a material resource more frequently and in more varied ways than may be true of other ethnic groups. (Baker, 1994:498)

In summary, my investigation of homelessness in America indicates that poverty is the central causal factor. Homelessness is exacerbated by the inability of social networks to provide the necessary resources to help those in need. These social networks themselves are overburdened and cannot subsidize homeless families. They can barely make it on their own. In the concluding chapter of this book, I will return to this topic and examine in some detail social policies in practice or being proposed that would help the homeless family in America.

BOX 6-3   The Contemporary American Family

The Human Face of Homelessness

How economic changes have impacted on families and have resulted in homelessness for so many is given a human dimension in the following passages. The first case is from an underemployed African American who saw his job designing and building conveyer belts end when the company he worked for went out of business. Faced with the job loss and a medical emergency, his family was forced out of their home in an affluent city east of Seattle and moved to temporary housing in a large public housing project in Seattle.

> "But minimum wage—that's insulting. I don't knock it for high school students. They're getting training, learning about working, making their pocket money. That's fine. But you take a person . . . I got six kids. $3.35, $4 an hour, I spend more than that wage in a day's time on a grocery bill. I mean you can accept some setbacks, but you can't tell a person, 'I don't care if you've been making $15 something an hour, the minimum is what you've got to make now.' If I hand you this letter, give you my resume, my military record, show you the kind of worker I am, talk about my family, how can you degrade me by offering me the minimum wage?" (cited in Vanderstaay, 1992:173)

The underemployed man's sentiments are echoed by a minister in a depressed industrial town in Pennsylvania. This Lutheran church leader witnessed the loss of hundreds of truck and auto manufacturing jobs when companies left the area. Families saw their savings dwindle, their unemployment benefits and pensions disappear at the same time food and rent costs rose, while their federal benefits declined.

> "Yes, there are new jobs . . . There's a new McDonald's and a Burger King. You can take home $450 in a month from jobs like that. That might barely pay the rent. What do you do if somebody gets sick? What do you do for food and clothes? These may be good jobs for a teenager. Can you ask a thirty-year-old man who's worked for G.M. since he was eighteen to keep his wife and kids alive on jobs like that? There are jobs cleaning rooms in the hotel . . . Can you expect a single mother with three kids to hold her life together with that kind of work? All you hear about these days are so-called service jobs—it makes me wonder where America is going. If we aren't producing anything of value, will we keep our nation going on hamburger stands? Who is all this 'service' for, if no one's got a real job making something of real worth?" (cited in Kozol, 1988:6).

Kozol, 1988; Vanderstaay, 1992.

CONCLUSION

In this chapter, I devoted attention to poverty families in both industrial and nonindustrial Western societies. Two theoretical orientations dominate the analysis of poverty families, and both have different consequences for social policies affecting the poor. In this chapter I analyzed the nature and circumstance of poverty and its implications for social policies.

The cultural position (the culture of poverty) emphasizes the cultural dynamics of poverty and is seen to have long-range effects on individuals' and families' behavior and values. This position argues that, although social conditions may be or may have been the underlying cause of poverty, emergent cultural conditions may lead to the development of self-perpetuating cultural patterns that are inimical to movement out of poverty. A self-perpetuating cycle is seen to come into play—broken families and low educational motivation lead to inadequate job preparation, which, in turn, perpetuates poverty, unemployment, despair, and broken families.

The second position, the situational approach, hypothesizes that although the behavior of poverty families is different than the middle-class pattern, the values of culture of the poverty group are basically the same. The behavior of poverty families is seen as adaptations and solutions to poverty conditions. The cultural similarity among generations is seen to result from the perpetuation of poverty conditions—no jobs, discrimination, inadequate housing, and so on—rather than the cultural transmission of a poverty culture.

The chapter continued with a discussion of the widening difference between the proportion of white and black families found in poverty and the proportion maintained by women. The restructuring of the American economy from production with its full complement of low-skill jobs to a service economy that has relatively few such jobs and demands a higher-skilled, more educated workforce has proven disastrous to those who lack the requisite qualifications for employment. This has led to disastrous consequences for those who have found themselves least able to compete in this new economic marketplace. The rise of homelessness in the 1980s, and particularly the appearance of homeless families, is largely attributable to this economic restructuring and the inability of kinship networks to provide the necessary "safety net" that the government promised but failed to provide.

By comparatively examining a diverse number of poverty families representing different races and different societal cultures, I reach a similar position with that of the situationalists. My position is that the culture of poverty perspective tends to put the blame of poverty on the very victims of poverty—the poverty families themselves. It downplays the societal factors and the debilitating consequences of inequality. I share the viewpoint of sociologists who have argued that the removal of the causes and consequences of inequality will also remove the "tangle of pathology" of poor people: If we want to change poverty families, we must end poverty.

III

GENDER ROLES, COURTSHIP, AND MARRIAGE AND THE FAMILY

7

GENDER ROLES
AND SEXUALITY

Chapter Outline
Biology and Gender Roles
Religious Views on Patriarchy and Gender Roles
Sociological Views: Cross-Cultural Evidence
Sexuality and the Family
Homosexuality and the Family
AIDS—Its Global Impact
   Moral Panics, Sexual Behavior, and AIDS
Conclusion

The first two parts of this book examined the changing family through a sweeping historical and cross-cultural analysis. It was the intention to provide a sociological perspective that would serve as the foundation for the understanding on how the family relates to the larger community and to the society. Of particular interest to us was the relationship of industrialization, urbanization, and modernization processes with the changing family. This analysis was broadened by an investigation of cultural and social class family diversity through a focus on immigration, ethnicity, and poverty.

In this and the next part of this book the emphasis is on how these macrolevel societal factors relate to changes within the family—what structural functionalists called internal family dynamics. More specifically, a major concern is on gender role relationships and how they are played out in the premarital, nonmarital, marital, and family context. The way we think about sexuality, love, dating, courtship, and mate selection is associated with broader societal structures and processes that are subject to processes of change. Further, our definitions, attitudes, and behavior towards marriage, work, and the family are linked with these processes of change. In Part IV, this analysis is extended to generational relationships. The generational members of the family—parents, children, grandparents—and their relationship to each other are inherently cultural defined and societal influenced and are also subject to change.

BIOLOGY AND GENDER ROLES

The social sciences make an important distinction between sex and gender. Sex refers to biologically determined differences between males and females, which is most evident in male genitalia and female genitalia. Maleness and femaleness are determined by biology. Gender refers to social and cultural definitions of masculinity and femininity based on biological differentiation. Gender involves socially learned patterns of behavior and psychological and emotional expressions and attitudes that socially distinguish males from females. Ideas about masculinity and femininity are culturally derived and provide the basis for differing self-images and identities of men and women.

Given this distinction between sex and gender, the term used to refer to the social behavior of men and women should be *gender roles*, not *sex roles*. However, in popular usage, the term *sex roles* is often used in place of the more accurate term *gender roles*. Keep in mind that the term *sex* refers to an ascribed status, in that a person is born either a male or a female. The term *gender* refers to an individual's psychological, social, and cultural attributes, and thus is an achieved status.

Are gender-role differences innate? The dominant view in most societies is that the learned gender identities are expressions of what is "natural." People tend to assume that acting masculine or feminine is the result of an innate biologically determined process rather than the result of socialization and social-learning experiences. Proponents of both the biological and the social-learning views have sought evidence from religion, the biological sciences, and the social sciences to support their respective positions. Whereas most religions tend to support the biological view, both biology and the social sciences provide evidence suggesting that what is "natural" about gender roles expresses both innate and learned characteristics.

In this chapter, I review the biological and religious views on gender roles and examine them in light of sociological viewpoints and the cross-cultural evidence. I indicate how patriarchy, the main ideological justification for the sexual division of males and females, manifests itself. Also in this chapter there is a historical analysis of sexuality, including homosexuality within the context of cross-cultural family systems and structures. A section includes an analysis of the gay community in contemporary America. Subsequent chapters in Part III are devoted to discussions of love; courtship; premarital relationships; mate selection; singlehood; the sexual division of labor, especially how it is articulated within the family; and marital intimacy.

Supporters of the belief that the basic differences between males and females are biologically determined have sought evidence from two sources: studies of other animal species including nonhuman primates—monkeys and apes—and studies of the physiological differences between men and women. I will examine each in turn.

Ethology is the scientific study of animal behavior. Ethologists have observed that there are sexual differences in behavior throughout much of the nonhuman animal world. Evidence indicates that these differences are biologically determined—that in a given species, members of the same sex behave in much the same way and perform the same tasks and activities. Popularized versions of these ideas in the 1970s, such as those developed by Desmond Morris in *The Human Zoo* (1970) or Lionel Tiger and Robin Fox in *The Imperial Animal* (1971), generalize from the behavior of nonhuman primates to that of humans. They maintain that in all primate species, including *Homo sapiens*, there are fundamental differences between males and females. They try to explain human male dominance and the traditional sexual division of labor in all human societies on the basis of inherent male or female capacities. They even have extended their analysis to explain other human phenomena, such as war and territoriality, through evolutionary comparisons with other species. A more sophisticated treatment of this same theme is found in the field of sociobiology, the study of the genetic basis for social behavior (Wilson, 1975, 1978).

Sociobiologists believe that much of human social behavior has a genetic basis. Patterns of social organization—such as family systems, organized aggression, male dominance, defense of territory, fear of strangers, incest taboo, and even religion—are seen to be rooted in the genetic structure of our species. The emphasis in sociobiology is on the inborn structure of social traits.

Opponents of this view use two types of arguments to criticize it. First, they note that sociobiologists have overlooked studies showing the importance role learning plays among nonhuman primates in their acquisition of social- and sexual-behavior patterns (Montague, 1973). Second, critics of sociobiology observe that those who generalize from animal behavior to human behavior fail to take into account fundamental differences between human and nonhuman primates, such as the human use of a complex language system. Even though they freely acknowledge the biological basis for sex differences, these critics claim that, among humans, social and cultural factors overwhelmingly account for the variety in the roles and attitudes of the two sexes. Human expressions of maleness and femaleness, they argue, although influenced by biology, are not determined by it; rather, gender identities acquired through social learning provide the guidelines for appropriate gender-role behavior and expression.

While not denying the impact of social and cultural influences on gender roles and sex-linked behavior, some investigators maintain that genetic and physiological differences between the sexes also influence (but do not predetermine) what types of things members of each sex can do and learn and the ease with which they do so (Rossi, 1977). According to this view, the study of gender roles should take into account well-established biological and physiological differences between the sexes in such traits as size and muscle development (both usually greater in males); physiological and mental development (males ahead in some areas, females in others); longevity (females live longer than men and have a lower death rate at all ages); and susceptibility to disease and physical disorders (generally greater in males). For instance, some diseases that primarily affect males have a genetic basis and are related directly to the male sex chromosomes (XY), which differ from the female sex chromosomes (XX). Among these sex-linked ailments are color-vision defects, blood-clotting disorders (hemophilia), deficiencies in immunity, and baldness.

While many differences between males and females have a biological basis, other physical conditions may be tied to cultural influences and variations in environment and activity. Men react differently to psychological stress than women; each sex develops severe, but dissimilar, symptoms. Changing cultural standards and patterns of social behavior have had a pronounced effect on other traits that formerly were thought to be sex-linked. For example, the rising incidence of lung cancer among women—a disease historically associated primarily with men—can be traced directly to changes in social behavior and custom, not biology; women now smoke as freely as men.

In sum, differing learned behaviors and activities do contribute to the relative prevalence of certain diseases and disorders in each sex. But, as has been pointed out, not all male-female differences in disease and susceptibility can be attributed to these factors. In addition to genetically linked defects, differences in some basic physiological processes—such as metabolic rates and adult secretion of gonadal hormones—may make males more vulnerable than females to certain physical problems.

Most scientists believe the way people are socialized has a greater effect than biological factors on their gender identities. Paleoethnologist Stephen Jay Gould (1981) sees them overstating the biological basis of human behavior by failing to distinguish between genetic determinism (the sociobiological viewpoint) and genetic potential. Indeed, sociobiologists in the more than a quarter of a century since they promulgated their theories have provided virtually no evidence of biological determinism. Rogers summarizes the criticism by noting that biological constraints on culture are so insignificant that "models of genetic evolution will be of little use in understanding variation in human behavior" (1988: 819).

Cross-cultural and historical research offers support for this view, revealing that different societies allocate different tasks and duties to men and women and that males and females have culturally patterned conceptions of themselves and of each other.

RELIGIOUS VIEWS ON PATRIARCHY AND GENDER ROLES

Many religions have given overt expression to the view that men are superior to women. Anthropologist Marvin Harris (1988) observes that in many cultures men are believed to be spiritually superior to women, who often are thought of as weak, untrustworthy, and dangerous. Further, religious rituals, organized and conducted by men, and spiritual myths are tied to a belief in the political, economic, and social supremacy of men. For example, the Judeo-Christian story of Creation presents a God-ordained sex-role hierarchy, with man created in the image of God and woman created as a subsequent and secondary act. This account has been used as the theological justification that man is superior to woman, who was created to assist and help man and bear his children. This kind of legitimation of male superiority is called a patriarchal ideology.

> For a man indeed ought to have his head veiled, forasmuch as he is the image and glory of God; but the woman is the glory of the man: for neither was the man created for the woman but the woman for the man: for this house ought the woman to have a sign of authority on her head. (I Corinthians 11:3-10)

Patriarchy has been the basis on which tasks, rights, and roles are allotted to the sexes, usually with the woman's position subjugated and inferior to the man's. Patriarchy often voices the belief that a woman's "proper" place is within the home and her role is devoted to domestic activities—housework and the bearing and raising of children. This is particularly true in Muslim countries and in early Western industrial societies. As societies have developed industrially and technologically and have moved further and further away from cultural patterns where tasks are distributed on the basis of physiological factors, patriarchal ideas are increasingly open to challenge. It is necessary to understand the multifaceted nature of patriarchy to understand gender-role relationships.

A patriarchal ideology has two components; the first emphasizes the dominance of males over females, the second the subjugation of younger males by older ones. The first component is of concern here; the second is examined in the chapters devoted to generational relationships.

The institution of patriarchy is anchored in an ideology of male supremacy and it is reinforced by traditional socialization practices that implement it in matters of status, role, and temperament. Patriarchy has been deeply entrenched in political, social, and economic institutions. Patriarchy can be seen in political terms as the domination of males over females. The term *sexual politics* was used by Kate Millett (1970) to emphasize the power-structured basis of the male-female relationship and the arrangements whereby one group of persons, females, is controlled by another, males.

Gender-role relationships are legitimated through the socialization of both sexes to the patriarchal ideology. Gender socialization is the way in which we learn the behavior and attitudes that are expected of males and females. For example, gender roles are associated with temperament, which involves the formation of self-concepts and is stereotyped along sex lines. Aggressiveness, force, intelligence, and efficacy are seen as "masculine" traits; passivity, ignorance, docility, and ineffectuality are "feminine" traits. Millett observes that gender role "assigns domestic service and attendance upon infants to the female, the rest of human achievement, interest, and ambition to the male" (Millett, 1970:26). Socialization practices are biased toward male superiority and male superior status. Women are viewed as inferior. Millett sees these three facets—status, temperament, and role—in terms of political, psychological, and sociological components. Each is interdependent and, in totality, they serve to support the patriarchal ideology.

The patriarchal ideology has dominated the Greco-Roman, Semitic, Indian, Chinese, and Japanese civilizations. It has also been the predominant pattern in Western Christian civilization. Many sociologists believe that the basis for the patriarchal pattern stems from the reproductive function of women, which serves as the justification for women's existence and the reason for their subordination. According to this view, it is women who are responsible for the continuation of a human group. For it is only women who can become pregnant, have children, and breastfeed them (Huber, 1990; Lerner, 1986). High infant mortality rates in non-modern societies required that women have many children so that some would survive into adulthood. Consequently, it was to women that household and child care was relegated. Men assumed primary responsibility for economic support and contact with other groups. This male involvement eventually resulted in their dominance and their control over the group and the society.

The European sociologist Evelyn Sullerot (1971) sees patriarchal rule as a coherent system linked by four elements—attitudes toward fertility and adultery, domestic confinement, property, and civic rights. She (1971:20-28) proceeds to show how these four types of restriction on women are elaborated in patriarchal civilizations.

1. *Fertility and adultery.* Sullerot observes that the primary function of the woman was "as a breeding machine to perpetuate the male line of the husband, the tribe, and the race" (1971:20). The entire rationale for the woman's existence was her ability to produce children, particularly male children. Failure to do so resulted in severe punishment. The Manu code of India stated that if a wife had no children after eight years of marriage, she would be banished; if all her children were dead, she could be dismissed after ten years; and if she only had produced girls, she could be repudiated after eleven years. Similarly, the Mosaic law of the biblical Israelites allowed a husband to repudiate his infertile wife and to father children with servants. The story of Abraham and Sarah is illustrative.

Female adultery was prohibited and punishments were extremely severe. Female adultery represented an attack against male dominance and the assertion of female individuality and free will. This was seen as a threat to the patriarchal system. Potentially, it was destructive to the patriarchal-based system of property, inheritance, and power. Common to the historical civilizations of Israel, China, India, and Greece was the norm that a husband could put to death his adulterous wife. It was this assault on patriarchy, not simply emotional jealousy, that was the underlying motivation for such extraordinary punishment.

2. *Domestic confinement.* The seclusion and separation of women were practiced to assure masculine dominance and to prevent the possibility of adultery. Their confined world had both actual and symbolic significance. Such confinement symbolized the inferior status of women. Domestic activities were viewed as less important than and subordinate to outside involvements. In traditional India, the Hindu religion conceived of women as strongly erotic and thus a threat to male asceticism and spirituality. Women were physically removed from the outside world. They wore veils and voluminous garments and were never seen by men who were not members of the family. Similar practices existed in China and Japan and in the Muslim Middle East. Only men were allowed access to and involvement with the outside world.

A screen is used to separate male and female students at the College of Islamic Studies in Peshawar, Pakistan.

3. *Property.* Stemming from the patriarchal ideology was the practice of excluding women from owning and disposing of property. The prevalent practice in traditional Hindu India was that property acquired by the wife belonged to the husband. Similarly, restrictions on the ownership of property prevailed in Greece, Rome, and in ancient Israel.

4. *Civil rights.* The general pattern was the exclusion of women from civic matters. This included, as is the case in Jewish tradition, the exclusion of women from the majority of religious observations. Islam uses as its justification for the exclusion of women from the city and religion the notion of female impurity and uncleanliness. Oriental religions share a similar philosophy. In ancient China, female infanticide was practiced through child neglect. The birth of a daughter was accompanied by a period of mourning. The low status and power of women are summed up in the following passage from the book *Several Articles Intended for Women*, written in the first century A.D. by a Chinese woman, Pan Hoei Pan:

> Never let us forget that we belong to the lowest form of human life. We must expect only contempt. There will never be disillusionment for a woman so long as she remembers that she will always be made to suffer by those with whom she lives. (Cited in Sullerot, 1971:27-28)

SOCIOLOGICAL VIEWS: CROSS-CULTURAL EVIDENCE

Cross-cultural and historical research reveals that societies allocate different tasks and duties to men and women. Among other animals the differentiation is biologically determined, and all the animals within a given species behave in the same way and take on the same tasks. Among humans, however, social and cultural factors account for variations in the roles and attitudes of the two sexes. The relationship between man and woman, although influenced by biology, is not determined by it; rather, gender identities acquired through social learning provide guidelines for appropriate behavior and expression.

Biological factors can be seen as having a great influence on gender-role relationships in less technologically developed societies. Physiological factors, periodic childbearing, and the relative physical strength of men and women play an important part in designating the role allocations within these societies. Clellan S. Ford, the noted anthropologist, argues that for preindustrial peoples, "the single most important biological fact in determining how men and women live is the differential part they play in reproduction" (1970:28). The woman's life was characterized by an endless cycle of pregnancy, childbearing, and nursing for periods of up to three years. By the time the child was weaned, the mother was likely to be pregnant again. Not until menopause, which frequently coincided with the end of the woman's life, was she free from her reproductive role. In these circumstances, it is not surprising that such activities as hunting, fighting, and building were usually defined as the male's task; the gathering and preparation of grains and vegetables were female activities, as was the care of the young.

In an early study, George Murdock (1937) provided data on the division of labor by sex, in which 224 preliterate societies divided their labor. Such activities as metalworking, weapon making, boat building, woodworking and stoneworking, hunting and trapping, house building, and clearing land for agriculture were tasks performed by men. Women's activities included grinding of grain; the gathering and cooking of herbs, roots, and seeds as well as fruits, berries, and nuts; basket, hat, and pottery making; and making and repairing clothing. D'Andrade (1966), after reviewing the cross-cultural literature, concluded that a division of labor by sex occurs in all societies. Generally, the male activities are those that involve vigorous physical activity or travel; the female activities are those that are less physically strenuous and require less geographical mobility.

We should not overestimate the importance of biological factors in gender-role relationships. Although physiological factors tend to play a more influential role in gender-role differentiation in preindustrial societies, that is not to say that biology *determines* these allocations. A classic illustration of the diversity of human behavior is Margaret Mead's (1935/1963) study of sex and temperament in three South Pacific societies.

Each society held a different conception of male and female temperament. The Arapesh were characterized as gentle and home loving, with a belief in temperamental equality between men and women. Both adult men and women subordinated their needs to those of the younger or weaker members of the society. The Mundugumor assumed a natural hostility between members of the same sex and slightly less hostility between the sexes. Both sexes were expected to be tough, aggressive, and competitive. The third society, the Tchambuli, believed that the sexes are temperamentally different, but the gender roles were reversed relative to the Western pattern.

> I found . . . in one [society], both men and women act as we expect women to act—in a mild parental responsive way; in the second, both act as we expect men to act—in a fierce initiative fashion; and in the third, the men act according to our stereotype for women—are catty, wear curls and go shopping, while the women are energetic, managerial, unadorned partners. (Mead, 1963; Preface to the 1950 edition)

Even if the premise is granted that physiological factors are contributing components in the distribution of tasks in preliterate societies, they are not as important in societies that are more technologically developed; that is, as technology develops, we move further away from cultural patterns where tasks are allocated on the basis of physiological justifications. Yet we continue to find the tasks, roles, and rights of men and women to be different. The justification for these differences has been moral and "sacred" arguments, combined with and stemming from the physiological argument.

In recent years, there has been a reexamination of the basis on which tasks and roles are allocated and their concomitant justification. Modernization processes, scientific and technological developments, rapid social change, and the women's movements have led to the questioning of traditional gender-role relationship patterns. In an earlier time marked by relative stability, little discussion or argument was made of the appropriateness of socially derived gender identifications and societal notions of masculinity and femininity. The "proper" roles, statuses, and attitudes for men and women were taken for granted. This has changed not only in the industrialized West but also in varying degrees throughout the world. This is a theme that I return to in later chapters.

SEXUALITY AND THE FAMILY

Cross-cultural and historical evidence reveals that every society controls the sexual behavior of its members. Further, in comparing sexuality in different parts of the world, we find an amazing variety of intercultural differences of practices, rules, and sentiments. In this section, I try to account for societal variations in sexuality norms and expressiveness through linkage with the manner in which sexuality is controlled.

Every society has a culture of sex, and the sexual sector of culture varies in the same ways as the total culture of which it is a part. The anthropologist William H. Davenport (1977), in his survey of sex in cross-cultural perspective, finds that there are constants within what seems the confusing complexity of variations. He states (1977:162-163) that in every society the culture of sex is anchored in two directions: "In one direction, it is moored to the potentialities and limitations of biological inheritance. In the other direction, it is tied to the internal logic and consistency of the total culture."

What this means is that, although human sexual behavior is directly based on inherited biological factors (genes, bodily organs, hormones, and so forth), every society shapes, structures, and constrains the development and expression of sexuality in all of its members. The difference between *sex* and *sexuality* is that the latter is socially structured and regulated. The rules for sexual conduct can only be understood within the broader context of customs and laws embedded within the cultural system and the social fabric of the society. These sexual conduct rules are inextricably linked with rules dealing with generational, gender, marriage, and family roles. Since sexual behavior is embedded within the complex web of societal rules, regulations, sanctions, and taboos, the change of one sector of culture has implications for other sectors, including sexuality. Within the context of social and cultural change, I examine sexuality and the family.

All societies have developed rules regulating premarital, marital, and extramarital sexual behavior. The reason for sexual regulation lies in two basic facts: Sexual intercourse has the potential for creating a new human being; and a person's desirability as a sex object is a valuable, but scarce and perishable, resource (Davis, 1976). As a consequence of the first fact, sexual norms and reproductive norms become intertwined. As a consequence of the second fact, sexual norms become linked with norms governing the distribution of goods and services. According to this functionalist viewpoint "sex norms contribute to the replacement of people in society and to the maintenance of an orderly distribution of rights" (Davis, 1976:225). The family, therefore, seeks to subordinate sex norms, since they can support or interfere with the formation and continuation of families.

Davis observes that the primacy of marriage and the family in sex regulation has great importance in the elaboration, importance, and universality of sex mores. These include the *principle of legitimacy*, which establishes a family by locating children through fatherhood and sanctioning a mother's childbearing. The *incest taboo* eliminates sexual rivalry from the nuclear family. The third rule makes coitus a mandatory obligation within marriage.

The primacy of the family is also seen to account for the concern regarding premarital sexual activities and relationships and why sex norms are different for men and women. Men usually have greater freedom and latitude, since it is women who become pregnant. Variations in the strictness of sex rules are seen to reflect the degree of their potential interference with the primacy of marriage, family formation, and continuance.

Political and economic differentiation is the second factor that explains sex norms. Societies, in addition to assuring orderly biological continuation into the next generation, must see to it that goods and services are generationally transmitted. Sexual access is seen as a good and service that can be politically and economically distributed. The nature of sexual rules is tied to the societal division of labor and "bargaining" regarding sexual favor and distribution is seen as being intrinsically linked with economic exchange. Davis notes that sexual desirability and economic capacity are age-graded and balanced. Youth have greater defined sexual attractiveness and middle or later aged having greater economic and political advantage. Similarly, Davis' argument is that the sexual division of labor is balanced, with the man's sphere primarily economic and the woman's primarily familial (Davis, 1976).

Following this structural-functionalist argument, Davis observes that—while conflict can arise between the primacy of marriage and family and the economic exchange in elaborating sex rules and regulations—there is often a balance between the two. "The exchange influence prevents familism from turning the society into an economically unproductive breeding system, and yet familism is strong enough to prevent economic domination from subordinating all sex to money, status, and pleasure" (Davis, 1976:228).

Davis' analysis reflects a somewhat sanguine functional view of the inherent equality in the articulation of sexual rules and regulations for people of different social classes and for men and women. It has engendered much criticism among theorists who point out that sexual rules and regulations often reflect the allegiance and domination of economically and politically powerful social-class groups and patriarchal authority figures within family systems. As a consequence, economically and politically disadvantaged groups and youth and women family members in all social classes are subjected to greater sexual restrictions and regulations. Further, there are factual errors in Davis' analysis. For example, it is simply not true that women's sphere was primarily familial. Throughout most cultures and most of history women's sphere is economic as well.

Randall Collins (1971), in his examination of the cross-cultural and historical evidence on sexuality and the sexual division of labor, develops a theory that bases the sexual-stratification system in terms of conflict theory and social exchange. Collins combines Sigmund Freud's proposition that human beings universally exhibit strong sexual and aggressive drives with Max Weber's proposition that humans strive to achieve as much dominance as their resources allow. This leads Collins to the conclusion that women will be the sexual prizes for men, since men are physically larger and stronger, are free from the biological limitations of menstruation and childbirth, and have greater economic advantages.

As evidence of this view that men will be sexual aggressors and women will be their sexual prizes, Collins describes how in some societies females are clearly viewed as sexual property, taken as booty in war, used by fathers in economic bargaining, considered to be owned by husbands, and so on. In our own society, as in virtually all other societies, men act as the sexual aggressors. He lists the following as additional evidence:

> Rape is defined as a crime only as committed by males, and cases of sexual assault by women are virtually unknown; men are the sexual aggressors in free courtship systems; men are much more motivated by sexual interests as a reason for marriage, whereas women emphasize romantic love, intimacy, and affection more highly than men; exclusively male culture has a heavy component of sexual jokes, bragging of sexual conquests, pinups, and pornography, which have little or no equivalent among women; prostitution occurs almost exclusively among women, and male prostitutes are sex objects for male homosexuals, not for women; men are much more likely to masturbate, experience sexual arousal earlier in life, and are generally more active sexually than women. (Collins, 1971:7)

Collins believes that historical changes in the structure of sexual dominance are the result of shifts in resources dealing with political and military force and economic power. These changes are supported by changes in sexual ideologies. The expectation of his conflict model is that, when economic resources and forces are equalized between men and women within a society, sexual conflict and marital bargaining will be individualized rather than divided across sex lines. Four types of social structures are analyzed in terms of male and female resources, sexual stratification, and dominant sexual ideologies. Let us review them, as outlined by Collins in Table 7-1.

Low-technology tribal societies are more commonly referred to as hunting-and-gathering societies. Their technology produces little or no economic surplus and as a consequence there is little economic, political, or status stratification. These types of societies are found in marginal forest, mountain, arctic, or desert environments. People live at subsistence levels in social bands of about 20 to 200 people. Premarital sexual behavior tends to be unregulated and, for the most part, egalitarian relations exist between women and men. Sexual practices are relatively permissive, with premarital sexual freedom for both males and females (Gough, 1971).

Ford and Beach's (1951) comparative study of sexual behavior found that equally active sexual behavior of men and women occurs in hunting-and-gathering societies. This has led sociologists, such as Betty Yorburg (1974), to speculate that this is attributable to the fact that these societies are poor and families are not greatly differentiated with respect to wealth. As a consequence, the sexual behavior of children and

TABLE 7-1   Types of Social Structure, Sexual Stratification, and Dominant Ideologies

Social Structure	Male and Female Resources	Sexual Roles	Dominant Ideology
1. Low-technology tribal society	Male: personal force, personal attractiveness. Female: personal attractiveness.	Limited male sexual property; limited female exploitation.	Incest taboos.
2. Fortified households in stratified society	Male: organized force; control of property. Female: upper-class women head lineage during interregnum of male line.	Strongly enforced male sexual property; high female exploitation; women as exchange property in family alliances.	Male honor in controlling female chastity.
3. Private households in market economy, protected by centralized state	Male: control of income and property. Female: personal attractiveness; domestic service; emotional support.	Sexual market of individual bargaining; bilateral sexual property in marriage.	Romantic love ideal in courtship; idealized marriage bond.
4. Advanced market economy	Male: income and property; personal attractiveness; emotional support. Female: income and property; personal attractiveness; emotional support.	Multidimensional sexual market of individual bargaining.	Multiple ideologies.

Source: Randall Collins. 1971. "A conflict theory of sexual stratification." Copyright 1971 by The Society for the Study of Social Problems. Reprinted from *Social Problems* Vol. 19, No. 1, Summer 1971, pp. 3–21 by permission.

consequent offspring would not be disruptive to the economic future of the family. Collins concurs in this belief. The lack of surplus combined with little economic and political stratification does not permit dowry or bride-price systems to develop. Further intermarriages are tolerated in that they have little effect on extended-family systems, since no families are powerful enough to be highly preferred for political alliances. Daughters are given sexual freedom and are not strongly controlled because they are not used as property in a bargaining system. As a consequence, "it is in low-technology tribal societies that most norms favoring premarital sexual permissiveness are found" (Collins, 1971:11).

The second type of social structure discussed by Collins is the *fortified household in stratified society*. Collins' classification is similar to Henry Sumner Maine's conceptualization of the "status" society and Ferdinand Tönnies' *Gemeinschaft*. In this type of society, economic and political organization coincides with the family community; force is not monopolized by the state. Work activities are integrated with familial activities, and authority over both is invested in the patriarchal head. In the case of preindustrial Europe, patriarchal households could vary in size, wealth, and power, from the holdings of a king or lord, through the households of merchants and financiers, to knightly manors, and down to the households of minor artisans and peasants. In addition to the subservience of family members to the patriarch, propertyless workmen, laborers, and servants were subservient as well.

This type of society, with its form of social organization, maximizes male sexual dominance and is characterized by the double-standard sexual ideology. These types of societies also include ancient Greek, Roman, and Arab societies. Sharp inequality among households can result in the upper classes practicing polygamy or concubinage and monopolizing more than their share of women. Males assert their rights in sexual property in these types of societies. The sexuality of women is strongly controlled and women are often exchanged on the basis of economic bargaining. Often in such societies, women "are closely guarded so as not to lose their market value" (Collins, 1971:11). This has given rise to customs such as wearing a veil, strict chaperonage, and the institution of the harem.

Similarly, Betty Yorburg observes that in agricultural societies where differences in wealth, power, and prestige between families become more extreme as the economic surplus increases, there is a greater desire by families to regulate premarital sexual behavior and control the sexual activity of women. "The mating of offspring is controlled (by arranged marriage) to increase family power and wealth. The sexual activity of women is more rigorously suppressed (confined, ideally, to procreation), and women come to be regarded, conveniently, as having a weaker sex drive" (Yorburg, 1974:31).

As observed earlier in this chapter, the patriarchal ideology views sexual property as a form of male honor. Collins believes that in a highly warlike patriarchal society like that of the Bedouin Arabs, the result is an almost obsessive desire to maintain sexual property and a concern for adultery and the institution of extreme controls over women. Women's sexuality was thought to be much greater than that of men. They were regarded as sexually amoral, unclean, and lacking in honor. The extreme reflection of this belief was the practice of clitoridectomy. By removing the clitoris, it was felt that temptation was being removed from women.

The rise of the centralized bureaucratized state, accompanied by the expansion of commerce and industry, led to the development of the third form of social structure, the *private household in a market economy* (Collins, 1971). The separation of the workplace from the home, another characteristic of this society, resulted in the development of the smaller and more private nuclear family. While men remained heads of households and controlled property, women gained a better bargaining position and were no longer under the control of their patriarchal family. Collins writes that "they become potentially free to negotiate their own sexual relationships, but since their main resource is their sexuality, the emerging free marriage market is organized around male trades of economic and status resources for possession of a woman" (1971:13).

The development of the smaller private household that lacked servants resulted in women being valued for their capabilities in homemaking and in providing emotional support for males along with their sexuality. Fostering this development was the ideology of romantic love, which included a strong element of sexual repression. Collins' argument suggests that the continuation of the double standard and the suppression of women's sexuality was upheld principally by the interests of women in contrast to the male-supported female chastity norm of traditionalistic patriarchal societies. Collins reasons that "the most favorable female strategy, in a situation where men control the economic world, is to maximize her bargaining power by appearing both as attractive and as inaccessible as possible" (1971:15).

An ideal of femininity was developed in which overt sexuality may not be used to attract the male but only indirectly hinted at as a sort of grand prize or ultimate reward, because "sexuality must be reserved as a bargaining resource for the male wealth and income that can only be stably acquired through a marriage contract" (1971:15). Femininity and female chastity are idealized because men and women are bargaining with unequal resources. A negative consequence of this idealization was the reinforcement of patriarchal ideology by the placement of nineteenth-century Victorian women on a pedestal that limited their involvement to the home and further excluded them from the world of work.

The movement to today's *advanced market economy* has resulted, in Collins' view, in a new shift in sexual-bargaining resources. The relatively high level of affluence combined with the increased employment opportunities for women has resulted in greater bargaining options for women. Those freed from economic dependence on males can be less concerned with marriage and more concerned with other kinds of exchanges. For example, dating can take the form of short-run bargaining, in which *both* sexes can trade their sexual attractiveness or social abilities for sexual favors and social involvements. Evidence for that is the rise, especially in the youth culture, of the ideal of male attractiveness.

In sum, Collins' conflict model asserts that political and economic factors play a determining role in influencing both sexual behavior and sexual ideology. The discussion highlights the cross-cultural and historical variations in which the dominant group (predominantly male) oppresses or exploits the other (predominantly female). The contemporary trend, as Collins speculates in his brief discussion of dating patterns, is one in which sexual bargaining between the sexes is beginning to occur on a more equal-exchange basis.

The following chapter is devoted to an in-depth historical analysis of the intersection of sexual behavior and sexual attitudes by examining changes in love, courtship, and premarital relationships. Before I move on, I would like to comment briefly on the contemporary gay-liberation movement as an extension of the discussion on sexuality and the family.

HOMOSEXUALITY AND THE FAMILY

Most societies strongly disapprove of homosexuality, although there is wide variation in its tolerance. Kingsley Davis (1976) attributes disapproval of homosexuality to its incompatibility with the family and the sexual-bargaining system; by this he means that it interferes with the norms and attitudes regarding the reproduction of societal members and the sexual allocation of males and females. He asserts that the negative attitudes toward homosexuality can be seen as part of the broader proscriptions concerning prohibited sexual partners—masturbation involves no partner at all; incest involves a kinsman; adultery involves a partner other than one's spouse; and homosexuality involves a partner of the same sex. In this section, I look at some of the cross-cultural variations in societies' views of homosexuality vis-à-vis the family, but first I briefly survey variations in its cross-cultural and historical prevalence.

Clellan S. Ford and Frank A. Beach (1951), in their pioneer cross-cultural survey, found that in 49 of 76 societies on which reports were available, some form of male homosexuality for some members of the community was approved. In 28 of them, adult homosexual acts were rare, absent, or so secret that they remained unknown. In general, homosexuality was found to be more prevalent among men than women; lesbianism was found to exist in only 17 societies. It is possible that the low rate of reported female homosexuality may be explained by the fact that female behavior may be less visible and less studied by anthropological research, which has been conducted primarily by men.

Societies that report male homosexuality as being rare have definite and specific social pressure against the disapproved behavior. This ranges from such lighter sanctions as ridicule among the Mbundu of Angola, Africa, and the condemning to death of male and female violators by the Rwala, a Bedouin tribe of the northern Arabian desert. Of the 49 preliterate societies in which homosexual activities are considered normal and socially acceptable, they tend to be limited to the roles of *berdaches* (transvestite homosexuals) and *shamans* (magicians or priests, in some societies homosexual).

It should be noted that Ford and Beach do not specify the actual incidence of homosexual activities. For example, it can vary from an isolated or occasional incidence of group masturbation among boys to regular anal intercourse by adult men. Nor are they clear on how given societies define homosexuality. Definitions can also vary in terms of type of activity or frequency of a given activity or whether it is "homosexual." Further, especially in regard to industrial societies—while laws may be liberal regarding homosexuality—public attitudes, especially among segments of the population, may be much more conservative.

Attitudes and behavior toward homosexuality have historically changed. Today, we are experiencing great debate on the nature and significance of homosexuality. Shedding light on the relativity of how homosexuality is conceptualized is a controversial book that looks at it from the standpoint of premodern Europe. John Boswell

(1994), a medieval historian, reports in his controversial book, *Same-Sex Unions in Premodern Europe*, that there is evidence for an early Catholic ritual for same-sex marriages. He examined medieval manuscripts that range from services for same-sex unions from the eleventh to the sixteenth centuries to Scripture and midrashim, to legal and ecclesiastical documents, to Greek and Latin romances and poetry, and to court chronicles and saints' lives. Boswell catalogs terms of affection like "brother and sister" and shows how they were used for siblings, heterosexual spouses, and homosexual couples. His case in point is an eighth-century Greek manuscript that lists four rituals. These included a ritual for the betrothal of a man and a woman, two wedding ceremonies, and a liturgical rite for the union of two men.

Boswell's analysis of same-sex unions works off the fact that in premodern Europe marriage was often an arrangement between families that had little to do with affection and more to do with economics and political alliances. Boswell implies that same-sex unions tended to be romantic in the modern sense. He warns against oversexualizing the relationship, preferring to stress their moral and social idealism. The controversy surrounding his research stems from assertions that these medieval documents indicate a ritual acceptance of homosexual attraction and perhaps sex by medieval Christianity.

The comic strip *Doonesbury*, by Gary Trudeau, devoted a week to Boswell's book. In one strip, a cartoon character reacts with nausea to another's summary of Boswell's research that found liturgies for same-sex ceremonies that included communion, holy invocations, and kissing to signify union. Critics believe that Boswell has misinterpreted liturgical books. The celebrations of "brotherhood" or "fraternity" are seen as being used for reconciling warring siblings, for adoptions and for establishing other fictive relationships, and not for promoting same-sex unions. Summarizing the controversy and its implications for the present-day Catholic church one commentator states that the purpose of the brotherhood ritual may have served as a cover for homosexual relationships but that there is no substantiation that it was created for that purpose (Woodward, 1994). "That its existence could lead to church-sanctioned gay marriages appears to be an empty hope" (Woodward, 1994:77).

The changing conceptualizations toward homosexuality from the middle ages to the present are reflected in the sweeping changes in the last quarter of a century to all facets of human sexuality. The "sexual liberation" era of the 1970s—which included the much-publicized communal marriage, mate swapping and swinging, and the rise in premarital heterosexual permissiveness and cohabitation, along with the gay-rights movement—has led to speculation that, taken together, these attitudes are symptomatic of a much larger change in our view of sexuality. This more comprehensive movement, anchored in the belief that human sexuality is learned, calls for a "liberation" of sexuality that transcends the "bias" of heterosexuality and advocates the encompassing of homosexuality into normative sexuality. Both those who advocate this view and those who condemn it see it as seriously undermining heterosexual relationships and ultimately marriage and the family.

However, there is no statistical evidence indicating that there has been a change in the rates of homosexuality of American men and women. In the 1940s, Kinsey found that 4 percent of men and about a third as many women were predominantly homosexual. According to studies by the Institute for Sex Research, the statistics are virtually the same today. The thought that the sexual revolution and the gay movement would have increased the incidence of homosexuality has proved to be wrong. Indeed, I could argue the opposite; that is, the same loosening of the norms governing heterosexuality may reduce homosexuality by permitting easier and earlier heterosexual experience. A cross-cultural illustration to provide support for this argument is the people of Mangaia, one of the Cook Islands in the South Pacific. The Mangaians are very permissive regarding heterosexual activities. They let their children begin sexual experimentation at an early age, including masturbation for both girls and boys. They view sexual exploration as a normal part of childhood. Even though there is little or no social pressure against homosexuality, almost no homosexual behavior is reported. This has led some (Sandler, Myerson, and Kinder, 1980) to speculate that "perhaps the general availability of heterosexual partners, as a result of the high degree of permissiveness toward heterosexuality, explains this low incidence of homosexuality among the people of Mangaia" (1980:28).

A lesbian couple expressing their love and affection for each other.

While the rate of homosexuality may not have changed in recent years, what has changed is the visibility of homosexuality from a largely private form of sexual activity to one that is more open and public. This change is most typified by the emergence of gay communities in almost every major city in Western Europe and America, a process that had its origins in the mid-nineteenth century. Furthermore, this movement from private to public homosexuality has been instrumental in changing the very way that our culture has conceptualized homosexuality in general and in the conceptualization of homosexual identity in particular. Let us trace this development.

Of particular interest to us is the scholarship that examines the cultural conceptualization of sexuality, heterosexuality, and homosexuality. A very influential study has been Michel Foucault's (1978) *The History of Sexuality, Volume I: An Introduction*. Foucault sees the modern conceptualization of sexuality as developing as a consequence of the decline of importance of kinship and extended-family ties in controlling individuals. He observes that beginning in the eighteenth century there was a shift in emphasis away from marriages that were constructed to control of individuals through the continuation and development of kinship and lineage ties. This movement was accelerated during the Industrial Revolution and continued into the Victorian era, and a new control system developed that placed emphasis on marriage and conjugality within a broader context of the control of sexuality and its modes of expression. Foucault writes: "The deployment of alliances (kinship ties) has as one of its chief objectives to reproduce the interplay of relations and maintain the law that governs them; the deployment of sexuality, on the other hand, engenders a continual extension of areas and forms of control. For the first, what is pertinent is the link between partners and definite statutes; the second is concerned with the sensations of the body, the quality of pleasures, and the nature of impressions . . ." (1978:106).

Foucault argues that Victorian society was not, as popularly depicted, a society that denied and suppressed sexual discussion; rather, it was a society that sexualized all social relations and was consumed with the study of sexuality and its control as part of its obligation to assume total responsibility for its citizens' lives and welfare. The study of sexuality becomes incorporated into the world of therapists, psychologists, social scientists, and educators as part of an all-encompassing attempt to shape and influence people not only in terms of their acting in socially, economically, and politically appropriate ways, but also in terms of their views of their bodies, their sex, and their human potentials. Foucault's analysis of sexuality shares a similar orientation to that of his French associate, Jacques Donzelot (1979), and of Christopher Lasch (1977a), all of whom call attention to the perceived intrusion of the state and subsidiary medical and social agencies (the "helping" profession) on the family beginning in the nineteenth century and continuing today. I examine this viewpoint later in the discussion of children; for now, let us see its applicability in regard to the conceptualization and policies regarding homosexuality.

In a book with the curious title *The Invention of Heterosexuality*, Jonathan Ned Katz (1995) examines the development of the conceptualization of *heterosexuality* in the nineteenth century. Katz is not arguing, of course, that sexual relationships between men and women were invented, but rather he refers to the way that this concept became distinct from the emerging concept of *homosexuality*. The concept of heterosexuality is seen to have changed over time and the current conceptualization is our particular historical arrangement of perceiving, categorizing, and imagining the relationship between the sexes.

Katz (1995) traces heterosexuality's conceptual development as a term meaning perverted desire to one of normal sexuality. Heterosexuality is seen to have been invented in Germany in the 1860s, and the concept appears in an American medical journal in 1892. It refers to a perverse desire for both sexes. In the ensuing decades the term is transformed, so by the 1930s it comes to mean normal sexuality manifested in sexual passion for one of the "opposite sex."

Katz picks up on the construct "opposite sex" to investigate this construct in broader terms that dichotomize things—such as black and white, good and bad, us and them. By referring to men and women as opposite sexes and homosexuality and heterosexuality as opposite sexual orientations, the tendency is to focus on differences rather than similarities. This is at a time when we have seen that men and women are more alike than different in terms of nurturance, aggressiveness, emotionality, and soon. The differences are more attributable to historical periods and cultural differences than to any innate biological differences. Katz further argues that while the media focus on biological differences between homosexuals and heterosexuals, the evidence shows a convergence in lifestyles, diverse family arrangements, and a sexual pleasure ethic. He believes that the desire for dichotomous labels of homosexual and heterosexual is fostered by the conservative elements of our society in a misguided determination to reinforce the "naturalness" and "superiority" of heterosexuality and masculinity as currently conceptualized.

As Katz sees the concept of heterosexuality as a recent social invention, other scholars [see Berube (1981), D'Emilio (1983a,b), Walkowitz (1980), and Weeks (1981)] on gay history have assembled evidence that homosexuality as it is currently conceptualized is also of relatively recent origin. John D'Emilio (1983b), in his excellent historical study of the formation of the gay community, reminds us that in colonial America there was no concept of "homosexuality." Erotic behavior between individuals of the same sex was viewed as a sporadic and exceptional activity that did not differ essentially from other sexual transgressions such as adultery, bestiality, and fornication. Heterosexuality was assumed to be the natural way of sexuality. Colonial society placed such a great emphasis on the family and on reproduction (the average pregnancy rate for white New England women was eight) to populate the vast American wilderness that "homosexuality" was inconceivable.

It was not until the second half of the nineteenth century, with the advent of full-blown industrial capitalism and the modern city, that gay and lesbian conceptualizations and identities emerged. D'Emilio traces the movement of large populations from kinship-dominated closely knit rural communities into the more impersonal urban centers. The family, in turn, shifted from a public community institution into a private insular one. For individuals, industrialization and urbanization created the social context for the development of a more autonomous personal life. Affection, intimacy, and sexuality became more a matter of personal choice than a determination by family members. Homosexually inclined men and women, who would have been visible and vulnerable in small rural communities, began moving into the city. In this setting, men and women who wished to pursue active and public sexual involvements with others of their own sex felt free to do so and began to fashion from this desire a new sexual identity and way of life (D'Emilio, 1983b).

D'Emilio astutely traces the development in urban settings of male homosexual bars, cruising areas, public bathhouses, and parks that enabled men to meet each other at the beginning of the twentieth century. Lesbians, more constrained in terms of both economic dependence on husbands and patriarchal ideologies, developed more private meeting places that included literary societies, social clubs, faculties of women's colleges, and settlement-house involvements. By the 1920s and 1930s, public institutions such as lesbian bars made an appearance, although they never assumed the size of their male equivalents.

World War II had a similar effect in developing gay male and lesbian community and identity. The war geographically mobilized young people—at the time that their sexual identities were just forming—from the heterosexual settings of their families, communities, and hometowns. D'Emilio asserts that "because the war removed large numbers of men and women from familial—and familiar—environments, it freed homosexual eroticism from some of the structural restraints that made it appear marginal and isolated" (1983b:38). This was the case not only for men and women in the sex-segregated armed forces, but also for nonmilitary females who entered the work force to fill America's labor needs. D'Emilio reminds us that this analysis should not let us think that heterosexuality did not continue as the predominant form of sexual expression, but the war did temporarily weaken the patterns of daily life that fostered heterosexuality and inhibited homosexuality. It provided a new situation in which those who were sexually attracted to their own sex but were previously constrained by their circumstances from acting on this attitude could do so. Further, the war reinforced the identities of gays and lesbians and strengthened their ties to homosexuality as a way of life.

By the 1950s, gay urban territories—such as Greenwich Village in New York City and similar enclaves in Chicago, Los Angeles, and San Francisco—were established. Gay and lesbian subcultures also came into existence in smaller cities such as Worcester, Massachusetts; Buffalo, New York; and Des Moines, Iowa. Activist groups such as the Mattachine Society and the Daughters of Bilitis formed to provide a vehicle for self-expression and protection against hostile actions and discrimination in government and the work world. Coinciding with and reinforced by the gay-rights movement, gay communities emerged in the late 1970s and early 1980s; in that short time period, they have made a significant impact on urban politics in the United States, with San Francisco being the most notable example.

In San Francisco and elsewhere, gays have moved into centrally located, but run-down, areas and have sought to transform them into hospitable neighborhoods. The most successful attempts have been marginal sections of New York's Greenwich Village and San Francisco's Castro Street area. However, gays have often faced the competition and hostility of other groups for control of the limited supply of cheap and moderate housing. Low-income gays have been the victims of street violence exacerbated by economic conditions and homophobia. In addition, in cities such as San Francisco that are undergoing massive downtown business development and high-cost condominium construction, gays are either being forced out or are depicted as the cause of the evaporation of affordable housing. Rubin notes that in San Francisco, "the specter of 'the homosexual invasion' is a convenient scapegoat which deflects attention from the banks, the planning commission, the political establishment, and the big developers" (1984:296).

John D'Emilio (1983b), in his analysis of the emergence of gay and lesbian identity and the creation of their respective communities, observes that structural changes in industrial urban society made possible the emergence of gay and lesbian identity and the creation of their respective communities. Yet, at the same time, the society is unable to accept homosexuality. He asks what accounts for societal heterosexism and homophobia and finds the answer in the contradictory relationship that exists between this form of society and the family. His analysis is provocative.

D'Emilio picks up on the theme shared by many sociologists that industrial capitalism shifted the family away from a productive economic unit into one that emphasized the affective function of the family in terms of the nurturance of children and the emotional happiness of its members. As a consequence, sexuality ceased to be defined primarily in terms of reproduction and instead became defined largely in terms of emotional expressiveness. Indeed, affection, intimacy, and sexuality became more and more a matter of individual choice and no longer were solely defined in terms of the family. This attitudinal and behavioral shift provided the setting and opportunity for people who wished to fashion their notions of sexuality with people of their own sex.

The increased reaction against the development of gay and lesbian identities and their communities stems from recent developments in heterosexual marriage that point to its failure to satisfy the emotional demands and needs of its members. D'Emilio points out that since the mid-1960s there has been a plummet in birthrates, a continuing decline in average household size, a rise in divorce rates, and an increase in the variety of living arrangements that people are choosing. The reason for these developments lies in the inherent contradictions of capitalism, which allows for individuals to live outside the family in relative economic independence and at the same time ideologically dictates that men and women marry and have children to assure the perpetuation of the society. As D'Emilio has indicated elsewhere (1983a), "[t]hus while capitalism has knocked the material foundation away from family life, lesbians, gay men, and heterosexual feminists have become the scapegoats for the social instability of the system. . . . The elevation of the family to ideological preeminence guarantees that capitalist society will reproduce not just children, but heterosexism and homophobia" (1983a:109, 110).

At the beginning of the Clinton administration in 1992 and 1993, the issue of gays in the military crystallized opinion about gay people and gay rights. Homophobia, like racism, anti-Semitism, and sexism, reflects a fear and intolerance toward others. An executive for a gay rights group observes that, "Homophobia . . . serves a purpose in society. It preserves privilege for some people, maintains an uneven playing field and limits who has access to the job market" (cited in Angier, 1993). Homosexuality, because of its linkage to feelings about sex and procreation, also provides a reason for homophobia. In Judaism and Christianity, especially Catholicism and Protestant fundamentalism, there is a clear separation between sex for procreation and sex for pleasure. The former is encouraged, the later rejected. Historians have observed that the religious injunction against homosexuality can be understood in the context in which the Bible was written. Lillian Federman, a historian on gay issues, states: "Fundamentalists refuse to see that whoever wrote the Old Testament was part of an endangered tribe. They had to emphasize procreation, and therefore homosexuality for men was taboo" (cited in Angier, 1993). Finally, AIDS, with its linkage of sexuality with pleasure and punishment, has exacerbated uneasiness about homosexuality (Angier, 1993). I will investigate this concern in the next sections of this chapter.

AIDS—ITS GLOBAL IMPACT

AIDS—an acronym for acquired immune deficiency syndrome—is a contagious disease that until mid-1985 was regarded as a disease largely confined to the United States that attacked specific "risk" groups: gays, intravenous drug abusers, and hemophiliacs. Persons stricken with full-blown cases of AIDS are victims of a virus that directly attacks a group of white blood cells that serves as one of the main coordinators of the immune system. As the disease progresses, these defensive cells are almost entirely destroyed. The immune system collapses, and victims fall prey to one infection after another. Ordinarily mild diseases become dangerous, even fatal, and many patients develop rare cancers—such as Kaposi's sarcoma, severe neurological disorders, and brain damage. There is an AIDS-related complex (ARC) that infects people who have been exposed to the AIDS virus but who have not yet developed the disease. The flu-like symptoms of ARC include swollen lymph glands, fatigue, malaise, fever, night sweats, diarrhea, and gradual loss of weight. In addition, science is finding that there are also human immunodeficiency viruses (HIV) that may eventually cause AIDS in unsuspecting healthy persons.

In June 1987, the Centers for Disease Control (CDC) in Atlanta recorded more than 36,000 cases of AIDS in the United States, with more than 20,000 deaths having occurred. In Africa, the figure is even higher. Only six years later, nearly ten times that number of AIDS cases (315,390) had been diagnosed in the United States. Since the start of the epidemic in 1981, 204,390 Americans have been killed by AIDS. By 1993 it was the number one cause of death in men aged 25 to 44 and was growing as a threat to women (Associated Press, 1993). Of those classified as having AIDS, 48 percent are white, 24 percent are black, 14 percent are Hispanic, and .05 percent are Asian Pacific Islander and Native American or Alaska Native (Centers for Disease Control, 1993).

While heterosexual transmission still accounted for a relatively small 9 percent of the total of 103,500 cases reported in 1993, a demographic shift of the epidemic became apparent. The proportion of gay men who contracted the disease through sex decreased from 66.5 percent to 46.6 percent in the period from 1985 to 1993. Also increasing during this period was the number of cases attributed to injecting drugs. A disproportionate number were among the urban minority (African American and Hispanic) populations, leading the Center for Disease Control to argue for the development of culturally and linguistically appropriate prevention measures for different racial and ethnic groups (Altman, 1994).

In 1985, four years after the disease first became known, the World Health Organization (WHO) conservatively estimated that more than 50,000 people had died from the disease. The worst hit countries all touched on the Great Rift Valley of east central Africa: Zambia, Zaire, Burundi, Rwanda, Uganda, and Tanzania. In Africa, half of all AIDS patients were women in their childbearing years, and AIDS was spreading predominantly through heterosexual relations. This fact led Dr. Alexandra Levine of the University of Southern California to comment: "[AIDS] is not really a disease of homosexuality at all. It is spread by sexual contact of any kind—homosexual or heterosexual. This is a disease of all of us" (quoted in *Time*, August 5, 1985). A similar belief was also articulated by Dr. Robert Redfield at the U.S. Army's Walter Reed Hospital: "As time goes by, it will be more evident that this is a sexually transmitted disease that is not limited to one sexual practice" (quoted in Clark et al., 1985).

In 1985, participants at a conference of more than 2,000 worldwide experts met in Atlanta, Georgia, for the U.S. Centers for Disease Control's international symposium on the deadly disease. Participants at the conference were predicting that AIDS threatened the world's general population and would assume the proportion of what epidemiologists call a "pandemic" as opposed to a "mere" epidemic (Clark, 1985). In mid-1992 the world's population reached 5.5 billion. While this global population picture was predicted at the start of the decade, the AIDS "pandemic" became evident. Nearly 13 million people were estimated to be HIV infected (Goldsmith, 1992). The United Nations' Population Division for the first time began to take account of the demographic impact of the AIDS pandemic. In the fifteen countries of Africa where AIDS has highest prevalence, life expectancies have been adjusted downward (Kalish, 1992). The most dramatic drop was in Uganda and Zambia. The United Nations found that the current life expectancy in Uganda and Zambia was eleven years lower than what was projected in 1990.

By 1995, the truth of the deadliness of AIDS was apparent throughout the world. The United Nations estimates that 6,000 people are infected every day. Nearly 20 million people worldwide have been infected, and an estimated 4.5 million have developed full-blown AIDS (Nullis, 1995). The head of the World Health Organization African office notes that in devastated Uganda, "You go to parts of Uganda now and see orphaned children and elderly people, and in between there's nothing" (cited in Nullis, 1995). By the end of the century the estimate is that nearly twice as many people, between 30 to 40 million, will become infected and about 90 percent of them will be from poor countries. For that reason the United Nations has developed a new international program—called UNAIDS—to battle the disease that has overwhelmed the Third World's medical system. The disease has wreaked social havoc and has seriously impacted its workforce.

UNAIDS is designed to be more streamlined and cost effective. However, many countries in the Third World—including hard hit Kenya, Tanzania, Uganda, Malawi, and India—fear that this program may not achieve its objectives. WHO and the World Bank are not directly involved in this program. Representatives of these developing countries believe that lending programs will not provide the necessary economic supports necessary to combat the impact of AIDS. They point out that at the grassroots level, programs in the past have ineffectively focused too narrowly on medical problems and vaccines without providing the necessary care and support. This has proved disastrous for these societies' economies. Zimbabwe's health minister reflects the bitterness of the developing nations to the World Bank for its perceived failures by stating: "The World Bank is dominated by monetary interests. In economic terms, it's worth more saving one American life than 100 African lives" (cited in Nullis, 1995).

Moral Panics, Sexual Behavior, and AIDS

Conflicts between the majority view on the "proper" expressions of sexuality and minority "deviant" expressions often become expressed as moral panics. Jeffrey Weeks (1981) coined this term to refer to important and consequential kinds of sex conflict. Moral panics are seen as the "political moment" of sex, in which diffuse attitudes are channeled into specific political actions that bring about social change. Examples include the hysteria regarding prostitution as a form of white slavery in the 1880s; the antihomosexual campaigns that were associated with the anticommunist activities of the U.S. Congress' House UnAmerican Activities Committee and of the Senate's Joseph McCarthy in the 1950s; and the outcry against child pornography in the late 1970s.

Similarly, the current medical and emotional attention regarding AIDS can be seen in terms of a moral panic. Gayle Rubin (1984), writing at the beginning of the AIDS phenomenon, astutely predicted that AIDS will have far-reaching consequences on both homosexuality and heterosexuality. She observed the effect AIDS has on sexual ideology regarding homosexuality at the very time that the taint of mental illness was being removed. "The syndrome, its peculiar qualities, and its transmissibility are being used to reinforce old fears that sexual activity, homosexuality and promiscuity led to disease and death" (Rubin, 1984:299). As we now see, her prediction has largely come true.

For the general public, the fact that AIDS was largely limited to the gay population led them, at first, to have a detached attitude toward the disease. This lack of concern was seen in the minimal amounts of government medical research money allocated to the study of AIDS. Anti-gay moralists saw AIDS as a fitting punishment for those who violated the "natural" way of sex. The political conservative Patrick J. Buchanan wrote in May 1983 in his syndicated column that "The poor homosexuals . . . have declared war on nature, and now nature is exacting an awful retribution" (quoted in *Newsweek*, August 12, 1985).

Rubin (1984) reports that homophobic columnists have viewed AIDS as appropriate punishment for violation of the Bible's Levitical codes and that moral conservatives in Reno, Nevada, sought to ban the annual gay rodeo. *The Moral Majority Report* of July 1983 ran an article with the headline "AIDS: HOMOSEXUAL DISEASES THREATEN AMERICAN FAMILIES." This article was accompanied by a photograph of a white family of husband, wife, son, and daughter wearing surgical masks. Rubin quotes from a passage in a pamphlet by the anti-women's-movement advocate Phyllis Schlafley that the passage of the Equal Rights Amendment would make it illegal for people to protect themselves from AIDS and other diseases associated with homosexuals.

However, as AIDS has continued to spread to many segments of the population including children and the famous, there has been an outcry for more research on this disease. As significant as the call for more medical research has been, the hysterical reaction—tinged in part by the moral panic first associated with AIDS and homosexual behavior—has been compromised by the fact that gays are the prominent victims.

AIDS has had a profound effect on sexual practices for both heterosexuals and homosexuals. In the first years of the outbreak the push for abstinence, marital fidelity, and "safe sex" was prevalent. *Newsweek* (1985), in a special report, "The Social Fallout from an Epidemic," reported that the immediate outcome was a "safe sex" movement and an aura of fear. For example, in San Francisco, the site of one of the country's largest gay communities, surveys found that among gay and bisexual men there was a substantial decrease in multiple sex partners and high-risk sexual activity. In many establishments catering to gays, pamphlets and fliers were distributed that urged the use of condoms, reduced promiscuity, or even the elimination of all "exchanges of bodily fluids" *(Newsweek*, August 12, 1985:29).

In the years since the *Newsweek* report, findings have in large supported the view that sexual behavior is changing among gay men. In a study of bars (Juran, 1991) 94 percent of the 71 gay men surveyed reported that their behavior has changes and 61 percent reported using condoms. Juran also reports that heterosexual men and women decreased their casual sexual contacts and one-quarter of the 65 lesbian and bisexual women in the sample reduced their casual sex involvements and no longer had sex with men. Anke A. Erhardt and associates (1991) reports that this change is reflected in the decline in the rates of HIV infections in this population. The urban areas on both coasts, "the epicenters of risk," has had a notable decline. But, there has been worry that safe sex practices may have declined in these gay communities.

At the end of 1994, health officials confirmed this fear in their observation of a second wave of AIDS rising in San Francisco, the "gay capital of America" (Gross, 1994). This front-page article in *The New York Times* reports that in the mid-1980s the infection rate dropped to less than 1 in 100 from a high of 18 infections in 1982. In December of 1994 it rose to 2 in 100, but more importantly, it was twice as high among men younger than 25. The young men are reported to have a sense of youthful invulnerability, a belief that AIDS is associated with older men, and a don't-care attitude based on a dread of growing old in a culture that prizes youth and beauty. For the older men what was once thought of as a short-term period of abstinence and safe sex has given way to the realization that they must live a life of circumscribed sex and they are unwilling to do so. In San Francisco, where nearly half of the gay population is HIV positive, infection seems inevitable. Because so many die each year from AIDS, a sense of resignation has crept in that is seen to affect sexual behavior. "Many gay men here, saying they are numb with loss, fatalistic about their own survival, unwilling to face a measure of sexual deprivation and eager for the attention showered on the sick and the dying, are again practicing unprotected anal intercourse" (Gross, 1994:1). And thus a self-fulfilling prophecy has taken hold.

In 1985, *Newsweek* (August 12, 1985) also speculated that the aura of fear will affect heterosexual behavior. The article reported that unmarried heterosexual women may be making behavioral adjustments by thinking twice before having a casual sexual encounter. Supporting this view is the statement by Dr. Donald Francis, a medical epidemiologist at the U.S. Centers for Disease Control, that even if there are only a few cases among heterosexuals, AIDS "will certainly end the sexual revolution. You can take your chances with herpes and hepatitis B, but you can't take your chances with this" (cited in *Newsweek*, August 12, 1985:29).

The Centers for Disease Control (1991) reports that AIDS was not a deterrent to early premarital sexual activity, which has substantially increased in the last twenty-five years. Social science research (Anderson, Kahn, Holtzman, Arday, Truman, and Kolbe, 1990; DeBuono, Zinner, Daaman, and McCormack, 1990; Forrest and Singh, 1990; Gray and Saracino, 1991) has confirmed that despite the threat of pregnancy, AIDS, and other sexually transmitted diseases, premarital sexual activity among teenagers, college students, and those in their early twenties has increased, and for the most part "safe sex" has not been practiced. DeBuono and colleagues (1990), however, do report that in a study of college women that there has been a substantial increase in the use of condoms during sexual intercourse. In another study, McNally and Mosher (1991) found that of the sampled sexually active unmarried women ages 15 to 44, sexual behavior in response to AIDS has been changed. This change includes the use of condoms, limiting the number of sexual partners, reducing the frequency of copulation, and abstinence.

In addition to their sexual behavior being affected, those afflicted with AIDS, and those viewed most susceptible to the disease—homosexual men and women—may involuntarily be tested, treated, and isolated. In the 1980s, stories appeared about deceased AIDS victims who had been refused proper burial by funeral parlors. For example, a Massachusetts mother dressed her dead son's body after funeral homes refused to handle the corpse. Fearful members of hospital staffs refuse to care for patients with AIDS and often neglect them. Patients have been discriminated against, including the pastoral care of those on their deathbeds. One particularly insensitive case illustrates this. A chaplain, introducing himself to AIDS patients, stated, "'I understand you're very sick because you've lived a very sinful life and God is punishing you. Without repentence,' the chaplain continued, 'you're going to die a terrible death'" (Ritter, 1985:15F).

When the cause of Legionnaire's disease was unknown, there was no comparable moral outcry (Rubin, 1984). Nor was there a call to quarantine members of the American Legion or to close their meeting halls. In the 1990s, civil liberties and our concepts of personal privacy have been threatened by those who call for mandatory testing of all those suspected of having HIV/AIDS and for all those who (which include most of us) can be a possible threat to others. The June 1995 decision of the Supreme Court allowing for random testing for drug use among high school athletes may be a preview in what the future has in store for mandatory testing for HIV/AIDS.

In summary, it has been the medical misfortune of the gay community to be the population in which the epidemic of the deadly disease AIDS first became widespread and visible. That community should not have to deal with the social consequences of moral panic. Rubin reminds us that "the history of panic that has accompanied new epidemics, and the casualties incurred by their scapegoats, should make everyone pause and consider with extreme skepticism any attempts to justify anti-gay policy initiatives on the basis of AIDS" (Rubin, 1984:300).

CONCLUSION

This chapter introduced the reader to an important theme of this book—patriarchal ideology and its effect on gender-role relationships. Patriarchy legitimates power and authority vested in the hands of men, with the eldest man usually wielding the greatest authority and power. I outlined the major components of patriarchal authority, emphasizing four types of restrictions for women: attitudes toward fertility and adultery, domestic confinement, property, and civil rights.

I began the chapter by observing that sociology makes a distinction between sex—the biological differences between women and men—and gender—the social and cultural definitions of femininity and masculinity. I then observed that two views of the nature of gender behavior have been proposed. The first sees it as innate and biologically determined; the second takes the position that it is acquired through socialization. Ethologists and sociobiologists are of the opinion that human social and gender-role behavior, like that of other animals, is biologically and genetically determined. Critics of sociobiology emphasize the qualitative differences of humans from other animals, particularly in terms of their use of language, and maintain that social learning is the important factor.

Cross-cultural and historical research offers support for the belief of most sociologists that socialization has a greater effect than biology on gender-role behavior. Studies indicate that every culture exhibits different, culturally patterned gender-role behavior and gender identities. Other studies show that in all preindustrial societies, there generally was a division of labor and activities by sex. Most scholars agree that in all societies, biology may influence, but does not determine, differences in gender roles.

My attention then turned to sexuality and the family. Here again, we saw from the cross-cultural and historical evidence how society, often influenced by patriarchal ideology, controls the sexual behavior of its members. The work of Randall Collins in this area was seen to be particularly important in understanding how political and economic factors play a determining role in influencing both sexual behavior and sexual ideology. The discussion of homosexuality illustrated the importance of social and cultural factors in determining the societal reaction. The chapter concluded with a discussion of AIDS. I showed how AIDS has become a "pandemic" as opposed to a "mere" epidemic. It now threatens the world's general population. I tried to demonstrate how the societal reaction to this dreadful disease is influenced and distorted by ideological factors relating to homosexuality. I also looked at the impact of AIDS on both heterosexual and homosexual behavior. The concept of a "moral panic" was used to frame my argument.

In the following chapter (Chapter 8), I comparatively examine how the patriarchal ideology manifests itself in the way we conceptualize love and courtship. I also examine premarital gender-role relationships. That chapter is followed by one (Chapter 9) on mate-selection processes. The following two chapters (Chapters 10 and 11) then focus on the sexual division of labor. Chapter 10 provides a cross-cultural view of men and women vis-à-vis their marital relationship and their respective involvements in the world of work and in domestic household and child-care activities. This discussion is followed in the concluding chapter of Part III by a historical examination of marital gender-role relationships, focusing on the United States.

8

LOVE, COURTSHIP,
AND PREMARITAL EXPERIENCES

> *Chapter Outline*
>
> **Romantic Love and the Double Standard**
>
> **Love and Courtship in Comparative Perspective**
>
> **Courtship and Love in America**
>
> **The Double Standard and Premarital Relationships**
>
> **From Dating and Rating to Cohabitation**
>
>   *Cohabitation: A Brief Cross-Cultural View*
>
>   *Cohabitation: An American Perspective*
>
> **Singlehood as an Alternative to Marriage**
>
> **Conclusion**

In this chapter, I build on the previous discussion of gender roles and sexuality conceptualizations by indicating how they are related to love, courtship, and premarital relationships. I begin with a discussion of how the conceptualization of romantic love was elaborated out of the conceptualization of patriarchy. As a consequence, the historical articulation of love, courtship, and premarital relationships took on a still recognizable character. In addition, the features that mark contemporary dating patterns and cohabitation among the young still exhibit vestiges of past conceptualizations.

I begin the chapter with a historical analysis of romantic love and the double standard, examining the Western historical experience of love and courtship and indicating the influence of patriarchal thought. I then proceed to a contemporary look at premarital relationships, focusing on college students. That discussion is followed by an in-depth examination of premarital cohabitation, where unmarried heterosexual couples live together and share the same household. Many sociologists believe that this is becoming a fundamental new state in premarital relationships and has implications for the way we think of marriage.

ROMANTIC LOVE AND THE DOUBLE STANDARD

The advent of Christianity in Europe after the fall of Rome witnessed a continuation of the patriarchal ideology. Reacting against the "corruption of Roman morals" and the increased freedom of women in imperial Rome, the Christian Church under the influence of St. Paul developed a very low regard for sexual relations, marriage, and women. Women were hated, feared, and degraded. The following passages from St. Paul illustrate this attitude. The first demonstrates the extent of the depreciation of heterosexual relations; the second enunciates the ideal of sexual abstinence and the subjugation of women.

> To avoid fornication, let every man have his own wife, and let every woman have her own husband . . . For I would that all men were even as I myself [a bachelor] . . . I say therefore to the unmarried and widows, it is good for them

if they abide as I; but if they cannot contain, let them marry; for it is better to marry than to burn. (I Corinthians 7:2-9)

For a man indeed ought not to have his head veiled, forasmuch as he is the image and glory of God; but the woman is the glory of the man. For the man is not of the woman; but the woman of the man; for neither was the man created for the woman, but the woman for the man for this house ought the woman to have a sign of authority on her head. (I Corinthians 11:7-10).

During the Middle Ages, Christianity adopted a strong ascetic morality. Sex was inherently evil and shameful. Abstinence was viewed as the ideal, with the proper role of sex being limited to procreation. In the fifth century, St. Jerome expressed this limited view of sex in marriage when he said:

It is disgraceful to love another man's wife at all, or one's own too much. A wise man ought to love his wife with judgment, not with passion. Let a man govern his voluptuous impulses, and not rush headlong into intercourse. He who too ardently loves his own wife is an adulterer. (Cited in Hunt, 1959:115)

Tied to the ascetic morality was an ambivalent attitude toward women. At one end of the continuum was the depiction of woman as Evil, the temptress Eve, and at the other end was the depiction of woman as Good, Mary, the Virgin Mother of Christ. Women, as the source of sin, were lesser beings who deserved subordination to men. They were not allowed to own or inherit property. However, certain females—nuns—were respected. They were often permitted to exercise vast authority and power within their convents.

Arising out of this dual conceptualization of women were the patterns of chivalry and courtly or romantic love among the nobility of the eleventh century. These sentiments flourished in the world of knights and ladies and were spread by troubadours and poets—finally to become the ideal of the European middle classes. The essence of courtly love was the belief in the distinction between love and lust. Love was seen as a pure and ennobling romantic ideal. It was anchored by the belief that one could become obsessed with the beauty and character of another. Romantic or courtly love occurred only outside of marriage. An integral feature was that it was asexual. It idealized a fantasy of unconsummated desire: Lovers were allowed to kiss, touch, fondle, and even lie naked together, but they could not consummate their love. It was thought that to consummate the love was to destroy it.

In contrast to love was the attitude of lust. Lust allowed sexual relations and was confined to marriage. It was viewed as an inferior emotion to romantic love. Morton M. Hunt (1959), who has written a delightful historical account of love in Western society, observes that marriage during the Middle Ages was primarily a business proposition. It involved the joining of lands, loyalties, and the production of heirs and future defenders (Hunt, 1959:137). Romantic love thus offered an alternative to the mundane relationships of marriage.

Courtly or romantic love was not a basis for marriage. In the twelfth century Andreas Capellanus (Andreas the Chaplain) (1969) wrote *The Art of Courtly Love*. This

BOX 8-1   The Historical Family

The Creation of the Romantic Ideal

Morton M. Hunt

When he was a mere lad of five, says Ulrich, he first heard older boys saying that true honor and happiness could come only through serving a noble and lovely women; he was deeply impressed, and began to shape his childish thoughts in that direction. Even at that tender age it was perfectly clear to him that such service, the keystone of courtly love, could be undertaken only for a woman one could never marry. True love had to be clandestine, bittersweet, and beset by endless difficulties and frustrations; by virtue of all this, it was spiritually uplifting, and made a knight a better man and a greater warrior.

The subject evidently dominated the thoughts of the boy, for by the age of twelve he put away childish things and consciously chose as the lady of his heart a princess. In every way, it was a perfect choice; she was far too highborn for him, considerably older than himself, and, of course, already married. He became a page in her court, and conscientiously cultivated his feelings of love until they commanded his whole being. He adored her in total secrecy, and trembled (inconspicuously) in her presence. When he saw her hands touch the petals of flowers he had secretly placed where she would see them, he was all but in a faint. And when she washed her hands before dinner, young Ulrich would sometimes filch the basin, smuggle if off to his room, and there reverently drink the dirty water.

Five years of this went by; his love affair progressed no further, however, since being totally unworthy of the lady he dared not even tell her of his feelings. At the age of seventeen he therefore took himself off to the court of the Margrave Henry of Austria, to raise his status; there he studied knightly skills for five more years, and at last was made a knight in 1222, during the wedding festival of the Duke of Saxony. By a marvelous coincidence, his ladylove, whom he had not seen but religiously dreamed of during those years, was one of the guests at the wedding, and the very sight of her so moved him that he immediately took a secret vow to devote his newly won knighthood to serving her. This decision filled him with melancholy and with painful longings, a condition which apparently made him very happy.

That summer, feverish and flushed with his infatuation, he roamed the countryside fighting in numerous tourneys and winning many victories, all of which he ascribed to the mighty force of love within him. At last, having compiled an impressive record, and feeling worthy to offer the lady the tribute of his devotion, he persuaded a niece of his to call on her and privately tell her of his desire to be an acknowledged but distant, respectful admirer of hers; he even got his niece to learn and sing for the Princess a song he had written. (Ulrich was already a competent *Minnesinger*—the German equivalent of the troubadour—as were many young noblemen of breeding.)

The heartless lady, unmoved by his ten years of silent devotion and his recent feats of valor, sent back a cruel and pointed reply: she considered him presumptuous, was scornfully critical of the high-flown language of his quite inappropriate offer, and for good measure, took the trouble to let him know he was too ugly to be considered even in the role of a very distant admirer. For it seems (and the lady was specific) that the unhappy young knight had a harelip. Undaunted—perhaps even inspired by this obvious proof that she had actually noticed him—Ulrich promptly undertook a journey to a famous surgeon and had his lip repaired. Considering the techniques of medieval surgery, this must have been both excruciatingly painful and quite dangerous; indeed, he lay feverish on a sickbed for six weeks. News of this, plus a new song he wrote for her, softened the lady's heart, and she sent word that he might attend a riding party and enjoy the rare privilege of speaking with her for a moment, if the opportunity should arise. And it did, once, when he had the chance to help her down from her horse, and could have uttered a sentence or two of devotion; unfortunately he was tongue-tied by her nearness and could say nothing. The lovely lady, considerably put out, whispered to him that he was a fraud, and gracefully indicated her displeasure by ripping out a forelock of his hair as she dismounted.

Not in the least angered by this, Ulrich reappeared the next day, this time found his voice, and humbly begged her to permit him to be her secret knight and to allow him to fight for her and love her. She accepted his service, but under the very minimum conditions, granting him no "favor" whatever—neither embrace, kiss, nor word of promise, and not so much as a ribbon to carry in his bosom. Ulrich, nevertheless, was filled with joy and thankfulness for her kindness, and sailed forth, tilting about the countryside with anyone who would break a lance with him, and composing many a song to his ladylove, which his secretary set down for him since writing was not a knightly accomplishment. The messages and letters that passed between him and the Princess at this time conveyed, in the one direction, his endless, burning, worshipful feelings and, in the other direction, her condescension, coldness, and criticism. But this was exactly what was expected of her in the situation, and he found each new blow a delicious pain; it even sounds somewhat as though a part of his pleasure lay in observing his own noble constancy under duress. If so, he must have had a thoroughly agreeable time for the next three years.

At the end of that period, Ulrich petitioned her forthrightly through a go-between to grant him her love, at least verbally, in return for his faithful adoration and service. The Princess not only sharply rebuked the go-between for Ulrich's unseemly persistency, but expressed her scorn that Ulrich had falsely spoken of losing a finger fighting for love of her. Actually, he had suffered a finger wound which healed, but an incorrect report had reached her. When the go-between related her scornful message, Ulrich paled for a moment, then resolutely drew out a sharp knife and ordered his friend to hack off the finger at one blow. This done, the knight had an artisan make a green velvet case in which the finger was held by gold clasps, and sent her the mounted digit as a keepsake, together with a special poem about the mat-

ter. Deeply impressed by this evidence of her power over him, she returned word that she would look at the finger every day from thenceforth, a message which, incidentally, he received as he did all other communiqués from her—on his knees, with bowed head and folded hands.

Determined now to earn her love by some stupendous feat, Ulrich conceived the scheme of the jousting-trip from Venice to Bohemia in the disguise of Venus. He went to Venice and there had seamstresses make a dozen white gowns to his own measurements; meanwhile he sent off a messenger with the open letter announcing the event. The northward march began on schedule on April 25, and concluded five weeks later, during which time Ulrich shattered an average of eight lances every day, made the notable record already mentioned, and acquired great glory and honor, all in the cause of love and for the sake of the Princess he so faithfully adored.

All this being so, it comes as something of a shock when one reads Ulrich's own statement that in the midst of this triumphal *Venusreise* he stopped off for three days to visit his wife and children. For the fact is that this lovesick Galahad, this kissless wonder, this dauntless knight-errant, had long had a wife to lie with when he had the urge, and a family to live with when he felt lonely. He himself speaks of his affection (but not his love) for his wife; to love her would have been improper and almost unthinkable. Like the other men of his class and time, Ulrich considered marriage a phase of feudal business-management, since it consisted basically of the joining of lands, the cementing of loyalties, and the production of heirs and future defenders. But the purifying, ennobling rapture of love for an ideal woman—what had that to do with details of crops and cattle, fleas and fireplaces, serfs and swamp drainage? Yet, though true love was impossible between husband and wife, without it a man was valueless. Ulrich could therefore unashamedly visit his wife during his grand tour, proud of what he had been doing and certain that if she knew of it, she too was proud, because *Frauendienst* made her husband nobler and finer.*

(continued)

Having completed his epochal feat of love service, Ulrich waited for his reward, and at long last it came: the Princess sent word that he might visit her. Yet he was to expect no warm welcome; she specified that he must come in the disguise of a leper and take his place among lepers who would be visiting her to beg for alms. But of course this monstrous indignity fazed the faithful Ulrich not in the least; nor did he falter when she knowingly let him, disguised in his rags, spend that night in a ditch in the rain; nor was he outraged when the next night he was finally allowed to climb a rope up the castle wall to her chamber, only to find it lit by a hundred tapers and staffed by eight maids-in-waiting who hovered about her where she lay in bed. Though Ulrich pleaded urgently that they all be sent out, she continued to be coyly proper, and when she began to see that this patient fellow really was getting stubborn at last, she told him that to earn the favor he would have to prove his obedience by wading in a nearby lake. She herself assisted him out the window—and then, bending to kiss him, let loose the rope, tumbling Ulrich to the ground, or perhaps into a stinking moat. (It is worth remembering at this point that this painful incident was not recorded by any enemy or satirist of Ulrich, but by himself, his purpose being to make clear the extent of his suffering for love and his fidelity in the face of trials.)

Even such torments cannot go on forever. The cruel Princess next ordered Ulrich to go on a crusade in her service, but when she learned that he joyfully and obediently received the direct command from her, she suddenly relented, bade him rather stay at home near to her, and finally granted him her love. What an outpouring of thankful verse then! What a spate of shattered lances, dented helmets, broken blades, humbled opponents! For having won her love, Ulrich was puissant, magnificent, impregnable; this was the height of his career as a knight. Regrettably, it is not clear in the *Frauendienst* just which of her favors she so tardily vouchsafed after nearly a decade and a half, but in the light of other contemporary documents concerning the customs of courtly love, one can be fairly sure that she permitted him the kiss and the embrace, and perhaps even the right to caress her, naked, in bed; but if she gave him the final reward at all, it was probably on extremely rare occasions. For sexual outlet was not really the point of all this. Ulrich had not been laboring nearly fifteen years for so ordinary a commodity; his real reward had always been in his suffering, striving, and yearning.

Morton M. Hunt. 1959. *The Natural History of Love.* New York: Knopf, pp. 134–139. Reprinted by permission of Morton M. Hunt.

*Ladies, too, were increased in value by being loved. In a fictional counterpart of Ulrich's relations with his wife, a lady in an old Provençal romance, reproached by her husband for having a lover, proudly replies: "My lord, you have no dishonor on that account, for he is a noble baron, upright and expert in arms, namely, Roland, the nephew of King Charles" (*Gesta Karoli Magni and Carcassonam et Narbonam*, p. 139).

work was written at the request of a countess and portrays life at a queen's court. The thesis is that love is an art and has an elaborate system of rules that govern the conduct of lovers. These include who may love whom, and the ways love may be acquired, kept, decreased, and retained. Of paramount note is his observation that love cannot exert its power between two people who are married to each other. Addressing himself to men, he observes that one cannot love one's wife but must love the wife of some other man. By necessity, then, the affair must be kept secret and that love cannot exist apart from jealousy. Love was extramarital and not apart of marriage.

Eventually, the ideal of romantic love with its nonconsummating characteristic was rejected; however, it was of extreme importance in the evolution of gender-role

Courtly love in the Middle Ages, in this case a picnic
scene in a garden with a wattle fence and a spring of
water (A.D. 1460).

relationships in Western civilization. Prior to its inception, the Middle Ages were distinguished by a pervasive male-dominant/female-subordinate society. Women were treated with hatred and contempt. Hunt (1969) believes that courtly love brought about three major changes in the male-female relationship. First, it introduced tenderness and gentleness into it. Courtly love developed an emotional relationship between men and women that eventually played a role in increasing the status of women. Second, it advocated the sexual fidelity of one partner to another, even though marital fidelity developed out of adulterous fidelity. Third, it introduced the revolutionary notion that love must be mutual and must involve respect and admiration. Thus, "the adulterous flirtation and illicit infatuations of the Middle Ages were the very instrument that began to enhance woman's status, and hence eventually to alter marriage" (Hunt, 1959:171-172).

Unfortunately, the dichotomization of love and lust and the "good" and "bad" woman, which was part of courtly love, continued to be manifest in the patriarchal ideology of the double standard. The double standard, which has been the dominating pattern of the gender-role relationship, is based on the notion of female inferiority. Women were divided into two categories: "good" women, who were premaritally chaste and thus were eligible marriage partners, and "bad" women, who were available to satisfy men's sexual needs outside of marriage. Men had access to women both in and out of marriage. "Good" women must restrain their sexual activities prior to marriage and in marriage. The double standard had a two-pronged basis: the notion of the lesser sexual interests of women and the idea of women as personal property. The argument was made that a woman was the personal property first of her father and second of her husband, and a woman had no right to give herself to another man without their consent.

In addition to the rights and privileges of men in regard to sexual activities, the double standard was extended to other spheres of life, including religion, politics, and economics. In all spheres, women had subordinated duties and obligations. Moreover, the placing of women on a pedestal (derived from romantic love ideology) further discriminated against them. Although supposedly protected from the harsh "realities" of the outside world, women were actually placed in a position of subservience and dependency. By viewing women as "delicate flowers" who must be protected and sheltered, men effectively removed women from these spheres in the outside world that would have made the equality of women possible.

I return to these themes in later chapters. Here, let us take a historical look at how patriarchal ideology influenced the way we conceptualize love and practice courtship. This discussion is followed by a contemporary examination of the double standard in its effects on premarital dating, courtship, and cohabitation. Our focus is on the American scene, with emphasis on college students.

LOVE AND COURTSHIP IN COMPARATIVE PERSPECTIVE

> Love and Marriage,
> Love and Marriage,
> Go together like a horse and carriage,
> This I tell you brother,
> You can't have one,
> No, You can't have one,
> Without the other.*

The above lyrics from a popular song of the 1950s that was sung in the small town are bittersweet, nostalgia play, *Our Town*, written by Thorton Wilder. It reflects the prevalent contemporary view of the inseparability of love and marriage. In the 1990s it was satirically revived as the theme song in the caustic view of marriage and the family in the television situation comedy *Married with Children*. In Western history, love and marriage did *not* "go together like a horse and carriage." In this chapter, I discuss the relationship of these two phenomena within the context of an examination of courtship and mate-selection processes. To frame my analysis, I work off the basic ideas of what has become known as the *sentiments approach* in family history (Anderson, 1980).

A few general remarks on the sentiments approach are desirable before proceeding more directly to the analysis of courtship systems and processes. The pivotal works in this area are Philippe Ariès' *Centuries of Childhood* (1962), Edward Shorter's *The Making of the Modern Family* (1975), J.L. Flandrin's *Families in Former Times*

---

*Love and Marriage, by Sammy Cahn and James Van Heusen © 1955 Barton Music Corp.
© Renewed, Assigned to Barton Music Corp. and Cahn Music Company. All rights o/b/o Cahn Music Company administered by WB Music Corp. All rights reserved. Used by permission. Warner Bros. Publications, U.S. Inc., Miami, FL 33014.

(1979), and Lawrence Stone's *Family, Sex and Marriage in England, 1500-1800* (1977). I will have more to say on Ariès' and Shorter's works in later chapters. Here, let me limit my attention to Stone and Flandrin within the context of courtship systems and processes.

The account begins by examining the influential work of Lawrence Stone (1977), who hypothesizes that the most important cultural change in the history of early modern Europe, and perhaps within the last thousand years of European history, was the rise of *affective individualism*. Stone discusses this conceptualization through a historical construction of three family types (the open lineage family, 1450-1630; the restricted patriarchal nuclear family, 1550-1700; and the closed domesticated nuclear family, 1640-1800) to explain change between 1500 and 1800. Anchoring his analysis is the sociological thesis that an inward-turning nuclear family gradually replaced the extended-kinship networks.

Stone's central argument is that family relationships are markedly different over the last 400 years. Similarly, Flandrin makes the point that the very concept of "family" has historically undergone major changes. The premodern English and French concept of the family reflected notions of kinship and co-residence. It referred both to sets of kinsfolk who did not live together and to all people who lived within a household and were not necessarily linked by ties of blood and marriage. Flandrin (1979:5) observes that this was still the case in the second half of the eighteenth century in both France and England, "that the members of the family were held to include both the kinsfolk residing in the house and the domestic servants, insofar as they were all subject to the same head of the family."

In the sixteenth century and extending into much later periods in many geographical areas and among certain social-class groups, the family is seen as being patriarchal and authoritarian, and demanding deference. Husbands had virtually absolute power and control over wives and children. This held true not only in economic terms but also in moral matters. Enforcement included the right as well as the duty to use physical force on those who disobeyed. Both women and children were relegated to subordinate legal positions that were based on the economic and political control of the husbands and fathers. Children were legally subordinate to their fathers to the extent that they could not enter into contracts until they were into their twenties (if even then). Similarly, children's rights either in law or in practice to select their own spouses were often strictly circumscribed (Anderson, 1980).

The "open lineage" family patterns are seen by Stone as a reflection of the overall patterns of people of premodern Europe who were typically violent, distrustful, and suspicious. People are characterized as having a markedly low level of affection and emotional interaction. The society is depicted as one in which everyone found it difficult to establish any emotional ties and there was a lack of warmth and tolerance in interpersonal relations. Privacy in this period is nonexistent. Concurring with Stone, Flandrin—basing his analysis on a study of confessors' manuals—finds no evidence of a duty to love either spouse or children. The prominent emphasis is on respect, deference, and obligation. Affection and sentimental attachments are treated with suspicion and seen as likely to lead to disorder.

This family system, with its emphasis on broad kinship ties and emotionally remote relations within the nuclear unit, changed in the mid-sixteenth century when the upper and middle strata of English society began to substitute loyalty to the state for loyalty to the broader kinship group that comprised the lineage. The resultant family form, the restricted patriarchal nuclear family, reconceptualized the family to its nuclear core while maintaining paternal authority. The result was a contradictory system that began to emphasize affectional ties between husband and wife, and between parents and children, within a nuclear family environment that continued to stress patriarchal obedience. In essence, Stone follows the recent historical interpretation that sees patriarchal authority within the nuclear family as being reinforced by the demands of the state and the church in the sixteenth and seventeenth centuries.

The final type of family, the closed domesticated nuclear family, rests on the belief in affective individualism. Stone observes that the change occurred first among the upper bourgeoisie and the affluent landowners. The emphasis in the nuclear family moved from absolute patriarchal authority to affectional ties. Children were seen as neutral and plastic beings who could best be molded by nurture and kindness. Prior affection was now an essential ingredient to a marriage, and young people were increasingly given the freedom to choose their own mates instead of having them selected by parents. Traditional patriarchy was replaced by romantic love, companionate marriage, and an affectionate and permissive mode of child rearing.

The various factors to which Stone attributes these eighteenth-century changes include Renaissance ideas about education, Reformation ideas of holy matrimony, and emerging ideas about liberty and the importance of the individual. The result was the rise of a more affectionate and more individualistic family type that is the direct antecedent of the contemporary conjugal family in both structure and emotional content. How this change in the closed domesticated nuclear family influenced changes in courtship processes concerns us here.

Stone views the period from 1660 to 1800 as one in which there was a shift in beliefs in how to assure that the interests of "holy matrimony" would best be served. By 1660, the belief moved from the previously held view of absolute parental decision making to the emerging opinion that children of both sexes should have the right of veto over a future spouse chosen for them by their parents. By 1800, the more radical view that children themselves should make their own choices prevailed. Accompanying this shift was the parallel one that moved the primary motive for marriage away from extended-kinship interest toward personal affection. Stone believes that the overall change to allow children much greater say in their choice of a spouse was a reflection of a new consciousness and a new recognition of the need for personal autonomy and for the individual pursuit of happiness.

There are three sociological conditions that are seen by Stone as essential for the development of relatively free mate selection. The first is the increased independence of the nuclear family from extended-kinship bonds. The second is the development of close parent-child bonds so that parents are assured that their values are shared by their children and that their children would make appropriate mate-selection choices. The third is the development of settings that would allow members of both sexes the opportunity to develop their own "courting rituals of conversation, dancing, etc." (Stone, 1977:184). The next section examines how courtship rituals and institutions were articulated in nineteenth-century America and how they reflected the ideology that Stone has called affective individualism.

COURTSHIP AND LOVE IN AMERICA

The historian Carl Degler (1980) reflects the current consensus among social historians that the modern American family emerged in the approximate fifty-year period from the Revolution to 1830. During that period, the family is seen to have changed not only in structure but also in internal dynamics. The four predominant characteristics of that family form as outlined by Degler embrace themes already discussed here. Marriage becomes based on affection and mutual respect, low fertility, child-centeredness, and, most important, what Degler calls the *doctrine of the two spheres*.

Degler's analysis emphasizes the importance of the doctrine of the two spheres or separate spheres in the articulation of husband and wife roles. Essentially, this doctrine held that, the primary role of the wife was child care and the maintenance of the household while the husband's was work outside the home. The very real potential of this doctrine is the belief that while the wife may be the moral superior in the relationship, the source of legal and social power rests with the husband. The consequence is the subordination of women's roles to their husbands. To deal with that subordination, women are seen to have carved out a source of power based on the emerging importance of mutual affection, love, and sexuality as integral components of modern marriage. The following discussion examines this development within an analysis of courtship processes.

Degler, influenced by such social historians as Lawrence Stone (1977) and Philip Greven (1970), developed his argument that prior to the American Revolution, fathers were not adverse to use "economic blackmail" to assure that their children married whom the fathers wanted. For example, as Greven has observed in his historical analysis of four generations in colonial Wendover, Massachusetts, the threat of withholding of land from their sons increased the influence of Puritan fathers over their sons during the 1700s. By the eighteenth century, however, there was a notable weakening of parental control over the marital choice and this form of coercion was less likely to occur. Degler traces similar historical developments in the freedom of mate-selection choices for both sons and daughters in other sections of preindependent America. The overall pattern is that by the beginning of the nineteenth century, parental control over the choice of marriage partners of their children was limited to a nonbinding veto much as it essentially is today (Degler, 1980).

The reasons for this change in the courtship decision-making process came as a consequence of the emerging belief that marriage should be based on personal happiness and the affection of the partners for each other. This attitude stems from the equating of marriage for love with individualism. "Love as the basis for marrying was the purest form of individualism; it subordinated all familial, social, or group considerations to personal preference" (Degler, 1980:15). Further, the growing acceptance of affection as the primary ground for marriage became an essential factor in the change in women's roles and a potential source of power and autonomy within the family. This was of particular importance because women in the nineteenth century had declining power or influence in the economic sphere.

> [M]ost relationships between people involve the exercise of power, and certainly the relationship of marriage is no exception. Yet once affection is a basis of marriage, the marital relation becomes significantly different from other relationships between superiors and inferiors. To begin with, unlike any other subordinate, such as a slave or an employee, a young woman contemplating marriage did have some choice as to who her new master would be. Clearly unsatisfactory possibilities could be ruled out completely, and from acquaintance at courtship, she had an opportunity to learn who were the undesirable partners. After the marriage, the woman also had an advantage that few slaves or employees enjoyed in dealing with their masters or employers. She was able to appeal to her husband's affection for her, and she, in turn, could use that affection in extracting concessions that a slave or an employee could not. In short, by the very nature of the relation, a woman in the family of affection had more power or influence than any other subordinate one can think of. (Degler, 1980:18)

Similarly, the expression of sexuality both within and outside of the courtship process took on a power component. Nancy Cott (1978), in an insightful article, sees that the Victorian notion of the "passionlessness" of women served to improve their status. The downplaying of sexuality was seen as a means of limiting male domination. At the same time sexuality was replaced by an emphasis on moral and spiritual superiority over males. "The belief that women lacked carnal motivation was the cornerstone of the argument for women's moral superiority, used to enhance women's status and widen their opportunities in the nineteenth century" (Cott, 1978:173).

Ellen K. Rothman—in a delightful as well as an insightful comprehensive history of courtship in America, *Hands and Hearts* (1984)—explains the interweaving of sexuality and courtship through an examination of three periods. Her account is drawn heavily from the analysis of unpublished courtship correspondence of 350 native-born, Northeastern, middle-class Protestants. Rothman acknowledges the limitation of this source of data in that it excludes large segments of the population—such as blacks, immigrants, and the poor—from her analysis. However, given that caveat, it is still of interest to see the courtship processes of that segment of American society to see what light it may shed on contemporary courtship and marriage practices.

Young males and females in the first period, 1770-1840, we are told, enjoyed a good deal of autonomy in regard to their dating. Places to get together included schools and churches, fields and factories, and dances and parties. Gender roles reflected a division of labor and did not, as yet, reflect the future development of the two spheres of work and home. Bundling, an eighteenth-century precursor to premarital sex in which couples would sleep together, albeit with their clothes on, was a common practice that allowed them to get to know each other better. Historians see it as a compromise between persistent parental control and the pressures of their children to subvert traditional family authority. A song written during that time period leads Rothman to conjecture that bundling may have been a practice that mothers and daughters favored because it was a ritual over which their sex had control.

> Some maidens say, if through the nation,
> Bundling should quite go out of fashion,
> Courtship would lose its sweets, and they
> Could have no fun till wedding day.
> It shan't be so, they rage and storm,
> And courtship girls in clusters swarm,
> And fly and bus, like angry bees,
> And vow they'll bundle when they please.
> Some mothers too, will plead their cause
> And give their daughters great applause,
> And tell them, 'tis no sin nor shame,
> For we, your mothers, did the same.
> (cited in Rothman, 1984:47)

The second period, 1830-1880, was so marked by the doctrine of the two spheres in almost all areas of life that Alexis de Tocqueville made a point to comment on this in his first visit to America in 1831 that "constant care" was taken to "trace two clearly distinct lines of action for the two sexes . . . in two paths that are always different" (quoted in Rothman, 1984:91). Clearly demarcated boundaries for men and women were developed in the community, the home, and in the world of work. Of equal importance was the commonly held view that women, while intellectually inferior to men, were their superior in terms of moral sensibilities. This definition of gender differences became the cultural context for the articulation of courtship processes and the transition into marriage during this period.

The essence of maleness was defined in terms of man's occupational involvement and the pursuit of worldly and material success. Women, on the other hand, were defined in terms of home—wife and mother—involvement and moral virtue. Ralph Waldo Emerson, the spokesman of New England transcendentalism, captures that sentiment as "Man's sphere is out of doors and among men—woman's is in the house—Man seeks for power and influence—woman for order and beauty—Man is just—woman is kind" (cited in Rothman, 1984:92).

Rothman believes that this idealization of masculine and feminine behavior affected courtship to the extent that romantic love took on greater importance as the criterion for marriage than ever before. Further, romantic love as a basis for marriage must go beyond transient passions but must serve as a base for sympathy and shared interests. It was vital that such a marital relationship be grounded on mutuality, commonality, and sympathy in order to overcome the gulf between men and women that resulted from their division in two different spheres. "The increasing isolation of married women in the home and the involvement of married men in the world made it imperative that lovers sympathize with each other; they must have a mutuality of tastes and interests because they might have little else to share" (Rothman, 1984: 107).

Candor became a dominant value in mid-nineteenth-century courtship ritual. It was seen as a vital link between people whose involvements were in two disparate worlds. Rothman observes that men were in constant struggle between the dominant masculine ideology of self-control and the felt necessity for self-exposure and intimacy in courtship. When it did occur, candor produced an intimate environment that was in direct contrast to the emotional reserve they experienced with other people. Further, courtship intimacy led to other changes; marriages took on a more companionate perspective and parent-child relationships—with particular emphasis on mother-child involvements—became a central focus of family life.

Candor also affected attitudes and behavior regarding sexual intimacy during courtship. Repeatedly, Rothman found in her examination of the correspondence of young people that erotic play, in both fantasy and reality, was a common component of mid-nineteenth-century courtship. Letters between separated lovers evoked the past and anticipated the future with images of sexual imagery. The following letter is illustrative:

> O happy hours when I may once more encircle within these arms the dearest object of my love—when I shall again feel the pressure of that "aching head" which will delight to recline upon my bosom, when I may again press to my heart which palpitates with the purest affection the loved one who has so long shared its undivided devotion. (cited in Rothman, 1984:122-123)

However, the achievement of candor and intimacy that was so necessary for the success of courtship and subsequent marriage and family patterns was severely handicapped by the continued prominence of the doctrine of the two spheres, which advocated the separation of male and female worlds. The third period, 1870-1920, was characterized by the beginning of the reaction against this doctrine and its offshoot, the doctrine of "female influence." This doctrine advocated the innate moral superiority of women while at the same time argued that women's place was at home. The doctrine of female influence soon fell under attack; for example, the women's suffrage movement pointed out the hypocrisy in the view that women did not need the vote because their innate superiority gave them so much influence over their enfranchised husbands and sons.

Yet the doctrine of female influence was part of the more encompassing doctrine of the two spheres. The consequence of these doctrines continued to foster obstacles to friendship between the sexes, often resulting in a reliance on friendships with their own sex. Further, it severely handicapped the development of emotional bonds within courtship. In the next section, I demonstrate how these historical changes in courtship affected the dating and courtship processes of middle-class Americans after 1930.

BOX 8-2   The Contemporary American Family

Home on the Range (and Lonely, Too)

Dirk Johnson

JAMESTOWN, N.D., Dec. 8—In the stillness of the frozen prairie, David Gasal walked along the snowy wheat fields with his constant companion, a rust-colored dog named Snickers, and ruminated about sunsets and songbirds and loneliness.

"I like to listen to the blue jays and watch the sunsets," said the 40-year-old farmer. "I like the quiet, too. I just wish I had somebody to share it with."

As women have become scarce in rural America, drawn to bigger towns and cities for careers, the men left behind on farms are facing a difficult time finding marriage partners. This epidemic of bachelorhood has led some towns, like Herman, Minn., to advertise their surplus of marriageable men in hope of attracting female suitors.

To help lonely hearts on the farm, several singles directories have emerged for rural people. One, published by Farm Journal earlier this year, drew more than 4,300 entries, nearly double the number in a similar directory published by the magazine a decade earlier.

"We had assumed—evidently wrongly— that rural America had become less isolated due to the explosion in communication technology," said Karen Freiberg, the managing editor of Farm Journal. "In matters of the heart, just the opposite appears to be occurring."

In Farm Journal's directory, about 77 percent of the entries came from men. In urban areas' dating directories, women typically outnumber men by a wide margin. Indeed, finding a decent, eligible man in his late 30's or early 40's, some women say, is about as easy as winning the lottery.

But in the remote corners of America, there is a good man or two left. Mr. Gasal, a fourth-generation farmer, seems to be one of them. A patient, well-spoken man with blue eyes and the rugged physique of a football player, at 6 feet 3 inches and 215 pounds, he does not smoke cigarettes, chew tobacco or take drugs. He frequents the church more often than the saloon. He takes good care of his mother. He even gave shelter to Snickers, who had been abused and abandoned. He is interested in art and photography and belongs to the Audubon Society. "I don't hunt animals," he said. "I would rather take pictures of them."

What does the bachelor farmer hope to find in a woman?

"Well, I don't care about hair color, as long as it's not dyed something weird," Mr. Gasal said. "Also, I wouldn't feel comfortable with someone who was interested in bodypiercing. And, I guess it would be nice if they're not really grossly overweight."

He would like to meet a woman willing to live on a farm. It would be nice if she would want to help run it. But if she wanted a career other than agriculture, he said, that would suit him just fine, too.

"Sometimes, I think the city gals find the farming life more appealing, since they sometimes have romantic ideas about it," Mr. Gasal said. "The gals who grew up in the country, they know a little too much about the struggles and hardship."

In fact, after Farm Journal compiled its directory, the magazine got a barrage of calls and letters from women in cities who complained that they would have liked a chance to participate in the directory in the hopes of meeting a nice farmer.

Mr. Gasal has lived all of his life on the farm, but has traveled throughout much of the United States. With other members of an art appreciation class he took at nearby Jamestown College a few years ago, he visited New York and was impressed by the art galleries in SoHo, the plays on Broadway, the architecture.

But he felt a bit uncomfortable that people in the big city did not make eye contact or make small talk, the way they do back home.

(continued)

Farmer, attractive and desperate, seeks life mate.

"I was walking up Broadway, and saying 'Hi' to people as I passed them," he said. "And some people looked back at me like, What are you, nuts? I don't know you."

As he neared 40, it started to bother Mr. Gasal that he might never find a partner.

"I don't want to be a bachelor, sitting around by myself," he said. "I'd really like to share my life with somebody. Maybe have kids. Have someone carry on my name, maybe even carry on the farm."

He lives in a 96-year-old farmhouse with his mother, Lois, who is also eager for him to marry.

"It's time, David," she has told him more than once.

"It's not as easy as it seems, Mom," he has replied.

A generation ago and more, there were many more farm families, and more ways for people to get to know each other. There were barn dances, church picnics, card parties. Most of that has gone by the wayside.

In Farm Journal's directory, the biggest share of entries came from Iowa, followed by Illinois. But there were bachelor farmers from Canada and all but two states, Rhode Island and Hawaii. The oldest entrant was an 88-year-old man from Indiana.

A 32-year-old from North Carolina wrote that he liked "fishing, hunting and car races." A divorced 52-year-old from Ohio signed himself, "Lonely." A 35-year-old man from North Dakota listed his interests as "motorcycles and guns," while a 48-year-old from that state listed "left-wing politics."

Dennis White, 36, a dairyman in Nashua, Iowa, had started to despair of his chances of finding the right woman. Two blind dates had gone badly when the women, both Iowans, learned he was a farmer.

"The agricultural connection was a turnoff," Mr. White said. "I guess they thought I'd be too tied down."

About the same time, Deb Renning, a 38-year-old dairywoman from Clarksville, Iowa, about 12 miles from Nashua, was starting to lose hope. A sister and brother-in-law had talked Ms. Renning into submitting her name to the Farm Journal's directory. "What do you have to lose?" her sister asked.

When Ms. Renning got the listings last June, her eyes lit up when she saw the entry from nearby Nashua and wondered whether he might want to meet her. She did not have to wait long. That same day, a letter arrived from that very Nashua dairyman.

The two agreed to meet at an ice cream shop between their two towns, figuring they would talk for 5 or 10 minutes. They talked for 5 hours.

The two were to marry this weekend in Clarksville.

"We're going to honeymoon out West—Iowa, that is," said Mr. White. "We're going to stay at a nice little bed and breakfast, on a farm."

The New York Times,
12 December 1995.

THE DOUBLE STANDARD AND PREMARITAL RELATIONSHIPS

In the United States, individual motives, particularly love, play an important role in the decision-making process related to whom we should marry. Yet falling in love is usually limited to someone who is socially approved by parents and peers; that is, through informal long-term socialization and through informal pressures, marriage is usually restricted to partners who share similar backgrounds, social class, religion, race, and education. I now discuss an additional factor that helps explain American dating, courtship, and mate-selection processes—the *double standard.*

The double standard is usually associated with sexual behavior. It allows greater freedom for men to have premarital and extramarital sexual experiences than for women. It originated in ancient Hebrew, Greek, Roman, and early Christian doctrines. Ira Reiss, who has done extensive analyses of premarital sexual standards and behavior, observes that the basis of the double standard involves the notion of female inferiority. Reiss (1960) argues that the double standard is not solely restricted to sexual behavior. The double standard allows men preferential rights and duties in a variety of roles. By and large, the more challenging, the more satisfying, and the more valued positions are awarded to men and not to women.

> It is not just a question of different roles—anyone looking fairly at the division of roles will see that women's roles are given low status as compared to men's roles. The particular role does not matter; whatever a woman does is valued less and whatever a man does is valued more, e.g., if men herd then herding is highly valued—if women herd it is not. (Reiss, 1960:92-93)

In later chapters, I examine in more depth the origins of the double standard and its implications for gender-role relationships in the family and in other spheres. Now I investigate its impact on mate-selection processes.

The double standard has had a pervasive effect on mate-selection processes. As Willard Waller (1938) has pointed out in his classic study of the family, double-standard-based courtship practices can be analyzed in terms of bargaining and exploitive behavior that denigrates both men and women. The stigma attached to being an unwed nonvirgin combined with the desire of women to marry, partly because of the lack of meaningful alternative options in the work sphere, promoted an atmosphere in courtship that was destructive for both sexes. In return for sexual "favors," women bargained for an ultimate marriage contract. But paradoxically, the loss of virginity lessened her marital desirability and eligibility (a man's wish to marry a virgin). The result was a frustrating relationship where there was a constant give-and-take revolving around sexual permissiveness and marital commitment. Ira Reiss (1960) has stated that the double standard results in a net of contradictory and unfulfilled desires:

> Many women very strongly resent this contradictory virginity-attitude on the part of men. These women feel it most unfair for a man to date a girl, try to seduce her, and then if he succeeds, condemn her and cross her off his marriage-possibility list. Many girls find themselves upset when they become fond of a particular boy and would like to be more sexually intimate with him, but must keep restricting their advances for fear of losing his respect. . . .
>
> Many girls who tease are merely playing the man's game. If men are so interested in sex, but dislike girls who "go too far," the logical thing to do, these girls feel, is to play up their sexual attributes to attract men and then restrict sexual behavior. The double-standard male creates his own "ene-

mies"—he makes women use sex as a weapon instead of an expression of affection; in this case, the weapon is in the form of the tease. This sort of situation leads to the anomalous case of a female who, on the surface, seems highly-sexed but who internally may be quite frigid—a sweet "sexy" virgin whose dual nature may well cause her much internal conflict. Such a virgin is similar to wax fruit—in both cases the appearance may be appetizing but the object is incapable of fulfilling its promise. (Reiss, 1960:106)

In the 1960s significant changes in premarital sexual and premarital relationships began to occur. Bernard Farber (1964) observed that mate-selection processes prior to the 1960s used to be characterized by a series of stages that culminated in marriage—dating, keeping company, going steady, a private agreement to be married, announcement of the engagement, and finally marriage. This pattern was seen as a reflection of the double standard, which placed a great deal of emphasis on "approved" sexuality confined to marriage and women's confinement to marriage as the only career possibility. In the 1960s this pattern was changing. Farber believes that these changes reflected the increased independence of women and their greater involvement in institutions other than the family; work, politics, religion, and education have provided them with career alternatives. Further, technological developments in controlling impregnation (the pill, the loop) combined with less stringent norms about sexual permissiveness for both sexes changed the courtship process. Farber pointed out that such a term as *keeping company* was no longer in the courtship vocabulary. As for the term *going steady*, it mainly referred to a person with whom one is currently involved. Since Farber wrote his monograph, such terms as dating and courtship have become antiquated. Farber concluded that with the whole system of courtship, which was based on the double standard, there was an ever-narrowing field of eligible spouses. This has given way to a series of personal "involvements," one of which may result in marriage (Farber, 1964:161).

Michal M. McCall (1966) continued the analysis of this new courtship pattern that was emerging in that pivotal decade of the 1960s. Sexual exploitation was no longer associated with courtship patterns. In this new relationship, there was an emphasis on intimacy and exclusiveness with a personal commitment. This commitment included sexual intimacy. Most men no longer expected women to be virgins at the time of their first marriage. The relationship was becoming more egalitarian and could be terminated by either partner if it turned out to be unsatisfactory. In this relationship, exploitation referred to the possible impregnation of the woman and the failure of the man to marry her. Analogous to the earlier pattern, where there was a legitimate expectation that marriage followed sexual intimacy, the emerging pattern had a legitimate expectation that marriage followed impregnation. The relationship of the couple was intensely personal. Given the greater equality of women, there was a greater tendency for either the man or woman to break the relationship and seek to form a new one. This is attributed to the fact that the notion of the "one and only love" (a main component of romantic love) was no longer as viable as before. It also helps explain why contemporary premarital relationships were less stable and enduring.

Darling, Kallen, and VanDusen (1984), reviewing historical changes in premarital sexuality in the twentieth century, report that in the 1970s a major change occurred.

Based on an analysis of thirty-five published studies that examined sexual behavior among never-married youths and young adults, the authors found that there was a dramatic upswing in premarital sexual activity after 1970. This was especially the case among women. Sexual involvement was now seen as being statistically normative among this age group. The authors conclude that the changes in sexual behavior for *both* sexes means that it may now have similar motives and meanings for *both* sexes. Darling and her associates working off Durkheim's schema of normal and deviant behavior, argue that it may mean that premarital sexual behavior may be seen as being normal behavior rather than deviant behavior. They reason that if the majority of the young are sexually involved, it is not possible to regard their sexual involvement as being socially deviant.

A major change occurring in the 1980s and continuing to the present time is a movement toward premarital cohabitation. The next section will review the historical changes in premarital behavioral practices.

FROM DATING AND RATING TO COHABITATION

To understand how the double standard operated in premarital relationships I turn to a classic article written in the 1930s. I then will expand on how the double standard and in turn dating practices changed in the ensuing years to our present situation. I begin with Willard Waller's (1937) famous study of what he called the dating and rating complex that existed at Pennsylvania State University in the later 1920s and early 1930s. I end with an analysis of nonmarital cohabitation.

Waller (1937) distinguished courtship from dating. Dating refers to the pursuit of sexual pleasure as an aim in itself, courtship involves interaction with a person who is seen as a possible marriage partner. Hedonistic considerations count for less in courtship than in dating, and the person's family and class background count for much more. Waller describes the dating process within the context of the fraternity system then in existence at Penn State. Half the male students lived in fraternities. These students were a homogeneous group predominantly from the lower-middle class. For these men, the dating system was highly competitive and based on a scale reflecting campus values. Males were rated highest if they were members of the better fraternities, were prominent in activities, had a large supply of spending money, were well dressed, were good dancers, and had access to an automobile. Girls were rated on their appearance, their popularity, their ability to dance well, and who they dated.

An integral aspect of the dating system was the boys' open antagonism toward the girls, the exploitative nature of their relationships, and what Waller calls "thrill seeking." The "thrills" varied by sex; men sought sexual gratification while women sought to enhance their prestige by going out with the more desirable men and gaining financial benefit, such as free admission to amusements, restaurants, theaters, and the like. This resulted in dating becoming a bargaining relationship with exploitative and antagonistic overtones. Waller illustrates this point by citing a woman student informant:

> A fundamental antagonism exists on this campus between the men and women students. There is an undercurrent of feeling among the men that the school really belongs to them, and that the coed is a sort of legalized trans-

gressor on their territory. A typical procedure of the college man is to give a coed a terrific rush, and then either drop her suddenly without any explanation whatsoever, or tell her that "Maryjane Whosis, the girl he is engaged to at home, is coming up for Senior Ball," or something of that sort. . . .

Against this sort of attitude the coeds build up a defense mechanism which usually takes the form of cynicism. "They're out for what they can get? That's fine. So are we." Everything is just one grand, big joke. Many of the girls really fight against liking a boy and try very hard to maintain this cynical attitude. One way in which they do this is the use of ridicule. Many coeds put on an act for their girlfriends after a date, mimicking certain characteristic actions of the boy she has been out with, and making a joke of the things he has said to her. Often the less a girl feels like doing this, the worse she will make it. It is her way of convincing herself that her armor of cynicism is as strong as ever. (Waller, 1938:252-253)

Waller attributes the development of the dating and rating system to the disappearance of community controls over the younger generation. Their loss is seen in the decline of the primary group community and in the reduction of such adult supervised activities as school and church socials. "From the sociological viewpoint, this represented social disorganization, a decay of older forms, a replacement of socially agreed-upon definitions of situations by hedonistic, individualistic definitions" (Waller, 1938:223). In short, Waller saw the dating and rating process being dominated by a desire for fun and amusement that was expressed in a system of exploitation, antagonism, and bargaining.

Waller saw dating becoming separated from courtship. The implications of Waller's study are that the gender-role antagonisms generated by the dating system are carried over to courtship and lead to undesirable emotional tensions in this relationship and in marriage. Waller developed the conceptualization of the "principle of least interest" to summarize this point. He believed that courtship grew out of dating as one or both partners became emotionally involved. But unequal emotional involvement could lead to the person with "least interest" exploiting the other, thus repeating the debilitating dating relationship:

Exploitation of sorts usually follows the realization that the other person is more deeply involved than oneself. So much almost any reasonably sophisticated person understands. The clever person, in my observation usually a woman, knows how to go on from that point. A girl may pretend to be extremely involved, to be the person wholly dominated by the relationship; this she does in order to lead the young man to fasten his emotions and to prepare the way for the conventional denouement of marriage, for, in the end, while protesting her love, she makes herself unattainable except in marriage; this is certainly not an unusual feminine tactic and is executed with a subtlety which makes the man's crude attempts at guile seem sophomoric. (Waller, 1938:276-277)

Waller sees love and marriage emerging out of courtship. Love is depicted as an outgrowth of the initial desire of one partner to get the other partner emotionally involved in the relationship. However, individuals, without being aware of it, may develop an idealized image of the other that takes on an irrational character, and thus they get caught up in an emotional surge that culminates in marriage. The consequences are that the couple must reorient their early stages of marital adjustment to a relationship based on the reality of each other, not on their idealizations of each other. For many, this becomes an impossible task, culminating in a marital relationship that is characterized by conflict and, in many cases, divorce.

Attempts to replicate Waller's finding of the existence of a "rating and dating complex" have not been successful. Christopher Lasch (1977a), in a review of the studies of the 1940s and 1950s, finds many flaws in their methodologies, particularly in the way they operationalized Waller's concept of rating and dating. Michael Gordon (1978) and Richard R. Clayton (1979), in their respective reviews of studies done in the 1950s, 1960s, and 1970s, report that personality factors may have played a more influential role than Waller's rating criteria in dating relationships. Gordon further develops the view that these more recent studies may reflect historical changes that have occurred in the attitudes and values that govern premarital heterosexual relationships, as well as the greater possibility that marriage may take place either during or immediately after college. Another factor that is emerging in the nature of premarital relationships is the dramatic increase in the number of college students who are now cohabitating. Cohabitation represents a significant movement away from the situation in which the dating relationship—according to Waller—was a means to an end, to a relationship that is an end in and of itself and characterized by personal involvements and commitments. My attention now turns to these new trends in premarital relationships.

Researchers [see Gordon (1978) and Leslie (1979) for reviews of these studies] have observed that in the 1950s, 1960s, and 1970s there was a movement away from pairing off in casual dating patterns to more informal group activities among high school and college students. Exclusive dating began at a later age and was more clearly associated with greater emotional involvements and commitments. Further, a more innovative development was occurring: the increasing number of nonmarried couples beginning to live together in a marriage-like situation. This development, nonmarital cohabitation, is characterized by greater informality, spontaneity, and intimacy outside the parameters of traditional dating and courtship relationships.

In her much cited research, Rebbeca S. Vreeland (1972a, 1972b) studied dating patterns among male Harvard University students during the 1960s and early 1970s. Her studies provided a baseline on the changes that occurred in dating during this period. She identified four dating patterns among the class of 1964. The *instrumental* pattern most clearly approximated Waller's rating and dating complex. The emphasis was on sexual exploitation and the enhancement of one's social reputation. Harvard students would take their dates to football games, dances, nightclubs, and so on, where they could be highly visible and "show off." In the second pattern, the *traditional* relationship, dating was ultimately designed to find a suitable wife. Women who ranked high by virtue of their good reputation, sexual inhibition, family background, and social status were the most sought after. In the *companion* pattern, the emphasis was on informal couple activities. The goal was to find someone with whom to share intimacies and engage in private activities. The fourth and last pattern that Vreeland thinks may be more typical of elite colleges was *intellectual* dating. Here, the emphasis was to find a woman who was the man's intellectual equal and with whom he would be able to share discussions and concerns.

Vreeland compared these patterns of the 1964 class with those of their 1970 counterparts. The companion pattern and the intellectual pattern still persisted. The former, while emphasizing friendship, broadened its activities to include recreational and social involvements. The latter became a defensive mechanism for intellectually gifted but socially inadequate men more than a means to form a mature relationship. The greatest changes occurred in the instrumental and the traditional dating patterns. The instrumental relationship became characterized by less emphasis placed on sexual exploitation and a greater concern placed on political activities, drug taking, and shared lovemaking. Men in the traditional dating pattern were now more concerned with finding women who were "liberated" and nonconventional, and who shared their rejection of traditional social patterns, than in becoming involved with socially acceptable women. Vreeland believes that these trends indicate that dating has become less formal and less exploitative. "Students in search of their own humanity have begun to treat their dates as persons and potential friends rather than as competitors or candidates for marriage" (Vreeland, 1972a:66).

Changing gender roles brought about changes in dating patterns in the 1970s, 1980s, and 1990s. Studies of dating in the 1970s and 1980s indicated additional changes in the traditional practice. The traditional "date" required it to be arranged ahead of time, with the male calling or inviting the female to accompany him. He would pick her up and take her to a place of his choosing with her agreement and he was expected to pay for all the expenses. The research revealed less structured and formal patterns of dating. Roger Libby (1977) reported that young people congregated in groups and paired off while retaining allegiance to the group. Knox and Wilson (1981), in a study of students attending a southeastern university found that many students met through friends, at parties, and at work. Surprisingly, the classroom was the least likely place for students to meet. Attending a public event—such as a movie, a football game, or a party—and then returning to the man's or woman's room was a common form of dating activity. Michael Gordon (1981) also found that a typical date involved spending the evening with a number of people, with pairing off occurring later in the evening. He also reported that females were more likely to initiate a date than their historical counterparts. In all, dating was seen to be less concerned with establishing and maintaining popularity, less gender-role-stereotyped, and less formal than the college students studied by Willard Waller in the 1930s.

The changing gender roles reported by Gordon and others in the 1980s (cf. Korman, 1983; Laner, 1989; and Whyte, 1990) help to explain the changes in the structure of dating. In addition, the increase in dual income families provides role models for the young adults on egalitarianism. Increasingly, young women and men were developing egalitarian gender-role preferences and this operationalized in more both-sex initiated dates and sharing of dating expenses. These changing gender roles may also have been responsible for changing sexual behavior in dating as well.

Knox and Wilson (1981), in their survey of college students, inquired on matters of sexual values and encouragement or discouragement of sexual intimacy. By the third date, after some initial reluctance by females, kissing was acceptable to all. Men were also more willing to engage in heavy petting and sexual intercourse earlier in the dating sequence than females. Sexual intimacy was tied to emotional involvement, particularly in the case of females.

An interesting study on premarital attitudes and behavior that reflect changes in both the double standard and the impact of the fear of AIDS and other sexually transmitted diseases was conducted by Ira Robinson and his associates (Robinson, Ziss, Ganza, and Katz, 1991). They found major changes over a twenty-year period in sexual behavior and attitudes at a large southern university. While they found that premarital intercourse was becoming more acceptable for both males and females, there was still evidence of the double standard, although it was somewhat in decline. Heavy petting, which included manual manipulation and oral-genital sex, had increased during this period, especially among women. While seven out of ten women felt that premarital sexual intercourse was immoral in 1965, a small minority (21 percent) felt that way in 1975, and only 17 percent shared that opinion in 1985. The respective percentages for men were 33 percent to 20 percent to 16 percent during that same period. The number of men having premarital sex steadily increased from 1965 to 1985 from 65 percent to 79 percent. The increase for women was more startling—from 29 percent to 1965 to 64 percent by 1980 with a slight drop to 63 percent in 1985.

Of particular interest were the changes in double standard sexual attitudes and the possible impact of the fear of AIDS and other sexually transmitted diseases on premarital sexual attitudes. A man having sexual intercourse with a great many women was thought immoral by 35 percent of the males and 57 percent of the females sampled in 1965. In comparison, a woman having sexual intercourse with a great many men was thought immoral by 42 percent of the males and 91 percent of the women. Ten years later, at the height of the "sexual revolution," both a small majority of men and women (20 percent and 30 percent) felt that many sexual partners for men was immoral. In 1985, at the beginning of the AIDS epidemic, there was a significant percentage increase in the number of men (now 32 percent) and women (now 52 percent) who felt such behavior was immoral. The same question asked about women who had sexual intercourse with a great many men reveals a similar pattern in which the double standard was breaking down while concern with AIDS was increasing their conservatism toward premarital sex. The figures for men in the three-decade survey years of 1965, 1975, and 1985 was 42 percent, 29 percent, and 51 respectively. For women it was 91 percent, 41 percent, and 64 percent.

Research specifically designed to compare the sexual practices of college women before and after the onset of the AIDS epidemic was conducted on women who had used the services of gynecologists at a college health center (DeBuono et al. 1990). In the three periods under investigation—1975, 1986, and 1989—relatively the same proportion of women, around 88 percent, were sexually active. Further, the number of partners and the type of sexual activity—sexual intercourse, anal intercourse, oral sex—remained the same during the three periods surveyed.

In comparison, in a more comprehensive study of sexually active, unmarried women between the ages of 15 to 44 years, there was a notable drop in sexual activity (McNally and Mosher, 1991). Nearly one-third of the women studied had changed their sexual behavior as a reaction to the threat of AIDS. These changes included having sexual relations with only one man or less men, restricting copulation, or refusing to have sex at all.

The above-mentioned studies reveal significant changes in heterosexual premarital relationships. The other change is the movement toward nonmarital heterosexual cohabitation, particularly among college students. Eleanor D. Macklin (1978), after reviewing the abundant research evidence that accumulated during the 1970s' sexual revolution predicts that: "Nonmarital cohabitation is fast becoming a part of the dominant culture in this country and it seems likely that in times to come a majority of persons will experience this lifestyle at some point in their life cycle" (1978:1). She estimated that about 25 percent of the undergraduate college population had engaged in living together under marriage-like conditions. In the years since her study, cohabitation has become even more commonplace. Before analysis is begun of this phenomenon in the contemporary American middle class, a brief examination of its historical and cross-cultural existence is appropriate to set the discussion in perspective.

Cohabitation: A Brief Cross-Cultural View

Cohabitation is not a phenomenon unique to contemporary America. Miriam E. Berger (1971) cites cross-cultural evidence to document its existence in non-Western societies. Traditionally, among the Peruvian Indians of Vicos in the Andes, cohabitation was an integral form of courtship. These parents made cohabiting arrangements for their children to test the work capabilities of the girl and the couple's compatibility. In modern Vicos, the young are free to choose their own partners with romantic love playing an important role—yet the men still value the traditional virtues of responsibility, hard work, household skills, and the willingness of the women to help in the fields. Trial marriage is still practiced. It lasts an average of about fifteen months and 83 percent of these arrangements are finalized in marriage. M.E. Berger notes that this practice seems to aid in the transition from adolescence to adulthood by virtue of the partners acquiring the social and sexual advantages of adulthood without assuming the full responsibilities of marriage.

Precedent also exists in Western Europe. M.E. Berger discusses the old Teutonic custom of trial rights, which is still practiced in the traditional community of Staphorst, the Netherlands. With parental acknowledgment, a man can spend three nights a week with his girlfriend. The hope is that the woman will become pregnant, for no marriage can take place if she is barren.

In the twentieth century, the incidence of cohabitation is often related to political pressure and social policy. While we must distinguish between brief periods of cohabitation and long-term marriage-like relationships (commonly referred to as common-law marriages) it would be of interest to look at how other countries deal with long-term marriage-like relationships. For example, in Mexico in 1950, 20 percent of the couples living together were unmarried (Trost, 1975). This figure is seen to have declined as a result of governmental pressure to get unmarried couples married officially and legalize their relationship. Through the efforts of a wife of a Mexican president, the Mexican government has sponsored "Wedding Days." These governmental proclamations have been promoted since 1955 and in twenty years an estimated 240,000 couples legalized their long-term relationships by getting married. In contrast, Scandinavian countries have liberalized their social policies and social sanctions against cohabitation and long-term marriage-like relationships. As a result there is less fear of social stigma and a resultant high cohabitation rate both for short-term as well as long-term relationships.

Jan Trost (1975, 1978), one of the leading specialists on changes in the European family, has observed that Germany, Sweden, Norway, Denmark, and Ireland have long traditions of cohabitation. However, beginning in the 1960s, there has been a startling change in the cohabiting rate that is also related to the marriage rate. During the period of 1970 to 1974, the number of lasting nonmarried cohabiting Swedish couples doubled (from 6.5 percent to 12 percent). Concomitantly, the number of marriages decreased steadily from 61,000 marriages in 1966 to 38,125 in 1973. Trost, in his 1970s' studies, argues that cohabitation is a kind of test or trial marriage to see if the couple are compatible or to be sure that the woman can conceive. He believes, if this view is correct, that the marriage rate in Sweden should eventually increase. Trost's prediction has not occurred—the cohabitation rate continues to rise and the marriage rate continues to fall.

This movement toward long-term cohabitation and away from marriage continued to accelerate in the 1980s and continues to the present. By the end of the 1980s, Sweden had the lowest marriage rate among Western societies and its men and women were marrying at a later age than elsewhere (Hoem and Hoem, 1988). And for those who did marry, virtually all couples lived together before marriage. By the end of the 1980s, nearly half of the children born were to unwed mothers (Sorrentino, 1990).

The relationship between social policy and marital and family attitudes and behavior is evident in present-day Sweden. Trost (1975, 1978) has observed that Scandinavian countries have liberalized their social policies and societal sanctions against cohabitation. As a result, there is less fear of social stigma and a resultant high cohabitation rate. By the end of the 1980s, the distinction between formal marriage and informal marriage was in decline throughout Western Europe and the United States and particularly in Sweden (Glendon, 1989).

Sweden has been a notable example in which the high incidence of cohabitation began taking the form of long-term informal marriage. Mary Ann Glendon (1989) has written a comprehensive comparative analysis of changes in marriage laws in Western Europe and the United States. She observes that in Sweden throughout the twentieth century there has been a strong movement away from formal marriage to informal marriage or "marriage-like relationships." The legal distinctions between formal and informal marriage have steadily been eroding. Likewise, the legal concept of "illegitimacy" was dropped in 1917 and by the 1970s even the less pejorative phrase "born out of wedlock" had no legal meaning (Popenoe, 1987).

While marriage may have lost its symbolic importance in Sweden, that does not mean that there is no value placed on long-term emotional and supportive relationships or that children are being abandoned or neglected (Moen, 1989). Men and women desire to live as couples in long-term permanent relationships. Children are wanted. An "unmarried" parent is not a "single" parent. Swedish governmental policies strongly support child care that includes paid maternity or paternity leaves (Popenoe, 1987).

Jan Trost (1975, 1978) thought that cohabitation would have an effect on future divorce rates—they would lower them. "The situation will arise that many marriages between two partners not fitting together will never be formed, those marriages being formed will be happier and thus the divorce rate, *ceteris paribus*, will be lower" (Trost, 1975). He was wrong. In an examination of data of Swedish women, Bennett and his associates (Bennett, Blanc, and Bloom, 1988) examined the linkage between cohabitation, incidence of marriage, and the subsequent success or dissolution of marriages. The survey was of almost 5,000 Swedish women between the ages of 20 to 44. It found that women who cohabited before marriage had marriage dissolution rates 80 percent higher than those who did not. If they cohabited more than three years prior to marriage, their divorce rates were 50 percent higher than women who cohabited for a shorter duration. For those who were married more than eight years, regardless of whether they did or did not cohabit, their divorce rates were identical.

Bennett and his associates found the possible explanation for these findings in a study by Philip Blumstein and Pepper Schwartz (1983) of American couples. Blumstein and Schwartz believe that cohabiting couples are more likely to be personally independent. Both partners work in the paid labor force. They are not likely to pool their incomes, jointly own property, or share leisure activities. The women tend to view themselves as responsible for their own economic support; they do not see their partners as the primary providers. Bennett and his associates speculate that these characteristics may be similar for their Swedish sample and this may explain why Swedish women who cohabited before marriage may have a higher marital dissolution rate than those women who did not.

A further analysis of the implications of these changes in Swedish cohabiting, marital and family dynamics for gender-role relationships and for children will be undertaken later in this book. For now, the discussion continues by looking at cohabitation in the United States.

Cohabitation: An American Perspective

Nonmarital cohabitation has been a topic of debate through most of the twentieth century in the United States. Miriam E. Berger (1971), in her historical account, mentions the controversy surrounding the beliefs of Ben B. Lindsay in the 1920s in his call for "companionate" marriage and the tumult surrounding the opinions of the philosopher Bertrand Russell. Russell advocated trial marriages for university students and believed that students could more easily combine work and sex "in a quasi-permanent relationship, than in the scramble and excitement of parties and drunken orgies" that prevailed during the 1920s Prohibition era (Russell cited in M.E. Berger, 1971:39).

Russell's beliefs aroused a storm of controversy when he was appointed to a professorship in New York.

In the 1960s Margaret Mead (1966) recommended a two-step marriage. The first step, "individual" marriage, provided for a simplified marriage ceremony, limited economic responsibility of each partner to the other, easy divorce, and no children. "Parental" marriage, the second step, would be undertaken only by those couples who wished to share a lifetime involvement in a marital relationship that would include children. Such a marriage would be more formalized with divorce more difficult to obtain. Mead argued that for too many young people their desire for sexual relationships led them into making premature decisions on marriage and parenthood and often led to unhappiness and divorce. Similar proposals have been voiced and have had wide publicity. These include Vance Packard's (1968) call for a two-year marriage confirmation period, after which the marriage could be finalized or dissolved, and the much publicized ideas of Robert H. Rimmer (1966) in *The Harrad Experiment*. Rimmer advocated a trial marriage period with group marriage overtones. His novel depicted Harrad as an institution where college-aged couples would live together under the benevolent guidance of a husband-and-wife team of sociologist and marriage counselor. This couple would require their students to become well versed in the subjects of marriage, love, sex, contraception, moral values, and philosophy. Rimmer's belief was that through a structured, socially approved form of premarital experimentation more viable and stronger marital and parental relationships would ultimately be developed.

These intellectual discourses on the desirability of nonmarital cohabitation reached behavioral fruition in the experiences of a significant number of college students by the late 1960s and increasing numbers through the 1970s, 1980s, and into the present. Paul C. Glick and Graham B. Spanier (1980), on the basis of national data from the Census Bureau's *Current Population Survey* (1975, 1977, and 1978), reported that there had been a profound increase in unmarried cohabitation from 1960 to 1980 with an accelerated rate increase since 1970. The United States Bureau of the Census has tracked this increase in cohabiting couples. Those who cohabit are given the acronym *POSSLQs*—pronounced "possel-kews"—persons of the opposite sex sharing living quarters. In 1960 the number of unmarried couple households was 439,000; by 1970 it was 523,000, jumping to 1,589,000 in 1980 and to 2,851,000. In 1993, more than 3.5 million unmarried couples were living together (U.S. Bureau of the Census, 1994a).

The National Center for Health Statistics conducted a nationwide study of women between the ages of 15 and 44 who had cohabited or were still doing so (London, 1991). They found that only about 40 percent of the respondents under the age of 30 had ever been married, reflecting a significant postponement of marriage for many American women. Slightly more than half (52.8 percent) of first cohabiting relationships ended in marriage. Thirty-seven percent were dissolved without marriage; and 10 percent were ongoing at the time of the survey. White and Hispanic women were more likely to marry their cohabiting partner than black women. For example, by the age of 44, 94 percent of white women had married compared to only 64 percent of African American women.

Commenting on the accelerating rate of cohabitation, Glick and Spanier stated: "Rarely does social change occur with such rapidity. Indeed, there have been few developments relating to marriage and family life which have been as dramatic as the rapid increase in unmarried cohabitation" (1980:20). These authors believe that the explanation for this increase is that young Americans are finding this emerging lifestyle attractive and that their parents are voicing little objection as long as the relationship does not end in childbearing and the couple is economically independent. The authors speculation on the future has proven correct:

> The rapid increase in the number of adults who choose to live with an unrelated person of the opposite sex has been showing no signs of diminishing.
> Increased freedom in adult behavior, less pressure to marry at traditionally normative young ages, and greater acceptance of unmarried cohabitation as a lifestyle are evidently providing a context in which this way of living is becoming increasingly accepted as an alternative to marriage or as a temporary arrangement preceding or following marriage. (Glick and Spanier, 1980:30)

Those working primarily with quantitative data are somewhat limited in their analysis of the qualitative nature of the relationship of the cohabiting couple and the internal dynamics of the relationship and their consequent effects. Eleanor D. Macklin's (1978) seminal review essay complements the quantitative data. Macklin was one of the first researchers (1972, 1978) to report on the rising incidence of nonmarital cohabitation on college campuses. Macklin argues that it is inaccurate to talk about the cohabitation relationship. She asserts that there are at least five types, which significantly vary, and that at this time there is insufficient data to say what proportion of cohabiting couples fall into each category. The following are the five types:

1. *Temporary casual convenience* . . . where two persons share the same living quarters because it is expedient to do so;
2. The *affectionate dating-going together* type of relationship where the couple stays together because they enjoy being with one another and will continue as long as both prefer to do so;
3. The *trial marriage* type, which includes the "engaged to be engaged" and partners who are consciously testing the relationship before making a permanent commitment;
4. The *temporary alternative to* marriage, where the individuals are committed to staying together, but are waiting until it is more convenient to marry; and
5. The *permanent alternative to* marriage, where couples live together in a long-term committed relationship similar to marriage, but without the traditional religious or legal sanctions. (Macklin, 1978:3)

Cohabitation is now so prevalent that the majority of the children of the baby boomers will cohabit before marriage (Cherlin, 1992). Increasingly, cohabitation is becoming part of the courtship process. The rapid rise in the number and extent of cohabiting unmarried couples lead Graham Spanier more than fifteen years ago to conclude that "it is incumbent on demographers and other social scientists to examine this living arrangement less as an alternative 'lifestyle' and more as a normative phenomenon" (1983:287).

The extent to which premarital cohabitation has become institutionalized as a new phase of the mate selection process in our society has been suggested by Patricia A. Gwartney-Gibbs (1986). The researcher examined marriage-license application data from a representative American county—Lane County, Oregon. She ingeniously compared data gathered from two years, 1970 and 1980, to answer the question, To what extent do couples who marry cohabit prior to marriage? Marriage applicants who reported identical home addresses were considered premarital cohabitants. The data findings indicate that the rise in premarital cohabitation, from 13 percent to 53 percent, reflected the national trend. Gwartney-Gibbs conjectures that the extensiveness of cohabitation in this county suggests that social norms regarding premarital sexual relations have relaxed substantially during this decade. She echoes the opinion of other investigators that "premarital cohabitation may indeed become institutionalized as a new step between dating and marriage for many couples" (Gwartney-Gibbs, 1986:433). Similarly, in a study of Canadian students, Charles Hobart (1993) found that those who favored cohabitation also favored marriage.

Macklin argued in 1978 that there should be no substantial decrease in overall marriage rates in the United States owing to the strong social supports for marriage. Rather, cohabitation will remain a part of the courtship phase for most people and will eventually culminate in marriage. Its most likely effect is to delay the age of marriage of those who cohabit. She was partially correct. While cohabitation has become a new stage in the mate selection process, for a significant number of others, there has been a movement away from legal marriage toward a movement toward nonmarital unions (Surra, 1991).

Indeed, the prevalence of cohabitation has led to a new classification of couples—*domestic partners*—that has gained legal recognition. Macklin predicted this outcome in 1978. She examined the implications of nonmarital heterosexual cohabitation for the society. Among her observations, she noted the need to change legal statutes and practices that view living together as man and wife without being legally wed a crime (in twenty states in 1976) and having sexual relations without being married a crime (in sixteen states in 1976). She also saw the necessity for changes in the financial obligations of the man and woman to each other if and when they decide to separate. The Lee Marvin/Michelle Marvin legal case is illustrative of this problem. Lee Marvin, now deceased, was a movie star, and Michelle Marvin argued that she gave up a potentially successful career to become his cohabiting partner. In that case, in which the term "palimony" was coined by the news media, the courts examined the question of the legality of agreements between unmarried partners regarding income and property. (They concluded that such agreements are legal but ignored the issue of whether a partner is entitled to support after separation.) Also, the rights of children born to unmarried couples needed to be clarified, as do the respective parental custody rights.

Today, domestic partnership laws that grant the protection of marriage to cohabiting partners are becoming more commonplace. Further, these laws are not being limited to heterosexual relationships. Cohabiting lesbian and gay couples are gaining legal rights as well. A number of cities across the United States have passed domestic partnership ordinances that cover adults cohabiting in a stable, intimate relationship and are financially interdependent" (Ames, Sulavik, Joseph, Beachy, and Park, 1992; Wisensale and Heckart, 1993).

At the end of the 1970s, the effects of cohabitation on the divorce rate was uncertain. Macklin (1978) speculated that with the long life span, changing views of marriage, and yet-to-emerge lifestyle options, it seems doubtful that whether a couple cohabited or not will have significance regarding their decision to divorce. An important research study conducted in the late 1980s indicates that prior cohabitation may be associated with higher divorce rates. Thomson and Colella (1992) analyzed the relationship between more than 700 couples who cohabited prior to marriage and their likelihood to divorce. Their data was gathered from a 1988 National Survey of Family and Households. In support of earlier speculations by Blumstein and Schwartz (1982) they found that individualistic attitudes and values may account for differences in marital commitment and satisfaction. They found that nearly two-thirds (61.2 percent) of those who had cohabited as compared to slightly more than a third (38.8 percent) of those who did not felt that a separation or divorce may occur in the future. Further, prior cohabitation was associated with less commitment to the institution of marriage and less satisfaction with their own marriages. Utilizing the same database, Schoen (1992) compared first marriages of women who cohabited with those who had not cohabited. For women who were born between 1948 and 1957 there was no differential risk associated with cohabitation.

Macklin urges that future research include longitudinal studies on noncollege and older populations. Finally, she sounds a different note: She questions the wisdom of placing too much emphasis on the legal status of heterosexual relationships. Instead, she calls for more emphasis on the study of relationships, regardless of whether the couple is legally wed or not.

> Knowing that an individual is living with someone to whom she/he is not married tells us little about either the relationship or the person. Rather than focus on the specific legal status of a given relationship, investigators should be concerned with how the particular individuals define their own relationship, their degree of commitment to and investment in that relationship, the quality of the interaction, and the emotional maturity and interpersonal skills of the individuals involved. (Macklin, 1978:11)

Larry L. Bumpass (1990) who has studied the changing contemporary dynamics of cohabitation, marriage, and family patterns, believes that there are several important implications of cohabitation for marriage. Bumpass (1990) observes that marriage and divorce have been significant *social markers* in a person's life. They indicated major life transitions; the first indicated the formation of a relationship, the second the dissolution of a relationship. However, increasingly, because of premarital sexuality, cohabitation, having children outside of marriage, marriage and divorce have lost their marker distinctiveness. Further, cohabitation, has in effect nullified the traditional meaning of being "single."

Cohabitation has required a new way of marking when a union that eventually ended in marriage began. Does it begin when the couple began living together or when they legally married? And, does "divorce" happen when cohabiting couples no longer do so? Finally, Bumpass observes that for many, cohabitation is not an alternative to marriage but rather a relationship of convenience in which marriage is not an issue.

Andrew Cherlin (1992), in his review of the effects of cohabitation on marriage and the family in the last twenty-five years, concludes that for many, cohabitation seems to be a new stage of intimacy that precedes or follows marriage. However, it has not produced major changes in patterns of marriage, divorce, and remarriage. For young adults this is especially true. Cohabitation has become a way of finding a compatible partner, rather than a permanent way of life for most people. In any case, cohabitation has significantly impacted on the nature of premarital and postmarital relationships and certainly reflects changes in the way we think of marriage itself.

SINGLEHOOD AS AN ALTERNATIVE TO MARRIAGE

In the concluding section of this chapter, I turn attention to a group of people who find singlehood a positive alternative to marriage. Singles are comprised of a number of different demographic groups. They include the divorced, the widowed, or the separated. The demographer Paul Glick (1984b) notes that the largest proportion of singles in the United States are those who never married. Since 1970, while the number of married couples has risen 19 percent, there has been a dramatic 85 percent increase in the number of singles. Forty-nine million Americans over age 25 are now single (DeWitt, 1992). In the thirty-year period of 1960 to 1990, increases in the proportions of men and women who have never married have occurred for each five-year age group between the ages 20 and 34 (see Figure 8-1) (U.S. Bureau of the Census, 1992b). While some view singlehood as a lifestyle, others view it as a temporary stage that eventually will lead to marriage. My discussion here focuses on those singles who either voluntarily or involuntarily have accepted singlehood as an alternative to marriage.

The reasons why many choose singlehood include the increased acceptance of sex outside of marriage; a rejection by many women of the patriarchal constraints of marriage, which places them in unequal and subservient roles; and a rejection by members of both sexes that the institutions of marriage and parenthood are absolutely mandatory to lead the "good" life. In any case, an increasing number of people are not only delaying marriage but also are choosing not to marry at all. Peter J. Stein (1981b), one of the leading researchers on singles, predicts that the number of individuals who will never marry will be twice as great for this generation (8 to 9 percent) as the previous generation. Three years later, the noted demographer Paul Glick (1984b) raises that estimate to 10 to 12 percent of young adults in the 1980s who will remain single, and these will be mostly by choice. Commenting on the relatively high number of young people who are single, Andrew Cherlin (1992), cautions that this may represent only a stage in their lives and that they eventually will marry. He does, however, note that those who are postponing marriage aren't necessarily postponing living with a partner. The increase in the number who are cohabiting, a topic I discussed earlier, is another demographic factor that one must take into consideration in determining the permanency of singlehood.

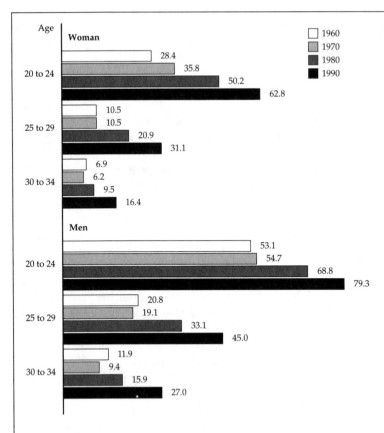

Just as age at first marriage has been rising, so are the proportions of men and women who have never married. Increases have occurred for each five-year age group between ages 20 and 34 in the proportions who have never married. For persons age 20 to 24, the majority of both men and women were never married in 1990. For women in this age group in 1990, 63 percent had never married compared to 28 percent in 1960.

The proportion of men in this age group who had never married has been over half since at least 1960, growing from 53 percent in 1960 to 79 percent in 1990.

The proportions never married at ages 25 to 29 also increased greatly between 1960 and 1990, more than doubling for men to 45 percent and tripling for women to 31 percent. At ages 30 to 34 years, the proportions never married have grown to 27 percent for men and 16 percent for women.

FIGURE 8-1   Number of never-married persons increase. Percent never married, by age and sex: 1960 to 1990.

(*Source:* U.S. Bureau of the Census, *Current Population Reports*, Series P23-181, "Household, Families, and Children: A 30-Year Perspective," U.S. Government Printing Office, Washington, D.C. 1992.)

Another important demographic statistic that has been an important factor in the rise in the number of singles, particularly women, has been the "marriage squeeze." Demographers have observed that between 1946 and 1957, each year's number of new babies was larger than the previous year. Since most women marry men who are several years older than themselves, women who were born during this period and who were looking to marry older men found that they far outnumbered the available pool. This caused a large number of women to postpone marriage or put it off entirely. Media in the mid-1980s, such as *Newsweek* (cf. Salholz et al., 1986) reported on the public reaction to a demographic study "Marriage Patterns in the United States" by Neil G. Bennett, Patricia H. Craig, and David E. Bloom that had received much attention. Extrapolating from marriage-squeeze statistics, these researchers state that college-educated women who are still single at the age of 35 have only a 5 percent chance of ever getting married. *Newsweek* states that "Within days, that study, as it came to be known, set off a profound crisis of confidence among America's growing ranks of single women" (Salholz et al., 1986:55). Being single was redefined from being a voluntary option to being a statistical mandate.

In January 1987, a new Census Bureau study (*Time*, 1987; Webb, 1987) reported that college-educated single women have nearly 2 to 1 odds that they will get married, not the 1 to 5 chance of the Bennett, Craig, and Bloom survey. Further, it stated that women who go to college are more likely to get married than those who have only a high school diploma. This is a significant change from past years, when getting a college degree often meant giving up marriage. The Census Bureau said its analysis of marriage, birth, and education rates indicated that a 30-year-old unmarried woman in 1985 who graduated from high school stood a 47 to 56 percent chance of getting married by the time she turned 65. The comparable rates for the same woman if she spent four years in college were even higher—58 to 66 percent. Jeanne E. Moorman of the Census Bureau was critical of the highly publicized Bennett, Craig, and Bloom study that received cover-story treatment in *Newsweek* and other publications. She argued that the study assumed that a woman who has not married within a narrow range of years had dealt herself out of the matrimonial pool. According to Moorman, college women "are spreading out their marriages over a longer period" (quoted in *Time*, January 26, 1987).

Nevertheless, as *Newsweek* did point out, the Bennett, Craig, and Bloom study reflects the impact of the marriage squeeze on "baby-boomer" women who have not as yet married. Further, the voluntary decision of many women not to marry is a reflection of the changing roles of women in our society and is not a consequence of the marriage squeeze. The acceptability of careers for women no longer requires them to have husbands for economic security and the sexual revolution no longer requires women to marry for sex.

Newsweek believes that singlehood is one manifestation of the struggle of men and women to reach a new gender-role accommodation. "Even though men say they respect women's career aspirations, many openly long for full-time wives and mothers. For professional women, the challenge is to remain independent without sacrificing companionship" (Salholz et al., 1986:56).

The stereotypes regarding singles range from the lusty swingers to the lonely losers. Peter J. Stein (1981b), addressing himself to these stereotypes, counters with a typology of singlehood. This typology contrasts four types of singles: (1) voluntary temporary singles; (2) voluntary stable singles; (3) involuntary temporary singles; and (4) involuntary stable singles. It would be instructive to look at Table 8-1 to see how these types of singles differ.

Being single is neither totally good nor totally bad; rather, there are both advantages and disadvantages. The benefits of deciding to remain single include freedom to have a variety of interpersonal relationships or not interact with others and less restrictions on having different sexual partners. Being single also gives one more mobility to move and this could be a benefit for career advancement. Responsibilities to others are much more limited; often one is responsible only for oneself. This would allow more spontaneous activities and greater freedom to go out and travel. The disadvantages of being single include not fitting into a society that defines marriage as normative. Being single may be viewed as deviant and can cast aspersions on an individual's character. For example, business and corporation personnel managers may be

TABLE 8-1   Typology of Singlehood

	Voluntary	Involuntary
Temporary	Never-married and formerly married who are postponing marriage by not currently seeking mates, but who are not opposed to the idea of marriage	Those who have been actively seeking mates for shorter or longer periods of time, but have not yet found mates Those who were not interested in marriage or remarriage for some period of time but are now actively seeking mates
Stable	Those choosing to be single (never-marrieds and formerly marrieds) Those who for various reasons oppose the idea of marriage Religionaries	Never-marrieds and formerly marrieds who wanted to marry or remarry, have not found a mate, and have more or less accepted being single as a probable life state

Source: Peter J. Stein. 1981. "Understanding single adulthood." In Peter J. Stein (ed.), *Single Life: Unmarried Adults in Social Context.* New York: St. Martin's Press, p. 11. Copyright 1981. Used with permission.

of the opinion that unmarried persons are "less stable" or "emotionally immature" and unwilling to take on "responsibilities." As a consequence, they may not be as eager to promote and advance such individuals.

Stein (1975) observes that the attitudes toward singlehood often are a reflection of attitudes toward marriage. In his early study, Stein found that singles believed marriage inhibited personal growth, provided inadequate emotional support, and promoted an unwelcome dependency on one's spouse. These singles believed that singlehood gave them greater freedom and greater opportunity to meet new people and experience more and better sexual encounters. The women interviewed felt that the psychological autonomy that they felt would be impossible within the context of marriage.

The greatest difficulty that these singles encountered was confronting a couple-oriented society. Married people tend to think in terms of couples. In the typical situation where people get together as married couples, married people felt that if they invited singles to their home, they must match them up. Stein's respondents report that they have few married couples as friends, and the circle of their friendships is generally restricted to other single people. To ward off feelings of loneliness, singles believe that they must have networks of friends who can provide them with their basic needs and satisfactions of intimacy, sharing, and continuity.

In this account of singles and in later works (1976, 1981b), Stein delineates the pros and cons of being single in terms of the "pushes and pulls toward marriage and singlehood" (see Table 8-2). Pushes represent negative factors and pulls represent attractions. The strength of these pushes and pulls is seen to vary according to a number of other variables that include stage of the life cycle, nature and extent of involvement with parents and family, availability of friends and peers, perception of choice, and sexual identity.

In conclusion, the increase in the number of young adults who are postponing

TABLE 8-2   Pushes and Pulls Toward Marriage and Singlehood

Marriage	
Pushes **(negatives in present situations)**	**Pulls** **(attractions in potential situations)**
Pressure from parents	Approval of parents
Desire to leave home	Desire for children and own family
Fear of independence	Example of peers
Loneliness and isolation	Romanticization of marriage
No knowledge or perception of	Physical attraction
alternatives	Love, emotional attachment
Cultural and social discrimination against	Security, social status, social prestige
singles	Legitimation of sexual experiences
	Socialization
	Job availability, wage structure, and promotions
	Social policies for favoring the married and the
	responses of social institutions

Singlehood	
Pushes **(to leave permanent relationships)**	**Pulls** **(to remain single or return to singlehood)**
Lack of friends, isolation, loneliness	Career opportunities and development
Restricted availability of new experiences	Availability of sexual experiences
Suffocating one-to-one relationship,	Exciting lifestyle, variety of experiences,
feeling trapped	freedom to change
Obstacles to self-development	Psychological and social autonomy,
Boredom, unhappiness, and anger	self-sufficiency
Poor communication with mate	Support structures: sustaining friendships,
Sexual frustration	women's and men's groups, political groups,
	therapeutic groups, collegial groups

Source: Peter J. Stein. 1976. *Single.* Englewood, Cliffs, NJ: Prentice-Hall.

marriage or who will never marry reflects important social developments that include the following:

1. The increase in the number of women enrolled in colleges and in graduate and professional schools
2. Expanding employment and career opportunities for women
3. The impact of the women's movement
4. The excess of young women at the currently "most marriageable" age, resulting in a marriage squeeze
5. A shift in attitudes about the desirability of marriage among both college and noncollege youth
6. The increasing divorce rate, which has led many people to question the traditional appeal of marriage and family life
7. The increasing availability and acceptability of birth-control methods (Stein, 1981a:5-6)

What is striking about the rise in the number of singles is the fact that more and more people remaining single may reflect a change in the contemporary attitudes toward marriage and the family. In the early 1990s, two national polls (Roper, 1990; Patterson and Kim, 1991) reported that significant numbers of singles felt that being single was a superior lifestyle and life-choice to being married. In comparison to their married friends, they felt they were better off. Many felt that too many of the people that they knew had unhappy marriages and they knew of too many who had experienced disruptive family lives.

For women, given career options, greater economic independence, and a no longer valid stigmatized "spinster" identity, singlehood has proven to be a popular life-choice. "Singleness" as a permanent lifestyle is also the choice of the gay and lesbian population as well. However, for many women, singleness may not reflect "popularity" but necessity given economic factors and male availability. This is particularly the case for many African American women. For men, many who see limitations in the exclusive "breadwinner" work role so predominant in the 1950s and 1960s or have feelings of uncomfortability in readjusting those traditional roles to the new career-option women's roles, singlehood may also seem an attractive alternative to marriage. In order to understand this phenomenon of the voluntarily unmarried more fully, I must turn attention to much broader concerns on the understanding of the patterns and structures of marriage and the family.

CONCLUSION

This chapter continued the investigation of patriarchal ideology and its effect on gender-role relationships. Here, the context of my discussion was on premarital relations. The double standard that epitomizes the patriarchal ideology was studied. I discussed how it became an integral part of the Westernized idea of romantic love. A historical analysis of the origins of romantic love was presented and detailed in our historical examination of courtship practices. I moved into the contemporary period by examining the movement of dating practices from the "rating and dating" methods of the 1930s to the more intimate patterns of today. The chapter examined premarital heterosexual cohabitation and its implications for gender-role relationships.

I concluded the chapter by discussing singlehood as an alternative to marriage. The involuntary factors, such as the marriage squeeze and the marriage gradient, were discussed. A good deal of attention was given to voluntary singlehood. I examined the factors that have caused the increase in the number of people in America who have chosen this lifestyle over marriage. In light of the prevailing sentiment that marriage is the "only way to go," those who voluntarily choose singlehood represent a perspective that casts a different light on this assumption.

The next chapter compares differences in mate-selection processes and examines how they are influenced by the pervasiveness of patriarchal ideology.

9

MATE SELECTION

Chapter Outline

Mate Selection: Free Choice or Arranged?
   Marriage Regulations

Why Marriages Are Arranged: Love and Marriage

Arranged Marriages and Dowry in India

Mate Selection in Feudal and Contemporary Japan

Institutional Matchmakers: A Comparison of Contemporary Japan and America

Conclusion

In earlier chapters, I discussed an important structural change occurring in family systems—the movement toward the conjugal family. The conjugal family emphasizes the importance of the marital relationship and the ties of parents with children. In contrast, the consanguineal family stresses the extended-kinship relationship based on a common ancestry. In this family form, the emphasis is on the reciprocal ties and obligations of individuals with their extended kin. The importance of the conjugal (marital) relationship is deemphasized, whereas the individual's involvement with the consanguineal (blood) family is emphasized.

A most dramatic piece of evidence of the movement toward the conjugal family system is in the areas of premarital sex, conceptions of love, and mate selection. In many societies, men and women were not expected to choose the person they would marry; marriages were arranged by their parents and kinsmen. The freedom to choose one's spouse is an emerging phenomenon. In this chapter, I investigate the whys and wherefores of arranged marriages and nonarranged marriages. I examine the factors that accounted for the prevalence of arranged marriages and the various forms these marital arrangements took. Of considerable interest is the relationship of modernization processes with marital-arrangement patterns and the contemporary modification of these patterns. Changing conceptualizations regarding premarital sex and love and the relationship of these to marital-selection arrangements attract attention. The consequences of the changes in attitudes and behavior regarding sex, love, and marriage for the individual, the family, and the society are investigated and analyzed. I conclude by looking at singlehood as an alternative to marriage.

MATE SELECTION: FREE CHOICE OR ARRANGED?

Who do people marry? One way this question can be answered is to look at how spouses are chosen. When persons have freedom to choose their spouses, individual motives account for marital decisions (Stephens, 1963). These can include romantic love, sexual desire, loneliness, desire for children, and the feeling of the attainment of adulthood. In some societies, individual motives are allowed to be the determinants in selection of spouses. However, the majority of the world's societies chose to have family elders arrange the marriage of the potential couple. Frequently, this occurred without the consent of the prospective marital couple, and in some societies, like Hindu India, China, and Japan, the couple did not meet until the marriage day. In these societies, individual motives, like romantic love, were not supposed to be factors in mate selection. For example, in classical China or in feudal Tokugawa Japan, love was viewed as a tragedy and at best as irrelevant to the family. The criteria for the selection of a spouse revolved around such matters as the size of the bride-price or dowry, the reputation of the respective kin groups, and traditional, customary, and obligatory marital arrangements.

In his now classic cross-cultural survey on family customs in other societies, William N. Stephens (1963) found that those societies that had extended-family systems or unilineal kin groups tended to give the heads of these families, who were usually men, a great amount of authority and power. They either had the entire responsibility for arranging the marriage of their children or did not allow children to choose for themselves without reserving the right to veto that choice. Further, those societies that were characterized by a nuclear conjugal-family system and bilineal kin groups were the only ones that allowed free choice of mate with parental approval not being necessary. Stephens concludes that "the form of mate choice is in part a function of extended kinship: when large kin groups are strong and important, then marriage tends to be a kin-group affair—it is taken out of the hands of the potential bride and groom" (Stephens, 1963:198).

This strong relationship between types of family organization, extended or nuclear, and the form of mate choice is consistent with earlier discussions of conjugal and consanguineal systems. The conjugal-family system, which takes the nuclear form, emphasizes strong husband-wife and parent-child ties. As William J. Goode (1963) has observed, the *ideology* of the conjugal family emphasizes the independence of the marital couple from extensive obligatory ties with extended consanguineal kin. It stresses individual choice in mate selection that is guided by romantic love and sexual attraction. On marriage, the couple set up their own independent household (neolocal residence), which symbolically and actually demonstrates their commitment to the development of strong conjugal ties and the desire to sever potentially dominating ties with either kin groups.

The consanguineal family, on the other hand, is a quite different form of family organization. Here, the stress is on the maintenance of extended blood relationships. On marriage, a couple may move into or near the household of either the husband's or wife's family (patrilocal or matrilocal residence). Children are socialized into the larger extended kinship group. The consequent strong blood ties of unilineal members of the consanguineal-family system thus account for the greater need and desire to control the mate choice of their members.

Marriage Regulations

There is a striking increase in the number of societies that now allow individuals to marry through free choice in contrast to their former predominant practice by which family elders arranged the marriage. The choice of eligible mates for their children was governed by two conflicting types of marital regulations. The first, *endogamy*, refers to the requirement that an individual marry someone within a particular group.

This group could be a kinship group, a clan, a religious organization, or any other social category. The second, *exogamy*, refers to the requirement that an individual marry someone outside a particular group.

Exogamous rules usually coincide with *incest taboos*—the prohibition of sexual intercourse between certain blood relations, for example, between father and daughter, mother and son, or brother and sister. Exogamous rules are primarily kinship based and generally prohibit sexual activities and marriage among people who are closely related. Frequently, exogamous rules are extended to apply to larger social units. In classical China, a man was not permitted to marry a woman who had the same surname, even though they were not kinship-related. Certain societies prohibit the marriage of members of the same village or the same tribe. Yonina Talmon (1964) reports that children raised in the same peer group on a collective settlement (kibbutz) in Israel are informally pressured against intra-kibbutz marriage. She suggests that the excessive familiarity of young people socialized together prevents them from falling in love.

There are numerous theories of incest and exogamy. This is a much discussed topic in the social sciences with many explanations proposed through the years. The explanations seem to fall into two main categories: First, there are theories that revolve around biological, genetic, and psychological factors to explain individual motivations; second, there are theories that deal with mate-selection patterns in terms of their effect on intragroup or intergroup solidarity with macrolevel analysis of the society.

Falling into the first category are such theories as (1) a horror instinct against incest, (2) Freudian psychoanalytical theory, and (3) genetic influences on the incest taboo. The first theory, horror instinct against incest, postulates that individuals have an instinctive horror of having sexual relations with close kin. To avoid such an occurrence, incest taboos were created to provide further social pressure against the commitment of such a "horror." This theory is somewhat contradictory in that if there was an instinctual dread of incest, there would be no need for the creation of incest taboos socializing individuals against it. This theory has been generally discarded.

The Freudian psychological theory in regard to the incest taboo was developed out of Sophocles' tragedy, *Oedipus Rex*. Oedipus, the son, unknowingly slays his father and marries his mother. On becoming aware of his actions, he blinds himself. Freud stressed the universal tendency of children to have a strong sexual attraction to the parent of the opposite sex. Incest taboos arise as a reaction to incestuous wishes and are a rejection of the forbidden and frightening sexual attraction of the opposite-sex parent. The Freudian theory is weak in that it does not explain the extension of incest taboos beyond the immediate family.

The genetic theory postulates that incest taboos were developed to prevent the potentially harmful effects of inbreeding, that is, madness, hemophilia, and so on. The theory emphasizes the real and imagined deleterious effects of inbreeding and ignores the positive ones; for example, the inbreeding of cattle to develop a superior strain of usable beef. Further, although there is some genetic evidence of the negative consequences of inbreeding, the theory assumes a level of biologic sophistication and knowledge that goes beyond that exhibited by most persons in most societies. An extreme example is the Arunta of Australia who were unaware of the role of the father in procreation.

There are several theories that focus on societal factors in regard to the incest taboo. George Murdock (1949) used psychological behavior theory, Freudian psychoanalytic theory, and previously developed theories in anthropology and sociology to construct his theory of the incest taboo. His ideas were enhanced by his use of his own cross-cultural data from 250 societies. He argues that the origins of the incest taboo arise out of the unwillingness of parents and siblings to satisfy personally the child's sexual desire. Further, the family, which provides important societal needs (economic cooperation, reproduction, education, and socialization), wishes to avoid anything that weakens it. It is thought that weakening the family would, in turn, weaken the larger social system. Conflict within the family resulting from sexual competition and jealousy would be highly disruptive. Thus, "the reduction of sexual rivalry between parents and children and between siblings consolidates the family as a cooperative social group, promotes the efficiency of its societal services, and thus strengthens the society as a whole" (Murdock, 1949:295).

Murdock then argued that the extension of the incest taboo to more distant and remote relatives beyond the nuclear family can be explained by the behavioristic psychology concept of stimulus generalization. According to this principle, any response evoked by one stimulus will tend to be elicited by other stimuli in direct proportion to their similarity to the original stimuli. Murdock sees that secondary or remote relatives who resemble a sexually tabooed member of the nuclear family will have the avoidance behavior extended to them. His illustration is that of a mother's sister (ego's aunt), who may possess similar features and other physical traits of the mother. This relative will be perceived as similar to the mother and thus will be sexually avoided. He states that there is a prevalence of applying the same kinship term to the two women in many societies (both referred to by the term, mother) and ego exhibits similar patterned behavior towards both.

Murdock does not answer the question on why the marital restrictions and taboos are extended further in many societies. The theory of reciprocity by Claude Levi-Strauss seeks to answer this question. Levi-Strauss (1957) believes that the prohibition of incest is one of the rules related to reciprocity. The marriage between individuals belonging to different nuclear families may be viewed as an exchange between two families, one providing the husband, the other providing the wife. The newly formed nuclear family is conceived of as a social organization that links several families in a chain of reciprocal exchanges. The cultural development of a society is seen to be dependent on the development of a more complex culture than can be developed by any given family. Cultural development is enhanced by the linking of families into wider social organizations through reciprocal social bonds.

To illustrate this, Levi-Strauss utilizes the following model. The prohibition of incest is a rule of reciprocity when it means that a family must give up a daughter or sister if its neighboring family will also do so. Marriage is viewed as an exchange between families in which, at one point in time, a given family gives up a daughter and at another point accepts one. Thus, there is a perpetual mutual obligation to supply women in marriage. If one looks at a hypothetical situation in which one family has a monopoly on desirable women, whereas the other family in the group has none available, a potential climate of hostility and tension can arise. Reciprocity thus serves to assure a more balanced state. This illustrative model assumes that women are treated as property and that there is a scarcity of women for marriage. It is based on an assumption of male polygyny and on the greater attractiveness and desirability of certain women. More important, the principle of reciprocity in regard to marriage is seen by Levi-Strauss as assuring the occurrence of social exchange and the establishment of alliances between families. The incest taboo serves as the basis for the development of groups larger than the nuclear family and is a key organizing factor in society. The family, then, is vital to society as it establishes broader social relationships through the patterned exchange of sexual relationships.

Rules of endogamy run counter to the rules of exogamy, or totem prohibition. To repeat, endogamous rules require a person to marry someone within a given social grouping. These social groups can range from the extended-kinship system, the tribe, community, social class, race, or nationality. Linton C. Freeman (1974), following the analysis of George Murdock, sees the basis for endogamous rules stemming from *ethnocentrism*, or group conceit, which is common to all social groups. Freeman observes that, almost universally, outsiders are suspect; people tend to distrust or to dislike people who are different from themselves. People discriminate on the basis of race, creed, and cultural backgrounds. Conversely, they accept members of their own family and community more readily, since they share a common background and heritage. In sex relations and mate selection, ethnocentrism is expressed by prohibiting marriage with outsiders through specified rules of endogamy. In the United States, endogamous rules are exhibited through pressures for individuals to marry someone of the same race, social class, ethnic group, religion, and age. The term *homogamy* has been used to refer to this governing principle of marital choice. Homogamy is the tendency to marry someone who is like ourselves in the important social attributes of race, class, education, age, religious and ethnic backgrounds.

Endogamy (marriage within a group) and exogamy (marriage outside a group) can be seen to delineate a "field of eligible mates" (Freeman, 1974:355). This field of eligible or approved marital partners can be large or small, depending on the relative strengths of the two complementary tendencies of endogamy and exogamy. Together, they are seen to make up the rules for preferential mating. In addition to preferential mating, a second principle is seen to underlie the process of mate selection: marriage arrangement. Marriage arrangement is defined by Freeman as referring to the degree to which persons other than the prospective bride and groom participate in the process of selection; for example, whether parents are involved in the mate-selection process. Here, again, a wide range of societal patterns exist, ranging from families having little involvement in the selection of a spouse to societies where families select the individual's spouse with little or no involvement by that individual in the decision-making process.

The question now arises, why should and how do people other than the man and woman immediately involved arrange marriages?

WHY MARRIAGES ARE ARRANGED: LOVE AND MARRIAGE

A more systematic analysis of the factors that have accounted for the widespread prevalence of arranged marriages is now undertaken. Of particular interest is the role of love in the arrangement of marriages.

Amlee, a 5-year-old bride, unties string knots of her husband, Ashok, 15, during their marriage ritual in the Indian desert village of Srirampur of the northwestern state of Rajasthan on May 14, 1994. Hundreds of children across the state were married on the Hindu auspicious day "Akha Teej" despite the government proclamation against such marriages.

Two different theoretical models have been put forth on why marriages are arranged. One theory, developed by Bernard Farber (1964), stresses the importance of rules regarding mate selection in terms of preserving family culture. The other, developed by William J. Goode (1959), stresses the restrictions placed on mate selection to maintain the social-stratification system through the emphasis on lineage and kinship obligations and involvements.

According to Farber (1964), family culture is seen to have as its constituent elements the norms and values that people hold regarding courtship, marriage, divorce, kinship identity and obligations, socialization of children, residence, and household maintenance. Exogamous rules may lead to individuals marrying outside of their family group; potentially the possibility does exist that one will marry someone with different norms and values and open the family system to external influences that can be damaging to the continuity of the culture of the particular family group. The choice of marriage partner, then, is controlled by the family of orientation to assure transmission of the family culture to future generations.

> Thus, at the point of marriage of the child both parental families are in danger of having their culture interrupted in transmission by the introduction of possibly contradictory values from the other family. Restrictions in the society on mate selection would delimit the direction of change in family cultures from one generation to the next. If certain families will permit marriage only with other families very similar to themselves in norms and values, then a general continuity of the cultures of both families can be expected. (Farber, 1964:63-64)

In his essay "The Theoretical Importance of Love," William J. Goode (1959) delineates the reasons on why marriages are arranged and the way love is controlled. Goode argues that allowing individuals the freedom to marry on the basis of individual motives, particularly love, can be potentially disruptive to lineage patterns and weaken kinship systems. When marriage involves the linking of two kinship groups and when kinship serves as the basis of societal organization, mate choice has important consequences for the social structure. Thus, when marriage affects the ownership of property and the exercise of influence, the issue of mate selection and love have been considered "too important to be left to the children" (Goode, 1959:43).

Goode states that, "Kinfolk or immediate family can disregard the question of who marries whom, only if a marriage is not seen as a link between kin lines, only if no property, power, lineage honor, totemic relationships, and the like are believed to flow from the kin lines through the spouses to their offspring" (1959:42). Societies that emphasize kinship find it necessary to control marriages.

Goode, then, distinguishes among several methods for controlling the selection of marital partners. First, it is controlled by child marriage, where, as in India, the young bride moves to the household of her husband and the marriage is not consummated until a much later date. This practice precludes the possibility of the child falling in love and also limits the resources for the opposition to the marriage. While much less common today and against the law, such child marriages still occur in India [Associated Press (1989) cited in Benokraitis (1993)]. In 1981 [Associated Press (1981) cited in Eshleman, (1994)], an estimated 40,000 to 50,000 children were married over a single weekend in violation of a law banning such marriages. In this rural section of India these marriages occurred in keeping with centuries-old Hindu traditions. Children as young as a 2-year-old girl and an 8-year-old boy were ceremoniously married in a ritual that usually is kept secret from outsiders. It was presumably publicized as a reaction to a law banning child marriages that was trying to be implemented.

Second, mate selection is controlled by kinship rules, which define a relatively small number of eligible spouses. For example, the Yaruros of Venezuela, a nomadic tribe of fisherman and hunters, is a society that restricts marriage to cross-cousins: That is, a man must marry the daughter of his mother's brother or the daughter of his father's sister. Incest taboos and ethnocentrism are employed to restrict the field of eligibles. Freeman (1974) observes that this practice fosters interfamilial solidarity by forcing marriage to people who live nearby but in different communities. The Hottentots of southwest Africa are a group of seminomadic herders. They too, require cross-cousin marriage. But, unlike the Yaruro, the Hottentots are free to choose for themselves which cross-cousin to marry (Freeman, 1974).

A third practice of mate selection is controlled by socially and physically isolating young people from potential mates. This makes it easier for parents to arrange the marriage of their children in that there is little likelihood that these children would have developed love attachments to conflict with their parents' wishes. In feudal Japan, the social contacts between members of the opposite sex were limited and were highly ritualized. They were permitted only in the presence of elders. This had the effect of minimizing informal and intimate social interaction. I shall return to a more in-depth analysis of this practice in feudal Japan a little later in this chapter.

Fourth, love relationships are controlled by strict chaperonage by duennas or close relatives. Here again, young people are not permitted to be alone together or in intimate interaction. This practice has existed in Spain, Portugal, Italy, and in Latin America. It has also prevailed among recently arrived Hispanic immigrants to the United States. The play—later made into a movie—*West Side Story*, is a tragic love story that updates *Romeo and Juliet* to the sidewalks of New York City. It depicts the influence of family and friends on a Puerto-Rican-born young woman and her forbidden love for a young white-ethnic man. The clash of youth gangs, battles over turf, and the questioning of traditional family cultures are used vividly depict the power of romantic love.

The fifth and final way in which love is controlled is typical in American culture. Although formally allowing individuals to choose their own marriage partners, parents control the field of eligibles through the influence of the informal contacts of young people. This is done through living in selected neighborhoods, asserting control over the schools that children attend, restricting guest lists to parties and informal gatherings, and making the children aware of their parents' ethnocentric biases relating to race, religion, ethnicity, social class, and so on.

In the United States, individual motives play an important role in deciding the question of whom one should marry. The common assumption is that two people marry on the basis of love. However, the determination of eligible lovemates is influenced by the principle of preferential mating. Incest taboos preclude the eligibility of immediate kin. Frequently, the incest taboos extend to the first-cousin relationship, but there are no clan or other kinship structure restrictions.

Rules of endogamy are expressed in ethnocentric beliefs that define "suitable" marriage partners to people of the same social class, religion, ethnic group, and race. The field of "suitable" partners is further limited to people of the same age group and to people who live nearby in the same neighborhood or community. Until recently, ethnocentric biases were supported by legal statutes in the most dramatic case—racial intermarriage. As late as 1967, almost twenty states still had antimiscegenation statutes, with penalties up to ten years imprisonment and fines up to $1,000. In that year, the Supreme Court declared that such laws were unconstitutional.

Although there has been some trend away from ethnocentric restrictions, the general pattern continues to be the marriage of people who share similar backgrounds, values, attitudes, and interests. Informal ethnocentric pressures, which still characterize American mate-selection processes, help account for the fact that marriages outside these norms tend to have greater difficulty and more frequently end in divorce. The result is that although the field of eligibles can be the entire unwed opposite-sex population, it is in fact significantly narrower because of these endogamous practices.

The choosing of one's spouse is ideally depicted as being solely within the province of the individual. Parents, friends, and others are normally not supposed to interfere in the mate-selection process. In addition, it is felt that such interference is not effective and can even backfire. For example, *The Fantasticks*, a long-running contemporary play, uses this normative guideline as the central theme: Two fathers scheme to keep their respective children apart in the hope that such interference will have the opposite effect and bring them together. In many cases, parents are not informed or consulted by children about their prospective spouse either prior to or after the wedding.

Although their formal input in the marital decision-making process is diminished, the parents have a strong indirect influence in the mate-selection process. By residing in selected areas and sending their children to selected schools, parents restrict the options of young people in forming friendships. Further, through parties and selective invitation lists and verbalizing their own ethnocentric biases, parents influence their children. By influencing the informal social contacts of their children, the parents indirectly control the mate-selection process. As William J. Goode states, "Since youngsters fall in love with whom they associate, control over informal relationships also controls substantially the focus of affection" (Goode, 1959:46).

The following passage from Peter L. Berger's *Invitation to Sociology: A Humanistic Perspective* nicely conveys American mate-selection processes:

> In Western countries, and especially in America, it is assumed that men and women marry because they are in love. There is a broadly based popular mythology about the character of love as a violent, irresistible emotion that strikes where it will, a mystery that is the goal of most young people and often of the not-so-young as well. As soon as one investigates, however, which people actually marry each other, one finds that the lightning-shaft of Cupid seems to be guided rather strongly within very definite channels of class, income, education, racial and religious background. . . . The suspicion begins to dawn on one that, most of the time, it is not so much the emotion of love that creates a certain kind of relationship, but that carefully predefined and often planned relationships eventually generate the desired emotion. In other words, when certain conditions are met or have been constructed, one allows oneself "to fall in love." (Berger, 1963:35)

In summary, where societies emphasize the importance of kinship lineage and its preservation—and support this by establishing strong ties between family interests and economic and social interests—marriages are arranged by the couple's respective consanguineal families. On the other hand, where societies emphasize the importance of the conjugal relationship between husband and wife and deemphasize their obligations and responsibilities to the extended-family system, the choice of marriage partners is more or less left up to the individuals involved.

ARRANGED MARRIAGES AND DOWRY IN INDIA

Contemporary matchmaking patterns in India has fascinated Americans. However, juxtaposed with these often humorous—to Western sensibilities—accounts of the attempt to use modern matrimonial want ads in newspapers with traditional concerns for matching astrological signs and caste groups has been a concurrent darker and horrific story of mate selection processes. These are the too prevalent and tragic incidents of wife abuse and bride-burnings that have become known as *dowry deaths*. In this section I will discuss these contemporary phenomena.

India has become an increasingly mobile, urban society. For the more highly educated, the centuries-old practice of arranging marriages has been transformed by modern technology. In New Delhi, on a typical Sunday, more than 1,500 "matrimonial" advertisements appear in the three largest newspapers. These ads are now appearing throughout India's urban centers and are placed primarily by affluent Hindi middle-class parents and grandparents and are designed to marry off their children. The typical ads detail the qualifications of the prospective groom's or bride's caste, education, income, and demands. The following ad is illustrative:

> "Beautiful, fair, slim, educated girl wanted for slim, 27 year old, 173cms respectable Punjabi Khatri project engineer. 2,500 [rupees] per month salary—plus perks." The salary would be about $215 U.S. dollars. (Fineman, 1985)

The ads are not confined to Indians living in India but include those who have migrated elsewhere. The periodical *India Abroad* has classified ads appearing on a regular basis that seeks to matchmake globally (see Figure 9-1). For both men and women the appearance of matrimonial advertisements promoting their marital qualifications are justified in that they believe that the ads give them a wider choice of potential spouses.

The matrimonial ads reflect the changing circumstances of modern times. As families migrate outside of the familiar social circles of the ancestral village to urban centers and to other countries, these ads have replaced the traditional matchmaker, socially connected relatives, and parental networks. While there has been an upsurge in Westernized love matches, the prevalent pattern are arranged marriages. They, however, have been tempered by the final veto power of the children, and prior to the marriage, children are allowed to date their future spouses between the engagement and the marriage (Moore, 1994).

FIGURE 9-1   Modern classified matrimonial ads in *India Abroad*.

Some years ago, social scientists David and Vera Mace spoke to a group of young Indian women. They discussed then-prevalent American dating patterns, going steady, courtship rituals, and engagement and subsequent marriage. The Maces elaborated on American romantic love traditions and expected the Indian women to express their envy of the superiority of American free choice versus Indian arranged marriage patterns. Instead, they received unexpected responses to their query: "Wouldn't you like to be free to choose your own marriage partners, like the young people do in the West?" (Mace and Mace, 1990: 130). These women felt that they would be put "in a humiliating position" by calling attention to themselves by trying to be attractive to men. If they did not attract a man, it would indicate failure reflecting their own shyness and inability to compete with other young women. Most importantly, they felt that they were incapable of judging the marital worthiness of the potential husband. As one woman put it:

"Besides, . . . how would we be able to judge the character of a boy we met and got friendly with? We are young and inexperienced. Our parents are older and wiser, and they aren't as easily deceived as we would be. I'd far rather have my parents choose for me. It's so important that the man I marry should be the right one, I could so easily make a mistake if I had to find him for myself." (Mace and Mace, 1960: 130).

The attitudes of the young women reported by the Maces so many years ago is still prevalent in today's India. It is based on a different view of love than that found in the United States. In the United States one is expected to fall in love before one marries; in India love comes after marriage. In India love is believed to develop out of social arrangements and is subservient to such arrangements. Love, in fact, is "created" between two people by arranging the right conditions for it. These "right conditions" is marriage based on shared backgrounds and interests (Bumiller, 1985). In a Laksmi Bai College study, 82 percent of all female students surveyed felt that arranged marriages with their consent was the preferred form of matrimony. Almost half opposed courtship before marriage (Moore, 1994).

Moore provides the following account of a woman, Dhoundiyal by name, who after rejecting two previous marriage candidates agrees to marry a third. Her decision was based on a brief exchange in which he expressed strong support for her studies, career, and intellectual pursuits. This was despite the fact that even a few weeks before her wedding, she confided, "I don't have a sense of who he is—he's not even totally a friend yet" (cited in Moore, 1994). Her wedding and married life is depicted as follows:

> The two were married in a lavish traditional Hindi wedding ceremony, and now Dhoundiyal leads a double life. In New Delhi she exemplifies the modern Indian career woman—in outlook, attitude and dress. But on weekends, as the train draws closer to Lucknow, where she visits her husband's family, Dhoundiyal pulls a veil over her face and slips rows of bangles on her arms, rings on her toes and bracelets on her ankles—the accoutrements of the proper Indian bride—and kisses the feet of her in-laws when she enters their home.
>
> "I don't feel a conflict," she said. "They are supportive of my job. This is my way of reassuring them I'm not going to break up the family." She paused. "I didn't marry for love. I married the family." (Moore, 1994)

Traditionally, Hindu marriage was considered sacred, based on the devotional worship of a wife for her husband. The ancient practice of *suttee* where a woman was expected to throw herself on the funeral pyre and burn to death with her deceased husband has been banned since 1829. It reflected a view that marriage was "based on the devotional worship of a wife for her husband, much like the love for a god" (Bumiller, 1985). This Hindu religious tradition still holds for many in the middle classes where girls are told from childhood that they will love the man that their parents select for her.

Unfortunately, increased incidence of wife abuse and even death among these urban middle-class elite has brought into question the traditional nature of mate selection and marriage. Another qualification not placed in the matrimonial want ads is the demand for a dowry—an Indian tradition in which the bride's family provides monetary incentives and gifts to the groom's family. As the cities have grown, so has materialism. The outcome is an increased demand for greater dowries. Often, this proves insufficient, and each year more and more young brides are found dead under mysterious circumstances. Soon thereafter, the groom's family advertises once again for a prospective second bride—and a second dowry (Fineman, 1983, 1985).

In the introductory chapter of Robin Morgan's (1984a) comprehensive collection of articles by leading feminists from seventy countries, *Sisterhood is Global: The International Women's Movement Anthology*, Morgan writes that the "woman as property" concept is epitomized by the dowry. Dowry is seen as "the price of a life (and a death)." The dowry in essence represents a payment for a woman.

The term "dowry" often is used interchangeably to refer to two types of marriage purchase. "Bride-price" involves payment to the family of the bride by the groom or his family. Often it is seen as payment that compensates the bride's family for loss of her services. "Dowry" is when the bride or her family provides payment to the groom or his family thus ensuring that woman will have a husband and ostensibly to enhance her marriageability and to provide property for her. In essence, both forms—bride-price and dowry—represent a payment for a woman. Morgan observes that the payment is almost never controlled by the woman herself; instead, it binds the bride to a marriage that she may never have wished to enter in the first place and prevents her from leaving.

George Murdock (1949), in his comprehensive cross-cultural survey of marriage and family practices, observed that payments for a bride can be seen as a compensation for the loss of work represented by the loss of a daughter. The practice occurs most frequently when the rules of residence for the new couple are patrilocal, especially when the bride is removed from her local community. In Murdock's (1957) *World Ethnographic Sample*, about 70 percent of the societies included have some form of marriage payment. By far the most common is the bride-price, in which the groom's family transfers some property to the bride's family.

Beyond its economic value, the bride-price serves as a symbol of the commitments of the families to one another. It gives the family a vested interest in the stability of the marriage, since the bride's family is more likely to adjust to the loss of the girl if it is accompanied by a gain in wealth and less likely to look forward to a cancellation of the dowry agreement. In marriage situations where marriage is purchased, economic considerations take precedence over romantic or emotional criteria both in the selection of mates and in the maintenance of marriage. For that reason, "[r]eturn of the dowry is one of the most frequent reasons families on either side oppose divorce" (Morgan, 1984c:11).

Murdock asserts that the bride-price "seldom if ever is regarded as a price paid for a chattel, or as comparable to the sum paid for a slave" (1949:21). Yet it must be emphasized that there is an economic component to both consanguineal and conjugal families. Indeed, the very term *family* comes from the latin *familia*, a term that referred to household property. This property included both people—wives, children, as well as slaves—and objects—fields, house, furnishings, and so forth. Given the economic reality that underlies dowry systems, it should not be surprising to find incidents of dramatic abuse.

The practice of dowry still exists in most parts of the world. In some countries, custom and even statute still require it. In other societies, even when legislation prohibits it, loopholes are often found to get around the law, or the practice takes on a contemporary guise. For example, in Kenya, such customs as the paying of a bride-price still continue to exist. The payment is determined by the girl's level of education and her ability to produce or earn money. Directly contradicting Murdock, Rose Adhiambo Arungo-Olende contends that "Today, bride-price makes the intended bride look like a chattel for sale" (1984:397). She observes that women never have a say on the subject of bride-price. In fact, there are cases in which the bride has to assist her husband financially in completing the payment of the dowry by the groom's family. The dowry can often leave the newly married couple in economic ruin, struggling to set up their new home in the face of the dowry's burden.

Interestingly, even in circumstances where a women has gained economic independence, traditional marriage through purchase practices can still exist. For example, in Lebanon, education and work have contributed to women's economic independence. The percentage of women in the labor force has increased from 17 percent in 1972 to 25 percent in 1981. In addition to the traditional careers of teaching, nursing, and secretarial work, women have been entering the professions of medicine, engineering, architecture, pharmacy, and law (Ghurayyib, 1984). However, women's gains are still modified by traditional-family practices. The family structure of both Christians and Muslims still adheres to tribal laws and clan loyalties that seek to perpetuate family control. The extended-family system remains the bastion of entrenched traditions which stand against change and women's rights. Notions of women's inferiority and subservience are still articulated. A woman who has achieved economic independence often finds herself "using her job as bait for attracting suitors, thus continuing the dowry tradition" (Ghurayyib, 1984:422). Bowing to family pressure and public opinion and the fear of living alone, women often accept compromises and sacrifice their ambitions.

In India, the rising incidence of dowry murders became so great that massive anti-dowry demonstrations have been a major focus of the Indian women's movement. The feminist journal *Manushi* has reported in both its Hindu and English versions on hundreds of attempted and committed dowry murders and has brought this to the attention of the Western press. Morgan concludes her denunciation of dowry with the following statement:

> Only by such indigenous women's activism will practices like these—whether so dramatically posed as in India or subtly preserved through "trousseau" commercialism and symbolic "giving the bride away" in the West—be eradicated, and with that eradication come the end of transacted love, and of women's marital servitude. (Morgan, 1984a:12)

BOX 9-1   The Global Family

Dowry: The Price of a Life (and a Death)

The horrible cases of murders or forced suicides, "dowry deaths," first reported in India in the early 1980s, have caught the attention of the media and have publicized the pervasiveness of continued abuses of the dowry system. To fully understand why these occurrences happened, it is necessary to provide some background. Traditionally, only sons inherited property, because they were the ones that perpetuated the patrilineal family system. To make the marriage of their daughters more enticing, families gave large dowries to the grooms' families. India has passed legislation that has sought to eliminate this form of gender discrimination. For example, laws pertaining to inheritance now give daughters equal rights with sons. Anti-dowry legislation was passed in 1961.

Unfortunately, families have virtually ignored the laws that attempt to change the system. Young women, whether they are illiterate, poor, and reside in rural areas or are educated and live in the more progressive cities, do not actively oppose the dowry system for fear that they will not marry. Nor do they actively claim their inheritance rights out of respect for tradition and to protect the economic interests and viability of their natal families. In contemporary India, the dowry system has taken on a modern form. A well-educated male of a higher-caste group can command considerable dowry payment (as much as $10,000 in some cases) from a prospective bride's parents. His parents view such payment as a proper reimbursement for their son's educational expenses. The bride's family sees it as important to marry her well even if the economic sacrifice is severe.

The Hindu family is patriarchal, patrilineal, and patrilocal. Men control the chief resources and family authority and inheritance is transferred to the sons. Daughters serve temporarily in their natal family and then move to the household of their husband's family. Their children are raised as members of the husband's lineage. As a consequence, male children are preferred because they will serve their consanguineal family for their entire lives. Sons also bring wealth into

their families through their wives' dowries. The birth of a son is viewed as a blessing; that of a daughter may be an occasion for sorrow and grief. As I discussed previously, female infanticide was a not unfamiliar occurrence in India's past and it continues today in the form of more subtle practices, such as medical neglect.

The dowry represents a payment to the groom's family; it is not a source of personal security for the bride. As evidence is the severe abuse of the dowry system that has resulted in increasing numbers of murders or forced suicides because of familial dissatisfaction with the value of the dowry, reported in villages as well as in urban areas. The 1975 Report from the Indian Commission on the Status of Women reacted to the growing commercial intensity of the dowry system and the growth of violence against brides. It declared that the dowry system was one of the gravest problems affecting women in India.

By 1980-1981, there were 394 cases of brides burned to death in New Delhi. Indian women's groups claim that this figure represents only a very small percentage of the actual cases that occur in Delhi and elsewhere. They believe that the police register only one out of every 100 cases of dowry murder or attempted murder and that for each of these cases six go unreported. In 1983, the number of dowry deaths in New Delhi nearly doubled to 690. In 1987, the government released data on the registered cases of dowry death nationwide as 999 in 1985, 1,319 in 1986, and 1,786 in 1987. In 1992, 4,785 women were killed by their husbands for not providing adequate dowries. On the United States National Public Radio's "Morning Edition" broadcast of July 6, 1995, they reported that the figure was an astonishing 6,000 deaths in the last year.

The increase in "dowry deaths" is a contemporary phenomenon. As I mentioned, the institution of dowry began in India largely because, under Hindu law, parental property was not allowed to be shared by female children. In compensation, parents would give their daughter a gift at the time of her marriage. In time, bridegrooms and their families made handing over the gift as dowry an institutionalized demand. Especially for younger Indians who covet a lifestyle and whose incomes do not allow them to achieve it, dowry has become a means of bridging the gap. The threat of dowry death has become a form of extortion. The husband and his family can harass, beat, or torture a bride to extract more money from her family. In the extreme case, the bride is murdered. Her death is made to appear accidental (for example, dousing the woman with kerosene and setting her afire and claiming that it was a cooking accident) or as a suicide. The bride's parents are reluctant to prosecute for lack of evidence, for belief that others would think they had reneged on the dowry, or if they have other daughters for fear that they will not be able to marry them off.

The prevalent attitude toward women is instrumental in the violence committed against them. Girls are seen as a responsibility that parents want to get rid of. An example is a man who, after paying off increased amounts of dowry toward his daughter's husband, is finally told that this is not enough and he must take her back. The father laments that the problems are not with the dowry system but with his daughter: "Girl children are a big headache, a big problem. Why this trouble? If we don't give birth to girl children, we wouldn't have these problems. What flows out of our eyes is not just tears, but blood" (cited in Gargan, 1993).

Bumiller, 1990; Fineman, 1983, 1985; Gargan, 1993; Morgan, 1984a; O'Kelly and Carney, 1986; Sharma, 1980

MATE SELECTION IN FEUDAL AND CONTEMPORARY JAPAN

Japan is a society that historically has permitted a wide range of marital eligibles. But the actual choice, especially in the past, was determined by the family, not the marrying person. In this section I will provide an overview of the historical changes that have occurred in Japan. Linton Freeman (1974) in his study of feudal Japan (Tokugawa Japan) in the eighteenth century, observed that it was divided into local small duchies, each ruled by a lord and supported by an army of knights (*samurai*). Governing the society was a hereditary military leader, with the emperor having little importance. As in most feudal societies, there was a clearly delineated social-class system, with each class restricted to designated dwellings, styles of clothing, food, and so on.

The family in feudal Japan was at the heart of an individual's activities. The family was ruled by a patriarch with the assistance of a family council, which included most of the mature males and the old women in the family. The extended family included the patriarch's wife, all his sons and their wives and children, his unmarried daughters, younger brothers and their wives and children, and finally the servants. As head of the family, the patriarch's approval was required for marriages and divorces, for adoptions, and for the expulsion of recalcitrant members. He was responsible for the family's fulfillment of its obligations to the state. Professor Kawishima, a Japanese social scientist, observes the following:

> As a means of emphasizing through external impressions the mental attitude of filial obedience, the head of a family (generally the father) enjoys markedly privileged treatment in everyday life. The family head does not do with his own hands even trifling things—or rather is prohibited from doing such

things because it is thought to compromise his authority. He must be served in everything by his wife, children or others subject to his patriarchal power. For instance, he should get his wife or servant to hand him anything which is right under his nose. The family head must be better fed and must not eat the same things as other members of his family (especially children), for it impairs his authority as such. When entering or leaving his house, he should be treated with special ceremony. In his house the head's room must be one fit for his authority. In all other trifles of everyday life the head of a family should enjoy special treatment becoming his position as absolute ruler. A parent's, especially a father's, position is majestic and supreme. (Kawashima cited in Mace and Mace, 1960:35)

The power of the patriarch was exercised in the name of the preservation and perpetuation of the lineage and the enhancement of family status. The independence of the individual was strongly deemphasized. The stress was on the importance of familial obligations and responsibilities as a member of the family and of the immediate community. Within the family, a rigid hierarchy existed that delineated social roles and responsibilities. David and Vera Mace (1960) illustrate this by noting that a rigid ordering of rank is exhibited in the sequence in which family members take turns in using the bathtub. The sequence reflects the rank order in the family and where the person stands in the official family hierarchy. The father has the first turn, followed by the eldest son and all other sons, according to birth order; then, the mother is followed by the daughters in birth order; finally, the servants take their turn.

The practice of subsuming individuality to the family system was most evident in socialization practices and in mate selection. Children were socialized relative to their position in the family hierarchy. Robert N. Bellah (1957) points out that the socialization of sons differed depending on whether they would inherit the property. The oldest son, who most likely would inherit, was trained to be responsible and cautious, befitting his prospective responsibilities. Younger sons were encouraged to be more independent and show initiative and cleverness, which would aid them in the outside world. Girls were raised with the expectation that they would marry and join their husband's family. Their training emphasized the fact that they would represent their family in the appropriate manner in their husband's household. Thus, children were socialized relative to their social positions in the family hierarchy. An intricate system of duties and obligations was taught, emphasizing an individual's position within the family and the position of the family in the larger society. Individuality was submerged in the family system.

Ideally, by the time they reached adulthood the Japanese had learned to view each other, not as individuals at all, but almost completely as stereotypes. If two people were members of the same family they treated each other in terms of their relationship. They met neither as personalities nor as persons, but only as representatives of particular relationships. All fathers treated, and were treated by, their sons in much the same way. Their interaction was based upon their kinship, not upon personal feelings. (Freeman, 1974:362)

With the great emphasis on family lineage and its perpetuation, it is not surprising to learn that marriages were arranged by the family. The marriage gained its importance in the fact that it established a reciprocal bond between the two families and in that it could enhance the prestige and security of each of the families. The concerns and choices of the young people were inconsequential in light of this feudalistic family model.

Marriages were arranged through the services of a family friend, who acted as a go-between. After consideration and negotiation about the respective worth of the families, the marriage ceremony occurred. As was frequently the case, the young couple did not meet until the wedding ceremony.

The feudalistic Japanese family dominated the mate-selection process. Although there was a wide choice of eligible marriage partners, the children were neither consulted nor involved in the decision-making process. This pattern is a logical development, given the importance of the extended kinship in Japanese society.

Contemporary Japanese society has emerged out of a feudal past that emphasized an elaborate formal hierarchical and authoritarian structure. Marital arrangements were determined by the respective family heads in the name of the preservation of lineage and the enhancement of family status. The marrying individuals had little or no say in the determination of their prospective marriage partners. Robert O. Blood, Jr. (1967), in a comprehensive analysis of Japanese marital arrangement patterns, reported that a revolutionary transition was occurring in post-World War II Japan. There is a movement toward greater equality between parents and children and between men and women. This change is reflected in the appearance of a new system of mate selection parallel to the older system. Further, the old system of marriage arrangement is gradually being transformed.

Blood presents the following illustrative case of a Japanese colleague's father on "what marriage was like in the old days" (Blood, 1967:4).

> In those days (the 1850s), marriage was a contract between families, not between individuals. My grandparents carefully investigated my mother's family background before choosing her to be my father's wife. They wanted to be sure that her background was of the same rank, was of good financial reputation, and had no hereditary diseases that might be transmitted to later generations of Kondos. After they decided she was suitable, they went around and got the approval of all their close relatives before entering into negotiations with the other family, using a relative as a go-between. The wedding was followed by a series of drinking parties lasting several days, first at the groom's home and then at the bride's home. The women attended these festivities, but only the men did any drinking. Every year after that, the two families got together at every festive occasion.
>
> My father and mother were from villages ten miles apart in an age when sedan chairs were the only means of transportation. They never met until the wedding ceremony. My own marriage was unusual in that my wife and I didn't meet even then. I was away from home at the Imperial University and studying hard for the civil service exam. Since I was the eldest son, my parents were

anxious to have me get married. My father's uncle and my mother's uncle were good friends and made the arrangements on behalf of the two families. My wife was 17 years old at the time of the wedding, and I was 27. She had seen my picture, but I had never seen hers—I was too busy to be disturbed. The wedding was unusual because I was presented by proxy. After the ceremony, the main relatives on both sides brought my wife to Tokyo to meet me, completed the formalities, and then left us to begin living together. In those days, love affairs were unheard of except in the lower class. (Blood, 1967:4)

Blood contrasts two major forms of marriage arrangement in Japan, the love match and the arranged marriage. Since the mid-nineteenth century, arranged marriages were negotiated through the *nakodo* ("go-between"). By using a go-between, families avoided direct dealings with each other and the possibility of losing face in the event that one family would reject the arrangement. It also protected the family who broke off the negotiation from any negative consequences of offending a family that by virtue of its social status was important to them.

The *nakodo* had three basic functions: introduce the participants, negotiate the conditions, and perform a ceremonial function at the wedding. The *nakodo*'s task was to assess the compatibility of the respective families in terms of lineage and socioeconomic status. In addition, a woman's physical appearance was important as was the fact of her proper instruction in marital and family affairs. If all proved satisfactory, a *miai* ("formal introductory meeting") was arranged for the prospective partners and their parents. Blood notes that although the meeting attempts to introduce the young people to each other in an informal manner and encourages them to converse, the underlying motive for the meeting makes such interaction difficult. The tension of the situation, a marital eligibility trial, makes conversation stiff and awkward if it occurs at all. He observes that *miai*s are standard fare for slapstick movies in Japan. David and Vera Mace discuss the *miai* in the following passage:

The atmosphere was very formal, and there was much bowing. Politeness forbade any mention being made of the object of the meeting, and the boy and girl had little chance to talk with each other. Even when attempts were made to get them to talk, these were not generally successful. "Some young couples are so shy that they keep silent from beginning to end. The matchmaker tries to make them talk but usually fails. Then when a daughter who has kept her eyes cast down on the tatami throughout the interview is later asked by her family how she likes the man, she says she cannot say because she didn't see him!" (Mace and Mace, 1960:144)

The arranged marriage was made with the sole aim of assuring the continuation of the family line. Although love might be expected to occur over time, the extended family household deemphasized the husband-wife relationship. Households consisted of three generations, with the emphasis on strong ties between mother and son. For the husband, sexual satisfaction and affection were more usually obtained through a concubine or mistress than through the relationship he had with his wife.

Arranged marriage still occurs in contemporary Japan, but its character has changed. Blood states that *miai kekkom* ("interview marriage") is no longer arranged by parents on behalf of unknowing children but rather by matchmakers on the behalf of the participating families. " 'Arrangement' now means primarily the formal introduction of potential marriage partners to each other and secondarily the follow-up message-carrying which cements a promising relationship" (Blood, 1967:12). The prospective husband and wife preview each other through personal and family credentials and photographs provided by the matchmaker. This provides the young people a chance to reject one another prior to the arrangement of a *miai*.

If the impressions after meeting at the *miai* are favorable, the couple is allowed to meet informally in limited contact for a period of up to six months. R.P. Dore (1965), who has written an interesting monograph entitled *City Life in Japan: A Study of a Tokyo Ward*, reports that it is not uncommon for the young couple to go to the cinema after the *miai* and to court each other for some weeks or months afterward. The continued involvement of the courting couple with each other provides the indication that the marriage is acceptable and usually, in less than six months after the *miai*, the marriage takes place within the guidelines of the traditional marriage ceremony and the exchange of betrothal gifts.

Blood (1967) believes that his findings indicate that the main function of the formal introduction was to allow the prospective couple the opportunity to meet and assess their interest in one another. It was not to arrange the marriage. Hardly more than 10 percent of the *miai*s led to marriage. Further, this modern version of the marriage arrangement usually occurs among young people who fail to contract a successful love match. They also tend to be confined to the "old-fashioned" (less-educated, less-emancipated) segments of the younger generation.

By contrast, the love match is defined as the falling in love of the man and woman prior to getting engaged. The love-match couples do not date much more than the arranged-marriage couples. The difference is that their relationship developed into love. It must be remembered that traditionally Japan has been a sex-segregated society and potentially eligible partners had little opportunity for informal socialization. Blood reports that almost 75 percent of the love-match couples met at work. The scarcity of coeducational colleges and congregational churches and the nonprevalence of using the homes of friends and relatives for informal meetings account for the importance of the place of work for the meeting of eligible singles.

The criteria for the selection of a spouse are different for the love-match couples and the arranged-marriage group. The traditional emphasis in arranged marriages is the wife's ability to fit into the husband's family, provided that the family background and status qualifications are met. In the self-selection process of love-match individuals, the emphasis is on personal qualifications. Those who are introduced through the *miai* stress the husband's income and the wife's health and housekeeping ability. Couples who meet through their own initiative emphasize the importance of love.

Blood (1967) then raises the question: Which of these two patterns of mate selection, the modernized version of arranged marriage or the love match, is superior in terms of the ultimate happiness of the couple and the stability of the marriage? This is a somewhat inappropriate question since, where marriages are arranged, the happiness of the spouses is not the primary purpose of the marriage. Yet Blood's answer is interesting. He found that the happiest arranged marriages were those in which the couple dated for an extended period of time after the formal introduction at the *miai*. These couples had the opportunity to get to know each other and to start developing a love relationship. The happiest love-match couples were those whose parents were enthusiastic about the pending marriage. When the parents viewed the love match negatively, the consequent marriage ran into the greatest difficulty. In general, Blood believes that those marriages that combined affectional involvement and parental approval tended to be the most successful. The combining of the positive sentiments of both generations, the parents and the children, gave the greatest assurance of the eventual happiness of the marrying couple.

Jane Condon (1985), a writer for *Life* and *People* magazines, interviewed a number of Japanese women about their lives, thoughts, and beliefs. What they had to say about mate selection and marriage is fascinating. Condon reports that contact between single men and women is still much more limited than in the West. Further, the Japanese tend to be shy, particularly in public places and especially with the opposite sex.

Another factor that limits the contact of singles is that for economic and traditional reasons most live at home with their parents until they marry. Housing is relatively scarce and expensive. In addition, customs that advocate dependency, particularly for the female, are still popular. Indeed, single women who live apart from their families are often stigmatized as being too independent or tainted by the opportunity to engage in sex without parental knowledge. Condon observes that some job notices specify that women not living with parents or relatives need not apply for them. As a consequence of all these factors, while some singles meet at school or at work, date, fall in love, and marry, for many others arranged marriage, or *omiai* (literally, "look" or "meet"), still serves as a safety net for those wishing to marry.

Condon reports that estimates of the percentage of *omiai* marriages range from as low as 25 percent to as high as 60 percent. The great fluctuation is that many arranged meetings turn into a love marriage and are counted as such. One woman comments:

> To my mind, *omiai* is just a first clue for *ren'ai* [love marriage] really. After our first meeting, we went to movies and restaurants a lot together. Then the *nakodo* began pressing us to make a decision. So two months later we held our engagement ceremony. (quoted in Condon, 1985:27)

The Japanese term for this new type of marriage is *omiai/ren'ai*, because the young people fall in love after they meet. Condon contrasts the differences in the courtship pattern of a contemporary *omiai* with the courtship pattern of a love marriage. She describes the first speaker, Noriko Aoki, and her husband as an upwardly mobile, prosperous young couple (the Japanese equivalent of American Yuppies). The second woman, Miwako Yamakawa, a friend of Noriko Aoki, comes from an aristocratic background, worked before marriage, and describes the days and the events leading up to her marriage.

Noriko Aoki states that prior to the *omiai* ceremony, through the offices of a matchmaker, families exchange photographs and documents that provide social background and personal interest information about the prospective couple. In some cases, private detectives are employed by families to assure that the future spouses have not had previous lovers or there are no criminals in the family. Neighbors may be interviewed to comment on the type of people they are, and indeed, such interviews are considered to be a normal occurrence when people marry through arrangements. Noriko Aoki's *omiai* was successful, and she was married after a two-month engagement.

Like Noriko Aoki, Miwako Yamakawa was college-educated. The death of her mother and the lack of extended-family support forced her to support herself after graduation. She met her future husband through her married sister who knew him in Houston, Texas. After a brief dating period they became engaged. Her father believed that changing attitudes and values no longer required the approval of relatives for marriage. Miwako Yamakawa's fiance was college-educated, as were his parents and siblings. They, too, believed that a love marriage was proper. Yamakawa comments on her married life:

> So we encountered no opposition to our marriage. Now I'm very happy to have married him. My husband and I agree that my most important job is to keep the house clean. I take care of the home, which means taking care of my daughter, too. My husband goes out any time he likes, but he thinks that his wife should always be home. I think he's right. You see, if a mother goes outside for a walk, there might be a phone call or a problem, and she wouldn't be there. I want to be home when my daughter comes home from school, and her school advised me to do so. I stay home because I don't want to disturb any other member of the family. (quoted in Condon, 1985:36-37)

Condon (1985) observes that although most young people prefer love matches, a potential difficulty is their future relations with their in-laws. In Japan there is a much greater chance for discord than in America, since parents have a strong say in their children's married life. Further, Japanese women are becoming less and less subservient to their in-laws. A popular post-World War II saying is, "Since the war, women and nylons have become stronger" (Condon, 1985:37). The result is often conflict between daughters-in-law and in-laws that reflects different generational expectations, as well as different expectations between the sexes.

In another insightful interview, Condon uses the experience of a young Japanese woman to highlight some of these difficulties. Miki Suzuki spent her senior year at a midwestern American high school and is now employed in Japan as a full-time professional translator working on magazines. Like Miki, her fiance graduated from Keto, one of Japan's elite universities. After much soul-searching, Miki Suzuki decided not to marry. Her story dramatizes some of the difficulties confronting young people who wish to marry on the basis of love.

Essentially, Miki Suzuki's prospective in-laws asked her parents to financially contribute to the setting-up of the newlyweds' household. Failure to comply would indicate a lack of commitment to the marriage and result in a termination of the engagement. Further, they wanted Miki Suzuki to forego her career as a translator and immediately have children. Suzuki comments:

BOX 9-2   The Global Family

Some Japanese Kiss in Public; Their Elders Are Shocked . . . Shocked!

T.R. Reid
WASHINGTON POST

TOKYO—You must remember this: A kiss is still a kiss—except in Japan, where it has become a social problem.

In a nation that loves to follow rules, the media are up in arms because some young people are violating one of the unwritten social rules that govern this decorous place: They are actually kissing each other right out in public.

It's not an everyday, or even an everyweek, event, but nowadays you can sometimes see young couples kissing goodbye at street corners and train stations. Media reports say there have even been instances of outright necking on the train, although this correspondent could not find a single person who had witnessed such behavior.

By American standards—or even by the standards of Japan's raunchy magazines and late-night television programs—puckering up in public is tame stuff indeed.

But the public kiss, or even the public hug, is rather shocking here. The Japanese have been raised to greet friends, spouses and lovers with a polite bow. Even soldiers coming home from months on distant duty are welcomed by their wives at the airport with nothing more than a smile and a bow.

"Kissing in public—it's ugly!" social critic Chiaki Aso said in the weekly magazine Shukan Yomiuri. "These people never give a thought to how others feel, the people who have to see them do it."

The aversion to public kissing is a little hard to comprehend in a country that has ubiquitous, if illegal, prostitution and a thriving pornography business. Even in mainstream publications, pictures of naked women are so common that United Airlines has been forced to ban some Japanese newsmagazines from its planes because of passenger complaints.

Nudity and pornography thrive. But an unshielded "choo-choo" is a no-no.

Video rental stores here offer countless films purporting to show high school girls stripping out of their sailor-suit school uniforms. There are stores where men can buy used panties, priced around $40, packaged with a photo of the high school girl who reputedly wore them.

Why, then, would anybody care if some college or high school students were seen kissing on the corner?

The difference seems to be the public nature of the kiss. It is commonplace here that shame in front of others—rather than a private sense of guilt—is the chief restraint on bad conduct. It follows that if people no longer restrain themselves in public, the whole society may soon go to pot.

"These young people have lost their sense of shame," housewife Shizue Tsutsumi wrote recently in one of many letters to the editor on the kiss question in the Yomiuri Shimbun, Japan's largest newspaper. "Without shame, there is no sense of restraint. If we lose that, we're no different from animals."

"Kissing in public is less shocking nowadays than it would have been, say, 40 years ago," said Hideo Sakamoto, an educator and author. "But it's still not accepted. There's a view that this is a sign of weakness. People see young people who do this as weak."

Despite many recent articles on the kissing controversy, shame still seems to be winning out over public passion.

A survey this summer of 400 Japanese men revealed that 71 percent had never kissed a woman in a public place. Of the 29 percent who admitted to kissing at train stations, airports or street corners, more than half said they were embarrassed to admit it.

But change is occurring, and it has extended even to the language of the kiss.

The Japanese have their own noun for kissing, composed of two characters that mean "approach the lips." But this old term is generally used only in highbrow literary contexts. The standard word for the touch of lovers' lips is *keesu*, the Japanese pronunciation of the English word *kiss*.

Recently, however, young people have invented a new Japanese word for kissing. It is the onomatopoeic noun *choo* or *choo-choo*, evidently adopted because *choo* is the sound of kissing to Japanese ears.

Accordingly, the most provocative moment on a Japanese date these days comes when the woman turns to her man and says, "Hiroshi-san, won't you choo me?"

Philadelphia Inquirer, 9 November 1994.
Reprinted with permission by the
Philadelphia Inquirer, 1994.

I couldn't believe it! His mother [stated that] all his family really wants in a wife for him (the fiance) is a healthy, obedient girl who could produce a baby boy—that is, a family heir! And listen to this. During the first year that he is away they insist that I move from my home in Tokyo to Osaka to live with them, so they can train me! Train me? These people are really old-fashioned. Their ideas seem to come from a time before *Meiji*. They are positively feudal. (quoted in Condon, 1985:39)

Ultimately, even the fear of her in-laws' continued interference and influence over her fiance could not offset her fear of humiliation if she ended the engagement. Condon did not feel it was her place to tell Miki that it was worth the risk to endure "the potential short-term embarrassment of not having the wedding compared to a lifetime spent with an unpleasant mother-in-law and a spineless husband" (1985:42). Despite her serious misgivings, Miki Suzuki, a woman torn between traditional and modern views of marriage and family, was married. Condon, who could not attend the wedding because of other obligations, concludes:

Eight days later, I was in the United States visiting my family, and I felt a sad twinge as I imagined Miki in her kabuki-white makeup, elaborate hairpiece, and elegant kimono standing at the Shinto shrine sipping sake from nuptial cups with her husband-to-be. It was supposed to be the day little girls dream of. I wondered how she felt. (Condon, 1985:42).

INSTITUTIONAL MATCHMAKERS: A COMPARISON OF CONTEMPORARY JAPAN AND AMERICA

In traditional Japan, the matchmaker (*nakodo*) provided an invaluable service for families in arranging the marriage of their children. The *nakodo* served as a go-between negotiating the delicate relations between families and providing a face-saving service in case the negotiations failed. Today, the Japanese matchmaker's primary function is to introduce young people formally and give them the opportunity to get to know each other rather than actually to arrange a marriage. Blood (1967) found that almost 90 percent of the formal introductions did not culminate in marriage. Further, despite the pressure of families on young people to marry as soon as possible, the remaining 10 percent who did eventually marry did so only after a considerable period of time and a considerable number of dates.

In a later book, Blood (1972) observes that urbanization and mobility have made it more difficult for Japanese families to find potential partners for their children. This has produced a gradual shift away from the personalized matchmakers toward municipal governmental sponsorship of matchmaking agencies. Marriage consultation centers in urban areas provide an inexpensive public service to individuals in search of marriage partners. He reports that the Tokyo center in the early 1960s arranged 1,000 marriages a year through its facilities. One problem was that twice as many women applied as men; the result was that men were more likely to find partners than women. An additional form of matchmaking agency was established by the segregated women's colleges in Japan for their alumnae. The general belief was that such alumnae would become "submissive" wives and this image attracted large numbers of men from the largely segregated men's prestige universities.

In a widely circulated Japanese poll conducted in 1992, Japanese women report low assessments of Japanese men (Itoli and Powell, 1992). Terms used to describe men include "unreliable," "self-centered," "boring," and "predictable" individuals who are "spoiled" by their mothers. In a later poll, both Japanese women and men had low assessments of each other—their poor ratings on love and romance were the lowest among the fourteen industrial countries polled (WuDunn, 1995). These difficulties have become associated with a term the "Narita divorce." This refers to a newlywed couple returning after their honeymoon to Narita Airport outside of Tokyo when the wife immediately dumps her husband because he so bored her.

These negative opinions of men are reinforced by the increased economic independence of Japanese women. Japanese women are putting more emphasis on careers. A feminist movement has developed in which women have organized pressure groups and national rallies to fight against economic discrimination. The traditional situation in which women were married and had children by the age of 25 is giving way to a startling increase in the number of single women and single men who are over the age of 30. This figure has doubled in the last two decades. As a reflection, the birthrate has dropped to 1.53 children per woman—below the population replacement figure. This has resulted in an aging population with less than a fifth (17.4 percent) under the age of 15. In comparison, in the years prior to World War II, 36 percent of the population was under 15. An aging population is forecast for the future. This would have serious economic ramifications with greater amounts of money being put into programs supporting the elderly with less money being available for economic investments.

Japanese women are not only calling for a change in female roles but in male roles as well. They want men to be more concerned with family matters and less involved with their careers. They refer to men who are as "seven-eleven"—those who work from seven in the morning to eleven at night (WuDunn, 1995). Reports indicate that single men, in an attempt to rectify the situation, are attending self-help classes that will make them better able to understand women and themselves.

The downside for men's "resocialization" is that the older generation may not be as readily accepting of the new ways. WuDunn provides the example of a man who now does the dishes as a matter of course even when he visited his mother's house. His parents were astonished and horrified, viewing dishwashing as women's work. To avoid future arguments and to keep within the good graces of her in-laws, the women reports: "Now when we go over there, it's constant work for me. I don't let him do anything; otherwise his family will hate me" (cited in WuDunn, 1995).

Blood (1972) observes that analogous institutional matchmaking agencies are to be found in the United States. Here, they take the form of computer centers or dating services, singles or date bars, summer resorts, and holiday cruises. Additional mating institutions include matrimonial bureaus, lonely hearts clubs, encounter groups, classified ads, and sexual liberation groups.

The American matchmaking institutions are somewhat different from the Japanese ones. Blood points out that the American pattern emphasizes personal qualities of the prospective partner, a natural consequence of the American system of self-selection. In Japan, the emphasis is on objective family-background criteria, an outgrowth of traditional kin-selected arranged marriages. In America, the couple arrange their own dates through correspondence or by phone; in Japan, the agencies set up formal introductory meetings at their establishments that are presided over by a staff counselor. However, as in Japan, more women in America avail themselves of these institutional matchmaking agencies than men. Again, this reflects the double-standard ethos that allows women less initiative than men in personally soliciting dates.

In the 1980s and 1990s a great deal of discussion has occurred on two important factors—the *marriage squeeze* and the *marriage gradient*—that have impacted on matchmaking institutions and mate selection practices in the United States. The marriage squeeze reflects demographic data that suggests an imbalance in the sex ratio, or the number of females and males available for marriage. There are more women look-

Young people enjoying themselves around a billiard table.

ing for men who are eligible for marriage and looking for a partner. This pattern began after World War II and continues today. The marriage gradient is the other factor that affects the availability of eligibility of potential marital partners. This is the belief that men should have higher income, education, status, and be older than women. The belief, in short, is that men should marry "down" and women should marry "up." Taken together, the result is that more women seek husbands than men seek wives.

The situation is reported to be particularly acute in large cities where there are more unmarried women than eligible men. Social scientists have observed that this marriage squeeze is particularly predominant among African Americans. This is a consequence of the lower life expectancy of black men coupled with the relatively high numbers of black men who are victims of homicide or who are incarcerated and who have dropped out of the economic job marketplace (Lindsey, 1994; O'Hare et al., 1991; Staples, 1981). O'Hare and his associates observed that at every educational level, and especially among women, the percentage of African Americans who are not married is higher than it is for whites. As a consequence, and one that we discussed in an earlier chapter, marriage is less common among blacks and there is a greater reliance on the mutual assistance patterns of an extended kinship network.

The city with its more transitory population and the large number of singles who flock to urban areas for economic opportunities is the site where new forms of matchmaking are taking place. The mass media in America have found that stories on such commercial matchmaking institutions as computer dating services and singles bars sell newspapers, and the tendency is to publicize them beyond their actual importance. Starr and Carns (1973), in an article titled "Singles in the City", made this point almost twenty-five years ago and it still holds true today. They report on a sample of seventy never-married male and female college graduates in Chicago. These people did not find singles bars the best place for making friends or for meeting persons of the opposite sex. They found that apartment dwellings and their neighborhoods were also unsatisfactory in this regard. The home and neighborhood were seen as havens for privacy in which the person did not have either the desire or the time to interact informally with neighbors. The work setting was most frequently mentioned as the place for developing personal associations (Starr and Carns, 1973). A two-stage process operates in the relationship between work and dating. Most graduates form friendships on the job. But they do not date their work associates, since they desire to avoid intimacy with those with whom they must interact regardless of whether a personal relationship succeeds or not. Rather, they use work friends to arrange dates through a friend-of-a-friend pattern.

The authors conclude that the popular image of the swinging singles developed and nurtured by the media is patently false. Singles bars and their ilk do not attract people looking for meaningful relationships. Further, singles do not lead lives of hedonistic abandonment. "They are people coping with the same problems we all face: finding a place to live, searching for satisfaction from their jobs and seeking friends, dates and ultimately mates in an environment for which they have been ill-prepared and which does not easily lend itself to the formation of stable human relationships" (Starr and Carns, 1973:161). In response to the lack of institutional supports found in the city environment, these people look to the world of work, much as their Japanese counterparts do, to provide them with opportunities to meet and to form friendships.

Since the 1980s a variety of institutionalized dating services have become prominent. They include personal ads, matchmaking consultants, computer matching, and video dating. Personal ads and mail-order catalogs were used in the late 1800s, as unattached men living in the American West sought wives through these sources (Steinfirst and Moran, 1989). The 1945 film *The Harvey Girls* is a story of unattached young women who go the "wild west," ostensibly to work as waitresses for a restaurant, but they also have prospective marriage as a goal. In a very interesting 1867 book, *Marriage in the United States*, Auguste Carlier (1972) comments on the regular appearance of matrimonial advertisements with the promise of dowries to make the proposal more enticing for prospective frontier wives. In the late 1900s, a return can be seen to commercial matchmaking services in the new urban frontier.

Personal classified advertisements have become an increasingly popular way for people to meet each other. They have increasingly appeared in newspapers, city-entertainment and dining guides as well as magazines, national magazines that appeal to a specialized audience such as *The New York Review of Books*, and suburban shopping guides. Bolig, Stein, and McKenry (1984) found that both men and women who place ads in singles magazines hope to find respondents who are physically attractive and have desirable personalities. The ad-placers view themselves as offering attractiveness, intelligence, good education, and stable careers. The use of this impersonal form of contact can be seen as indicating the difficulty that many people feel in finding ways to meet others.

Computerized dating services are a mushrooming business. Individuals fill out lengthy questionnaires dealing with family background (for example, religion, race, social class, and so forth), interests, and attitudes. Men and women are then matched on the basis of similar backgrounds and likes and dislikes. By and large, the computer is a gimmick since matchings can occur by other sorting techniques. Its basic function is a legitimizing one, giving "scientific" credibility to the sorting procedure. The computer simply sorts data coded with biographical information and pairs individuals on the basis of "compatible" areas of interests, attitudes, and desires.

The entire procedure rests on the quality of the questionnaire data. In-depth, detailed questionnaires, if properly utilized, can match individuals on common interests, attitudes, and backgrounds. Such match-ups do not necessarily guarantee that the two people will be attracted to each other.

> The most obvious weakness of the system, however, is its inability to gauge attraction. At its scientific best it can only weigh a certain limited range of psychological and physical factors and conclude that two people are *compatible*. Frequently this means nothing whatsoever in terms of human relationships. How little compatibility may count was shown by this letter addressed to another dating outfit:
>
> "Your computer was right. Mitzi W. and I like all the same things. We like the same food, we both like the opera. Mitzi likes bike riding and so do I. I like dogs, and so does Mitzi. Actually, there was only one thing we didn't like—each other." (Goodwin, 1973:87)

Computer dating services and other formalized introduction agencies can provide a service for those people who cannot or will not find dates or prospective marital partners on their own. Although many find the use of such agencies repugnant and artificial, they can be helpful to others. As they are currently operated, the initiative to develop the relationship rests solely on the participants. Thus, the individual decision-making process on the compatibility and attraction of the matched individual still remains a personal matter. Unfortunately, a significant number of these "mating trade" organizations have been guilty of exploitation. The charges against them run from the charging of exorbitant fees to fraudulently based "computer" match-ups. Some have exploited the weaknesses and desires of their clientele. If the abuses of the system can be minimized, perhaps through effective governmental legislation, these agencies can provide a service for those so inclined to use them.

Major characteristics of singles bars include the predominant sexual undertones of interaction, the underlying competitive aspects of that interaction, and a preoccupation with first impressions and appearance. In one of the first studies of single bars, Natalie Allon and Joan Fishel (1981) observe on what has proved to be a constant feature of them. In the eight singles bars in Manhattan observed, participants were constantly monitoring their appearance and comparing it to others in attendance. Games of staring and touching were played. Women would try to establish eye contact with men whom they wanted to meet but left it up to the men to initiate the relationship. Touching was used frequently to initiate conversation, signal approval, or as a gesture of affection, and often took on sexual connotations. Gender-role stereotypes were much in evidence—men would light women's cigarettes, buy them drinks, offer them bar stools, and so forth. Men were expected to be the initiators of interaction and of asking for phone numbers.

A twin phenomenon of alienation and sociability was observed by the researchers. The atmosphere seemed strained and forced, with participants acting defensively and on guard and not naturally. Allon and Fishel noted that in their interviews, participants often expressed surprise with how differently people whom they met in singles bars acted on a date:

> Everyone knows why you're here; you want to meet people. But at the same time no one wants to seem overanxious. You have to be very cool about it, and the tougher you act the cooler people will think you are [man].
>
> I do want to meet new men to go out with, but I don't want them to think I'm hard up for a date. I try not to seem too excited if a guy asks for my number or asks to take me out. . . . Guys can be real smart asses, especially if they think you really want them [woman]. (Allon and Fishel, 1981:119)

Pepper Schwartz and Janet Lever (1976) summarize the alienating nature of singles bars in the title of their article "Fear and Loathing at a College Mixer." In their study of college mixers at Yale University where women from Vassar, Smith, and Mt. Holyoke "mixed" with Yale men at Saturday parties, Schwartz and Lever found that underlying the social activities were interaction processes that impacted on participants' concepts of self and identity. This was a consequence of a structural setting where strangers met with the express purpose of evaluating each other. They observe the following:

Rather than seeing the event as "pure fun," to the contrary, the participants feel the tension and anxiety associated with a situation where high personal stakes are involved. Interactions with the opposite sex occur in a predominantly conflict-ridden context where mutual satisfaction rarely occurs. Noncooperative strategies to protect face are accepted as rational by nearly everyone, and the "battle of the sexes" becomes more than a metaphor. (Schwartz and Lever, 1976:430)

The single bars of the 1970s, 1980s, and 1990s have become more of a "meat" market than a "meet" market. They have given way to multi-use clubs that feature dancing facilities and game rooms as well as dining and drinking facilities. Many cities, such as Philadelphia, Baltimore, and Denver, have seen rebirths of former commercial and industrial areas that have been transformed by public social clubs catering to singles. There is a conscious attempt to desexualize the setting—although it has not been completely successful. The noise level of the music and the frantic pace of these establishments often make them an undesirable setting to "meet" someone. The complaint is that appearance rather than substance prevails. The use of the local supermarket for "singles nights" that is promotionally tied in with local young-adult-focused radio stations had a period of popularity in the 1980s (O'Reilly, 1986). Alternative sites that have recently appeared are coffee houses and large book emporiums that have coffee and snack areas set aside for less hectic interaction.

Another means of getting people together has taken the form of videotape dating. A dating service videotapes an interview and casual conversation with a client, which is then placed in a file along with a personal profile and a photograph. Other clients then select from this video file people whom they would like to meet. On mutual agreement after seeing each other's video, arrangements are then made for the male and female to meet.

Video dating organizations are popular in many countries, including England and Japan, as well as in many cities and states in America. For example, as early as 1974, one agency in Japan had a roster of 4,500 clients and about 100 couples a month met through this modern-day *nakodo* (*Newsweek*, 1974). Video dating services have increasingly been used in the United States. Over 600 such services were reported in 1992 (Ahuvia and Adelman, 1992). The video, which lasts between two and ten minutes, is supplemented by a brief biographical sketch and a photograph. Its popularity stems from a more "life-like" opportunity to prescreen potential dating partners. They have not proved all that effective in promoting long-term relationships (Woll and Cozby, 1987; Woll and Young, 1989).

An emerging form of matchmaking services has been electronic/phone communication networks that include computer-based networks and telephone party lines (Ahuvia and Adelman, 1992). With the increased use of computer-based networks such as Compuserve and Internet and e-mail, the potential is there for usages beyond computer singles ads and bulletin boards. As of this writing, the potential for initiating relationships through this medium is there. How and the extent to which it will be operationalized and utilized remains to be seen. I would, however, expect that if trends toward longer periods of singlehood and later ages of marriage continue, computer usage as well as other institutionalized matchmaking services discussed will continue to prove popular.

BOX 9-3 The Contemporary American Family

Seeking Fine Mind/Body. Dog Lovers a Plus.

Eric Asimov

With its promise of young love, Valentine's Day may be the first harbinger of spring. Buds are not yet visible on trees, but personal ads sprout everywhere, evidence that no matter how many seasons of deprivation pass, the mating sap rises eternal.

In alternative weeklies and intellectual journals, in buttoned-up conservative reviews and buttoned-down liberal newsletters, common ground can be found in the back of the book, where DPF's (divorced professional females) seek SNSM's (single nonsmoking males), and uninhibited kinky couples seek anybody.

The Internet is fertile ground for the seeds of love, from Webpersonals (http://www.webpersonals.com) to Cupid's Network (http://www.cupidnet.com). Nuance and delicacy are not strong points of Internet discourse, however, and alt.personal.ads is never far from alt.sex.wanted.

Here is a selection of current personal ads. While there may not be somebody for everybody, at least there's a lot to choose from. Pucker up.

The quest for love knows no political bounds. Concerned Singles is a newsletter based in Stockbridge, Mass., that "links single men and women who are concerned about social justice, peace, gender and racial equality."

DWF, 5'8", entering my 60's, another beginning, the ripple effect of a smile, the tickle of laughter, the beat of a rhumba, the flight of a tennis ball, the exchange of ideas, the colors of a palette, looking for someone with passion to share.

Would that woman be willing to take a chance on this gentleman advertising in National Review, the conservative journal?

TAKE MY HAND. Wind, rain, wildflowers, autumn leaves, galleries, footprints in the sand, wonderment, library nook, ideas—that's me. Death, silence, solace, rebirth—also me. Tennis balls, laughter, absurdities, podiums, moves, patterns, fountain sprays—again me. Lithe, comely, playful, evolved, sensuality engaged. That's me too! Active 60's to 70.

Too subtle? Check out these ads from Russia, available at http://www.f8.com/FP/Russia/Personal-ads.html.

TALL, beautiful woman, 32, temperamental and sexually knowledgeable, urgently seeks a rich lover not younger than 42.

SWEET ladies! Thin and fit ladies! I offer you sessions of love. Will also respond to lesbians with pleasure. Decency guaranteed. Your telephone gets a quicker response.

YOUNG MAN, 29, tired of loneliness in this world. Seeking acquaintance with young men who feel that spending time with men is more interesting than with women.

The Internet can offer visual aids, with full-length color photographs sometimes accessible. Occasionally, it is difficult to reconcile words and pictures, as in the case of one Brazilian woman whose photograph in a very brief bikini can be seen on Cupid Network's Women of the World's service, http://www.cupidnet.com/womenwld.

I am serious, not liberal or "hot." I am reserved and shy. I want a husband and family, North American or European man, serious with good character who will respect my values, honest and responsible.

Some people may place personals because their requirements are so, well, specific.
From New York magazine:
ANGEL SOUGHT, 18-25, who believes

her spiritual and physical beauty can only be preserved by following Plato in his Laws, Book 8, verses 839-841. The girl I seek is Old Testament believer, organic believer in green international tech disarmament and, like David Copperfield's Agnes, will always point upward.

From Interrace magazine:

LIBERAL, HIPPIE, eclectic, pacifistic, passionate, educated, humorous, tall, independent mother of multicultural toddler, seeks intelligent, compassionate, peaceful male, 25-40ish. Should know the differences between: Kachina and Kokopelli; Spirituality and Religion; Race and Racism; Henley and Van Morrison; Emerson and Thoreau; Truisms and Ideology; Disposable and Cloth; Mutilation and Art; Zimbabwe and Rhodesia; or possess a willingness to learn.

From the Cupid Network:

I want a man who has sweet odors, body and breath, no snoring who will be good to me, gentle and kind, elegant and professionally secure with virtues, just as I have, for marriage (Spanish or Portuguese only).

Literary and historical allusions are a good way of weeding out the incompatible:

From The New York Review of Books:

GORGEOUS AND GUTSY, tender and tough. Beautiful female writer, brainy, funny, built like a Hemingway femme fatale, passionately involved in world affairs, seeks *real* man: sharply intelligent, witty, attractive, 30-50 passionate about his *own* life's work. Wimps, nerds, and Republicans need *not* reply.

From New York Press:

CHALICE OF THE SUCCUBUS awaits your thirsts. Beautiful BiWF, long hair black as a hundred midnights. Spiritual, satyrical, surreal, sybaritic, into literature, 4 A.D./gothic stuff, body adornment, weird films, exploring museums, and the darker alleys of lower Manhattan. Seeks long-haired, like minded sloe eyed M/F

shapeshifter for intense and intelligent esoteric quenchings. Asian a plus.

Knowledge of recent movies can be important, as in these ads from New York Press:

NOT WAITING TO EXHALE We enjoy life fully, but will make room for right friend/lover/mate. We both bring a lot to the party. SBPF, 5'4" 128 lbs., fine mind/body, varied interests ISO SM, 45-55, financially/emotionally secure.

SENSE AND SENSIBILITY wanted by pretty SWPF (36) ISO SWPM for LTR. I'm up and offbeat, articulate, with eclectic sense of humor, a steadfast, stalwart friend, world traveler, career yet beach-oriented, seriously into world/reggae/surf music. You: any variation/complement to the above, especially steadfast, stalwart. Dog lovers a plus.

Beyond loneliness and desire, the personals are sometimes one of only a few options for some people.

From New York magazine:

I'M LONELY, in the witness protection program. That's why I'm seeking a 23-34, Jewish female who is smart, warm and attractive. The F.B.I. says I'm a Jewish male, 33, funny, smart, attractive and kind.

Placing an ad may go well beyond one's usual role. From Harper's:

SON SEEKS BOYFRIEND FOR MOM. I have a terrific mom. She's thin, pretty athletic, funny and works hard but still goes to all my weekend games. If you're like her, between 45-55, like to travel, entertain at home and wouldn't mind playing ball with me too, then send a picture and a note so we can check you out.

Then there's the casual approach, as seen on Cupid Network's Women of the World:

I am not searching but if some really nice guy comes along then I am available.

CONCLUSION

In this chapter, I looked at different marital-arrangement structures in different societies. I examined the social factors that account for the wide prevalence of arranged marriages in many of these societies and the reasons that a relatively small proportion of societies allow for free choice of spouse. A predominant correlation exists between types of marital arrangements and types of family systems. Generally, where a consanguineal-family form exists—one that emphasizes the rights, obligations, and duties of family members to the larger extended family—there is a tendency for such families to control the marriages of their members. On the other hand, where a conjugal-family form exists, there is a greater emphasis on individual motivations and, consequently, a greater freedom is allowed family members in choosing their partners.

Of particular interest to us was the effect of modernization on traditional arranged-marriage structures. The arranged-marriage phenomena that has emerged in India frequently utilizes modern technology—for example, newspaper advertisements—to help attract suitable spouses for their children. However, I also saw that the increased materialism of the urban elite may be associated with the horrible practice of wife abuse and bride deaths that has become so prevalent. Marriages, increasingly based on bride dowries rather than on any marital and kinship relationships, was seen to be the contributing factor. The emerging pattern, as seen in Japan, is the breaking down of arranged marriages and the development of free-choice systems based in large part on romantic love. I took a longer look at the mate-selection procedures of Japan and compared them to the United States. Japan is a society that historically has controlled the marriages of its youth; the United States has emphasized the importance of individual decision making. Our analysis has indicated that both societies are moving along the same path; both are emphasizing the free-choice system. And, in both societies unhappiness with prospective spouses helps account for an increasing decision by people in both societies to either postpone marriage or remain single.

I looked at the emerging phenomenon of institutionalized matchmaking institutions including singles bars, classified advertisements, and video and computer dating services. Arising out of the needs of an increasingly urbanized society, these agencies seek to be the contemporary counterparts of traditional matchmakers. Their limitations are insurmountable to a society that views romance as the cornerstone of marriage; although they can match people's interests, they cannot guarantee that the one ingredient deemed essential for marriage will surface in the relationship—love. This leads us our next concern: the changing nature and patterns of marital relationships.

10

A GLOBAL VIEW
OF GENDER ROLES

Chapter Outline
Work and the Family in Nonindustrial Societies
Gender Roles in Male and Female Farming Systems
Gender Roles, The Family, and African Modernization
   Living under Apartheid and Its Aftermath
Gender Roles in Industrial Societies: Russia
   Gender Roles and the Family before and after Perestroika
The Western Experience: Sweden
The Western Experience: Israel
Conclusion

In Chapter 8, we pointed out that sex-linked factors based on physiology as well as patriarchal ideology served as the philosophical and moral justification for discriminatory gender-role differentiation. We observed that variations on the patriarchal theme predominated in Greco-Roman, Semitic, Indian, Chinese, Japanese, and Western Christian civilizations. We also mentioned that in recent years there has been a reevaluation of patriarchal ideology. Modernization processes, scientific and technological developments, rapid social change, and ideological revolutions have led to questioning of the ways that tasks and roles are allocated on the basis of sex. Traditional gender-role relationship patterns and their ideological justification have been undergoing scrutiny and change. In the past, societies marked by relative stability, socially derived gender identifications, and role allocations were nondebatable and were taken for granted. In a rapidly changing world, this is no longer the case.

Our orientation in this discussion is on the activities of males and females in public and private or domestic spheres. The differentiation of these spheres has been seen by many researchers as a factor dominating the expression of marital roles. They are seen to be important in determining power, privilege, respect, and deference patterns within the family. We begin our discussion by looking at this differentiation in preliterate societies.

We then turn our attention to societies with different economic systems and examine the relationship between patriarchy and values about the sexes in work and in the family. First, we look at agricultural societies. Some of them are patriarchal, some are not. However, those in non-Western societies that are not based on patriarchy were forced to adopt such an ideology through the policies of European colonial administrators. These agricultural societies provide interesting illustrations of how patriarchy influences men and women.

Then, we explore gender-role relationships in highly industrialized societies. The focus will be on the relationship between the sexes, particularly as it revolves around the areas of work and the family. This relationship is examined by looking at societies that have officially espoused an antipatriarchal ideology: the former Soviet Union,

Sweden, and Israel. The former Union of Soviet Socialist Republics (USSR or Soviet Union) had a government that used Marxist principles in its policies regarding the status of the sexes. The major goal of these policies was to bring about equality of women and men in all spheres of life. We will look at the history of gender-role, marital, and family relationships in the former Soviet Union and what is now happening in post-Communist Russia. Both Sweden and Israel have developed highly elaborate social-welfare systems. They, too, share a desire for equality of the sexes. Unlike the former Soviet Union, they start from different ideological points of view that stem from their different philosophical positions and their different societal circumstances. Yet they are striving to change the patriarchal ideology and practices still inherent in their societies. Further, because all these countries have attempted to bring about equality of the sexes, they should provide a useful perspective for looking at future problems and their possible solutions that countries such as the United States may face as they seek to change the formal and traditional barriers to women's full participation in society.

WORK AND THE FAMILY IN NONINDUSTRIAL SOCIETIES

William N. Stephens (1963), in his excellent cross-cultural survey of the family, examined three aspects of husband-wife roles: togetherness versus separateness, men's work versus women's work, and power and privilege. Stephens used existing ethnographic data and interviews with ethnographers on family deference customs and power relations. These data comprise the "ethnographer-interview" and total fifty-three cases. Stephens found that traditional barriers curtail the intimacy, sharing, and togetherness of husbands and wives. Many nonindustrial societies practiced avoidance customs in public: The ethnographers interviewed said that these societies did not allow husbands and wives to share affection in public. Only 111 societies allowed this. Further, in over half of the reported cases, husband and wife may not even touch each other in public (Stephens, 1963:275). These avoidance customs were carried over into the private sphere. In the home, traditional barriers ordained that the husband and wife sleep in separate beds, live in separate houses, own separate property, eat separately, and go separately to community gatherings.

Stephens also found that the sexes worked at separate tasks. This task differentiation was not based on biologic capabilities or limitations of the two sexes. Yet, the women's capacity for bearing and nursing children tends to influence the work allocations of men and women. Stephens uses George P. Murdock's (1937) cross-cultural survey of the division of labor by sex and his own ethnographer-interview data. He finds that men were assigned the following tasks: metalworking, stonecutting, lumbering, and killing or herding large animals. They were also given tasks that required geographic mobility: hunting, fishing, warring, and trading away from home. These tasks were allocated to men not so much because of their alleged superior physical strength or ability but because of their exemption from childbearing and child care. This was a chronic condition for women in precontraceptive eras. A wife's work was centered in the home and in nearby locations because she could tend to her babies at the same time she completed other tasks. These tasks were nearly always done by women: cooking, water carrying, and grain grinding as well as housekeeping and care of young children. Stephens also notes that in most preliterate societies women's work was not solely confined to the home; they also were involved in the subsistence work of getting, growing, and processing food. In hunting-and-gathering societies, women gather plant food while the men hunt. In agricultural societies, particularly those that practice shifting agriculture, women do a large share of the farm work. Table 10-1 shows some data on the division of labor by sex.

The third aspect of husband-wife roles examined by Stephens was power and privilege. He found that power tends to be controlled by men.

> If there are social inequities between the sexes, women tend to be the "underprivileged minority group" in matters of marriage form (polygyny), sex restrictions, marital residence (moving far from home), and access to public gatherings and public office. (Stephens, 1963:305)

Stephens concludes that traditional rules having to do with power relationships tend to be made for men: deference patterns (the ritual expression of cultural expectations of an unequal power relationship) and real power (who dominates and who submits, who makes the family decisions, who commands, who obeys, and so forth, in the family) are in the majority of cases determined by men. Stephens examines some of the widespread transcultural discrimination against women. The following findings are based on his ethnographer-interview sample:

The Double Standard

In a good many societies, sex restrictions are more severe for women than they are for men. For thirteen sample societies, premarital sex restrictions bear more heavily on girls than on boys. . . . For no society is it reported that premarital sex regulations are stricter for men than for women. Likewise, I know of no society in which restrictions on adultery are more severe for men than for women. On the other hand, in eight cases, husbands are free to practice adultery, but wives are supposed to remain faithful. . . . For two other cases, adultery rules seem to be stricter for wives than for husbands.

Deference

In six societies in my ethnographic notes, a wife must kneel or crouch before her husband. . . . In six societies, the woman is reported to walk behind her husband. . . . For five cases, the husband is said to get the choice food. . . . For no society in my ethnographic notes is there any mention of husband-to-wife deference customs.

Power

In the language of politics, husbands and wives may be viewed as two separate and opposing interest groups. If a husband gains in power, his wife must lose power; if he gains in privilege, his wife loses privileges, and vice versa.

TABLE 10-1   Comparative Data on the Division of Labor by Sex

	Number of Societies in Which Activity Is Performed by				
	Men Always	Men Usually	Either Equally	Women Usually	Women Always
Metalworking	78	0	0	0	0
Weapon making	121	1	0	0	0
Pursuit of sea mammals	34	1	0	0	0
Hunting	166	13	0	0	0
Manufacture of musical instruments	45	2	0	0	1
Boat building	91	4	4	0	1
Mining and quarrying	35	1	1	0	1
Work in wood and bark	113	9	5	1	1
Work in stone	68	3	2	0	2
Trapping or catching of small animals	128	13	4	1	2
Work in bone, horn, and shell	67	4	3	0	3
Lumbering	104	4	3	1	6
Fishing	98	34	19	3	4
Manufacture of ceremonial objects	37	1	13	0	1
Herding	38	8	4	0	5
House building	86	32	25	3	14
Clearing of land for agriculture	73	22	17	5	13
Net making	44	6	4	2	11
Trade	51	28	20	8	7
Dairy operations	17	4	3	1	13
Manufacture of ornaments	24	3	40	6	18
Agriculture—soil preparation and planting	31	23	33	20	37
Manufacture of leather products	29	3	9	3	32
Body mutilation—for example, tattooing	16	14	44	22	20
Erection and dismantling of shelter	14	2	5	6	22
Hide preparation	31	2	4	4	49
Tending of fowls and small animals	21	4	8	1	39
Agriculture—crop tending and harvesting	10	15	35	39	44
Gathering of shellfish	9	4	8	7	25
Manufacture of nontextile fabrics	14	0	9	2	32
Fire making and tending	18	6	25	22	62
Burden bearing	12	6	33	20	57
Preparation of drinks and narcotics	20	1	13	8	57
Manufacture of thread and cordage	23	2	11	10	73
Basket making	25	3	10	6	82
Mat making	16	2	6	4	61
Weaving	19	2	2	6	67
Gathering of fruits, berries, and nuts	12	3	15	13	63
Fuel gathering	22	1	10	19	89
Pottery making	13	2	6	8	77
Preservation of meat and fish	8	2	10	14	74
Manufacture and repair of clothing	12	3	8	9	95
Gathering of herbs, roots, and seeds	8	1	11	7	74
Cooking	5	1	9	28	158
Water carrying	7	0	5	7	119
Grain grinding	2	4	5	13	114

Source: Adapted from George P. Murdock, 1937. "Comparative data on the division of labor by sex," Reprinted from *Social Forces,* vol. XV, May 1937 p. 552. Copyright The University of North Carolina Press. Reprinted by permission.

Marriage—seen in these terms—is a power struggle. The husband may "win" (and become a dominating patriarch) or "lose" (and be a hen-pecked husband), or they may "tie" (and have an egalitarian marital relationship). One gets the impression that men usually have an initial advantage in this struggle. It looks as if men often make the rules to suit themselves; the deference customs, the jural rights, generally point in the direction of a power advantage for the husband. (Stephens, 1963:290, 294, 302)

Many investigators have asked why there is almost a universal classification of women to secondary status. Sherry Ortner (1974:69), an anthropologist, observes that "everywhere, in every known culture, women are considered in some degree, inferior to men." She provides some answers when she observes the types of criteria particular cultures use to assign women inferior roles. The first type of data are the statements of cultural ideology that explicitly devalue women, their roles, their tasks, and their products. Second, there are the symbolic devices, such as the attribution of defilement, associated with women. Last, there is the exclusion of women from participation in or contact with areas believed to be most powerful in the particular society, whether religious or secular. We concentrate our discussion on the third element in this analysis.

An explanation on the universality of women being allotted secondary status is offered by sociologists and anthropologists who see this stemming from the relegation of women to the domestic, private domain of the household, whereas men remain in the public sphere of activities. The greater involvement of women with childbearing and child rearing leads to a differentiation of domestic and public spheres of activity. Michelle Zimbalist Rosaldo (1974:36) argues that "women's status will be lowest in those societies where there is a firm differentiation between domestic and public spheres of activity and where women are isolated from one another and placed under a single man's authority in the home."

Rosaldo believes that the time-consuming and emotionally compelling involvement of a mother with her child is unmatched by any single involvement and commitment made by a man. The result is that men are free to form broader associations in the outside world through their involvement in work, politics, and religion. The relative absence of women from this public sphere results in their lack of authority and power. Men's involvements and activities are viewed as important, and cultural systems give authority and value to men's activities and roles. In turn, women's work, especially when it is confined to domestic roles and activities, tends to be oppressive and lacking in value and status. Women are only seen to gain power and a sense of value when they are able to transcend the domestic sphere of activities. Societies that practice sex discrimination are those in which this differentiation is most acute. Those societies in which men value and participate in domestic activities tend to be more egalitarian.

Rosaldo points out that in contemporary America—although giving perfunctory lip service to the idea of sexual equality—society, nonetheless, is organized in such a way that it heightens the dichotomy between private and public, domestic and social, female and male. Further, through the restrictions of the conjugal family, women tend to be relegated to the domestic sphere. Yet, when the society places values on men's work and women's work, the tendency is to place greater value and higher priority on the public work associated with men rather than the domestic work associated with women. This is symbolized by the phrase "only a housewife." This dichotomization is encouraged by the admonitions placed on women to cease work and take almost exclusive care of small children and to sacrifice their career aspirations to those of their husbands. These normative strictures perpetuate the assignment of women to the domestic, private sphere, whereas men are almost exclusively involved in the higher valued and higher status activities of the public sphere.

Rosaldo's domestic (or private)/public model articulated more than twenty years ago became very influential in gender studies. However, over the years, various reinterpretations have been developed [cf. Sharistanian (ed.), 1987]. The criticisms stem from an overall belief that the model overgeneralized and did not accurately assess the cross-cultural and historical heterogeneity in gender relationships. The criticism fall into three categories. The first examines the domestic/public model in terms of cross-cultural diversity. The second in terms of transhistorical variation and change. The third argument is in the comparison of different classes and races within a given society.

Sharistanian (1987) citing the literature on cross-cultural diversity observes that in some societies—for example, in traditional and contemporary West Africa—many political and economic activities are intertwined with domestic ones. In these societies women have power, authority, and influence in public spheres and in effect the domestic/public dichotomy is not valid. (We will examine the West African experience in the next section of this chapter.)

Historical comparisons of women who were unmarried and childless may provide evidence on the limitations of the domestic/public dichotomy. The sexual division of labor may not indicate sexual subordination. Sharistanian (1987) argues that an investigation of women's activities based on their own perspective may negate the significance of the domestic/public dichotomy. In both the nineteenth century and into the contemporary period, many women in the West are actively involved in both the public sphere of work and in the home. These "people with two jobs" have their feet in both spheres and it would be inaccurate to depict solely in terms of domestic world involvements (Sharistanian (1987).

Finally, in terms of intrasocietal analysis, the experience of contemporary African American women who have traditionally had high labor force participation, albeit often in menial and low-paying jobs, provides further evidence on the limitation of the domestic/public model (Sharistanian, 1987).

In summary, while the domestic/public model has its limitations, it has generated a vast amount of research that has sought to investigate the factors that account for the variability in gender-role relationships and the underlying sexual stratification processes. We continue by investigating, in more depth, societal variations in which women play an active role in both the domestic and the public spheres. We begin by looking at the West African experience as part of a broader examination of agricultural societies. Then we turn our attention to the industrial societies of Russia, Sweden, and Israel. In the next chapter we shift our attention to a social historical examination of the worlds of work and the family in Western Europe and the United States.

GENDER ROLES IN MALE AND FEMALE FARMING SYSTEMS

Anthropologists distinguish between two types of agricultural systems: *shifting agriculture* and *plowing agriculture*. *Shifting agriculture* is practiced by clearing an area of trees and brush, burning them, and planting seeds. Rainfall waters the growing crops and the ripened foods are harvested. The cleared fields are used for two or three years and, when the soil becomes depleted, they are abandoned and allowed to lie fallow. The people then move on to cultivate a new area that has been cleared, and the cycle is repeated. The technology is rather simple: Digging sticks serve as the most common agricultural implement.

Plowing agriculture uses either the plow and fertilizers or irrigation works in permanently cultivating the land. Domestic animals are raised on those parts of the land that are not being cultivated. This is a more advanced technological form of agriculture and is the most widespread form of farming found throughout the world today. Shifting agriculture was found most frequently in Africa, the Pacific, and the Americas.

Ester Boserup (1970), a researcher and consultant with the United Nations and other international organizations, refers to shifting agriculture as the female farming system and plow agriculture as the male farming system. Using Africa as an illustration of a shifting agricultural culture, Boserup observes that this farming system dominated the whole of the Congo region, large parts of southeast and East Africa, and parts of West Africa. Men and young boys helped to fell trees and hoe the land in preparation for the planting of the crops. The bulk of the work with the field crops, including sowing, weeding, and harvesting, was done by women. Before European colonization and involvement, the men devoted their time to hunting and warfare.

Closely tied to the female farming system, shifting agriculture, is a widespread pattern of polygyny that is closely related to economic conditions. In such farming communities, the more wives a man has, the more land he can cultivate. This adds to his wealth and prestige. In the typical polygynous marriage arrangement, a husband has two or three wives, each residing in a separate household, cultivating her own land and feeding her own children. The economic advantage of having multiple wives leads to an increase in the status of women. This is evident in the payment of a bride-price to the prospective wife's family by the bridegroom. Women have relatively high status, enjoy considerable freedom, and have some economic independence derived from the sale of some of their own crops.

The ability to sell one's own crops is an important aspect of the female farming system. The regions in Africa where women dominate the food trade of rural and urban markets are usually those regions that are characterized by a tradition of female farming. Such agricultural products as fruits, vegetables, milk, eggs, and poultry are sold by the women. Associations of women traders are formed and wield considerable power. Boserup (1970) points out that the cultural tradition of female farming and involvement in traditional market trade accounts more for her relatively high status and placement in the modern trade sector of contemporary independent African states than does the stage of modernization achieved by any given country.

Although shifting cultivation is quite prevalent in Africa, it is not exclusively found there. It also occurs in Latin American communities and in regions of India and

Laos. Here, too, agricultural work is solely within the province of women. The lazy-man label applied to African males by Europeans is also applied to the males of shifting agricultural communities by both Europeans and by the people of the plowing agricultural communities (Boserup, 1970).

> Thus, the Vietnamese find that the Laotians, with shifting cultivation and female farming, are lazy farmers, and the Indians have a similar opinion of the tribes of Manipur (in northeast India) which likewise practice shifting cultivation and female farming. They are said to take it for granted that women should work and it is quite usual to hear that men wile away their time doing nothing very much. (Boserup, 1970:24)

The value judgment implied in such lazy-men labels reflects an ethnocentric bias by those who do not believe or practice this form of agricultural system. The gender role allocations reflect not a lazy attitude but, rather, a distinctive form of economic enterprise.

According to Boserup, in regions that practice plow agriculture, the division of labor between the sexes is quite different than that in shifting agricultural societies. The agricultural labor force is primarily composed of men, with women being almost completely excluded from field work. Most of the techniques associated with plow agriculture, for example, sowing the land by using draft animals, are done by the men. Women are confined to domestic duties and the care of some of the animals. It is for this reason that Boserup labels plow agriculture as the male farming system (1970:16).

Associated with the male farming system is the low status and treatment of women. Whereas in female farming systems men pay a bride-price to the prospective wife's family, in societies where plow culture predominates, a dowry is usually paid by the girl's family. With the lessened economic importance of women, there is a concomitantly lower number of polygynous marriages. Where polygyny does occur in plowing cultures, particularly in Asia, it is not closely related to economic conditions associated with agriculture. A further factor contributing to the low status of women is their almost complete economic dependence on their husbands.

Huber and Spitze (1988) observe that polygyny takes two different forms in shifting and plowing cultures. The polygamous system of marriage in shifting agriculture is called *populist polygyny*; in plowing cultures it is called *elite polygyny*. In populist polygyny nearly everyone marries. The sex ratio problem is solved by women marrying at a young age and men marrying at an older age. The need for women's productive farm work ensures that they have a measure of freedom and control over their own affairs. In the elite polygynous system only those men who have access to a large food supply has more than one wife. In contrast to the wives in the shifting agricultural systems of sub-Saharan Africa, the wives of elite polygynists tend to be secluded, as in the Arabic Middle-East, and are only free to interact with other wives and children.

Women's low status in plowing cultures may be seen as a result of their low economic value. In contrast to a shifting cultivation system where women have high status and economic value, in a plowing cultivation system, women's primary status is in their reproductive role particularly giving birth to sons, who are considered to be more valuable than daughters.

The low economic value of women is attributed to the fact that female births are not welcome. In some extreme cases, China and India being prime illustrations, female infanticide was practiced. In northern Indian communities where women did little work in agriculture, parents bemoaned the birth of daughters, who were considered economic burdens and would eventually cost their parents a dowry. It therefore became customary to limit the number of surviving daughters through infanticide. Although this practice has virtually disappeared, vestiges of it still remain in a more subtle form: Boys are treated better than girls in matters of nutrition, clothing, and medical care. The result is a much higher mortality rate for female children than for male children. Thus, although female infanticide is no longer prevalent, the neglect of female children continues. An Indian social scientist in a district in central India that had a deficit of women explains why this is:

> The Rajputs always preferred male children.... Female infanticide, therefore, was a tolerated practise.... Although in the past 80 years the proportion of the females to males has steadily risen, yet there was always a shortage of women in the region.... When interrogated about the possibility of existence of female infanticide, the villagers emphatically deny its existence.... It was admitted on all hands that if a female child fell ill, then the care taken was very cursory and if she died there was little sorrow. In fact, in a nearby village a cultivator had twelve children—six sons and six daughters. All the daughters fell ill from time to time and died. The sons also fell ill but they survived. The villagers know that it was by omissions that these children had died. Perhaps there has been a transition from violence to nonviolence in keeping with the spirit of the times. (K.S. Bhatnagar cited in Boserup, 1970:49).

Not only were women barred from field work in plow agriculture, they were also barred from public life. The loss of economic function was replaced by a rise in the sexual value of women. Most ironically, the increased value placed on women's sexuality was interpreted by the belief in the necessity of controlling it. This was done in a variety of ways: from secluding women, to mutilating their bodies, and to killing them. Taking the worse first, in Indian plow culture, *suttee*, the burning to death of a wife on the husband's funeral pyre was a common practice before its legal banning in the nineteenth century. In China, footbinding was a common practice for constraining women. And, in Muslim societies various forms of genital mutilation have been practiced.

In the prevailing practice of Chinese footbinding, young girls between the ages of 5 and 7 had their feet bound. This practice, which was introduced into China in the tenth century, continued well into the 1940s, although it was officially banned in 1911. Ostensibly the bound foot was romanticized as a mark of femininity and beauty; in actuality it became a symbol of the subordinate role of women in China. An old Chinese proverb states its essential purpose: "Feet are bound, not to make them beautiful as a curved bow, but to restrain women when they go out of doors" (Curtin, 1975:10). The binding process, which was excruciatingly painful, required the flexing and pressing of four toes over the sole of the foot. The feet were then bound in bandages, and the girl was forced to walk in shoes that became progressively smaller until, after a two- or three-year period, the feet were reduced to three or four inches in length from heel to toe.

Clitoridectomy occurs in Muslim countries of mixed plow and herding cultures (Huber, 1993). Clitoridectomy—the removal of the clitoris—can be seen as a means of reducing women's sexual desires, and thereby ensuring premarital chastity and conjugal fidelity (Bryden and Chant, 1989). It has also been viewed as a procedure used to control the lives of women and is part of an all-pervasive male sexual violence against women that is an undercurrent of family life (Levinson, 1989). Levinson cites *The Hosken Report; Genital and Sexual Mutilation of Females* (Hosken, 1982). The report details the effects that this and other forms of genital mutilation has had on millions of women "that include death resulting from the operation, lifelong health problems, such as urinary infections and childbirth complications, and the emotional trauma caused by an inability to reach orgasm, painful intercourse, and chronic menstrual pain (Levinson, 1989:77-78).

The barring of women from public life, at the same time increasing their sexual value, often resulted in a practice of guarding women. This was evident in the physical isolation of women from the outside world and their virtual segregation in the household. In Muslim societies the wearing of the veil symbolized this segregation; in northern India, Hindus adopted the Muslim practice of female isolation. Their custom *purdah*, which literally means a curtain, segregated women from all outside contact. Women were locked up out of sight in the *zenana*, or women's private quarters of the household.

> Women were shut away in crowded, airless and isolated rooms at the back of the house, or screened in by shuttered divides through which only faint glimpses could be obtained of the life outside. These rooms were usually overcrowded, poorly lit and ventilated—the barest and ugliest in the whole house. Under such crowded conditions, shut away from all cultural life, with no stimulation from outside, how could women preserve a sense of beauty? It grew to be an envied boast for a Hindu woman to be able to assert that not even the eye of the sun had ever beheld her face. (Freida Hauswirth, cited in Mace and Mace, 1960:68).

David and Vera Mace (1960) report that estimates place the number of women in *purdah* at the close of the eighteenth century at 40 million. As late as 1930, the number of women restricted to their households was estimated at between 11 and 17 million.

The phenomenon of the seclusion of women from the outside world and the restriction of their appearance in public is associated with plow cultivation and is virtually unknown in regions of shifting cultivation where women are involved in agricultural work (Boserup, 1970:25-27). To illustrate, the seclusion of women was more prevalent among rich families than poor families in northern India. The reason was that poor women were involved in agricultural work and this economic necessity helped to break the custom. Similarly, in Pakistan, a Muslim society, the wearing of the *burqa*, or veil, was and is a more common sight in Pakistani cities than in villages. The *burqa* envelops women from head to foot in a cloaklike garment. It even covers the face, leaving only holes or an open mesh through which the women can see. However, in the villages, where 85 percent of the people live, women do not wear the *burqa* or observe *purdah*. The reason for this is that they have to work in the fields. The *burqa* would be too restricting and *purdah* would be economically unfeasible (Aziz-Ahmed, 1967:48).

In general, then, the movement from shifting agriculture to plow agriculture is accompanied by a rigid gender-role differentiation, with women becoming more isolated and confined to the domestic sphere and more dependent on the male. In shifting cultivation, where women are involved in economic production, they are highly valued as both workers and mothers. In plow cultivation, where women take little part in field work, they are valued less and their value tends to be restricted to their reproductive role of bearing sons.

GENDER ROLES, THE FAMILY, AND AFRICAN MODERNIZATION

The coming of the European colonizers to Africa initially benefited women in societies that were based on shifting agriculture. The foreign powers ended intertribal warfare and built roads. This gave women greater geographical mobility and increased their trading profit. Missionaries and colonial government policies alleviated some of the harsher treatment of women—they suppressed the slave trade, reduced the husbands' power of life and death over their wives, and rescued women who were abandoned after giving birth to accursed twins (Van Allen, 1974:61).

As time passed, however, the colonial imposition had detrimental impact on women. Foreign powers did not recognize or approve of the practice of women being primarily responsible for the cultivation of crops. Europeans had little sympathy with the role allocations of shifting agriculture. They came from plow cultivation societies where men were primarily responsible for agricultural cultivation. They viewed men in shifting agricultural societies as lazy and, with the decline in the importance of tree felling and hunting and the prevention of intertribal warfare, there was little work remaining for the men to do. A self-fulfilling prophecy thus operated—men are lazy because they do not do anything, and they do not do anything because the Europeans were instrumental in the decline of the male-role tasks.

A dramatic change in the relative status of men and women occurred through the colonial imposition of modern agricultural techniques. Europeans saw a need to introduce modern commercial agriculture and its accompanying technology. The crops produced were designed for export to European markets. The Europeans were ethnocentrically biased against women's involvement in agricultural work. They believed that cultivation was a job for men and that men could be better farmers than women. This bias led the colonial male technical experts to train only men in the new farming techniques. Female cultivators were neglected and ignored.

As a result of these practices, the women were at a distinct disadvantage. Whereas men were cultivating crops by applying modern methods and equipment, the women were confined to using the traditional methods of cultivation—hoes and digging sticks. The inevitable result was that cash crops became a completely male enterprise. The men were able to expand their production; women who produced the food crops for the family had no cash income for improving their farming techniques. The result was an inevitable decline in the status of women and the enhancement of the status of men. Men were involved with modern technology; women with traditional drudgery. "In short, by their discriminatory policy in education and training the Europeans created a productivity gap between male and female farmers, and subsequently this gap seemed to justify their prejudice against female farmers" (Boserup, 1970:57).

Further, the European policy of recruiting men to voluntary or forced work in road building, mining, and other heavy construction was detrimental to women as well as men. The migration of husbands and sons to cities or plantations or mines increased the agricultural workload of women. Their independence was not increased. Men still retained the rights to land, to cattle, and to the sale of the cash crops that women cultivated. Women were responsible for cultivating their own land and that of their husbands without any personal benefit.

These practices continue in independent African states, like Kenya and Zambia, where Europeans control mining companies and plantations. Judith Van Allen (1974: 61) reports that wages to migrant laborers are set too low to support a whole family. The husband, then, treats his wages as his alone and does not, and cannot, spend them for housing and food for his family. Where provisions are made for nearby housing of workers' families, farm plots are provided so that women produce food for the family. In both situations, then, women are primarily responsible for the feeding and housing of their families. The economic pattern is one of exploitation. Wages are kept at a minimum and women's farming subsidizes both the mining company and plantation wages. The companies, in their turn, make exorbitant profits.

Western legal systems that have been imported to the countries of southern Africa have often worked against women. Alice Armstrong (1994) has been involved in a project looking at the relationship between law and women's family involvements. She observes that the legal definition of the family and the concept of marriage is problematic as a consequence of contradictions between official and customary law. In customary law all property belongs to the husband's extended family. Thus, when a man dies, all property passes on to his male children or to his brothers; his wife is not entitled to any inheritance. Land ownership is also held exclusively by men but not women. Men, therefore, are free to leave the land and work elsewhere, knowing that it is in their possession. However, women's rights to land depends on their use of it. Women are deprived, then, of the greater economic opportunities that nonagricultural subsistence work provides. In addition to these advantages, men have greater access to educational opportunities which they can use in urban areas.

The high incidence of male migration away from the rural areas often means that there is little family life in the form of common household or pooled financial resources that is presumed in the Western legal system. As a consequence, women often found themselves with little maintenance resources for themselves and for their children. The maintenance laws that do exist are not enforced. Maintenance laws are

BOX 10-1   The Global Family

African "Market Mommies"

Michelle Singletary

WASHINGTON POST

ACCRA, Ghana—In the West African countries of Togo and Benin she is popularly called "Nana Benz," a name coined because of the kind of car she drives. In Ghana she is called a "market mommy."

Whichever term is used, such women are a part of a growing class of African entrepreneurs who are staging their own economic emancipation.

Diana Amekudi, 35, is one such businesswoman. Amekudi employs several woodcarvers in Accra to make fertility masks, statues and other hand-carved sculptures that she then sells to an African art dealer in Chicago. She imports, exports, and runs several other small businesses. Amekudi calls her company Flyover Limited G.H. because she will fly over any West Africa country to find a product for a customer.

"In Ghana, we have a saying: 'Little drops of water can make a mighty ocean,'" Amekudi said, explaining the economic potential of African women.

Afie Agbenyega, 32, employs 12 workers who produce tailor-made traditional African clothing that she designs. She exports some dresses to the United States and this year won the title of best designer in Ghana and a free trip to Paris.

"It's like an awakening," Agbenyega said. "There are so many social problems in Africa. There isn't enough money, and so many men are out of work. The African woman is tired of living in poverty."

Across sub-Saharan Africa—from Angola to Gambia to Zambia—black businesswomen are creating national trade associations and encouraging one another to become better trained so they can move from operating small-scale businesses to running taxpaying, large-scale business ventures. Women business leaders implore fellow female entrepreneurs to incorporate their businesses to gain better leverage to change the social, economic and cultural obstacles that prevent their growth.

These women dominate the informal business sector. In the local marketplaces, they hawk vegetables and fruit grown on plots of land that village chiefs allow them to cultivate. They make and sell tie-dyed cloth and batiks.

Hours after sunset here in Ghana's capital city, they sew by candlelight in small shacks the size of telephone booths set up on sidewalks.

"It's women who predominately keep the African economy going, and there is no argument about that," said Aba Amissah Quainoo, a manager of a savings and loan program operated by Women's World Banking in Ghana. The program is designed to help women obtain small loans and save some of their income.

In these countries, where many women are married off by the time they are 15, generally don't own any land and are largely illiterate, their dominance in dozens of cottage industries testifies to their business acumen, Quainoo said.

In the agriculture industry—the mainstay of most African economies—women account for about 75 percent of the total labor expended and produce more than 60 percent of food consumed in Africa, according to estimates from the World Bank, the United Nations Development Program and a recent report on women in Africa by Rita Byrnes, a research analyst for the State Department's Office of Research and Analysis for Africa.

Quainoo and other experts say it is hard to determine how much money circulates among the women, but most agree that they are turning over millions of dollars by trading everything from avocados to wood carvings.

However, if the women are to become an economic force in the next century, they must be incorporated into the formal economy, according to Lucia Quachey, president of the Ghana Association of Women Entrepreneurs (GAWE). The association is affiliated with the Federation of African Women Entrepreneurs, formed four years ago to foster cooperation among women business owners in sub-Saharan Africa.

Quachey said her organization seeks to help more businesswomen become legitimate by encouraging them to register their businesses and by getting them to pay corporate income taxes.

By joining the formal economy, the women's contribution to the gross national product will be officially recognized, and formal credit channels could open up to them, Quachey said. Most important, African women can begin to influence governmental policies, she said.

Quachey said she started her own dressmaking business in 1969 after high school because she wanted economic independence. At its peak, Lucia Manufacturing Industry Ltd. employed 40 people and had revenues of about $3 million a year. However, since the devaluation of Ghana's currency, the cedi, Quachey said, business has fallen and she now employs about eight workers.

I didn't realize I didn't have the resources to meet such changes in the economy," said Quachey, who now operates her dress shop out of her home.

Although more women are running their own enterprises, they still face tremendous obstacles.

In African countries such as Benin, Burundi, Chad, Mozambique and Nambia, the constitutional prohibition against gender discrimination is ignored, according to Byrnes' report.

Although Ghana has passed a succession law that calls for a more equal distribution of a husband's assets, many women are reluctant to challenge the traditional inheritance system in which assets are passed to males in the family, Quainoo said. In the end it means most women don't have a chance to own land, which could be used to obtain bank financing.

Women also are hindered by a lack of formal education. In an economy where the average person earns about $400 a year, families often decide they cannot afford to send their girls to school. Although education is supposed to be free, there are fees for uniforms and books that families often cannot afford. If there is extra money, boys attend school first. More than two-thirds of all illiterate adults in Africa are women.

But despite the barriers, market mommies can still be savvy saleswomen and entrepreneurs, experts agree. "These women have a lot of potential, and it's just a matter of tapping into it," Quainoo said.

Washington Post, 10 October 1994.
© 1994, Washington Post Writers Group.
Reprinted with permission.

---

important in reinforcing a man's responsibility in the domestic sphere. When a man is not involved in the family, the woman is prevented from being involved in the public sphere. Maintenance laws are also important in assuring that women will not have to personally plead with their husbands for support, but that they are legally entitled to that support. Armstrong concludes that enforced maintenance laws would "when combined with other strategies such as increasing women's education and employment opportunities and improving their legal status in other areas of the law, will improve women's position in society, and in that way contribute to the development of the counties of southern Africa" (1994:60).

In summary, the problems associated with the implementation of Western legal systems and the loss of women's rights and status can be seen as a result of agricultural land-reform policies of colonial European administrations. The Europeans were against the involvement of women in agricultural work, which they viewed as antithetical to the proper roles of men and women. This discriminatory policy continues in independent African states that are dependent on foreign aid and investment. The result is that for women in Africa, "modernization means more dependency" (Van Allen, 1974:60).

Living under Apartheid and Its Aftermath

The word apartheid was coined as an election promise by the powerful Nationalist party of South Africa in 1948 and literally means "separatehood." It was a segregationist policy designed to restrict and enforce strictly the control by the state over blacks in their movement to urban areas and in their employment and residential opportunities. Anchoring the policy was the creation of ten quasi-independent "homelands" (or *Bantustans*), based on the former tribal reserves. The establishment of the homelands also enabled the white government to legally force blacks out of designated white areas into resettlement camps or other inferior living arrangements. Between 1960 and 1980, an estimated 1.75 million blacks were relocated in the homelands from just the "white" rural areas (Browett, 1982). The policy of the white government was to grant "independence" to these homelands and create "national states." This has occurred in the Transkei (1976), Bophuthatswana (1977), Venda (1979), and Ciskei (1981).

The homelands enabled the white ruling government to use the blacks as a cheap and disenfranchised labor force. Three kinds of laborers were represented in the black population (Smith, 1982). The first and most numerous were workers who permanently and legally resided in "white" South Africa. They resided in townships attached to the "white" cities. The second were the migrant laborers who contracted to work for extended periods of time in white-run businesses, factories, mines, and agricultural farms. They returned to the homeland to visit their families for short spells.

The third form of migrant labor was what had been called "frontier commuters" (Smith, 1982). These were people who lived with their families in the homelands and traveled on a daily basis across what apartheid ideology depicted as national borders into "white" South Africa. These townships were just within the homelands in areas adjacent to the "white" urban areas. They experienced extremely rapid growth and had taken on the character of squatter settlements. Within the township itself, there was little economic opportunity. That was only available in the "white" urban areas, and, even here, it could not handle the burgeoning township population.

The extended family was used to produce cheap labor. The male worker on his annual return to the homeland for short spells between work contracts provided the minimum amount of family continuity that was required for his involvement in taking care of the very young and very old, the sick, and the education of the young. During the rest of the year, the wife and other members of the extended family were expected to take care of the everyday needs of family members. Apartheid used the extended family in terms of a "social security" function (Smith, 1982). The apartheid homeland policy transformed the traditional family system from its precapitalist mode of production to a reproduction system and used it to control a cheap African industrial labor force. In effect, the poor, rural, black homelands subsidized the white, urban, industrial, economically advanced areas.

The wages paid to the migrant laborers did not meet the needs for family support (Lemon, 1982). Joseph Lelyveld (1986), in his Pulitzer Prize-winning book, *Move Your Shadow: South Africa, Black and White*, observed how the legalization of apartheid laws affected the more than 800,000 black migrant workers. The law psychologically pressured black family members to succumb to a feeling of resignation that their lot in life was to be separated and fragmented. He speaks of the impact of apartheid as being measured not in dollars and cents but in "dead souls."

Black men were given jobs in white areas, including the major cities. They also worked as migrant laborers in the mines or on sugar plantations, many for extended periods of time. Their wives and children, however, had to live in the designated black homelands. The law was designed to prevent black families from living together. Housing accommodations for the black men were in single-sex, prison-like hostels (Browett, 1982). For those increasingly smaller number of blacks who had chosen to continue living together, illegal life was very hard.

One such "illegal" described by Lelyveld had lived in Cape Town for twenty years, where he, his wife, and their six children had moved from one squatter camp to another in their constant attempt to escape the authorities. They slept in a church hall that was used as a nursery school during the day. His original home was in Transkei, a black homeland. Since then, like himself, his extended family had dispersed all over South Africa. He found himself with no land, no extended family, and no place to go back to. He commented: "My heart is not feeling nicely. I'm the same like dead. I think of these things, the government and all, and sometimes I cry" (quoted in Lelyveld, 1986:109).

In the 1990s, bowing to worldwide condemnation and being treated as a pariah nation, the apartheid system gradually was abolished. In April 1994 democratic elections were held and Nelson Mandela became president of the first black-majority government. Change has been slow and continuous but lags behind expectations (Keller, 1995). The South African Institute of Race Relations warns that progress will be impeded because the impoverished black majority lacks the resources, money, and education to get ahead (Matloff, 1995).

A year after the elections, the African National Congress had begun making changes that supporters praised and critics felt were insufficient (Keller, 1995). A relatively stable peace has been secured, the economy is growing, and there is a concerted effort for changing race relations and in transforming the institutions of the former all-white controlled society. Critics complain that only a very small number of houses have been built to overcome the acute housing shortages. Squatter settlements are continuing to grow outside the major South African cities. It has been estimated that as many as 10 million blacks have no formal shelter (Keller, 1993). These homeless people are the remnants of the millions who were forcibly removed from their homes during the apartheid years and dumped into poor rural areas and are now seeking to return to areas where there is greater potential for economic advancement. For example, in the suburbs of the city of Durban, squatters have built shacks right next to modern apartment buildings (Lewis, 1995).

Another problem is the transition that is occurring in the struggle to redistribute land that black tenant farmers have farmed for generations. Eighty percent of the farmland is in the hands of just 60,000 white farmers; a result of the seventy years of racist policies. Prior to the end of apartheid, 1 million black tenant farmers were evicted and forcibly removed to the overcrowded black homelands. With the installation of the Mandela government, 30 percent of the white farmland was earmarked for redistribution. White farmers, as a defensive maneuver, have forcibly evicted thousands of tenant farmers in anticipation of the time when Parliament passes a redistribution bill (Daley, 1995).

These black tenant farmers have suffered severe poverty under the apartheid policies. They lived in hovels without electricity or running water. These conditions have persisted. Their workday is from 6 A.M. to 6 P.M. seven days a week with a few hours off on Sundays. They do not work for a cash wage; they are provided just one meal a day. The proposed legislation would allow tenant farmers the right to buy land whether or not a farmer wants to sell. The aim of the white farmers, therefore, is to remove these tenant farmers from their ancestral homes and thus reduce their claim to the land. Protest marches and boycotts have occurred but have not changed matters. Both blacks and whites have been slain in this somewhat brutal transition period.

Throughout South Africa, the black population still finds education lacking. Apartheid deliberately degraded education for blacks so that they would only be able to serve in menial jobs in the white-supremist system. Now, as new economic opportunities are developing, the country finds itself in need of a large education-trained workforce. Instead, they have a large poorly trained workforce not able to handle the high-level skill jobs needed. The result is that the black joblessness rate—41 percent—has not measurably improved. Adding to these economic problems are political ones. Tensions still exist among the white minority and the black political minority. Further, those ethnic leaders who held power in the former black homelands have been reluctant to relinquish it. So tension has developed between the Government of National Unity and regional governments that often reflect latent ethnic hostilities.

Yet, there is a sense of optimism in the air and only time will tell on how this emerging country will meet the needs of its citizens and its families. Caspar W. Weinberger, an influential conservative member of the Reagan administration, spoke of the sense of the possible in South Africa: "South Africa is embarked on the most invigorating, hopeful voyage any country has attempted since the American Revolution—and we all have a moral obligation to help it succeed" (cited in Lewis, 1995).

GENDER ROLES IN INDUSTRIAL SOCIETIES: RUSSIA

It is beyond the scope of this book to document fully the entire range of social historical changes in male-female relationships that have accompanied the advent of the Industrial Revolution over the last 200 years. But certain changes have been especially significant in how they affected gender-role relationships. The demographic revolution, the changing nature of economic life, and the changing ideology pertaining to gender-role and family relationships are important factors.

The demographic revolution includes the lengthened life span and the lowered mortality rate of mothers and infants during childbirth. Before industrialization, women were defined primarily in terms of their reproductive and maternal roles. The scientific advances in medicine that accompanied industrialization had a qualitative effect on the conceptualization of women. No longer need they be defined solely in terms of their maternal role. Their life span has increased to the extent that they no longer devote their longest phase of life to maternity. They are now free to pursue additional roles, both in the family and outside it in the economy.

Industrialization has also been a factor in changing gender roles. Children are no longer the economic necessity that they are in nonindustrial agricultural or hunting-and-gathering societies. They are an economic burden, since they are unable to participate in the economic sphere until they complete a long period of training. This has resulted in the loss of the importance of women's reproductive role as the entire rationale for their existence. Also, the economic value of the housewife has declined; her economic contribution no longer justifies the housewife role. The increased use of labor-saving and relatively inexpensive prepared-food items has made the housewife a consumer rather than an earner through her production in the home. The result is that for women who wish to contribute to the economic well-being of their families, it is more efficient to do so by becoming wage earners than by staying housewives.

In addition, the increased economic demand for labor in industrial societies increases the involvement of women in the economy. Women particularly have found a place in the tertiary sector (office work and service jobs) of the Western industrial economy; they hold jobs in occupations that are clearly related to traditional female gender-role activities and personality traits. There is an overwhelming concentration of women in canning and clothing factories, teaching, nursing, social work, and dietetics, and at occupational levels that require little or no organizational leadership or organizational characteristics. As we will see, the pattern is somewhat different in the former Soviet Union and Eastern Europe.

The third element, the changing ideology pertaining to gender-roles and family relationships, intersects with the other two factors in influencing the changes in the relationship between men and women. The lessened economic importance of children as producers has fostered a shift in values regarding children. Children are socialized in a more permissive manner than when they were of high economic value. The increased life span of the husband and wife has also allowed for the development of a more romantic love ideology, the development of a companionate notion of marriage, and the seeking of erotic gratification within the marital relationship. This has been concomitant with the increase in the number of years that the husband and wife can spend with each other in activities other than childbearing and child rearing.

Given this cursory overview, let us turn our attention to the examination of the relationship of men and women within the economy and the family in industrial nations. The discussion of the demographic revolution and its impact on parent-child relationships is a theme discussed more fully in later chapters. To put the examination of occupations into perspective, we review recent developments in Russia and contrast them with those in the United States, Sweden, and Israel. These industrial societies, which are based on varying ideological perspectives, have differentially involved men and women in the economy. Yet, there are basic similarities underlying all of them.

For those old enough to remember the Cold War that began shortly after World War II, the collapse of the Soviet Union in 1989 was an unbelievable occurrence. For nearly forty-five years, the colossus that was the Union of Soviet Socialist Republics was as Winston Churchill described it "a riddle wrapped in a mystery inside an enigma." In this section we will focus on the history of gender roles and the family in what was the Soviet Union, what occurred just before and after *perestroika* (reconstruction of society and economy) and *glasnost* (openness, candor) and what the future now holds for the family in Russia.

The traumatic birth of the Soviet Union in the Russian Revolution of 1917 ushered in a communist society that was designed to implement the economic, political, and social policies of Marxism. An integral part of Marxist ideology was a stated belief to bring women into positions of equality in the economy. The Soviet Union from 1917 to 1989 was in many ways ahead of Western industrial societies in this endeavor. But, at the same time, it experienced major setbacks and problems that ultimately played a significant role in undermining the confidence of the people in the Communist government. The experience of the Soviet Union and now Russia can provide guidelines for Western societies in their attempts to bring women into full participation in the occupational world. Two major elements, ideological and economic considerations, have been the historical forces behind this movement. Let us examine each in turn.

Ideology was a prime factor influencing the relationship between the sexes in the Soviet Union. The Marxists, and particularly Friedrich Engels in his *The Origin of the Family, Private Property, and the State* (originally published in 1884), saw monogamy as a tool of economic capitalism. The division of labor between men and women in the monogamous household, according to this argument, has as its effect the subjugation of women and children to the capitalistic patriarchal system. The division of labor between the sexes is viewed as the prototype of the class struggle between the men who own the means of production and those who toil in their behalf. Engels conjectured that the socialist revolution would dissolve the monogamous family system. Women would be able to achieve equality by entering the economic system and there would be created public household services and public centers for the socialization of children.

> At all events, the position of the men thus undergoes considerable change. But that of the women, of all women, also undergoes important alteration. With the passage of the means of production into common property, the individual family ceases to be the economic unit of society. Private housekeeping is transformed into a social matter. (Engels, 1884/1972:83)

The Marxists believe that the housewife role is alienating. Work and social interactions outside the household are necessary to realize one's full potential. Housewives who are cut off from such outside contacts are cut off from the creative source and thus can never realize their full capabilities. Ultimately, the family and the society are the losers by this underutilization of women. This philosophy serves as the foundation for the policies of the Soviet Union after the Russian Revolution of 1917. Lenin, echoing Marx and Engels, saw the necessity of removing women from the "slavery" of the household to full participation in the socialist economy:

> You all know that even when women have full rights, they still remain downtrodden because all housework is left to them. In most cases, housework is the most unproductive, the most savage and the most arduous work a woman can do. It is exceptionally petty and does not include anything that would in any way promote the development of the woman. . . . To effect her complete emancipation and make her the equal of the man it is necessary for house-

work to be socialised and for women to participate in common productive labour. Then women will occupy the same position as men. (Lenin, 1919/1966:69)

Following the Russian Revolution, legislation was passed that aimed to achieve the liberation of women from the household and their equality in all spheres of life. Laws regulating family relationships and questions concerning divorce and abortion were designed to aid in this task. Marriage and divorce regulations were simplified. Abortions were legalized in 1920. The goal was to bring women into full participation in the social economy and into government. The means to accomplish this were seen in the transfer of economic and educational functions from separate households to the society as a whole. Barriers to educational institutions were removed for women. Communal household services, kitchens, dining halls, laundries, and repair shops were established. Infant-care centers, kindergartens, and educational institutions for older children were expanded.

However, economic considerations and demographic realities caused vicissitudes in Soviet family law and the implementation of many programs. Throughout Soviet history women have constituted a majority of the population. The Soviet Union had over 25 million war deaths in World War II. These were mostly men. This was in addition to the massive losses in World War I, the revolutionary civil war, the famine and epidemics of the 1920s, the industrialization drive, the forced collectivization of agriculture, and the purges of the 1930s—all brought about a most uneven sex ratio. For the post-World War II population, this difference was at its highest in the marriage-age groups because so many men died during the war. In human terms, the loneliness of Soviet women is reflected in the poem by Vladimir Semenov addressed to a Soviet girl:

You tried to find him everywhere
He must exist
He is someplace.
You asked:
Where is he? Where?
There was no answer.
Your youth is gone.
You paled and withered.
You, whose beauty shone once,
You do not know the verity
That a wife to no one
You long since are
A widow . . .
You do not know that he was killed
in War
Before you met him.

(Semenov, 1959, cited in Field and Flynn, 1970:261)

In addition, then, to the ideological factors, the severe shortage of men in the Soviet Union necessitated women's involvement in the economy. This involvement was not as in Western societies where women constitute a reserve labor force, but rather women were integrated into and indispensable to the Soviet labor force. Although the labor shortage encouraged the employment of women, it also required an emphasis on childbearing to replace the decimated population. The stress placed on childbearing modified the application of the Marxist ideology.

In 1936, abortions were once again made illegal, except in exceptional medical circumstances. Divorces were made more difficult and costly. Unregistered marriages lost their validity and equality with registered marriages. In 1944, a decree was passed encouraging large families by establishing the honorific title, heroine mothers. These were women who had more than five children. They received special economic rewards and honors.

At the onset of these changes, child-care facilities proved inadequate. Eventually, they were expanded, particularly in industries that employed a large percentage of married mothers. Since 1953, the end of the Stalinist era, there was a return to a more ideological implementation of the Marxist principles regarding male and female relationships. But the general pattern through Soviet history has been one of vacillation in ideological implementation, which has depended on the needs of the Soviet economy.

This discussion gives us some overview of the history of the factors that have influenced the involvement of Soviet women in the labor force. The labor history of women during the nearly half century that elapsed after World War II found women heavily concentrated in certain types of economic activities and significantly underrepresented in others (Lapidus, 1982). In the service sector, public health, social welfare, education, and culture, women account for three-fourths or more of the labor force. Only one-fourth of the labor force is female in construction and transportation. In industry, where women represent almost half of all production personnel, they constitute over 80 percent of food and textile workers and over 90 percent of garment workers.

Women were underrepresented in occupations that entail directive, managerial, and executive functions (Lapidus, 1982). They also tended to be overrepresented in subordinate and minor positions, as well as in menial jobs. Occupationally, women predominated in the lower and middle levels of white-collar employment and the paraprofessions. Virtually all nurses, technicians, librarians, typists, and stenographers were female. Yet, women were underrepresented in supervisory and managerial positions. There was also much disparity in male and female earnings, with women frequently making less money for doing the same work as men (Mamonova, 1984).

Explanations on why women do not fare as well in the labor force focus on social factors and not biological constraints as the most salient factors. Soviet social scientists are recognizing the fact that differential educational opportunities and family responsibilities work against women. Lapidus observes how all these social factors create a "vicious circle" that severely retards and restricts women's economic equality and advancement:

> . . . women have lower expectations of occupational mobility than their male counterparts; they gravitate toward jobs which are most compatible with their domestic responsibilities; they have less time available for study and are

not able to improve their qualifications as rapidly as men; they tend to become stuck in less rewarding and stimulating jobs with few incentives or opportunities for upward mobility; and they are viewed by enterprise managers as less promising and productive, which reduces their leverage and opportunity still further. (Lapidus, 1982:xxv)

However, if we compare the Soviet figures for professions—including law, engineering, and medicine—with those of Western countries, one is astonished by the greater proportional participation of Soviet women (Mamonova, 1984). This was particularly true in the 1960s when the women's movement was first beginning in the West and when there were virtually very few Western women in the medical, legal, and engineering professions. For example, in the Soviet Union there were more women surgeons, specialists, and hospital directors than in all the Western countries put together (Sullerot, 1971). Similarly, more than a third of the lawyers and engineers were women in the Soviet Union; in contrast only 3 percent of the lawyers in the United States were women and less than 1 percent were engineers.

Despite the great progress that women made in the Soviet Union, there still remained problems in the achievement of complete equality. As mentioned previously, a greater proportion of women were found in subordinate positions and menial labor. They also tended to be discriminated against in jobs that demand directive, managerial, and executive skills. Women did not reach the upper echelons of responsibility in occupational institutions, the professions, or in government politics. They were overrepresented in the lower ranks where the prestige and pay were less. To illustrate, although over 80 percent of school teachers were women, nearly two-thirds of the principals were men. Similarly, in the medical profession, which is 77 percent composed of women, the heads of hospitals and other medical facilities are usually men. It was men who were in charge of formulating all national health policy (Gray, 1989).

Thus, although the Soviet Union had advocated a public policy designed to stimulate women's involvement in the economy, and although it had pioneered in the development of maternal and child-care services, it still did not have full equality of women in the work sphere. There are a number of reasons to explain why this situation existed. Examination of these reasons may prove instructive to Western countries in their attempts to develop policies and procedures. They include the aforementioned economic problems that constantly beset the government. These often resulted in inadequate day care, education, housing, and consumer goods and services.

A major contributory factor was the continuation of patriarchal attitudes from the pre-Soviet period. Traditionally, the people of the Soviet Union shared the patriarchal ideology that has characterized Western countries. Even at the end of the Soviet era, despite the introduction of Marxist egalitarian principles over seventy years earlier, patriarchy still flourished. The remarkable achievements of women in the Soviet economy came despite the fact that many men and women shared patriarchal assumptions of women's intellectual inferiority and emotional frailty.

This attitude was most representative in the women's dual role, which demands that they continue to keep a home (without expecting much help from their husbands) at the same time that they hold down a full-time job. The result was that women worked longer hours than their husbands; in addition to their full-time jobs, they put in an additional five to six hours a day in household activities. Their task was complicated by the fact that there are few labor-saving devices available, little domestic help, and few conveniences, such as supermarkets and prepackaged food. A common word heard among women was *peregruzhennost* ("overburdening") (Gray, 1989:33). Gray (1989) illustrated this by examining a typical day of household work that is in addition to the full day of occupational work for a Russian women as depicted in Natalya Baranskaya's novella, *Nedelya Kak Nedelya* ("A Week Like Any Other"):

> Olga's mornings are a typical nightmare. The children are two and four, her husband helps but grudgingly to get them washed, fed, dressed in the many layers needed in a Moscow winter . . . In the evenings, if there has been a late meeting at the lab, Olga runs back toward the subway and bus stops, flies across empty lots, runs up the stairs to find her hungry children ruining their appetites by munching bread while her husband remains buried in technical journals. After dinner, while he continues reading, Olga does the dishes, washes and mends her children's and husband's laundry, prepares their clothes for the morning, sweeps the kitchen. In constant terror of the 6 A.M. alarm clock, she is seldom in bed before midnight, and must often get up during the night to soothe a child made sick by the nursery school diet (Gray, 1989:30-31).

Traditional sexist attitudes persist in the household. Soviet men view household tasks as "feminine" and refuse to do their fair share. David Shipler, a reporter, observes that "it is common to go into the homes of Moscow intellectuals and discover women professionals with their own careers, who participate fully in conversation and are accustomed to having their views respected. Yet it is rare to see men clearing tables, shopping for food or doing housework" (1976:9).

Gender Roles and the Family before and after Perestroika

The impact of women's occupational involvements on the family has remained a constant concern in the years immediately preceding *perestroika* and in the years after the collapse of the Soviet Union. The focus is on three broad areas: its effects on patterns of marriage and divorce, on fertility, and on the sexual division of labor. The widely held view that female education and employment was inversely associated with family stability was supported by statistical data (Lapidus, 1982). High divorce rates were associated with women, who were more likely to initiate divorces. This is, in part, attributed to their greater economic independence and relative unwillingness to hold together an unsatisfactory marriage. Divorce rates varied by region, age, and ethnic makeup. From 1940 to 1987 divorce rates increased threefold. The overall divorce rate for the entire Soviet Union was 3.4 divorces per thousand population. This figure is exceeded by the 4.9 figure for the United States (Doherty, Hogan, Foteeva, and Zaikina, 1994). However, for the European parts of the USSR and particularly in the major Russian cities like Moscow (5.1) and Leningrad (5.6), the divorce rate was much higher.

In the 1980s, experts of the family interpreted the divorce rate as a sign of greater family instability that has troubling implications for the demographic situation in the Soviet Union (Juviler, 1984). These experts estimated that about 15 percent fewer children will be born because of family breakup. Further, family strains may serve as a deterrent against having children. This problem was seen as being particularly acute in the Russian Soviet republic rather than in the less European Asian Soviet republics with their large Islamic population.

The high divorce rate for urban couples reflected the fact that these couples represented the technological and professional elite of Soviet society (Bowen, 1983). They were characterized by dual-careerism, conjugal-family systems, and neolocal residence—all factors that cause high divorce rates. In comparison, rural families in the Soviet Union continued to be characterized by lower divorce rates, reflecting the continued prominence of extended-family networks and stable familial and traditional cultural values.

Some authorities believed that the high divorce rate reflected an ordinary phenomenon in contemporary family life. Bowen observed that, "in some ways the marital pattern presently found in the Soviet Union reflects that which Engels envisioned: one based on true love with the capacity to be dissolved when this love ceases" (1983:309). Indeed, Lapidus (1978) cited one Soviet sociologist who interpreted the rising divorce rate not in terms of marital disorganization but as a sign of strength and adaptability to new conditions.

Other authorities were more alarmed. By the end of the 1980s, judges in the Soviet legal system saw the divorce rate as most troubling and suggested that the underlying contributing factors should be dealt with. These included (in rank order): "(1) Improve financial and housing conditions for families; (2) build more child care centers; (3) enhance the preparation for marriage; (4) treat alcoholism more vigorously; (5) make divorce procedures more complicated; (6) raise the age of eligibility for marriage; and (7) improve the lives of employed women" (cited in Doherty et al., 1991:81).

V.A. Sysenko, a leading family scholar from Moscow University, saw divorce as the deplorable consequence of women's double burden at work and at home (Danes, Doudchenko, and Yasnaya, 1994). The pressures of the dual responsibilities sharply decreased women's satisfaction with their marriage. He and others felt that women's employment also affected the family through its influence on childbearing. The urban and industrial areas where there was a declining birthrate were also the areas where there was a high level of female employment. Lapidus (1982) observed that some officials had suggested that to counter this trend there should be a reduction in female employment. "Deploring the fact that the one-child family has become the norm in the urban regions of the European USSR, a number of Soviet authors call for reducing the level of female labor force participation and even restricting abortions in order to increase birthrates to a socially optimal level" (Lapidus, 1982:xxxiv).

In addition to the full-time employment of many urban women, the trend of having small families was also explained by the general lack of living space and the low standard of living for many families. The Soviet government was particularly concerned with the low fertility rate and the trend toward single-child families. It goes counter to the ideological belief that children of such families are likely to be indulged and fail to develop the intellectual and emotional characteristics of self-discipline, joint participation, and unselfishness that are necessary for integration into a socialist society (Bowen, 1983).

In the post-Soviet period, a leading Russian sociologist, Anatolyi I. Antonov believes that the low birthrate and the high death rate is evidence of the decline of the Russian family (Hogan, Maddock, Antonov, and Matskovsky, 1994). He attributes this decline not so much to the economic chaos that preceded the breakup of the Soviet Union or to the economic uncertainties of the contemporary situation as it moves from a communist economic system to a capitalism market economy. Rather, he attributes the decline in birthrates to a fundamental change in social values that has had a profound negative effect on the family. The Russians' intrinsic value toward children has lessened to the extent that individuals no longer see as part of their responsibilities the bearing and nurturing of future generations. Antonov places the blame of this change in social values on the depersonalized bureaucracy that characterized the Soviet period.

Antonov faults Marxist ideology that expected both men and women to be employed by the state. According to his view of socialism, women who devoted their lives to the family did not fulfill society's needs and were seen as "sponges" on society (Hogan et al., 1994: 223). Socialism viewed child rearing as a responsibility of the state and housework itself had little intrinsic value. For an individual to be involved in meaningful work, that work must take place outside the home. Antonov concludes that "surely these social norms have a direct relationship to the low fertility rate and weak intrafamily commitment that currently exists, and particularly to the burden it places on women" (Hogan et al., 1994: 223).

Antonov argues that unless there is a revival of the family as the principal mediator between the state and the individual, post-Soviet society will continue to experience social problems. He advocates multiple children families with more involvement of parents in their children's lives. He also calls for supportive programs including public health services, housing programs, cultural activities, and increased attention by the mass media on the importance of children for a society's ultimate well-being.

The third way in which female employment was seen to impact on the family was on the sexual division of labor within the family. The consensus among Soviet authors in the 1980s was that working women were developing greater authority within the family. A more democratic pattern of family decision making—including a more equal sharing of family responsibilities—was seen as another consequence of women's employment (Lapidus, 1982). Juviler supported this observation: "Women these days are making greater demands than their mothers did for equality in family burdens, decency and sobriety on the part of their husbands, and emotional supports. They have more options and make more demands than their mothers and grandmothers did" (1984:98). He also attributes this rise in family equality to the elimination of illiteracy and cultural backwardness and to the movement from village to city and the breakdown of the extended family. This movement effectively destroyed the power and social control of the villages over couples, while it also removed the nuclear family from extended-family controls.

Lapidus (1982), however, cautioned us not to exaggerate this movement toward gender-role equality. She cites voluminous Soviet time-budget investigations that reveal that while men and women devote equal time to paid employment, women are

BOX 10-2   The Global Family

Russian Mothers, from All Walks, Walk Alone

Alessandra Stanley

MOSCOW, Oct. 20—The collapse of the Soviet state has changed everything in Russia—except the relationship between the sexes. Expectations are low, but divorce rates remain high and the numbers of single mothers, either divorced or never married, keep growing.

Yelena Polyakovskaya, 32, has two small children, by two fathers, and never really expected either man to stay or help her financially.

"People tell me I'm so strong, such a heroine," she said of her struggle to hold down a demanding job as a television reporter while raising children.

"I'm not strong. It's our men who are weak. They seem to have no sense of responsibility at all."

In a trend that is as unmistakable to sociologists and social workers as it is distressing, millions of maids, factory workers, and university professors alike have grown inured to raising their families without men. Instead they have come to rely on mothers, sisters and aunts in the kind of matriarchal society—and downward spiral of poverty and limited horizons—that in the United States has become a hallmark of the poorest urban areas.

Here, however, paternal absence and neglect is a reality shared widely by Russian women, regardless of background, aspirations, or income.

"As I understand it, in the United States, single mothers are mostly teenagers with very low education," said Marina Kiyenya, 35, a professor of Spanish who started a support group here five years ago for single mothers like herself. "Most of our single mothers have a university degree, some are very active in their professions."

She, too, detects something deeply wrong with the way men and women relate in her country. "Seventy years of Soviet rule taught men to be selfish and passive," she said. "The biggest problem I see is the total lack of responsibility of our men."

Even in Communist days, the unhappiness of Russian families was hard to hide. The divorce rate in the 1970s was 46 percent (now it is 51 percent) and alcoholism, though never officially quantified, was blamed.

Communism gave women the right, and necessity, to work as equals, but a notion of male superiority clung despite 70 years of official propaganda. Women worked at their jobs, then did nearly all the housework and child-raising. Men did not help, and were not expected to help. They were expected to drink, and they did.

Sociologists blamed Soviet life, its regimentation, oppression, and lack of individual freedom, for men's alcoholism and apathy to work and family. Nowadays, many people blame democracy, or rather, the economic free fall many Russians find themselves in, for those same things.

"There is so much economic uncertainty and real fear," Ms. Kiyenya said. "Men feel humiliated that they cannot provide for their families, and they just walk away."

With a bitter laugh, she said her own story was typical. "When I got pregnant," she explained "my boyfriend promised to marry me, then he changed his plans and disappeared." He lives in Moscow but never sees their 10-year-old daughter and provides no support, she added.

One thorn of Russian society is that while single mothers complain of isolation and social disapproval, men who abandon their families—or even several families—do not appear subject to much censure.

"Its a strange thing, but fathers who don't pay child support are not ill favored by public opinion," said Aleksandr Sinelnikov, a researcher at the State Institute of the Family. "His friends say that it is her own fault for throwing him out. And if a mother goes to the police to try and force him to pay up, well, police officers are men, and they tend to side with the father. Ms. Polyakovskaya lives with her 6-month-old baby, relying on friends and baby sitters to watch Aleksandr when she is at work. The father, an unmarried journalist, has never seen his child. Her 6-year-old son, Simeon, is being raised by his

(continued)

grandmother and great-grandmother in Kiev. Ms. Poliakovskaya says she hopes to bring him to Moscow, but cannot even afford train fare to visit him.

She loves her job covering music and ballet, but it is ill paid. In her bare one-room apartment, she sleeps on a tiny, fold-out couch next to the baby's crib. An ironing board serves as a desk. But like many women raising children alone, she said she does not want to marry again.

"My life is difficult," she said, "but God, if I had to come home from work and clean, cook, and iron for a husband who keeps telling me I am doing it wrong, it would be even worse."

Russians can be wildly romantic, but few seem to harbor much sentimentality about marriage.

Nina Vasiliyeva, 40, a single mother who is twice divorced, runs a matrimonial agency for Russian women seeking American husbands. Called Russian Romance, the agency matches American men who seek traditional wives with Russian women who want a dependable husband.

There are dozens of such agencies in Russia today, many of which use high-tech tools of the mating game, like computer match-ups, electronic mail, and videocassettes.

"American men are more polite, they don't drink as much, and they accept responsibility for their families," Ms. Vasiliyeva said of her American clients' reputation among her Russian clients, many of whom are single mothers who despair of finding a reliable husband here.

So does Ms. Vasiliyeva. She left her first husband after he became the leader of his local Communist Party organization and he began acting like a tyrant at home. She divorced the father of her son, an unemployed alcoholic, after he went to jail for drug dealing.

In addition to her matrimonial agency, which she runs out of her apartment, she works as an office manager in a French photo agency, and makes $1,300 a month, enough to raise her 5-year-old son and pay her husband's $250 monthly rent—the price she pays to keep him at bay.

A teacher turned business executive, Ms. Vasiliyeva says women are adapting better to Russia's new market economy than most men.

"In Soviet times, our men had it easy," she explained. "They went to work, but they didn't have to work hard, they put in two hours and spent the day smoking, drinking, and playing chess, then came home and lay on the sofa. Women did everything else. We were already used to working hard. Men are having problems because nobody wants to pay you for doing nothing anymore."

Demographers at the State Institute of the Family who have studied a 1994 microcensus, estimate that 15 to 20 percent of all Russian families are run by a single parent, and that 94 percent of those parents are women, either widowed, divorced or never married.

The numbers of single mothers are not significantly higher than those in Western and Eastern Europe and are far lower than in the United States, where sociologists estimate that 27 percent of mothers are single. What distinguishes single mothers in Russia is that they come in all ages and evenly span the social spectrum.

Some sociologists, like Mr. Sinelnikov, say single mothers are not much worse off than married ones because so many single mothers (31 percent) live with their mothers or relatives and rely on them for assistance.

At the Center for Gender Studies in Moscow, Olga Zdravomyslova dryly disagreed. "The women we surveyed don't want to live with their mothers—it's just that they have no choice," she said.

Ms. Zdravomyslova worked on a study begun in 1991 comparing single mothers in Russia to those in Eastern and Western Europe, and found that the plight of Russian women was different. Half the single mothers in countries like Switzerland were living with boyfriends. Only 5 percent in Russia had found a new partner. "They are not just legally single—they are absolutely alone," she said.

The study also found that Russian fathers had far less contact with their children than those in any other country. "We found there was almost no relationship at all," she said.

Russian divorce law does not allow for joint

custody. Child support payments, while required by law, are difficult to collect, and increasingly, given the nature of Russia's free-market economy, men can better hide their real income from tax collectors and ex-wives.

Ms. Kiyenya, the professor, said it was better to be a single mother than a divorcée. "I still get a Government stipend, even though it is only $12 a month," she said. "I could never drag that out of an ex-husband."

But many single mothers in Moscow, including Ms. Polyakovskaya, the television reporter, do not have residency permits and cannot apply for welfare.

Parliament is drafting a new law aimed at providing deadbeat fathers with more flexible child support payments. But few expect the Government to make a dent in so deeply rooted a social problem.

"We must help ourselves," Ms. Kiyenya said firmly. "If our children's fathers don't want to help us, why would the state want to do it?"

still devoting an additional 28 hours per week to housework. Men's contributions are only an additional 12 hours. As a consequence, men have 50 percent more leisure time than women. She further observes that a reduction in the time that women spend on housework is not a consequence of husband involvement but rather the result of the use of labor-saving household appliances. In short, she argues that the "double burden" still exists. Research conducted at the end of the decade report a continuation of this pattern (Danes et al., 1994). The fundamental problem is that the household continues to be viewed as the female's domain and the family is her responsibility. As long as this assumption holds, fundamental improvements in women's positions and the Russian family cannot occur. In the post-Soviet period, the new democratic society will be tested on how well it can redress the gender inequality still prevalent in the society.

In summary, the Soviet Union had to a large extent been in the forefront of the effort to establish equality between the sexes and had made giant steps toward the accomplishment of that goal. Yet, formal and traditional barriers to women's progress still existed. However, in light of the relatively minor advances of Western countries in the quest for sexual equality of opportunity, the achievements of the Soviet Union were notable. Its failures have been noted, and it will be of great interest to see how post-Soviet Russia copes with the continuous changes in gender roles and the family in the years ahead. This country will continue to provide a useful perspective from which to compare the development of problems and ultimate solutions of Western countries in their movement toward achieving sexual egalitarianism.

THE WESTERN EXPERIENCE: SWEDEN

The worldwide depression of the 1930s had a profound affect on Sweden and the Swedish family. From that time to the present, Sweden has created one of the most progressive social-welfare systems in the world. Comprehensive governmental programs and services exist in the fields of health, education, and welfare. Parents receive family allowances for their children. Education is free and universal. Old-age pensions and benefits are available to all citizens, regardless of the amount of their prior contributions. Day-care facilities are numerous and are well utilized. Birth-control information, contraceptive devices, and abortions are readily available.

Sweden has made great strides in bringing about gradual equality between men and women in politics, education, employment, and the family. To accomplish this goal, the Swedes approach the problem through far-reaching policies carefully conceptualized and pragmatically implemented. Yet, by the middle of the last decade of the twentieth century, the Swedish family has been seen by some critics as representing the ultimate decline of the family as a consequence of such social policies. In this section, we will investigate the Swedish family experience.

To illustrate how the Swedish government dealt with family issues, let's begin by looking at the dramatically declining birthrate in the 1930s and how social policies handled it. During the depression, people could not afford to have children. The Swedish government realized that if it wished the population to rise it must implement a comprehensive and supportive social-welfare program. This was essential to encourage marriage and child bearing and to protect the lives and health of both the parents and the children. The policy that was developed was multifaceted and included the following elements: "encouragement of sex education and contraception; state-financed housing; a child-allowance benefit for all families; the creation of mother-baby health clinics throughout the country; a commitment to feed every schoolchild every day; and medical services for all" (Herman, 1974:77).

Although Sweden has been notably successful in its attempt to equalize the relationship between the sexes, vestiges of traditional patriarchal ideology still are manifest. In work, women are predominantly employed as office workers and sales help. They are overrepresented in the lowest civil service grades and under-represented in the highest-paid grades. Women's income is less than men's. This variation reflects women's lower job status and the proportionately greater number of women who are employed part-time. This persistence of part-time employment and lower-echelon positions for women reflects the traditional viewpoint that women's place is in the home.

The double burden of the employed wife has been as prevalent in Sweden as it was in Russia. The old idea that women have greater responsibility in the home for both domestic activities and child care still predominates. This has handicapped the drive for the advancement of women in the field of employment, in labor unions, and in political organizations.

The Swedish approach to bringing about changes in these traditional ideas has been to broaden the discussion concerning women's rights and "the problem of women" in relation to the overall problem of gender roles. In 1962, a controversial book was published that stimulated this debate. This book, *Kvinnors Liv och Arbete [The Life and Work of Women]* (Dahlstrom, 1962)], consisted of a series of essays by noted Scandinavian sociologists, social psychologists, and economists who center their attention on the overall problem of gender-role discrimination in society. The book was a major breakthrough in that it placed the discussion about the "women's question" into the larger social context. One of the contributors to this book, Rita Liljestrom, summarizes by alluding to the similarity between gender-role discrimination and racial discrimination:

> If a society shows sexual discrimination in the labor force, if its decision-making bodies, councils, and parliament contain an overwhelming majority of men, if sexual discrimination is practiced in connection with household tasks, it is as unreasonable to talk about "the problem of women" as to lay the blame for racial prejudice upon the Negro. (Liljestrom, 1970:204)

The placing of the "women's problem" into the broader social issue relating to discrimination and civil rights was a significant turning point in changing traditional ideas. The widening of the debate beyond the conventional focus of discussions on the conflict between women's two roles—family and work—to encompass the two roles of men has also had an effect on men. Liljestrom (1970:200-201) notes the use of the expression "men's emancipation" means the rights of husbands and fathers to become involved in child care and domestic activities. Further, the phrase is taken to mean that options for men and women should be expanded in both economic and family institutions.

In the ensuing thirty-five years, Sweden developed many programs designed to help the family. They recognized that families with children were at an economic disadvantage compared to individuals or married couples who were childless. Liljestrom (1978) spoke of a "new kind of poverty" characterizing families who cannot make ends meet. Childless individuals or couples are able to maximize their spending and investing power. Through their ability to focus their economic resources, they are driving up the price of commodities, including housing, transportation, and other consumer goods. Families with full-time employed husbands and wives are finding that they cannot economically compete given the financial costs of child rearing. In turn, seeing this, younger people are making decisions either to postpone or to never have children. As a consequence of this trend, Sweden experienced a declining birthrate.

The Swedish government was concerned that if this trend continued unchecked, it would produce more childless couples and accentuate the divergence in living styles. To combat this problem, Sweden adopted the family allowance as a "pronatalist" measure. The government pays a fixed allowance to all parents with children. It also advances payments of private child support that are due.

Sweden was also aware of the impact that these programs have on the lives of women. Taken by itself, a family allowance could easily function as a strong incentive to remain at home for the married woman. If she subsequently divorces, she may find herself ill-prepared, lacking the necessary job skills and experience to enter the job market. To combat such eventualities, Sweden has developed a parent-insurance program that allows either or both parents to take a nearly fully paid employment leave of up to nine months after the birth of a child. This system is financed through taxes and employers' contributions.

The Swedish system reflects a substantial commitment to child-care responsibility. In addition to cash allowances, the government has undertaken to provide widespread public child-care services. This is very important for women who are divorced; the burdens of child care are shared with the state. The government does not operate under the principle of equalizing the financial burden with the father. However, the state, rather than women, absorbs much of the impact of divorce.

In an examination of parental leave social policies in Sweden, Linda Haas (1992) found that Swedish couples shared parenting and domestic roles to a much larger extent that their American counterparts. However, gender-role equality is still wanting with practice lagging behind the egalitarian ideology. As evidence, a national study of working parents reports that men continue to be engaged in physical labor and in supervisory positions. Women are still more likely to be found in jobs that are monotonous and less prestigious (Moen, 1989). Finally, women are still expected to be the primary caretaker of children and responsible for the upkeep of the home. As a consequence, the majority of women with young children put in a shorter occupational work week than the fathers of their children.

Sweden has been in the forefront of sociological investigations that seek to understand marital and family trends in that country and project if similar changes may occur in the United States. Sweden has the lowest marriage rate of any country in the Western industrial world. The median age of first marriage, 27 for women and nearly 30 for men, is also one of the highest (Hoem and Hoem, 1988). However, about one in four Swedish couples live in nonmarital cohabitation classified in Sweden as a "marriage-like relationship." This compares to about 5 percent in the United States (Popenoe, 1991).

The large number of childbearing couples of nonmarital cohabitation relationships has given Sweden one of the highest percentages of children born out of wedlock in the industrial world. Over 50 percent of all children born are "illegitimate" as compared with about 22 percent in the United States. We place the term "illegitimacy" in quotations to reflect the fact Sweden dropped the term in 1917 and that legislation in the 1970s banned the concept of children born out of wedlock (Popenoe, 1988). Further, it must be pointed out, that unlike the situation in the United States where the majority of unwed mothers are unattached, the vast majority of Swedish out-of-wedlock children are born to attached albeit unmarried couples (Popenoe, 1991). And, as the Swedish sociologist Jan Trost (1985) observes, nonmarriage cohabitation does not have negative connotations and is viewed as equally acceptable as marriage.

The high percentage of nonmarital cohabitation relationships and children born out of these relationships is partly attributable to changes in Swedish family law introduced in the 1960s. This legislation, which has been amended over the years, is based on several fundamental principles that in effect removes legal marriage as the only legitimate form of cohabitation (Kaplan, 1992):

1. that every adult ought to be responsible for his/her own support independent of marital status;
2. that marriage is a voluntary form of cohabitation;
3. that no form of cohabitation is superior to another; and
4. that the child's needs ought to be fulfilled irrespective of circumstances and social (family) constructs into which the child is born (Wistrand, 1981:18 cited in Kaplan, 1992:68).

The American sociologist David Popenoe (1987, 1988, 1991), in a number of highly interesting and controversial works, uses Sweden as the bellwether on the future of the family. Popenoe (1991) sees an ominous "family decline in the Swedish welfare state" that is also occurring in the United States albeit at a slower pace. He argues that Sweden, one of the most advanced, if not the most advanced, modern society in terms of its welfare policies, has seen its family system grow weaker than any family system anywhere else in the world. He argues that the result of the Swedish welfare system, rather than strengthening families, has actually weakened them. He strongly cautions that if the United States continues to emulate the Swedish model the same family decline will occur here.

Popenoe (1991) identifies five aspects of Swedish family decline. First, parental authority has declined as the state has taken over traditional family concerns. As illustrations, he mentions the Swedish law that prohibits parents from striking their children and the fact that social workers often have the power to remove children from parents and place them in foster care. Second, the economic dependence of children on their parents has declined as a consequence of state-run programs of free or low-cost medical care, public transportation, and education. These programs, tied with state guarantees of a part-time job to anyone over the age of 16, leads to a lowering of the economic bonds of children to parents. Third, the economic interdependence of spouses declines as a result of Swedish policy that nonhandicapped adults are responsible for their own economic well-being. As a consequence, Swedish spouses have almost no mutual economic obligations. Fourth, comprehensive programs for the elderly have removed the need for the nuclear family to provide economic care for their aged relatives. Fifth, familism, the "belief in a strong sense of family identification and loyalty, mutual assistance among family members, and a concern for the perpetuation of the family unit; the subordination of the interests and welfare of the family group" is in decline (Popenoe, 1991:68). This decline is attributable to Swedish family legislation that is "almost exclusively concerned with the situation of the individual family member" (Popenoe, 1991:69).

In essence, Popenoe attributes the decline in the family to welfare policies that put the emphasis on the individual rather than the family. He has argued (1988:329) that these policies reflect the underlying processes of "late modernization" in the last fifty years that reflect the ideas of progress in terms of self-fulfillment and ultimately to unbridled individualism over the interests of the family. ". . . [S]wedes have apparently become the least willing to invest time, money, and energy in family life. Instead, the main investments are increasingly made in the individual, not in the family unit" (Popenoe, 1991:69).

The Australian sociologist Gisela Kaplan (1992) takes issue with Popenoe's view. She argues that the Swedish emphasis on individuals over the family represents a recognition of individual responsibility and maturity. Swedish legislation that makes no moral decisions on forms of cohabitation reflect a society that believes that individuals can act responsibly without need of coercion by law. As evidence, she observes that virtually universal family planning and the widespread use of contraceptives has not lowered the country's birthrate as compared to other European countries. Kaplan concludes: "This means that most children both in and out of wedlock are wanted children, which is indeed a worthwhile outcome, though still so much opposed in some other countries" (1992:69).

In conclusion, what has been occurring in Sweden can be insightful for other

Western industrial countries and the United States. Sweden is far ahead of the United States in achieving the ultimate goal of gender equality. Its government has been progressive and farsighted. It has supported and led meaningful programs and reforms. However, the traditional idea of masculine dominance still persists and hinders the drive for equal opportunity for men and women. And, its family system is moving into new forms that place greater stress on individual initiatives and responsibilities. The full implications for both individuals and families still awaits as these processes unfold. While sociologists such as David Popenoe are highly pessimistic about the future, others, including this author, are much more optimistic.

THE WESTERN EXPERIENCE: ISRAEL

Our last societal illustration in this chapter is that of Israel. We focus on the kibbutz movement, which is a prime illustration of communities whose major goal is the emancipation of women and the establishment of complete equality between men and women in all aspects of life. The kibbutz is a collective agricultural settlement comprising between 100 to 2,000 inhabitants. There are some 230 kibbutzim (plural of kibbutz) in Israel, with a total population of about 100,000. This is a little less than 5 percent of Israel's population.

Parents take a break from their jobs at Kibbutz Tuval, Galilee, in northern Israel to feed their children a midmorning meal at the children's house nursery center.

The kibbutz movement originated in the beginning of the twentieth century by East European Jews who settled in what was then Palestine. It represented an attempt to implement the ideologies of Zionism (the belief in a Jewish homeland), socialism, and the ideals of Tolstoy and his disciples concerning the virtues of agricultural pursuits and the belief that the greatest happiness is a return to mother earth.

There are a great number of different types of kibbutzim in Israel. Politically, they range from mild social democratic ideologies to extreme left Marxian positions. Generalizations, therefore, must be made cautiously. Most, generally, try to maintain the belief in economic collectivism. Essentially, this principle eliminates private property and the opportunity to accumulate wealth. The common feature of these collective settlements is the shared ownership of property and the communal organization of production and consumption. Except for a few personal belongings, all property belongs to the community. All income goes into the common fund. Everything is provided by the community, based on the collective decision of the community. Through a general assembly and an extensive committee system, the members' needs are provided on an egalitarian basis.

A most striking feature of the kibbutzim is their attitudes and practices regarding the family. Kibbutz founders expounded their revolutionary and collectivist ideology toward the family. The kibbutz philosophy demanded the complete commitment and involvement of all its members (kibbutzniks). It was felt that this goal could be best accomplished if family and kinship ties were minimized. The late Israeli sociologist Yonina Talmon (1965b:146) stated that the kibbutz founders saw the family as an obstruction to the desired collectivist community. Individuals' attachment to the family and their intense emotional involvement with family members were seen to infringe on the loyalties to the kibbutz. They also believed that involvement with the family members might impede the ideological and work goals of the kibbutz. Finally, it was felt that "inasmuch as they act as buffers and protect the individual from the direct impact of public opinion, they reduce the effectiveness of informal collective control over members" (Talmon, 1965b:261).

With this antifamily ideology, the kibbutz founders rejected the double standard for men and women and the traditional patriarchal structure of the Jewish family. This traditional structure required women and children to be subservient to the husband and father in the family. The division of labor was rigidly segregated in the Jewish family. Women had little involvement with external family matters in the social, cultural, religious, and economic life of the community. Women were confined primarily to the house; their activities revolved around children and domestic chores.

The kibbutz movement seeks to counter the debilitating effects of the family on women and its accompanying double standard through a series of dramatic steps designed to limit drastically the function of the family. Men and women are given jobs based on egalitarian principles. Although husbands and wives are housed in separate household units, their meals are cooked in communal kitchens and taken in the communal dining room. Clothing is purchased, washed, and ironed by assigned kibbutzniks. The community is run as a separate household. From infancy, children are raised in a separate children's house with other children of their own age group. They sleep, eat, and study in these houses. The children are allowed to visit their parents and siblings for several hours daily, but they are raised as a group by community members assigned to this task. Thus many of the tasks traditionally performed by the wife-mother are transformed in the kibbutz into occupational roles requiring trained and professional staffs.

This, then, is the philosophical basis of the kibbutz movement and the implementation of that philosophy. However, the historical and contemporary evidence is that the collectivist system is losing ground to the reemergence of individual values and patriarchal patterns. Manifestations of this change are apparent in the development of discriminatory gender differentiation patterns in the work sphere and the reestablishment of family and kinship ties. Talmon, who had done extensive studies on the kibbutz movement before her untimely death, examined (1965a) the developing division of labor between the sexes in both the internal system of the family and the external system of the occupational and leadership areas. She found that whereas the predominant egalitarian ideology is formally applauded, in reality a segregated gender division of labor exists.

In the sphere of the family, there has been a gradual increase of family functions. Parents are now taking a more active role in raising their children. This is a partial reversal of the collective's role in the care and socialization of the children. Further, although the role differentiation between the mother and the father is not as segregated as it is in the United States, there is a trend to a division of labor between the parents. Women become more involved in taking care of the children in the home. Women also are becoming more involved in the domestic activities of the home; cleaning, washing clothes, and so on. Men, in turn, have their responsibilities geared to work outside the home—in the yard, on the farm, and in dealing with communal affairs of the kibbutz. The result is that "in the eyes of the growing child, the father emerges gradually as the representative of the kibbutz, and its values within the family, while the mother acts primarily as the representative of the family in the kibbutz" (Talmon, 1965a:147).

Gender-role differentiation is also developing in outside-work assignments and in the involvements of kibbutz committees. Men's work activities are concentrated mainly in agriculture and in the production services, transportation, equipment- and machinery-maintenance shops, and the like. Women are found in extensions of traditional women's occupations. Workers in the communal kitchens, in the clothing shops, and stores are almost exclusively women. In education, women are found teaching in the primary grades, men at the high school level.

Talmon found a gradual trend toward growing gender-role differentiation in the participation on committees and in the overall leadership of the community. Generally, men predominate in overall leadership and in the central governing committees. The committees on which women are predominant are those involving education, health, and consumption. Thus, here too, the gender-role division of labor begins to follow traditional patriarchal male-female patterns.

Talmon attributes the growing gender-role differentiation in the kibbutz to two major reasons. First, there are the vestiges of traditional patriarchal thought that surfaced again in the kibbutzim. Second, there are the factors attributed to pregnancy and lactation. Childbearing necessitates that women become involved with activities that do not jeopardize their child-care role. Tied to pregnancy and child rearing is the overall increase in family function. The family thus regains some of its lost functions and becomes more active in internal activities. In addition, "the identification with the specifically and typically feminine role of mother undermines the masculine image of the feminine role upheld by the official ideology and weakens the resistance to sex-role differentiations" (Talmon, 1965a:151).

The role differentiation within the family gradually exerts pressure and influences the work sphere. Lines between appropriate work for men and women become more sharply delineated. The egalitarian basis for the designation of occupations becomes lost. The result is the continued acceleration of gender-role differentiation. Today, sociologists are in agreement that the assigning of women to work in the service areas and with children ultimately led to the sex stereotyping of job roles in the contemporary kibbutz (Safir and Izraeli, 1991).

Another interpretation, albeit a minority view, of the kibbutz experiment was that the differentiation of gender roles was ultimately based on physiological factors—the reproductive function of women. The argument is that even when a social group desires to construct a community based on sexual equality, the biologic differences between the sexes have a determining role. Tiger and Shepher (1975), in a polemical study of women in the kibbutz, continue this argument by postulating that biologic reasons may ultimately be the determining causal factor in the allocation of gender-role patterns. It is our opinion that biology, although influential, is not deterministic; that is, although it would be negligent to ignore the influence of biology on human activities, we believe that the pervasive influence of the traditional patriarchal ideology combined with other social factors can best account for the reemergence of discriminatory gender-role differentiation patterns.

While gender equality on the kibbutz and in Israel has not been achieved, it is wrong to put the blame on women. It must be emphasized that the kibbutz movement is not an isolated social phenomenon. It occurs in a society that is predominantly a Western-oriented capitalistic system. A study by Dorit D. Padan-Eisenstark (1973) found that women have not achieved an appreciably higher degree of equality in Israeli society than their counterparts in other Western industrial societies. More specifically, the findings based on a secondary analysis of surveys and studies conducted in Israel from 1930 through 1971 reveal that women's employment is concentrated in various service occupations. Almost three-quarters of the women held jobs in teaching and nursing occupations, clerical and service occupations, and the catering industries. These occupations are those that have been traditionally linked to women and represent the professionalized form of the domestic household tasks. In addition, a large number of women held jobs that had flexible hours and were part-time. This allowed them to be less committed to employment and more involved with family and domestic tasks. Finally, Israeli women were underrepresented in all managerial and high-status professional occupations.

Paden-Eisenstark's study supports the view that the kibbutz pattern can be seen as a reflection of the larger societal pattern. Similarly, other sociologists have observed that while there is a rhetoric of gender egalitarianism that favors the increase in status of women: "the overwhelming thrust of Israeli public policy is toward reinforcing women's traditional roles" (Boneparth, 1986; cited in Lindsey, 1994:138). *The Bluff on Equality in Israel* is the title of a book (Swirski and Sapir, 1991) whose contributors examined the way that gender inequality manifested itself throughout Israeli life. In the late 1980s there developed a movement by kibbutzim women that demanded greater access to higher status jobs and away from the self-perpetuating lower positions that have been traditionally assigned to them (Lindsey, 1994).

One final note, Hartman and Hartman (1993) found interesting differences in a comparative examination of gender equality among Israeli and American Jews. Their findings speak to an emerging reconceptualization of Israeli marital and family roles. In Israel today, family roles carry more prestige and institutional support than in the United States. In the United States more people, including American Jews, never marry, remain childless, and have alternative lifestyles that are acceptable to the general populace. In addition, the multiple arenas of social activity, including occupational and military roles that both Israeli men and women are involved in, are other factors that influence perceptions of gender equality. Hartman and Hartman conclude that "the greater compatibility of family and economic roles outside the home and a greater value placed on familism are suggested explanations for the relatively higher gender equality found in Israel" (1993:48).

In conclusion, the kibbutzim were not isolated from the dominant Israeli society that continued to discriminate against women following patriarchal sexist guidelines. Nor were its members immune to this ideology. The kibbutz movement cannot be studied and treated as if it were a totally autonomous and independent entity. The kibbutz movement can be viewed as a noble experiment, and although it has not achieved the long-sought goal of sexual equality, its failure in this area can be attributed to specific social factors rather than to unproved biologically determined theories of causality. Indeed, recent behavioral and attitudinal changes in Israeli society regarding gender roles and marriage and family dynamics provides further evidence of how malleable gender roles are.

CONCLUSION

This chapter presents a broad range of topical areas regarding gender-role relationship patterns. We began the chapter with an examination of the arguments that seek to explain the almost universal female subordinate patterns that exist cross-culturally and historically. Two factors—one physiologically based, that is, women's reproductive role and their lesser physical strength; and the second ideologically based, that is, patriarchy—have served as the philosophical and moral justifications for discriminatory gender-role differentiation. These ideologies have held sway in Greco-Roman, Semitic, Indian, Chinese, Japanese, and Western Christian civilizations.

Next, investigation of different economic systems and the accompanying gender-role differentiation patterns was undertaken. We found that in shifting agricultural economies the prevalent pattern was egalitarian. On the other hand, in plow agricultural systems the patriarchal ideology held sway. As a result of imperialistic colonization, many shifting agricultural systems, most notably in Africa, were forcibly transformed to plow agricultural systems. In addition, the Western patriarchal ideology accompanied this transformation. The result was a decided loss of feminine status and power. Our concern was also how modernization processes have impacted on African women. We observed that often "modernization means more dependency." Our final topic in this section of the chapter was what living under apartheid in "white" South Africa meant to black families. The debilitating, demoralizing, and exploitative system was analyzed and we concluded with the difficulties that are occurring in that country's post-apartheid present.

The nature of the male-female division of labor in industrial societies was then investigated. To dramatize the continued impact of patriarchal sexist thought, we looked at societies that have adopted the goals of female liberation and of sexual equality as official policy. Russia (and the then Soviet Union) and the Western societies of Sweden and Israel espouse the egalitarian ideology, but they have not achieved total equality. They still are plagued by vestiges of the discriminatory ideology of patriarchy. Although great strides have been taken by women in the occupational economy, they are overrepresented in service occupations and underrepresented in managerial and executive positions. Further, they are burdened by a dual role that expects that in addition to their full-time occupational involvements they must also be involved full-time with home tasks—domestic and child-care activities. Husbands and fathers, although equally involved in the occupational sphere, continue to be relatively noninvolved in the home sphere.

The examination of gender-role differentiation patterns occurring in these industrial societies provides Americans with an interesting comparative perspective. The pitfalls, problems, and experiences of these societies, more advanced than we are in sexual equality, can serve as important models in our own drive toward gender-role liberation. By profiting from the experiences of other countries, we may be able to develop alternative strategies in assuring sexual equality.

11

INTIMACY, WORK,
AND MARRIAGE

This chapter is a continuation of the previous one, since many of the same underlying issues that were discussed there are also pertinent here. In the previous chapter, we emphasized different types of economic systems and how they are related to the male-female relationship. These underlying conditions, which have influenced the differentiation between the sexes, are notably manifest in the marital relationship. The economic-variable framework will allow further exploration and insight into the relationship between the sexes in marriage.

Our orientation in this discussion is on the activities of males and females in public and domestic/private spheres. The differentiation of these spheres of activities has been a factor dominating the expression of marital roles. They are important in determining power, privilege, respect, and deference patterns within the family. They have also played a significant role in affecting the articulation of intimacy in marriage. We begin our discussion by looking at this differentiation in the preindustrial Western family, and then shift our attention to a social-historical examination of marriage in Western Europe and the United States since the Industrial Revolution.

THE PUBLIC WORLD OF THE PREINDUSTRIAL WESTERN FAMILY

In earlier discussions we have observed that there was a heightened dichotomization between private, noneconomically productive domestic work and the public world of finance, industry, commerce, and wage-earning work after the industrial revolution. It would be instructive to contrast the preindustrial world of Western Europe at the advent of industrialization with our contemporary era.

Philippe Ariès, a French social historian, has written a seminal work on the analysis of the historical evolution of the Western family. Ariès' *Centuries of Childhood: A Social History of Family Life* (1962) traces the developments in the conceptualization of the family from the Middle Ages to the present. His data sources include paintings and diaries, the history of games and pastimes, and the development of schools and their curricula. Ariès' basic thesis is that the contemporary conceptualization of family life and the modern image of the nature of children are recent phenomena. He argues that the concept of the family did not emerge until the seventeenth century. He does not deny the existence of the family prior to that time but makes a critical distinction between the family as a *reality* and the *idea* of the family, which is sensitive to change. Ariès states that the physical existence of the family is not in question: Fathers and mothers and children exist in all societies. But the point is that the ideas entertained about family relations can be radically dissimilar over lengthy periods of time.

> . . . it would be vain to deny the existence of a family life in the Middle Ages. But the family existed in silence: it did not awaken feelings strong enough to inspire poet or artist. We must recognize the importance of this silence: not much value was placed on the family. (Ariès, 1962:364)

The low valuation placed on the family in preindustrial Europe occurred because of the individual's almost total involvement with the community. People lived in their communities; they worked, played, and prayed in them. The communities monopolized all their time and their minds. They had very little time for their families. The gathering point for the community was the "big house," which contained up to twenty-five people, including families, children, and servants. They fulfilled a public function by serving as places for business and sociability. Here friends, clients, and relatives met and talked. The rooms of the house were multifunctional: They were used for domestic activities as well as for professional purposes. People ate, slept, danced, worked, and received visitors in them.

> They ate in them, but not at special tables: the "dining table" did not exist, and at mealtimes people set up folding trestle-tables, covering them with a cloth. . . . It is easy to imagine the promiscuity which reigned in these rooms where nobody could be alone, which one had to cross to reach any of the communicating rooms, where several couples and several groups of boys or girls slept together (not to speak of the servants, of whom at least some must have slept beside their masters, setting up beds, which were still collapsible in the room or just outside the door), in which people forgathered to have their meals, to receive their friends or clients, and sometimes to give alms to beggars. (Ariès, 1963:394-395)

The general situation was one in which most activities were public and one where people were never left alone. The density of social life made isolation virtually impossible. Families were part and parcel of the society and were intertwined with relatives, friends, clients, proteges, debtors, and so on. Ariès argues that the lack of privacy attributed to this overwhelming community sociability hindered the formation of the concept of the family. The concept of the family developed as other specialized institutions relieved the home of its multifaceted functions. The growth of taverns, cafes, and clubs provided alternative outlets for sociability. The establishment of geographically distinct business and occupational places freed the family from its business functions. The strengthening of the family was to be seen in the increased privacy for family life and a growing intimacy among family members. Gradually, the family cut itself off from the outside world and a separate and distinct family life emerged. As we see, this isolation has had critical implications for women and children.

A formal portrait of a seventeenth-century Flemish family. Note how the children are dressed in adult clothes and are depicted as small adults.

Edward Shorter—in a provocative book, *The Making of the Modern Family* (1975)—continues the general theme of Philippe Ariès. He sees the family tied integrally with the community. Shorter states that ordinary families in western and central Europe from 1500 to the end of the eighteenth century were "held firmly in the matrix of the larger social order" (Shorter, 1975:3). The family was secured to the community by two ties: One was the intricate web of extended kin, including uncles, aunts, and cousins; the other was to the wider community. The family had no sense of privacy or separation from the community. The marital roles were not viewed as independently important. Marriage was frequently arranged on the basis of advancing the extended family's economic interests.

Shorter's central argument is that the history of the family can be seen in the shift in the relationship between the nuclear family and the surrounding community. During the preindustrial period, the physical matrix discouraged privacy and intimacy within which the traditional family found itself. However, unlike Ariès—who presents a rather rosy, idealized depiction of preindustrial life, where all peoples of different ages, sexes, and classes intermingled in a Bruegelesque scene—Shorter stresses the negative characteristics of marital and family life. Shorter argues that family life was characterized by emotional coldness between husband and wife and an emotional isolation through a strict division of work assignments and gender roles. The emotional detachment of the marital pair and their demarcation of tasks are seen to be revealed in the following French regional proverbs:

- "Mort de femme et view de cheval font l'homme riche." (Brittany) (Rich is the man whose wife is dead and horse alive.)

- "Deuil de femme morte dure jusqu'a à la porte. " (Gascony) (Your late wife you so deplore until you enter your front door.)
- "L'homme a deux beaux jours sur terre: lorsqu'il prend femme et lorsqu'il l'enterre." (Anjou) (The two sweetest days of a fellow in life are the marriage and burial of his wife.)
- "Les femmes à la maison, comme les chiens, les hommes à la rue, comme les chats." (Gascony) (Women belong at home, like the dogs; men belong in the streets, like the cats.)
- "Jamais femme ni cochon ne doivent quitter la maison." (Dauphine) (Never let go out the doors either the women or the boars.) (Shorter, 1975:58, 73)

Unlike other social historians—who stress the importance of women in domestic industry in preindustrial England—Shorter sees the life of women in preindustrial continental Europe as being relatively removed from economic enterprises and confined to having children and doing household tasks. The significance of this is spelled out in the considerable inequality between working men and domestically confined women. This finding is a notable contrast to the status and treatment of working women in England.

Shorter finds women having considerable power within the household but "women's control over certain domestic spheres, which were isolated from the economy as a whole, did not free them from subordinate social rules" (Shorter, 1975:66 - 67). Women's roles were subservient and they were expected to be inferior. Three specifically feminine roles are delineated: passivity of women in external relations and with men in general, self-abnegation and personal sacrifice for the family, and finally "women's work was found in sex and reproduction: sleeping with husbands on demand and producing babies to the limits set by community norms" (Shorter, 1975:75).

Both Ariès and Shorter, then, observe that the preindustrial family was one that was characterized by a lack of privacy and intimacy. However, Ariès emphasizes the positive qualities of preindustrial community life, which compensated for the lack of marital "togetherness." Shorter, on the other hand, decries the lack of emotional involvement as being detrimental to the individual well-being of men and women; he does not regard community involvement positively. For our purposes, a more rounded picture of the nature of husband-and-wife relationships can be seen when we examine the couple's lives in terms of their involvement in work and in the home and the impact of their marital relationship on the power and status of women.

In the preindustrial period, the family was the unit of production. Men, women, and children worked in the home and in the fields. Life was characterized by an interweaving of the husband's and wife's involvement with domestic life and with a productive work life. Women were involved in both the care of the home and the children as well as being participants in the family's basic economic productive system. Family industry was common. The food or goods produced did not yield much more than a bare subsistence. The family was the unit of production, with its members tied together in economic partnership. With the husband working in the home as well as the wife and children, there existed an integration of the public and private spheres of activities.

Alice Clark, in 1919, wrote an important work entitled *The Working Life of Women in the Seventeenth Century*. She examined women's work in agriculture, textiles, and the woolen trade in England during this period. All these activities were performed under a system of family industry. All goods and services produced by the family were intended for either family consumption or for sale or trade. Work, then, was not distinguished between that for domestic consumption or that for sale or trade. Cotton production illustrates this. The home was set up like a miniature factory; the entire process of cotton production from raw material to finished cloth was contained within the home. Men and women worked side by side. Both were actively involved in all aspects of the work. Clark summarizes her observations on the role of women in the preindustrial economy in the following manner:

> Under modern conditions, the ordinary domestic occupations of English women consist in tending babies and young children, in preparing household meals, and in keeping the house clean. . . . In the seventeenth century [the domestic role] embraced a much wider range of production; for brewing, dairy work, the care of poultry and pigs, the production of vegetables and fruit, spinning flax and wool, nursing and doctoring, all formed part of domestic industry. (Clark cited in Oakley, 1974:15)

Ann Oakley (1974), who has written a valuable work of the social history of the housewife, observes that women at the time of marriage were expected to be economically productive, whether in agriculture or in the handicraft trades. The notion of women's economic dependence was foreign to the family system. Men were not viewed as the economic supporters of women. To demonstrate, Oakley (1974:22) examined the list of the occupations of married couples taken from the Sessions Papers of the Old Bailey. These were couples who were either witnesses, prosecutors, or prisoners of the court. She found that only 1 out of 86 married women did not have an occupation of her own. The remaining 85 women's occupations ranged from plumber to poultry dealer to seller of old clothes.

Traditionally, the husband was seen as the head of the household. He presided over the division of labor in various work and domestic tasks. Michael Young and Peter Willmott (1973) argue that the doctrine of St. Paul—"Wives submit yourself unto your own husbands, as it is fit in the Lord"—was still the canon in the seventeenth century. The husband's power was tempered by the importance of the wife's economic contribution and also that of the children. Thus, although most wives were in fact beaten (some beaten severely), it was not to the husband's economic advantage to antagonize his wife too much. "Her economic value was her saving, especially if she not only worked herself but also produced for her employer other workers, so putting him in the state recognized in the words of the psalm 'Happy is the man who hath his quiver full of children' " (Young and Willmott, 1973:67).

In summary, traditional life in preindustrial Europe can be seen as being characterized by a much greater involvement of the family with the surrounding community. The relationship between husband and wife was not as intimate or private as it is in today's contemporary industrial societies. In addition, the status and treatment of women can be seen to vary with their involvement in economically productive work. When a woman contributed, she had more power and control over her own life. When she did not, her life was that of a domestically confined slave; servile and subservient to her master—her husband.

FROM PUBLIC TO PRIVATE: THE EARLY INDUSTRIAL WESTERN FAMILY

The Industrial Revolution shattered the domestic economy centered in the household. Looking at mid-eighteenth-century England, we are best able to observe its impact. England was primarily rural with men and women largely engaged in some form of domestic industry. This activity occurred within the home. In the cities, women as well as men were involved in some form of trade, frequently serving as partners in joint work activities. The agrarian revolution at the end of the eighteenth century saw the lessening of the necessity for productive work at home. Industrial development deprived them of their involvement in the older domestic industries and trades:

> If you go into a loom-shop, where there's three or four pairs of looms,
> They are all standing empty, encumbrances of the rooms;
> And if you ask the reason why, the older mother will tell you plain
> My daughters have forsaken them, and gone to weave by steam.
> (J. Harland, *Ballads and Songs of Lancashire*, 1865. Cited in Thompson, 1963:308)

Family members were absorbed into the new economy as wage earners. This led to the differentiation between work and the home. E.P. Thompson, the English historian, in his *The Making of the English Working Class* (1963) comprehensively examines the changes occurring in people's ways of life between 1780 and 1832. In the following passage, he contrasts the differences between two economies:

> Women became more dependent upon the employer or the labour market, and they looked back to a "golden" period in which home earnings from spinning, poultry and the like could be gained around their own door. In good times the domestic economy supported a way of life centred upon the home, in which inner whims and compulsions were more obvious than external discipline. Each stage in industrial differentiation and specialisation struck also at the family economy, disturbing customary relations between man and wife, parents and children, and differentiating more sharply between "work" and "life." It was to be a full hundred years before this differentiation was to bring returns, in the form of labour-saving devices, back into the working woman's home. Meanwhile, the family was roughly torn apart each morning by the factory bell. (Thompson, 1963:416)

During this period, the family lost its productive function to industry. Work was now separated from the family. The differentiation of the family from the economy necessitated by the new industrial economy was accompanied by the differentiation of roles within the family. For men, it meant involvement in the outside world and in the expanding occupational marketplace; for women, it increasingly meant confinement within the home. "The woman became the nonemployed, economically dependent housewife, and the man became the sole wage or salary earner, supporting by his labour his wife—the housewife—and her children" (Oakley, 1974:34).

At the outset, women gained by the transference of economic production from the home to the workplace. It was instrumental in improving domestic conditions. The grime, filth, and industrial wastage associated with industrial production were now being removed from the home. Ivy Pinchbeck (1930), another English historian, observed that with the home no longer a workshop, women for the first time in the history of the industrial age were now able to turn their attention to homemaking and the care of children.

Shorter (1975) also is impressed by the positive consequences of industrialization. Shorter believes that the family underwent some major changes with the advent of market capitalism. By market capitalism, Shorter is referring to the development of the modern marketplace economy with the linking of local markets with regional and national ones. The effect was that local tradesmen, artisans, craftsmen, and small shop owners developed a less parochial orientation. For the family, this translates into a more cosmopolitan attitude with a lessening of importance given to local lineage concerns. Further, market capitalism contributed to the growth of the philosophy of individualism and freedom. The wish to be free emerges in gender-role relationships as romantic love and conjugal marriage.

Shorter is concerned with the changes in the relations between husbands and wives and parents and children since 1750. He believes that there was a great onrush of emotions and sentiment in family life and he examines changes in three areas: courtship, the mother-child relationship, and the relationship of the family with the community.

In courtship, he notes the emergence of sentiments of affection and friendship and the romantic love ideology. The result was that marriage became more and more a matter of free choice rather than an arranged concern determined by the parents on the basis of economic and social considerations.

The second area, mother-child relationships, is depicted as of secondary importance to the needs of domestic work and activities in the traditional preindustrial era. Shorter presents a shocking picture of mothers' neglect and disinterest in their children. The result is an all-too-frequent occurrence of unattended children burning to death or being eaten by the pigs or succumbing to the indifference of wet nurses. The absence of bereavement at the death of the infant or child supports Shorter's belief that mother-child relationships were unimportant. Although his description of events is parallel, in some respects, to Ariès' social history of childhood, it is embroidered with horrific analysis and commentary.

Shorter downplays the importance of economic factors. He deemphasizes both the fact that "ordinary" families were living under bare subsistence conditions as well as the lack of medical sophistication needed to combat the epidemic diseases rampant throughout Europe. Instead, he stresses the prevalence of an ideology of maternal neglect and indifference. "The point is that these mothers did not care, and that is why their children vanished in the ghastly slaughter of the innocents that was traditional child-rearing" (Shorter, 1975:204).

Shorter believes that attitudes toward children began to change in the nineteenth century. New sentiments of affection and love emerged and neglect and indifference became less common. The result was an increase in the growth of maternal care, defined in terms of maternal breast-feeding and the development of a more loving attitude toward children by their mothers.

The relationship of the family to the community is seen to have undergone dramatic changes with these shifting sentiments. The family became more of an emotional unit rather than a mainly productive and reproductive one. The affectional and caring sentiments tied the husband-wife relationship tighter. It began to replace lineage, property, and economic considerations as the foundation of the marriage. Simultaneously, there was a lessening of the couple's involvement with the community. Peer-group pressures lessened and with it the ending of community controls on the young couple. The emphasis was on a value system that exalted personal happiness and self-development as opposed to a value system that emphasized generational allegiances and responsibility to the community.

These new sentiments manifested themselves in the rise of the companionate family and domesticity. The companionate family is one in which the husband and wife become friends rather than superordinate and subordinate, and equally share tasks and affection. Domesticity, which Shorter (1975:227) defines as "the family's awareness of itself as a precious emotional unit that must be protected with privacy and isolation from outside intrusion," is a central feature of the companionate family. Domesticity serves to sever the involvement of the family from the surrounding community. Thus, two processes are at work: The first is the couple's almost complete withdrawal from the community; the second is the corresponding strength of the ties of the couple with each other and with their children and close relatives.

Shorter has been criticized on both methodological and theoretical grounds. Reviewers, notably Richard T. Vann (1976), have criticized the inadequacies and inconsistencies of Shorter's analysis of admittedly impressionistic data culled from contemporary accounts by physicians, priests, local magistrates, and family members. For our purposes the criticisms of Shorter on theoretical grounds (Gordon, 1977; Plumb, 1975; Vann, 1976) are more relevant. These critics question the theoretical conclusion on the relationship among sentiment, the family, and industrialization. A basic viewpoint is that Shorter overemphasizes the importance of the "sentimental revolution." He tends to overlook the enormous impact the loss of women's economic involvement and their confinement to the home have for their power and status. Let us look at another perspective on the relationship between early industrialization and the family. This orientation differs from Shorter's in two ways. It stresses the negative consequences of both the Industrial Revolution and the Victorian patriarchal ideology, which sought to fight the evils of industrial labor practices with a highly protective philosophy that secluded and confined women and children to the household.

We have discussed the fact that the family ceased to be a productive unit in society. The world of work was separated from the family household, and there was an increased differentiation of roles between husband and wife. These changes had dramatic effects on the family. The separation of workplace and home meant that husbands and wives were also physically separated during working hours, which were quite long. Husbands' work became isolated from family contact. The wife no longer knew what the husband was doing or how much he was earning. The lack of occupational visibility also meant that children could not be socialized into their father's profession by their father. People no longer worked as a family; now men were employed as individuals for a wage. If the wages were good the husband could support his family; unfortunately, too often, they were low and inadequate to provide for the family.

Young and Willmott (1973) observe that this new economic system had disastrous consequences for the family. They cite nineteenth-century sources in England to argue their case. They note that the husband as the prime breadwinner controlled the economic resources of the family. All too frequently this was much to the family's detriment. There was an extraordinarily high consumption rate of spending on such items as betting, tobacco, and liquor. The quantity and quality of food purchased for the home was also disproportionately distributed, the husband getting the most and the choicest. Physical abuse of the wife and children, which was held in check by their economic contribution in the preindustrial family-oriented economy, now occurred with greater frequency and duration. The husband's actions become more understandable if one takes into consideration the relatively low wages that these men were paid. Employees were not paid according to the number of dependents that they had. The inadequate income of these men combined with the low status and power of women and children led to the last two being a convenient scapegoat for the former.

The subjugation and subordination of women during the nineteenth century were a central concern of the great English humanists of the Victorian era: Henry Mayhew, John Stuart Mill, and Friedrich Engels. Mayhew, in his investigations of the poor in London, reported on the great prevalence of wife beatings in his classic work, *London Labour and the London Poor*:

> They can understand that it is the duty of the woman to contribute to the happiness of the man, but cannot feel that there is a reciprocal duty from the man to the woman. The wife is considered as an inexpensive servant and the disobedience of a wish is punished with blows. She must work early and late, and to the husband must be given the proceeds of her labour. Often when the man is in one of his drunken fits—which sometimes last two or three days continuously—she must by her sole exertion find food for herself and him too. To live in peace with him there must be no murmuring, no tiring under work, no fancied cause for jealousy—for if there be, she is either beaten into submission or cast adrift to begin life again—as another's leavings. (Mayhew cited in Young and Willmott, 1973:76)

John Stuart Mill (1869/1966), in his essay "The Subjection of Women," attacks the condition of legal bondage and debilitating education, and the oppressive ethic of "wifely subjection." Mill views the home as the center of a system of domestic slavery, the wife a bondservant within marriage. He observes that under Victorian law women have fewer rights than slaves. Women and children are owned absolutely by the husband-father. Unlike slaves, who were sometimes spared coercion into sexual intimacy, wives could not be entitled to any household items and, if the husband so desired, could be compelled by the courts to return to him. There was little legal opportunity for women's freedom through divorce. Mill also observed the prevalence of physical brutality in marriage, it being the logical conclusion of women's subjection.

> And how many thousands are there among the lowest classes in every country, who without being in a legal sense malefactors in every other respect, because in every other quarter their aggressions meet with resistance, indulge

the utmost habitual excesses of bodily violence toward the unhappy wife, who alone, at least of grown persons, can neither repel nor escape from their brutality; and toward whom the excess of dependence inspires their mean and savage natures, not with generous forbearance and a point of honor to behave well to one whose lot in life is trusted entirely to their kindness, but on the contrary with a notion that the law has delivered her to them as their thing, to be used at their pleasure, and that they are not expected to practice the consideration towards her which is required from them towards everybody else. (Mill, 1966:467-468)

Mill advocated legal change—suffrage and a just property law—to alleviate the debilitating conditions of women. He also saw the need for women to enter the labor market and the professions and urged the right of women to work.

Friedrich Engels, as you recall, took a more radical approach. He argued that the monogamous family system was created by the industrial capitalist economy to enslave women and use them as a cheap source of domestic labor. He felt that the attainment of legal equality for women was not enough unless it was also accompanied with total social and economic equality. Further, it was necessary to broaden the opportunities of women to assure personal fulfillment in productive work. The dependent status of women was seen as antithetical to equality. And equality can only be assured with the end of masculine dominance over economic production and the entrance of women into the economic world on a parallel level.

Contributing to the lowly position of women during the Victorian industrial period was the development of an ideology whose explicit goal was to assure the safety and well-being of women but that implicitly added to her political and social demise—the ideology of domestic confinement. A central tenet of this philosophy was the belief in women's natural domesticity. This belief prevented and restricted the employment of women outside the home. It advocated the economic dependence of married women on their husbands and their sole involvement with household tasks and child care. This ideology was in direct contrast to the practices of the preindustrial era when women were a part of domestic industry. It can be seen as the Victorian answer to the harshness and severity of early industrial labor practices. Numerous laws were passed that restricted or prevented female and child labor in mining, factories, and the textile industries. This protective legislation led to the creation of the modern housewife role that has become the prime source of feminine subservience. It is ironic that this legislation passed by "chivalrous" Victorian gentlemen to alter the brutality of industrial work had as its ultimate effect the substitution of a different form of subjugation.

Ann Oakley (1974) investigated contemporary Victorian documents to find the rationale for the confinement of women to the household and their restriction or prevention from seeking outside employment. Four main reasons are delineated: "female employment was condemned on moral grounds, on grounds of damage to physical health, on grounds of neglect of home and family, and lastly, simply on the grounds that it contravened the 'natural' division of labour between the sexes" (Oakley, 1974:45).

Oakley reports that from 1841 to 1914, housewifery increasingly became the sole occupation of women. She cites figures from England to show that 1 of 4 married women were working in 1851, compared to only 1 in 10 by 1911. The ideology of women's confinement to the home originated in the middle and upper classes. A woman's idleness was seen as a mark of prosperity. The leisured lady at home was the ideal. The development and elaboration of society and rules of etiquette became the epitome of the later Victorian era. For the working classes, the doctrine of female domesticity began to crystallize in the last quarter of the nineteenth century. It ran counter to the economic needs of the family, yet became prevalent. For the working classes, too, "the idea that work outside the home for married women was a 'misfortune and a disgrace' became acceptable" (Oakley, 1974:50). A closer look at Victorian society and its accompanying etiquette rules can be enlightening, for it was these rules, established by the emerging bourgeois upper class, that proved to be influential in effecting gender-role relationships not only for that class but also for the entire society.

Victorian rules of etiquette controlled interaction between the sexes in public places.

BOX 11-1   The Historical Family

Sexual Politics in Victorian Etiquette

During the nineteenth century, England saw a radical transformation of its ruling classes. As newly rich families began to gain eminence, these families—through individual achievement in industry and commerce—were supplanting the traditional rich whose positions were based on heredity and family connections. To govern the social mobility of these new personnel, an elaborate formalized society developed. The rules of etiquette set down in housekeeping books, etiquette manuals, and advice columns in magazines were most relevant for highly structured social gatherings. The behavior of all participants in presentations at court, country and city house parties, and the round of afternoon calls was strictly regulated.

The rules of "society" were created to control entrance and involvement within social classes. This was viewed as necessary, since Victorian "society" was undergoing unprecedented social change; rigid rules of social acceptance provided a haven of stability. The elaborate code of etiquette created barriers to social entry. Ceremonial behavior can be seen as rites of passage, especially during certain important events such as births, marriages, and deaths. The introduction of new individuals and families into group membership and activities was also a sensitive area and it, too, was marked by etiquette rules. Introductions, visits, and dining patterns became formalized and vastly elaborate.

The home became increasingly an important area for social gatherings. It served to control and regulate the contacts that the "ins" wished to have with their equals and the new people seeking entrance into their group. The private clubs served a similar function. The "society" can be seen as controlling access to and involvement with those of the upper classes. For the newcomer it necessitated the abandonment of old allegiances, family and nonfamily, for this new prestigious social group.

The role of women was paradoxical. Influenced by the male-dominant patriarchal ideolo-gy, Victorian "society" was elaborated by its women. Women were exhorted to act as guardians of the home; men were exhorted to leave the home for the struggles of the business world, the army, the church, or politics. Women's duties were to regulate and control social gatherings and thus keep order in the ever-changing social scene. However, their sequestration in the home, and the confinement of their activities to domestic and "society" matters, occurred at the same time that men were expanding their influence and involvement in the new industrial world. This, ultimately, proved disastrous for women's independence and autonomy.

Socialization practices reinforced this dichotomy. Men were being socialized to operate in the ever-changing and complex world of industry, finance, and commerce. Women were socialized into the complexities of etiquette and the running of the home with its hierarchy of servants. Dress was a sign of social position and achievement. It serves as a good illustration of the extent to which etiquette rules were elaborated:

> Every cap, bow, streamer, ruffle, fringe, bustle, glove and other elaboration symbolized some status category for the female wearer; mourning dress being the quintessence of this demarcation. A footman, with long experience in upper-class households, said "jewelry was a badge that women wore like a sergeant major's stripes or field-marshall's baton; it showed achievement, rank, position." It is not surprising, then, that girls and women of all classes were preoccupied with dress. (Davidoff, 1975:95)

The rules governing sexual behavior for women were also paradoxical. The emphasis was on respectability through control of sexual behavior and desire. Victorian women gained status by denying their own sexuality and treating the Victorian masculine sex drive as sinful. Purity beliefs and the elaborate etiquette norms that stressed modesty, prudishness, and cleanliness— as well as the rules governing demeanor and appearance—served to provide a sense of order, stability, and status in the everyday world. However, they also served to be psychologically stultifying. Further, the placing of women on a virginal pedestal, limiting their involvement to the home, and excluding them from the economic sphere served to reinforce the patriarchal ideology. Through idolatry, subservience emerged.

Davidoff (1975) and Bartelt and Hutter (1977)

GENDER ROLES IN THE INDUSTRIAL WESTERN FAMILY

Industrialization and a patriarchal ideology led to the development of a conjugal-family system with a clear delineation of roles between husband and wife. The breakdown of larger community involvements was supposed to be compensated for by an increased intimacy and emotionality between family members. Unfortunately, many husbands, burdened by inadequate wages to support their families and finding themselves isolated from domestic everyday activities, did not provide the necessary emotional as well as economic supports for their wives and children. An all-too-frequent occurrence was family neglect and physical abuse. Thus, the breakdown of community involvement with the family and the disintegration of the traditional extended family, which characterized preindustrial rural life and domestic industry, led to an intolerable situation for women and children. They were dependent both economically and emotionally on the whims of detached, autocratic, and often despotic husbands.

Young and Willmott (1973), in their astute history of the family in England, developed the thesis that women—after acclimating themselves to industrial-based city life—eventually developed a family organization based on mother-daughter maternal bonds. They did this to protect themselves and their children from the unreliability and indifference of their husbands. With the husband absent from the household and working elsewhere, daughters developed strong ties with their mothers. They lived near them and mothers served as an oasis of security for both married daughters and grandchildren. In addition, mothers could provide day-care services if their daughters got jobs, and they were also able to pass on gifts and money during periods of need.

We have discussed this family system earlier in our analysis of working-class communities and families in England and the United States. Young and Willmott base their thesis on the working-class community of Bethnel Green in London (cf. Marris, 1958; Townsend, 1957; Willmott and Young, 1960; and Young and Willmott, 1957). As you may recall, these communities were labeled *closed communities* by John Mogey (1964) and *urban villages* by Herbert Gans (1962a). These communities were depicted as ones in which intense interfamilial cooperation exists. They also are cohesive and homogeneous in cultural values and are closed to nonmembers. In our discussion of working-class family life in Bethnel Green, we saw that husbands and wives performed a separate set of household tasks. In times of emergency, aid for either the husband or wife is provided by other husbands and wives in the area. Frequently, these are same-sex relatives. Under these conditions, a strict role segregation of tasks is maintained. Leisure-time activities are similarly segregated. Within segregated role-pattern families, mother-daughter relations tend to be stronger than father-son relations. This is particularly the case when the married couple takes up residence in close proximity to the wife's mother. Intimate, emotional, and isolated conjugal families did not live in these communities.

When we examine these internal family structures in more detail, we find the opposite of the conjugal-family form. Elizabeth Bott (1957), in an interesting typology, focuses on the husbands' and wives' involvement with social networks comprised of kin, friends, and neighbors in the community as well as their relationship and involvement with each other. Bott found that if neither family member maintained ties with a network of friends, neighbors, and relatives who knew one another and interacted, husband-wife ties would be minimal. Husbands and wives who are members of such close-knit networks when they marry and continue to maintain such relationships during their marriage have a marital-role organization based on a clear differentiation of tasks with few shared interests or activities. If either needs assistance, whether economic or emotional, he or she does not ask the spouse but rather seeks help from network members. The result is that the husband-wife relationship is not close. The couple lives in relatively separate worlds with different involvements and activities.

The picture presented is quite different from that drawn by Edward Shorter (1975) of families emotionally and intimately involved with each other. It is a family that has weak marital ties and strong lineage ties. It is an industrial-age version of the community dominating the family pattern, which was characteristic of preindustrial society. This developed out of the felt need of economically and emotionally dependent women and their children to assure some stability and continuity in their lives. Young and Willmott (1973) observe that this family system becomes self-perpetuating. Once the female-centered system developed, it served to exclude men from the intimacies of domestic family life and forced them to seek other ways to satisfy their needs:

> This sort of structure—weak on the family of marriage, strong on the family of origin—tended to perpetuate itself. Husbands were often squeezed out of the warmth of the female circle, and took to the pub as their defence against the defence. They had to put up with mothers-in-law who were constantly interfering, as the man might see it, with the arrangements in his own home. His wife could seem more her daughter than his wife, and both of them belonged to a group which did not award men a high place in its order of values. He could find himself undermined, in a hundred ways, subtle and unsubtle. He could be pushed into becoming an absentee father, so bringing on the insecurity which the extended family in this form was established to counter. (Young and Willmott, 1973:92)

In this section, we have seen that the Industrial Revolution had important and long-lasting effects on the family. It meant the separation of men and women into two isolated worlds—the world of work and the world of the household. This had the effect of setting apart the life of the husbands from the intimacies of everyday domestic activities and estranging them from their wives and children. Women found themselves outside of the workforce and involved solely in housework and child care. Economic factors coincided with a misguided Victorian patriarchialism that saw economic employment as a threat to womanly virtue and bad for her from both a physical and emotional standpoint. Not, incidentally, that a woman working for wages was seen as an indication of her husband's failure to earn sufficiently to support her and the family. The increased sentiments, emotions, and intimacies of the newly emerged conjugal family did not compensate for women's economic dependence on their husbands and their resultant decline in social status. Particularly, this became a problem as it occurred at the same time that the ties with extended kin and with the surrounding community diminished. Thus, the emotional supports of these "outsiders" collapsed, and the increased emotional dependency of the marital couple on each other—heretofore called on far too infrequently—occurred. To help compensate for their loss, working-class women in England developed an alternative family system that emphasized mother-daughter ties and deemphasized the ties between husband and wife.

However, the predominant ideology was focusing more and more on the belief in the primacy of the conjugal family with its accent on intimacy and emotionalism between husband and wife. At the same time, an integral aspect of the ideology of the conjugal family, female domesticity, worked against it. Thus the conjugal family system found itself in a dilemma. Its advocacy of differentiated spheres of activity—masculine public life and feminine private life—was antithetical to the very intimacy it sought; that is, female dependency ran counter to conjugal intimacy. It is now time to examine the contemporary conjugal-family system and see how it attempts to resolve this issue.

From Private Family to Symmetrical Family

The theme running through this chapter is the distinction between public and domestic/private spheres of activity and their respective implications for male and female marital relationships. The trend has been gradual, from a more public family system with high community involvement to a more private closed family system. The public family was one in which there was little distinction made between work and the home and where community played a major role in shaping and determining family relationships. Community control and scrutiny was primarily responsible for the limitations on family intimacy and privacy. Women in the preindustrial period were actively involved in work. In fact, the distinction between work and domesticity hardly existed.

The ideology of the private family emerged during the Industrial Revolution. Work was separated from the household and there was a greater differentiation and specialization of the roles of husband and wife. Coinciding with industrialization was the development of an ideology that stressed the importance of sentiments regarding emotionality, intimacy, and privacy among conjugal family members. However, through much of the history of industrialization, the reality of the private family was relatively uncommon, since it was restricted to the more affluent middle classes of the society.

The upper classes, desiring to maintain and control their family wealth and power, continued to maintain a family system that placed great importance on extended kinship lines. For the working classes, especially in the city, maternal-centered, three-generational family systems developed to compensate for the husband's emotional distance and the too frequent economic unfeasibility of the conjugal-family form.

Certain conditions have become prevalent in contemporary industrial society that have had great significance for family relations. Demographic changes, the lengthened life span, the decline in infant and child mortality rates, the decline in maternal deaths in childbirth, lower birthrates, the dissociation of reproductive from sexual activities, and the decline in the period of life devoted to maternity in relation to the total life expectancy have contributed to attitudinal and behavioral changes in the family. For example, the typical couple now spends a great number of years together outside of parental concerns. This has helped foster the emergence of the conjugal role ideology. The emphasis on love, emotional support, friendship and companionship, and erotic and sexual gratification can transform the marital relationship into the ideal conjugal family.

Feminism has also been influential in the reshaping of the family. Through the twentieth century, women have been gaining in legal equality. Areas of legal change include the women's suffrage rights, rights of separation and divorce, and rights of equal employment and opportunity. Although equality has not been fully realized, as the struggle over the Equal Rights Amendment (ERA) can testify, there has been marked improvement in the power and status of women compared to life in the nineteenth century. The result has been a growth of female independence.

The higher standard of living for ordinary families and the migration of families from rural to urban and from urban to suburban residences has contributed to these changes. As we saw in our earlier discussion on suburban families, the emphasis became more and more focused on conjugal family ties at the expense of the extended family. The acquisition of better homes has made the household a more attractive place in which to spend time and on which to spend money. Husbands are devoting more time to their families, and there is a diminishing of the segregation of marital couples that characterized working-class couples of the earlier industrial period.

Observing these changes in England, Young and Willmott (1973) have postulated the emergence of a new family form that epitomizes the ideals of the conjugal family but with some notable differences. This is the symmetrical family. The *symmetrical family* is seen as one in which there is recognition for the continued differences in the work opportunities and ways of life of husbands and wives but in which there is marked egalitarianism between the sexes. Young and Willmott note a similarity between this family form and the family of domestic industry. Both families emphasize the relationships among husband, wife, and children. However, unlike the domestic industrial family, which functioned as a productive entity, the symmetrical family functions as a unit of consumption:

> When husband, wife, and children worked together on a farm or in handicrafts the family was *the* productive unit even if it did not yield much more than a bare subsistence to its members. When individual wage-employment became almost universal (except for housewives), the family had to give way to a wider division of labor. But in the course of time the family has re-established a new kind of primacy, not as the unit of production so much as the unit of consumption. (Young and Willmott, 1973:xxi)

Couples, particularly husbands, see themselves as no longer having to devote as much time to earning a living and providing for a family. They are now able to spend more time with their families in leisure and home-centered activities. The new egalitarianism is realized in the assumption of joint responsibility in the planning of children and the increased tendency for greater husband involvement in the rearing of the children. Feminism is evinced in the symmetrical family as the belief that there should be no monopolies for either husband or wife in any sphere of activity. Women, then, are entitled to the same rights as men to become involved in work outside the home as well as in it. The result has been a movement of women back to the labor force, the usual pattern being the wife staying at home during the early years of child rearing, then taking first a part-time job, and later a full-time job as the children grow older.

Young and Willmott (1973), however, believe that the traditional pattern of the husband being the primary wage earner will continue. They observe a similar phenomenon to the one that we discussed in our analysis of the Soviet Union/Russia, where the wife has become responsible both for her outside work and for all domestic tasks. This dual role or double burden for women is practiced among the London families interviewed by Young and Willmott.

Notably, Young and Willmott see positive gains in the strength of the feminist movement. They believe that just as the worlds of work and leisure are merging, so too will the worlds of men and women merge. The result will be an eventual sharing of the tasks by men and women in both domestic and outside work. They recognize the strains that will have to be overcome: the caring of children as well as arrangement of work and leisure schedules so that the family can spend time together. Generally, they are optimistic for the future: Technology and family wants can both be fulfilled.

Problems of the Dual-Career Family

In the nearly quarter of a century since Young and Willmott wrote *The Symmetrical Family*, in the United States the dual-income family had become the normative family system. In 1960, fewer than one-third of married women (30 percent) were in the paid labor force. By 1990 the proportion of married women in the labor force had nearly doubled (see Figure 11-1), reaching 58 percent (U.S. Bureau of the Census, 1992b). But, rather than ushering in a new wave of egalitarian spousal relationships, many problems developed and still plague the family. These concerns revolved around the tensions between occupational career commitments for both men and women and for their marital, familial, and household commitments.

Since 1970 women in increasing numbers entered the labor force, so by 1990 more than half of all women with children under the age of 6 were in it. Nearly three-quarters of all divorced mothers also were involved in labor-force participation. The experience of women in the labor force follows that of their counterparts in Russia, Sweden, and Israel. They too found themselves making less for the same work as men. The gender gap in wages is one source of evidence of economic discrimination based on sex. Generally, women who work full time earn only about three-quarters as much as men. Another source of discrimination is the fact that women usually experience occupational segregation where they only can find employment in such extensions of traditional "women's work" as food services, teaching, social work, and in "pink-collar" low-skill clerical and sales work. In the more skilled professions, including medicine, law, and engineering, women traditionally had supportive jobs such as nursing

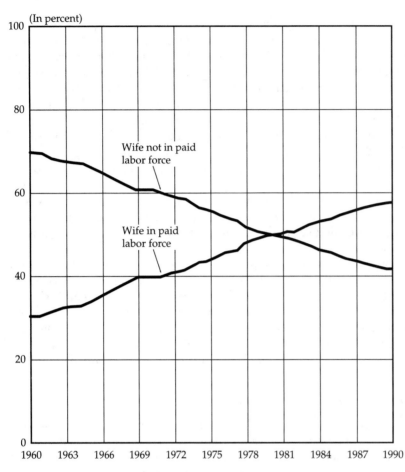

Wives' Labor Force Participation Rises

The labor force participation rate for married women has increased dramatically during the last 30 years. In 1960, fewer than one-third of married women (30 percent) were in the paid labor force. By 1990 the proportion of married women in the labor force had nearly doubled, reaching 58 percent.

Source: U.S. Bureau of the Census, *Current Population Reports*, Series P23-181, "Households, Families, and Children: A 30-Year Perspective," U.S. Government Printing Office, Washington, D.C., 1992.

FIGURE 11-1   Married-couple families with wives in the labor force: 1960 to 1990.

and legal stenography. Even today, when there has been a major movement of women into these professions they tend to specialize in pediatrics, obstetrics and gynecology, anesthesiology, and social and family law. In higher education, where more women are entering and gaining tenure track positions, they continue to experience lower wages and more difficulty in promotions into the higher ranks of associate and full professorships (Business and Professional Women's Foundation, 1992).

Two terms that have entered the language in recent years summarize women's experiences in the labor force—the *mommy track* and the *glass ceiling*. The mommy track was a term coined by media in response to a controversial article written by Felice Schwartz (1989) that appeared in the influential *Harvard Business Review*. The article recognized that wives take greater responsibility for taking care of their children and spend more time on housework than their husbands. They also experience greater role conflict than do their husbands when it comes to commitments to occupational careers and family involvements. Schwartz argued that this familial and household commitment, especially in the years of child bearing and early childhood, necessitated corporations to develop two parallel career path options for women. The first track, or what became known as the "mommy track" would seek to achieve a balance between career and family commitments by lessening a women's involvement with her job.

The second track, or "fast track," would make no concessions to familial involvements. Women who were primarily career oriented would be expected if necessary to assume high-powered demanding positions that may often include travel and may also require sixty or seventy hours of work per week. The response to Schwartz's proposal was instantaneous (cf. Day, 1989; Ehrlich, 1990; Kantrowitz, 1989; Lewin, 1989). The corporation response was largely positive. However, many critics saw that Schwartz's proposal reified the societal practice that relegated women, but not men, to family and domestic responsibilities. The mommy track would also encourage women to lower their career aspirations and to provide justification for employers to promote fewer women. Further, a "spill-over" effect will also impact on women on the fast track.

The implementation of this two-track system would only reinforce male stereotypes of women and would provide justification for relegating all women into lower-paying and inferior-echelon positions in corporations. In effect, then, the "mommy track" would serve to reinforce the already prevalent "glass ceiling." The "glass ceiling" refers to the practice in which corporations set a barrier that prevents women from advancing to higher executive positions. While companies argue that no such barrier exists, U.S. Department of Labor findings confirm that gender-related biases do exist (Segal and Zellner, 1992). This study provides support for women executives who participated in a *Business Week*/Harris poll who believed that a male-dominating corporate structure curtailed their career advancement (Vamos, 1992). The Business and Professional Women's Foundation (1992), in a report on the status of women working in corporations, academia, and government, determined that the dearth of women in middle and senior level management positions was due to "*organizational, attitudinal,* and *societal* barriers that kept women and minorities from advancing up the career ladder" (1992:1). They observe that 7 out of 10 women ages 25 to 54 are currently in the labor force. This constitutes nearly half of the entire workforce. "Discrimination, whether intentional or unintentional, prevents women and minorities from truly benefitting from their training and efforts and from fully contributing their abilities and knowledge to the productivity of our country" (Business and Professional Women's Foundation, 1992:10). They conclude that if nothing else it is bad business to underutilize this large segment of the workforce that has become increasingly essential.

When we turn our attention to how women have fared in the domestic sphere, we find that the hopeful and sanguine portrait of family life prophesied by Young and Willmott has not materialized for many dual-career families. One of the major sources of difficulty for husbands and wives is how family roles need to be reallocated in light of the fact that both spouses have full-time involvements in their jobs. Joseph Pleck (1985) found that women experienced "role overload." In addition to her outside work involvements, the major burden of family and domestic work fell on her shoulders. However, Pleck did see some movement by men to pay more attention to family matters. Pleck believes that this is indicative of a value shift in which men will develop greater family involvements, particularly taking a more active father role.

Arlie Russell Hochschild (1989a) in her widely praised book, *The Second Shift*, is concerned with how cultural definitions of "appropriate" domestic roles and labor force roles affect marital dynamics. She observes that contemporary economic trends have altered women's lives much more so than they have altered men's lives. Women have found themselves in new circumstances: They are working full time in the paid labor force, yet, at the same time, they are seen as primarily involved in domestic work. As a result, women are experiencing a "cultural lag" in the larger world, and a "gender lag" in the home. There is a lag regarding both attitudes and behavior toward women's paid work and domestic work. Hochschild speaks of a "stalled revolution" that does not recognize that women have changed but "most workplaces remain inflexible in the face of the family demands of their workers and at home, most men have yet to really adapt to the changes in women" (Hochschild, 1989a:12).

Women are confronted with a "second shift" of domestic labor because husbands are generally not increasing their work involvement with the home. Further, men have not emotionally supported women's role change to the same extent that women have. Similar to Pleck's findings, Hochschild found that while couples indicated that they "wanted" to share the domestic tasks of the second shift, less than 20 percent of the couples actually did so. Even when sharing does occur, women feel greater responsibility for caring for their homes and children. The "sharing" is also often inequitable: Men get to do the more "fun" things like taking children to the movies or the zoo; women often do the more tedious household tasks such as vacuuming or cleaning the toilet.

Hochschild (1989b) analyzes the second shift through her concept of the "economy of gratitude," which was elaborated in an article by the same name. This concept is used to analyze whether husbands and wives have the same reality definitions about whether a given act requires an expression of appreciation and gratitude or not. The following examples of housework in a dual-career marriage demonstrate the implications of differential reality definitions can impact on marital dynamics:

> A husband does the laundry, makes the beds, washes the dishes. Relative to his father, his brother and several men on the block this husband helps more at home. He also does more than he did ten years ago. All in all he feels he has done more than his wife could reasonably expect, and with good spirit. He has given her, he feels, a gift. She should, he feels, be grateful. However, to his wife the matter seems different. In addition to her eight hours in the office, she does 80% of the housework. Relative to all she does, relative to what she expects of him, what she feels she deserves, her husband's contribution seems welcome, but not extra, not a gift. So his gift is "mis-received." For each partner has perceived this gift through a different cultural prism. By creating different cultural prisms for men and women, larger social forces can impoverish a couple's private *economy of gratitude* (Hochschild, 1989b, 95).

In an insightful article, Hunt and Hunt (1982) observe that an examination of the contemporary dual-career family provides important insights on social-change processes and their impact on the family. They are not as sanguine about the future of the dual-career family. They challenge the view that dual-career families—in which both husbands and wives have significant and fulfilling occupational careers as well as meaningful, intimate, and involved family roles—represent the wave of the future. Instead, they theorize that *both* men and women will have to make decisions regarding their commitments either to occupational careers or to the family. The result will be a polarization of the worlds of career and family, and institutional separation of the world of work and the world of the family will be even more complete. "[T]he movement of women into careers and of men into family involvement will break down the integration of these spheres and promote the evolution of more distinct lifestyles organized around either careers or families" (Hochschild, 1982:508).

The dual-career family since the late 1960s has been characterized by the unequal distribution of self-commitments to careers and to families by men and women. (By careers we mean work involvements that are continuous, developmental, demand a high level of commitment, and have intrinsic value and reward). Essentially, while both men and women worked, men have given differential commitment and involvement to their careers, while women have toned down their career aspirations and have given differential commitment to their familial roles. Women, especially highly educated women, have pursued a "career of limited ambition" (White, 1979). This family form has not challenged the male role and has departed little from the conventional domestic division of labor among dual-career couples. The career wife has worked the "second shift" and performed dual roles or the "double burden" through skillful allocation of her time and resources.

We have seen how the "mommy track" and the "glass ceiling" have contributed to this phenomenon. Profamily coercion by employers has further reinforced this pattern. Women often find themselves in dead-end careers with restricted employment, fewer professional opportunities, and lower salary scales. Implicitly, this has been legitimated by beliefs that wives' careers are secondary, with their primary identification being the family, and that their wages were supplemental family income. The consequence of this pattern is a dual-career family form that "permitted the lives of dual-career men to be similar to those of other career men, while the lives of dual-career women were carefully balanced to provide a measure of career involvement as long as the family was not inconvenienced" (Hunt and Hunt, 1982:501).

However, a countermovement has been emerging that has questioned this family form and alternative patterns are emerging. Many women are entering the labor force and are making greater commitment to their occupational careers. This factor, combined with the occasional enforcement of antidiscrimination laws, has pressured and forced employers to move away slowly from discriminatory gender employment practices. At the same time, many women are also choosing to avoid the stresses of dual commitments by postponing or permanently deciding against marriage and parenthood. Concomitantly, men observing the continued erosion of the acceptance of women's double burden may themselves be reluctant to assume greater commitment to familial and domestic roles and may make similar decisions regarding marriage and parenthood. Hunt and Hunt observed in the early 1980s that the incidence of the two-person career family was decreasing. They believed that growing employment for women may actually cause a decline in the formation of the family. We have commented elsewhere in this book how such a movement is actually occurring with more and more women and men postponing marriage and having children by living in less permanent cohabiting relationships or living a single lifestyle.

A major motive for those not marrying is that the appeal of marriage has become weaker (Espanshade, 1985). Economist Gary Becker (1991) sees it as the "gains of marriage" becoming less appealing. For women, in particular, increased financial independence and reproductive control makes singlehood or cohabitation a viable option. The potential difficulties of balancing a career, children, and the home combined with an uncertain economic marketplace that makes coordinating education and career objectives with potential spouses more problematic makes marriage a less attractive life option. For men, current economic uncertainties makes it increasingly unlikely that they can solely support a family. We have seen how these economic pressures have had a particularly strong effect on African Americans where male-joblessness is an everyday reality and marriage is increasingly not a viable option.

While these trends continue for a significant segment of the population, many other people continue to marry and have children. However, Hunt and Hunt speculated that the men and women who are family-oriented will tone down their career aspirations. This will occur as a realization that they cannot effectively compete occupationally with their counterparts who have made decisions to be solely committed to their careers. The consequent result will be two dominant lifestyles. Men and women who pursue careers will begin to resemble each other and the world of work will become more gender-neutral. For those who marry and become family oriented, there will also be a blurring of the lines of gender-role differentiation. In some families, men may take on traditional female roles and will spend more time with their families and limit their career aspirations and goals, while women will do the opposite. In Hunt and Hunt's terms "women can become 'sociological men'—persons who emphasize their public lives and enjoy the resulting power and independence—and men can become 'sociological women'—persons who invest themselves primarily in their families and forfeit power and control of their personal destinies" (Hunt and Hunt, 1982:503). Yet these changes do not threaten the underlying polarization of public power and family involvement.

The polarization of career and family has wide-ranging family policy implications. Polarization will result in a widened gap between parents and nonparents. Those without children will monopolize the highest-paying jobs. Without worrying about the costs of raising children, singles or "child-free" couples will be able to afford the bounties of an affluent consumer society. The Yuppie movement and the gentrification of many cities points to the growing disparity in resources between these professionals and their family-oriented, less economically successful counterparts. Family-oriented couples may find themselves priced out of the market for the more attractive rewards, housing, automobiles, and consumer goods available to the wealthy. It will become apparent to families that they cannot compete effectively in a consumer market stimulated by the spending and investing power of child-free adults. As a consequence, more and more people may reach the decision that parenthood is too costly an option that prevents them from pursuing other attractive lifestyles.

A significant decline in a nation's birthrate has the potential to become a serious social problem. "The birth of fewer children and/or their failure to develop into healthy and productive adults would be economically depressing and would increase the ratio of non-employed to the population of employed adults" (Hunt and Hunt, 1982:508). This could ultimately undermine the viability of benefit systems such as social security. It is for that reason that Hunt and Hunt argue for social policies that would support family life. They call for policies that would subsidize family incomes to reduce the disparity in

BOX 11-2   The Contemporary American Family

Redefining Motherhood on the Edge of the Millennium

Rosalind C. Barnett and Caryl Rivers

As Mother's Day 1996 approaches, we are beginning to see the outlines of what might be called "The New Motherhood." Neither the traditional image of the blissful, all-sacrificing mother, nor the revisionist image of the unhappy, depressed mom who regrets she gave up her life for her kids, it is a "motherhood as part of normal life" image that's coming into focus.

The new motherhood may be in fact the *old* motherhood. It harks back to the hunter-gatherer days when women cared for children while ranging across many miles to collect food—a rigorous life far different from the modern notion of the passive female. Motherhood as "No Big Deal" may be hard for us to swallow, but it is the picture that emerges from our major new study of American couples funded by the National Institute of Mental Health.

Tradition decrees that motherhood transforms the world for a woman—in one way or another. In the Freudian tradition, motherhood is so central to a woman's psyche that everything else in her life pales. In the 1950s, that image became happy suburban mom, driving the station wagon, dusting the table.

Or, there's the opposite message from the behavioral sciences that we began to hear in the late 1960s, when studies of women with children began to emerge. "There's nothing more depressing than a houseful of young children," psychologist Marcia Guttentag wrote. Mothers were seen as overburdened, depressed, anxious, generally in bad shape. A spate of books by mothers appeared, confessing anger and sadness because they had put their own lives on hold and invested so much in being mothers.

In either view, the most important fact about a woman was that she was a mother. Today, the either-or image is outdated. For women in our study, becoming a mother was just not a big deal, at least as far as emotional health was concerned.

For these women, whose average age was 35, having either a first child or other children simply had no impact on their level of stress. This is not to say that having a child isn't a wonderful experience, or that it doesn't deepen a woman's understanding of life. But it is no longer the great event that is utterly life-transforming. It is simply an important event in the continuum of her life, which continues in many ways as it did before.

In another study, sociologists Elaine Wethington and Ronald Kessler reported that having a child per se was not related to distress, but leaving the labor force was. Thus, *only* when a woman had a child *and* reduced her labor force commitment significantly did her distress increase.

We did not find the anxiety and depression associated with motherhood that earlier studies found. Indeed, women who were mothers reported *lower* distress than women who were nonmothers. In our study, 80 percent of the women went back to work in the first year after the birth of a child. So, many of the issues facing women who find themselves home alone with children—isolation, boredom, loss of freedom, curtailment of activities—were for these women only a time-limited phenomenon. They did not pine for their colleagues at work or miss the challenge of a job in a way that would press their mental health. Even when they were at home, they felt themselves connected to the workplace.

Clearly, it is time to redefine motherhood as one important and rewarding part of a woman's life, but not *the* totally defining event on which her emotional well-being depends. Today and in the years ahead, women will choose from a number of options as far as parenting is concerned.

How to mother has changed dramatically. Many women will stay in the workforce after a maternity leave and combine mothering and working for their entire lives. Some may take time out when their children are young, keeping their skills honed, staying connected to work, and planning for a return. Some will choose shift work so that each parent will share parenting time with the children. Few women will be in the mothering mode common during the 1950s—leaving the workforce after the birth of a first child, never to return.

(continued)

Today, with the reality that most mothers are in the labor force, we are seeing a gradual change in cultural beliefs as well. Gone is the belief current in the 1950s that one must have a child to be an authentic woman. But gone as well is the prevailing belief of the 1970s that to have a life of work and accomplishment, one has to give up on having children.

When sociologist Kathleen Gerson studied women who were born in the 1950s—a sample close in age to our study—she found that these women did not feel they had to choose between a career and motherhood. The struggle that gripped women in the 1960s and 1970s has evaporated. It has been replaced with another, perhaps more difficult struggle: *How* to combine motherhood and a paid job. What was considered *unnatural* for most 1950s mothers is now a fact of life. And while old ideas linger, the debate about whether a woman can both be a mother and be employed is moot. The question of *how* to do both is very much alive.

The problem with our tradition of seeing work as peripheral to a woman's well-being has been that we have paid scant attention to the *quality* of her work. We have to change this focus.

For a mother, having a good job may affect not only her life, but the lives of her children as well. New research is finding that a woman's work may have a profound impact on the resources and skills she brings to being a parent. One series of studies shows that the complexity of a mother's job affects her child's verbal ability. Its authors—Toby L. Parcel and Elizabeth G. Menaghan of Ohio State University—suggest that inequality can be passed from generation to generation when a mother is stuck in a dead-end, repetitive job.

They looked at a study of 795 children, aged 3 to 6, and their employed mothers in the National Longitudinal Youth Survey Cohort study. The more complex the work activities in the mother's occupation and the better paying her job, the higher was her child's verbal ability, they found.

But the woman whose work involves simple, repetitive tasks has more problems with her children than the woman who has a more complex job. The employee who is given little autonomy and is subject to rigid supervision tries to

handle her children the same way, with less-than-wonderful results. Here is an example of how the disappearance of complex, high-wage jobs from the economy can affect families. To the degree that those jobs are replaced by low-level, routine service jobs, and to the degree that work for more adults becomes routine, unskilled and deadening, children's problems are likely to increase.

It is chilling to think that the dead-end jobs many women wander into will affect the next generation. But the researchers argue just that: Inequality may be passed to children from mothers whose own jobs stunt their potential—and their children will reflect that lack of potential.

Researchers have known for some time that conditions of work for men affected their child-rearing. Routinization, low autonomy, heavy supervision and little opportunity for complex work in low-paid jobs erode intellectual functioning and exacerbate psychological distress. This is true as well for women. Both men and women whose distress is high are less attentive and responsive as parents and can give their children little intellectual stimulation.

Young women who drop out of school, who get tracked into the least challenging, least complex jobs, are those whose children may not be able to get the stimulation they need to develop to their maximum intellectual potential. By letting women be tracked into a low-wage, dead-end "pink-collar ghetto," we may be hobbling the next generation at a time when the nation will need an educated, articulate work force to compete in the increasingly global and competitive world economy.

All this research screams out at us that we had better be paying a lot more attention to the nature of women's jobs. One aspect of a New Motherhood we *don't* want to see is a parenting style that is the echo of a dead-end job.

Rosalind C. Barnett of the Murray Research Center at Radcliffe and Caryl Rivers of Boston University are the authors of "She Works, He Works: How Two Income Families are Happier, Healthier and Better Off," published by HarperSan Francisco.

Philadelphia Inquirer, 3 May 1996.
Reprinted with permission by the Philadelphia Inquirer, 1996.

living standards between families and nonfamilies. These policies provide for greater sharing of the costs of children through such programs and policies as publicly funded child care and health care, family allowances (payments per child), housing allowances, and paid maternal (or paternal) leave to care for infants and sick children. Such tax-financed services and income-transfer policies are in effect in European societies like Sweden, which has a large proportion of the female population in the workforce. Unfortunately, the policy of the U.S. government has been less enlightened. The consequences will be the further dichotomization or polarization of the worlds of work and the family, with particularly negative consequences for the American family.

> Families will survive, but not thrive. They will be idealized like motherhood and ignored like mothers. They will be forced to trade efficacy for security. Under these conditions, people will be free to choose families, but those who do so will continue to suffer the age-old effects of being women in a man's world. (Hunt and Hunt, 1982:510)

THE SEARCH FOR BALANCE: INDIVIDUALISM AND FAMILY COMMITMENT

The problems of the American family are seen most vividly in the tensions that exist within the dual-career family as men and women seek to balance occupational work and family commitments in the face of economic conditions that require employment for both of them. For the last twenty-five years, many sociologists have placed the problem as stemming from the dichotomization of public and private worlds and the growing privatization of the family.

In the 1970s critics of the conjugal family pointed to its deficiencies in coping with the needs of women, children, and elderly. In the 1980s and into the 1990s critics have continued to find fault with the conjugal family in its inabilities to handle the concerns of individual family members including wives/mothers, husbands/fathers, children. However, there has been a major countermovement that extols the conjugal family and bemoans the perceived decline of the family in the last thirty years. In this section we will investigate contemporary sociological thinking on the current state of marital and family relationships.

In 1973, Barbara Laslett wrote an influential article that observed that the private family was a central feature of contemporary life. Its development was a consequence of the separation of work and family activities. The privatization of the family resulted in less community and social control over how family members behaved toward each other as well as providing less social support for family members. Barbara Laslett speculated that the experimentation with alternative family styles, such as communal living, group marriages, and single-parent families, were adaptations to the strains of nuclear family living. This view saw the final development of the intimate *private* conjugal family as not achieving the long-sought needs of individualism and equalitarianism. Instead, the private conjugal family was seen as mired with problems. Let us look at this position in some detail.

The Homeless Mind

The above argument by the critics of the conjugal family bear a striking similarity to those of Peter L. Berger and his associates in *The Homeless Mind: Modernization and Consciousness* (1974). By integrating Berger's analysis with those of the scholars we discussed, we may be better able to grasp the dynamics of contemporary marital dynamics.

The Homeless Mind is concerned with the consequences of modernization and the privatization of the family. The argument is as follows. Modernization was supposed to free the individual but has, instead, increased feelings of helplessness, frustration, and alienation and has beset individuals with threats of meaninglessness. A condition similar to that expressed in sociological parlance as *anomie* (Durkheim, 1951/1897; Merton, 1957). Technology's primary consequence has resulted in the separation of work from private life. Further, work is characterized by anonymous and impersonal relations; individuals interact with each other in terms of the functions they perform in their jobs. There is no need to be aware of each other's uniqueness as individuals. To combat this situation, private institutions like the family are developed. In them, individuals can express their subjective identities and the individualism that is denied them in the work situation.

The reality of the world is sustained through interaction with significant others; an individual who is deprived of relationships with significant others will feel a sense of anomie and alienation. This is the case of the individual at work. However, the marriage relationship is designed to provide a *nomos* versus an *anomic* situation. Here intimacy can occur and a meaningful world can be constructed. Marriage is viewed as a "dramatic" act in which the two participants come together and redefine themselves through the unfolding of the marital relationship and the involvement they have with others.

The contemporary character of middle-class marriage, then, has its origins in the development of a private sphere of existence that is separated and segregated from the controls of such public institutions as politics and economics. It is designed to be a haven of security and order. It is a world in which the husband and wife can create their own social reality and social order. This is seen to be of crucial importance to wage earners—it provides them with an environment in which they can gain a sense of control in contrast to their jobs, which are often viewed in terms of powerlessness and unfulfillment, or to politics, which is viewed cynically.

It is important to note that in an earlier work Peter L. Berger, in collaboration with Hansfred Kellner (1964), saw marriage as accomplishing these outlined objectives. In that work, "Marriage and the Construction of Reality," the marital relationship is viewed as a *nomos institution* that helps establish a meaningful reality sustained through the interaction of the marriage partners. However, Berger and Kellner's view of the positive nature of marriage is seen from the man's perspective. They virtually ignore women in their analysis. Although noting how the family may serve as a refuge for men from the debilitating reality of the workplace, they do not address themselves to the problems of domestically confined housewives who have no refuge from their mundane and repetitive household chores or from the unceasing demands of their children. Further, they overlook the greater demand placed on women to satisfy the demands and morale of their husbands than the reverse.

In *The Homeless Mind*, the authors come to the realization that marriage is insufficient to satisfy the demands of all family members, including the husband. In this book, they also come to the implicit recognition that the *ideology of* marriage as a *nomos institution* is one thing and that *reality* is another. That is, marriage, which was seen as providing a meaningful world for the participants, is in fact unable to overcome the modern condition of "homelessness," which results from the separation of work and the family. This "pluralization of life-worlds," which is distinguished by the dichotomy of private and public spheres of activities, fosters both a world of work that is insufficient to give people a feeling of worth and a world of marriage that is unable to provide ample satisfactions in people's private lives.

Berger and his associates conclude that the modern private family is in trouble. Evidence of this is the development of processes of demodernization that manifest themselves in various forms of rebellious movements, such as the youth rebellion and feminism. Further evidence is apparent in the dramatic rise in the divorce rate, which reflects the desire of individuals to seek more satisfactory private meanings and relationships than those that exist within the marriage.

Current thinking has sought to balance the concerns with individual self-development and family welfare and commitment. The constant debate centers on the merits and demerits of the contemporary conjugal family as the family form that best maximizes the ideology of individualism and egalitarianism. This discussion reflects to a major extent continuous social changes experienced both by the family and American society in the last quarter of a century.

Criticism of the conjugal family especially as depicted in terms of the "traditional" roles of husband/father as breadwinner and wife/mother as homemaker and childcarer with children being supported and protected from a perceived hostile world has been countered by a strong conservative force in American society that extols "traditional family values." This major countermovement glorifies this form of the conjugal family and bemoans the perceived decline of the family in the last thirty years.

The decline or "breakdown of the family" is seen as a primary factor for the rise of a host of social ills including the extensive use of drugs, startling increases in teenage pregnancies, family violence and child neglect, the decline in educational standards, and the overall decline in societal morality and ethics (cf. Popenoe, 1988). The debate is closely linked with "decline of community" and "self-centered" or "self-development" arguments. This perspective argues that close-knit bonds of moral reciprocity have declined and have been replaced in its stead with a vocabulary of individualism. As a consequence, the middle class finds itself without a language of commitment in which to create their moral discourse (Bellah et al., 1985).

Robert Bellah and his associates (1985) emphasize that one theme has been of central concern to sociologists since the nineteenth century: the debate about individualism versus social commitment and individual rights versus civic responsibility. America's moral dilemma is seen to revolve around the conflict between the desire for fierce individualism on the one hand and the need for community and commitment on the other. The basis for their discussion stems from the work of the French social philosopher Alexis de Tocqueville, who in his analysis of American character and society, *Democracy in America*, described the mores, the "habits of the heart," that helped form American character:

[Tocqueville] singled out family life, our religious traditions, and our partici-pation in local politics as helping to create the kind of person who could sus-tain a connection to a wider political community and thus ultimately support the maintenance of free institutions. He also warned that some aspects of our character—what he was one of the first to call "individualism"—might even-tually isolate Americans one from another and thereby undermine the condi-tions of freedom. (Bellah et al., 1985: vi)

These analysts see that the failure of contemporary Americans is in their weaken-ing of motivational commitments to collective purposes of families, communities, and the nation. The unchecked growth of individualism, "inside the family as well as out-side it" is the cause of the society's general decline (Bellah et al., 1985:90). An all-powerful market economy is seen to have fostered individualism and achieved its first manifestation in the family by allowing its members to freely choose love matches. More recently, individualism appears in the form of the quest for personal growth, which is not necessarily associated with commitment and emotional bonds. As a con-sequence, the security of lasting relationships and stable marriages is in jeopardy as individuals seek self-knowledge and self-realization. The meaning of one's life is no longer seen to be anchored or derived from one's relationships with one's parents or children. As a consequence, there is a loss of historical connectedness. Further, they cite a Tocqueville prediction that Americans would come to forget their ancestors and their descendants. This would lead to an inability to think positively about family con-tinuity (Bellah et al., 1985).

David Popenoe (1988) builds on Bellah's assessment of the decline of American character by seeing its counterpart in the decline of the American family. Popenoe argues that four major social trends emerged that called into question both the "ideal and the reality" of the traditional nuclear family (the conjugal family). These are the decline in fertility, the sexual revolution, working married mothers, and the increased divorce rate. The traditional nuclear family is seen as one that is "focused on the pro-creation of children" and consists of "a legal, lifelong, sexually exclusive, heterosexual, monogamous marriage, based on affection and companionship, in which there is a sharp division of labor (separate spheres) with the female as full-time housewife and the male as primary provider and ultimate authority" (Popenoe, 1988:1).

Five aspects of family decline are articulated by Popenoe. First is the deinstitu-tionalization of the relationship between family members, resulting in a weakening of economic interdependence ties and a concomitant lessening of effective control over family members. Second, the family's traditional functions of procreation, child rear-ing, and the control of sexuality are becoming less effectual. Third, the power of the family is being lost to other groups, notably the state. Fourth, the family is not only decreasing in size but is becoming increasing unstable. Fifth, and finally, Popenoe believes that the family as a unit is giving way to the increasing importance of the indi-vidual. Popenoe attributes the decline of the family to underlying processes of mod-ernization, particularly to what has been occurring in the last fifty years—a period he labels as "late modernization." Late modernization is characterized by the idea of progress as self-fulfillment, which creates a situation of unchecked individualism. As should be apparent, Popenoe in effect builds on Goode's analysis of world revolution and family change and sees it reaching its ultimate end not in the supremacy of the conjugal family but rather in its decline. In a later chapter, we will examine in more detail Popenoe's comparative perspective in his analysis of the most developed advancement of this process of decline in Sweden, a country in an even more advanced stage of late modernization.

This countermovement on the negative effects of modernization on the family as articulated by such scholars as Bellah and his colleagues and Popenoe in turn has its critics. The changes in the American family that have occurred in the last thirty years are seen as not representing a decline of the family but rather the opportunity for the empowerment of women (cf. Skolnick, 1991, Stacey, 1990).

Skolnick points out that Popenoe's argument is not so much a debate about the decline of the family but of a particular form of family life. This particular form is based on traditional nineteenth century notions of father as breadwinner and mother as homemaker gender roles. She believes that "traditionalists like Popenoe place too much emphasis on family structure and not enough on the emotional quality of family life" Skolnick, 1991: 204). She cites sociologist Dennis Orthner, who observes that structural characteristics like divorce or maternal employment "'are weak predictors of the consequences most of us really care about: personal and family well-being, economic mobility, educational attainment, children's health'" (cited in Skolnick, 1991:204).

Dennis Orthner (1990) in his assessment of the contemporary family calls for increased attention to underlying family processes particularly in terms of how the family deals with new stresses, reaches out for assistance, adopts new roles, alters patterns of courtship and sexuality, and satisfactorily adapts to social change.

One sociologist who gives these emerging processes such attention is Judith Stacey (1990). Stacey (1990) presents a powerful portrait of American working-class families and how they have been impacted by the feminist and post-industrial revolutions. She observes that contemporary patterns of economic insecurity and the sexual revolution have led to the development of the "postmodern family." A "recombinant" family life is being created in which new gender, kinship, and cultural patterns are being created through the "feminization of kinship."

Stacey discusses how new relationships are arising that supplant the traditional family. For example, divorce becomes the opportunity for the development of kinship resources composed of households that incorporate new and former marriage partners, their multiple sets of children, step-kin, and friends. Further, she examines how the impact on families of working mothers, high divorce rates, institutionalized child care, and sexual liberation has resulted in the adaptation of working-class women to a continuous commitment to sustaining kin ties, especially in the light of economic and familial uncertainties.

In a later analytical treatment of her groundbreaking study, Stacey states: "In an era when most married mothers are employed, when women perform most 'working-class' jobs, when most productive labor is unorganized and fails to pay a family wage, when marriage links are tenuous and transitory, and when more single women than married homemakers are rearing children, conventional notions of a normative working-class family fracture into incoherence" (1991: 29).

One final argument in this debate will be put forth. Francesca Cancian (1987) observes how the separation of males and females into two separate worlds of involvement—work and the home—has misshapened marital love and intimacy. She argues that those scholars who extol the virtues of the conjugal family do not fully appreciate the negative aspects of the separation of the worlds of work and the home has on these family dynamics. She further argues that many, like William J. Goode (1963), who have made the argument that the modern (conjugal) family is characterized by more affection and equalitarianism than the preindustrial Western family, failed to recognize its deficiencies.

Cancian takes note of those who link the rise of industrial capitalism with "affective individualism" (Stone, 1977) or the "sentimental revolution" (Shorter, 1975). As you recall, Lawrence Stone argued that the rise of industrial capitalism was associated with the new values of "affective individualism" that emphasized self-development and intimate interpersonal bonds. Affective individualism was associated with romantic love, companionate marriage, and an affectionate and permissive mode of child rearing. Edward Shorter's (1975) notion of the "sentimental revolution" essentially reports the same thing. He observed an increase of emotions and sentiments in courtship, marital dynamics, and mother-child relationships.

Cancian however argues that the dichotomization of the worlds of men and women, in effect, had not achieved the intimacy and love that these analysts have suggested. Rather, love was defined in feminine terms that handicapped both men and women in understanding and loving each other.

The feminized perspective defines love in terms of emotional expressiveness, verbal self-disclosure, and affection. Women are identified with this perspective. In contrast, the definition largely ignores love manifested by instrumental help or the sharing of physical activities that has been identified with masculine behavior. She argues that by conceptualizing love in this manner, polarized gender role relationships that contribute to social and economic inequality occur. She calls for an androgynous perspective that rejects the underlying ideologies of separate spheres and validates masculine as well as feminine styles of love.

Cancian makes use of earlier research conducted by Lillian Rubin (1976) in developing her ideas. In *Worlds of Pain*, Rubin recounted the experiences of fifty white working-class families. Major family decisions—whether to buy a house or a car, where and when to take vacations, and how to spend money—were seen by men as their prerogative. Economic concerns were a major factor in the general level of dissatisfaction that both felt, but women in particular felt trapped in their houses and with their never-ending housework. Rubin wanted to know the extent to which these problems and conflicts had affected their sexual adjustment. She found strong dissatisfactions felt by both men and women that were seen to reflect the fundamental differences in the ways that these men and women conceptualize sexuality and emotional expressivity.

Rubin's interviews with these blue-collar couples provide evidence of Cancian's notions of masculine and feminine love. Women express longing for more communication and emotional closeness; husband's responses are often baffled, not knowing what this means. Men's views that women do not understand the masculine way of loving through instrumental help is conveyed by this husband's discussion of his wife's complaints that he does not communicate with her:

What does she want? Proof? She's got it, hasn't she? Would I be knocking myself out to get things for her—like to keep up this house—if I didn't love her? Why does a man do things like that if not because he loves his wife and kids? I swear, I can't figure what she wants. (cited in Rubin, 1976:120)

The wife, who has a feminine notion of love, explains:

It is not enough that he supports us and takes care of us. I appreciate that, but I want him to share things with me. I need for him to tell me his feelings. (Rubin, 1976:121)

Cancian argues that women and men define love differently, and that society tends to define love from a feminine point of view. This cultural definition puts both women and men at disadvantage. For men, love as expressed through such instrumental tasks as providing for their families and sexual intercourse too often is not recognized as such. For women, the yearning for love through intimate communication and companionship does not manifest itself in their spousal relationships.

Cancian believes that this is changing. Beginning in the 1960s there has increasingly been a movement to incorporate both male and female views of love—instrumental and expressive—into a more androgynous framework. This movement has accelerated in recent years as a consequence of women's increased educational achievements and involvement in the labor force that have gained for them greater societal resources.

She notes that Bellah and his associates see two separate and distinct categories of love. The first defines "love as an expression of inner freedom, a deeply personal, but necessarily somewhat arbitrary choice," and the second is "the image of love as a firmly planted, permanent commitment, embodying obligations that transcend the immediate feelings or wishes of either partner" (Bellah et al., 1985:93). According to Cancian, this definition implies a conflict between self-development and commitment to others. Bellah and his colleagues are seen to argue that love as commitment requires " 'a version of the traditional distinction between the sphere of men and the sphere of women' " (Cancian, 1987:107). Cancian, in effect, disputes this view. She sees that changes in male-female relationships, in part due to the changing and increasingly interwoven nature of career and family involvements, have led to an interweaving of the masculine and feminine conceptualizations of love. Also, the new definition of love that is emerging, androgynous love, reflects how self-development strengthens commitment. It is through individualism that androgynous love is made possible. The emerging androgynous definition of love is when people:

(1) express affection, acceptance, and other positive feelings to each other, and (2) provide each other with care and practical assistance. Love also includes (3) commitment—an intention to maintain the affection and the assistance for a long time, despite difficulties; and (4) specialness—giving the loved person priority over others. (Cancian, 1987:70)

CONCLUSION

This chapter concludes my five-chapter analysis of the effects of patriarchy on male-female premarital and marital relationships. It can be seen as a continuation of the previous chapter's analysis that emphasized the interrelationship of patriarchy and economic systems and how they influence the division of labor of husbands and wives.

I demonstrated how the differentiation of activities of males and females in public and domestic/private spheres has been a dominating factor in establishing marital roles and responsibilities. The differential involvement of men and women in the worlds of work and in the household is important in determining the power, privilege, respect, and deference patterns within the family. Comparatively, I examined cross-cultural and Western historical evidence to develop our thesis. I concurred with the views of a significant number of social scientists that the greater and more exclusive the involvement of women is in the domestic sphere, devoting their time to household tasks and child rearing, then the less freedom, authority, and power women have in relation to men. Concomitantly, the more exclusive the involvement of men in the outside world of work, politics, and religion, the greater is their authority and power over women.

A large segment of this chapter was devoted to a historical analysis of the effects of the Western Industrial Revolution on male-female relationships. I discussed the relationship of modernization processes to the privatization of the family (referring back to our opening chapters) and saw striking parallels in the conclusions reached by social scientists coming from different subdisciplines. The common thrust of this presentation was on the negative consequences of the dichotomization of private and public spheres of activities and the privatization of the family. I argued that such developments as the youth counterculture and women's movements of the late 1960s and 1970s, and the new family form (perhaps idealized) of the symmetrical family represented reactions against the privatized family. I then presented a detailed discussion of dual-career families. The optimism that initially greeted this family form has been tempered by the realization that family members may withhold some of their commitments to careers because of familial obligations. The implications of this potential problem in terms of economic and career competition with single individuals or couples without children was noted.

The chapter concluded with a discussion of the debate on the supposed "decline of the family." However, this debate in part reflects the attempt by social scientists to come to grips with the fundamental changes in gender relations that have emerged in marriage and the family in the last twenty-five years. This change was precipitated by women, in increasing numbers, entering the labor force. This was necessitated by ideological, personal, and economic factors. It has necessitated a reworking of gender relationships both in the world of work and in the world of the home that has still not been resolved.

In Part IV, I examine the family in terms of generational relationships. These represent a different expression of patriarchal ideology, authority, and power differentiation. Of particular interest is an analysis of the changing conceptualizations of the statuses of children, adolescents, and the elderly and how this is related to changes in generational relationships in the family.

IV

GENERATIONS AND THE
CHANGING FAMILY

12

FERTILITY PATTERNS
AND PARENTHOOD

In this part of this book we continue to look at how macrolevel societal factors affect microlevel family structures and processes. Here, the topic of concern is on generational familial relationships. The generational members of the family—parents, children, grandparents—and their relationship to each other are inherently culturally defined and societally influenced and are also subject to change. In the three chapters devoted to fertility patterns and parenthood, childhood and adolescence, and the elderly we integrate a global view of the generations to shed light on the diversity of the American family experience with generational relationships. We begin the discussion with an observation on contemporary population growth.

An inescapable fact of contemporary life is the overwhelming increase of the world's population. Today's population is increasing at a rate faster than ever before in history. It is taking less and less time for the world's population to double. During the Stone Age, when man was hunting and foraging for subsistence, the total world population is estimated to have been about 10 million. By the beginning of the Christian era, the world population was about 250 million people. If it took about 35,000 years for the first one-quarter billion people to appear, it took only about 1,650 years for the population to double to one-half billion. But, in a mere 200 years (A.D. 1850), it doubled again. Then, in a time span of only eighty years—from 1850 to 1930—the population increased to 2 billion. By 1975, forty-five years later, the population again doubled to approximately 4 billion people. Demographers expect by 1997 or 1998 the world's population will reach 6 billion. By the year 2050 the United Nations predicts that 10 billion people will be living on this planet. Figure 12-1 shows this growth pattern. Most of the population growth will occur in the poorest and least developed countries located in Africa, southern Asia, and Latin America.

Rapid population growth and the size of the contemporary world population are among the most urgent concerns of the twentieth century. The consequences for the quality of life and for the future are subject to extensive analyses, discussions, and

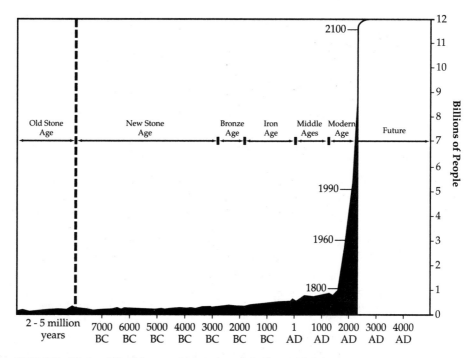

FIGURE 12-1   **World population growth through history.**

(Source: Joseph A. McFalls, Jr. "Population: A Lively Introduction," *Population Bulletin* 46(2), October 1991.)

speculations. Population-control programs have been implemented throughout the world. Within the contexts of modernization and the family, my analysis will examine some of the elements that account for this phenomenon. In addition to examining the broad demographic trends, I discuss changing attitudes and values regarding parental roles and the transition to the parenthood period of Americans. I conclude the chapter by studying the impact of abortion on the family.

FERTILITY PATTERNS IN PREINDUSTRIAL FAMILY LIFE

Earlier, I noted a distinction between mating and marriage. Mating refers to a biological phenomenon, whereas marriage, as a sociological concept, refers to a social institution. Marriage controls sexual activity and reproduction. Throughout the world, we find copulation and reproduction reinforced by cultural norms. Reproduction, which is vital to a society's continuation, is always controlled by cultural norms about family size and such related matters as marriage, frequency of intercourse, and abortion. It is never a matter left up to the individual couple alone.

There are notable differences in fertility rates for underdeveloped preindustrial societies and more developed industrial societies. Demographers (cf. Davis, 1955; Freedman, 1963/1968; Goldscheider, 1971) have long observed that, generally, underdeveloped societies have higher fertility levels. These fertility levels are related to various factors found in these societies. High fertility can be seen as an adjustment to high mortality and to the centrality of kinship and family structures to community life. Let us examine each factor in more detail.

High infant and child mortality along with a relatively short and precarious life expectancy require a high fertility rate to assure a society's perpetuation. Many families have "extra" children as a hedge against infant and child death and the probable early death of one of the parents. Thus, families may have had a large number of children so that some of them would survive.

The second element that accounts for the high fertility rate in preindustrial countries is the dominance of kinship and family groupings. Prior to modernization, a wide range of activities involved interdependence with kinfolk, especially children. Economic production and consumption along with leisure activities and assistance to the elderly and the infirm occurred largely within family and kinship structures. Large numbers of children are desired when the society is based on and its values are achieved through kinship and family ties rather than through other social institutions. Under high-mortality conditions, high birthrates become desirous to assure the survival of the kinship groupings.

In kinship-dominated societies pronatalist sentiments are prevalent. Children are a source of protection and prestige. The social strength of a given kinship unit is dependent on its size. Tied to this attitude is the domination of the kinship group over the individual. Children enable families and the kin group to achieve socially desired goals.

In such instances, high value is placed on large families. Further, the viability of extended-kinship involvements diminishes the personal responsibilities of the couple for the care and maintenance of their children. The burdens of a large family, economic and social costs, and social and personal care are shared and controlled by the larger kinship-family structure: "Parents not only had personal rewards for having large families but they could escape from direct responsibilities of their many children" (Goldscheider, 1971:142).

The gender-role segregation that predominates in these kinship-based societies is another important facet in encouraging a large family. The role and status of women is clearly linked with their childbearing function. Prestige and other social and economic rewards and benefits can only be obtained through motherhood. The production and survival of healthy offspring for the continuation of kinship lines provide the chief source for rationalizing a woman's existence.

The familial-based economic system found children to be important productive assets. Children were an integral part of the labor force. Thus, the more offspring, the more workers within the family. Further, the larger the number of offspring, the greater the chances of their providing for their parents when they got old. Children, then, represented one type of old-age insurance. The lack of geographic and social mobility combined with the lack of personal aspirations also increased the desire for large families.

Taken altogether, the kinship-based society was dependent on high fertility for the perpetuation of its social system. Demographic, social, familial, and economic conditions resulted in the institutionalization of high fertility. The entire society—its values and goals as well as the various aspects of its cultural and religious life—were organized around high-fertility values and behavior.

The rate of population growth has decreased after an earlier rapid increase in the industrialized nations of the world. Demographers have referred to this phenomenon as the *demographic transition*. Simply put, the demographic transition refers to the movement from high-fertility and high-mortality rates to low-fertility and low-mortality rates. Demographers have traced the historical sequence of population growth in the Western world over the last 200 years. They observed three broad stages of population dynamics.

During the preindustrial period, birth- and death rates were high, variations occurring during periods of famine and epidemics. Population size was relatively stable. Industrialization ushered in the second stage. It was accompanied by improvements in sanitation and sewage systems, better transportation systems for shipping foods, and more productive family techniques. Improvements in these conditions led to a reduction in the death rate. Although the death rate was reduced, there was no commensurate reduction in the birthrate. This resulted in a period of rapid population growth. By the end of the nineteenth century, through the twentieth century, and continuing until today, the high birthrate has been reduced. The disparity that existed between birthrates and death rates, which was characteristic of the second stage, is reduced in this, the third stage. Today, the industrialized nations of the world have a low, steady death rate and a low, but somewhat fluctuating birthrate.

How can this dramatic decline in the rate of population growth in contemporary industrial societies be explained? Goldscheider (1971) has developed an argument that is similar to that articulated by William J. Goode (1963) in his *World Revolution and Family Patterns*. Goldscheider (1971:148-151) believes there are three key social processes that can account for the transition from high to low fertility and family size. First, there is the shift from kinship dominance to the conjugal-family unit. He sees the breakdown of the dominance and centrality of the kinship-based consanguineal family as one of the significant features of modernization. The extended-family system can no longer dictate the number of children that a given nuclear family should have. Individual couples emphasize their family of procreation rather than their family of orientation. They have their own economic and social responsibilities and the welfare of their children is primarily in their hands. The break with the extended-family system allowed for the development of new behavioral and value patterns. It coincided with the processes of migration, urbanization, and social mobility.

Second, there is a marked improvement in living standards accompanied by increased economic opportunities. These contribute to rising aspirations for social mobility. This aspiration is frequently in conflict with the desire for a large family. These social and economic changes are seen to have exerted direct pressures toward fertility control and reduction. The decline in family-based agricultural and preindustrial enterprises diminished the importance of children. Children are no longer productive assets. The decline in fertility is accentuated by the rapid urbanization that accompanied industrialization. Urban conditions contribute to the decline of the traditional classical extended-family system. It frees the conjugal family from the socioeconomic controls of the extended-family system. Further, urban lifestyles, living standards, and aspirations all run counter to the traditional values that encouraged large family size and high fertility.

The third and last factor is the development of new values and attitudes that stress individualism, secularism, and rationalism. These values all share a common belief in the desirability of limiting family size. Values in favor of smaller families are also shared by the emerging value of achievement versus ascription. Together, these three processes greatly affect the decline in fertility and family size in industrialized societies. Attention will now be turned to examine how these factors operate in developing nations undergoing major population growth. India and China will serve as case studies.

POPULATION GROWTH AND THE POSITION OF WOMEN IN THE FAMILY

The highest birthrates occur in the less developed countries that make up the Third World. Consanguineal family and kinship systems that are still predominant in the Third World have resulted in women having families that average between three and six children with more children typically found in rural areas (United Nations, 1991). The total fertility rate (TFR) is more than six children in many parts of sub-Saharan Africa, North Africa, and West Asia. Thirty percent of women are either pregnant or lactating at any given time.

Improved sanitation, a more dependable food supply, and the introduction of Western medicine have drastically lowered death rates. The result is a most startling and dramatic population rise in Third World countries. Major efforts at family planning have had limited success in curbing population growth. India and China, to be discussed in more detail in the following sections, have developed centralized government controlled family planning programs that seek to control fertility, often through coercive measures. In Latin America, economic factors, patriarchal ideology, and the religious doctrines of Roman Catholicism have discouraged the use of birth control devices. In much of the Islamic world birth control advocates are few and far between. In Africa, confronted with ethnic tensions, political instability, and cycles of famine and starvation, birth control programs have not been systematically implemented. In this section, rather than focus on abstract demographic and population rates and figures, we wish to focus on the impact of reproduction on these women's lives.

In much of the Third World, patriarchal ideology still dominates and the consanguineal family system prevails. Decisions regarding the family are collective decisions; this includes decisions regarding childbearing. Women are perceived primarily in their childbearing and child-rearing roles. Most are deprived of the educational and economic opportunities increasingly available to men. Illiteracy rates are associated with fertility rates; the more education a women has, the fewer children she is likely to bear (Abernathy, 1993). In the world, some 960 million people are illiterate, two-thirds of them women; 90 million young women are denied primary education (Elliott and Dickey, 1994). In Latin America the illiteracy rate for women 25 and older is 20 percent; it gets progressively higher as we move to Southeast Asia (40 percent), and to sub-Saharan Africa and West Asia (70 percent). Within these regions, the illiteracy rates are highest in rural areas, where women are two to three times more likely to be illiterate than their urban counterparts (United Nations, 1991).

Economically, women have less opportunities than men. In most situations, women are expected to and do spend the central part of their lives involved with reproduction. When they do work in the paid labor force, they are usually paid less, have fewer benefits, are more likely to work part-time, and have fewer opportunities for advancement (United Nations, 1991). Agricultural work is a predominant occupation for women in sub-Saharan Africa, but it is often combined and integrated with domestic responsibilities. In Latin America, a small minority are so employed and in Asia, where nearly 50 percent are so involved, they have less control than men of what they produce. Regardless of their occupational involvement, women are expected to be primarily responsible for child care and domestic work.

The large number of children that women of the Third World bear has had a major impact on their health. Births are a dangerous activity and inadequate or no health care is often the case. These women are 80 to 600 times more likely to die during pregnancy and childbirth than women in industrial countries. Adolescents whose bodies are still in transition are particularly vulnerable; their risk of maternal or infant mortality is nearly twice that of women from the ages of 20 to 24 (United Nations, 1991). Women much more than men experience malnutrition and are recipients of inferior health care. Pregnant women and women with young children are even more vulnerable to illness and disease. Given the high infant and young child mortality rate, many women continue to have children as long as they can. In effect, they find themselves in a constant cycle of nutritional deprivation and great bodily stress (United Nations, 1991).

The United Nations Conference on Population and Development

The detrimental impact of large families on women was a major factor in orienting the concerns of the United Nations International Conference on Population and Development that met in Cairo, Egypt, in September 1994 (Elliott and Dickey, 1994; Hedges, 1994; Linden, 1994, Sipris, 1994). The conference included representatives from more than 170 countries. A twenty-year United Nations plan was developed for stabilizing the world's population at about 7.8 billion people by the year 2050. The United Nations estimates that in the absence of such a family planning program the population of the world may accede 10 billion and could reach 12.5 billion. Such a large population growth would most likely cause mass poverty and starvation in the developing world as well as unsustainable human pressure on the planet's resources.

The plan, prepared by the United Nations Population Fund, involves quadrupling the amount of money allocated to poor nations for family planning to some $4.4 billion dollars by the end of the century. An integral part of the plan is to promote social changes, especially in the treatment of women.

By the year 2015, the projections are that expanded family planning programs will reach an estimated 350 million people who now do not have access to these programs. These programs are also designed to improve general health care for women and children. Infant mortality rates will hopefully be reduced from their present level of 69 deaths for every thousand births to the 12 deaths for every thousand births, which is the current rate of industrialized societies.

The second goal of the document was recommendations for a broad program of social measures to improve the living conditions and status of women. The plan advocates that women's rights and opportunities must be improved. This would primarily be done by providing universal primary education for girls as well as for boys throughout the Third World. Secondary education would become available to 50 percent of all girls. The plan calls for efforts to give women equal participation in politics and public life. It calls for initiatives to eliminate gender discrimination in the workplace and the providing of meaningful employment opportunities. Other forms of economic inequality would be challenged including women's ability to obtain credit, hold property, or receive an inheritance. The premise of the strategy is that if women are "empowered to control their own reproductive lives, they will choose to have fewer children" (Linden, 1994).

The United Nations program also enshrines the right of women to make independent decisions regarding their families and their relationships. The document declares that women have the right to decide the number of children that they will have and when they will have them. The document declares that in all matters related to reproduction women have the right to sexual or *reproductive health*, which is defined as "a state of complete physical, mental and social well-being" (cited in Hedges, 1994).

The accord reached at the conference was not without considerable acrimony. The most controversial chapter that provoked numerous heated exchanges between Islamic and Catholic leaders and many liberal delegates from Western industrial countries was the one on "reproductive rights and reproductive health." Muslim leaders, in particular, objected to specific wording that referred to "marriage, other unions, and the family." Muslims objected to the reference to "other unions" outside of marriage as endorsing homosexual unions. Some Caribbean and African states sought the inclusion of this phrase as a means to protect the rights of couples in common-law marriages, prevalent in some societies. The final decision was to delete the entire reference to marriage, other unions, and the family and substitute in its stead a broad injunction against discrimination.

The Vatican had objected to mentioning the need for "fertility regulation," for fear that it would imply the sanctioning of abortion. The compromise reached was a word shuffling to "regulation of fertility" that was seen to carry a more ambiguous meaning. Another issue revolved around a paragraph that pertained to abortion in the context of hazards to women's health. Catholic delegates from several large countries, with support of the Vatican, campaigned against this passage, which had implications that abortion in any context could be legal or safe. Faced with overwhelming opposition, they backed off with their objection. They were successful in ensuring that the document proclaim that abortion should not be promoted as a means of family planning. They also succeeded in the inclusion of a reference regarding parental responsibility in the section of adolescent sex counseling.

This was the third world population conference. The first was held in 1974 in Bucharest, Romania. That conference was notable for the opposition of developing nations to population control. They argued that population control was a coverup for the enormous economic inequalities that existed between the developed and the developing nations. The phrase "development is the best contraceptive" was coined to highlight their view. The second world population conference was held ten years later in Mexico City, and by that time the developing countries saw the need for family planning programs. This conference occurred during the Reagan administration. At that time, the United States government expressed severe reservations against United Nations family planning programs and initiatives and stopped contributing to them. The Cairo conference had the support of the Clinton administration. Despite the initial opposition to many facets of the United Nations documents, the Roman Catholic Church, which opposes artificial means of birth control, and Muslim groups that oppose the emphasis being placed on improving women's status in society as a means of limiting family size, reached agreement with the vast majority of the delegates for the necessity of an effective population plan for the future. At the end of the conference, not one country voted against the final draft.

> Whatever the practical benefits of the conference, few denied its symbolic importance. One delegate likened the event to an Alcoholics Anonymous meeting: countries drew comfort from the plight of other countries, and together they resolved to deal with the mutual problem. As this delegate saw it, "Muslim nations said to other Muslim nations, 'It's O.K. to support family planning,' as did Catholic nations to other Catholic nations." Thus, the consensus in Cairo may allow the world community to move beyond divisive debates about abortion and contraception in dealing with the population juggernaut. The accord may signal a new, more mature approach to confronting a potential global disaster. (Linden, 1994)

INDIA: A CASE STUDY

India is one of the world's largest nations. It is also one of its poorest. Second only to the People's Republic of China in population size, in mid-1975 India had a population of 608.5 million (Population Reference Bureau, 1976). Nearly twenty years later its population was at 882,600,000 (Chen, 1994). In a land area one-third the size of the United States, India has three times as many people. India's population represents one-eighth of the entire world's population. Demographers predict that unless the current growth rate is substantially reduced, by the end of the century India will have a population of well over 1 billion and its population will double by the year 2028.

Since its inception as an independent country in 1948, the Indian government has viewed its population growth as a major deterrent to economic and social development. Initially, however, Mahatma Gandhi, Jawaharlal Nehru, and other government leaders were ambivalent about the need to reduce fertility, but eventually family planning programs became more and more important, culminating in the coercive sterilization policies of Indira Gandhi and the Congress Party during the "emergency" of 1976-1977. The general position held is that the economic development of the country is dependent on the investment of the national income. However, a rapidly increasing birthrate diverts income to food consumption, housing, education, and other social needs. A lower birthrate would allow for greater modernization, economic development, and increased total production. Population, then, is seen as being a crucial variable in the complex interrelationships of economy, social structure, and culture. In the transition to a modern industrial state, the population growth of the society must be regulated through governmentally sponsored population-planning programs.

In 1952, India became the first country to adopt an official family planning program. At the outset, the program was poorly funded. This reflected the ambivalence of Indian officials to reduce fertility. The census of 1961 provided a major impetus for the government to develop population-control programs. The continued rapid growth of the population was seen as having detrimental economic and social consequences. Initially, the government was very conservative in its advocacy of means of contraception. It first favored the rhythm method and *coitus interruptus*, which proved ineffectual. Next, diaphragms and spermicide were advocated, but soon thereafter they also were viewed as being inappropriate. An oral contraceptive, the pill, was too expensive and the general feeling was that women would forget to take it daily. In 1965, two new techniques were introduced: male sterilization (vasectomy) and the intrauterine device (IUD).

Shortly after its introduction, the IUD fell into disfavor. Increasingly, male sterilization was gaining favor by government officials. During 1965-1966, 600,000 men had vasectomies. Through various cash-incentive payments, the number rose in the following year but started to decline toward the end of the 1960s and the early 1970s. The low vasectomy rates did not approach the governmental goals. Further, most of the men who underwent the operation had already fathered as many children as they wanted.

The failure of the vasectomy program paralleled the failure of the other population-control programs. India's programs have been continually hampered by bureaucratic inefficiency, inadequate funds, poor planning, and the monumental size of the task. Further, India has never been able to convince its people about the necessity for population limitation. As previously noted, although the birthrate has dropped somewhat since the implementation of these programs, the population is still increasing by a rate of 57,000 new births every day. In 1974, a panel of Indian social scientists predicted that by the year 2000 half the Indian population would be homeless and the country would be stripped bare of its resources for fuel and food (McKee and Robertson, 1975:45).

To combat this trend, the Indian National Congress, the ruling party of India since independence, accelerated its family planning programs. A multitude of programs were implemented. IUDS, condoms, and other contraceptive devices were distributed free. The oral birth-control pill was available only through pilot projects and distribution had begun in rural and urban family planning centers. The mainstay of the program was sterilization.

During the authoritarian "state of emergency" of Indira Gandhi and the Congress Party, a mass vasectomy campaign sterilized millions of Indian males. Although ostensibly a voluntary program, the government pressured, cajoled, and forced people to undergo sterilization. The national campaign set a target of 4.3 million sterilizations. Over 7.8 million sterilizations were actually performed in the "emergency" between April 1976 and January 1977. The excessiveness of the aggressive birth-control program led to a high number of forcible operations. The sterilization issue was one of the major factors contributing to the dramatic defeat of the ruling Congress Party and of Indira Gandhi in the elections of March 1977. In the so-called vasectomy belt, the populous states of north and central India, which felt the full brunt of the aggressive family planning campaign, the Congress Party suffered overwhelming defeat.

Soon after the election, the government ended its sponsorship of sterilization and the cash-incentive payments to individuals who underwent sterilization operations. Politicians downplayed population policies until 1994 when population was once again upgraded as a matter of grave importance and a population-planning cabinet-level ministry was founded.

In 1988, 68 percent of all Indian couples planned to have two sons (Chen, 1994). These sons would be expected to contribute their labor to family-owned farms, care for their parents when they reached old age, and inherit land. Social pressures remain strong for women who don't produce sons and they are often deserted by their husbands.

The circumstances today are that 40 percent of the population is under 15 years of age. It is estimated that if effective population control measures are not implemented the population could triple in size in the next fifty years. Sterilization still remains the birth control method favored by government, and it still is the one that most people reject (Chen, 1994).

The 1994 Cairo Population Conference of the United Nations has particular meaning to India. While the "green revolution" in agriculture has kept pace with India's swelling population, it has depleted the soil and has resulted in environmental degradation (Stevens, 1994). In a major study, "The 'Second India' Revisited," which was conducted by a team of demographers led by Robert Repetto (1994) is pessimistic about the future ability of the food supply to meet population demands. The term "second India" refers to the near doubling of its population in the last twenty years.

India's population growth rate was only slightly lower in the period between 1970 and 1990 than it had been in the preceding twenty-year period. However, in some sections of India, the population growth rate was moderated. This moderation was largely attributed to the rising status of women. The case in point was the state of Kerala in southern India. Twenty-five years ago, the women of Kerala had a high birthrate. In the ensuing time period, their status has risen considerably. Women's literacy rate approaches 90 percent. The *demographic transition* has occurred—the birthrate has now stabilized at the replacement level. In other sections of India where women have relatively low status, even those who are using contraception devices, their birthrate is over 2.0. Women not using contraceptives have increased the number of their children from six to about nine primarily as a result of better health care.

In the debate of how best to control population the relative worth of two factors had always been debated. One position contends that economic development and rising incomes would be the way to lower the birthrate—development is the best contraceptive. The second advocates widespread access to family planning services. The study by Repetto and his associates highlights a third factor—the improved status of women. All three are seen necessary for a rapid demographic transition and the consequent lowering of the birthrate. To achieve the improved status of women, it is seen that changes in the tradition of the consanguineal extended family must occur. This family and kinship system has long had power over women's reproductive rights as the

International Conference on Population and Development held in Cairo, Egypt, in 1994 makes clear. An Indian delegate to that conference, Kavel Galhati, asserts: "Tradition is great, but if tradition is putting women down, it must be changed. Unless women can manage and control their own fertility they cannot manage and control their own lives" (cited in Elliott and Dickey, 1994).

This examination of population dynamics in India reveals that it is interrelated with family conceptualizations and dynamics along with social, political, and economic factors. The next section deals with how the interrelationship of these factors is manifested in another Asian country, China.

CHINA AND ITS ONE-CHILD POLICY

In 1980, China passed a new marriage law that aroused worldwide attention. This law has had important implications for family reform and for population policy. The new law is particularly focused on family planning. China has a population of more than 1 billion people—about 22 percent of the total world population, yet China has only 7 percent of the world's arable land (Redmond, 1986). Her land mass, however, is only slightly larger than that of the United States. Further, only a small portion of the land is suitable for growing crops, while there is plentiful agricultural land in the United States. In essence, China has half the usable farmland that America has and five times as many people.

China's huge population and the continued growth of that population has aroused much concern. It is for that reason that a "one couple, one child" policy has been implemented. This policy, in the first five years after implementation, prevented an estimated 100 million births (Redmond, 1986). The goal is to hold the population down to 1.2 billion by the year 2000 (Haub, 1993). If the policy fails, and family size stays at just over two children, it will have a population of 1.4 billion. In mid-1994 it was estimated that the population was 1,165,800,000 (Chen, 1994). In 1993 the Population Reference Bureau reported that China's population program has remarkably achieved a below-replacement fertility rate in the short twenty-year period after first declaring that the birthrate was a problem. Even so, China has added twice the population of the United States during this time period.

The new marriage law raised the minimum age for marriage by two years to 22 for men and to 20 for women, and made family planning mandatory. It made family planning the duty of both husband and wife and articulated a new statement of obligation among family members (Stacey, 1985; Wolf, 1985a). The principle of equal status of men and women was reaffirmed and neither spouse was allowed to restrict or interfere with the other's production, work, study, or social activities. The norm of extended-family relations was shifted from a patrilineal form to a bilinear direction. Family members now have obligations to both maternal and paternal relatives extended over three generations; that is, grandchildren, parents, and grandparents have reciprocal obligations to support and assist each other. The motive for this change was to diminish and undermine the social and economic logic of son preference and thus alleviate the potential problem of the birth of a daughter in the new birth limitation program of one child.

Restrictive measures and incentives are combined to augment the new population policy. In urban areas, workers must meet the new age requirements and have their facto-

A contemporary street scene in China with a family-planning billboard advocating the one-child policy.

ries' permission to get married. They must have received instruction in family planning and passed a written test. Once married, they have to get the permission of the family-planning officer for when they can try to have children. A bureau chief of the factories in the city of Changzhou expresses the goals of the factory in fulfilling the policy this way:

> Recently we have met all our targets 100 percent. Couples using birth control is 100 percent. One-child families is 100 percent. Late marriage is 100 percent. We have attained the so-called "three withouts." "Without" permission, no one is pregnant. We are "without" any second child. We are "without" early births. We have no under age mothers. ("China's Only Child," Nova, February 14, 1984)

BOX 12-1 The Global Family

China's Only Child

Edward Goldwyn

NARRATOR

In Mrs. Wu's neighborhood there are some 200 women whose contraceptive is an intrauterine device.

She sees that they are all checked regularly every four months. The check is said to be necessary to see the I.U.D. is in the right place. But the check also shows if there's an accidental pregnancy underway—or if the I.U.D. has been removed, which would be illegal and very serious.

Mrs. Wu always goes along, both to be friendly and to see that there's no deception, that a woman is not hiding a pregnancy by sending a neighbor along as a stand-in.

Hospital Worker: A coil check? This way.

Mrs. Wu: I'll tell you a joke to show why I love birth control work.

NARRATOR

Early one morning Mrs. Wu was in the street. She saw Mr. and Mrs. Li on their way to work. She overheard Mrs. Li say, "We've just had our wage increase. Why don't we have another baby."

That was at seven o'clock.

MRS. WU

After I overheard that I rushed to her factory. I was there at nine o'clock. I looked for the party secretary, that's Party Secretary Wang. At 12 o'clock he went to find her and have a talk. He asked her very seriously, "Is it true you want another child?" She said, "I'm not going to, I use contraception all the time." He asked again. That made her cross and she said, "No! Of course I'm not going to!" "But this morning you said you would, that you could afford it now." She said, "I was only making a joke." Afterwards she found me. She apologized and said it was a joke. Then she asked me: "Why did you take it seriously?" But I must, the minute you let go, someone's tummy starts to get fatter.

MR. MING

We of Zuang Tang brigade have done well in family planning and been rewarded. But we must be modest and work even harder next year.

NARRATOR

Mr. Ming is the leader of a brigade of 500 families in a commune in the country close to Changzhou. His 100 percent record is being threatened by a couple who has fought very hard to have a second child.

Jinghu—and his wife ManXue have just given in after weeks of "persuasion." ManXue is six months pregnant, but she has agreed to have an abortion tomorrow.

The person who had to make ManXue agree is Mrs. Feng—the brigade's family planning official.

Mrs. Feng's duties are to control the quota and to see no one breaks the rules.

She's just decided which women can have a child. So she moves their names from "being on pills" to "waiting to be pregnant."

They are the last two women to get places in this year's quota of 32 babies.

Who gets them is worked out from a simple formula that gives priority to couples who are older and who have been married longest.

MRS. FENG

You've been allocated a birth permission card. Here it is. I hope you have an intelligent healthy child. Here's your book.

NARRATOR

The book is called "How to Have Healthy Child," and it's given to couples when they get their permission so they can get off to a good start.

Mrs. Feng has to tell six couples they must wait.

In this household the young couple live with the husband's parents.

When Mrs. Feng came to tell them the new wife was out.

The woman is his mother.

Mrs. Feng: You are one of the youngest couples. I'm asking if you can wait? What do you have to say?

Husband: I have nothing to say. The important thing is the country's call. We have to give emphasis to work and study. Don't you agree, mother?

Mother: Yes.

NARRATOR

Most people accept the new rules. The defiance that their neighbor, ManXue, has been showing is very unusual.

The story of how Mrs. Feng made ManXue agree to an abortion shows how the persuasion is done.

ManXue and Jinghu work their fields under the new "responsibility system." That means they hand over to the commune a fixed amount of the vegetables as payment for using the field. They sell in the market any extra they grow.

They have made a great deal of money this year—from the work they've put into the crops—from the chickens ManXue keeps and because Jinghu not only has a factory job as a carpenter, but makes furniture in the evening.

They have become quite wealthy, and have made for themselves about three times an average salary. They already have a son aged one-and-a-half but they felt they could afford a second child. They had not taken out a one-child certificate.

JINGHU

Go to mummy. Dad is going to work.

NARRATOR

Six months ago Jinghu and ManXue stopped using birth control. The thick winter clothing made it easy to hide her swelling figure.

ManXue is an outspoken woman. Just a month ago she went to Mrs. Feng and said, "I'm pregnant and I'm having this baby."

Next day Mrs. Feng came by and said, "I have to tell you why you mustn't have this child."

ManXue said, "Fine, come back and tell me after the baby is born."

Mrs. Feng brought along the leaders of the brigade who spent several evenings telling her, "One child is good for the country. It's also good for you. Why won't you agree to an abortion? If you're worried about your health, we'll guarantee you get the best doctors. Why won't you agree!"

ManXue said, "No."

The next night more senior officers of the commune came to the house. They went through it all again and again very slowly. The next night

an even more senior official came and he said the same things.

So it went on night after night. Repeatedly she was asked, "Why *won't* you agree?"

In the end ManXue got worn down. She said, "After a while I knew they would just keep on and on and on."

None of her friends stood up for her—they kept silent.

She offered a deal to Mrs. Feng. "I'll have the abortion if you get me a job in the commune shoe factory."

Mrs. Feng tried to arrange that. She came back to report, "They'll agree provided you agree to be sterilized too."

ManXue said, "No—I don't want that."

But finally she agreed to have the abortion in her sixth month of pregnancy.

Hospital Worker: So she wants an abortion but not to be sterilized?

Mrs. Feng: That's right.

Hospital Worker: Bring her at eight o'clock tomorrow.

Mrs. Feng: ManXue, are you in?

Jinghu: Should we bring a quilt?

Mrs. Feng: Just a change of clothes. Let me carry it.

NARRATOR

ManXue will be given an injection into her womb that will kill the fetus and cause its premature delivery within 24 hours.

MRS. FENG

Personally I feel sympathy for couples wanting a second child. It's reasonable to want two. But in the interest of the country, we can't let them have it. If one couple is allowed, too many others will want a second. That would make our work impossible. So we must do our job well. Don't let second children be born. But personally, I sympathize.

NARRATOR

Why do the rebels in the end give in?

Why is it that these women don't get support from friends and neighbors?

(continued)

Why do the people of this town accept these intrusions?

And why are the persuaders so proud of their work?

Madame Chen says it's because of the huge effort she has made with public education and propaganda.

The thing she proudly shows her visitors is the first ever neon sign in Changzhou. It says, "Please practice contraception carefully."

Over the last three years she has filled Changzhou with slogans for the one-child policy. "Fewer people but higher quality." "Birth control is every citizen's responsibility." "One child allows us to modernize."

It says on this boat: "Take pride in your single child." And "Have fewer children but raise the quality."

"A single child is cause to be proud."

NEIGHBORHOOD WORKERS (SINGING)

Neighborhood workers are in high spirits. We grasp the work of birth control. We work together with one aim. We shall never waver.

CHILDREN (SINGING)

Ee-yo-ei-hai-ei-hai-yo. Mummy only had me. We don't want brothers or sisters. Everyone is happy. The whole house rejoices, laa . . . , la, la.

NARRATOR

Each brigade is told monthly one couple—one child, and why.

MR. MING

If the one-child policy is followed to the year 2000, it guarantees that food and industrial production will first double and then redouble.

NARRATOR

Afterwards they break into their production teams to say what they think, and to discuss local problems.

This meeting of Mrs. Feng's group was attended by ManXue and her neighbors. They all knew of her fight.

Mrs. Feng: Now we've heard Comrade Ming's speech, are there any questions? Anything to discuss?

Brigade Member: The whole country and the party should concentrate on family planning work. The members of our team must answer the government's call. I respond to the government's call strongly, I want only one child.

Young Brigade Member: We young people have strength. Now the government asks us to marry late and use birth control. This is good for young people.

NARRATOR

Nobody mentioned ManXue's recent ordeal. What they felt, they hid. ManXue said, "The hardest part of the last weeks has been that no one stood up for me—or said anything."

ManXue agreed to take out the one-child certificate, but she has remained adamant that she won't be sterilized.

So Mr. Ming's brigade has met all of this year's targets—and he'll receive another certificate at the Changzhou award ceremony for birth control.

On the platform sit the mayor and the other important bureaucrats who will present the awards.

The audience are all delegates from units which have met their targets—it's an honor to be invited.

The applause and awards conclude a year of difficult—often painful—work and persuasion.

These efforts have made China the only developing nation in the world today to significantly slow its population growth. And with one-fourth of the people on earth, China's success is crucial to controlling world population.

Changzhou is the Chinese dream.

It's had a huge investment of government money to develop its factories.

Most of the old people here have pensions. They don't need sons to support them.

Elsewhere that's not so.

Eighty percent of the Chinese live in the countryside. They are peasants who must have a son. The officials there understand—and turn a blind eye when a couple has two children. In the countryside, results fall short of 100 percent.

But in Changzhou people can actually see the wealth the publicity promises.

Changzhou is not a typical city, it's the

ideal. It's to show the Chinese people what the sacrifice is for—the wealth there could be for all in two generations.

If they don't control the population, the future will be catastrophic.

It's very rare to see a government trying to deal with problems 30 years ahead. The Chinese are saying this: if the population were reduced to 700 million, they would have twice today's living standards.

If it steadies at one billion, they can continue to keep people fed and housed. At one-and-a-half billion they see a descent to poverty. Above that, severe hardship. Above two billion, it's a fight for food.

This will be their future at three children per family. This for 2.3 children per family. Two children each. One and a half children each.

One child.

If we were faced with this future, how would we try to deal with it?

First, we would educate and convince everyone there is a problem. Then limit births. And finally ensure the rules are applied equally to all.

That's what the Chinese are doing. It is harsh. But is there an alternative?

MADAME CHEN

To be honest, my own opinion is if couples had two children, it would be quite all right. Two children is very desirable and people would easily accept it. Our work would be easier if we could allow two children. But we think of our country's future. We have to keep our population under 1.2 billion in the year 2000.

Nova. 1984. "China's only child." Edward Goldwyn and Terry Kay Rockefeller BBC/WGBH.

Married couples who obtain a "one-child certificate," which pledges their intention not to exceed the norm, are rewarded in terms of wage increases, preferential housing assignments, and special considerations for their child in terms of free education and priority for a university place and priority for a job. Unauthorized pregnant women who are carrying either their first or their second child are pressured to have abortions. Those that have a second child lose these rewards and various sanctions are applied including the loss of wages, promotions deferred, maternity leaves denied, loss of preferential housing and educational supports for their children, and reductions in their food allotments.

The "one couple, one child" law is not as stringently enforced in rural areas; bowing to the importance of the family, a two-child norm is the goal. Similar collective pressure tactics are used to reach this goal. Those who voluntarily restrict their family size to one child become eligible for preferential treatment regarding work, grain rations, and private land plots. There are inducements for women who agree to be sterilized after the birth of one child that include sewing machines, additional food allocations, and money. Couples who do not enter such agreements experience social and economic pressures and are required to wait for at least five years to have a second child. Forced sterilization after the birth of a second child or becoming contractually obligated to abort unauthorized pregnancies has been practiced in a number of different regions (Stacey, 1985).

Stacey (1985) believes that one of the consequences of the "one couple, one child" policy may be a dramatic shift in family structure and gender relationships. "A one-child family system could level a serious challenge to patrilineality by making parents as dependent upon their daughters as their sons. . . . This could significantly raise the family status of daughters and dissolve the patrilocal marriage system" (Stacey, 1985:279). However, the strength of the patrilineal system continues to be evident—in 1988 China relaxed its one-child policy and put in effect a one-son policy that has become operationalized in many rural areas of China (Chen, 1994). In these agricultural regions, wealth passes through sons not daughters. A rural couple may have a second child if their first was a girl.

The rise in the family status of daughters is not seen as likely to materialize in the near future. A two-child norm is seen to be feasible, and this would tend to weaken, but not to destroy, the patrilineal base of rural family structure. However, the overall consequences of this new marriage law and population policies should in the long run diminish the power of patriarchal interests.

In summary, this examination of population dynamics in India and China reveals that it is interrelated with family conceptualizations and dynamics along with social, political, and economic factors. In the next section I seek to demonstrate how the interrelationship of these factors is manifested in Western societies, particularly the United States. The focus of concern centers on the conceptualization of parenthood and its influence on marital and parental relationships.

FERTILITY PATTERNS IN THE WEST: PARENTHOOD AND IDEOLOGIES

Two somewhat contradictory ideologies characterized the emerging industrial system of the nineteenth century. The first ideology argued for low fertility and small family size. At the same, the other ideology emphasized domesticity and motherhood as the "natural" roles for women. Doctrines, then, placing high value on women's exclusive involvement with housework and child rearing were being set forth at the same time forces were motivating couples to want fewer births and to restrict their family size. Thus, women's entire functions were being defined in terms of motherhood at the same time the societal demands for children were diminishing. This situation was of course inherently unstable. The women's movements, the delay in marriage and childbearing, and the increased participation of women in the labor force can all be seen as protests to the untenable position of women in industrial society. I have previously discussed some of these ideologies and the conditions underlying them. A brief review would be beneficial to help put this discussion of fertility and parenthood in perspective.

The rise of industrialization in the mid-nineteenth century saw a vast migration of people from rural areas to the factories and bureaucracies of a modern urban society. Work became more and more removed from the family setting. Men took jobs away from the home. They became increasingly independent of the previous prevailing domestic economy. With work becoming independent of the home, so did men.

These processes had an opposite effect on women and children. They became more economically dependent on the financial contributions of husbands and fathers. Domestic constraints, household tasks, and the care of children became solely the province of women. They were prevented from participation in extrafamilial occupations. Increasingly, they became cut off from the outside world of work. The resultant picture was that women and children were now economic liabilities who were almost totally dependent on the economic viability of men. Ann Oakley (1974:59) summarizes three lasting consequences associated with industrialization: "the separation of the man from the intimate daily routines of domestic life; the economic dependence of women and children on men; the isolation of housework and child care from other work."

Patriarchal ideology advocated the domestic confinement of women in the Victorian era. Its basis was the desire of more affluent men to shield the family from the perceived evils of industrialization and urbanization. The isolated home was to provide a safe shelter and protection for the wife and the children. In this cloistered home the mother was to shield and protect the man's children. It was each man's castle and sanctuary. The home and women took on a sacred quality; they became the repository of goodness in a world of evil. John Ruskin has made the classic statement on the nature of the domestic scene as the province of mothers in his essay "Of Queen's Gardens" first published in 1865:

> This is the true nature of home—it is the place of Peace; the shelter, not only from all injury, but from all terror, doubt, and division. In so far as it is not this, it is not home; so far as the anxieties of the outer life penetrate into it, and the inconsistently-minded, unknown, unloved, or hostile society of the outer world is allowed by either husband or wife to cross the threshold it ceases to be home; it is then only a part of the outer world which you have roofed over and lighted a fire in. But so far as it is a sacred place, a vestal temple, a temple of the hearth watched over by Household Gods . . . so far as it is this, and the roof and the fire are types only of a nobler shade and light, shade as of the rock in a weary land, and the light as of Pharos in the stormy sea— so far as this it vindicates the name and fulfills the praise of home. (Ruskin, 1865/n.d.:151-152)

The Victorian model, then, depicted women as the repository of virtue. The home was seen as the sanctuary protecting women and children from the evils of the outside world. The home was the working man's castle; his refuge from "the jungle out there."

The Victorian idealization of motherhood continues to linger in contemporary society. The nineteenth century "cult of true motherhood" (Welter, 1966) was the expectation that women would stay at home, have children, and be the moral guardians of the family. It was updated in the twentieth century by what Betty Rollin refers to as " 'The Motherhood Myth'—the idea that having babies is something that all normal women instinctively want and need and will enjoy doing—they just think they do" (Rollin, 1971:346). The motherhood myth is seen to have grown in strength after World War II. The economic prosperity and growth of postwar America was in striking contrast to the years of want and sacrifice during the Great Depression and the uncertainties of the war years. Rollin cites Betty Friedan who, in *The Feminine Mystique*, saw the late 1940s and 1950s as a period when the production of babies became the norm and motherhood turned into a cult.

Psychoanalysis was influential in the development of the mystique surrounding motherhood. Psychoanalysis placed undue emphasis on the mother-child relationship, oversentimentalizing it. It argued that only the biological mother was capable of providing the emotional satisfaction and stimulation necessary for the healthy development of the infant. For the individuals involved, parenthood represented a necessary step on the road to maturation and personality development. For women, parenthood was necessary for them to achieve normality and avoid neuroticism. Freudian psychology insisted that the reproductive potential, that is, childbearing, must be actualized if women were to achieve mental health. Motherhood represented the realization of women's basic psychological and biological needs.

Rochelle Paul Wortis (1977) critically reexamined the concept of the maternal role as expressed in psychoanalytic theory. She concluded that the evidence used in psychological studies for the importance of the mother-child relationship was based on scientifically inadequate assumptions. The overemphasis on parenthood and particularly on motherhood encouraged "the domestication and subordination of females in society" (Wortis, 1977:361).

Wortis observed that the psychological studies centering around the mother-infant bond reflected the provincialism of Western psychology and psychiatry. She argues that they turned a cultural phenomenon into a biological one. Wortis notes that there are diversified ways in which children around the world are raised. Our society is relatively unique in insisting that child development lies solely within the province and responsibility of the mother. Wortis augments her argument by citing from the work of Margaret Mead:

> At present, the specific biological situation of the continuing relationship of the child to its biological mother and its need for care by human beings are being hopelessly confused in the growing insistence that child and biological mother, or mother surrogate, must never be separated, that all separation, even for a few days, is inevitably damaging, and that if long enough it does irreversible damage. This . . . is a new and subtle form of antifeminism in which men . . . are tying women more tightly to their children than has been thought necessary since the invention of bottle-feeding and baby carriages. Actually, anthropological evidence gives no support at present to the value of such an accentuation of the tie between mother and child. . . . On the contrary, cross-cultural studies suggest that adjustment is most facilitated if the child is cared for by many warm friendly people. (Mead, 1954, cited in Wortis, 1977:366)

The anthropological literature provides numerous examples on the variability of child-rearing practices. In the now classic study of six cultures by Minturn and Lambert (1964), the researchers found that only in the New England suburb of Orchardtown were there isolated households and exclusive mother-infant child rearing. In the five more "primitive" societies, there was a greater involvement by other kin and outsiders in the raising of the child. Thus, among the Nyansongo of Kenya, the child is cared for by an older sibling when the mother is working in nearby fields. Among the Rajputs of India, a caretaker, either an older sister or a cousin, cares for the child. Old men and, eventually, other male relatives—fathers, uncles, or grandfathers—assist in the child's care. Similar shared involvements characterize the Taira in Okinawa, the Mixteans of Mexico, and the Tarong of the Philippines. It is only in our society that women solely have this task.

Henrietta L. Moore (1988) has observed that the concept of "woman" is not elaborated through ideas about motherhood, fertility, nurturance, and reproduction in much of the world's cultures. Collier and Rosaldo (1981), in their analysis, find that among hunting and gathering societies throughout the world the themes of motherhood and sexual reproduction are not central to such peoples conception of "woman." "Woman the Fertile, the Mother and Source of All Life, was quite remarkably, absent from all available accounts" (Collier and Rosaldo, 1981:276).

The emphasis in American society on motherhood being the ultimate achievement and fulfillment and a woman's highest calling is seen to apply primarily to middle-class white women and does not apply to the realities of African American women. This is the argument put forth by Patricia Hill Collins (1994) [See also Berry (1993)]. In contrast to what she defines as a "eurocentric view of white motherhood" is a model of African American motherhood that consists of four basic themes.

The first theme—"bloodmothers, othermothers, and women-centered networks"—emphasizes the importance of a community network of women who share responsibility when conditions warrant for each others' children. These responsibilities range from temporary child care arrangements to long-term care or informal adoption. "Providing as part of mothering" paid work and being economic providers is an important dimension of the Afrocentric definition of motherhood in contrast to the white conceptualization. The third theme is an extension of the first. "Community othermothers and social activism" refers to black women's social activism and their belief in looking out for the well-being of all children in the community. The fourth theme—"Motherhood as a symbol of power"—reflects the fact that a substantial part of black women's status in African American communities is through their roles of mother to their own children or serving as community othermothers and contributing to community development (Collins, 1994).

While economic conditions as well as ideological views regarding the relationship between family and home and paid work and career are changing in the larger white community as well, the majority of women in America have lived their lives being fundamentally defined as mothers. Judith Blake (1972), who was a world-famous demographer, argued that in contemporary Western society motherhood is actualized in *coercive pronatalism*. Blake believed that motherhood, rather than being a voluntary option for women, is in fact a mandatory directive. This directive assures that women will bear children. Two pronatalist coercions characterize modern American society. The first is the prescribed primacy of parenthood in the definition of gender roles. The second is the prescribed congruence of personality traits with the demands of the gender roles as defined. Adult gender roles are defined in terms of parenthood. Americans socialize girls and boys to become the proper kinds of people they say that mothers and fathers should be.

Blake believes that the emphasis on the primacy of parenthood limits the accessibility of alternative roles. This is particularly the case for women. Nonfamilial roles are seen as deviant and pathological. Challenges to the role of motherhood arouse widespread opposition since they are viewed as threats to the gender-role expectations relegating women to domesticity and parenthood. Female labor-force participation, higher education for women, and feminism are viewed negatively by society as they run counter to the desired goal of motherhood. Motherhood is seen to represent the fulfillment of a woman's destiny.

BOX 12-2 The Contemporary American Family

The Murphy Brown Trend: Older, Richer Single Moms

Donna St. George

HERALD WASHINGTON BUREAU

WASHINGTON—Teenage pregnancy is still a problem in America—but the Murphy Browns are gaining on the teens.

That's right, the unmarried mother in America is slowly shifting profiles: More and more, it's a 30-something college grad with a professional job, says Amara Bachu, author of a Census Bureau study released Wednesday.

"It's a common belief that it's the teenagers and the poor that are having more babies," she says. But the biggest jump in out-of-marriage pregnancies, she says, is coming from the older and better-off.

"It's women who have postponed their childbearing to have a career," she says. "They are economically independent, they can afford to have a baby. Their biological clock is ticking, and they probably could not find a suitable partner."

The other motivating force, she suggests, is waning social disapproval. "Society has changed, and there is no stigma attached," Bachu says.

Her report, "Fertility of American Women," shows that the country continues to have more out-of-marriage births than ever—with one of five never-married women giving birth.

Teenagers are still a major part of that baby boom. They had more than 28 percent of the children born last year to unmarried mothers. And many fertility experts warned that their plight should not be overshadowed by the phenomenon of older, more secure women having babies outside of marriage.

"It's true that there are these women, but they are not common," says Stephanie Ventura, a fertility expert with the National Center for Health Statistics. "Only 5 percent of the never-married mothers are managers."

But in the Census Bureau report, Bachu focuses on three separate statistics:

In the past 12 years, the birth rates have more than doubled for never-married women with at least a bachelor's degree and never-married women with professional and managerial occupations. And they have almost doubled for never-married white women.

In her view, the portrait that emerges is one of Murphy Brown, the fictional television character played by actress Candice Bergen, who became pregnant and decided to have the child.

"It's really interesting how many women are very clear that they want to be mothers—they want to raise a wonderful child, they want to make that contribution to the world," says Leslie Wolfe, president of the Center for Women Policy Studies. "They haven't found the right man, but they aren't going to let that stop them."

"Their first choice is to get married and have kids and live happily ever after," Wolfe said. "But that doesn't happen for everyone, and if their second choice now is, they can have a child and live happily ever after."

For many women, she suggests, "this wedlock thing is not all its cracked up to be."

But on the conservative side, Patrick Fagan, a senior policy analyst for Heritage Foundation in Washington, calls the Census report "a sign of the continuing breakdown of the family and the culture. I think it's very serious because it means it's getting deeper into the mainstream."

"Marriage," Fagan says, "is the center beam of society."

The Miami Herald, 9 November 1995.
Reprinted with permission of The Miami Herald.

Myths about motherhood provide the supportive ideology for the above view-point. Motherhood is seen to provide a woman with her most rewarding status. Fatherhood demonstrates the masculinity of the man. E.E. LeMasters (1957) has out-lined several folk beliefs about parenthood that have been popular in American cul-ture. (A folk belief is one that is widely held but that is not supported by facts.) Here are some of LeMasters' examples of these beliefs:

1. Rearing children is fun.
2. Children are sweet and cute.
3. Children will turn out well if they have "good" parents.
4. Children will improve marriage.
5. Childless couples are frustrated and unhappy.
6. Parents are adults.

LeMasters believes that these myths have been disproven by scientific evidence. However, they still serve to promote parenthood. Further, they downplay the prob-lems associated with the transition to parenthood. Indeed, the transition to parent-hood is a period often marked by crisis and marital disruption. Alice S. Rossi (1968), in an enlightening article, argues that the tensions and problems accompanying parent-hood can be seen as an outgrowth of the isolation of the nuclear family and the almost exclusive involvement of the mother with infant and child care. An examination of the transition to the parenthood period is revealing in that it highlights the nature of parental roles in our modern industrial society.

Father as the Good Provider

The following discussion reviews the sociological character of men's lives in American families. Invariably, in the study of the family, greater attention is paid to the female roles of wife and mother than is paid to the male roles of husband and father. Given the dichotomization of the worlds of work and the worlds of the family, with men and women having corresponding influence in each, this is not surprising. However, the women's movement of the last thirty-five years has resulted in a serious reconsidera-tion of the allocation and appropriation of the given roles of *both* women and men and their relative place in the public and private spheres of work and the home.

Jessie Bernard (1981), in an insightful article, "The Good Provider Role: Its Rise and Fall," traces the historical development and changes in male roles in the family in the United States. She observes that the Industrial Revolution and the transition from a subsistence economy to a market economy in the 1830s led to the development of a specialized male role, that of the "good provider." This role can be seen as the coun-terpart to the "cult of true motherhood." It remained in effect for almost 150 years. Then, in the late 1970s, forces precipitated by the women's movement brought about changes symbolized and reflected in the 1980 census. That national census no longer assumed that a male should automatically be considered to be the head of the house-hold. Essentially, the good provider role defined a man as one whose wife did not have to, or should not, enter the labor force. Bernard cites Webster's second edition, which defines the good provider as "one who provides, especially (colloq.) one who provides food, clothing, etc., for his family, as he is a good or an adequate provider" (cited in Bernard, 1981:2).

The good provider role has implications for both men and women. Bernard reminds us that in the colonial period, women such as Abigail Adams, the wife of John Adams, managed estates and were active in business and professional pursuits. Women were expected to provide for the family along with men. They were involved in the running of stores, shops, and businesses. The domestic economy of preindustrial America saw the household as a center for the production of food, clothing, furniture, bedding, candles, and other accessories. Women's involvement in the economic well-being of the family was taken for granted.

The development of a specialized male role devoted to economic activity had as a consequence the removal of women from labor-force participation and income-producing activities. Instead of looking after themselves and their families, they had to devote their attention to obtaining a "good provider" who would "take care of" them and their children. Throughout this book, I indicate the psychological and sociological consequences of this viewpoint for women's lives. Now it is time to turn attention to the consequences for men.

Men were told to concentrate on their jobs and careers; emotional expressivity was not to be their concern. The expression of emotion was to be in the women's realm. Lack of expressivity became a defining characteristic of the good provider role. It was even reflected in the criteria for marriage. A man was defined as a good marriage prospect if it was felt that he would be a good provider, not that he would be gentle, loving, or tender. Being a good provider was the essential quality that was looked for. While being a "family man"—setting a good table, providing a decent home, paying the mortgage, feeding and clothing wife and children—was important, loving attention and emotional involvement with the family were not necessarily seen as a part of the package. As Bernard puts it: "If in addition to being a good provider, a man was kind, gentle, humorous, and not a heavy drinker or gambler, that was all frosting on the cake" (1981:3).

A consequence of the good provider role was the development of a predominant concept of male identity in terms of work and career activities. Success was measured by an economic criterion. The worth of a man and the meaning of his life became defined by the workplace and his success and failure there; they were not measured in terms of his being a caring, loving, and nurturing husband and father. The consequence was that failure to provide economically for the family resulted in negative identity feelings regardless of how successfully the man may have fulfilled the emotional and expressive needs of family members.

Also involved in attitudes regarding the good provider role was the belief that a wife employed was evidence of the male's failure to provide. A working wife was also viewed as ultimately undermining the man's position as head of the household.

Bernard historically examines the different ways that males have confronted the good provider role. Two categories of males—the "role rejectors" and "role overperformers"—are delineated. The role rejectors are epitomized by the fictional character Rip Van Winkle, who slept through the twenty crucial years of marriage and child rearing. The tramp, the hobo, and today's homeless men on skid row are men who dropped out of the role entirely. The social historian John Demos (1974) depicts the tramp as follows:

> Demoralized and destitute wanderers, their numbers mounting into the hundreds and thousands, tramps can be fairly characterized as men who had run away from their wives. . . . Their presence was mute testimony to the strains that tugged at the very core of American family life. . . . Many observers noted that the tramps had created a virtual society of their own . . . based on a principle of single-sex companionship. (Demos, 1974:438)

Conversely, we speak of the overperformers as "workaholics" or men so intoxicated by work that they lose sight of the ultimate goal of providing for the family with a compulsive striving for occupational and career achievement. This often results in the complete neglect of family members. They epitomize the intrinsic strain and contradiction in the good provider role. For, by epitomizing it, they highlight the inherent limitations of defining good providing solely in economic terms. And as Bernard points out: "Their preoccupation with their work even at the expense of their families was . . . quite acceptable in our society" (1981:7).

Beginning in the 1970s, the good provider role underwent dramatic changes. Ideological changes brought about through the women's movement questioned male family roles. Further, the simultaneous occurrence of recession and inflationary economic conditions often necessitated a two-income family to maintain the family's standard of living. Ideological factors combined with economic conditions resulted in more and more wives and mothers entering the workforce. One consequence was a welcome relief for the husband-father from the economic burden of being sole provider. Attached to women's work realities was a consequent demand for two modifications in the traditional male good provider role. Bernard identifies these as a call for more intimacy, expressivity, and nurturance on the part of males in the family and sharing of household responsibility and child care. To some extent, changes are occurring, albeit painfully for some. Bernard closes by raising a number of questions regarding the impact of the large influx of women into the workforce, the large number of men who will increase their participation in the family and the household, and the subsequent demise of the good provider role:

> Will men find the apron shameful? What if we were to ask fathers to alternate with mothers in being in the home when youngsters come home from school? Would fighting adolescent drug abuse be more successful if fathers and mothers were equally engaged in it? If the school could confer with fathers as often as with mothers? If the father accompanied children when they went shopping for clothes? If fathers spent as much time with children as do mothers?
>
> What does the demotion of the good provider to the status of the senior provider or even mere co-provider do to him? To marriage? To gender identity? What does expanding the role of housewife to that of junior provider or even co-provider do to her? To marriage? To gender identity? (Bernard, 1981:11)

BOX 12-3   The Contemporary American Family

The New Dad Works the "Second Shift," Too

Caryl Rivers and Rosalind C. Barnett

The image of family men isn't exactly sterling these days, especially in the American media. Either they're "deadbeat dads" who are creating a fatherless America, or lazy slobs who come home, put their feet up and watch TV while their working wives do all the scut work on the "Second Shift."

The latter notion was enough to make working women furious: men retreating, in mulish stubbornness, from doing their fair share. It was believed that men were accepting the money and the perks from working wives, but being total male chauvinist pigs when it came to work at home.

But it's time to say a good word about the American male. And new research shows that there is good news to report.

First of all, there may be a Second Shift, but it's not just women who are on it. The image of the overworked woman and the man who won't dry a dish is simply inaccurate. Our study of full-time, employed, two-earner couples, funded by the National Institute of Mental Health, looked at the housework patterns of 300 couples. We asked them how many hours per week they spent planning and preparing meals, shopping, doing laundry, taking out the garbage, paying bills, looking after the car, and caring for the yard. The women spend more time each week on home work than their husbands—but not much more: 26 hours for the women and 21 hours for the men. Altogether, women spend more time on household chores (about 3.7 hours a day) compared to the men (about 3 hours a day). So while women still do roughly 55 percent of the housework, men do 45 percent. This picture is a lot closer to equality than it is to the Second Shift scenario.

When we looked at hours on the job, however, we found the reverse picture. men put in more hours than did their wives: 48.5 hours a week compared to 42 hours for their wives. Considering jobs and housework, both partners are putting in roughly 70 hours a week! No evidence of male sloth here. Men and women alike are very busy pulling the load.

And while the image of the gun-toting, macho guy is at the forefront of the American consciousness these days, he's far from typical. The man changing a diaper is more the norm. Fathers today are very involved in their children's lives. When researcher John Snarey of Emory University reviewed data from a major, four-decades-long study of fathers and sons, he concluded that the traditional image of Dad as the shadowy figure who stands in the background while the mother does all the nurturing is erroneous. Snarey says that old—and widely quoted—studies showing that fathers spend few hours each week with their children and mainly "help out" as parents are passe.

Dads provide 25 percent of primary child care for preschool kids.

"These findings are historically dated and culturally limited," he says. He notes that U.S. census data indicate that fathers now provide 25 percent of primary child care for preschool age children, and one study showed that in two-earner families, fathers take sole responsibility for child care at double the rate of men who are single-earners.

In our study, women did more parenting when children were very young, but by the time they reached school age, mothers and fathers put in equal time. And a major new study in Sweden shows no gender differences at all in parenting hours. So our findings are not isolated. A new trend is clearly emerging.

When men do get involved with their children, the effect is beneficial. Psychologist Leslie Brody, a professor at Boston University, found that with such fathers, boys are able to show more vulnerability, and girls more competitiveness.

Fatherhood has moved back closer to center stage in men's lives today. A 1991 Gallup poll shows that a clear majority of men today derive a greater sense of satisfaction from caring for their family than from a job well done at work. And when sociologist Kathleen Gerson studied a group of 138 men for her book *No Man's Land*, she found that the men who seem happiest with their lives are the group Gerson calls the "new fathers"—a group very much like the men we studied. While they often enjoy their work, they don't put the entire burden of their identity and happiness on their jobs—as men often did in the past. Since the mid-'60s, the number of fathers who are becoming highly involved in rearing their children is growing.

We are now entering what might be called the Era of the Involved Father. Men in two-earner families are very connected to their children. They care for children in ways that fathers have rarely done in the past.

Not just a breadwinner, not just a "pal" to his kids, the new father is deeply involved with his children from infancy onward. In fact, today's fathers spend considerably more time rearing their children than did fathers in the '50s—the vaunted "togetherness" era.

Several recent studies have documented this change in men's attitudes. A major 1993 study by the Families and Work Institute shows that American workers are willing to trade bigger paychecks and the fast track for more time with their families. One-third of men under 40 said they would consider giving up raises and advancement for a better home life—twice the number of men who felt that way five years ago. A survey by Du Pont found that 56 percent of its male employees favored flexible schedules allowing more family time, and 40 percent would consider working for another employer who offered more flexibility.

A number of studies, including ours, show that flexibility on the job—or lack of it—to deal with family issues affects a man's stress level as much as it does a woman's.

Still, we have the idea that a man is an automaton who never thinks about his kids when he's at work, who doesn't need paternity leave or flexibility to deal with his family. Those things are "women's issues."

Until we can start to think about "family friendly" corporate policies and such issues as parental leave and flexibility as men's issues, they are never going to get much attention. And if they don't, it is the fathers of America—and their children—who will be the losers.

Caryl Rivers, a Boston University journalism professor, and Rosalind C. Barnett, of the Murray Research Center at Radcliffe, are the authors of *She Works, He Works: How Two Income Families Are Happier, Healthier and Better Off*, just published by HarperSan Francisco.

Philadelphia Inquirer, 16 June 1996.
Reprinted with permission by the Philadelphia Inquirer, 1996.

THE TRANSITION TO PARENTHOOD

Parenthood, rather than marriage, may be the crucial role transition for men and women. Parenthood necessitates the reorganization of economic patterns of earning and spending the family income. It demands the reallocation of space, time, and attention. It necessitates the reorganization of marital decision making and the reorganization of occupation-role commitment—particularly for the wife. It calls for the reworking of relationships with extended family, friends, and neighbors. Finally, it demands the reestablishment of marital adjustment and intimacy, which have been disrupted by the period of transition to parenthood.

The behavioral sciences have almost exclusively confined their attention to the child when studying the husband-wife-child relationships. Thus, a vast body of data has been accumulated in the field of child development. There is a great deal of literature concerned with the effect parents have on their children. The corresponding issue—the effects children have on their parents—has received relatively little attention. This reflects the parenthood myth that having children is an enriching and maturing experience. The myth says parenthood enhances personality growth, solidifies the marriage, and indicates the achievement of adult status and community stability. With such positive attributes, the impact of parenthood on the parents was not seen as problematic and was, therefore, not defined as a subject worth studying.

At the height of glory of the traditional family in the 1950s, a groundbreaking study appeared that put forth the argument that parenthood is not always positive. In a widely cited article, "Parenthood as Crisis," E.E. LeMasters (1957) found that 83 percent of the 46 couples interviewed experienced extensive or severe crisis in adjusting to the birth of their first child. Some of the problems of adjustment most frequently mentioned by mothers were chronic tiredness, extensive confinement to the home with resulting curtailment of social contacts, and the relinquishing of satisfactions associated with outside employment. Women felt guilty about not being better mothers. Fathers mentioned decline in sexual response of the wife, economic pressures resulting from the wife's retirement, additional expenditures necessary for the child, and a general disenchantment with the parental role.

The amount of crisis experienced by these couples was found to be unrelated to the planning of children, to prior marital adjustment, or to the personality adjustment of the couples. Couples seemed to experience crisis even when they actively wanted the child and had a good marriage. The only variable that LeMasters found to distinguish crisis from noncrisis reactions was professional employment of the mother. All eight mothers with extensive professional work experience suffered severe crises. LeMasters concludes that parenthood is the real "romantic complex" in our culture and that this romanticizing of parenthood and the attendant lack of training for the role are crucial determinants of problems.

Subsequent research (Dyer, 1963; Hobbs, 1965, 1968; Hobbs and Cole, 1976; 1977; Jacoby, 1969; McLanahan and Adams, 1989; Russell, 1974; Voydanoff, 1989) found greater role transition problems for middle-class parents than working-class parents. The factors that account for the more difficult transition of the middle-class parent include higher standards and greater expectations, career aspirations interfering with family involvements, less experience with raising children, and greater commitment and involvement of the husband-wife relationship (Jacoby, 1969).

A very interesting approach in the investigation of marital interactions after the birth of a child argues that the study of the allocation, utilization, and commitment of time can be useful in the analysis of the transition-to-parenthood period. Ralph LaRossa and Maureen LaRossa (1981) have made the argument that researchers have been so involved in the measurement of the attitudes that people have toward the transition to parenthood that they have neglected to study the actual behavior that occurs during this transition period. They described the experiences of twenty white upper-middle-class couples, half of whom had just had their first child and half of whom had other children in addition to their newborn one. The key variable in explaining the character of the transition into parenthood was how the couples allocated time. In answer to questions on how their lives had changed since their babies were born, the constant theme echoed by these parents was the loss of time for such everyday activities as sleep, communication, sex, and even using the bathroom. Paradoxically, they also reported that they were more likely to be bored; weight gain and television soap-opera addiction were unwanted consequences.

LaRossa and LaRossa attribute the simultaneous feeling of time being both scarce and abundant to the nature of infant care and its related activities. New infants require constant supervision and care and the parents have to be constantly available. "It is this basic pattern—child dependency resulting in continuous coverage, which means a scarcity of free time, which leads to conflicts of interest and often conflict behavior—that cuts across the experiences of all the couples in our sample" (LaRossa and LaRossa, 1981:46-47).

Among these affluent couples the distribution of time allocation for the infant is different for the mother and father. They make a distinction between playing with the infant and caring for the infant. Men are much more likely to play with their babies, while mothers are more likely to bathe, feed, dress, and change them. The spending of time at play is seen to require less attention on the part of the father than care on the part of the mother. Of course, there is also a qualitative difference in the nature of the interaction between parent and infant than between adults. Infants are unrelenting in their demand for the satisfaction of their needs, whether it be the changing of a diaper or being fed. Infants also demand that parents be present during their waking hours. This again severely restricts the activities of the parent.

In addition to the parental division of labor in infant care, LaRossa and LaRossa found that mothers are primarily responsible for their infants. When fathers assume the caring role, it is invariably defined as "helping" their wives. They found that "every couple would, at least once in their interviews, refer to the husband as 'helping' the wife with the baby, whereas not a single couple defined the wife's parental responsibilities in these terms. Clearly from the start, the mother is the one who is 'in charge' of the baby" (1981:57).

In a later article, Ralph LaRossa (1983) makes the theoretical distinction between "physical" time and "social" time as an explanatory variable in understanding the transition to parenthood. Physical time is astronomical time; it is quantitative, continuous, homogeneous, and objective. The examples provided include the speed of light and the rate of decay of the body. Social time, on the other hand, is qualitative, discontinuous, heterogeneous, and subjective. Here, the examples include courtship, small talk, and the sequences and durations of friendship. LaRossa builds on William J. Goode's (1960) sociological approach to time put forth in his theory of role strain. Goode conceptualizes time as being a relatively scarce resource. People face a problem in trying to meet their total role obligations given their overall activities and given the finite nature of time. LaRossa focuses on one of the twenty couples that he (along with Maureen LaRossa) studied earlier to demonstrate the utility of this distinction between physical time and social time.

LaRossa shows how both the mother and father find difficulty in fulfilling their total role obligations as a consequence of the birth of their third child. The wife-mother has to balance caring for the two other children, her career, housework, and marriage with the demands of infant care. The husband-father, who travels a lot, must make every second count when he returns home and spends time with his family. The demands of the infant, who will not socially accommodate to the temporal rules of the parents' schedule, complicates matters. LaRossa states, "Thus, the transition to parenthood makes a family more aware of their schedule—formerly a taken-for-granted system (who questions the validity of not getting up at 4:00 A.M.?)—which in turn makes them more aware of the clock, which then makes them feel that they are constantly running out of time" (1983:585-586).

Further, when, as in the case of this case-study family, the couple have an overcommitment to their work and their home, additional problems may be felt. LaRossa believes that this couple may be a prime candidate for what he calls "marital burnout," a belief that they do not have enough time to make love or have a meaningful conversation. Their overcommitment to other activities leaves them less time than they wish for their commitment to each other. They are then forced to justify their undercommitment to their relationship in terms of these other involvements. "[T]hey find themselves excusing and justifying their misconduct (i.e., their conduct that is at odds with their shared belief that they are still in love) by citing their lack of time" (LaRossa, 1983:587).

I concur with LaRossa's opinion that the future investigation of the transition to parenthood would be aided by examining it within the context of the social reality of time. By so doing, we would be able to find out how time is allocated and its trajectory and effect on the transition-to-parenthood period. Social-time analysis would also be a significant conceptual tool in understanding differential commitments, role allocations, and the definition of infant care as a scheduled event. Variations in societal norms and subcultural families' commitments to the social construction of the transition to parenthood should also be studied. Finally, the study of the resolution of apparent contradictions between articulated commitments and actual behavior of new mothers and fathers would aid in the analysis of the transition to parenthood.

In summary, I believe that the dissatisfactions and problems associated with parenthood, particularly for the middle class, ultimately stem from the very nature of the conjugal-family system. In middle-class American society, the family is relatively isolated from the supports of extended kin and the surrounding community. They are not available to assist in the care of infants and young children. This is quite different from conditions in our historical past or in other societies.

Historically, the family was a part of the community. Philippe Ariès (1962) has observed that the contemporary family has withdrawn into the home. It has become a private place of residence for family members. The former extended-family group, who lived in common residence, is gone. The family is segregated from the rest of the world, and the home is isolated from external involvements. This has had profound effects on the wife-mother who has been relegated to domestic tasks and childbearing. She has the major responsibility for the well-being of the child. Fathers are not required to be involved in child care. The community provides minimal institutional supports and assistance. The result has been the increased dissatisfaction with parenthood and particularly motherhood.

This has been the traditional pattern. But, as I have observed, there are movements of change. Increasingly, husbands are becoming involved in domestic activities, including relationships with their children. Another is the increased demands for child-care facilities outside the home. This would allow both the husband and the wife to pursue outside family careers. As of this writing, child-care facilities are still woefully inadequate. Finally, and most dramatically, there is the development of ideological arguments for increased options for women. The motherhood myth is less acceptable to many. This should result in a more satisfying and more productive parenthood and childhood. My thoughts echo those of Betty Rollin:

> When motherhood is no longer culturally compulsory, there will, certainly, be less of it. Women are now beginning to think and do more about development of self, of their individual resources. Far from being selfish, such development is probably our only hope. That means more alternatives for women. And more alternatives mean more selective, better, happier motherhood—and childhood and husbandhood (or manhood) and peoplehood. It is not a question of whether or not children are sweet and marvelous to have and rear; the question is, even if that's so, whether or not one wants to pay the price for it. It doesn't make any sense any more to pretend that women need babies, when what they really need is themselves. If God were still speaking to us in a voice we could hear, even He would probably say, "Be fruitful. Don't multiply." (Rollin, 1970:17)

ABORTION AND THE FAMILY

There are a seemingly endless variety of laws, restrictions, customs, and traditions that affect the practice of abortion around the world. Globally, "(a)bortion is probably the single most controversial issue in the whole area of women's rights and family matters" (O'Connell, 1994:32). It is an issue that inflames women's rights groups, religious institutions, and the self-proclaimed "guardians" of public morality. The growing worldwide belief is that the right to control one's fertility is a basic human right. This has resulted in a worldwide trend toward liberalization of abortion laws. Forty percent of the world's population live in countries where induced abortion is permitted on request. An additional 25 percent live in countries where it is allowed if the women's life would be endangered if she went to full term with her pregnancy. The estimate is that between 26 and 31 million legal abortions were performed in 1987. However, there were also between 10 and 22 million illegal abortions performed in that year (Nam, 1994).

Feminists have viewed the patriarchal control of women's bodies as one of the prime issues facing the contemporary women's movement. They observe that the definition and control of women's reproductive freedom have always been the province of men. Patriarchal religion, as manifest in Islamic fundamentalism, traditionalist Hindu practice, orthodox Judaism, and Roman Catholicism, has been an important historical contributory factor for this and continues to be an important presence in contemporary societies. In recent times, governments, usually controlled by men, have "given" women the right to contraceptive use and abortion access when their countries were perceived to have an overpopulation problem. When these countries are perceived to be underpopulated, that right has been absent. Robin Morgan (1984b:6), a leading advocate of worldwide women's rights, states, "The point, of course, is that this is *the right of an individual woman* herself, *not a gift to be bestowed or taken back*" (1984b:6).

Examples of Morgan's position include changes in policies in some nations that comprised the former "Eastern block" of communist societies and in the former Soviet Union. In Poland, under the Communist regime abortion was legal. After the fall of communism, the new government, strongly influenced by the Roman Catholic Church, changed its policies. At the beginning of 1992 abortion was legal up to 12 weeks for a variety of reasons. In early May of that year the Polish Doctor's Guild implemented a controversial code under which doctors performing most abortions risked loss of license (Lacayo, 1992). By 1995 it had become outlawed.

In the former Soviet Union, the Russian government policies changed as political and economic conditions changed. Abortion was legalized in 1920, soon after the Revolution. In 1936, it was made illegal, and policies strongly encouraging unrestricted childbirth came into force that lasted until Stalin's death in 1953. Morgan reports in 1984 that the average Soviet woman has between twelve and fourteen abortions during her lifetime, because contraceptives, although legal, are extremely difficult to obtain. Now, in post-communist Russia, an emerging anti-abortion movement is linking up with physicians who are disturbed by the large number of abortions that women have (Vrazo, 1995).

The Abortion Controversy in the United States

Until the nineteenth century, a woman's rights to an abortion followed English common law; it could only be legally challenged if there was a "quickening," when the first movements of the fetus could be felt. In 1800 drugs to induce abortions were widely advertised in local newspapers. By 1900, abortion was banned in every state except to save the life of the mother. The change was strongly influenced by the medical profession, which focused its campaign ostensibly on health and safety issues for pregnant women and the sanctity of life. Its position was also a means of control of nonlicensed medical practitioners such as midwives and women healers who practiced abortion.

The anti-abortion campaign was also influenced by political considerations. The large influx of eastern and southern European immigrants with their large families was seen as a threat to the population balance of the future United States. Middle- and upper-class Protestants were advocates of abortion as a form of birth control. By supporting abortion prohibitions the hope was that these Americans would have more children and thus prevent the tide of immigrant babies from overwhelming the demographic characteristics of Protestant America.

The anti-abortion legislative position remained in effect in the United State through the first sixty-five years of the twentieth century. In the early 1960s, even when it was widely known that the drug thalidomide taken during pregnancy to alleviate anxiety was shown to contribute to the formation of deformed "flipper-like" hands or legs of children, abortion was illegal in the United States. A second health tragedy was the severe outbreak of rubella during that same time period, which also resulted in major birth defects. These tragedies combined with a change in attitudes towards a woman's right to privacy led a number of states to pass abortion-permitting legislation.

The United States has witnessed a revolution in the abortion situation for the last quarter of a century. In the late 1960s and early 1970s, seventeen states liberalized their abortion laws. Then, in January 1973, the Supreme Court issued landmark rulings that virtually wiped out both the old laws and most of the more liberal new ones. In *Roe v. Wade* and *Doe v. Bolton*, the court held that any woman anywhere in the United States can legally receive an abortion if she wants one.

Legal challenges that attempt to change the Supreme Court decisions have been continuous. In 1977 the Hyde Amendment was passed by Congress. This amendment restricts funding for abortions for women who also receive Medicaid (unless the pregnancy is life threatening). In 1989, in *Webster v. Reproductive Health*, the Supreme Court allowed for additional controls for abortion. The Court upheld the state of Missouri's law that said life begins at conception and requires physicians to conduct viability tests on fetuses of twenty weeks or more before abortions could be performed. In 1992, in *Planned Parenthood v. Casey*, the Court upheld the law on the right to abortion, but at the same time permitted states to pass various laws to restrict the practice. The Pennsylvania law required a woman to wait 24 hours between the confirmation of pregnancy and abortion and women under the age of 18 had to have the consent of one parent before they could have an abortion. The law also required that women had to be informed about options to abortion and to be given materials that described the fetus. The Supreme Court in that same case ruled that a woman did not have to inform her husband if she intended to have an abortion.

Since *Roe v. Wade* the annual number of abortions performed in the United States has risen from 744,600 in 1973 to 1.5 million in 1980. That later figure has remained fairly constant since then (U.S. Bureau of the Census, 1993). A little more than one out of every five (21 percent) of women of reproductive age have had abortions. The Census Bureau reported that the abortion rate per 100 women was 2.3 for white women and 5.6 for African Americans. The court's decisions and the rise in the abortion rate that followed it has provoked a crusade of unrelenting commitment. This "right to life" movement has become perhaps the most powerful single-issue force in American politics in the last fifteen years.

On one side of the controversy are those who call themselves "pro-life." They view the fetus as a human life rather than as an unformed complex of cells; therefore, they hold to the belief that abortion is essentially murder of an unborn child. These groups cite both legal and religious reasons for their opposition to abortion. Pro-lifers point to the rise in legalized abortion figures and see this as morally intolerable. On the other side of the issue are those who call themselves "pro-choice." They believe that women, not legislators or judges, should have the right to decide whether and under what circumstances they will bear children. Pro-choicers are of the opinion that laws will not prevent women from having abortions and cite the horror stories of the past when many women died at the hands of "backroom" abortionists and in desperate attempts to self-abort. They also observe that legalized abortion is especially important for rape victims and incest victims who become pregnant. They stress physical and mental health reasons why women should not have unwanted children.

To get a better understanding of the current abortion controversy, let us examine a very important work by Kristin Luker (1984), *Abortion and the Politics of Motherhood*. Luker argues that female pro-choice and pro-life activists hold different world views regarding gender, sex, and the meaning of parenthood. Moral positions on abortion

BOX 12-4   The Contemporary American Family

Abortion Fight Here Like None in World

Fawn Vrazo

PHILADELPHIA INQUIRER

From her office in Canberra, the capital of Australia, family-planning worker Rowena Childs has given some thought to the American obsession with abortion. She has heard about clinic blockades. She has been horrified by clinic shootings. She is up to date on the Henry Foster uproar.

She can only feel relief that the scene in her country is so much calmer—a rare rally outside a clinic is about the biggest thing that happens.

Abortion "is very obviously a hot issue" in America, Childs observed last week. Perhaps, she conjectured, it's because "the religious groups in America are a lot more vocal, more deeply seated in society. In Australia, religion doesn't come to the fore so much."

Abortion is certainly debated abroad. Only in America has the argument resulted in murder.

As America struggles through yet another abortion controversy—the passions raised over abortions once performed by surgeon general nominee Foster—the rest of the world watches in wide-eyed amazement and wonder.

In Russia, in Great Britain, in Latin America, in every other part of the world, abortion does not come close to being the political hot-button issue that it is in the States. And in no other country have abortion clinic workers been murdered. The United States holds that gruesome record, with five slain in the last two years.

No one can say with certainty why this is so. Experts here and abroad, those for abortion rights and those against, cite a wide range of the-

ories: It may be because America has a stronger fundamental religious streak, or more guns, or a more vocal democracy, or because it has one of the world's most liberal abortion laws.

Or maybe it's just a wilder place. "In Canada, they call it the 'Excited States,'" said the Rev. Paul Marx, a Maryland priest who has traveled worldwide for the group Human Life International. Touting his anti-abortion message in England, Father Marx found people there to be "very sedate." In Germany, they were blase. Anti-abortion bumper stickers, "little feet" lapel pins— "they just don't work," he said.

On abortion, the French think Americans "are bonkers," said Marie Bass of the Washington, D.C., lobbying firm Bass & Howes, which has worked closely with the French to bring the so-called French abortion pill, RU-486, to the United States. "They think because our society is so violence-prone . . . that it lends itself to the potential for more violence around a controversial issue."

It is not that abortion is not controversial elsewhere. In many places, while it may not dominate the news, it is at least Topic B or C. Countries grappling with abortion issues include:

- Poland, where women's groups favoring abortion rights are fighting the government's sudden turnaround on abortion. Under communism, it was legal; now, under a non-Communist government strongly influenced by the Catholic Church, it has been outlawed.
- Ireland, where a right is brewing over a referendum that would legalize distribution of information about foreign abortion clinics. Abortion is strictly outlawed in Ireland, and about 4,000 women a year leave the country to seek abortions in Britain and other countries.
- Australia, where anti-abortion activists are campaigning against testing of RU-486.

• Russia, where a nascent anti-abortion movement is attempting to forge a link with doctors who are upset about the high number of abortions—eight on average—that Russian women have.

But despite those controversies and others, no other country comes close to challenging America's preoccupation with abortion—if only because anti-abortion movements elsewhere are relatively small.

The National Right to Life Committee in Washington, just one of dozens of American anti-abortion groups, has 3,000 affiliates throughout the nation. In Russia, Association Life "has just a few branches—it's just getting started," says Committee president Wanda Franz, who has given speeches in Moscow.

In France, anti-abortion activists recently marched in Paris to protest the 20th anniversary of the legalization of abortion in that country, which occurred in 1975. About 10,000 turned out. In America last month, a less significant anniversary—the 22nd—of the 1973 *Roe v. Wade* decision brought 45,000 marchers to Washington.

In many other countries, including Muslim nations and most nations in Latin America, abortion is illegal. While clandestine abortions—both safe and unsafe—are common, there is not much on a public policy level for anti-abortionists to get excited about. Potential abortion-rights activists are concerned about other things.

"In a lot of developing countries, [many believe] until you get family planning accepted you can't start working on the abortion issue," said Judith Helzner, director of program coordination for the International Planned Parenthood Federation.

She compared Latin America, where all but Cuba and Barbados outlaw abortion, to America in the 1950s and 1960s, when artificial contraception was just beginning to gain acceptance.

"There is a huge debate" among abortion-rights supporters in developing countries where abortion is illegal, Helzner said. "Should they [push for] legalization or not? Some people think it would be totally counterproductive, that legalizing it would give a lightning rod for all the opposition in the entire world to be focused on."

Meanwhile, in countries where abortion has been legal for many years, there is growing fear among abortion providers that anti-abortion activists there will increasingly begin imitating their more aggressive American counterparts.

Great Britain, which legalized abortion in 1967, has been largely silent on the issue for years. Only a small group in Parliament is attempting to restrict the abortion law, and clinic demonstrations, when they occur at all, "are maybe three, four people standing outside with placards," said Ann Furedi of Birth Control Trust, an organization that advises the government and media on abortion rights.

Furedi credits the difference in Britain's abortion law for the public's calmness on the issue. Unlike America, where a woman decides on her own to get an abortion, women in Great Britain must first get approval from two doctors.

"What that does is medicalize the issue," she said. "It's not seen here as an issue of women's rights. . . . It takes it a little out of the political arena."

But recently, the picture has changed. In the last year, cars in the parking lot of one abortion clinic in Brighton were sprayed with a corrosive acid. In Manchester, the doctor at a clinic had his picture and name publicized on a widely distributed flier—a tactic used extensively by America's Operation Rescue organization. According to Furedi, both actions were unprecedented.

"We're aware in this country that whatever happens in your country, gradually comes here," Furedi said. And when it comes to harassment and shooting of abortion clinic doctors, "you don't need a mass movement and hundreds and thousands of people to carry it out."

Philadelphia Inquirer, 19 February 1995.
Reprinted with permission by the Philadephia
Inquirer, 1995.

The issue of abortion has aroused great emotions among pro-life and pro-choice advocates.

are seen to be tied intimately to views on sexual behavior, the care of children, family life, technology, and the importance of the individual. Luker identifies "pro-choice" women as educated, affluent, and liberal. Their contrasting counterparts, "pro-life" women, support traditional concepts of women as wives and mothers. It would be instructive to sketch out the differences in the world views of these two sets of women. Luker examines California, with its liberalized abortion law, as a case history. Public documents and newspaper accounts over a twenty-year period were analyzed and over 200 interviews were held with both pro-life and pro-choice activists.

Luker found that pro-life and pro-choice activists have intrinsically different views with respect to gender. Pro-life women have a notion of public and private life. The proper place for men is in the public sphere of work; for women, it is the private sphere of the home. Men benefit through the nurturance of women; women benefit through the protection of men. Children are seen to be the ultimate beneficiaries of this arrangement by having the mother as a full-time loving parent and by having clear role models. Pro-choice advocates reject the view of separate spheres. They object to the notion of the home being the "women's sphere." Women's reproductive and family roles are seen as potential barriers to full equality. Motherhood is seen as a voluntary, not a mandatory or "natural," role.

Views on sex and sexuality also differ between the two groups of activists. Pro-life people are more likely to view the proper role of sex in terms of procreational love, not amative (recreational or pleasurable) love. "Sex as fun" is an ideology not shared by pro-life activists; rather, the emphasis is on the sacred and the transcendent—to bring into existence another human life. They tend to oppose most forms of contraception. Natural family planning or periodic abstinence is the preferred form of fertility control. According to the pro-lifers, highly effective contraception would subvert the reproductive functions of marriage and would subordinate the role and value of children.

In regard to sexuality, differing attitudes toward premarital sex, particularly among teenagers, highlight the differences between the two groups. For the pro-lifers, those who feel that sex should be procreative, premarital sexuality is very disturbing. Teenage sexuality is seen as both morally and socially wrong, as it is not directed in terms of having children. But to provide sex education, contraception, and abortion services for teenagers goes against everything in which pro-life advocates believe. It is a clear threat to their belief systems on the procreative function of sex.

Pro-choice advocates take diametrically opposite positions to these views regarding sex and sexuality. The central concern of sex should be on intimacy. Contraception enhances intimacy by allowing people the freedom to focus on the emotional aspects of sex without worrying about the procreational aspects. A belief in the procreational supremacy of sex is seen to lead to an oppressive degree of regulation of sexual behavior, particularly the behavior of women. Luker states that "In the pro-choice value system, both the double standard and 'purdah'—the custom of veiling women and keeping them entirely out of the public eye, lest they be too sexually arousing to men—are logical outcomes of a preoccupation with protecting and controlling women's reproductive capacities" (1984:177).

In regard to teenage sexuality, pro-choicers have no basic objection to sexual activity provided that the people involved are "responsible." Their main concern is about teenage parenthood. Like the pro-lifers, they take the position that teenagers are not prepared to become good parents. But given their view that sex helps create intimacy, caring, and trust, premarital sex (whether with different people or with the one person with whom they intend to make a long-term commitment) is desirable. Sex education and the availability of contraception and abortion services are deemed as proper and important for teenagers.

Luker believes that the essence of the abortion debate and the reason that it is so passionate and hard-fought is "because it is a referendum on the place and meaning of motherhood" (1984:193).

> Motherhood is at issue because two opposing visions of motherhood are at war. Championed by "feminists" and "housewives," these two different views of motherhood represent in turn two very different kinds of social worlds. The abortion debate has become a debate among women, women with different values in the social world, different experiences with it, and different resources with which to cope with it. How the issue is framed, how people think about it, and, most importantly, where the passions come from are all related to the fact that the battle lines are increasingly drawn (and defended) by women. While on the surface it is the embryo's fate that seems to be at stake, the abortion debate is actually about the meanings of women's lives. (Luker, 1984:193-194).

Luker found significant social-background differences between the pro-choice and pro-life women whom she examined. Pro-life women had less income than pro-choice women; 44 percent of them had incomes of less than $20,000 a year. In comparison, one-third of the pro-choice women reported incomes in the upper end of the scale, $50,000 a year. Tied to income levels are a number of interconnecting factors. Pro-choice women tend to work in the paid-labor market; earn good salaries; and, if married, have husbands with good incomes. Pro-life women were less likely to be employed; when they were, they made less money for less skilled work or part-time or less structured activities like selling cosmetics to friends. The education levels of these two groups also significantly differed. The pro-choice group had attained higher levels of education that often translated into employment in the major professions, as administrators, owners of small businesses, or executives in large businesses. Pro-life women were likely to be housewives, and the few who worked did so in the traditional jobs of teaching, social work, and nursing.

Women in the two groups also made different choices regarding marriage and the family. A greater percentage of the pro-choicers were not married, and for those who were married, they had fewer children than their pro-life counterparts. Religious affiliation and involvement were significantly different as well. The majority (63 percent) of the pro-choicers who were active in the movement reported that they observed no religion; the majority (80 percent) of the pro-life women were Catholic; the minorities of both groups contain Protestants and Jews. However, the major difference in regard to religion is the active involvement of the pro-lifers with their respective religions both in terms of church attendance and in terms of how religious doctrines govern their attitudes and behavior.

In summarizing her findings, Luker (1984) believes that women become activists in either of the two movements as the end result of lives that center around different conceptualizations of motherhood. Their beliefs and values are rooted to the concrete circumstances of their lives—their educations, incomes, occupations, and the different marital and family choices that they have made. They represent two different world views of women's roles in contemporary society and as such the abortion issue represents the battleground for the justification of their respective views.

Brigitte Berger and Peter L. Berger (1983), in their book *The War Over the Family*, also observe the importance of the abortion issue in coalescing differing opinions on the meaning of children, marriage, and the family. They see abortion as a strategically important moral issue that raises fundamental questions of human and civil rights and not just as a topic of family policy. They see the two antagonistic and opposing groups being at loggerheads with little shared ground and with little likelihood that a consensus can easily be reached. They refer to the two warring camps as "pro-abortion" (pro-choice) and "anti-abortion" (pro-life).

They call to task the pro-abortionists who fail to see the "awe" of human reproduction in terms of the fundamental metaphysical questions of birth and death. Similarly, they are critical of the anti-abortionists who fail to recognize our ignorance about the very foundations of human life—what human nature is and when it begins. That is: When does the fetus become human? Berger and Berger observe that pro-abortionists often try to avoid the reality that the fetus has the potential to become human. They illustrate this by noting that pro-abortion advocates become infuriated when anti-abortionists parade color photographs of fetuses or (as has happened at least once) dump aborted fetuses literally in their laps. On the other hand, anti-abortionists' certainty—by virtue of divine revelation or traditional religious authority—that human nature begins at the moment of conception does not recognize our ignorance on this matter.

To arrive at a consensus on the abortion question, Berger and Berger (1983) suggest a general policy direction. This would recognize the awe of conception by setting a fairly narrow time frame (not beyond the first trimester) as the period when the abortion would be permitted. The law would lean to the side of conservatism when the fetus is to be regarded as a person. The decision on whether to abort must be left to the pregnant woman, in consultation with whomever she chooses. They reason that if the fetus is presumed to be a person, no one—neither the mother nor any other individual—has the right to kill that person. But if the fetus is not presumed to be a person, it must be presumed to be considered as part of the pregnant woman's body. This being the case, no one other than the woman has the right to make decisions regarding it.

Given the extreme moral and metaphysical positions taken by the opposing groups, whether such a consensus can become operative remains in question. Further, given the extreme contrasting social positions regarding gender roles, sex and sexuality, and the nature of parenthood, the abortion debate promises to continue as a major political issue for years ahead.

Sex Choice: Amniocentesis and Abortion

Another issue regarding abortion that has become prominent is the social ramifications of biological technology that provides alternative means of aborting. One such technology that has impacted on the abortion controversy is the development of *menses-inducing* drugs. They can be taken soon after menstruation has ceased and there is medical certainty that the joining of sperm with the ovary has occurred. These drugs serve to cause expulsion of the uterine contents and menstruation. The French-produced drug RU-486—the French abortion pill—has been adequately tested for its effectiveness in France. However, pro-life and pro-choice groups have argued on whether it should be viewed as an abortifacient or be considered as a contraceptive. This disagreement has spilled over into the courts and has seriously limited its use. As of this writing, anti-abortionist groups have been successful in preventing its use in many countries, including the United States.

Another issue regarding abortion that has become more prominent is the social ramifications of biological technology to predict the sex of the fetus. One such technique is *amniocentesis*. After finding out the sex of the fetus, a decision could be made on whether to abort. At the time of this writing there is no data on how many abortions are based on sex selection in the United States.

Amniocentesis is a biological technique that takes a sample of the amniotic fluid surrounding the fetus. A needle is inserted through the pregnant woman's abdomen into the amniotic sac. A small amount of the fluid surrounding the fetus is withdrawn. The amniotic fluid contains cells sloughed off from the fetus. These cells can be examined to detect some seventy genetic disorders such as sickle-cell anemia, Tay-

Sachs disease, cystic fibrosis, hemophilia, and trisomy-21 or Down's syndrome or mongolism. Amniocentesis is usually performed at 14 to 16 weeks of pregnancy, and is often used with women over age 30 or 35 because of the increased risk of trisomy-21. It is also indicated if the couple already have a child with a genetic affliction, or if either parent is a carrier of a genetic disorder. If the woman so desires, an abortion would be performed.

The technique can also determine if the cells have XX chromosomes (girl) or XY chromosomes (boy). Some women have had the procedure done in order to discover the sex of the fetus and then have chosen abortion if the fetus was not the desired gender (Franke, 1982). There has been much speculation on the consequences of such sex-control if it were to become prevalent (Campbell, 1976). For example, the demographer Charles Westoff suggests that sex-control could lead to smaller families, defuse the population bomb, and lower the incidence of sex-linked hereditary diseases.

Proponents of sex-control foresee that it could lead to a growing satisfaction with the composition of the family. Parents would no longer have two or three children of the same sex if they no longer wished to have them. They could choose their family composition—a boy or girl, two boys, two girls, and so forth. The late anthropologist Margaret Mead believed that such technology would finally mean that female children would at last be wanted, since they will have been chosen.

Less optimistic is the sociologist Amitai Etzioni, who paints a scenerio of a world populated with boys, or a society locked into a pattern of first-born boys and second-born girls. Westoff counters by suggesting that an increase in males will eventually lead to a baby boom in girls and ultimately a balance in the sex ratio. Westoff believes that in American and European countries, the preference for boys is relatively mild and therefore the shortage of one sex will increase its value; for example, a shortage of girls would lead to a rising demand for them and presumably an increase in production. But I would argue that there may be serious problems in patriarchal societies where there is a strong preference for boys and where people would have the ability to control the sex of their population.

More specifically, many patriarchal societies place much greater emphasis on the birth of a son than on the birth of a daughter. This preference is explained by the fact that in patriarchal societies in which descent is reckoned through the male line and where patrilocal residence is practiced, males play a more prominent and more continuous role in the consanguineal-family structure. A female severs her involvement with her natal family (family of orientation) after marriage and, in effect, becomes part of her spouse's family system. As a consequence, the birth of a male often brings joy while the birth of a daughter is accompanied by feelings of sorrow. I have noted earlier that in some cases female infanticide has been practiced.

This family-planning decision has become a major problem in some patriarchal societies, such as India. Since amniocentesis has become readily available, there have been a number of reports from India that it has been used to detect and abort unwanted girl children. The All India Institute of Medical Sciences found that as early as 1974-1975, the test had been used in this manner extensively. Since then a forum of women's organizations has called for a ban on the test and disciplinary action against doctors who perform it (Morgan, 1984a). In the summer of 1986, United States news services reported that there still was a high incidence of amniocentesis being used to abort female fetuses. More recent speculations by Western social scientists believe that such practices are still continuing especially among the more affluent in India. And, in China, where the one-child policy is in effect, amniocentesis is also used by many, albeit covertly, to terminate a pregnancy of an unwanted female.

CONCLUSION

This chapter has sought to integrate demographic analysis into a sociological perspective on social change and the family. It opened with a discussion of fertility and family size, comparing extended-family systems, which emphasize kinship ties, with conjugal-family systems, which emphasize the marital and parental relationships. I observed that kinship-dominated societies were dependent on high fertility and large family size for the perpetuation of their social system. In contrast, in industrial societies where conjugal-family units prevail, there is an appreciable lower fertility rate and family size.

A sociological perspective was then applied to understand population dynamics in India. The high birthrate was seen to be detrimental to Indian modernization, economic development, and increased total industrial, commercial, and agricultural production. The failure of family-planning programs reflects governmental policies that run counter to the economic viability of large family size for the joint-family system and the village-based caste system. It was emphasized that demographic changes could only occur when the class and caste systems are changed and when technological development makes it economically feasible for these families to limit their family size.

China and its one-child policy is experiencing similar demographic problems as India's. Here again, family culture has played an instrumental role in shaping the administration of fertility control legislation. This examination of population dynamics in these two countries revealed that it was interrelated with family conceptualizations and dynamics along with social, political, and economic factors.

Attention was then turned to an examination of fertility patterns in the West. Ideologies relating to parenthood and particularly motherhood were of concern. I pointed out that contradictory demands were placed on women. On the one hand, doctrines placed high value on their confinement to the home and their exclusive involvement in household tasks and child rearing; on the other hand, doctrines were being propounded that encouraged families to restrict their family size.

Coercive pronatalism, a term coined by the demographer Judith Blake, was introduced to point out how social institutions forced women to assume exclusively the everyday parental role. Discriminatory practices in education and in work, reinforced by the myth of motherhood, relegated women to the wife and mother roles. I pointed out how supportive parental ideologies contributed to the obscuring of the possibility that the transition to parenthood can be problematic.

The next topic was the transition to parenthood. This transition necessitates the rearrangement and reorganization of marital roles; relationships with kin, friends, and neighbors; economic patterns; and the reallocation of space, time, and attention. Some of the problematic areas of concern were indicated, and it was pointed out that changes are beginning to take place in the nature of motherhood and fatherhood and in society's responsibilities.

The concluding discussion dealt with the social issues of abortion. I presented a cross-cultural overview and indicated that abortion policies often reflect patriarchal ideologies; that is, in societies where patriarchy still predominates, anti-abortion policies are adhered to. Where patriarchal interests are losing strength, more liberal policies regarding abortion exist. Religious, economic, and political factors also play a role in legal attitudes toward abortion. In the analysis of abortion in the United States, the contrasting and conflicting views of pro-life advocates versus pro-choice advocates were delineated. A related theme regarding abortion was its utilization of amniocentesis to abort unwanted fetuses who were of the "wrong" sex. As of yet, this has not been a major concern in the United States. However, amniocentesis and abortion may seriously impact male-female sex ratios in other societies where strong preferences are made.

In the next two chapters, the investigation of generational relationships is continued. Chapter 13 concerns childhood and adolescence; Chapter 14 focuses on the role of the aged in the family.

13

THE FAMILY AND CHILDHOOD AND ADOLESCENCE

Chapter Outline

Social Change and Generational Control

Childhood and Adolescence Conceptualizations: Comparative Perspectives
> *Cross-Cultural Views*
> *Historical Views*

Contemporary Implications of the Western Conceptualization of Childhood and Adolescence

The Family and Child-Welfare Institutions
> *Parental Autonomy versus Children's Rights*
> *Threatened Children: The "Face on the Milk Container"*

From Economic Asset, to Priceless Treasure, to Responsible Family Member
> *Working Children in Changing Families*

Conclusion

All human societies are differentiated on the basis of age and sex. Throughout history, the social roles of men and women have differed, as have the roles of children, adults, and the aged. Always, these differences have been linked to status differences in power, privilege, and prestige. The previous chapters examined sex differentiation structures and processes. A power dimension was seen to be inherent in the differentiation between the sexes. Generations are part of the permanent nature of social existence. And, likewise, conflict between generations has been a perennial force in the history of humanity.

In earlier discussions, the family was viewed as the primary form of social organization that stratified people according to sex. It can also be seen as the basic form of social organization that stratifies people according to age. Basically, families are hierarchical social structures in which older generations or older siblings hold positions of power, authority, and prestige over their younger counterparts. There are different degrees of stratification by age. But the universal tendency is for the elders to exercise control over younger family members.

The degree of generational control also varies by the tempo of social change in given societies. Generally, in societies that are relatively stable, patterns of generation control become traditionalized. In societies undergoing patterns of rapid social change, the normal relationship between generations is disrupted and can be destroyed.

In this and the next chapter, I examine different forms of family systems and the relationships between family members of different ages. I am particularly interested in the manifestation of the power dimension that underlies the age hierarchy. I look at children, adolescents, and the aged within different forms of family life. Of noted concern is the role of social change on age differentiation within the family and its influence on generational controls.

SOCIAL CHANGE AND GENERATIONAL CONTROL

Ann Foner (1978) discusses what she has labeled an age-stratification perspective and applies it to a historical examination of nineteenth- and twentieth-century American families. This approach emphasizes that age must be conceived as a social process as well as a biological one. Age is seen as a key component in social structure and social change. This age-stratification perspective incorporates both structural and dynamic elements that have implications at both the individual and societal levels for the analysis of the family.

Structurally, age stratification affects how people of different ages relate to each other and influences the individual's attitudes and behavior. People of different age groupings are stratified into different role complexes with differential rewards, duties, and obligations. Dynamically, individuals pass through the different age strata as they move through the life cycle. The transition through stages in the life cycle and the transitions of a particular age cohort are historically unique. Thus, the age-stratification structure of the population is constantly subject to change.

The family is composed of members of different ages who are differentially related. The dominant perspective in sociology, structural functionalism, has stressed that the age differentiation of family members enhances the solidarity of its members. The interdependence of family members fosters emotional attachments, structural solidarity, and family cohesion. However, as Foner points out, family conflict is also a basic component of family life. Inherent in the differential age structure of family members is the potential for conflict and tension:

> For the family is itself stratified—not merely differentiated—by age. Not only do family members of different ages have diverse functions, but they also receive unequal rewards.... There are age differences in power, privilege, and prestige in the family. And these inequalities can generate age-related dissension—for example, resentment about the exercise of power or the way family resources are distributed—in the family unit. (Foner, 1978:S347)

The nature and rate of social change has been associated with the nature and type of generational control parents have over their children. Robert Redfield (1947), in his classic work "The Folk Society," contrasts the slow changing of rural folk society with the dynamic tempo of urban industrial societies. The tempo of change is associated with the attitudes and behavior patterns between the generations. It has also been observed that the authority and power of parents is correlated with the societal pattern that emphasizes the maintenance of tradition. S.N. Eisenstadt (1971) points out that societies that emphasize traditional practices are characterized by strong intergenerational bonds. These societies are also characterized by a strong central authority.

These tradition-oriented societies have been characterized by the rule of the old. The nineteenth-century and early twentieth-century British anthropologist Sir James George Frazer called these societies "gerontocracies." Using the Australian aborigines as the case in point, Frazer described the authority structure of that culture as

> an oligarchy of old and influential men, who meet in council and decide on all measures of importance, to the practical exclusion of the younger men. Their

deliberate assembly answers to the senate of later times: if we had to coin a word for such a government of elders we might call it a "gerontocracy." (Frazer, 1922/1960:96)

In contrast, in societies that are undergoing rapid social change, generational continuity is deemphasized. Concomitantly, the older generation has less control over the younger one. Indeed, some social observers argue that the pattern in contemporary Western society is characterized by such an appreciable loss of parental control that the family has become largely irrelevant in influencing the behavior and attitudes of children and adolescents. At the same time, and somewhat paradoxically, the argument is also being made that the family is a detrimental force that acts to frustrate and deny the fulfillment of the needs of the younger generation. Margaret Mead's *Culture and Commitment: A Study of the Generation Gap* (1970) reflects the former position. After this work is examined, I look at the latter position, which derives from the contemporary conceptualization of the family, childhood, and adolescence.

Margaret Mead in her monograph (1970) comparatively examines the "generation gap" in contemporary societies. She wrote her book at the height of the hippie and anti-Vietnam War youth culture movement. This was a period when the United States was undergoing major trauma; a cultural reexamination was in full force, generated also in part by the Black Power revolution; the women's movement; as well as the antiwar movement. Mead tries to understand the differences in generational relationships in three broad societal types. Her analysis is still most pertinent.

She begins with a historical explanation of why the elders of traditional, stable societies exert such powers over the younger generations. She calls these societies *postfigurative*. In postfigurative cultures, children are socialized by their forebears. The children are raised so that the lives of the parents and grandparents "postfigure" the course of their own. That is, the children will be living their lives in much the same matter as their parents and grandparents lived theirs.

Postfigurative societies are small religious and ideological enclaves. They derive their authority from the past. Their cultures are conservative and resist change. There is a sense of timelessness and all-prevailing custom. Continuity with the past is a basic premise underlying the social order. The sacredness of custom and the lack of a written history makes the elders the repositories of societal wisdom and knowledge. The elders have high status because they know best the traditions of the past. Generational turmoil is rare. Adolescent and youth rebellion is almost entirely absent.

In postfigurative cultures, the emphasis is on generational continuity. The experiences of the young repeat the experiences of the old. Events that have occurred and that question the traditional order are redefined and reinterpreted to deny changes. To preserve the sense of continuity and identification with the past, occurrences that have caused change are culturally blurred and innovations are assimilated into the traditional past. Mead provides some illustrations of elders who edit the version of the culture that is passed to the young. They mythologize or deny change:

> A people who have lived for only three or four generations in tepees on the great American plains, who have borrowed the tepee style from other tribes, may tell how their ancestors learned to make a tepee by imitating the shape of a curled leaf. In Samoa the elders listened politely to a description of the long

voyages of Polynesian ancestors by Te Rangi Hiroa, a Polynesian visitor from New Zealand, whose people had preserved a sacrosanct list of the early voyages which was memorized by each generation. His hosts then replied firmly, "Very interesting, but the Samoans originated here in Fitiuta." The visitor, himself half-Polynesian and half-European, and a highly educated man, finally took refuge, in great irritation, in asking them whether or not they were now Christians and believed in the Garden of Eden. (Mead, 1970:18)

The postfigurative society socializes the young so that they behave in accordance with the mores and values of the older generation. They do not question the way things are or the way things were. Indeed, they have a lack of consciousness of alternative ways of life. This sociocultural quality explains the great stability of postfigurative society. It also accounts for the minimal internal change from one generation to the next.

Mead emphasizes the importance of three-generational households in the socialization of children. In such households, parents raise their children under the eyes of their parents. This arrangement emphasizes cultural continuity and strengthens the power of the older generation. The power of the aged was institutionalized in the extended-family system. The high priority and status of the aged gave rise to the extended-family system and was, in turn, supported by this form of family structure.

In societies undergoing social change, there is a break in generational continuity. The experiences of the younger generation are significantly different from those of their parents and grandparents. Mead characterizes these cultures as *cofigurative*. American society experiencing urbanization and massive industrial growth in the later part of the nineteenth century and into the twentieth century is a prime illustration.

Cofigurative cultures can be brought about by rapid technological development; migration to a new country and separation from the elders; military conquest and the subsequent forced acculturation of the captured society to the language and ways of the conqueror; religious conversion, where the younger generation is socialized into a new religious world view; and planned revolutionary changes in the lifestyles of the young. The consequent differential experiences of the younger generation necessitate the development of different attitudes and behavior. The elder generation cannot provide the necessary emulating models and the younger generation must find these models among their generational peers.

One illustration that Mead provides on how these changes have affected family relationships is of particular interest to us. Earlier in this book, I examined the Western urban family and suggested that the diminished importance of extended kinship of city families may have resulted from the differential socialization processes experienced by different-generation family members. Those who were raised in rural areas of European societies and who migrated to the United States will have had a quite different upbringing than their urban Americanized children and grandchildren.

Mead points out that the immigration situation is typified by the concentration on the nuclear family, with grandparents either absent or having very little influence. Grandparents are no longer the models for their grandchildren; parents have little control over grown children's marriages or careers. Characteristic of cofigurative American culture is the relinquishing of responsibility for the elderly. This is associated with the breakdown of sanctions exercised by the elderly over the second and third generations.

In its simplest form, Mead sees cofigurative culture as one in which grandparents are absent. The result is the loss of the individual's links with the past. The future is not anticipated through the traditional past but by the contemporary present. The result is that parents and grandparents no longer serve as dominating socialization agents. Formalized educational institutions take over this task. Concomitantly, the elders are no longer authority figures or models for youths' future behavioral and attitudinal patterns.

However, Mead emphasizes that in cofigurative cultures the break is never complete. Elders still have influence to the extent that they set the style and set the limits within which cofiguration is expressed in the behavior of the young. Thus, to a certain extent, the elders, along with youths' generational peers, develop a new style that will serve as the model for others of their generation.

Writing at the height of the social unrest of the late 1960s and being particularly influenced by the extensiveness of youth counterculture movements, Mead saw an emerging pattern that made both the postfigurative and cofigurative cultural models inadequate. In this newly emerging era of extreme rapid rates of change, Mead saw the development of a *prefigurative* culture. In prefigurative society, the future is so unknown that change within an elder-controlled and parent-modeled cofigurative culture, which also includes postfigurative elements, is inadequate.

> I call this new style prefigurative, because in this new culture it will be the child and not the parent and grandparent that represents what is to come. Instead of the erect, white-haired elder who, in postfigurative cultures, stood for the past and the future in all their grandeur and continuity, the unborn child, already conceived but still in the womb, must become the symbol of what life will be like. (Mead, 1970:68)

Mead's analysis of permanence and social change demonstrates how it affects different cultures and their respective generational dynamics. The conceptualizations that exist to define the nature of particular age groups also play a significant role in the manifestations of generational attitudes and behavior. A careful examination of the different conceptualizations of young people and the family will now prove instructive.

CHILDHOOD AND ADOLESCENCE CONCEPTUALIZATIONS: COMPARATIVE PERSPECTIVES

As observed, societies define sets of people according to age. These age categories influence people's relations to one another. Expectations differ on what involvements, activities, and accomplishments are expected for each age grouping. Societies differ in the age distinctions they make. For example, among the Kikuyu of Kenya, age distinctions are prominently defined and explicit, and elaborate rites of passage mark the transition periods that carry the individual from one age category to the next. Age differentiation also has consequent implications for the conceptualization of persons placed in particular age groupings. Further, we must realize that the conceptualizations of childhood and adolescence are reflections of the conceptualization of the family, and together they must be seen in a cross-cultural and in a social-historical contexts.

Cross-Cultural Views

Anthropologists have long observed the cultural relativity of age roles. They have noted that the conceptualization of childhood and adolescence varies cross-culturally. Probably the most famous research study in this area was done by Margaret Mead in her *Coming of Age in Samoa* (1928). Mead was concerned with the relationships between adolescents and culture. She contrasted the development of girls in the United States with patterns in Samoa. She was particularly concerned with whether the psychological disturbances and the emotional crises characteristic of Western adolescents were due to the nature of adolescence itself or to the culture. She wanted to ascertain if these disturbances were due to physiological changes occurring at puberty or were largely brought about by social and cultural conditions.

To test the universality of developmental psychological stages of childhood and adolescence, Mead went to the South Pacific and lived for nine months in Samoa, where she studied fifty adolescent girls. Among the adolescents of Samoa, she found no period comparable to the storm and stress that characterize their American counterparts. Samoan adolescence was not characterized by tension, emotional conflict, or rebellion. Indeed, Samoan culture did not even recognize the developmental stage of adolescence: It had no concept of adolescence. Mead concluded that the source of such characteristics in American youth stemmed from the social institutions and traditions found in the United States.

Anthropologists have also compared societies in regard to the conceptualization of childhood. Mead (1949), herself, examined societies that viewed the child as a small adult, with responsibilities similar to those of an adult, versus societies like the United States, where the child is thought to be qualitatively different. Ruth Benedict (1938/1973), in her classic study "Continuities and Discontinuities in Cultural Conditioning," has argued that there is less continuity in treatment and development from childhood and adolescence to adulthood in societies such as the United States than there is in those societies that employ the little-adult conceptualization.

Benedict sees as a distinctive feature of American culture the dichotomization of value patterns between those applicable to the child and those applicable to the adult. "The child is sexless, the adult estimates his virility by his sexual activities; the child must be protected from the ugly facts of life, the adult must meet them without psychic catastrophe; the child must obey, the adult must command this obedience" (Benedict, 1938/1973: 100). Benedict points out that the more discrete and isolated the status of the child is from the status of the adult, the more difficult and ambiguous is the transition from one age group to the other. Further, this dichotomous pattern intensifies the status discontinuity experienced by the adolescent.

She argues that children are segregated from the adult world. This is especially the case for work and sex. The children's world is organized around play; little attention is given to the adult world of work. Similarly, strong taboos exist regarding sexual repression and children are required to be submissive to adult authority. As adults, they are expected to work, to be sexually mature, and to be assertive and autonomous. This disjunction between the role of the child and the one he or she is expected to perform as an adult makes the transition painful, awkward, and traumatic.

In contrast, Benedict reports that in nonliterate societies, the cultural discontinuities that characterize American society do not exist. For example, in contrasting cultural variations regarding responsibility and nonresponsibility, she finds that nonliterate societies encourage children to engage in adult activities and responsibilities as soon as possible. Among the Ojibwa Indians of Canada, boys accompany fathers on hunting trips and girls share the responsibility of preparing the meat and skins of animals trapped by their brothers and fathers in much the same manner as their mothers. Ojibwan children are consistently taught to rely on themselves and to see the world of the adult as not much different from the world of the young.

Similarly, among the Papago of Arizona, children are trained from infancy and are continuously conditioned to responsible social participation while, at the same time, the tasks that are expected of them are adapted to their capabilities. To illustrate, Benedict cites an observer who tells of sitting with a group of Papago elders when the man of the house turned to his little 3-year-old granddaughter and asked her to close the door.

> The door was heavy and hard to shut. The child tried, but it did not move. Several times the grandfather repeated, "Yes, close the door." No one jumped to the child's assistance. No one took the responsibility away from her. On the other hand, there was no impatience, for after all the child was small. They sat gravely waiting till the child succeeded and her grandfather gravely thanked her. It was assumed that the task would not be asked of her unless she could perform it and having been asked the responsibility was hers alone just as if she were a grown woman. (Benedict, 1938/1973:102)

Benedict sees American culture as viewing the adult-child or, specifically, the parent-child relationship in terms of a dominance-submission arrangement. In contrast, many Native American tribes explicitly reject the ideal of a child's submissive or obedient behavior. To illustrate, Benedict reports on the child-training practices among the Mohave Indians that are strikingly nonauthoritarian:

> The child's mother was white and protested to its father (a Mohave Indian) that he must take action when the child disobeyed and struck him. "But why?" the father said, "he is little. He cannot possibly injure me." He did not know of any dichotomy according to which an adult expects obedience and a child must accord it. If his child had been docile he would simply have judged that it would become a docile adult—an eventuality of which he would not have approved. (Benedict, 1938/1973:104)

Benedict then contrasts how children are socialized into sexual awareness in different societies. She notes that in virtually all societies the norms concerning sexual conduct are not identical for children and adults. This is explained by the relatively late onset of puberty and physiological maturation in human beings. Benedict defines continuity in sexual expression as meaning that the child is taught nothing it must unlearn later. Societies can, therefore, be classified in terms of whether they facilitate continuity or impose discontinuity regarding sexual matters. Adults among the Dakota Indians, for example, observe great privacy in sexual acts and in no way stimulate or encourage children's sexual activities. Yet there is no discontinuity since the child is not indoctrinated in ways it has to unlearn later. The Zuni in New Mexico regard premature sexual experimentation by children as being wicked. The sexual activity of adults is associated solely with reproduction. Our society, in contrast, associates the wickedness of a child's sexual experimentation with *sex* itself rather than as wickedness because it is sex at a child's age. The result is that adults in our culture must unlearn the belief taught them as children that sex is wicked or dangerous.

In concluding her analysis, Benedict examines age-grade societies that demand different behavior of the individual at different times during the life cycle. Persons of the same age grade are grouped into a society whose activities are oriented toward the appropriate behavior desired at that age. Although there is discontinuous conditioning, Benedict believes that cultural institutions provide sufficient supports to persons as they progress through the age-grade life stages.

In striking contrast, Benedict argues that Anglo-American culture contains discontinuous cultural institutions and dogmas that exert considerable strain on both the interpersonal processes and the personality systems of young individuals. The result is that American adolescents face serious problems during this transition period; problems of readjustment and ambiguity are experienced in activities, responsibilities, and the allocation of power: The result is an adolescent period of *Sturm und Drang* ("storm and stress") that is caused by our culture rather than any physiological characteristic of adolescence.

Historical Views

Ruth Benedict's thesis anticipated the arguments advanced by the social historian Philippe Ariès in *Centuries of Childhood: A Social History of Family Life* (1962). In this classic study, Ariès applied a similar kind of analysis to medieval European society and its evolution to the present. He sought to document how in medieval life the child was integrated into the community and how it was not until the development of bourgeois society that the segregation of children occurred. Implicit within his discussion is a condemnation of the consequences of this segregation.

The theme of *Centuries of Childhood* is how the Western ideas about childhood and family life have changed and developed from the Middle Ages to modern times. Ariès examines the paintings and diaries of four centuries; documents the history and evolution of children's dress, games, and pastimes; and analyzes the development of schools and their curricula. This leads him to conclude that the concept of childhood as a distinct stage in the life cycle is a rather recent development, as is the conceptualization of the private family.

He argues that in the Middle Ages, children were treated as small adults. As soon as they were capable of being without their mothers, children interacted in the adult world. They shared the same world of work and play. By the age of 7 or 8, they were treated as if they had the same mental capacities for understanding and feeling as their adult counterparts and peers. In a particularly notable use of historical resources, Ariès points out that medieval painters portrayed children as "miniaturized" adults. Children were depicted in adult clothes and looked like adults, but on a reduced scale. The failure of the artists to draw children as we know them was not due to their incompetence or lack of artistic skill but rather to the lack of a conceptualization of the notion of childhood:

> In medieval society the idea of childhood did not exist; this is not to suggest that children were neglected, forsaken or despised. The idea of childhood is not to be confused with affection for children; it corresponds to an awareness of the particular nature of childhood, that particular nature which distinguishes the child from the adult, even the young adult. In medieval society this awareness was lacking. That is why, as soon as the child could live without the constant solicitude of his mother, his nanny or his cradle-rocker, he belonged to adult society. (Ariès, 1962:128)

The lack of awareness of the particular nature of childhood and the full participation of children in adult life is associated with the nature of the family and the community. Ariès pictures medieval community life as intense; no one was left alone. The high density of social life made isolation virtually impossible. Life was lived in public. The "sociability" of medieval life was lived on the public streets. The private home was virtually nonexistent. The street was the setting of work and social relations. This sociability hindered the formation of the concept of the private family. The medieval family was embedded in a web of relatives, friends, workmates, and neighbors all living in close proximity and in public. The distinct sense of privacy so characteristic of modern-day families was absent. In the following passage, Ariès dramatically provides an illustration of this point:

> The traditional ceremonies which accompanied marriage and which were regarded as more important than the religious ceremonies (which for a long time were entirely lacking in solemnity)—the blessing of the marriage bed; the visit paid by the guests to the newly married pair when they were already in bed; the rowdyism during the wedding night, and so on—afford further proof of society's rights over the privacy of the couple. What objection could there be when in fact privacy scarcely ever existed, when people lived on top of one another, masters and servants, children and adults, in houses open at all hours to the indiscretions of callers? The density of society left no room for the family. Not that the family did not exist as a reality: it would be paradoxical to deny that it did. But it did not exist as a concept. (1962:405-406)

The transition to the modern conceptualization of the child began to emerge during the seventeenth century. There was a revival of interest in education. This, in turn, introduced the idea that a period of special preparation was necessary before individuals could assume their place as adults. Childhood became defined as a period in which to train children. Children began to be treated differently, they were expected to behave differently, and their nature was viewed as being different. Children were now coddled, and a greater interest and concern for their moral welfare and development became common.

Although Ariès recognizes that this change reflects declines in mortality rates and the growing division of labor in the society, he believes that this concept of childhood developed and was given expression in the emergence of the bourgeois family. He argues that from a relatively insignificant institution during the Middle Ages, there developed a growing belief in the virtue of the intimate and private nuclear family. The rise of the private family and the growth of the sentimental bonds among its members came about at the expense of the public community.

> The more man lived in the street or in communities dedicated to work, pleasure or prayer, the more these communities monopolized not only his time but his mind. If, on the other hand, his relations with fellow workers, neighbors and relatives did not weigh so heavily on him, then the concept of family feeling took the place of the other concepts of loyalty and service and became predominant or even exclusive. The progress of the concept of the family followed the progress of private life, of domesticity. (Ariès, 1962:375)

The continued inward development of the family and its creation of a private sphere of life removed from the outside world was intertwined with the increased importance given to children. The outside community came to be viewed with suspicion and indifference. Proceeding into the industrial era, the family began to withdraw its nonproductive members, women and children, from involvement with the surrounding community. The increased division of labor of family members and the consequent isolation of women and children within the home was the result.

Ariès ends on a pessimistic note. He is highly critical of the contemporary private family. He believes that it has stifled children's autonomy and independence. He views medieval childhood as a period of free expression and spontaneity. The separation of the child from the larger community leads to the development of youths who are deprived of much experience in the outside world. They are increasingly dependent on their parents. The result is the ultimate loss of their individuality.

> The evolution of the last few centuries has often been presented as the triumph of individualism over social constraints, with the family counted among the latter. But where is the individualism in these modern lives, in which all the energy of the couple is directed to serving the interests of a deliberately restricted posterity? Was there not greater individualism in the gay indifference of the prolific fathers of the ancient regime? . . . It is not individualism which has triumphed, but the family. (Ariès, 1962:406)

Similar historical analyses on the changing conceptualization of adolescence have been made by Frank Musgrove (1964) and Joseph Kett (1977). Musgrove traces the historical changes in the status of adolescents from the mid-seventeenth century, when adolescence was "invented," to the present. England provides his case in point. Kett examines how youths have viewed themselves and how these views have coincided or clashed with adult expectations in America from 1790 to the present.

Musgrove believes that youths are increasingly segregated from the adult world. This has diminished rather than enhanced their social status. He develops an argument that is similar to the one developed by Ruth Benedict. Musgrove sees the inconsistency and discontinuity of training youths for adulthood by excluding them from the world of adult concerns, and of training youths for the exercise of responsibility by the denial of responsibility. The result is the development of compliant, accommodating, and conservative security-conscious adults. He attributes this changing status to economic developments and demographic changes, and to psychological theories on the nature of adolescence that have helped to justify it.

Joseph Kett (1977), in his historical study of adolescence in America, observes that the economic and social relationships between youth and adolescents have significantly changed since 1790. Today's youths are characterized as being consumers rather than producers. They have been largely removed from the workforce, spend most of their time in school, and tend to be segregated from adult society. The causes of these changes are traced to urbanization, industrialization, demographic changes, and child-rearing practices. It is his concern with the moral values associated with child-rearing practices that attracts his and our attention.

Kett places particular attention to the period between 1890 and 1920, when the society came to classify the time between 14 and 18 years as a distinct period of youth and labeled it adolescence. Kett seeks to demonstrate that the moral values associated with this conceptualization were subsumed under supposedly universal psychological laws and determined by a biologic process of maturation. These laws provided the basis for the subsequent development of a number of adolescent "helpers," such as educators, youth workers, parent counselors, and scout leaders. Through their efforts, they gave shape to the contemporary concept of adolescence, which necessitated the massive reclassification of young people as adolescents: "During these critical decades young people, particularly teenage boys, ceased to be viewed as troublesome, rash, and heedless, the qualities traditionally associated with youth; instead they increasingly were viewed as vulnerable, passive, and awkward, qualities that previously had been associated with girls" (Kett, 1977:6).

Kett observes that the most influential study on the nature of adolescence written during this period was by G. Stanley Hall (1904). Hall was profoundly influenced by the theories of Sigmund Freud and sought to link Freud's theory with that of Darwinian evolutionary theory. Hall developed a psychological theory of adolescence that emphasized the significance of hereditary determinants of personality. His theory of the socialization of adolescents was based on the principles of recapitulation theory, which held that every individual repeated the history of the species in his or her own development; that is, Hall took the viewpoint that children passed through the various stages of development from savagery to civilization that had already been traced by the race.

Hall, like the anthropologist Ruth Benedict, postulated a "storm and stress" (*Sturm und Drang*) interpretation of adolescence. Although anthropological studies, like Margaret Mead's *Coming of Age* in *Samoa* (1928), strongly suggested that adolescence need not be a period of turmoil and psychological disruption, Hall's viewpoint—combined with changes in industrialization, urbanization, and the developed intimacy and privatization of the nuclear family—led to the basic forms of today's concept of adolescence and to the treatment of adolescents in society.

Kett examines three dominating moral values that have continued to be influential in society's response to youth. The first is the belief that youths should be segregated according to their own age, both in school and in work. No longer were mixed-age groups of younger and older children to be allowed in the same classroom. Similarly, children were segregated out of the labor force. Increasingly, their work was restricted to part-time or summer employment. The second belief was the characterization of youth by passivity. The view was that adolescents should be easily moldable by grownups into the grownups' definition of adulthood. A third belief was the necessity for adult-directed activities for adolescents. Kett cites August de B. Hollingshead in his landmark sociological study of adolescence, *Elmtown's Youth: The Impact of Social Class on Adolescents* (1949), on why the discontinuity in the socialization of youth can be so devastating.

> By segregating people into special institutions, such as the school and Sunday school, and later into youth organizations such as Boy Scouts and Girl Scouts for a few hours each week, adults apparently hope that the adolescent will be spared the shock of learning the contradictions in the culture. At the same time, they believe that these institutions are building a mysterious something variously called "citizenship," "leadership," or "character," which will keep the boy or girl from being "tempted" by the "pleasures" of life. Thus the youth-training institutions provided by the culture are essentially negative in their objectives, for they segregate adolescents from the real world that adults know and function in. By trying to keep the maturing child ignorant of this world of conflict and contradictions, adults think they are keeping him "pure." (Hollingshead, 1949:149)

I am struck by the parallel conclusions and opinions reached by such anthropologists as Margaret Mead and Ruth Benedict and by a sociologist such as August Hollingshead—also shared by the social historian, Joseph Kett—on the negative consequences of this conceptualization of adolescence. It remains for me to now delineate fully how these conclusions and opinions on the contemporary definition and treatment of adolescents fit into my conceptual orientation on the nature of social change and the family.

CONTEMPORARY IMPLICATIONS OF THE WESTERN CONCEPTUALIZATION OF CHILDHOOD AND ADOLESCENCE

To assess properly the contemporary condition of childhood and adolescence in the family and the society, it is necessary to re-present a brief historical sketch on the changes that have occurred. Preindustrial societies were characterized by a minimal differentiation of age groupings. Childhood and adolescence were not separated as separate and distinct chronological stages; rather, children were conceptualized as miniature adults. As they proceeded through childhood, they increasingly took on more and more adult responsibilities. There was no psychological conceptualization that prescribed an extended moratorium period when adolescents would be segregated and not be allowed to take on responsibilities. Life from childhood through adulthood to old age proceeded in a continuous process without cultural and institutionalized disruptions. The "adult" roles of parenthood and work participation were a culminating

Child labor was very prevalent in turn-of-the-twentieth-century United States. Lewis Hine, a prominent photographer, during this period documented many such incidents before child labor laws were enacted.

occurrence that flowed out of this nondifferentiated conceptualization of childhood and adolescence.

Demographic changes, industrialization, urbanization, and the changing conceptualizations of the family and of childhood and adolescence combined to produce the differentiation into the stages of life that characterizes today's population. Let me now be more explicit in my delineation of the contemporary condition of young people. I also observe how social scientists, coming out of different ideological persuasions, develop different assessments on what effect these changes have had. By necessity, I refer to previous arguments on the nature of the marital relationship in this discussion. By so doing, I hope to present a more developed analysis.

Industrialization meant the loss of economic participation by young people in the labor force. Having once assumed economically viable positions in the family, they now became economic dependents. In the eighteenth and nineteenth centuries, the American family acted as a self-sufficient economic unit. Boys and girls were involved in work activities on the farm and in the home. They participated in the growing and harvesting of crops, the storing and cooking of foods, the caring for domestic animals, and the making of clothes. In short, the children were an economic asset contributing to the economic well-being of the family. By the end of the nineteenth century, the family economy was disappearing, giving way to a cash industrial economy. Today children are an economic liability, whereas in the preindustrial period children not only were able to pay their own way by working but also were expected to be the chief source of their parents' support when they got older. There was no government old-age assistance such as social security. Today, children can no longer be counted on to provide such an economic resource.

This historical change in the character of childhood and adolescence captured our attention. For modern children and adolescents are faced by a dilemma: the desire for the development of personal freedom and autonomy in the face of dependency situations, both in the home and in social institutions. To understand the contemporary situation it is necessary to look at the actions of late nineteenth and early twentieth centuries social reformers. They were concerned with protecting children from the perceived evils of urbanization and industrialization. Often, they felt that the only way to "save" children was to remove them from their environment, which often included their families as well. Manifestations of their social welfare policies will be shown to be prevalent to this day.

THE FAMILY AND CHILD-WELFARE INSTITUTIONS

In previous discussions, I showed that there has been a systematic movement among the bourgeois middle class, begun several hundred years ago, to segregate and remove children from adult life. It was based on a belief that children and adolescents did not have the psychological capacities, intellectual abilities, and the requisite maturity to participate on an equal footing in adult affairs. Coinciding with this conceptualization was the development of the notion of the private family system.

This conceptualization was fostered by the emergence of the new industrialized urban society, which was viewed as threatening and unpredictable by the emerging middle class. For them, the same ideological currents that sought to protect women—by removing them from active participation in the outside world and sequestering them within the home—was carried over to the younger generation. Ostensibly, the desire was to protect both women and children from abhorrent labor conditions and their abuse by industry. In effect, however, this resulted in the subordination and dependence of both women and children. Before examining its effect on the middle class, we can best understand how it came about by examining the child-welfare movement, which developed out of concern for the conditions of poor children of the nineteenth century. It was then that social policies regarding children developed and were carried over to the contemporary era.

Child labor and the abuse of children in industry were common occurrences in the burgeoning factories of the late eighteenth and early nineteenth centuries of England. The prospering middle classes, aghast at the treatment of women and children in these factories, removed their own families from these harsh and brutal work conditions. Unfortunately, the children of the poor, the destitute, and the abandoned were not as fortunate. Economic and political realities resulted in their being victims of social injustice and forced employment in work situations that were inhumane and barbarous.

> With the coming of the machine age . . . mere babies were subjected to terrible inhumanity by the factory systems . . . Children from five years of age upward were worked sixteen hours at a time, sometimes with irons riveted

around their ankles to keep them from running away. They were starved, beaten, and in many other ways maltreated. Many succumbed to occupational diseases, and some committed suicide; few survived for any length of time. (Helfer and Kempe, 1968:11)

To illustrate, poor city children in England who were employed as chimney sweeps worked day and night. Death from cancer of the scrotum was frequent and pulmonary consumption was so common that it became known as the chimney sweep's disease.

The children who worked under these oppressive conditions were from the poorer classes. They were the young paupers from the workhouse, children without parents to protect them, many as young as 4 or 5 years of age. They also included the children of poor families who could not support them and reluctantly allowed their children to work in the mills and factories. Piven and Cloward (1971), writing on the societal functions of public welfare, note that pauper children relegated to parish poorhouses became an ideal labor source for the English textile industry. Parishes and orphanages supplied children to factories as cheap labor. They were motivated by both greed and the self-serving moral belief that idle children would grow up to be shiftless, idle adults. The manufacturers negotiated with them for lots of fifty or more children at a time. These children provided a very stable labor force because they were obligated to work until they fulfilled the terms of their indentures. For many, the terms of their indentures did not expire until the age of 21 and many children did not survive until that age.

In the beginning of the nineteenth century, the child-labor reform movement started in England with the passage of the First Factory Act in 1802. The act broke up the factory pauper-apprentice system, but it did not interfere with traditional parental rights over children. It did not apply to children whose parents were living and who allowed them or sent them involuntarily to work. Throughout the nineteenth century, the laws that were passed to curb the abuses of child labor in industry did not infringe on the Victorian premise that the family was a private and sacred institution into which outsiders had little right to intrude. It was not until the end of that century and the beginning of the twentieth that social-reform legislation was passed to protect children of the poor who did not pass the moralistic muster of middle-class reformers. An examination of events in the United States during this period will prove instructive.

In the last quarter of the nineteenth century, increased attention was given to the ways in which children were being abused. The first American legal action for child abuse was not brought about until 1874. In fact, laws to protect animals were enacted before laws to protect children. Indeed, the first child-abuse case was actually handled by the New York Society for the Prevention of Cruelty to Animals. In this first case, the child was treated under the rubric (legal rule) concerning a small animal.

By the turn of the century, a basic philosophy was developed on how best to handle abused and neglected children. These tenets have affected the way we look at abuse and neglect today and so deserve our attention. Muckraking journalists and social reformers argued that these children could best be "rehabilitated" by placing them under the jurisdiction of state industrial schools, reform schools, and the juvenile court system. Through their influence, such special judicial and correctional institutions were created for the labeling, processing, and managing of "troublesome and destitute" youth. An interesting twist is observed in this philosophy. The victimized child has in effect become the victimizer who must be incarcerated and rehabilitated. It is a nineteenth- and early twentieth-century version of "blaming the victim."

Anthony Platt (1969) has written a fascinating account of the child-welfare movement and the development of the conceptualization of abused children as delinquents. The social reformers—or, as he calls them, the child savers—believed that children who were brought up improperly by negligent parents were bound for lives of crime unless taken out of the parents' hands at a very early age. The child savers succeeded in the creation of rehabilitation institutions that were designed to prevent the development of criminal and deviant tendencies.

These reformers were influenced by the prevailing antiurban bias prevalent during that period and by their own middle-class Protestant morality. They reacted against the perceived "social disorganization" of the city. The city became the symbol of all the evils of modern industrial life. It was depicted as the main breeding ground of criminals. The children of the European peasant immigrants were seen as the victims of cultural conflict and technological revolution.

The social reformers extolled the virtues of the rural community and placed high value on religion, home, work, and the family. Parental discipline and women's domesticity were advocated to control children. The hope for children living in the city slums, who were described as "intellectual dwarfs" and "physical and moral wrecks," was to remove them from these debilitating surroundings (Platt, 1969). Platt cites a nineteenth-century reformer who reported to the National Prison Association in 1898 that philanthropic organizations all over the country were

> making efforts to get the children out of the slums, even if only once a week, into the radiance of better lives. Seeing the beauties of a better existence, these children may be led to choose the good rather than the evil. Good has been done by taking these children into places where they see ladies well dressed, and with their hands and faces clean, and it is only by leading the child out of sin and debauchery, in which it has lived, into a circle of life that is a repudiation of things that it sees in its daily life, that it can be influenced. (Platt, 1969:40-41)

The child savers were middle-class moralists who emphasized the values of home and family as the basic institutions of American society. They defined the problems of neglect as attributable to faulty hygiene and lax morality. They minimized or ignored the economic and political-power realities of the urban poor. By extolling such values, they fostered the movement of children out of the homes of the poorer classes that did not meet their standards. Middle-class families, of course, were by and large not affected by their zeal.

Unfortunately, the rehabilitation institutions did not function in the manner intended. They were overcrowded punitive institutions that physically punished boys and girls and that often had them working in industries contracted by their custodians. Platt describes the "educational" program of the Illinois State Reform School, which consisted of boys laboring 7 hours a day for a shoe firm, a brush manufacturer, and a cane-chair manufacturer. He argues that what were purported to be benevolent institutions for the intervention and prevention of crime became themselves abusive, punitive, and authoritarian, breeding their own abusive patterns. He summarizes his view by making four points (1969:176):

1. The reforms of the child-saving movement did not usher in a new system of justice, but rather they reaffirmed and expedited traditional policies.
2. A "natural" dependence of adolescence was promulgated. The creation of a juvenile court imposed sanctions on "premature" indulgence and behavior "unbecoming" a youth.
3. Paternalistic and romantic attitudes were developed but were anchored by authoritarian force. No conflicts of interest were perceived between the vested interests of agencies of social control and those of "delinquents."
4. Correctional programs were implemented that required long terms of forced imprisonment, involuntary labor, and militaristic discipline. Middle-class values and lower-class skills were inculcated.

The child-saving movement resulted in the forced incarceration of many urban poor children. Platt points out that the programs, which were rhetorically concerned with protecting children from the physical and moral changes of increasingly industrialized urban society, diminished the children's freedom and independence. Rather than provide remedies, they aggravated the problem. Platt makes an interesting observation on the relationship of this reform movement and Philippe Ariès' analysis of European historical family life that is worth repeating. It nicely summarizes a major point of this discussion—that ideological and moral biases often have a detrimental effect on the people they are designed to benefit.

> The child-saving movement had its most direct consequences on the children of the urban poor. The fact that "troublesome" adolescents were depicted as "sick" or "pathological," were imprisoned "for their own good," and were addressed in a paternalistic vocabulary and exempted from criminal law processes did not alter the subjective experience of control, restraint, and punishment. As Philippe Ariès observed in his historical study of European family life, it is ironic that the obsessive solicitude of family, church, moralists, and administrators for child welfare served to deprive children of the freedoms that they had previously shared with adults and to deny their capacity for initiative, responsibility, and autonomy. The "invention" of delinquency consolidated the inferior social status and dependency of lower-class youth. (Platt, 1969:177)

The child-saving movement, in summary, was based on the assumption that physical abuse and neglect were associated almost exclusively with poverty, slums, industrial exploitation, and the cultural deprivation of the poor and immigrant populations. As the physical conditions associated with abuse and neglect began to improve by the second decade of the twentieth century, the attention began to shift to concerns of the emotional neglect and abuse of children.

The 1920s and 1930s were a period in which the child-welfare movement increasingly turned its attention to the implementation of the new ideas of Freudian psychoanalysis and psychiatry. The emphasis shifted to the advocacy of the utilization of various forms of social services, either voluntary or by judicial intervention, in the hope of assuring the emotional well-being of children. This increasingly led to difficulties as the acceptable legal definition of emotional neglect and abuse was and is more difficult to define or prove than is its physical counterpart. The result was the development of an antagonism between affected families and social institutions that continues today.

Parental Autonomy versus Children's Rights

In the 1970s a number of major studies appeared that examined the nature of the relationship among children and adolescence, the family, and social welfare policies and institutions. In *All Our Children: The American Family Under Pressure* (1977), the Carnegie Council on Children, headed by Kenneth Keniston, the psychologist known for his study of youth in the 1960s, reported on a five-year examination on the way children grow up in America. The Council debunks the myth that the family is self-sufficient and self-sustaining as well as the widely held belief that parents alone are responsible for what becomes of their children.

The researchers believe that this myth developed in the nineteenth century out of the economic doctrine of laissez-faire capitalism and was built on images of the independent farmer and entrepreneur. The authors pick up a theme, which was reported in this book, on how the family defined itself as a refuge that guarded women and children from the incursions of an increasingly alien and hostile urban environment. In the preceding preindustrial era of the seventeenth and eighteenth centuries, the family was defined by the Puritan conceptualization of the "little commonwealth." The family was viewed as essentially similar to the surrounding community and governed by the same standards of piety and respect. With the emergence of an industrialized and urbanized society in the nineteenth century, the belief developed among the affluent and privileged classes that the home must serve as a refuge protecting its frailer members, women and children, from the temptations and moral corruptions of a threatening outside world.

The Council pointed out that, in reality, this family system was an ideal one that was perhaps realized by only a small segment of the upper-middle-class segment of the population. Poor families, immigrants, slaves, Indians, and growing numbers of factory workers rarely achieved this ideal of self-sufficiency and independence. Today, it is even less real for all segments of the population. Yet, the myth still persists. It fails to see that the family has been deeply influenced by broad social and economic forces over which it has little control. The Council argues that the family's authority and influence are constantly eroding and dwindling as that of outside institutions increase. Economic and social pressures of parents' jobs, the cost of raising children, the increased involvement of institutionalized health-care services and schools, and the entire social ecology—from television programming to the packaging of foods—define and limit parents' autonomy and independence.

The Council concluded that the family is changing, but it is not collapsing. They believe that "families—and the circumstances of their lives—will remain the most crucial factors in determining children's fate" (Keniston and The Carnegie Council on Children, 1977:xiv). But to do this, there is a need to remedy the greatest enemy of the family—poverty. To remedy this poverty, the Council recommends a major overhauling of America's economic structure and sweeping reforms in social policies, work practices, laws, and services. Their proposals were designed to return to parents the authority they should have to raise their children, with the ability to do so under better circumstances than now exist. Among their specific recommendations was a guaranteed family income that was no lower than one-half the national median, full employment, income supplements for the working poor, and a national health-insurance plan.

Christopher Lasch (1977a, 1977b, 1979) was also concerned about the usurpation of family authority by professional social agencies. Lasch, a historian at the University of Rochester, believed that a work such as The Carnegie Institute's *All Our Children* reflects the growing disillusionment with the public institutions and welfare agencies that have taken over the functions of the family—the school, the hospital, the mental hospital, the juvenile courts, and the rehabilitation institutes. But, he argues, Keniston and his colleagues do not go far enough in their criticism of professionalism. He sees a contradiction in Keniston's advocating governmental expansion of services to the family, which includes a federal guarantee of full employment, improved protection of legal rights of children, and a vastly expanded program of health care, while also proposing to strengthen the family by its participation in these programs. He argues that the helping professions have systematically appropriated parental authority by demeaning the capabilities of parents, by arguing that only they have the scientific expertise to know what is best for the child, and by their piecemeal allowance of parents' decisions that only serve to perpetuate feelings of inadequacy and dependence.

Lasch developed his argument through a social-historical analysis of the family and helping agencies. He asserts that the privatization of the family in the nineteenth century was short-lived. The bourgeois family did try to establish itself as a refuge, a private retreat, where it could become the center of a new form of emotional intensity between parents and children. Following the lines of previous historians, Lasch saw the nineteenth-century middle-class family developing a cult of the home, where the woman cared for her husband and sheltered her children from the perceived corrupting influences of the outside world. But—and this is the crux of his argument—at the same time that the glorification of private life and the family was occurring, a realization was developing that the family was inadequate to provide for its own needs without expert intervention. This led to the development of the helping professions.

Lasch stated that the helping professions of the nineteenth and early twentieth centuries played on bourgeois fears by inventing and defining social needs only they could satisfy. He is particularly concerned with demonstrating how these professional social agencies condemned and appropriated parental authority and competence. They did so deliberately, and rather than defend the family, they contributed to the deterioration of domestic life. He picks up on a topic I discussed earlier to make his point. He argues that educators and social reformers saw that the family, especially the immigrant family, as an obstacle to what they conceived as social progress—the "homogenization" and "Americanization" of its citizens.

The [immigrant] family preserved separatist religious traditions, alien languages and dialects, local lore, and other traditions that retarded the growth of the political community and the national state. Accordingly, reformers sought to remove children from the influence of their families, which they also blamed for exploiting child labor, and to place the young under the benign influence of state and school. (Lasch, 1977a:13)

He goes on to discuss how the schools and social-welfare services expanded under the justification that the family could no longer provide for the needs of its children. Likewise, children's aid societies, juvenile courts, and visits to families by social workers became commonplace as the result of this belief that the family was not prepared to take care of the physical, mental, and social training of the child. Lasch believed that the result of these forces has been the usurpation of the family by outside professionals, doctors, social workers, the helping professions, and the schools.

Lasch was particularly critical of contemporary social scientists—sociologists, anthropologists, neo-Freudian psychoanalysts, and most of all, Talcott Parsons and his school of functionalism. He believed that their theoretical framework was responsible for the decline of the family. This occurred through their advocacy of "the family's indispensability while at the same time providing a rationale for the continued invasion of the family by experts in the art of social and psychic healing" (Lasch, 1977a: 115-116). He maintained that Parsonian theory, although arguing the sociological justification of the family's importance because of the intensification of the emotional climate of the family, nevertheless undercuts this importance with another line of argument that sees the family creating strains that only the helping professions' experts know how to handle.

Lasch saw this development as undermining the family with severe repercussions for its children. He reasons that, with the rise of the helping professions, parents become reluctant to exercise authority or to assume responsibility for their children's development. This, in turn, results in the weakening of the child's ability to develop an autonomous personality and prevents the development of moral values. In another work, *The Culture of Narcissism* (1979), Lasch asserted that these developments have undermined American values and that the young are being socialized into a fake world of easygoing, low-keyed encounters. This culture of narcissism represents the decadence of American individualism and the end of the Protestant virtues of hard work, thrift, and capital accumulation. Today, the concern is with personal survival and hedonism.

In summary, both The Carnegie Council on Children report and Christopher Lasch's analysis provide a welcome shift away from the emphasis of debates on the family's psychological structure to the impact of society on the family and children. The policies advocated by the Council are designed to develop comprehensive and universally accessible public services to support and strengthen, but not to replace, families in the rearing of their children. However, to accomplish this, a fine balance must be achieved between the family's desire for autonomy and privacy and the public policies that seek to help and protect the child. Far too frequently, as Lasch emphasizes, the government acts not as a helping agency but as an opponent that seeks to legislate the family out of existence and to undermine its independence and autonomy.

This tension also dominated the analysis of the family and social policy of Mary Jo Bane.

In her study *Here to Stay: American Families in the Twentieth Century* (1976), Mary Jo Bane, after careful statistical analysis, concluded that the contemporary American family is still quite viable and persists in its commitment to its children. She takes issue with the widely held notion that the American family of the past was an extended one. She supports the conclusions I reported, namely, that the nuclear family has been the predominant family form.

She opposes the belief that the declining birthrate reflects disintegration within the family. Rather, she observes that it indicates decreasing size of individual families and not the collective decision of the population to stop having children. As for divorce, she views it as a safety valve for families; it assures that only those who desire to stay together do so. Ultimately, it improves the quality of American marriages. Further, although the divorce rate has risen dramatically, most people remarry. Those that do not tend to keep their children with them. Compared to a century ago, the loss of a parent is less disruptive to the family today.

The major thrust of Bane's study centers around the tension between public social policies designed for the protection of individuals, including children, and the desire for family privacy. She presents a detailed examination of such issues as mandatory day care for all, the Equal Rights Amendment, and Aid to Families with Dependent Children. She is particularly concerned that the rights of minors be protected from abusive and negligent adults and that the rights of children to economic sufficiency not impinge on and destroy the family's right to privacy and its viability. The argument is made that the tensions between family privacy and values pronounced in social policies can be resolved by a public stance that emphasizes the rights of individuals and assures the working out of family roles within the privacy of the family.

In conclusion, Bane argues for the view that Americans persist in their deep commitment to the family. Family ties continue to remain as persistent manifestations of human needs for stability, continuity, and nonconditional affection. Paradoxically, the greatest danger to the American family may lie in social policies that reflect the erroneous belief that the American family is dying. Consequently, those who hold that belief may advocate programs that, rather than attempting to supply helpful choices, may actually contribute to the family's decline and demise.

> Family ties and family feelings are integral to the lives of most Americans. The ethic that governs relationships between people who love and care for each other inevitably intrudes into public life, coloring people's perceptions of what they and others ought to do. Policies that ignore this ethic—that imply that public facilities can replace parental care or that the public welfare system is responsible for supporting children—will almost surely be either widely resented or essentially disregarded. Even when family service programs respond to real needs, they are often perceived as undermining the fabric of society. Until such programs are designed to incorporate the very real and very strong values that underlie family life in America, and until they are perceived as doing so, they are doomed to failure. (Bane, 1976:142-143)

BOX 13-1   The Contemporary American Family

Study of Welfare Families Warns of Problems for Schoolchildren

Tamar Lewin

A new study of 790 Atlanta-area families receiving welfare has found warning signs that their young children are likely to have problems in school.

On average, the children, ages 3 to 5, correctly answered only slightly more than half the questions in a test of concepts and skills—such as shapes, colors, and understanding relationships like "under" or "behind"—needed for school readiness.

"These are things kids should know to start school, so it's disturbing to find how many of them don't," said Kristin Moore, one of the writers of the study by Child Trends Inc., a nonprofit research group in Washington for the United States Department of Health and Human Services. "Our discussion of welfare reform has focused mostly on mothers, and how they can be moved into the work force. But the basic message of this report is that we need to attend to the children as well."

The children, almost all of them black, scored lower on vocabulary tests than either a national sample of black children, or in an unexplained finding, somewhat lower than a sample of black children on welfare. In the Atlanta study, the longer their families had been on welfare, the lower their scores were.

But the writers cautioned that the study did not measure the effects of welfare policy, and, indeed, that earlier studies of children living in poverty showed very similar problems.

"There is lots of research showing that long-term poverty is especially destructive," said Martha Zaslow, another of the writers. "This does not damn the mothers, but rather, says these mothers are facing very serious circumstances."

Most of the homes in the study were rated as safe and orderly. But most were also characterized as providing little cognitive stimulation and emotional support to young children, based on both independent interviewers' findings and the mothers' own reports on indicators like how often they read to their children or spanked them.

Some experts read the findings as evidence that the current thrust of welfare overhaul—requiring mothers of young children to work—is the right one.

"When you start with a baseline like this, you can be relatively sure that these children won't be worse off when their mothers work," said Douglas Besharov, a resident scholar at the American Enterprise Institute. "This study is an early signal that mandatory work, even for mothers of young children, is wise social policy."

A new report finds widespread depression among welfare mothers.

Isabel Sawhill, a senior fellow at the Urban Institute, and Ms. Zaslow agree that the study supports the idea that these children can benefit from high-quality child care.

"Poor mothers do a worse job of helping their children, cognitively and emotionally, than better-off mothers," Ms. Sawhill said. "There really is a difference. We know that cognitive development starts earlier than we used to think, way before the child is 4. Maybe the best situation for a lot of these families is if the mom works and the child is in high-quality child care."

But children's advocacy groups point out that the current welfare overhaul plans being proposed by the governors and in Congress would cut the Federal money earmarked for improving child-care training and quality.

"These plans cut by nearly half the funds to improve the quality of child care for these at-risk children, and eliminate even the most basic health and safety standards to protect them," said Nancy Ebb, a senior staff lawyer at the Children's Defense Fund.

The new study also found widespread depression among the mothers, all of whom are participating in the JOBS program, a Federal

(continued)

welfare-to-work program. On a standard screening test for depression, 42 percent of the mothers had symptoms of clinical depression, more than twice the proportion of the general population. Several previous studies have shown that maternal depression has a negative effect on children's well-being.

Just what the high incidence of depression means for welfare policy is unclear. In some cases, depression may be ameliorated by a steady job and income; in others, the depression might make employment impossible.

"My speculation is that for some people having more control over their world, their own paycheck, their own job, might help," Ms. Sawhill said. "But the notion that some policy-makers have, that everyone can work, is just wrong. Some segment of the welfare population, whether it's 15 percent or more, is not going to be able to cope with the world of work. And pushing them in won't help them or their children."

More than half the mothers also have poor reading and math skills.

The study found great diversity among the families, and identified both maternal risk factors, like depression or low literacy, and protective factors, like help from the father's family and contacts with other caring adults, that influence children's well-being. It confirmed previous research showing that women raising children on welfare receive little help from their children's father, either in child support or in non-cash assistance.

Most of the women had positive views of work, with 8 out of 10 agreeing with the statement that having a job makes life interesting, and more than half agreeing that even a low-paying job is better than being on welfare.

The families in the study, the first part of a five-year evaluation of the JOBS program, had been randomly divided into three groups—one assigned to job-searching, one assigned to improving their education, and one serving as a control group.

"The study's supposed to find out what impact the JOBS program has on children," Mr. Besharov said. "But we'll never find out from this project. As soon as welfare reform is passed, it'll get defunded."

The data in the current study was collected just a few months after the families were divided into the groups. But already, one important difference had emerged. The percentage of children in child care grew by more than 50 percent in the work and study groups, but increased only slightly in the control group.

Threatened Children: The "Face on the Milk Container"

Bane's optimistic view of the future of the family has in more recent years given way to a more pessimistic outlook. Lasch's *The Culture of Narcissism* and Robert Bellah et al.'s *Habits of the Heart* both spoke to a "me" generation characterized by unbridled individualism that was seen to have dire consequences for families and the children raised in them. David Popenoe, as I discussed earlier, has become a leading family studies proponent of the decline of the family. Working off his analysis of the experience of the family in Sweden, four major trends' criteria are delineated by Popenoe that highlight "family decline." These are declining birthrates, the sexual revolution, the movement of wife/mothers into the workforce, and the divorce revolution. Popenoe calls for a return to a more traditional conjugal family system where the male was the prime economic supporter and where women spent their full time in child rearing and housework.

Arlene Skolnick (1991) and Dennis Orthner (1990) are leading family analysts who believe that Popenoe represents a group of traditionalists who place too much emphasis on family structure and give insufficient attention to the emotional quality of family life. Skolnick observes that the traditional nuclear family advocated by Popenoe, conservatives, and the New Right is not shared or lived by the majority of Americans. The two-worker family is becoming the new cultural norm. Associated with this new family type is a pro-family belief system anchored in a more symmetrical version of marriage. Orthner concurs by noting that too much attention is focused on the structural properties of marriage and insufficient attention is being paid to emerging forms that enable the family to adapt to new roles, alter its patterns of courtship and sexuality, and adapt to societal changes. Further, Orthner observes that by focusing on divorce patterns and maternal employment as factors that have caused the decline of the family is misplaced. "(T)hese structural changes are weak predictors of the consequences that most of us really care about: personal and family well-being, economic mobility, educational attainment, children's health, and antisocial behavior" (Orthner, 1990: 94).

Skolnick, citing national polls, finds that the anxiety about the state of the family often focuses on the state of children. The media has picked up on this concern by creating "'epidemics' of teen pregnancy, suicide, and drug use, and of the increasing poverty of children, the dire effects of divorce, the plight of latchkey children" (Skolnick, 1991: 207). The face of the missing child on the milk container captures this media frenzy. Skolnick points out that while the underlying concerns of the impact of changes in children's lives is warranted, much of the claims about threats to children are wildly exaggerated. She also points out that the family in effect is not the central agency that is responsible for much of the current child issues that include the state of children's health, the deterioration of the education systems, the predominance of sex and violence in the media, drugs, and unsafe schools and streets.

Joel Best (1990) notes that the "child-savers" of earlier epochs were guided by their own images of childhood, children's needs, and children's problems. The history of the American child-saving movement reveals several different images of children. The *rebellious child* was the most common image. This was the child who ran away from home, broke the law, was sexually active, and adopted disturbing tastes in music or dress. These were all forms of rebellious behavior that represented the rejection of the adult world. Reformers and the development of the juvenile justice system were designed to control and reform this group of children and put them on the proper adult paths. The *deprived child*, often the victim of poverty, was another common image. The task of the child-savers was the development of social welfare institutions to minimize the negative effects of childhood deprivations that were a result of circumstances, not choice. The third image was that of the *sick child*. It emerged with the development of medical science. Here reformers turn to the medical profession to aid in the solving of problems associated with childhood illnesses. The success against polio, whooping cough, smallpox, and other childhood diseases has its contemporary counterparts in campaigns designed to solve such problems as sudden infant death syndrome. The *child-victim* menaced by deviants and suffering from child abuse, incest, child molestation, Halloween sadism, and child pornography is a fourth image. Here the child is threatened by deviants who intentionally want to harm children. This image played a relatively minor role in the child-saver movement. However, in recent years it has taken on a more prominent place. Best attributes this development to recent concerns about the strength of the family, the economy, and other central institutions. It also reflects concerns about rising crime rates and the widespread fear of crime. The sophistication of social action groups such as MADD—mothers against drug drivers—feminists drawing attention to domestic violence and sexual exploitation, the rediscovery of child abuse, concerns of missing children (often the result of custody disputes between mothers and fathers), and other grassroots social action groups are combined with successful tactics that include demonstrations, sit-ins, and so on to draw media attention. The media then provides the press coverage through newspapers, weeklies, news broadcasts, and weekly television news documentaries that help create and inflame concerns.

Best observes that "because children seem to embody the future, doubts about America's future course translates easily into concerns about threats to children" (1990: 181). The importance of children has moved from a period when they had economic functions both within the household and as child laborers. In more recent years, the importance of children resides in their "sentimental" importance. As will be seen in the next section, the child as a "priceless treasure" conveys an image of childhood as a period of innocence that must be protected. Deviants who have the potential to menace children become the focus of natural concern.

The child as victim is seen as a part of the sentimental view of childhood. For example, Best illustrates this by pointing out how representatives of the New Right in their social agenda to protect the nuclear family and preserve parents' traditional authority over children are particularly concerned about threats to children. The New Right advocates that a society that does not emphasize religion and "family values" endangers children. The result are policy recommendations that emphasize the need to minimize the contact of strangers and outsiders with children, and the need to restrict the authority of protective service workers to interfere within families.

A second example of those who advocate the protection of children from perceived threats is the feminists, who saw that threats to children lie in the larger problems of society. These include family violence, sexual exploitation of children through pornography and prostitution, and concerns about the safety of children in preschool and daycare centers. The underlying belief about the vulnerability of children underlies the concerns held by both the New Right and feminists as well as other claim makers. That innocent children should not be harmed seems like a goal that should be held by all. However, Best observes that the undue stress given to this theme is misplaced. "A society which is mobilized to keep child molesters, kidnappers, and Satanists away from innocent children is not necessarily prepared to protect children from ignorance, poverty, and ill health" (Best, 1990: 188).

FROM ECONOMIC ASSET, TO PRICELESS TREASURE, TO RESPONSIBLE FAMILY MEMBER

Sociologists see the potential beginning of a trend toward the reconceptualization of childhood and adolescence. This changing viewpoint is seen to have been ushered in by such recent family changes as the outside work of both husbands and wives and the continued rise in divorce rates. The argument follows that these changes have necessitated that children and adolescents assume more responsible family roles. These include household activities and involvements and, when necessary, outside employment. The reconceptualization is reflected in this section's title.

As we saw, between the 1870s and the 1930s there was a profound change in the attitudes toward children. Viviana Zelizer (1985) has traced the emergence of the modern child by documenting a shift in the value of children during this period from economically useful assets to economically "useless" but emotionally "priceless" love objects. To illustrate her thesis, Zelizer contrasts two legal cases:

> In 1896, the parents of a two-year-old child sued the Southern Railroad Company of Georgia for the wrongful death of their son. Despite claims that the boy performed valuable services for his parents of $2 worth per month, "going upon errands to neighbors . . . watching and amusing . . . younger child," no recovery was allowed, except for minimum burial expenses. The court concluded that the child was "of such tender years as to be unable to have any earning capacity, and hence the defendant could not be held liable in damages." In striking contrast, in January 1979, when three-year-old William Kennerly died from a lethal dose of fluoride at a city dental clinic, the New York State Supreme Court jury awarded $750,000 to the boy's parents. (Zelizer, 1985:138-139)

In the 1896 case, both the parents and the court argued solely on the basis of the child's economic worth. However, with the passing years, traditional forms of child's "work" were reconceived as illegitimate child "labor" and became a moral issue. Child-labor laws and compulsory schooling further reduced the economic contribution of children. Zelizer argues that by the 1920s, the strict economic approach to children's worth and judging the value of children by their potential earning power came to be seen as degrading, even immoral.

Children were redefined as precious, priceless objects of love and affection. Children's insurance became big business. It came to be viewed as protecting parents against the incalculable loss of a child by death or accident. This was an idea that would have been unimaginable half a century before. By the same token, in the 1870s there was no economic market for unwanted children. Baby farms, generally homes for illegitimate children, were paid fees to take in these unwanted children. By the 1930s, a market was created for babies that was based on their emotional worth. Adoption agencies for healthy white babies commanded fees of as much as $10,000 in the 1950s and even more today. Zelizer observes: "This startling appreciation in babies' monetary worth was intimately tied to the profound cultural transformation in children's economic and sentimental value in the twentieth century" (1985:170). And the change in the conceptualization of children is intimately tied to the historical change in the relationships of husbands and wives to a more expressive and more affectional pattern.

There have been a number of social commentators on the family who state that the conceptualization of children is once again undergoing transformation. Marie Winn (1983), in her book *Children Without Childhood*, and Neil Postman (1982), in his book *The Disappearance of Childhood*, advance the position that children are not allowed to be children. Instead, they believe that adults are rushing children into adult-like concerns. Winn attributes this to the disintegration of family life due in part to divorce and to the return of women to the workforce. Further, the emphasis on sex on television, in the movies, and in other forms of the media, adult clothing designed for children, and the proliferation of drugs lead Winn to ponder, "What has happened to childhood innocence?" Similarly, Postman decries the "disappearance of childhood." Both advocate the restoration of a "real" childlike childhood.

Other social scientists have long advocated that letting children assume responsible roles has positive consequences for children. Zelizer picks up on an earlier discussed chapter theme on the necessity for giving children real responsibility and productivity in their lives. Citing anthropological evidence (Whiting and Whiting, 1975) that examined child-rearing practices cross-culturally, she finds that children who are taught responsibility develop a sense of worth and involvement in the needs of others. Glen Elder (1974), in his study of Great Depression children, found that children working to help fulfill some of the economic needs of their poor families developed independence, dependability, and maturity in money management.

Today, two views of childhood are being disputed that literally reverse the reform and traditional positions of the early twentieth century. "Once again, as at the turn of the century, two views of childhood are being disputed; but this time, the reform group proposes to selectively increase children's useful adult-like participation in productive activities, while traditionalists cling to the progressive ideal of a separate domestic domain for children" (Zelizer, 1985:221). The major factor that has precipitated this development has been the rapid increase in mothers entering the occupational workforce.

Zelizer takes the position that as more and more women enter the workforce and devote less time to domestic activities, and as more and more husbands become involved in household tasks, so too will children become more involved with, and responsible for, the maintenance of the household. "The demise of the full-time housewife may create a part-time 'househusband' and 'housechild'" (Zelizer, 1985: 223). Indeed, she notes that a manual [Eleanor Berman (1977), *The Cooperating Family*] has already appeared that provides guidelines for how to get children to become actively involved in assuming household responsibilities including shopping, cleaning, and cooking. Popular magazines such as *Working Mother* and *Seventeen* have published advisory materials on how to define, negotiate, and establish rules for children's work. These articles are targeted for working mothers, divorced parents, and children on the necessity and means of establishing a new working relationship among family members. Zelizer quotes from a *Seventeen* article—"Do Your Parents Ask Too Much of You?" written by Sally Helgesen—which offers the following advice:

> Try to look at things from your parents' point of view. If you don't do certain chores, who should do them? Do your parents, with all their responsibilities, really have time? Examine the situation to see what really is fair, and try to think of your family in terms of a unit with everyone having something to contribute. (Helgesen, 1982:176-177)

With children assuming new household responsibilities, the question arises of just compensation for their labor. Many families do not consider household chores as deserving of monetary rewards; others pay their children in the form of allowances. However, we know very little about the nature and extent of children's domestic work.

Further, more research is needed on the lives of children living under poverty. Estimates indicate that at least 300,000 migrant children work in the United States. In total, more than 11 million children live in poverty and many of them live in female-headed families (Zelizer, 1985). The meaning of work and money to these children, as well as their meaning to more affluent children, is vital. Ethnic and racial variations and boy-girl variations and the age that work begins need to be investigated. Zelizer concludes on a hopeful note that the new family system that includes working parents and responsible children may well result in children becoming invaluable participants in a cooperative family unit. The result will also be a new integration of sentimental attitudes with a new appreciation of children's instrumental value.

> The world of children is changing and their household responsibilities may be redefined by changing family structures and new egalitarian ideologies. The notion, inherited from the early part of the century, that there is a necessary negative correlation between the emotional and utilitarian value of children is being revised. The sentimental value of children may now include a new appreciation of their instrumental worth. (Zelizer, 1985:227)

Working Children in Changing Families

How much work do children do in the contemporary household? Are the domestic workloads of boys different from girls? What are the implications of children's household chores experience for their own future marital and familial divisions of labor? These are the questions posed by researchers Frances K. Goldscheider and Linda J. Waite (1991). They note that the study of children's work involvements in the paid labor force ended with passing of legislation banning much of this form of child labor. But, there was no interest to then study the nature and extent of children's labor in the home. Now in the face of major transformations in the home as a result of the emerging dual income family, Goldscheider and Waite (1991) believe that it is necessary to understand the nature and extent of children's household involvements and what it may tell us about the future of marriage and the family in America.

Reviewing the small amount of research literature on children's roles in household tasks, they observe that the data on the changing nature of the domestic division of labor between wives and husbands is only beginning to be accumulated. Historically, we know that rural and farm children have historically been more involved in household chores than urban children. In the urban environment, children are seen to have taken on more responsibility in dual income families than in families where one parent, usually the mother, stays home. However, the relative amount of their involvement is much less than children in mother-only families.

Goldscheider and Waite's own research is based on data that comes from the National Longitudinal Surveys of Young Women and Mature Women conducted by the Ohio State University Center for Human Resource Research. These surveys included information gained over a fifteen-year period on more than 10,000 women. The authors are concerned with the implications of the increased movement of women into the paid labor force. They see two revolutions confronting the family precipitated by women's increased commitment to and involvement in the paid labor force. The first revolution is a movement toward changes within the household as more women are confronting severe limits in time and energy to traditional household tasks. The result is the necessity for a movement to "new families" that is characterized by men and women sharing economic and domestic responsibilities. The second revolution is a movement toward an increased number of women and men who remain unmarried and live independent lives. In this "no-families" option, marriage and family are avoided and the choice is not to marry and have children. The no-families option is becoming increasingly utilized as women and men see a reluctance of the opposite sex to restructure their traditional gender roles. Rather than battle for such a restructuring within marriage they decide to not marry at all.

The research on the impact of the rise of dual income families and on the possible restructuring of the domestic division of labor, for the most part, has been limited to spousal reconfigurations that virtually ignore children as contributing participants. Further, even less information is known about the extent of contributions and the proportion of boys and girls who do a given task.

Goldscheider and Waite (1991) in their own study report that in many families, parents are reluctant or ambivalent about their children assuming household chores. Parents' expectations usually center on their belief on how beneficial such activities would be in their children's character development and gaining a sense of responsibility. The performance of households chores as a form of anticipatory socialization for adult roles is mentioned by a relatively few number of parents and only for their daughters not their sons. Waite and Goldscheider point out for those parents who pay their children to do such tasks, they are really reinforcing a view that such work is optional and not part of a child's everyday activities. They speculate that the experiences that children have in childhood and adolescence are very important for their own future family experiences. These childhood experiences will only serve to reinforce an already traditional division of labor for the next generation of families. "If children, particularly boys, have little experience with the tasks associated with maintaining a home, it is difficult to expect them to feel comfortable taking them on as adults" (Goldscheider and Waite, 1991:143).

Working from their database, they examine the emerging family forms of the 1970s and 1980s to see what they portend for the future. Of particular interest is their view that children's experiences in the home will be instrumental in shaping the families that they will form in later life. They speculate that if children are asked to substantially contribute to household tasks men will also more likely share responsibility for the maintenance of the household. The result will be that a family that develops egalitarian gender roles will not only not experience the wife's "double burden" but that the children of such a family will lead them to form "new families" when they marry.

The researchers found that younger couples were moving to a pattern in which husbands were assuming more responsibility in domestic chores. This increase in men's household involvements was correlated with increases in women's paid employment and the development of egalitarian gender-role attitudes. However, and most interestingly, these young couples were reluctant to involve their sons *and* daughters with domestic chores. These children were less involved in dishwashing, laundry, shopping, and cleaning up. Teenage daughters' participation in chores, while relatively low, was still much higher than that of teenage sons. There was a noticeable decline in children's involvement in the productive work of the household compared to their counterparts whose parents were of the depression and World War II generation. Further, higher education levels of the parents and living in larger, more urbanized communities—levels of modernization—are associated with a reduction in household tasks by children.

While the overall movement is to less work for both girls and boys in dual income spousal households, Goldscheider and Waite (1991) found that children who live in mother-only families do play a key role in the household economy. This is true for both boys and girls. These boys' greater involvement than boys in dual income families is attributed to the fact that they may take on the tasks normally performed by the absent father. Daughters, too, take on more responsibility for housework than their two-parent counterparts.

In summary, Goldscheider and Waite (1991) feel that despite the trend to lower sons' and daughters' household-task involvements and responsibilities, a "gender factor" still operates. Daughters still take on differential responsibility throughout their teenage years and into young adulthood. Sons contribute very little and are virtually exempt from any contribution as they approach adulthood. Most importantly, however, the researchers see that the relative decline in the overall imposition of domestic responsibilities on daughters reflects the parents' realization of the changing nature of the future lives of women as they become more involved in occupational roles outside the home. They no longer are being socialized into the adult housewife role. But, boys shielded from almost any household-task involvements and responsibilities are not only not being socialized into the egalitarian gender roles that their parents are trying to develop for themselves, they are not being socialized into living an independent life. Thus boys, as they become men, will be unfit both for the "new families" or "no families" options of the future. The irony is that while their parents still want their children to marry and have families they are not socializing them into that path. Goldscheider and Waite (1991) conclude:

> But while they probably want their *daughters* to marry liberated men, who will share in the housework so that these daughters can be successful, they are preparing their *sons* to marry traditional women, who will carry the household burden themselves to further their son's career. They are not yet ready to prepare their sons for someone else's ambitious daughter. (1991:171)

CONCLUSION

The relationship between family members of different ages captured the attention of this chapter, as it will in the following one. Here, a power dimension was seen to be inherent in the differential relationships among family members of different ages. Children and adolescents were examined within an age-stratification perspective.

The nature and rate of social change was shown to have been associated with the nature and type of generational control parents have over their children. Margaret Mead's *Culture and Commitment* (1970b) was analyzed for its cross-cultural contribution to the understanding of what has been popularly labeled as the generation gap.

Mead's work led to an examination of how conceptualizations of childhood and adolescence are important factors in the way generational attitudes and behavior become manifest.

The comparative analysis drew on research in anthropology and social history. It stressed the common elements in these research studies and this led to the conclusion that the contemporary Western conceptualization of childhood and adolescence emphasizes the removal of the younger family member from the outside world into the private family.

The implications of these conceptualizations for children and adolescents were discussed in the section on child-welfare institutions. The idea of juvenile delinquency developed by child-saving professionals was analyzed. This was part of the larger discussion on the tension that exists between the sometimes conflicting concerns for preserving family; autonomy while protecting children.

The chapter continued with a discussion of the ideas of Kenneth Keniston and the Carnegie Council on Children, Christopher Lasch, and Mary Jo Bane. These researchers asserted that the belief that the family is self-sufficient and self-sustaining is a myth. Public institutions and welfare agencies have had a strong impact on family autonomy and its authority over family members. Christopher Lasch, the most vocal opponent of the helping professions, is highly critical of structural functionalism and neo-Freudianism as forces that are undermining the family. Mary Jo Bane emphasized the tensions that exist between public social policies designed for the protection of individuals, including children, and the desire for family privacy. This was followed by a discussion of the differing positions on the relationship between individualism and the state of the family and the state of children. It led to an analysis of "threatened children"—the "face on the milk container."

The concluding section reflected the growing recognition among social scientists that dual income families and high divorce rates may foster a change once again in the way we conceptualize childhood and adolescence. More specifically, there are demands now being placed on younger family members to take on responsible positions in the family. One factor for this change is the belief that by assuming responsible roles the child and/or adolescent will be able to become a more responsible and ultimately a more successful adult. Another significant factor is structural change in the American family. Children and adolescents are becoming involved in the everyday activities of the household including shopping, cleaning, and cooking. With both parents working, many families need such help. Likewise, the single-parent family resulting from divorce often means that children and adolescents must take a more responsible family role, including entering the job market while still attending school. The implications of these changes for the future are just beginning to be thought through.

The ways society conceptualizes childhood and adolescence are also factors in the phenomenon that we call child abuse, which becomes one of my concerns in the chapter on family violence. In the following chapter, I continue the analysis of generational relationships in the family by examining the relationships among older family members, their adult children, and their grandchildren. The four-generation family is also discussed and analyzed.

14

THE FAMILY AND THE ELDERLY

In the previous chapter, I examined relationships within the family, with particular focus on the relationship between children, adolescents, and their parents. I also looked at how social policies affect the generational relationships between parents and children. In this chapter, I extend the analysis of age differentiation and age stratification by looking at the relationship between elders and their married children. Here again, my concern lies with the structure of family status and authority patterns within the context of social change.

We focus our investigation by examining age differentiation in preliterate societies and contrasting it with the contemporary Western pattern. To highlight the differences in the conceptualization of age, I begin with an analysis of those preliterate societies that use age groupings rather than kinship as a basis for organizing social relationships. I then seek to demonstrate how age conceptualizations influence generational involvements in preliterate societies that do not employ age-set groupings. An in-depth examination of contemporary Western European and American societies follows. I show how these conceptualizations have implications not only for family relationships but also for government-based social policies that affect these relationships. I conclude by examining contemporary grandparenthood and the rise of the four-generation family.

THE AGED IN PRELITERATE SOCIETIES

Age differences are biologically based. They are universally recognized. Age categories help shape people's relations to one another. Expectations vary, depending on the age of the person in question. Yet the categorizations of childhood, adolescence, youth, adulthood, and old age are social categories. They are not a mere product of biology. The social roles of child, adult, and the aged, for example, have varied from society to society and within given societies historically.

Yet one consistent pattern exists throughout the world. In all family systems, the superiority of parents to children is striking. Authority is vested in the parents, and children legitimate that authority. Thus, although parents treat their children " 'like children,' . . . children treat their parents with respect" (Blood, 1972:457).

Robert O. Blood, Jr. (1972), lists three general reasons for the superiority of parents in generational relationships. First is the biological dependence of infants on their parents. This subsequently is transformed into social dependence, which continues indefinitely. Next, parents have had more experience and, concomitantly, they are wiser than their children by virtue of having lived longer. This especially holds true in nonliterate societies that depend on memory for the transmission of cultural knowledge about the proper ways of doing things. The third reason is that age gives parents a head start in achieving positions of power in the outside world. This, in turn, increases the resources that they can bring to the family. Together, these factors strengthen the power that parents have over their children.

There is a great deal of variability on the relative importance of age in a given society and on the degree to which age forms the basis of a separated social group. The importance of age as the determining factor in social relations varies with the total degree of differentiation in a given society. The extent of age differentiation varies by societal complexity and amount of industrialization. Generally, complex differentiated societies, especially industrial societies, place less emphasis on age. Differences in work, socioeconomic status, ethnicity, religion, and the like are the more important determinants of group membership. In contrast, simpler societies with non-technologically based economies tend to place primary emphasis on kinship, sex, and age. Kinship, sex, and age serve as the social-organizational basis of the society and provide the societal framework for the differentiation of relationships.

Robert Redfield (1947) has defined *folk societies* as slow-changing and emphasizing tradition and ceremonialism. They tend to be conservative and resist change. Continuity with the past is a basic premise underlying the social order. There is a sense of timelessness and all-prevailing custom. The sacredness of custom and the lack of a written history makes the elders the repositories of societal wisdom and knowledge. The elders have high status because they know best the traditions of the past.

In folk societies, the population clusters in small homogeneous communities. The community structure is fairly explicit, and it is anchored by stable values that are sacred rather than secular. The relationships among different age groups tend to be governed by explicitly delineated roles. These relationships are face to face and personal. Relationships among group members are multifaceted; they interact in different contexts, including work, home, and religious settings.

However, Leo W. Simmons (1945), who was one of the first anthropologists to attempt a large-scale cross-cultural study of aging, cautions us to be aware of the wide range of differences in attitudes toward and adaptations made to the problems and opportunities of aging. In a later article, Simmons (1960) observes that there is great diversity in cultural norms in terms of neglect and abandonment of old people on the one hand, and for their succor, support, and even glorification in death on the other. He finds that the influence and security of the elderly varies with the stability of the given society. Generally, the establishment of permanent residence, the achievement of a stable food supply, the rise of herding, the cultivation of the soil, and the increase of closely knit family relationships are all positively associated with the status and treatment of the old.

The status of the old tends to be inversely related to their numbers in the population. Simmons (1960:67-68) states that it is rare to find more than 3 percent of a primitive people 65 years of age and over. He also observes that in more primitive and rudimentary forms of human association there are fewer old people. Further, old age is attributed to these peoples at an earlier chronological date than in modern industrial societies. To illustrate, he cites a 1905 monograph on the Bontoc Igorot in the Philippines:

> A woman reached "her prime" at 23, at 30 she was "getting old," before 45 she was "old," and by 50 if she was so fortunate to live that long, she had become a "mass of wrinkles from foot to forehead." . . . Probably not more than one or two in a hundred lived to be 70. (Simmons, 1960:67)

Further, even though the number of those who did attain old age in some societies was small, the aging years came to be regarded as the best part of life. In fact, some preliterate peoples try to appear and wish to be regarded as older than they are. The anthropologist Leslie Milne (1924) reports that the Palaung in North Burma is one such society where privilege and honor is given to the old:

> The older a person becomes, the greater is the respect that is paid her. The young women are expected to do a great deal of hard work along with the girls, such as bringing wood and water to the village before any festival; so married women are a little inclined to make out that they are older than they really are, in order that they may evade the extra work. (Leslie Milne cited in Simmons, 1960:68)

Simmons hypothesizes that when the old can participate and fulfill themselves in the society, they tend to be treated with respect and deference. He examines their roles in the economic system, in government, and in the family to test his belief. He finds that when the aged have accumulated experience and familiarity with special skills, they retain directive roles in labor. For example, in the arts and crafts of basketry, pottery, house building, boat construction, and the manufacture of cloth, tools, weapons, and other implements, the old take on leadership roles based on their expertise. They are also highly valued for their roles of magician, healer, shaman, and priest. Midwifery is a prime illustration of a specialty associated with older women.

When they do not take on leadership roles, they can still find positions of usefulness. These usually involve engaging in secondary economic activities in field, camp, shop, and household. The underlying philosophy is the belief that all members of the society should participate in the society as long as they are physically and mentally able. By such activities, no matter how menial, the aged retain a sense of place and purpose in the society. The Hopi, a herding and farming people in northeastern Arizona, illustrate this principle:

> Old men tend their flocks until feeble and nearly blind. When they can no longer follow the herd, they work on in their fields and orchards, frequently lying down on the ground to rest. They also make shorter and shorter trips to gather herbs, roots, and fuel. When unable to go to the fields any longer, they

sit in the house or kiva where they card and spin, knit, weave blankets, carve wood, or make sandals. Some continue to spin when they are blind or unable to walk, and it is a common saying that "an old man can spin to the end of his life." Cornshelling is woman's work, but men will do it, especially in their dotage. Old women will cultivate their garden patches until very feeble and "carry wood and water as long as they are able to move their legs." They prepare milling stones, weave baskets and plaques out of rabbit weed, make pots and bowls from clay, grind corn, darn old clothes, care for children, and guard the house; and, when there is nothing else to do, they will sit out in the sun and watch the dying fruit. The old frequently express the desire to "keep on working" until they die. (Simmons, 1960:73)

Property rights is an important area for prolonged and effective participation. The ownership or control of property on which younger people are dependent helps maintain the independence of the aged. Property rights also permit the aged to govern the opportunities of the young. Simmons, then, sees property rights as providing benefits to the old when they become sedentary and are not involved in direct economic production.

The high prestige and high status of the aged are supported by the extended-family system. The extended family is the basic social group providing economic security for the aged. It is central to the social structure. The obligations to the aged are institutionalized as formal rights; they are not simply generous benefactions of the young. In patriarchal societies, the eldest male possessed rank and authority. He had absolute authority over his wife (wives) and children. He determined what they should do and whom they should marry. Disobedience meant disinheritance or even death.

The role and treatment of elderly women could be diametrically opposite that for elderly men. Simmons (1960) provides a vivid illustration of this in his discussion of the Ainu of Japan. The Ainu were a technologically primitive society before they were influenced by Japanese civilization. They lived in a very cold coastal area where they subsisted largely on raw fish. Fathers possessed great authority. They could divorce their wives or disinherit their children. The elder fathers received filial reverence and obedience to their dying days. Women throughout their lives were treated as outcasts and their fate grew harsher with advancing age. A.H.S. Landor (1893) relates his visit to a hut in 1893 in which he found a feeble old woman crouched in a dark corner:

As I got closer, I discovered a mass of white hair and two claws, almost like thin human feet with long hooked nails. A few fish bones were scattered on the ground and a lot of filth was massed together in that corner. . . . I could hear someone breathing under that mass of white hair, but I could not make out the shape of a human body. I touched the hair, I pulled it, and with a groan, two thin bony arms suddenly stretched out and clasped my hand. . . . Her limbs were merely skin and bones, and her long hair and long nails gave her a ghastly appearance. . . . Nature could not have afflicted more evils on that wretched creature. She was nearly blind, deaf, dumb; she was apparently suffering from rheumatism, which had doubled up her body and stiffened her bony arms and legs; and moreover, she showed many symptoms of leprosy. . . . She was neither ill-treated, nor taken care of by the village or by her son, who lived in the same hut; but she was regarded as a worthless object and treated accordingly. A fish was occasionally flung to her. (Landor cited in Simmons, 1960:81-82)

Simmons (1960) states that one tactic used by the old men to maintain their advantages in the family was to marry younger women. By so doing, they assured the continuation of their power. The following passage written by the anthropologist W.C. Holden in 1871 describes the position of an aged Xosa or Kafir in Africa:

> The man is then supported in Kafir pomp and plenty; he can eat, drink and be merry, bask in the sun, sing, and dance at pleasure, spear bucks, plot mischief, or make bargains for his daughters; to care and toil he can say farewell, and go on to the end of life. As age advances he takes another young wife, or concubine, and then another, to keep up eternal youth, for he is never supposed to grow old as long as he can obtain a youthful bride; she by proxy imparts her freshness to his withered frame and throws her bloom over his withered brow. (Holden cited in Simmons, 1960:80)

The fate of the aged in preliterate societies was ultimately determined by the balance between their contribution to the society and their dependence on it. As long as the productivity of the old exceeded their consumption, they found places for themselves. However, for those who were regarded as a living liability—the overaged; those at the useless stage; those in the sleeping period, the age-grade of the dying; and the already dead—actual neglect or even abandonment was rather common. In Simmons (1945) cross-cultural investigation of thirty-nine tribes in which definite information was available, neglect and abandonment were customary in eighteen tribes. He reports that among the Omaha, a nomadic North American Indian tribe, the very feeble were customarily left at a campsite provided with shelter, food, and a fire. Similar practices occurred among the Hopi, the Creek, the Crow, and the Bushmen of South Africa (de Beauvoir, 1973). The Eskimo persuaded the old to lie in the snow and wait for death or put them on an ice floe and abandoned them when the tribe was out fishing or shut them up in an igloo to die of the cold.

Yet, the abandonment, exposure, or killing of the aged was not necessarily disrespectful. It occurred out of dire necessity rather than from personal whims. It came from the hardness of preliterate life, not the hardness of the preliterate heart. Environmental necessity forced the rather drastic deaths of the few helplessly aged persons (Simmons, 1960). Simone de Beauvoir, in her comprehensive study *The Coming of Age*, cites anthropologist Paul-Emile Victor's dramatic example of a sick Amassalik Eskimo man in Greenland who was unable to get into his kayak. The man asked to be thrown into the sea, since drowning was the quickest way to the other world. His children did as he asked. But, buoyed up by his clothing, the man floated over the freezing water. A beloved daughter called out to him tenderly, "Father, push your head under. The road will be shorter" (cited in de Beauvoir, 1973:77-78).

My final illustration from Simmons serves to conclude this discussion. Simmons indicates that the abandonment of the sick and very old was a reciprocal process with the "victim" actively participating in the process without harboring feelings of ill will toward the young. He quotes from J.A. Friis' (1888) monograph on the Lapps of Finland:

To carry the sick and disabled persons on such a long journey is impossible, and so there is no choice but that he or she, whoever it may be, perhaps one's own father or mother, must be left behind, provided with food, in some miserable hut on the mountain, with the alternative of following later or else of dying entirely alone. . . . But a father or mother does not think this being left alone on the mountain a sign of cruelty or ingratitude on the part of their children. It is a sad necessity and a fate that perhaps had befallen their parents before them. (Friis cited in Simmons, 1960:85-86)

Simmons (1960:88) concludes by outlining five universal interests of aging people:

1. To live as long as possible.
2. To hoard waning energies.
3. To keep on sharing in the affairs of life.
4. To safeguard any seniority rights.
5. To have an easy and honorable release from life, if possible.

These five wishes are seen to be shared by people living in the most primitive societies and the most complex. (It is important, however, to note that in the 1990s the elderly do not want to live as long as possible if that means, as it often does today, that the extension of life is the result of long years of severe disability or nursing home residence). Simmons believes, however, that the ability to obtain these wishes becomes more problematic with social change. He argues that in stable preliterate societies a pattern of participation becomes relatively fixed for the aged. A structured framework for participation is developed in which statuses and roles are defined, sex-typed, aptitude-rated, and age-graded. With permanence, the pattern solidifies and the aged are able to entrench themselves. However, all becomes upset with social change:

In the long and steady strides of the social order, the aging get themselves fixed and favored in positions, power, and performance. They have what we call seniority rights. But, when social conditions become unstable and the rate of change reaches a galloping pace, the aged are riding for an early fall, and the more youthful associates take their seats in the saddles. Change is the crux of the problem of aging as well as its challenge. (Simmons, 1960:88)

We now investigate the impact of social change on the aged by looking at a type of society that differs radically from the so-called primitive societies—Western industrial societies.

THE AGED IN THE WEST

Irving Rosow, a contemporary American social scientist, has written persuasively and elegantly on the status of the old in the industrial United States. In a thoughtful article, Rosow (1973) contrasted the role of the aged in preindustrial societies with their role in America. He wished to explain the societal variations in the welfare of the aged. He outlined seven contributing factors: property ownership, strategic knowledge, religious links, kinship and extended family, community life, productivity, and mutual dependence. All seven involve the resources that old people command, the functions they perform, and the state of social organization. I use them as the organizational framework for our discussion. In the following pages I point out how social changes relating to these factors have affected the role of the elderly in Western industrial societies.

Property Rights

Preindustrial agrarian Western societies were characterized by the elders' ownership, control, and direct operation of the principal form of productive property—the farm. In such circumstances, the aged maintained their independence at the same time that their offspring were dependent on them.

Conrad M. Arensberg's *The Irish Countryman* (1937/1959) and his *Family and Community in Ireland*, written with Solon T. Kimball (1968), are classic works on the family in a farming economy. The studies are concerned with rural Irish communities of the 1930s, consisting of families with small farms. They demonstrated the importance of the relationship of property rights, the elderly, and the family in the rural Irish countryside.

Gordon F. Streib (1973) reported on Ireland since Arensberg and Kimball's famous work of the 1930s. Streib found that for many parts of rural Ireland, the old pattern of prestige, recognition, respect, and power conferred on the old farmers still held. The elder males relinquish authority very reluctantly. They retain firm control over their sons until a late age. The sons commonly delay their marriages until they have gained control of their inheritance; they consequently marry late. When the transfer of power and ownership of the land does occur, it is done formally and legally with the older man retaining only specified limited rights and prerogatives.

However, change is occurring and is attributable to both indigenous and alien influences. More specifically, the back and forth emigration of Irish emigrants and British tourists and the media's penetration into the rural Irish hinterland have altered traditional patterns. Further, there is a rise in influence of young farmer organizations and rural community groups that promises to continue the change in traditional thinking. Streib believes that the result of these changes may be a "shift of Irish

---

BOX 14-1   The Global Family

The "Boys" of Ireland

Conrad M. Arensberg's *The Irish Countryman* (1937/1959) and his *Family and Community in Ireland* written with Solon T. Kimball (1968) are classic works on the family in a farming economy.

The rural Irish communities of the 1930s consisted of families with small farms. The family's total existence was centered around the pos-session and maintenance of the family farm. "Keeping the name on the land" was the central value that governs the family. The Irish farm is too small for feasible economic subdivision. Family continuity demands that the farm pass to the next generation intact. Economic necessity means that the inheritance of the farm can only be passed to one child, usually one of the elder sons. All the other sons "must travel" and seek their fortunes elsewhere. Likewise, daughters who were not provided with dowries were forced to leave the farm.

Until the time when the father died or retired and gave one of his sons the family farm, he controlled the life of his children. Even though his sons did the major work on the farm, he mandated the direction of farm work and the distribution of the farm's income. The farm bore his name in the community and his sons were spoken of as his "boys." The subordinating of sons could continue even to the ages of 45 and 50. As long as the father had not given up the farm, the sons remained "boys" both in farm work and in the rural vocabulary:

> In 1933, a deputy to the Dail raised considerable laughter in the sophisticated Dublin papers when he inadvertently used the country idiom in expressing country realities. He pleaded for special treatment in land division for "boys of forty-five and older"—boys who have nothing in prospect but to wait for their father's farm. For "boyhood" in this instance is a social status rather than a physiological state. A countryman complained to me in words which tell the whole story. "You can be a boy forever," he said, "as long as the old fellow is alive." (Arensberg, 1937/1959:39)

The change in the "boy's" status occurred when he married and inherited the farm. Country marriages were made through "matchmaking" and involved parental negotiations and a dowry. Marriage symbolized the transfer of economic control and the attainment of adult status. The marriage and the transfer of land to the son accomplished a drastic transformation in the relationships of household members. Other sons and daughters had to be provided for elsewhere. They felt themselves entitled to some form of inheritance, either in the form of dowries to marry into another farm or of some other form of aid to help establish themselves. Typically, they had to leave the farm.

The "old people" had to abandon their power and move into a new status of old age. They relinquished the farm and their economic direction of the family properly passed to the young people. For the father, it meant the abandonment of the farm ownership; for the mother, it meant that she was no longer the woman of the house.

Marriage was a central focus of rural life. It represented a universal turning point in individual histories. Marriage coincided with the transfer of economic control and land ownership. It meant the reformation of family ties, advance in family and community status, and entrance into adult procreative sex life. For this reason, we can understand why Ireland had the highest rate of late marriage of all record-keeping societies in the 1930s. When Arensberg first reported on his research in 1937, 62 percent of all men between the ages of 30 to 35 were still unmarried, as were 42 percent of the women in this same age group. Late marriage can be associated with the reluctance of the old couple to renounce their leadership.

In many instances, a smooth transition occurred and father and son continued to work together. This happened when the son showed deference and respect to the accumulated knowledge of the parent. One such family was described by a neighbor who observed the old man working by the side of his son, "Look at the Careys; old Johnny gives his boy a hand in everything. You wouldn't know which one has the land" (Arensberg, 1937/1959:86). The old woman could also have been of help in assisting the son's wife with domestic chores and the raising of the children.

In cases where there were disagreements between the old couple and the new farm-couple owners, it was the old people who must leave. It was only in this way that the family continuity, the giving their "name to the land," could be continued. In summary, rural Irish family life maximized the importance and the power of the aged. The Irish rural community could be viewed as a virtual gerontocracy.

Arensberg (1937/1959); Arensberg and Kimball (1968)

culture from one that was more traditional and oriented to slow changes to one which stresses youth orientation, more rapid changes, and technological development" (1973:181). The result may be that "the veneration of the old may be one of the casualties of 'progress' " (1973:181).

In recent years, the rural Irish practice of older males holding property not only to ensure their own security but also to hold adult sons in a subordinate role has been changing. In parts of western Ireland, where the land has become very unproductive and a high proportion of the farmers have no visible heirs, this system has broken down. Scheper-Hughes (1983) found that these old men are portrayed as unenvied scarecrows watching over wasted, worthless land. She refers to these people as "deposed kings."

In comparison to the control of property by the elders in an agrarian society, property ownership by the elderly is not typically found in industrial American society. Property ownership has spread broadly through the American population. Further, capital ownership and management is not centered in the hands of elderly people. The expanded industrial economy has created new jobs occupied by younger people. Higher education also provides further opportunities for the young.

Together, these developments have increased the opportunities for the young and reduced the young's dependence on the old. Rosow concludes: "While an old property owner may be financially independent, he no longer has significant control over the life chances of the young; and they have less need to defer to him" (1973:230).

Strategic Knowledge and Religious Links

The elderly are viewed as the repositories of societal wisdom and knowledge in traditional societies. They have full understanding and knowledge of occupational skills and techniques, as well as a virtual monopoly of strategic knowledge regarding healing, religion, warfare, cultural lore, and the arts.

Now things are vastly different. The proliferation of new occupations and newer knowledge diminishes and minimizes the elders' control of strategic knowledge. Different universes of discourse are created between the generations. This, in turn, lessens the communication between the generations. For who among the young wants to hear from the old and their "old-fashioned" and "out-of-date" ideas and opinions?

Formal education has taken on the job of teaching the young occupational and other skills. The popular media teach the new attitudes and values of the society. The peer group, not the elderly, socializes the young. The result is that the elderly are no longer considered "strategic agents of instruction nor founts of wisdom" (Rosow, 1973:230).

In the past, the aged were seen as the links to the past and were venerated. In tradition-oriented societies, classical China being the prime example, old age was honorific and the aged were religiously revered. Ancestor worship of the dead parents was the norm.

The movement from the sacred order of the traditional society to the secular one of contemporary industrial society sees no corresponding role for the elderly. In practice, the old are venerated neither by religious tradition nor as links to ancestors, gods, or the hallowed past.

BOX 14-2　The Global Family

The Community, the Elderly, and the Family in Holland

The rural agrarian population of Achterhoek is one of the sandy districts of eastern Holland. The large majority of farms in Achterhoek are small. The labor is provided entirely by the farmer and his immediate family. Before 1875, Achterhoek was a relatively isolated regional community. Loyalty and identification were restricted to neighborhoods located within the district. The community was homogeneous with intensive social controls. The population was stable. Individuals were born there, were raised there, were married there, and worked on the land there until their death. The church, the neighborhood, and the family influenced every aspect of an individual's life.

The church was influential in religious concerns. In addition, it played an important role in the social life of the community. It kept the population informed on who was selling livestock. Before and after services, it gave the people an opportunity to meet and exchange bits of news and gossip. For the young, it gave them a chance to see each other, a rare occurrence in a life geared to isolated farm work. The moral standards of the people were not solely determined by the church. Rather, morality was defined within the broader rubric of proper social behavior that was set by the community's normative structure.

The extended family had a great deal of power over individuals. This included such issues as deciding on whether a child should marry and whom. Marriage was defined primarily in economic terms with young couples remaining subordinate to the parental generation even after marriage. In this small communal situation each marriage has a tremendous influence on every member of both families. Marriage would cause significant changes in the personal, economic, and social relations of many cooperating relatives. Grandchildren, too, were strongly influenced by their grandparents. In sum, the extended family with its generations and relatives, not the parent-child unit, controlled the

education and dominated the behavior of the family members.

The family system was interlocked with the neighborhood. Neighborliness was not social in nature nor was it based solely on friendship. Common law mandated mutual duties among neighbors. Neighbors assisted at births, weddings, and funerals. They helped when help was needed, including the disciplining of others' children.

The traditional neighborhood in Achterhoek began to change around 1876. Improvements in transportation and communication systems opened the district to outside influence. New farming methods and the development of educational facilities fostered the district's integration into the larger Dutch society. The result was the gradual loss of control by the neighborhood. Neighborhood stability was undermined. Today, although the tradition of the neighborhood still persists, its group loyalty is weakening. Younger members of the community view "neighborliness" as a communal burden rather than as a duty.

These changes affected the position of the aged and the nuclear family. In the traditional neighborhood, the elders held influential positions relating to all aspects of life. The elders were the embodiment of customs and traditions. Economically, they controlled the extended family system. Socially, they held sway not only over their own children but over their grandchildren as well. They were integrally connected to all facets of communal life.

Today, although still influential, their previous all-encompassing power and high status is eroding. The rise of the power of the individualized nuclear family is a major contributing factor to the decline of the importance of the aged. Traditionally, the nuclear family was incorporated into the all-embracing extended family, which, in turn, was closely integrated with the neighbor-

(continued)

hood and church. A new ideology has now arisen that emphasizes the independence of the nuclear family and the opposition to the extended family role. This sentiment is expressed in the following statements of farmers and countrywomen between the ages of 25 and 45:

Father does not trust anything beyond his hands, and the other generation never gets a chance. Such a life does not have any advantage.

Marriage can be fully enjoyed only when husband and wife are together. Living with relatives is entirely wrong because a young women feels like a maidservant. Previously she accepted this, but the younger generation does not.

In the households I know the atmosphere shows that these people should not live together. The person who has married into this extended family suffers the most. The older people do not give up their authority. The younger ones are (treated) no better than servants.

A woman taken into an extended family loses her personality. Very often she cannot lead her own life because of the domination of her in-laws, especially her mother-in-law. The loss of personality is common.

In my opinion only a mother and father should have authority over their children.

Kooy (1963:52–53)

Elderly, and the Family in Holland, based on the work of Gerrit A. Kooy, a Dutch sociologist, who has done a number of empirical studies of family life in the Netherlands.

In Kooy's account the breakdown of the traditional community, the increased importance of the nuclear family has resulted in the loss of status and the decline in institutional-role participation by the elderly. Instead of old age meaning higher rank in the community, it now signifies the loss of rank. Further, older persons are becoming defined as outsiders in community affairs. The loss of traditional supports has affected the elderly's need of self-maintenance and self-development. As modern ideas continue to become predominant, older people's feelings of frustration and uncertainty will increase. In the next section, we will see how the development of a welfare system and a pension system designed to assure the well-being of the elderly in their old age is itself now under attack as Holland experiences the graying of its population.

Productivity

In preindustrial societies, especially those at a bare subsistence level, the elderly play a significant role in economic productivity. In such societies—which have a minimal division of labor and low technological development—each individual, regardless of age, can be of value as long as he or she is able to contribute to the small gross product. Every little bit helps. This fact explains Rosow's somewhat paradoxical finding that "the greater the poverty and the struggle to survive, the *relatively* better off old people are by the standards of their group" (Rosow, 1973:229-230).

When we turn our attention to highly developed and technologically advanced societies, we find a minimally productive role for the elderly. The increased emphasis in these societies is to retire people who are defined as having little value in the labor market. An examination of the historical development of the conceptualization and implementation of retirement highlights the relationship of old people to productivity.

Industrial development in the West has seen a transformation in the age makeup of the work population. During the eighteenth and nineteenth centuries in America, individuals worked throughout their lives. Work involvement only ceased with illness or death. With increased specialization, the demand heightened for productive efficiency. The emerging belief in the late nineteenth century was that old people were not as productive as the young. This was in fact the case for many physically demanding jobs. In these cases, the growing practice was to shift older workers into less demanding and less productive work. The automotive industry with its notorious assembly line was a prime illustration. Its workers were relegated to nonproductive positions as soon as they were thought to be unable to keep up with the pace of the assembly line. Ely Chinoy, in his study of automobile workers, quotes a worker who complained bitterly of this practice:

> You see the fellows who have been there for years who are now sweeping. That's why most of the fellows want to get out. Like you take Jim, he's been there for thirty years and now he's sweeping. When you aren't any good any more, they discard you like an old glove." (Chinoy, 1955:84)

Soon, however, even this practice gave way to the retirement of the older worker, bowing to the demands of industrial efficiency.

The swift growth in technological knowledge also contributed to the dislodgment of old people's involvement in the economy. The emergence of many new specialized occupations with new knowledge requirements proved disadvantageous to the old. The young benefited with educational improvements; the elderly fell behind. The exposure of the younger generation to new educational, technological, and industrial ideas heightened the inequality between the generations. New jobs and new occupations had higher status than the old ones. The younger generation filled them. As people got older, they became more and more confined to the older, less prestigious, and, sometimes, obsolete occupations.

Accompanying the notion of elderly nonproductivity was the emerging belief in the cult of youth. No longer were older people venerated and exalted. The growing disparity between generations in occupational skills helped account for this change. So did the loss of the strategic knowledge of the elders. Stemming from the Protestant work ethic—with its emphasis on efficiency, productivity, and progress—the society increasingly placed emphasis on the virtues of modern youth as opposed to the old-fashioned ways of the elderly. The result was disparagement of the elderly. Increasingly, the older individual was being defined as useless and a drain on the social and economic well-being of the society.

The cumulative result was that by the end of the nineteenth century age-related standards of usefulness and productivity began to be implemented. And, by the beginning of the twentieth century, retirement at a specific age became commonplace. Thus, paradoxically, although men found themselves living longer than ever before, they also found themselves being forcibly retired to a stigmatized status at an earlier age than ever before.

Older women were not directly affected by the growth of the retirement movement since relatively few women were actively involved in the workforce. Yet, they, too, were affected by the demographic social and economic changes of the nineteenth century. This resulted in what best can be described as maternal retirement (Fischer, 1977:146). The great demographic changes in fertility and mortality rates of the nineteenth century had a profound effect on women's lives. More and more women began to survive childbirth and the childbearing years. Earlier, their life span coincided with the period when they were raising their children. As the life span of women increased, a proportionately greater number of years were spent outside the maternal period. For example, a woman today with a life expectancy of approximately seventy-five years can look forward to a period of about twenty-five years after her youngest child leaves home.

Women whose lives had been defined almost exclusively by their maternal role were now faced with a stage in the life cycle where no explicit norms or rules existed to govern their behavior and to provide meaningful direction for their lives. The post-parental period, coinciding with the physiological changes of menopause, proved to be a period characterized by depression and alienation for many women. Trained solely for domestic activities and child-rearing roles, women suddenly found themselves "retired" at a much earlier age than their spouses. Thus, although men were being retired in their late 50s and 60s, women were confronted with the fact that their last child left home before they were 50.

For many older Americans, mandatory retirement is a blessing in disguise. It frees them from boring and tedious jobs. It provides them with the opportunity to pursue leisure activities, travel, and hobbies that they could not pursue when they were employed. But, too many old people find themselves more victims than beneficiaries of mandatory retirement. Often the mental and physical health of many people is seriously hurt by the loss of status, lack of meaningful activity, fear of becoming dependent, and the isolation that may accompany involuntary retirement. Suicides reached a peak in upper age brackets, 70 years and over, after retirement normally occurs (Flaste, 1979:62). Since the early 1980s the suicide rate has risen among the elderly (Weeks, 1994).

To combat the debilitating effect of compulsory retirement, the aged in America have organized into pressure groups, such as the Gray Panthers, the National Council on the Aging, the National Association of Retired Federal Employees, and the National Council of Senior Citizens. Probably the most influential lobbying group is the American Association of Retired Persons (AARP). These groups successfully sought the passage of social legislation in 1986 to bar mandatory retirement ages. Leading the legislative battle was Congressman Claude Pepper, who was born in 1901. He was a leading proponent of this type of legislation to halt discrimination by age. He argued:

> Ageism is as odious as racism and sexism. Mandatory retirement arbitrarily severs productive persons from their livelihood, squanders their talent, scars their health, strains an already overburdened Social Security system and drives many elderly persons into poverty and despair. (*Time*, August 8, 1977:67)

However, modifications and even the banning of compulsory retirement have profound implications for the society. Many businesses are alarmed at the prospect of changes in compulsory retirement practices. They are concerned that promotion opportunities for hired younger workers will be severely limited—the longer older people hold their jobs, the slower the job advancement for younger people. They also believe that, despite a few exceptions, a significant number of older workers may just be deadwood. These proposed changes would hinder the productivity and progress of their businesses.

In education, for example, the extension of the mandatory retirement age coupled with the tenure system will result in schools and colleges being increasingly staffed by older faculties. Younger generations of scholars will be frozen out of academic positions. It will also hamper efforts of universities and colleges to comply with affirmative action programs for hiring women and minorities. The result will be a continued and increased predominance of older white men on the nation's academic faculties.

To counter this argument, critics of involuntary retirement argue as follows: Everyone should be judged on ability and no one should be refused work because of an arbitrary age limit. Such an age barrier is discriminatory and should be rejected, just as it is for sex and race. Old people need work, too, just like everybody else.

Various tactics have been implemented to get rid of unwanted employees. Some instituted "buy-out" incentive programs that include months or years of severance pay and continued health care benefits. These benefits would enable the employee to take "early retirement." By so doing, the perceived social and often economic burden by the continued employment of such individuals is alleviated. Closing down plants and "downsizing" are other tactics that institutions employ. Further, the hiring of new employees on "temporary" or part-time lines often means that they do not have to provide these individuals the financial and health care packages that they provided and continue to provide their long-term employees. Such tactics often result in bitterness of both young and old employees to their employers and to each other.

Also, and ironically, changes in mandatory retirement age legislation are gaining some support from younger people. They are concerned with the rise in the elderly population in America as a result of demographic changes and its impact on the Social Security system. Younger workers, whose taxes support those who are retired under Social Security, have seen a constant rise in the money needed to provide benefits. A raising of the retirement age at which people can claim benefits will serve to cut down on the monthly deductions of younger workers. This economic fact may persuade many that it is costing too much to discriminate against older workers.

At a Senate confirmation hearing held in February 1995, in a clever political attention-grabber, Senator Alan Simpson of Wyoming reported on a national poll that showed that more people under the age of 35 believed in flying saucers than in the prospect that the Social Security system will pay them benefits upon their retirement. Simpson was calling attention to the fear that the Social Security system will soon be in severe crisis or collapse when the "baby boomer" generation of the 1940s and 1950s reaches retirement. In 1995, for the first time in its history, some retirees began to receive benefits that were less then what they had paid in Social Security taxes, plus the interest those taxes might have earned if the money had been invested in a savings account. These more affluent retirees are the forerunners of many younger workers who will experience a personal deficit between what they will contribute to Social Security and what they will ultimately receive (Church and Lacayo, 1995).

The crisis in Social Security is a reflection of the fact that while it now takes five workers to support the pensions and health care for each retiree, by the year 2025, there will be only 3.2 workers for each recipient. In Western Europe the problem is even more severe; there will be only 2 workers for every retiree in 2025. The high tax system that supported the bountiful welfare systems is not able to cope with the strain of a rapidly aging population.

Unlike the United States, most European countries did not experience a post-World War II baby boom. They had very low population birthrates for most of the decades since the war. The United States post-war baby boom was followed by a precipitous drop in the birthrate since the 1970s. The result is that many European societies have high percentages of their total population represented by the elderly. Indeed, eighteen of the twenty countries with the highest percentage of population over the age of 60 are found in Europe.

In the Netherlands (Holland), where the problem is not even as acute as in other European countries, the government is forced to consider very politically unpopular options (Polman, 1995). These include raising the age for pension eligibles, cutting future pensions, denying pensions to the more affluent elders, and/or raising the tax contributions of present-day workers to support their generational elders. Earlier in this chapter I discussed the transformation of generational relationships in the Dutch town of Achterhoek. We saw the decline in the significance of extended family relationships and the concomitant decline in the responsibility that the younger generation had to the old. The generation now coming of older age was no longer able to count on traditional supports.

For this generation of elders a welfare system and its benevolent pension system was developed and counted on to assure its economic independence. These elders have become a potent political force, just as their American counterparts. Lulu van Egmond, a former United Nations aide who works with the elderly in The Hague, observes that in the past the old people of Holland lived with their extended families or got help from the church. This generation of elderly does not want to be dependent upon their families' or the church's "handouts." "This was an emancipated generation, and now they see themselves as emancipated elderly" (Egmond cited in Polman, 1995).

The elderly in Holland have founded their own political party, the Old People's Union, and had elected five members to the Dutch parliament in 1994. Their political clout has resulted in the fall of one government that had proposed the idea of freezing pensions. A political battle based on age stratification has emerged. One member of the Old People's Union who has a seat in Parliament reflects the militant attitude of the elderly:

> We have a right to be respected. I see this lack of respect all the time now in the streets. The other day, some youngsters were riding by on a motorbike, and they shouted to me, "Get aside, old fool!" You never used to hear such things in Holland. If I was younger, I would kick them in the butt, oh yes. Today there is little solidarity, more competition between groups, so we must stand up for ourselves. (cited in Polman, 1995)

BOX 14-3   The Contemporary American Family

She's on the Way Up, While He's on the Way Out

Shelly Phillips

PHILADELPHIA INQUIRER

When Barbara Vail-Carocci was growing up in New York, the Bloomingdale's furniture department was like opening night at the theater for her—change, drama, excitement. Now she gets her decorating highs from Main Street Furniture Galleries, which she opened nearly two years ago in Manayunk.

There's just one problem: She's spending 12-hour days nurturing her business baby, but her husband, Rick A. Carocci, 64, is planning to sell his business next door, Transamerican Office Furniture, to his employees. He wants to kick back and relax.

That's not on her agenda right now.

"Our roles have reversed entirely. I work more hours than he does," said Vail-Carocci, 54, who headed the design department at Transamerican for 15 years. "He goes home at the end of the day and prepares dinner. Very often he's angry at me because the chicken is burning or something, and I'm not there yet."

There are many couples like the Caroccis, all struggling to make sense of a flipped domestic code, a blip on the sociological screen. It didn't happen with women now in their late 60s and 70s, who may have had careers to the exclusion of family life; it's not happening to dual-career couples in their 50s who began working at the same time; and it won't happen to many younger couples, who have negotiated their own very different sets of ground rules, according to sociologists.

But women in their 50s who began careers late because they stayed home to raise families—or married older men the second time around—are out of sync with tradition, marital expectation, and their husbands: Their career trajectories are peaking just when their husbands are ready to retire.

"We're talking about a trend happening everywhere in the United States," said Phyllis R. Stein, director of Radcliffe Career Services, an office of Radcliffe College in Cambridge, Mass.

This is definitely new territory for those raised in the 1950s, when men were breadwinners and women were homemakers. Now, women this age who put their own work first are switching the stereotypical male and female roles of their youth. This isn't what their husbands bargained for. This is not how the original contract was written. And even in the best of marriages, some renegotiation must take place.

"Gender conflict is inherent in this relationship because it's counterintuitive to what most people have learned," said James M. O'Neil, professor of educational psychology and family studies at the University of Connecticut in Storrs. When there's perceived unfairness over time, resentment builds, and relationships break down, said O'Neil, who has written articles on dual-career couples.

From 1974 to 1994, the number of women ages 45 to 54 in the labor force increased by 20 percent. However, there are no studies on this group of women who are rosy from their own professional achievements and loath to give it all up.

For years, they put the needs of their husband and children first. Now the children are grown, they've tasted success, and love it. "Women say, 'Now it's *my* time,'" said Rosalind C. Barnett, visiting scholar at the Murray Research Center at Radcliffe College, who studies sex roles. "It's a real problem when their husbands, whom they've been caretaking, want something very different."

Women in this situation often are confused about their choices. Many wind up in the office of Beth Ann Wilson, senior career consultant at Options, a Philadelphia career advising and human-resources consulting firm. "Many people can't verbalize why they're not satisfied. Then,

(continued)

when it comes down to it, they're caught in this sort of conflict," she said.

Sometimes, women in second marriages who have married older men are reluctant to give up the financial independence they've achieved.

Jane Stewart, 53, definitely feels conflicted—not about finances, but about spending time with her husband, Ron, 63. Eighteen months ago, Jane Stewart became director of educational services in a Minnesota school district; her husband continues as a California county superintendent of schools. For now, they have a commuting marriage, but Jane Stewart, who was widowed in her late 20s and remarried 11 years later, thinks about the future.

"When Ron retires [in three years], do I keep working and miss out on all the travel and time together and then look back if something happened to him and say, 'Oh, I wish I hadn't kept working so we could have spent more time together'? And yet, you have the energy and you've reached a point in your career where you're being rewarded for your work just as he was at his age earlier."

It's not the shopping or the cooking that bothers Rick Carocci. It's the time and attention his wife, Barbara, lavishes on her 45,000-square-foot store, drafting interior designs, discussing fabric swatches with decorators, and forever moving furniture around. Only the birth of grandchildren takes priority over work. "She used to accuse me of being a workaholic. All of a sudden the roles are reversed. We haven't had a vacation in four years. Do I resent it? Of course. I worked so hard to attain these comforts, and now I can't enjoy them."

He's certainly proud, but has definite misgivings. "I'm very tolerant of her. I don't understand why she wants to work so hard," he said. "I felt that was *my* role in life."

Barbara B. Wood, director of client service for Work/Family Directions, a Boston-based provider of corporate work and family services, sees similar scenarios played out before her. In one couple, the husband sold his business five years ago, and his wife is still working. Now, because he's "driving her crazy," she is furiously

trying to procure business partners for him, so he will once again have outside interests.

Yet some couples find that this new lifestyle works just fine. Robert R. Marshak, 72, professor emeritus of medicine at the University of Pennsylvania School of Veterinary Medicine, gleefully relishes his role as trailing spouse, following his wife, Margo Post Marshak, 51, from her job as vice dean of the University of Pennsylvania Law School to her job as vice president for student affairs at New York University.

Robert Marshak, former dean of the veterinary school, continues to work on projects for Penn, hooked up electronically from his study. "I'm her greatest booster," said Marshak, who shops, cooks, cares for their standard poodle, and enjoys a lively social life with his wife. "I thought when she got this chance to come to NYU [in 1991], it was just extraordinary, and I was all for it," he said.

Experiencing this zest for difference is always good for a marriage, according to Wynnewood psychotherapist Richard J. Shapiro. "The marriage can be enriched when both partners bring in new experiences in an open, sharing environment, and the marriage can grow," he said.

Career peaks are also characterized by increased vacation time. When the husband has had a 15-year career head start, he often has significantly more time than his wife. A female Center City lawyer guards her vacation time tightly. "I'm pretty chintzy with every single day that I have," she said. This disparity forces her husband to vacation alone at times. "I like being alone for about a day and a half, to be really honest, and then I can't stand it," he said. "But it's just a fact of life."

On their own, this Philadelphia couple have discovered what Arthur Kovacs, a Santa Monica psychologist who specializes in family-life transition, advises his clients: "Nobody's right or wrong. They need to treat the aspirations of their partner as precious and important as their own."

Penny Bilofsky, 52, and her husband Allan, 55, literally sat down and renegotiated their marriage contract after she finished her graduate degree 15 years ago. "Midlife divorce is very high, and it is because people will not allow their partner to grow and change," said Penny Bilofsky, a psychotherapist in Cherry Hill and Philadelphia.

She tells distraught clients that they must appreciate where their partner is at the moment. "It's not that she doesn't want to be with you," she tells the man, "but this is her need to make her mark in the world. He's not discounting the important of your job," she tells the woman, "but he's interested in having a more intimate relationship at this point."

Penny Bilofsky has started a managed-behavioral-care company and fully expects her husband of 32 years to respect the energy and drive she's putting into her new venture, which is exactly what she used to do for him when he was building his mailing-list brokerage firm.

Barbara Vail-Carocci's marriage is important to her, and so is her business. She and her husband are gingerly edging their way along the crevasses of their role reversals, taking care that no irreparable damage is done.

"He was extremely supportive at first," said Vail-Carocci, who has relinquished her black-belt shopping title for lack of time. "Now I think he's beginning to resent it a little bit because I'm not sharing the amount of time that he would like me to. It's growing into something that he didn't anticipate. He's very empathetic because I'm working as hard as I am. He understands the motive—he just doesn't enjoy the result."

Her husband, Rick, emphasizes: "Our marriage is very important to us. We have a wonderful family. We're not going to do anything to hurt it." And yet, he notes ironically, "she always acknowledged the fact that the most important thing in my life was my business. She understood that. Now that's become the most important thing in *her* life."

Philadelphia Inquirer, 11 October 1996.
Reprinted with permission of the Philadelphia
Inquirer, 1996.

Mutual Dependency

The development of retirement as a new stage of the life cycle has necessitated a major readjustment for men and women in our society (cf. Friedan, 1993). Unlike other transitional periods that occur throughout the life cycle, the retirement stage is one that lacks a clearly defined social position in the structure of society. In a society that places its strongest emphasis on the necessity of work for the establishment of a man's sense of identity, retirement is almost antithetical. For a woman, the maternal role has served as a primary source of self-conceptualization. As she gets older, this role is no longer viable.

In addition to these social concerns, retirement is problematic because of financial uncertainties and increasing health concerns. In earlier times, children were obligated to care for their aging parents. Often, it is true, that this "obligation" was self-serving in that the elders also made important contributions to the well-being of their children. But, since the new ideology of nuclear family privatization and independence emerged in the nineteenth century, this obligation has receded in importance. The result has been that the government is becoming more and more involved in providing financial aid and health-care facilities for the elderly. Unfortunately, governmental programs have proven to be woefully insufficient in providing adequate help to these people. Further, the welfare programs developed by the government have not proved to be viable alternatives to the involvements, obligations, and satisfactions that were inherent in the kinship ties that the elderly had with their children and other relatives in the preindustrial period.

As a consequence, many families are faced with the increased dilemma of care for their elderly parents. While it is true that the rise in living standards has allowed for more working-class families to take care of dependent elders just as their more affluent counterparts could do, many do not. Those adult children who do take care of their parents often find that they are being overwhelmed by the responsibility due to the extensive care needs as a result of increased longevity and increased years of disability. I will have more to say on the costs and burdens that these families face today in providing care for the elderly in the concluding section of this chapter.

In preindustrial societies there was a high mutual dependence between age groups. This great interdependence promoted the mutual aid and reciprocity between the generations. In contemporary industrial society, the relative economic affluence of the population and the rise in living standards have undermined this mutual dependence (Rosow, 1973). The result has been a growth in individuality and independence at the expense of solidarity and reciprocity.

Tamara K. Hareven (1976) takes a somewhat different approach to explain the decline of mutual dependency. She believes that the transformation and redefinition of family functions have been instrumental in the growing isolation of older people in our society. The privatization of the middle-class family with its emphasis on internal sentimentality and intimacy precludes the involvement of extended kin, including aged parents. The modern family has also withdrawn from community involvements. The result has been an intensification of the segregation of different age groups within the family and the community, and the elimination of older people from viable family roles.

Suburbanization has also contributed to the geographic segregation of older people. As you recall from our discussion of families in the city, after World War II there was a marked increase in the number of conjugal families that migrated into new suburban communities. These middle-class families emphasized privatism and independence from both community and extended-kinship involvements. John Mogey's (1964) distinction between closed communities and open communities provides us with a framework to discuss these variations and the relationships that exist between the generations. A closed community is characterized as one where scenes of intense interfamilial cooperation exist. The involved relationships between mother and married daughter in the English working-class community of Bethnel Green is a prime example. Open communities are those where families have selective attachments to a variety of associations or secondary groups. These families interact with individuals and extended kin in other areas as well as in their own area. Yet, these relationships do not share the same degree of intimacy or involvement as that characterized by the families of the closed community.

Open communities and conjugal family privatism have resulted in the increased geographic segregation of old people. The age segregation of the elderly is either in new suburban retirement communities, in old institutions, or, and most often, in the deteriorating neighborhoods of cities. Herbert Gans (1962b) referred to the latter group as *the trapped.* These are less affluent old people who have been forced to remain in former homogeneous working-class communities that have become dilapidated and into which poorer families of different ethnic or racial backgrounds have moved.

The plight of *the trapped* was dramatically conveyed in a series of criminal incidents that occurred in the Bronx, New York City, in 1976 (Klemesrud, 1976). Criminals, many as young as 12 and 13, terrorized old people. Unable to defend themselves and afraid to go to court because they feared retaliation, the old fell unwitting prey to a vicious cycle of mugging, beating, rape, and murder. At the time that the newspaper article was written, twenty old people had been reported murdered in the Bronx. (The Manhattan and Brooklyn figures were thirty-four and twenty-five murders, respectively.) The headlines tell the story best: "Youth Held in Murder of Bronx Man Locked in Closet Three Days," "Grandmother Is Raped and Robbed by a Burglar in Her Bronx Home," "Elderly Bronx Couple, Recently Robbed, Take Their Own Lives, Citing Fear," "Two More of the Aged Killed in the Bronx," and "Many Elderly in the Bronx Spend Their Lives in Terror of Crime."

The sections of the Bronx that were the scenes of these horrible occurrences were once almost exclusively white. Today, their population is about 80 percent African American and Hispanic and 20 percent white. The blacks and Hispanics tend to be a mixture of working-class people and welfare families with few elderly members. The whites tend to be elderly Jews living on Social Security payments. They have remained in the area because they cannot afford to move or for sentimental reasons. The racial pattern of crime against old people varies through the city, depending on the makeup of the neighborhood. Elderly African Americans and Hispanics have also been victimized. It is apparent that these elderly people portray the worst consequences befalling the elderly as the result of community and familial abandonment.

The rapid rise in the number of retirement communities in the last thirty years reflects the situation of elderly people in our society. As early as 1942, Talcott Parsons reflected on the circumstances that brought this phenomenon about:

> In view of the very great significance of occupational status and its psychological correlates, retirement leaves the older man in a peculiarly functionless situation, cut off from participation in the most important interests and activities of the society . . . Not only status in the community but actual place of residence is to a very high degree a function of the specific job held. Retirement not only cuts the ties to the job but also greatly loosens those to the community of residence. Perhaps in no other society is there observable a phenomenon corresponding to the accumulation of retired elderly people in such areas as Florida and Southern California in the winter. It may be surmised that this structural isolation from kinship, occupational, and community ties is the fundamental basis of the recent political agitation for help to the old. It is suggested that it is far less the financial hardship of the position of elderly people, than their social isolation which makes old age a problem. (Parsons, 1942:616)

Retirement communities were developed out of a felt need by the aged for more satisfactory community involvement. They also sought to provide residents with meaningful interpersonal relationships, which the aged were not experiencing with their former non-elderly neighbors and extended kin. The most prominently visible retirement communities are located in warmer regions of the country and have such names as "Leisure Village" and "Retirement World." These communities restrict residency to those in their retirement years, about 55 or older. In the more affluent communities, residents tend to be white, middle- to upper-class persons with professional backgrounds. The goal of these communities is to provide their members with sufficient opportunities to become participants with "people like themselves" in a number of leisure and social activities.

In addition to the more affluent communities, residential housing projects and urban apartments have been set up to provide a supportive social environment for older people. Over the years, studies on age-segregated residential communities of all types have found high morale and social involvement of residents (Chudacoff, 1989; Kart and Manard, 1976). Critics, however, view them as too homogeneous and confining. They feel that life in a retirement environment is artificial, boring, and that residents have few meaningful involvements and activities. Betty Friedan (1993) observes that the voluntary placement into an "age ghetto" makes a "self-fulfilling prophecy of isolation" (1993:59).

Another critic is Jerry Jacobs. Jacobs (1976) studied a planned retirement community of approximately 6,000 affluent residents over the age of 50. This community, "Fun City," is located ninety miles from a large metropolitan area on the west coast. The sterility of everyday life is revealed in the following interview that Jacobs had with one of the residents:

MR. N. Well, for me a typical day is—I get up at 6:00 A.M. in the morning, generally, get the newspaper. I look at the financial statement and see what my stocks have done. I generally fix my own breakfast . . . because my wife has, can eat different that I do. So I have my own breakfast—maybe some cornflakes with soy milk in it—milk made out of soybeans that they sell in the health food store. And uh, then at 8:00 A.M. my wife gets up. The dog sleeps with her all night. And uh, she feeds the dog. Then the dog wants me to go out and sit on the patio—get the sun and watch the birds and stuff in our backyard and have quite a few rabbits back in there. And I finish my paper there. And then she sits and she looks at me. She'll bark a little bit. And uh, then she'll go to my wife, stand by my wife and bark at her. She wants me to go back to bed. So I have to go back to bed with her. So about 8:30 I go back to bed again with my dog for about an hour. And then I get up and I read.

And then I walk up around here and I go over to oh, the supermarket and sit there and talk to people. We go over to the bank. They have a stockroom over there, for people that own stock. We discuss stocks and events of the day. And then I come home and maybe have lunch if I want to or not—it doesn't make any difference. *In fact, down here it doesn't make any difference when you eat or when you sleep because you're not going any place. You're not doing anything. And uh, if I'm up all night reading and sleep all day, what's the difference.* [Emphasis added.] But, then, I'll sit around and read and maybe a neighbor will come over or I'll go over to a neighbor's and sit down and talk about something. And then, lots of times, we go over to a neighbor's and play cards 'til about 5:00 P.M. and then we come home and have our dinner. And the evening is . . . we are generally glued to the television until bedtime comes. And that's our day.

DR. JACOBS. Is that more or less what your friends and neighbors do?

MR. N. Some of them do. Some of them don't do that much. (Jacobs, 1976:389-390)

BOX 14-4 The Contemporary American Family

For More and More Job Seekers, an Aging Parent Is a Big Factor

Judith H. Dobrzynski

Just over a year ago, after much soul-searching, Robert W. Crispin turned down a plum job as one of the top three executives of a prestigious company on the West Coast. He decided instead to stay in Hartford, within easy visiting distance of his ailing 90-year-old father-in-law in northwest Pennsylvania.

"We tried to figure out ways to deal with this," Mr. Crispin said. "We talked about opportunities to travel back to the East. But traveling transcontinental every couple of weeks is not easy, and I was very concerned about how my wife would agonize, and how much she would have to be away from me and my 14-year-old daughter."

The company even offered to move Mr. Crispin's in-laws, but he thought that would be too disruptive.

Just when corporations were getting used to the "trailing spouse"—the wife or husband whose career puts obstacles in the way of business moves—a new problem is cropping up. The graying of America is starting to create "trailing parents," who pose even bigger relocation hurdles.

Nobody knows the exact extent of the problem. But already an estimated 10 to 12 percent of the work force is responsible for caring for an aging relative, said Andrew Scharlach, a professor at the University of California at Berkeley. By 2020, Mr. Scharlach projects, one in three people will have to provide care for an elderly parent. The Conference Board, a business research group, estimates even more people will be affected—as many as 40 percent before 2000.

With many more elderly parents to care for, more employees will face tough choices in deciding whether to move. "This is a new factor in the job equation," said Durant A. Hunter, president of Pendleton James & Associates, a search firm.

It is also a new wrinkle for the American economy, which has always depended on a high degree of mobility.

Like that first laugh line or gray hair, the problem is barely attracting notice—yet. But as baby boomers start turning 50 in 1996, their parents, who are expected to live longer than any previous generation, will ascend into their 70s and beyond. Soon, more and more Americans will find themselves in the same position as Mr. Crispin, who is 48.

Companies are only beginning to deal with the implications of trailing parents. A few, like Apple Computer Inc., have sometimes agreed to foot the bill for moving elderly relatives rather than settle for a second choice in important personnel appointments. But many, fearing high costs, do not want to acknowledge the problem.

Besides, no matter who pays, moving elderly people to unfamiliar surroundings often causes problems. Whether they live with a child, in a nursing home, or on their own, they risk social isolation and increased dependence on their children.

"This was not on our radar screen a few years ago," said Cris Collie, executive vice president of the Employee Relocation Council, a business-supported organization in Washington. "But the growth in concern is astronomical."

Meanwhile, corporations are ever-eager for a mobile work force. In a study released in May, 80.9 percent of the 147 companies surveyed by Atlas Van Lines said they expected to transfer more employees in 1995 than in 1994. Sixty-two percent said they expected to move more people in 1999 than in 1994.

And those numbers do not include the outside talent that companies increasingly seek to fill crucial slots. But with a larger number of people looking after elderly relatives, corporations are likely to see some of their choices stymied—even at top levels.

(continued)

"I have had two or three cases in a row where it was definitely a factor," said Mr. Hunter, the corporate headhunter.

Frederick W. Wackerle, a recruiter at McFeely Wackerle Shulman in Chicago, echoed the concern. In each recent search by his firm for a chief executive, "there's been one candidate who has needed to stay close to an elderly parent in their 80s or 90s."

Usually, recruiters said, such candidates temporarily drop out of the job-changing market, restrict how far they will move, or both. Mr. Crispin, for example, did move to a new job after his father-in-law died last spring. But the post— as executive vice president and chief financial officer of the UNUM Corporation—is in Portland, ME, still a relatively short flight from Pennsylvania, where his mother-in-law and his own parents, all in their 80s, live.

Not everyone is fortunate enough to stay in the running for a job. John F. Johnson, a recruiter at Lamalie Amrop International in Cleveland, said his firm recently considered candidates for a $500,000-a-year job. "One executive told us that he'd look at the opportunity, but might not pursue it because of elder-care responsibilities," Mr. Johnson recalled. "We decided not to pursue him."

Mr. Johnson said the issue currently affects "a very small minority of individuals in our work." But he added, "I don't always know if they will tell me about this."

Relocation specialists agreed that people often do not volunteer the information, lest they be left out of the running for promotions. Even so, in a survey of employees at eight large companies conducted by Rodgers & Associates, a research firm in Boston, 37 percent of those who identified themselves as providing care for an elderly relative said they were not interested in relocating. By comparison, 26 percent of all employees said they would not be interested in such jobs.

And in the 1995 Atlas Van Lines survey, "family ties" edged out "spousal employment" for the second consecutive year as the primary reason employees turned down a relocation. It was cited by 64 percent of respondents. Concern for elderly relatives was undoubtedly a large part of that, relocation experts said.

Recent Census Bureau statistics show that Americans over all are moving less frequently in the 1990s than they have in decades past, though they still relocate more often than people in Western Europe and Japan. In a one-year period ending in March 1994, 16.7 percent of the population changed residences, down from the 20 percent that was typical in the 1950s and 1960s.

Many companies have not yet decided how to respond to the elder-care problem. "People are starting to voice it, but it has not become an outcry yet," said T.J. Chiles Jr., director of work force diversity at the International Business Machines Corporation. Like many companies, I.B.M.—whose initials, it was often said, stood for "I've Been Moved"— has no policy on moving elderly parents, unless they live with the employee. Then, they move with the household.

Sometimes, though, the rules are bending to circumstances. "We do not move multiple households," said Kathleen Curtis, relocation manager at Apple Computer. "But we don't grill employees either. If they say parents are living with them, we do it."

Other trend-setting companies are winking at the rules, too. "We will move the new hire or the transferee and their dependents living at home," said Burke Stinson, a spokesman for the AT&T Corporation. He said if he were a transferee with a parent in a nursing home, "I'd just make arrangements to move him or her into my home for a month before the move."

In the Atlas survey, only 3 percent of the companies said they would move an elderly person who would not share the employee's home at the new location. In reality, though, these decisions are often made on an individual basis.

"Most companies are at the point where if someone's supervisor says, 'I want this to happen for this person,' they make an exception and pay for it," said Steve Mumma of Atlas Van Lines.

But there are few hard-and-fast rules in this sensitive area. Before setting a policy, "we'd have to see that people who are critical to us in managing our business are unable to accept assignments because of this," said Mr. Chiles of I.B.M.

The trouble is, employers may not know how an employee's personal responsibilities affect his or her professional life. "Transferees are not requesting help because there are so many other things that they are asking for," said Donna J. Malinek, president of Forward Mobility, a relocation consulting firm in Bernardsville, N.J. "They either turn down the transfer or they cope with moving the elderly parent themselves."

That, in turn, can create family tensions, Ms. Malinek said. "The spouse tends to do all the legwork to reconnect the elderly parent with the community, and that's an awful lot of work," she said.

Help with those tasks—already provided for employees who need to find schools for their children and job opportunities for their spouses—may be as important to transferees with responsibilities for parental care as paying for the moving van.

When one man was transferred from Cupertino, Calif., to Modesto, Calif., last year, his ailing mother-in-law, a stroke victim in her mid-70s who was living in a convalescent home, moved with the family. The employer, a large consumer products company, paid for the move and also for Forward Mobility to identify appropriate nursing homes in Modesto. As part of its package, Forward Mobility also researched doctors, hospital contacts, and home health aides.

But "this is not standard policy among corporations," said Bonnie F. Graziano, a manager at Forward Mobility. "It's usually done on a case-by-case basis." Companies that pay for help with child-care and other family issues are the most likely to approve it, she added.

There is no question that demand for such services will grow. "It's when people reach the 70s," said Dana Friedman, co-president of the Families and Work Institute, "where problems start arising."

Jacobs argues that retirement communities can be false paradises. His example, "Fun City," had few employment opportunities and few gainfully employed persons. It was geographically isolated with no intercity or intracity public transportation and no police department. Impatient and outpatient health-care facilities were inadequate. The failure lies ultimately in the residential community's denial of the individuality of the residents and the lack of meaningful activities and events.

On a more optimistic note, Arlie Russell Hochschild (1973/1976) reported on an old-age community in a small apartment building that had a viable communal life. There were active involvements among the residents. Friendships and neighboring and social-sibling bonds were prevalent. There was little feeling of alienation or isolation. Hochschild believes that the community life found here counters societal disaffiliation. It fosters a "we" feeling among the residents and an emerging old-age consciousness. Generalizing from this community, Hochschild summarizes the major virtues of retirement communities:

Communal solidarity can renew the social contact the old have with life. For old roles that are gone, new ones are available. If the world watches them less for being old, they watch one another more. Lacking responsibilities to the young, the old take on responsibilities to one another. Moreover, in a society that raises an eyebrow at those who do not "act their age," the subculture encourages the old to dance, to sing, to flirt, and to joke. They talk frankly about death in a way less common between the old and young. They show one another how to be, and trade solutions to problems they have not faced before. (Hochschild, 1973/1976:383-384)

GRANDPARENTHOOD IN CONTEMPORARY AMERICA

There has been a significant decline in the mortality rate in the twentieth century. Since the turn of the century, we have seen a decrease in infant mortality from about 140 infants out of every 1,000 dying in their first year of life to only about 14 out of 1,000 today. At the same time, the average life span has increased from less than 50 years to about 75 years. In an insightful article, the demographer Peter Uhlenberg (1980) observes: "Many of the most significant changes in the American family—the changing status of children, the increasing independence of the nuclear family, the virtual disappearance of orphanages and foundling homes, the rise in societal support of the elderly, the decline in fertility, the rise in divorce—cannot be adequately understood without a clear recognition of the profound changes that have occurred in death rates" (1980:313). This mortality rate change has had a major impact on family structure. I have addressed many of the significant changes in the American family attributable in part by Uhlenberg to this mortality decline. In this section, I investigate the changes in grandparenthood and the four-generation family as a consequence of these demographic changes.

The decline in mortality rate has caused a profound change in the relationship between grandparents and grandchildren. Mortality rate change has greatly increased the potential for family interaction across more than two generations. There was only a one in four chance that a child at birth in 1900 would have all four grandparents alive; three-quarter of a century later, almost two-thirds of all children at birth had all four grandparents still alive. By the time that 1900-born child was 15, there was only a 15 percent probability that three or more grandparents would still be alive; seventy-five years later, that probability increased to more than half, 55 percent. Uhlenberg (1980) points out that the demographic data cannot determine the actual role of grandparents in the lives of children. But they do indicate the increased possibility of the presence of grandparents in their grandchildren's lives.

To begin this analysis of grandparents and the relationship with their grandchildren, the age of people when they first become grandparents must be taken into account. In our society, the modal age of becoming a grandparent is around 49 to 51 years for women and 51 to 53 years for men (Troll, 1983). The onset of grandparenthood can be much earlier in the case of teenage pregnancies. This often produces grandparents in their 30s. Given increased life expectancy, many people can now experience not only grandparenthood but great-grandparenthood as well. By the same token, many young people can have grandparents well into their adult years.

The ages of grandparents cover much of the human life span—from the early 30s to the 100s. Obviously, there will be a great variation in the relationship of grandparents with their grandchildren, depending on their respective ages. Much of the research on grandparenthood covers the period of people from 50 to 70 years of age and the birth to teenage years of grandchildren. It is in this period that most people are most comfortable about being grandparents. People much younger and much older with grandchildren are not as satisfied with that role (Troll, 1983).

Active patients in a personal care residence enjoy a board game.

Andrew J. Cherlin and Frank F. Furstenberg (1986) investigated the role of the "new American grandparent" and the subtitle of their book indicates some of their findings—"A Place in the Family, A Life Apart." Their study is based on a representative nationwide study of American grandparents. They note that improvement of the quality of life of many older people has brought about changes in the grandparent-grandchild relationship. Better health and the generally improved standard of living that older adults enjoy because of such things as Social Security combined with technological improvements in transportation (for example, automobiles and airplanes) and communication (for example, the telephone) have fostered the reshaping of the grandparental "career." They further observe that class is relatively unimportant in grandparenthood.

Another factor that has had a positive impact of the grandparental role is that due to the lower fertility rate many people have completed raising all their children by the time they become grandparents. There is less likely to be role conflict among grandparents, their children, and their grandchildren. Also contributing to changes in the grandparental role is the relaxing of the formal roles among the generations. Reflecting the societal trend toward informality and personal gratification, the grandparent-grandchild relationship can be characterized more by affection than by obligation.

There is a difference in the nature of the involvement of grandparents and grandchildren, ranging from intense involvement to remoteness. In their classic article, Neugarten and Weinstein (1964) categorize five styles of grandparenthood. They include grandparents who are formal, fun-seekers, surrogate parents, reservoirs of family wisdom, and distant figures. Variations in styles of grandparenting differed by age categories. Younger grandparents ranged from fun-seekers to distant figures with a significant number of them in the fun-seeker category. Older grandparents were more consistent in their style of behavior. They were almost always formal and distant. Cherlin and Furstenberg (1986), based on their own findings, believe that the variations in grandparental involvements are more than simply a reflection of the age of the grandparents. The age of the grandchildren is a prominent factor as well. "The fun-seeking pattern failed to emerge in our data not because our grandparents did not like fun but rather because it was not an appropriate style with older grandchildren: no matter how deep and warm the relationship remains over time, a grandmother does not bounce a teenager on her knee" (Cherlin and Furstenberg, 1986:85).

Variations in grandfather and grandmother roles seem to follow traditional patterns of male-female family roles (Troll, 1983). Gunhilde O. Hagestad (1981) has found that grandmothers seem to be more nurturant and are more likely to have warm relationships with their grandchildren. Grandfathers tend to take on the role of the "reservoir of family wisdom." Further, grandfathers usually give more attention to grandsons than to granddaughters. Grandmothers make less gender distinction in their involvements with their grandchildren. Conversational topics among grandmothers and grandchildren center on interpersonal and intrapersonal topics such as dating, family, and friendship concerns; grandfathers' conversations are more focused on wider social issues and external family concerns regarding work, education, and time management. Similar findings lead Cherlin and Furstenberg to reflect that "These gender differences can be summed up in one principle: grandfathers are to grandmothers as fathers are to mothers or, indeed, as men are to women in our society" (1986:127).

Cherlin and Furstenberg (1986) observe that the revolution in the health conditions of the elderly, combined with their economic independence, enable them to pursue independent lives and live apart from the family. Indeed, this is the tension and central concern of many grandparents. They see a conflict between their desires to remain self-reliant while at the same time to establish and maintain affectionate ties with their descendants.

Cherlin and Furstenberg (1986) believe that divorce has the potential to restructure the relationships among grandparents, their children, and their grandchildren, and ultimately to alter the structure of American kinship. A special concern of grandparents, affecting their desire to be a part of the family while living a life apart, is the impact of divorce of a child, particularly a daughter, on their lives. This event often has an impact on the grandparents and they must make a decision to sacrifice some of their independence to aid their child and grandchildren. Usually, the young woman wins custody of the children and often has a hard time coping with her situation. Emotional and economic readjustments often accompany divorce. The grandparents serve as a form of insurance providing economic support and playing a larger role in the rearing and disciplining of grandchildren.

Maternal grandparents may, as a consequence of divorce, have stronger ties to some of their grandchildren than grandparents whose daughters remain married. Concomitantly, divorce can have different effects on paternal grandparents when given current patterns of child custody, the grandchildren remain in the custody of their mother, the daughter-in-law. The authors believe that if these current patterns continue, divorce may result in a "matrilineal tilt" in intergenerational continuity (Cherlin and Furstenberg, 1986:164). However, should joint custody become more common in the future, this tilt would be minimal and paternal and maternal intergenerational ties would become more equal.

The longevity of old people, their independence, and their ability to provide support in times of crisis are all seen to contribute to the emergence of a new American kinship system that often encompasses four generations. This is a development to which attention is now turned.

Four-Generation Families and the Sandwich Generation

Ours is an aging society. Demographic trends reveal that there will be a sharp rise in the elderly population in the foreseeable future. In 1900, around 3 million people in the United States were over the age of 65. They represented 4 percent of the population. In 1980 there were 25.5 million people over 65 years old. This was a 28 percent increase since 1970. Ten years later, in 1990, 31.7 million people representing 12.7 percent of the population were in this age group. This group is expected to increase to nearly a quarter of the population by the year 2050. The median age at which half the population is younger and half is older, rose in the decade that ended in 1990 from 30 years to 32.7 years. The factors accounting for this rise were that the proportion of people age 65 or over is increasing while the proportion of people under the age of 15 is decreasing (Thorson, 1995). These statistics indicate a sharply rising median age over the next three decades and have major implications for the elderly, for families, and for society.

Ethel Shanas (1980), in a ground-breaking lead article in the *Journal of Marriage and the Family*, centers her attention on the "new pioneers" among the elderly and their families. These are the members of four-generation families. Half of all persons over 65 in the United States with living children are members of such families. The prevalence of four-generation families is a new phenomenon; earlier in this century, such families were rare.

The relationship among members of these different generations can be quite problematic. Some of the difficulty stems from the fact that the great-grandparent generation is composed of old people whom the society views as residuals and somewhat useless. Irving Rosow (1976) has astutely observed that our society has deprived old people both of responsibility and of function. By so doing, it has provided the basis for the roleless position of the elderly. In Rosow's terms, the lives of the elderly are "socially unstructured" (1976:466); that is, these people in their 70s, 80s, and 90s have no role models that they can use to fashion their own present-day roles.

Shanas observes that the one place that the old people can find refuge and can have a role is within the family. Yet that role is not clearly defined and often the great-grandparent generation is found to strain the emotional as well as the economic resources of the younger generations in the family. Particularly caught in the middle is the grandparent generation. Known in the popular literature as the *sandwich generation*, they are sandwiched between their own children who need care and their older parents needing care. These people are experiencing their own stresses associated with their own stage in the family life cycle (Thorson, 1995). Many are contemplating their own aging, facing retirement, and perhaps their own financial and health problems. This generation has the brunt of generational responsibility thrust on it. They often are asked to assist their own children as they enter early adulthood and married and family life, while at the same time they are expected to care for their aged parents. Shanas speaks for this generation: "I've raised my family. I want to spend time with my husband or my wife. I want to enjoy my grandchildren. I never expected that when I was a grandparent, I'd have to look after my parents" (1980:14).

Gelman and his coauthors (1985), in a feature study in *Newsweek* citing studies of family functioning and stress among elders and their caretakers, found high psychological stress among the caretakers. This took the form of depression and anger as they coped with their parents. One respondent, a member of the American Association of Retired Persons, sums up these feelings this way: "There is a constant feeling of depression in the inability to bring happiness to the older person whose friends are gone, whose body is worn down and who knows he is disrupting his child's life" (Gelman et al., 1985b:64).

Women within that grandparent generation are the ones who often take on a disproportionate share of the time and emotional involvement with their elderly parents. In 1988, a U.S. House of Representatives report observed that the average women will spend even more years—eighteen years—taking care of elderly parents as they did—seventeen years—raising their children. *Newsweek* (1990), commenting on this fact, observes that the *mommy track* is being replaced by a *daughter track*. The shift is from balancing work, career, and child rearing to balancing work, care, and elder-caring. Indeed, these women are often working mothers and caretakers. They provide both for their parents and for their children while often holding down a full-time job.

Elaine Brody of the Philadelphia Geriatric Center has found that among her clientele, working wives are taking on the same responsibilities as nonemployed women. "They don't give up caring for their parent. They don't slack off on responsibility to their jobs or their husbands. They take it out of their own hides" (Brody, quoted in Gelman et al., 1985b:68). This book has talked about the "double burden" or "dual roles" of women. For these women, we can now see a "triple burden." And yet, as Brody laments, there is little attention paid to the problems of these women by the government, industry, and the women's movement.

Many elders are managing their own lives. Those that are more affluent live in retirement communities and senior-citizen homes. Others live in their own homes. An estimated 75 percent of the old remain in independent living situations. Eighteen percent live with an adult child. A relatively small number live in isolation. About 80 percent of older people see a close relative every week, according to Dr. Franklin Williams, director of the National Institute on Aging (Gelman et al., 1985).

Shanas (1980), however, cautions that we still know relatively little about the quality of the living arrangements of the elderly. "In much the same way, we do not know whether the visits between older parents and their children and relatives are brief or lengthy, friendly and warm, or acrimonious and hostile" (Shanas, 1980:13). We know that they do occur and that there is social exchange, but "[t]he nature of such an exchange may just be, as people say, 'a visit,' or it may involve actual help and services between the generations" (1980:13).

In a review of the literature on adult children with aging parents, Victor G. Cicirelli (1983) found that among the approximately 80 percent of all elderly people that have living children, 78 to 90 percent of them see their children once a week or more often. They also are in frequent contact with them via the telephone. Most adult children feel very close to their older parents and the feeling is shared. While the relationships are seen as gratifying and compatible, there is rarely much sharing of intimate details of life or consultation over important decisions. Cicirelli conjectures that this may be accounted for by the fact that interpersonal conflict between adult children and their parents is reported by only a very small percentage of them. "It may be that most parents and adult children are able to avoid conflict by limiting the scope of the relationship to less intimate and important areas of their personal lives. At the same time, they manage to enjoy certain satisfying aspects of the relationship, such as the sense of shared warmth and affectional closeness" (Cicirelli, 1983:35).

Cicirelli also found much evidence that a mutual helping relationship continues throughout life. The exchange of aid is both instrumental (for example, transportation, housekeeping) or affective (for example, companionship, sympathy). Early in life, parents are primarily donors of both types of aid and continue to help and provide for their children through early adulthood. As they get elderly and experience disability, illness, or economic stress, the balance of help shifts from parents to their adult children. The exchange of help between parents and adult children shifts through the life cycle depending on who needs help and who is able to offer help.

The support and helping patterns between adult children and aged parents are most likely to occur when the elder generation is still relatively healthy and economically independent. Unfortunately, it is in circumstances when the elders become dependent (whether because of illness or financial matters) that adult children will develop negative feelings toward them. This would especially be the case when there is a potential for conflict between adult children's commitments to their children or their own lives and their aged parents.

A daughter is usually the family member who takes on the responsibility of caring for aging parents and other elderly kin (Brody, 1990). Elaine M. Brody and her associates (Brody, Litvin, Hoffman, and Kleban, 1992) have investigated the effects of women's marital status on their parent care experience. They found that the stress of caregiving is lessened for women who had husbands, had more socioemotional and instrumental support, were financially well off, and had less financial strain from caregiving. Brody and her coauthors found that the changing lifestyles of women—the higher divorce rate and higher rates of not ever marrying—increase the difficulties of the parent-care years. A never-married daughter expresses the concerns and anxieties of these women without extensive kin involvements and who have taken on the major responsibility of parental care: "It's an awesome responsibility. It's scary to think what would happen if anything happens to me" (Brody et al., 1992:65).

Sandra J. Litvin (1992), a colleague of Brody's, is concerned with elderly care receivers' status transitions that include the loss of good health and declining social activities with friends and family members. She is also concerned with the effect that these status transitions have on the elderly and their caregivers. Such a status transition can cause considerable fears and anxiety over the future for both the care receiver and the caregiver. Their relationship, itself, is susceptible to breakdown.

Based on her research, she observes that the caregiver experienced conflict when the care receiver had a lack of social participation with family and friends. Many of the caregivers perceived their care receivers as in better health and participating more than did their care receivers. Litvin explains, "If caregivers can rationalize that their infirm elderly kin are independent and have adequate social interaction with family and friends, then the burden is temporarily lifted from their shoulders" (Litvin, 1992). The caregivers know that if their elderly kin participate less with others, then they will focus more of their expectations on increased emotional and instrumental support on these caregivers.

Litvin observes that as the aging population continues to grow, and where a major part of this growth is among the very old, it becomes essential to understand the changing nature of intergenerational relationships when status transitions occur. Litvin calls for the need for more studies to examine variations in the care giving/care receiving experience by race, gender, and social class.

Of crucial concern in the years ahead is the increasing number of people over the age of 65 and the increased number who will live beyond 85. The prospects, then, are of an aging population taking care of a very old population, with all the consequent emotional and financial strains. Given these demographic trends, the problems of the elderly and the sandwich generation will multiply in ways that we really are only first beginning to comprehend. There is an obligation for cooperation between the government and the family to care for our old. Nursing care and nursing homes will become even more significant in the future as more elderly people find that they do not or cannot live with their families. The cost for such care, as well as the increased share of the national budget needed to be devoted to health care for the old, must be confronted now. And yet, we find little systematic governmental attention to this future problem.

Shanas is optimistic that the four-generation family and the emerging kinship ties will continue to demonstrate the amazing resiliency that they have through the centuries. "They may be different for old people in the future from what they are now, but they will continue to provide safe harbor for their members however long they may live" (Shanas, 1980:14). The *Newsweek* article concludes:

> If a society can be judged by the way it treats its elderly, then we are not without honor—so far. But as we all grow older, that honor will demand an ever higher price. (Gelman et al., 1985:68)

CONCLUSION

This analysis of age stratification focused on the role of elders in the family. The chapter opened with an examination of age set, a system of age groupings in which paramount importance is given to age in defining and regulating social, political, economic, and family and kinship relationships.

The main emphasis was to compare the statuses and roles of elders in preliterate societies with their Western industrial society counterparts. Following the approach of Irving Rosow, I identified seven contributing factors that influence the position of older people in given societies. These factors are property ownership, strategic knowledge, religious links, kinship and extended family, community life, productivity, and mutual dependence.

The effects of family privatization once again proved to be a key factor in the generational relationships of the elderly with other family members. The elderly have little importance in an industrial society that emphasizes individual welfare, social and economic progress, and change, and that is opposed to the ideology of family continuity and tradition. The elders of an industrial society—in contrast to elders of a nonindustrial society, which views its elders as the embodiment of the societal customs and traditions—are too often treated as unwanted and unknowledgable representatives of a bygone era who have little function in contemporary society. The deemphasis of the role of the elderly, both in the family and in the society, has led to the general erosion of normative patterns of conduct and behavior between generations. The result has been the creation of a sense of futility and uselessness by the elderly and is typified by the development of institutions catering to the elderly. These range from old-age homes with minimal social and medical facilities for the poor to the segregated "leisure towns" for the elderly rich to lead atemporal and often purposeless lives.

Research has demonstrated that the significant decline in the mortality rate in this century has changed the character of contemporary grandparenthood and accounts for the rise of the four-generation family. This demographic change has greatly increased the potential for family interaction across more than two generations. For those who are grandparents, this time in their life cycle represents a period when there is a desire to maintain autonomy while at the same time participate in the family life of their children and grandchildren. The increase in longevity has resulted in the emergence of a four-generation-family system whose implications are not fully appreciated. Opportunities exist for the development of innovative and satisfying kinship ties across the generations, but the disruptive potential of the great-grandparent generation straining the emotional and economic resources of the younger generations in the family is quite real. Given these demographic trends, the study of gerontology within the context of the sociology of the family should prove to be a most important area of research and investigation in the years ahead.

V

FAMILIES IN CRISIS
AND CHANGE

15

FAMILY VIOLENCE

A major aim of this book is to demonstrate that the concepts of power and stratification are crucial in explaining familial relationships. In the discussion of marital gender roles and generational differentiation patterns, I sought to demonstrate that those who had higher status, power, and authority often used these to dominate and control relationships. Thus, in regard to gender-role relationships, a patriarchal ideology, supported by economic, social, political, and religious institutions enables men to have the upper hand in most aspects of the marital relationship. This is particularly manifested in their control of the public world of work, politics, and religion. Women are relegated to the less powerful and less prestigious private world of the household and of child rearing. Similarly, the domination of the older can be seen in age-stratification patterns in political, economic, and religious organizations.

In this chapter and the next, I examine two topics that focus on some of the negative consequences of family life. The first deals with the ultimate abuse of stratification and power differentials—family violence. The analysis of family violence includes two predominant patterns, wife battering and child abuse. It is only within the last twenty years that sociologists and the lay public alike have become increasingly aware of the frequency of family violence. Why it has so recently been discovered when all apparent evidence indicates that it has prevailed for centuries will be studied. I also examine the factors that account for its prevalence.

The second topic of concern is divorce. Divorce is a major form of marital dissolution. It represents an ultimate manifestation of marital and familial instability. Divorce has been viewed by some as an indicator of the breakdown of the American family and as a reflection of societal decline. Conversely, others see it as the outcome of a positive individual act, ultimately beneficial to all family members and as such, therefore, a sign of societal strength. A comparative analysis of divorce is undertaken. I look at divorce patterns and processes in the United States and in Islamic Iran. Muslim divorce patterns and processes were selected as the comparative illustration because they are a prime example of a Western stereotype—the patriarchal wish fulfillment for simplicity in divorce associated with the "I divorce thee" three times edict (Rosen, 1973). By debunking this stereotype, the hope is that a better understanding of this phenomenon will be gained.

VIOLENCE IN THE FAMILY: COMPARATIVE
AND THEORETICAL PERSPECTIVES

Throughout this book, I examined different theoretical orientations that have been applied to the study of the family in change. I noted how certain perspectives, such as structural functionalism, have tended to view family conflict and disruptions as somewhat deviant phenomena. Other perspectives, notably conflict theory, have seen such disturbances as natural outgrowths of family dynamics. Until the early 1970s, conceptualizations that viewed family consensus and cooperation as the "natural" state predominated in sociology. In a ground-breaking article published in 1971 in the most prestigious sociological journal devoted solely to the study of the family, *Journal of Marriage and the Family*, John F. O'Brien pointed out that from its inception in 1939 through 1969, not a single title in this journal contained the term violence (O'Brien, 1971). He argued that this absence may reflect a desire by sociologists to avoid an issue that may be too touchy or may be thought of as too idiosyncratic a feature of "normal" families.

The entire issue of the *Journal of Marriage and the Family* containing O'Brien's article was organized around the common theme of "Violence and the Family." It was an outgrowth of the 1970 meeting of the National Council on Family Relations, which was also oriented around this theme. In the years since that conference, social scientists have become increasingly involved in the study of the phenomenon of family violence. It is part of the more general realization that those orientations that view family disorganization as peculiar, abnormal, or as a strange deviation are limited. Instead, violence appears to be an expectable event and process and, therefore, has some legitimacy for study. The popular media also have turned their attention to this concern with particular emphasis on the most dramatic forms of family disorganization: violence between husbands and wives and between parents and children. In this section, these concerns will also be ours.

Prior to the 1970s, the social sciences had given relatively little attention to the extent that violence occurs within the family. Suzanne K. Steinmetz and Murray A. Straus (1974) surveyed the literature on violence and the family. They compiled a bibliography of over 400 sources and found little material on everyday domestic violence between husbands and wives, which includes fights, slaps, or the throwing of things. The most extensive and accurate data available was on more extreme forms of violence—murder and child abuse.

The avoidance of this topic was shared by anthropology. The prominent anthropologist Paul Bohannan suggested two possible reasons for this neglect: Middle-class anthropologists share the middle-class horror of violence, and—possibly more significant—people in cultures under colonial situations did not conduct their family quarrels in the anthropologist's presence; nor did they discuss the violent episodes that might characterize their private lives for fear of governmental-agency intervention (cited in Steinmetz and Straus, 1974:v).

Data has been accumulated on the prevalence and extent of intrafamily violence within the last twenty-five years as a consequence of the notable increase in the scholarly attention given to this concern. One of the most active pioneer scholars on family violence, Murray A. Straus, reviewed most of the early literature and presented certain tentative formulations to account for its cross-cultural prevalence. His formulations have proven to be quite accurate. Straus (1977) believes that aggression and violence of all types are so widespread that they can almost be labeled as a cross-cultural universal.

Straus examined the cross-cultural evidence on the most dramatic form of conjugal violence—murder. He found that for many societies, a high proportion of homicides occur within the family. Further, other less drastic forms of aggression are quite common. Straus conjectures that high rates of conjugal violence occur in urban-industrial, agrarian, and nonliterate societies, but the highest rates of conjugal violence occur in societies that have high violence rates in other institutional spheres. He develops this supposition by examining six factors that provide some explanations for the ubiquity of intrafamily violence.

The first three factors regarding family violence are the extent of time involvements of family members with each other, the number of overlapping activities and interests that the members share, and the intensity of their involvement and attachment. The development of the private conjugal family, particularly in Western industrial societies, can thus be seen as latently contributing to the increased occurrence of intrafamily violence. Because the traditional nuclear family is more involved in community and consanguineal extended family activities, aggressive incidents can less frequently be attributed to these factors.

The fourth factor is sexual inequality. Straus observes the linkage between male dominance and wife beating. He attributes this to the high conflict potential built into a system that ascribes a superior position to the husband, and the likely possibility that not all husbands may be able to achieve leadership roles or have wives who will be submissive and subordinate. Segregation by gender contributes to this problem by further aggravating and heightening the antagonism between the sexes. Straus presents the argument, which I have discussed elsewhere, regarding the detrimental effects of such segregation, showing how it leads to the inability of women to escape from a violent husband, particularly in Euroamerican societies:

> Such societies throw the full burden of childrearing on women, deny them equal job opportunities even when they can make alternative child-care arrangements, inculcate a negative self image in roles other than those of wife and mother, and reinforce the dependency of women on their husbands by emphasizing the idea that divorce is bad for children. Finally, in most societies, there is a male-oriented legal and judicial system, which makes it extremely difficult for women to secure legal protection from assault by their husbands except under the most extreme circumstances. (Straus, 1977:723)

Straus (1977) illustrates this point by describing a pattern of male behavior labeled as protest masculinity, which has been examined in the machismo pattern of

Latin American mates. Joseph P. Fitzpatrick (1971) states that *machismo*, literally maleness, refers to a combination of qualities associated with masculinity. It professes a style of personal bravado by which one faces challenges, danger, and threat with calmness. Through machismo, the individual seeks to develop a personal magnetism that attracts and influences others. It is associated with sexual prowess and power over women. This, in turn, is reflected in vigorous romanticism and jealousy of lover or wife, and it fosters premarital and extramarital sexual relationships.

Machismo fathers may have little importance or saliency in mother-child households or when the father may be physically present but not psychologically relevant. This often occurs in the extreme gender-role differentiation of the urban lower class. It is a pattern that is often associated with frequent wife beating and the glorification of physical aggression (Straus, 1977).

The privacy of the family is listed as the fifth factor to help account for family violence. The private family insulates the family members from the social control of neighbors and the extended family. Here again, the conjugal family found in Western industrial societies would be the family type most affected by this factor. The strength of the communal norm regarding the sanctity of family privacy is such that even when neighbors overhear family arguments and see the physical results of family aggression they try to ignore such evidence. More than likely they will neither contact appropriate public agencies nor make personal inquiries of the abused family member on the circumstances of the injury. Nor will they offer assistance.

The sanctity of family privacy is an important variable in Murray A. Straus' analysis of family life. He argues that cultural norms often legitimize the use of violence between family members, even if such aggression is illegal or a serious breach of normative proscriptions in nonfamilial circumstances. "In Euroamerican societies, to this day, there is a strong, though largely unverbalized, norm that makes the marriage license also a hitting license" (Straus, 1977:720).

Straus then builds on the relationship between family violence and aggression and various societal patterns. Citing cross-cultural research, Straus argues that the more pervasive the existence of societal violence, the higher is the level of family violence. More than this, Straus postulates the existence of a reciprocal relationship between the aggression and violence in the society and the level of violence within the family: "As societal violence increases, there is a tendency for intrafamily violence to increase; and as intrafamily violence increases, there is a tendency for societal violence to increase" (Straus, 1977:725).

One final point that I wish to emphasize in this summary of Straus' article is his assertion that there is a strong link between violence in one family role with violence in other family roles. Thus, in families where violence between husband and wife is prevalent, there is more likely to be violence by parents toward their children. Further, battered or abused children often become parents who batter and abuse their children.

Straus (1983), who has become a leading figure in the cross-cultural investigation of family violence, raises the question of whether physical aggression between family members is frequent enough to be considered a "near universal." That is:

Does intrafamily violence occur with such frequency in all societies that it must be related to the most fundamental aspects of human association? Such speculation essentially places the causes of family violence outside the individual and demands that the understanding and assessing of violence and abuse is best found by studying a given society's structure and its operations. Straus (1983) himself believes that the level of interfamily violence is related in part to the ecological conditions in which a society is operating and the society's technical and economic adaptation to these environmental realities. It is also influenced by societal changes in the subsistence basis of the society.

A classic anthropological example of this point of view is Colin Turnbull's (1972) study of the Ik, a small group of nomadic hunters in the mountains separating Uganda, the Sudan, and Kenya. This is an extreme case where the change of the subsistence base resulted in a descent into poverty. The Ik were driven from their natural hunting grounds, where they were a group of prosperous and daring hunters, into a barren mountainous waste where they were forbidden to hunt the animals that once were their food. The National Game Reserve sought to change them into farmers in a land without rain, without providing them with the technology and the social organization that would make farming possible.

As hunters and foragers, the Ik were nonaggressive and practiced food-sharing reciprocity. In less than three generations, they became a scattered band of hostile people whose social bonds disintegrated, and the only goal was individual survival. To survive, they learned that the price to pay was to give up compassion, love, affection, kindness, and concern—even for their own children. They lived in fear of their neighbors and were indifferent to anything but their own individual welfare. Turnbull depicts a society that has evolved whose ethics and beliefs derived from their ecological predicament. He chronicles episodes of almost unspeakable cruelty and callousness. Ik children steal food from the mouths of their aging parents; throw children as young as 3 years out to fend for themselves; and abandon the old, the sick, and the crippled. Turnbull accounts in one unforgettable passage how, for amusement, children and young men pushed and threw to the ground old men, and shrieked with laughter as the old men struggled to stand up.

However, Straus does not go so far as Turnbull, who in effect argued that the destruction of the Ik economy and the resulting cruelty and inhumanity reveal the basic features of human nature. Straus argues that Ik aggressiveness in the face of economic hardship is just one component of human nature as was their peacefulness and cooperative sharing when the ecological structure was more bountiful and when food was plentiful. Straus summarizes his position this way: "Rather, what the Ik tell us is that the level of aggression within families is governed by the complex interrelation of the constraints and resources of the particular ecological niche occupied by a society, the social organization of that society that evolved in relations to their particular ecological niche, the position of the family in that social organization, and the behavioral and personality characteristics that are congruent with these life circumstances" (1983:36).

Richard Gelles (1983), in a review of studies of wife abuse in East and Central

Africa and in Scotland, sees some underlying shared patterns that provide insights into cultural patterns and wife battering. Marriage customs often support the male point of view and wife abuse is highly correlated with domination, control, and chastisement of women due to the inferior position of wives. There is also a relationship between cultural legitimacy and extent of spousal violence. Where abuse is not positively sanctioned, the rates of wife victimization tend to be lower than in societies where violence against wives is positively sanctioned.

David Levinson is an anthropologist working with the Human Relations Area Files. Using these files he wrote *Family Violence in Cross-Cultural Perspective* (1989). The Human Relations Area Files (HRAF) was developed more than forty-five years ago by George Peter Murdock. They contain 800,000 pages of ethnographic materials on 330 societies around the world. Levinson utilized the literature available on ninety preliterate and peasant societies and worked off theoretical models developed by Murray Straus and others. He sought to investigate the causes of wife and child abuse through an examination of worldwide family violence data.

Levinson found that family violence, while fairly common, was not a universal problem. In fifteen of the ninety societies that he studied, violence was rare or entirely absent. Following Straus, he found that family violence did not occur in societies that had monogamous marriages, economic equality between women and men, and where there was equal access to divorce by both sexes. In these societies, alternative caretakers for children were readily available. Community and kinship network involvements were factors in maintaining a low violence rate. Neighbors and kin were expected to become involved when domestic disputes arose. The general normative expectation was to encourage the nonviolent settlement of disputes outside the home. The factors associated with wife abuse included male domestic and economic power and authority. There was also a tendency for adults to settle conflicts violently outside the home. Levinson's research, in essence, provides support for the belief that gender inequality is associated with family violence, and that societies can develop a culture of violence.

I conclude this discussion of intrafamily violence by examining one extreme manifestation of violence that occurred both within the family and outside it. I am referring to the destruction, in the later Middle Ages, of a large part of the female population because they were labeled witches. Misogyny, the hatred of women, is one outcome, albeit extreme, of the sexist patriarchal view that asserts the superiority of men over women in all spheres of life. This ideology was evidenced in marital-role relationships and the sexual division of labor, both in the home and in the workplace. Before discussion is begun of the persecution of witches, a most dramatic form of patriarchy that is associated with familial and nonfamilial violence, I would like to inform the reader of the origin of the commonly used term "rule of thumb." It derives from Blackstone's codification of English common law in 1768 that legally sanctioned the practice of disciplining one's wife with a switch or rod—provided it was no wider than the husband's thumb. However, as is discussed in the box, Violence Toward Women: The Case of Witches, more severe beatings and discipline were common in the Middle Ages.

BOX 15-1   The Historical Family

Violence toward Women: The Case of Witches

Probably the most extreme example of the violence toward women was the persecution of women during the later Middle Ages for allegedly being witches. Courtly love during the medieval period demonstrated the dichotomy that existed in the conceptualization of women. On the one hand, they were seen as the embodiment of the virtues of goodness reflected by the Virgin Mary; on the other, they were seen as evil incarnate, the temptress Eve, who formed pacts with the devil, Satan. At the same time the ideology of courtly love was developing, there was a countermovement based on the inherent evilness of women that grew from the eleventh to the fourteenth centuries and reached its violent peak in the Renaissance belief in witchcraft.

To counter the threat of "evil" women, the church sanctioned the absolute subjection of women to their husbands. The supremacy of the husband was espoused and the physical punishment of nonobedient and nonsubmissive wives was condoned. A wife's loyalty to her husband was likened to the fidelity of dog to master; all the husband's orders—whether just or unjust, important or trivial, reasonable or unreasonable—had to be obeyed. Implicit obedience was part of the ideal of marriage. Disobedient wives could be brought to compliance by force. Canon law specifically allowed wife beating. Divorce was impossible; even obtaining a separation from a brutal and violent husband was extremely difficult. Noblemen and squires beat their wives with such regularity that a fifteenth-century priest, Bernard of Siena, took pity on the lot of wives and urged his men parishioners to exercise a little restraint and treat them with as much mercy as they would their hens and pigs. However, to encourage women to win their husband's goodwill, the church urged that they be submissive, devoted, and obedient.

By the later Middle Ages and the Renaissance, the violent treatment of women reached its most extreme form in the belief in witchcraft and the resultant persecution and execution of witches.

A manual of witchcraft written near the close of the fifteenth century—at the request of the reigning Pope—reached the following conclusions:

> A woman is beautiful to look upon, contaminating to the touch, and deadly to keep . . . a foe to friendships . . . a necessary evil, a natural temptation . . . a domestic danger . . . an evil of nature, painted with fair colors . . . a liar by nature . . . [She] seethes with anger and impatience in her whole soul. . . . There is no wrath above the wrath of a woman. . . . Since [women] are feebler both in mind and body, it is not surprising that they should come under the spell of witchcraft [more than men]. . . . A woman is more carnal than a man. . . . All witchcraft comes from carnal lust, which is in women insatiable. (*Malleus Maleficarum* cited in Hunt, 1959:177)

The cited document, *Malleus Maleficarum* (The Witches' Hammer) [that is, a hammer with which to strike witches], was very influential for the next two centuries. It professed to document actual testimony of witnesses and confessed witches on the evil doings of women, ranging from summoning plagues of locusts to causing sexual problems (including infertility, impotence, frigidity, painful coitus, nymphomania, and satyriasis), to drying up a mother's milk. Witches allegedly were able to fly at night, could turn themselves into beasts of burden, and would kidnap, roast, and eat children. The belief in witchcraft was the culmination of the ideology of the evilness of women. Witchcraft was seen as a women's crime, and the ratio of women to men executed has been variously estimated at 20 to 1 and 100 to 1. Estimates on the number of executions that may have occurred during this period range from 100,000 to 1 million. In any case, although the exact number of victims of the witchcraft mania is unknown, judicial records for particular towns and areas provide some statistical indicators of its prevalence:

In 1975, more than 2,000 (2,143 to be exact) married or cohabiting adults with children between the ages of 3 and 17 living with them were interviewed. The 1985 survey was larger; it contained over 3,500 couples. Violence was reported in one form or another in 16 percent of the homes surveyed in 1985. Marital violence was reported to have occurred in some point during the marriage in more than a quarter (28 percent) of all households surveyed. Violence was defined as instances in which one spouse threw something at the other person, pushed, grabbed, shoved, slapped, kicked, bit, beat up, or hit the other with a fist or something else, or threatened with or used a knife and gun.

The Straus and Gelles study did find that there was a drop in severe violence by men toward their partners when they compared the 1985 data with that taken ten years earlier. But the authors conclude that the decline is not that large to indicate a major trend in decline in spousal abuse. Rather, the downturn may be indicative of greater awareness of domestic violence and reflections of improvements in the national economy. Another explanation may be that the increased attention that is focused on domestic violence may make people reluctant to report it.

The accumulated research over the last quarter of a century reveals that violence in the family is indeed widespread. Actually, this research may have only uncovered the tip of the iceberg of family violence. Gelles (1972), in his pioneer study of physical aggression between husbands and wives, emphasized that violence may be more wide-

A mother and daughter suffering from the battering of a troubled husband/father.

spread and severe than previously thought. His conclusions reached then are only reconfirmed by later research evidence:

> Taking into account the figures on the extent of conjugal violence we estimate that violence is indeed common in American families. Furthermore, these incidents of violence are not isolated attacks nor are they just pushes and shoves. In many families, violence is patterned and regular and often results in broken bones and sutured cuts. (Gelles, 1972:192)

He argued that the extent of conjugal violence and its intensity indicate that violence between family members is a social problem of major proportions. Further, he points out that marital violence, even if frequent and severe, may not lead to divorce or separation. The reasons why marriages continue are complex. Steinmetz (1977) observes that the physically violent are also more likely to be highly demonstrative in affection, engaging in a great deal of kissing, hugging, and embracing.

Del Martin (1976) suggests that fear may account for battered wives staying married. The predominant reason may be fear. Fear may immobilize them and rule their actions, their decisions, and their very lives. Martin illustrates with this dramatic account:

> When he hit me, of course I was afraid. Anybody would be if somebody larger than you decided to take out their anger on you. I really couldn't do anything about it. I felt as if I was completely helpless. (Martin, 1976:76)

The fear of reprisal also prevents the abused wife from seeking help. She may be afraid of endangering her children or any neighbors that may become involved. She sees only one alternative—sacrificing herself.

Martin (1976) also sees the contemporary definition of the woman's role in our society as being highly influential in the decision to stay married. A woman assumes that she is accountable for the failure of the marriage, even if she is the one being beaten. The failure of the marriage represents her failure as a woman. Probably even more important than the loss of a woman's self-respect is the fact that more often than not, she is economically dependent on her husband. Even in those circumstances where the wife is working, she frequently is forced to surrender her paycheck to her husband. Martin argues that although women's roles are changing and women are increasingly establishing new values for living on their own, the changes are not occurring fast enough for many women who have long ago given up hope: "Only by bringing the buried problems of wife-beating and financial exploitation into the open can we begin to inspire the imaginations of those women who silently wait out their time as scapegoats in violent marriages" (Martin, 1976:86).

Gelles and Straus (1988) in their report on findings from their national survey found that 70 percent of abused women did seek help. Those who were most likely to do so were married previously, had experienced conflict over a few rather than many issues, were healthy, and had experienced both verbal and physical abuse. Women who reported the greatest degree of stress and depression were also more likely to seek help.

John M. Johnson and Kathleen J. Ferraro (1984) are two sociologists who are concerned with how battered women continually adapt to situations and how these adaptations affect self-concepts. They studied the experiences of battered women who found themselves living through episodic outbursts of violence from their mates. The consequences of that victimization on their sense of identity is the focus of their concern. They found that women of repeated violence or abuse who did not feel victimized made use of rationalizations and belief systems that allowed them to perceive their marriage as being good, normal, or at least acceptable.

However, battered women who began to experience a turning point when the violence or abuse was seen to escalate perceived it to be a direct threat. Changes in feelings and interpretations occurred and a new sense of self developed—a victimized self. The victimized-self conception, in turn, begins to change when actions are taken to construct a new and safer living situation. Johnson and Ferraro's research was of women who passed through a shelter. The shelter served as a site where a new conceptualization of self had the opportunity to emerge. The authors make the point that such shelters are important in that they can provide the individual with a support structure that will enable her to take an active role in ending her sense of victimization.

The prevalence and severity of family violence is particularly acute in our society because of the ideology that stresses the privacy of the family. Throughout this book, I have observed that the rise of the private family is one of the major characteristics of contemporary times. Increasingly, the family has withdrawn from community and extended kinship involvements. Granted that this withdrawal is not absolute and that viable relationships do exist for most families with relatives, friends, and neighbors, nonetheless, the privacy and sanctity of the household is normative and usually nonviolated. The result is that violent outbursts usually occur in private and outside witnesses are rare. Del Martin (1976) refers to the book *Scream Quietly or the Neighbors Will Hear*, written by Erin Pizzey (1974), to illustrate this point:

> People try to ignore violence inside the home and within the family. Many abused wives who came to Chiswick Center told Pizzey that their neighbors know very well what was going on but went to great lengths to pretend ignorance. They would cross the street to avoid witnessing an incident of domestic violence. Some would even turn up the television to block out the shouts, screams, and sobs coming from next door. (Martin, 1976:16-17)

Richard J. Gelles (1974) observes that the sociologist Erving Goffman's concept of "backstage" is quite relevant in understanding domestic violence. It is in the home, away from the prying eyes of the community, that violent family members find a place where they can fight in private: "Protected by the privacy of one's own walls there is no need to maintain this presentation of family life as harmonious, loving, and conflict-free" (Gelles, 1974:96). Gelles finds three rooms in the house as centers of family violence: the kitchen, the living room, and the bedroom. The first two rooms are focal points of family activity and as such are scenes of much nonlethal violence. It is in the bedroom where most homicides occur and where much nonlethal violence also is prevalent: Conflicts regarding sex and intimacy are frequent; it is a room, used at night, from which many undressed victims find it difficult to leave. For where are they to go? The bathroom, the most private room for family members, sees relatively few violent episodes.

Family violence also occurs during particular periods of time of the day and the week. Gelles (1974) found that aggression usually occurs in the evening or late evening during the weekend. He accounts for this by observing that it is at these times that the family is usually alone and when the abused family member feels that there is no one to turn to. It is an inconvenient time to disturb neighbors, friends, or relatives with domestic quarrels. All too frequently, the only alternative is the police, and most are reluctant to take this step.

The pattern that emerges is that violence is often associated with the presence or absence of other people. The more alone the couple, the more likely violence will occur. The violent family member is often reluctant to abuse his spouse in the presence of others. Further, neighbors not wanting to intrude or become involved in domestic arguments actively seek noninvolvement in what we define as the private affairs of others.

Gelles (1974) also found that the isolation of the family from the community is a contributory factor in family violence. He contrasts his respondents who had viable neighborhood ties with those who had few friends in the community and rarely visited with neighbors or friends. He found that violent families tended to be those isolated from their neighbors; nonviolent families had viable neighborhood ties and had many friends in the neighborhood. The result was that the victims of a violent family member had minimal social supports and resources in the community to which they could turn for help when they encountered family problems. To highlight the effect of neighborhood involvements on family violence, Gelles compares two neighbors— Mrs. (44) and Mrs. (45). Mrs. (44) owns her own home and has never hit nor been hit by her husband. Mrs. (45) lives across the street and has been involved in some serious knockdown, drag-out physical brawls with her husband. Mrs. (44) discusses her neighbors:

MRS. (44): I like the neighborhood quite well, surprisingly well for just having moved here two years ago. They have been quite friendly and hospitable. The woman next door is my close friend. She is quite a bit older and has children who are married and are my age. But she has been a very good friend. It's a friendly neighborhood.

In contrast, Mrs. (45) knows few neighbors, has few friends, and does not socialize much with her neighbors:

MRS. (45): I don't bother with them and they don't bother with me. I don't mean it that way. . . . we say hello or they might wave. I'm not the type that goes from one house to the next. I'm not that type of social gatherer anyway. We help them, they help us, things that are needed. They are good neighbors.

Mrs. (45) thinks that they are good neighbors, but does not know the first thing about them. Mrs. (44), however, was able to inventory the family problems in many of her neighbors' families (Gelles, 1974:133-134).

One final series of factors associated with family violence stems from sexist patriarchal ideology. A number of investigators—Gelles (1974); Goode (1971); O'Brien (1971), Straus, Gelles, and Steinmetz (1980)—report that the role people play outside the family is important in understanding family violence. Husbands who have not achieved the societal definition of success in their occupational roles frequently take out their frustration on their wives. The investigators' explanation for this occurrence is that although patriarchy asserts that husbands should have a superior position in the household, that position must be legitimated by the husbands' achievements in the outside world of work. In situations where the husband has failed to achieve the necessary societal criteria of success, this can precipitate a conflict situation within the home.

Goode (1971) theorized that family violence is likely to occur in situations where the husband fails to possess the achieved statuses, skills, and material objectives necessary to support his ascribed superior status within the household. John E. O'Brien's (1971) research investigation supported this hypothesis. Likewise, Gelles (1974) found in his study of physical aggression between husbands and wives that it is most likely to occur when husbands have lower educational and occupational statuses than their wives. Gelles believes that in such circumstances the husband's inability to measure up to his and his wife's expectations are compounded by the husband's frustration over his inability to provide adequately for his family, and thus leads to outbreaks of aggressive behavior. Steinmetz (1987), in her exhaustive review of the literature, reports similar conclusions.

In summary, I investigated some of the dominating factors that are associated with conjugal violence. It is beyond the scope of my discussion to include such additional elements as socialization processes, psychological factors, and societal stress factors, which include unemployment and financial and health problems. I emphasized those factors that have governed attention throughout this book. They include gender-role relationships influenced by patriarchal ideology and the family's relationships and involvement in the community. Continuing with this same orientation, attention now focuses on child abuse.

CHILD ABUSE IN CROSS-CULTURAL PERSPECTIVE

The abuse of children denotes a situation ranging from the deprivation of food, clothing, shelter, and love to incidences of physical wounding and torture, to selling and abandonment, to outright murder. Although it has received an unusual amount of attention in recent years, violence toward children is as old as humankind. Historically, parents have had the prerogative to wield absolute power over their children's life and death.

Violence against children is not a recent phenomenon; it is the term abuse that is relatively new. Abortion, abandonment, and infanticide—the willful killing of children, usually infants—have been practiced in varying degrees throughout history and in most of the world's societies. One scholar argues that infanticide "has been responsible for more child deaths than any other single cause in history other than possibly the bubonic plague" (Solomon, 1973).

The most extreme form of child violence, infanticide, was usually related to beliefs concerning religion and superstition. But throughout human history, a more prevalent reason for infanticide has been population control or maintenance of a physically healthy population. William Graham Sumner, in his classic work *Folkways*, describes the common solution to overpopulation.

> It is certain that at a very early time in the history of human society the burden of bearing and rearing children, and the evils of overpopulation, were perceived as facts, and policies were instinctively adopted to protect the adults. The facts caused pain, and the acts resolved upon avoiding it were very summary, and were adopted with very little reasoning. Abortion and infanticide protected the society, unless its situation with respect to neighbors was such that war and pestilence kept down the numbers and made children valuable for war. (Sumner, 1906:308)

Sumner also observes the differential treatment given to boys or girls, depending on their importance for the family. Where girls were valuable and could bring a bride-price to the father, they were treated well. In circumstances where they were economic burdens, they might be put to death. Another common practice was to kill newborn babies with congenital weaknesses and deformities. Sumner reasons that this occurred "in obedience to a great tribal interest to have able-bodied men, and to spend no strength or capital in rearing others" (1906:313).

Class variations also played a determining role in infanticide decisions. David Bakan (1971), in his *Slaughter of the Innocents*, discusses the ubiquity of infanticide and abortion. He cites the observations of Reverend J.M. Orsmond who visited Tahiti in the late 1820s. Orsmond noted the relationship between infanticide and social class. The members of the higher social class were not obligated to kill their children, whereas the lower caste were obligated to kill their babies after the first or second. Failure to do so brought shame and disgrace: "More than two-thirds of the children were destroyed generally before seeing the light of day. Sometimes in drawing their first breath they were throttled to death, being called *tamari'i hia* (children throttled)" (Bakan, 1971:31).

A common reason for infanticide was to avoid shame and ostracism of unmarried mothers. Up to the dawn of the industrial era about 200 years ago, the killing of illegitimate children was extremely common in Europe. The unmarried woman was confronted with two negative options. If her maternity was discovered, she was excommunicated and lived as a social outcast. Nathaniel Hawthorne, in his American classic *The Scarlet Letter*, novelizes this situation in his account of Hester Prynne in colonial Salem, Massachusetts.

Bakan reports that in eighteenth-century Germany, the most common punishment for infanticide was sacking. The mother was put in a sack and thrown into a river accompanied by a live animal or two to make the death more painful. Frederick the Great, the King of Prussia in 1740, felt that this practice was too inhumane and substituted decapitation as a more acceptable alternative.

Women who committed infanticide were tried and prosecuted as witches. In the seventeenth century, Benjamin Carpoz was credited with the execution of over 20,000 women for witchcraft, a large number having committed infanticide. The manner of execution ranged from sacking to burning, to burying alive, to impalement (Bakan, 1971). Bakan cites a very popular English ballad, "The Cruel Mother," which appeared in B.H. Bronson's (1959) definitive work on child ballads, that illustrates the relationship between illegitimacy and infanticide:

1. There was a lady came from York
   All alone, alone and aloney
   She fell in love with her father's clerk
   Down by the greenwood siding.
2. When nine months was gone and past
   Then she had two pretty babes born.
3. She leaned herself against a thorn
   There she had two pretty babes born.
4. Then she cut her topknot from her head
   and tied those babies' hands and legs.
5. She took her penknife keen and sharp
   and pierced those babies' tender hearts.
6. She buried them under a marble stone
   And then she said she would go home.
7. As she was (going through) (agoing in) her father's hall
   She spied those babes a-playing at a ball.
8. "Oh babes, oh babes if (you were) (thou wast) mine
   I would dress you up in silks so fine."
9. "Oh mother dear when we were thine
   You did not dress us up in silks so fine,
10. "You took your topknot from your head
    And tied us babies' hands and legs.
11. "Then you took your penknife (long) (keen) and sharp
    And pierced us babies' tender hearts.
12. "It's seven years to roll a stone
    And seven years to toll a bell.
13. "It's mother dear oh we can't tell
    Whether your portion is heaven or hell. (Bronson, cited in Bakan, 1971:39)

Phyllis Palgi (1973), in her report of a case of infanticide in contemporary Yemen, demonstrates the continued prevalence of this theme in patriarchal societies. In Islamic Yemen, premarital pregnancy is viewed as a horrible, shameful tragedy that disgraces the entire family. A young woman who was able to hide her pregnancy up to the birth of the baby killed the just-born infant at the prodding of her mother. The baby was then wrapped in a bundle and was given to the young woman's brother and uncle, who were not told the contents of the package. They were told to bury the bundle. They did not carry out their task, and the next day the infant's body was discovered and the mother was arrested:

The [young woman's] father first threatened to kill himself and his daughter, and then he fell ill. Later he said he could not understand what had happened: perhaps something supernatural caused the pregnancy. If not, it was rape by design—this other family, the family of the baby's father, wished to have revenge upon him. Furthermore, he stated categorically that a child produced from rape is dirt, a sinful object, and must be destroyed. In Yemen the authorities would have no problem in understanding this, he claimed. The mother remained bitter and angry, although she agreed that it would have been impossible for her daughter to tell what happened that night. She felt cheated that she had always managed her family, and life in general, so successfully and now events had been stronger than she. It appears as if the family held council and it was decided that the mother would change her evidence. It was not her idea to kill the baby, she now maintained; the daughter was solely responsible. The daughter apparently obligingly changed her evidence accordingly. The rationale was simple: the mother was needed at home to look after her husband and small children. And in any case it was only Sara who really felt guilty. She told how she had sat opposite the baby, not seeing it until it sneezed. Suddenly she was confronted with the concrete evidence of her sin which she had denied for nine months and so blindly plunged with knife to destroy it and, perhaps, all her bad thoughts as well. (Palgi, 1973)

The child was killed to avoid a family scandal. In this patriarchal society, the killing of the child was a less onerous task than to bear the child and suffer the shame and ostracism that would inevitably occur not only to the unmarried woman but also to her entire family.

BOX 15-2   The Global Family

In Jordan, Killing for "Family Honor"

Rana Sabbagh

REUTERS

AMMAN, Jordan—When a Jordanian teenager stabbed and shot his handicapped sister to death in front of their parents for having a child out of wedlock, the family ululated in a traditional display of joy.

The killing in September of 18-year-old Jizia was not a rarity in a country where "family honor" is often defined by what happens to its women—willingly or otherwise.

Months earlier, Ayed, 32, slit the throat of his 16-year-old sister, Kifaya. She had been raped by a younger brother, forced to have an abortion, and married off to a 50-year-old man who divorced her six months later.

"I have cleansed my family's honor," declared Ayed when Kifaya lay dead on the floor. The official report said the family fired weapons in the air in celebration.

Those two were among 23 female victims of "honor killings" in Jordan this year, of a total of 86 cases of premeditated murder recorded by police.

Lawyers say the figure could be much higher, as many cases are never reported in an Islamic kingdom torn between strict ethnic traditions and rapid modernization.

In addition, there are hundreds of cases of abuse, beatings and marriages forced on women accused of "immoral" behavior in the male-dominated society.

Although honor killings have been carried out for centuries in the region, only now are such crimes being publicly debated.

"People have become more daring in discussing these crimes, which are a flagrant violation of human rights," said lawyer Asma Khader, a leading feminist and head of the Jordan Women Union. "The media is also dedicating more coverage on that."

But for most officials, the topic remains taboo.

Social and family pressure makes it unacceptable for any Jordanian couple to live together unless married. The majority of conservative families encourage segregation of sexes at an early age.

But, sociologists say, rapid social change, including greater urbanization and the rising number of women in the labor force where they meet men, has altered the social dynamic and contributed to the number of honor crimes.

Lawyers and officials say that in many cases, women were killed because male relatives had proof of "immoral" behavior, ranging from losing their virginity before marriage to mere flirting. Others were simply victims of rumors and even anonymous letters.

"People tend to do these acts because society is intolerant of any defiance, especially when it relates to sex," Sabri Rbeihat, a U.S.-educated sociologist, said in an interview.

"People who commit this are usually conservative, religious and tribalistic in thinking and behaving, and intolerant and hostile toward modernization and modernity."

Rbeihat encountered many honor killings in his former job at Jordan's general police headquarters. Most crimes take place in crowded areas where people are in close contact and news travels fast.

"They believe that through these acts they restore their status and role in their society," Rbeihat said.

Many killings are justified as honoring Islamic law, but most Muslim scholars deny that there is any law that justifies killing a woman in the name of family honor.

"Killings by individuals are rejected even if the justification is to protect honor," said Sheik Ahmed Hlayel, King Hussein's foremost advisor on Islamic affairs. "And there should be no leniency in implementing penalties related to such crimes."

Jordanian courts follow a mixture of sharia, or Islamic, and civilian law. But lawyers say most killers are regarded sympathetically in their communities and receive light sentences because of penal-code provisions concerning such crimes. Some men have been jailed for as little as three months.

One law, for example, reduces the sentence imposed on a man whose crime was committed "in a fit of fury caused by an unrightful and dangerous act on the part of the victim."

Khader's Union recently formed a committee to track violence against women. It will study court cases against women, operate a hotline for legal counseling, and campaign to amend laws.

But there is no organized movement against honor killings. Instead, most human-rights activists hope the crimes will become a thing of the past as the society moves from its tribal origins into the modern world.

Philadelphia Inquirer, 18 December 1994.
Reprinted with permission by the Philadelphia Inquirer, 1994.

Infanticide continues to prevail in contemporary industrial societies, such as Japan, despite the prevalence and acceptability of abortion. It can be seen as one consequence of modernization and the breakdown of the traditional extended family system. Naomi Feigelson Chase (1975) reports that the Japanese have practiced infanticide for over 1000 years. During the feudal era, the seventeenth through the nineteenth centuries, infanticide served as a means of population control. The scarcity of resources and the economic burden of a large number of children caused farmers to kill their second and third sons at birth. Many females were spared because they could be sold into prostitution, servitude, or—for the more fortunate—they could become *geishas*. This practice, *Mabiki*, an agricultural term that means thinning out, accounted for the death of 60,000 to 70,000 infants each year for a period of over 250 years (from about 1600 to 1850s) in northern Japan alone. The practice was prohibited with the onset of industrialization. The national policy encouraged population growth for industry and the army.

After World War II, infanticide reappeared briefly, reaching a peak of 399 cases in 1948, but it then dropped for the next ten years. In 1958, the incidence of infanticide began to rise. By 1973, more than 100 deaths were reported and an additional 110 children were found abandoned in Tokyo alone. Chase believes that the rise of infanticide and abandonment, despite the existence of a liberal abortion law and the widespread availability of contraceptives, is attributable to rapid urbanization and the shift from the traditional extended family to the more segmentalized nuclear family. Most cases of infanticide occur in nuclear families. A second factor is the belief that the young mother lacks the confidence to raise her children without the supports of the extended family. Infanticide in Japan is not due to promiscuity (illegitimacy) or cruel stepmothers. Chase observes that it is likely in families where the mother spends a lot of time alone with the baby. Chase cites another study that suggests that infanticide or abandonment may be one way of coping with unwanted children by unprepared Japanese mothers. In comparison, their American counterparts are more prone to child abuse.

In summary, infanticide may be seen as an extreme reaction to the stress of having children. It has been a basic practice for the handling of overpopulation. Sumner provides an apt concluding remark on the inherent conflicting relationship between parents and children:

> Children add to the weight of the struggle for existence of their parents. The relations of parent to child is one of sacrifice. The interests of children and parents are antagonistic. The fact that there are, or may be, compensations does not affect the primary relation between the two. It may well be believed that, if procreation had not been put under the dominion of a great passion, it would have been caused to cease by the burdens it entails. Abortion and infanticide are especially interesting because they show how early in the history of civilization the burden of children became so heavy that parents began to shirk it. (1906:309-310)

The considerable attention spent on examining infanticide should not perplex the reader. For infanticide is logically related to child abuse. As David Bakan (1971) observed, there is a similar underlying motivation for both. The largest category of abused children is the very young. Abused children also suffer from systematic neglect. The result is that, over time, the injurious treatment of the child has a cumulative effect with a high proportion of abused children dying as a result of their injuries:

> Thus, the most parsimonious explanation of child abuse is that the parents are trying to kill the child. However, in our culture murder of children is a serious criminal offense. The method of cumulative trauma allows infanticide to take place with relative immunity from detection, prosecution, and conviction. (Bakan, 1971:56)

Gelles and Cornell (1983), reviewing the cross-cultural literature on violence and abuse toward children, observe that there are variations in cultural meanings and norms concerning children and family life. Further, there are social-structure variations and family-structure variations. Variations also pertain to the definitions of violence and abuse. Given this caveat, they report that the accumulated evidence from both empirical studies and position papers is that child abuse is probably most common in Western, industrialized, developed nations. China and the Scandinavian countries are notable in that they are characterized by very little child abuse. Violence and child abuse are relatively rare in developing countries. However, the problems that do exist in the Third World are seen to stem from social disorganization caused by modernization and the resulting changes in family, clan, tribal, and social situations.

In their review of the factors that account for the low rate of child abuse and violence in Scandinavia, Gelles and Cornell (1983) point to some key factors that also account for positive parent-child relationships. They report that when social conditions are relatively good relatively little violence occurs. Poor economic circumstances have been associated with child abuse and violence. When there is widespread use of contraceptives and free abortions are readily available, thus reducing the number of unwanted babies, child abuse declines. Premature infants are kept in neonatal wards until they achieve sufficient weight and strength. Parents are taught how to handle the newborn, alleviating some of the tensions that often accompany the transition to parenthood. Finally, many mothers work, and day-care institutions are provided. This also lessens some of the difficulties experienced by working couples who require day-care facilities for their young children.

Researchers who study abuse in developing nations place considerable emphasis on social change, social disorganization, and cultural attitudes toward children in generating explanations regarding child abuse (see Gelles and Cornell, 1983; Levinson, 1989). These researchers voice concern that urbanization and industrialization are breaking down traditional values and family structures, leading to increases in abuse and neglect. Studies in Nigeria, Zululand, and Kenya have focused on the hypothetical increase in child-abuse problems as a consequence of the disruption of traditional clan life. Research in Africa also examines the impact of poverty and malnutrition on the impaired development and even the death of children. For example, "nutritionally battered" children is a term referred to by A.K. Bhattacharyya (1983) for a form of abuse stemming from severe protein-energy malnutrition in India and other Third World countries. Indeed, any adverse environmental factors that could have been prevented by way of scientific knowledge or adequate health services often fall under the definition of abuse.

We close this section by observing that there are other forms of child abuse that need to be given increased attention. Taylor and Newberger (1983) have observed that in many countries children are used as soldiers and are victims of wars they do not choose to fight. News reports in the 1980s have documented that children, some only 7 and 8 years old, served in the militia in Uganda, and teenagers fought in the Iran-Iraq war. The horrors of warfare are commonplace in the everyday life of many children in Ireland, Lebanon, Cambodia, and South Africa. Children, more than 50 million under the age of 15, are in the international labor force. Forty-two million of them work without pay. The murder of an 11-year-old rug weaver in Pakistan in 1994 as retaliation for his protest actions against child labor exploitation is a recent manifestation of this problem.

Finally, corporal punishment still remains a time-honored and sanctioned form of discipline in most countries, although it is increasingly undergoing scrutiny given current concerns (Taylor and Newberger, 1983). The caning of an American youth in Singapore in 1994 as punishment for malicious mischief deeds gained worldwide attention on the prevalence of this phenomenon. The United Kingdom and other members of the Commonwealth that include Australia, Barbados, Canada, New Zealand, South Africa, Swaziland, Trinidad, and Tobago, as well as forty-six states in America still permit corporal punishment in the schools. The practice is illegal in most Western and East European countries. Japan, China, and the Soviet Union view corporal punishment as an unsatisfactory form of discipline. Attempts to extend the ban to the home often meet with resentment. For example, even an enlightened country like Sweden has aroused controversy among its citizens when it made corporal punishment at the hands of the parents illegal.

In concluding their analysis of child abuse conducted in 1979—the "International Year of the Child"—Taylor and Newberger (1983) call for worldwide action that will help to prevent child abuse. This would include international exchanges of information to generate better understanding of child rearing throughout the world. This would help in the understanding of how people could make life better for all children. They plead for a sustained and increased effort to further the rights of children in the years to come. "At a time when enough weaponry exists to destroy the population of the world, we have everything to gain by rearing the next generation in peace" (Taylor and Newberger, 1983:56).

CHILD ABUSE IN AMERICA

The ideology that argues for the sanctity and privacy of the family household not only hides the extent of domestic violence between spouses but also prevents the full examination of the prevalence of child abuse. In 1972, only 60,000 child-abuse incidents were brought to the attention of governmental agencies. Five years later, the number passed the 500,000 figure. In 1977, the National Center on Child Abuse and Neglect projected that between 100,000 and 200,000 children are regularly abused and assaulted by their parents. Reports of child abuse dramatically increased from 669,000 cases in 1976 to 2.5 million cases in 1990. The National Council for the Prevention of Child Abuse (NCPCA) estimates that this is approximately 39 of every 1,000 children in the United States (NCPCA, 1991). Compounding the problem of the reporting of incidents of child abuse is the fact that agents of social institutions—physicians, nurses, social workers, teachers, police, and judges—tend to report actual cases differentially. Particular statistics from given agencies and institutions may be typical only for them or for their geographic locality and may not be an accurate representation of the national rate.

As previously discussed, Straus and Gelles (1985), two of the leading researchers and scholars in the area of family violence, compared statistics in the areas of child abuse and conjugal violence. The two studies, one conducted in 1975 and the other conducted in 1985, used nationally representative samples containing 2,143 families and 3,520 families, respectively. The researchers found extremely high incidences of severe physical violence against children and a high incidence of violence against spouses in both samples.

An encouraging note, however, was that there were substantially lower rates (47 percent) of child abuse in the more recent study. There was a similar decline (27 percent) in the wife-abuse rate. Straus and Gelles note that some of the differences may be accounted for by different methodology of the studies and an increased reluctance to report incidences of abuse. But they are encouraged that some of the reduction in intrafamily violence is due to the effectiveness during the ten-year period of efforts of prevention and treatment. They are also of the opinion that changes in American society and family patterns may have contributed to the reduction of intrafamily violence even without the help of ameliorative programs. These changes include a more favorable economic outlook, a more negative assessment of family violence, increased marital and familial alternatives for women, better social processes, and greater availability of treatment and prevention services.

While pleased that the national effort to do something about intrafamily violence was showing results, they caution against too much optimism. They observe their findings indicate that an intensified effort is still needed. For, even with the reduction in rates of child abuse and wife beating, there still leaves a minimum estimate of over a million abused children aged 3 through 17 in two-parent households and a million and a half beaten wives each year in the United States.

Studies of abused children and their parents find it difficult to identify conclusively the traits of the abusive parent. Such parents come from the complete range of socioeconomic classes, although there is increasing evidence that those parents who feel the weight of economic uncertainty are more prone to be violent. Many potential child abusers are "normal" parents who overreact to the normal frustrations of being a parent:

> Is there any mother or father who has not been "provoked" almost to the breaking point by the crying, wheedling, whining child? How many parents have not had moments of concern and self-recrimination about having, in anger, hit their own child much harder than they had expected they would? How many such incidents make a "child abuser" out of a normal parent? (Zalba, 1974:412-413)

Steele and Pollack (1968), in one of the early studies of what they termed the battered-child syndrome, found no particular psychopathological or abnormal character types among the parents. What differentiated the abusive parent was an exaggeration of the contemporary pattern of child rearing:

> There seems to be an unbroken spectrum of parental action towards children ranging from the breaking of bones and the fracturing of skulls through severe bruising, through severe spanking and on to mild "reminder" pats on the bottom. To be aware of this, one has only to look at the families of one's friends and neighbors, to look and listen to the parent-child interactions at the playground and the supermarket, or even to recall how one raised one's own children or how one was raised oneself. The amount of yelling, scolding, slapping, punching, hitting, and yanking acted out by parents on very small children is almost shocking. Hence we have felt that in dealing with the abused child we are not observing an isolated, unique phenomenon, but only the extreme form of what we would call a pattern or style of childrearing quite prevalent in our culture. (Steele and Pollack, 1968:104)

Some of the prevalent characteristics of abusers are parents who were social isolates having few or no contact with relatives, friends, or neighbors. The father infrequently participates in community activities. Both parents use physical punishment in disciplining children (Straus et al., 1980). Work patterns and child abuse are seen to be related. Women in the paid labor force have lower rates of child abuse than mothers who stay at home. Gelles and Hargreaves (1987) also found that fathers whose wives are employed also have lower rates of violence toward children. Fathers in blue-collar occupations are more violence-prone than their white-collar counterparts, as are those who are unemployed compared to those employed (Gelles and Cornell, 1983).

The realization of the extent of this social problem reflects our increased awareness that the contemporary private conjugal American family is not as conflict-free as previously idealized. Thus, although the privatization of the nuclear family has maximized emotional intensity, it has also made it problematic and difficult.

As I discussed earlier, the battered-child syndrome is not a new problem; it existed historically and it exists cross-culturally. What is new is the attempt to control child abuse legally. And, as described previously in my analysis of the child-welfare movement, it has its drawbacks and deficiencies. An examination of the law regarding child abuse also reveals similar problems.

In the nineteenth century, the law supported the premise that the family is a private and sacred institution into which outsiders have little right to intrude. As mentioned in an earlier chapter, the first American legal action for child abuse was not brought about until 1874. Laws, in fact, were enacted to protect animals before there were laws to protect children. Indeed, the first child-abuse case was actually handled by the Society for the Prevention of Cruelty to Animals. In this first case, the child was treated under the rubric (legal rule) concerning a small animal. At about this time, problems of child abuse were handled loosely by various voluntary agencies. When court action was deemed necessary, the child was treated as a "neglected" or "dependent" child under the juvenile court laws.

Despite the recent enactment of laws to protect the legal rights of children, the child-abuse statutes do not protect children adequately. There is great reluctance on the part of governmental agencies to prosecute parents or to remove the child from the home. Further, there is a natural queasiness by social agencies and by doctors and medical institutions to report cases: It is exceedingly difficult to accuse a parent who brings in a child for treatment. This is especially the case in incidents of child abuse among the middle class, where the parents may have the legal access to contest the issue.

Most of the reported cases are from hospital admissions. Generally, these are clinic cases, where the parent or foster parent (of the poorer class) rushes a badly injured child to a hospital. Pediatricians in private practice are reluctant to report child-abuse cases. Some researchers question whether private doctors even ask questions about how the child's injury occurred. One possible motive is the physician's desire to avoid the possibility of spending time in testifying in family courts. Further, they share the prevalent viewpoint of family court judges that public placement for the child may be far worse than returning the abused children to their parents.

Aggravating the problem is the lack of a unifying policy. This reflects the prevalent belief that deemphasizing the extent of child abuse and the reluctance to handle this problem. Social-welfare people argue for joint planning and cooperative arrangements between government and private sectors, between agencies and voluntary groups. There is also a need on both the administrative and case level for parent training and self-help for abusing parents.

But, we are reluctant to invade the privacy and sanctity of the home. If and when we do, we have become increasingly aware that the prosecution of negligent and abusive parents does not solve the problem of the victimized children or their parents. Programs designed to treat these parents to maintain the structural integrity of the family are woefully inadequate. In addition, the removal of children from their homes and placement in foster homes or other placement facilities may have negative consequences.

Related to the issue of parental versus social control is the extent to which our society is willing to make investments in broad-based social services that are supportive of the family structure and protective of children. Unfortunately, caught in the dilemma of values supporting parental privacy, control, autonomy, and desire to avoid overzealous intervention by social agencies, the child is all too frequently victimized.

Although it is beyond the scope of this discussion to present comprehensive solutions to the problem of child abuse, the following passage written by Serapio R. Zalba more than twenty years ago still provides some initial guidelines:

> What, then, is to be done about child abuse? We cannot wait for all men and women to become angels to their children. One sensible, concrete proposal has been made to offer preventive mental and social hygiene services at the most obvious points of stress in the family. One such point is reached when a child is born and introduced into the family. This may be especially true for the first child, when husband and wife must now take on the additional roles of father and mother. Assistance for men and women who seem under unusual strain because of this role might lead to fewer incidents of child abuse. More effective remedial efforts will await our willingness to spend greater sums of money on community-based health and welfare services. Protective

BOX 15-3   The Contemporary American Family

To Spank or to Spare

Murray Dubin

PHILADELPHIA INQUIRER

Richelle Phillips of Overbrook spanks her children.

"I spank and I love my children, too . . . . We can't be afraid to set limits with our children. I think society tries to lump spanking in with all the violence in our society. I think they're confused."

Steven Winokur of Upper Dublin *used* to spank his children.

"It was not teaching the values I really wanted to teach. It was not teaching *why*, not teaching the reason for the rules. I'm not saying let the child do whatever he wants. We are still in charge, but spanking is not the way to show that."

Add Phillips and Winokur to Proverbs in the Bible and the rhymes of Mother Goose, all contributors to the centuries-long commentary about disciplining children.

That commentary has become a cultural debate in recent years. Five countries—Finland, Sweden, Norway, Denmark, and Austria—have outlawed physical punishment of children, including spanking. Some want to see spanking outlawed here.

Central to the debate are questions such as this:

Are children spoiled if they are *not* spanked? Are they psychologically damaged if they are? Does spanking lead to child abuse? Does spanking encourage children to use physical force? Does spanking work?

And what—exactly—are people talking about when they discuss spanking?

Winokur and Phillips would agree on one issue—most parents spank their children.

The most recent federal study, conducted in 1988, found that 88 percent of parents had spanked their 3- to 6-year-olds one to five times in the past week. Only 5 percent had not spanked their children at all during the week.

"Eight-five to 90 percent believe it is some-times necessary to spank," says Murray Straus, sociology professor and co-director of the Family Research Laboratory at the University of New Hampshire. Spanking frequency diminishes as a child ages, but "there's no cutoff date." Parents spank less as children get older, Straus says, "but 25 percent of college freshmen we talked to were still being hit when they were 17."

"Foolishness is bound in the heart of a child, but the correction shall drive it far from him."—Proverbs 22:15 (King James Version).

"The most enduring and influential source for the widespread practice of physical punishment . . . has been the Bible," writes Philip Greven in his book, *Spare the Child—The Religious Roots of Punishment and the Psychological Impact of Physical Abuse* (Knopf, 1991).

The frequent references in Proverbs to why parents should not spare the rod is "embedded in the Middle Eastern cultures," says Greven, a professor of history at Rutgers University. "Scholars have talked about Proverbs as part of the 'wisdom literature.' They were . . . widespread and part of the folk wisdom."

While people point to the Bible as a rationale for the physical punishment of children, Greven says that they ignore what *isn't* in the Bible.

"What's astonishing to me is that Jesus never talked about it. And there's nothing in the four Gospels on the discipline of children," says Greven. Nor, he writes, is there any Biblical hint if Jesus, as a child, was spanked or physically punished.

"The rod and reproof give wisdom, but a child left to himself bringeth his mother to shame."—Proverbs 29:15.

John Rosemond is less interested in what the bible says than what extremists on both sides of the spanking debate are saying.

"What's happening is very dangerous because we are being polarized," says Rosemond, a Gastonia, N.C., family psychologist who writes a syndicated parenting column and who recently devoted three columns to spanking.

"What prompted me to write the columns was the awareness that there is a growing movement in the professional community whose purpose is to see to it that there is a criminalization of spanking.

"Quite a number of people are jumping on that bandwagon and failing to make the distinction between a pop on the rear and a beating. . . . These people don't accept that a pop on the rear under any circumstances is benign."

Rosemond insists that the overwhelming number of spankings with an open hand on a child's bottom are not abusive.

"If popped on the rear with an implement, like a paddle, that is a step closer to abuse and risky," he says. "Let's not kid ourselves. I see no indication that spankings of a traditional sort— 'Have you learned your lesson, yet?'—are effective. I see no indication children learn from that.

"What I do see is spanking as a means of terminating an undesirable behavior and focusing the child's attention. Spanking will not, in and of itself, stop a child from losing control. What will stop it is the message and consequences following the spanking."

As for all the studies that show terrible things happening to children who were spanked, Rosamond says, "The studies are bad science. They fail to distinguish between parents who spanked and parents who beat the hell out of their kids."

"My father was a gentleman and he expected us to be gentlemen. . . . If we acted disrespectfully, if we did not observe the niceties of etiquette, he took us over his knee and whopped us with his belt. He had a strong arm, and boy, did we feel it."—Prescott Sheldon Bush Jr., elder brother of former President George Bush, from *Spare the Child . . .*

"We are going through a change, from when people were proud of spanking and wanted to talk about it, to now when people feel uneasy and are having second thoughts about it," says Straus, the family violence expert from New Hampshire.

"In 1986 or '87, we surveyed the 10 most widely sold advice-to-parents books and none of them said don't ever hit your child. Most said almost nothing about hitting kids. In the last two or three years, several books have appeared that say a child should never be hit under any circumstances. That's new."

"Half the states say it is illegal for teachers to hit kids. That would have been unthinkable 75 years ago. Twenty-five years from now, a law will say parents will be breaking the law if they hit their kids."

Straus agrees with Rosemond that there is confusion about definitions. Most of Straus' studies are about corporal punishment, which he defines as: "an act carried out with intent to cause a child physical pain but not injury, with the purposes of correction or control."

Straus says that individuals define spanking differently. Some use the term to mean any sort of hitting of a child. Others just use it to describe hitting the buttocks, sometimes with a ruler or a stick, sometimes not.

"No one has ever established what's too much," says Straus, "and it is my observation that people seldom confine corporal punishment to just one thing."

He adds that there are numerous studies that show that the more children are corporally punished, the more likely they will be physically aggressive as they grow older.

He says he's done a study of college students that suggests a relationship between corporal punishment and occupational success—the more of one, the less of the other.

"It is hard to find parents who truly never spank," says Straus. "Parents who never, ever spank get a lot of heat from their mothers, fathers, brothers, sisters, neighbors. Kids inevitably misbehave. If they don't get spanked, these parents get advice. Spanking is morally expected. That's what a good parent does. . . ."

Winokur, the dad who used to spank, believes he is a good parent.

Father of a 6- and an 8-year-old, Winokur, 34, used to spank his oldest son. "If my older son reached for something he wasn't supposed to, he got his hand slapped. It stopped the behavior, but it was not effective at teaching him anything."

(continued)

Then he and his wife attended a course on effective discipline given by Parents Network.

"Now I've learned new skills. The classes didn't talk about spanking. We learned about being calm, clear and confident."

Diane Wagenhais, program director of Parents Network, a nonprofit educational support organization based in Fort Washington, says the key issue is options.

"Often, if they step back and think about it, parents will say they spank because they don't know what else to do. Sure, there are philosophical issues, but rarely do parents go through philosophical issues in the midst of frustration and anger. Especially if spanking has been the accepted practice in one's family."

A group of parents sat in the Parents Network office and talked about spanking.

"I was hit severely by my parents . . . and I didn't learn anything by it, just sheer terror. I don't remember what I did," says Jamie Lattimer, 32, of Plymouth Meeting, mother of two boys, ages 3 and 1. "Sure, I want to hit my kids sometimes. It's so easy. There's no thinking. Not spanking takes thinking, creativity."

"I was spanked and I hate my parents for that aspect of their parenting," says Deanna Bosley, 31, from Abington, mother of a 4-year-old son a 19-month-old daughter.

"They had a stick hung by the basement door. I hated that as a kid.

. . . My husband and I are both opposed to spanking . . . I have felt angry enough to swat, but I haven't."

Her mother sometimes baby-sits. What would she do if her mother struck her grandchildren?

"If my mom spanked my kids, I don't think I'd leave them in her care again," she says.

"One of my sisters is a parent. She spanks, but I haven't talked to her about it. It's a touchy subject."

Parents often do not want to talk about spanking because it makes public the momentary rages that all parents feel. "I think it's the dirty little secret of parenting," says Susan Anthony, 28, mother of 2-year-old twin boys in Fort Washington.

The parents who ask Adele Faber questions about spanking rarely do it in public. "It comes up, but I have the feeling that parents are embarrassed to ask me in a public forum," says Faber, a best-selling author of parenting books who speaks around the country.

"Parents come up to me afterwards, I get it in private questions."

Faber is against spanking, but she realizes that "it happens. There's that moment of instant rage. When that happens, something has to be said. 'I was angry, I hit you. I don't like to do that.'"

She says parents should try hard to eliminate spanking, even as "a casual part of your disciplinary repertoire. . . . If not, what are you modeling in your household? That I have the right to hit you . . . even once, that your body doesn't belong to you?"

In a late 1980s edition of *Baby and Child Care*, originally written in 1946, Dr. Benjamin Spock comes out against spanking, says New Hampshire's Straus.

But in the 1976 version, here is what Spock says:

"You come to punishment . . . once in a while when your system of firmness breaks down. . . . The best test of punishment is whether it accomplishes what you are after, without having other serious side effects.

"In the olden days children were spanked plenty, and nobody thought much about it. Then a reaction set in, and many parents decided it was shameful. But that didn't settle everything. If parents keep themselves from spanking, they may show their irritation in other ways; for instance, by nagging the child for half the day, or trying to make him feel deeply guilty.

"I'm not particularly advocating spanking, but I think it is less poisonous than lengthy disapproval, because it clears the air. . . . You sometimes hear it recommended that you should never spank a child in anger, but wait until you have cooled off. That seems unnatural. It takes a pretty grim parent to whip a child when the anger is gone."

Bill Chodoff, a pediatrician with the Greater Atlantic Health Plan, deals with questions about controlling children's behavior every day.

"I usually tell them not to spank because it doesn't work very well, and you could easily cross the line and lose your temper. It can be difficult to keep that boundary straight.

"But if a parent comes to me and says I gave him a smack on the butt, I do not think it's terrible if it isn't the only strategy they have used. I ask if it works. Does it stop the behavior? Was it with an open hand? What else are you doing?"

Again, Chodoff repeats, he is not an advocate of spanking, but in the real world, it is not the worst thing he sees.

If he's spent time with parents and is confident that they will not cross that line, then . . . "very seldom, very lightly, with an open hand, to get attention. . . ."

Philadelphia Inquirer, 22 September 1993.
Reprinted with permission by the Philadelphia Inquirer, 1993.

services are understaffed for the number of cases requiring their help and surveillance. And, the additional child care resources—whether they are institutions or paid individual or group foster homes—require additional sources if they are to be adequate either in terms of the number of children they can handle or in the quality of personnel. (Zalba, 1974:408)

In summary, what complicates the treatment of child abuse is the prevailing tension between the rights of parents and the intervention of social agencies. Since the privatization of the family, parental rights regarding the rearing of children have been of paramount importance. However, as I have been indicating, there has been a gradual encroachment of helping agencies, which provide "expert" advice and which ultimately subvert the autonomy of the family. In cases of child abuse, society finds itself in a dilemma. It is reluctant to interfere with parental prerogatives and often leaves the child in the family and subject to further neglect and abuse. Taking the child from the home, on the other hand, often means subjecting the child to inadequate foster-care programs and institutional facilities.

OTHER FORMS OF FAMILY VIOLENCE

Violence against the Aged

"Granny-bashing" is the starkly graphic phrase coined in England to refer to the abuse of elderly parents by their grown children. In an English study, Freeman (1979) found a cycle of violence in operation. Family members who were exposed to a high degree of physical punishment as children were more likely to resort to family violence as adults. Children who were reared in an environment of everyday violence later tended to batter their children and spouses and in turn found themselves exposed to violence later in life from their own children—who, in effect, had been brought up by violent parents. Suzanne K. Steinmetz, in her study of battered parents, remarked: "It may well be that the 1980's will herald the 'public' awareness of the battered aged-elderly parents who reside with, are dependent on, and battered by their adult, caretaking children" (1978:54-55). She was right; the study of elder abuse began in earnest during that decade. However, much of the research is on small, nonrandom samples or official police and social service agency reports and is not generalizable to the larger population (Renzetti and Curran, 1995).

Richard Gelles and Claire Pedrick-Cornell (1990) estimate that from 500,000 to about 2.5 million parents are abused by their children in America. Of this number, about 1 million are seriously injured. Steinmetz (1981) estimates that 10 percent of the aged are at risk of abuse, which takes many forms that include verbal harassment, physical assault, withholding food, theft, threats, and neglect. It is present at all socioeconomic levels.

Researchers (Giordano and Giordano, 1984; Pedrick-Cornell and Gelles, 1982; Rathbone-McCuan, 1980; and Steinmetz, 1981) point to a number of unique characteristics of this form of abuse. Many of the caregivers are women who, as the ones primarily responsible for aged parents, are also the ones most likely to abuse them. One explanation is that the caretaker, overburdened with other family responsibilities coupled with the additional stress of an aged parent, resorts to violence as an emotional outlet. The scenario is that of a 60-year-old daughter taking care of an 85-year-old parent while trying to help her children and grandchildren at the same time. Another unique characteristic is that the victim may at an earlier time have been the abuser; that is, the aged parent may have abused the child at earlier stages in the family life cycle and may now be reaping the sad consequences of that earlier abuse—chickens coming home to roost. While there is some research evidence of this (Kosberg, 1988) and given the cyclical nature of violence, Gelles and Pedrick-Cornell (1983) caution that more knowledge must be gained before firm conclusions can be drawn.

Lau and Kosberg (1979), in a retrospective study of thirty-nine cases of elder abuse (thirty of whom were women), suggest three possible reasons for abuse. The first is that the abuser was himself or herself harmed. A second reason for physical and emotional abuse lies in the possibility of financial gain. The third reason is laid to the societal placement of little value on the aged that is reflected in a misconstrued belief that this condones abuse.

Rape

Rape is the ultimate form of male sexual coercion. It is an act of pure violence. It can happen to any woman. In many societies, including our own, rape in marriage was not a crime, nor was it generally disapproved (Dubois and Gordon, 1984). In this section, I discuss rape with particular focus on rape in marriage.

In a review of some of the ethnographic studies on rape, Scully and Marolla (1985) conclude that culture is a factor in rape. They note that cross-cultural data from preindustrial societies on variations in rape are somewhat suspect, given the fact that in traditional ethnography researchers rarely systematically collected data on sexual attitudes and behavior. When they did, the information was often sketchy and vague. Ethnographic evidence does show the existence of rape-free cultures (Broude and Green, 1976; Sanday, 1979). Where rape and other forms of sexual violence do occur, Sanday attributes it to cultural values that manifest contempt for female qualities. She suggests that rape is part of a culture of violence and an expression of male dominance. Blumberg (1979) takes a similar view, believing that the physical and political oppression of women in preindustrial societies is more likely to occur when women lack important life options and economic power relative to men; that is, women win some immunity from men's use of force against them only when they have relative economic power.

In a cross-cultural study of 156 tribal societies, Sanday (1981) found strong support for an association between the level of nonsexual violence in the society (for example, whether warfare is frequent or endemic) and rape. Sanday argues that "where interpersonal violence is a way of life, violence frequently achieves sexual expression" (1981:18). There is cross-cultural evidence on the relationship of cultural support for violence and physical punishment in child rearing (Lambert, Triandis, and Wolfe, 1959), lighter murder rates (Archer and Gartner, 1984) and higher rates of child abuse (Shwed and Straus, 1979). Based on this evidence, Larry Baron and Murray A. Straus (1985) articulated a "cultural spillover" theory to explain the relationship of cultural support for rape with cultural elements that indirectly legitimate sexual violence.

They observe that in addition to beliefs and values that directly refer to rape, there are aspects of culture that indirectly serve to increase the probability of rape. The central proposition of their theory is that "the more a society tends to endorse the use of physical force to attain socially approved ends (such as order in the schools, crime control, and international dominance), the greater the likelihood that this legitimation of force will be generalized to other spheres of life where force is less socially approved, such as the family and relations between the sexes" (Baron and Straus, 1985:3).

Baron and Straus wished to test their theory by examining variations in the rape rate of all the American states and the rate of "legitimate violence" (for example, the cultural approval of violence) for each of those states. To do this, they utilized the 1980 rape rate as recorded in the annual FBI *Uniform Crime Reports*. They then developed an instrument to measure "legitimate force." The "Index of Legitimate Force" combined twelve indicators of noncriminal violence that fell into three broad groups. These were (1) mass-media preferences of television programs and magazines with a high violence content; (2) governmental use of violence, such as state legislation permitting corporal punishment in the schools, prisoners sentenced to death per 100,000 population, and executions per 100 homicide arrests; and (3) participation in legal or socially approved violent activities that included such indicators as hunting licenses per 100,000 population, National Guard expenditures per capita, and lynchings per million population during the period 1882 to 1927.

They found a positive association of states that ranked high on the Index of Legitimate Violence and the rape rate. (The five highest ranked states were the District of Columbia, Nevada, Alabama, California, and Florida. The five states that had the lowest rates were Wisconsin, Iowa, Maine, South Dakota, and North Dakota with the lowest ranking.) Other factors that also contributed to the rape rate were the degrees of social disorganization, urbanization, economic equality, and percentage of single males. They concluded that their findings support structural theories explaining the origins of violent cultural orientations and for a "cultural spillover" theory of rape.

Given this cross-cultural and societal overview, what about the individual rapist and the victim? What are they like? And under what circumstances does rape occur? Contrary to popular belief, most women are raped by people they know, not by strangers. These include coworkers, neighbors, dates, friends, and family members. Let us look at two groups of people who are often not associated with rape—dates and husbands.

Physical (including sexual) abuse can take place in dating relationships, especially committed relationships before marriage (Cate, 1982; Makepeace, 1981; Roscoe and Benaske, 1985). Date rape usually occurs over issues precipitated by jealousy or rejection (Strong and DeVault, 1995). Date rapes are often not planned; they usually occur over conflicts between dating partners over sexual issues. When the date does not go as expected the man, angered by this turn of events, takes out his frustration by forcing his sexual objectives on the date. He further often does not feel apologetic as sex was seen as the planned outcome.

"Date rape" accounts for about 60 percent of all reported rapes, but the actual percentage is probably much higher (Seligmann, 1984). Barrett (1982) observes that it is one of the least reported and potentially one of the most emotionally damaging forms of sexual assault. Ellen Doherty, coordinator of a Rape Intervention Program at a New York City hospital, observes that women find rape under these circumstances very hard to talk about, even with close friends, because "Not only has her body been violated, but her trust in another human being has been betrayed, and her faith in her own judgment has been shaken" (quoted in Barrett, 1982). Amy Levine, the director of the Rape Prevention Program at the University of California at San Francisco, observes that "It's hard to make women understand that if they get raped while they're in college, it's more likely to be on a date than in a dark alley" (quoted in Barrett, 1982:48).

Mary P. Koss (1988) conducted a large-scale study of 6,159 college students, both male and female, in a random sample of thirty-two colleges. Fifteen percent of the female students reported that they had experienced rape; an additional 12 percent had experienced attempted rape. More than half (54 percent) reported that they had been sexually victimized in some form. Eighty-four percent of the victims knew their assailants, and about half of the rapes were by dates or romantic acquaintances.

The respondents in Koss's study felt that in more than three-quarters of the occurrences their assailants had been drinking or had used drugs. The high reported usage of alcohol and drugs supports earlier research studies on the prevalence of these stimulants during these occurrences. Finally, almost three-quarters of the raped women did not identify their experiences as rape even though they met the legal criteria for rape in their locales. Further, only 8 percent made a police report.

Studies have reported that at least one-third of battered women have also been sexually abused by their partners (Finkelhor and Yllo, 1985; O'Reilly, 1983). Finkelhor and Yllo observe that often a marriage license is considered as a license to rape. Although at least seventeen states now have laws permitting the prosecution of husbands for raping their wives, a number of states expressly prohibit women from charging their husbands in these cases. In twenty-six states, husbands may be exempt from charges of rape if they have sexual intercourse with their wives by force but with no additional violence, such as threatening with a weapon, or if the women is asleep, drugged, or ill (Russell, 1990). When California adopted a marital rape law, Senator Bob Wilson protested, "If you can't rape your wife, who can you rape?" (O'Reilly, 1983). Marital rape has been a particularly difficult violent situation to legislate against because sexual intercourse is considered a right, of marriage. The states that have passed laws recognize that forced intercourse by a husband as being no different than forced sexual acts by someone else.

Richard Gelles (1979) calls attention to two violence situations where wives are particularly at risk—marital rape and beatings during pregnancy. He views married men who rape their wives as lacking resources, including economic resources, that could act positively in the power balance in marriage. They use marital rape as a way to exercise nonlegitimate power. Gelles believes that these men see this act as a way to coerce or humiliate or dominate their wives. These men react violently to the possibility that they may be forced to relinquish the power and privilege inherent in the traditional male role. Wife battering during pregnancy is associated particularly with tensions brought about by anticipated economic and social stresses as a consequence of the birth of a child. Another explanation offered is that it may result from sexual frustrations by the uninformed belief that abstinence is required during pregnancy. Also, husbands may batter their wives because the prospective child is unwanted.

Gelles points out that research indicates the lowest rates of marital violence are found in those families where decision making is shared by husbands and wives. He argues for a reconsideration of marital roles in terms of interest or ability rather than the assignment of tasks and responsibilities on the basis of sex and age as a way of reducing family violence. "An elimination of the concept of 'women's work,' elimination of the taken for granted view that the husband is and must be the head of the family, and an elimination of sex-typed family roles are all prerequisites to the reduction of family violence" (Gelles, 1979:19).

Rape traditionally was blamed on the victim, reflecting the sexist biases of many societies. If a man committed rape, it was somehow the woman's fault for provoking him. This belief was reinforced by a parallel belief that women expected or enjoyed being forced into sexual relations. This unfortunate view contributed to the massive underreporting of rape; victims feared disapproval from family and friends. In recent years, however, the feminist movement has vigorously challenged this false assumption. Through the operation of antirape groups, attempts have been made to reeducate people and to counsel rape victims and persons close to them. Groups such as these have fought the mistreatment of rape victims by the police, the courts, hospital personnel, the media, and the society as a whole. Still, despite changing attitudes and public policies many women believe that it is best not to report rape. In a *Good Housekeeping* (1982) article on rape, the Federal Bureau of Investigation estimates that in 1980 there were 165,000 to 700,000 unreported cases of rape compared to the reported 82,000 cases.

The traditional view of the rapist has also been under challenge. In two papers reporting on their research with convicted rapists, Scully and Marolla (1985) provide evidence that seriously questions the belief that rape is committed by a relatively few "sick" men who have idiosyncratic mental disease and uncontrollable sexual urges. Rather, they found evidence that rapists viewed and understood their behavior from a popular cultural perspective that condones or underemphasizes rape as violent abuse against women. They are led to the conclusion that explanations of this form of sexual violence must include culture and social structure as predisposing factors. From this perspective, rape is seen as the endpoint in a continuum of sexually aggressive behaviors that reward men and victimize women. Through an analysis of interview data of 114 convicted incarcerated rapists, Scully and Marolla report that "[E]vidence indicates that rape is not a behavior confined to a few 'sick' men but many men have the attitudes and beliefs necessary to commit a sexually aggressive act" (1985:251).

Through an analysis of interview data of 114 incarcerated rapists, Scully and Marolla found that rape was frequently a means of revenge and punishment. Victims were often substitutes for the woman they wanted to avenge or women whom the offenders perceived as collectively responsible and liable for their problems. In other cases, rape was used as a means of gaining access to unwilling or unavailable women. It often occurred during a robbery or burglary and was seen as an added bonus. Finally, rape represented a recreational activity and excitement. "Gang" rape is an example of rape being viewed as a recreational activity. Impersonal sexual violence was exciting as it gave the offenders a sense of power and control over their victims. It also gave some a feeling of elation and even elevated their self-image. For these men, women are objectified. They are seen and treated as sexual commodities, not as human beings with rights and feelings. One rapist who murdered his victim because she would not "give in" expressed this contemptuous view of women this way:

> Rape is a man's rape. If a women doesn't want to give in, the man should take it. Women have no right to say no. Women are made to have sex. It's all they are good for. Some women would rather take a beating but they always give in; it's what they are for. (Quoted in Scully and Marolla, 1985:261)

Scully and Marolla see as very significant the rapists' belief that they would never go to prison for their actions. Many did not fear imprisonment because they redefined their behavior as not being rape or a sexually violent act. They knew that many women would not report it, and if they did, the likelihood of their being convicted was very low. These offenders perceived rape as a low-risk act that was rewarding. Scully and Marolla conclude that these men have "learned that in this culture sexual violence is rewarding" (1985:262). They end by raising the question that given the apparent rewards and cultural supports for rape, why is it that all men do not rape or sexually assault women? "Instead of asking men who rape 'Why?' perhaps we should be asking men who don't 'Why not?'" (Scully and Marolla, 1985:251).

CONCLUSION

This chapter was concerned with different manifestations of family violence. Predominant attention was given to wife battering and child abuse. Both were depicted as irrational outgrowths of the excesses of patriarchal authority. In the first case, wife battering, I sought to demonstrate that the legitimation of male prerogatives, privilege, authority, and power can be abused, and too often it is. This results in the severe mistreatment of women. Both cross-cultural and historical evidence was cited. However, the predominant concern was to study contemporary American society and its recent "discovery" of the prevalence of the marital abuse. I indicated that structural conditions inherent in the private conjugal family plays a contributory role. Further, the belief that "normal" conjugal marriages are happy and well adjusted and that violence is an aberration has led to the underestimation of such abuse and to the treatment of it erroneously as a psychologically determined pathology and not as a social phenomenon.

In many ways, my discussion of child abuse can be seen as a continuation of my previous analysis of childhood and adolescence. I stressed that the conceptualization of children and adolescents as essentially inferior and subordinate human beings makes them particularly vulnerable to child abuse. Structural characteristics of the conjugal family play important contributory roles. Governmental policies and the underlying assumptions of the helping professions too often work against the best interests of children.

The chapter's concluding section included discussions of violence against the aged and date and marital rape. The growing concern of abuse of elderly parents by their grown children can be explained by a number of salient factors. Here again, we saw that inadequacies of the conjugal family in their treatment and regard for the elderly is a significant contributory explanation of this abhorrent phenomenon. Likewise, in the discussion of rape I stressed how it is a manifestation of an ultimate form of male sexual coercion. What may have surprised the reader is that rape in dating and marriage is not uncommon. Finally, the update pointed out the devastating impact that intrafamily violence has on the character of the contemporary American family.

16

DIVORCE, SINGLE PARENTHOOD, AND REMARRIAGE

There are many internal and external situations, events, and activities that require major readjustments on the part of the family. These include death, physical disabilities, and illnesses; social and psychological maladjustments, such as mental illness, alcoholism, and drug abuse; marital infidelity, separations, desertions, and divorce; and family violence. External factors that also play a role in family instability include war, unemployment, poverty, and such catastrophes as floods and earthquakes. All of these require changing conceptualizations by family members of their marital and family-role definitions. For example, the women's movement has necessitated the rethinking of family roles for all members of the family as has new-role conceptualizations regarding the aged, children, and youth. In this section, I focus on divorce and see how divorce processes and outcomes are responded to by different family systems.

Greater attention is given to divorce than other forms of marital dissolution because it often represents the culmination of other types of family disruption. In this, I follow the example of William J. Goode (1976)—one of the few structural functionalists who has given extensive attention to family disorganization—who reasons that differential consideration should be given to the study of divorce "because so many other types of family disorganization are likely to end in divorce sooner or later, because it is the focus of so much moral and personal concern, and because changes in the divorce rate are usually an index of changes in other elements in the family patterns of any society" (Goode, 1976:517).

The United States has the highest divorce rate among industrialized societies. In Europe, Sweden's current rate of divorce is highest. Sweden, which has been in the forefront of profound changes in family patterns in the last quarter of a century, has also seen its marriage rate drop appreciably. This trend has also been observed in the United States (Glick, 1990). Because of this fact, the divorce rate itself as a measure of family dissolution is no longer as useful as it once was. In the 1960s and 1970s the Soviet Union, Hungary, and Cuba had high divorce rates (Glick, 1975). Other societies that have had high divorce rates in the recent past include Japan (1887-1919) and Islamic societies, including Egypt (1935-1954) (Goode, 1976).

In the West, beginning in 1890, there was a startling *increase* in the divorce rate (Goode, 1976). For example, the United States went from 55.6 divorces per 1,000 marriages in 1890 to 424.0 in 1974. During that same period, France went from 24.3 to 117.0. The divorce data from Germany in 1900 was 17.6 to 186.0 in 1974; Sweden's figures are 12.9 to 380.0. However, in Japan during this same period there was a startling *decrease* in the divorce rate from 335.0 per 1,000 marriages in 1890 to 98.0 in 1974. Islamic Egypt also saw a similar *decrease* in the period from 1930 (269.0) to 98.0 in 1974. I will examine why divorce patterns differ by focusing on Japan and Iran where the divorce had declined and in the United States where the divorce rate had increased.

Our attention is drawn to the common opinion that the high frequency of divorce is associated with the decline of marriage and threatens the very existence of the family. Tied to this belief is the feeling that contemporary marriages are less harmonious and gratifying than "traditional" marriages. Further, the argument follows that a lowering of the divorce rate would enhance the stability of the family. I examine the assumptions underlying these beliefs and test their validity by looking at the implications of divorce for the individual, the family, and the society.

I conclude by analyzing changes in divorce laws that reflect changes in traditional concepts of marriage and the family. Coming under scrutiny are the consequences of divorce for the resultant single-parent family. My analysis ends with a discussion of family structures and the dynamics of remarriage.

DIVORCE

In Non-Western Societies

This analysis begins by looking at divorce in preliterate societies. George Murdock (1950) has compiled systematic cross-cultural descriptive data on divorce in forty small and preliterate societies in Asia, Africa, Oceania, and North and South America. In all but one society (the Incas), institutionalized provisions existed for dissolving marriages; in three-fourths of these societies both sexes had equal rights to initiate divorce. Murdock estimates that divorce rates in about 60 percent of all preliterate societies are higher than in the United States. On the basis of these findings, he concluded that: "Despite the widespread alarm about increasing 'family disorganization' in our society, the comparative evidence makes it clear that we shall remain within the limits which human experience has shown that societies can tolerate with safety" (Murdock, 1950:197).

The higher divorce rates in preliterate societies does not mean that divorce is associated with social disorganization. The society reintegrates the divorced person into the family and that person is not stigmatized and can remarry. Many societies have mechanisms to care for the children or, as in Japan, the divorce took place before children were born. Further, a variety of devices are employed to preserve the stability of marital relationships. These include prohibitions against incest, dowries and bride-prices, and parental influence and supports. A most important stabilizing practice is the custom of vesting parents with the right to arrange the marriage for their sons and daughters. In societies where marriages are arranged, marriage is usually not defined by characteristics associated with Western romantic love. These marriages do not exhibit the same degree of intimacy and emotionality as their Western counterparts for they are not based on the personal attraction between the persons getting married. Their solidarity derives from the obligations, duties, and rights of members of consanguineally related extended families.

High divorce rates can be, and often are, associated with stable extended-family systems. Goode argues that stable high-divorce rate systems use divorce as a "way of 'sifting' candidates for family membership (1993:16). When divorce does occur, there are clear norms that specify what will happen to family members after the separation. Many societies have provisions for the reintegration of the divorced husband and divorced wife back into their respective kinship groups. The children usually remain within the prevailing unilineage's locality. Further, high divorce rates do not necessarily mean that the family system is being undermined nor is it necessarily associated with societal disorganization. High divorce rates may not reflect family breakdown; in fact, they may reflect culturally prescribed ways of eliminating disruptive influences.

Family sociologists have found it useful to distinguish between the instability of the family unit and the instability of the family system in a given society. Both types of instability must be distinguished from social change and family disorganization (Goode, 1976). High divorce rates have been common in many Arab Islamic societies for centuries, and they did not reflect, until recently—when the divorce rate declined—changes in the family system. The high divorce rate remained unchanged for many generations and the essential structure of the Arab family created it and has coped with it.

Goode (1962, 1976) observes that the direction of change in the divorce rate of a given family system depends on the characteristics of the system prior to the onset of change. For example, the divorce rate in Arabic Islam and in Japan were decreasing rather than increasing when the reverse pattern was occurring in the West. Thus, he reaches what at first glance seems to be a somewhat paradoxical conclusion that social change, rather than bringing about disorganization, may actually reduce the rates of occurrence of such disorganizational phenomena as divorce.

These conclusions bring us to my next concern: Why are divorce rates changing in contemporary societies? Goode (1963), in his influential *World Revolution and Family Patterns*, put forth the explanation that still prevails. He attributes the relatively high divorce rates in the West to the emergence of the conjugal-family system and the decline of the consanguineal extended-family system. The large kin groups associated with unilineage systems in non-Western societies subordinate their younger members and arrange their marriages. Love as a basis for marriage is discouraged as the affectional ties between the couple may undermine their loyalty to the extended family. Nothing is permitted to conflict with the obligations and loyalties one has to the larger kin group. The development of the conjugal family leads to the assumption that greater emotional ties between husband and wife will be present. The diminished importance of the larger family group removes the alternative source for emotional sustenance and gratification. The conjugal relationship now becomes all important. The consequent mutual dependence of spouses on one another for support combined with the comparative isolation of the conjugal unit from kin fosters a relatively more unstable relationship with a concomitant rise in the divorce rate.

> Thus the emotions within this unit are likely to be intense, and the relationship between husband and wife may well be intrinsically unstable, depending as it does on affection. Consequently, the divorce rate is likely to be high. (Goode, 1963:9)

Goode cites the experiences of the Japanese and Arabic Islamic people to provide the illustrative cases of cultures whose high divorce rates have declined in the twentieth century. He attributes this decline to the development of the independent conjugal family. An examination of Japan and the impact of the Islamic Revolution in Iran demonstrates some of the dynamics operating in the lowering of the divorce rate.

In Japan

Goode (1963, 1993) reports that in the early Meiji period of the late 1860s and 1870s, as well as for many prior generations, Japan had a high divorce rate in a very stable society. Marital instability did not affect the stability of the family system nor did it undermine Japanese social structure.

The Japanese conception of marriage and divorce differed from that of the West. They were neither sacramental affairs nor a concern of the state. Marriage was arranged by extended families through go-betweens. The typical pattern after marriage was for the wife to move into her husband's family's household. This was especially true for the wealthier families. But, regardless of wealth, the wife was expected to accommodate herself to her in-laws. This included showing deference, respect, and obeying them by performing all the assigned tasks. Failure to comply or meet the approval of in-laws would result in the termination and repudiation of the marriage. This was done without regard to the relationship between the woman and her spouse.

This system permitted rather free divorce and the divorce rate was higher in the lower social strata than in the upper strata. Goode (1963) attributes this to a system that allowed noblemen to obtain concubines if marital problems existed. If a wife got along with her in-laws and if she bore sons, the marriage continued. The purpose of marriage was not for the emotional gratification of the couple, but rather for the development of the extended family alliances. Divorce could be too disruptive and could cause unnecessary conflict between the two families.

In the traditional Japanese family, members of the family included only those who actually lived and worked together. Children were viewed as the property of the father, and he almost always retained custody of the children after separation and divorce. He was the one who initiated divorce, and after divorce the mother left, severing all ties with her husband, his family, and her children. The children would be raised by the women in the patrilineal family. Thus, from the man's perspective, divorce had little impact on his everyday life. He could divorce without much regard to its future consequences for himself or his children.

Divorce was an option that could be exercised by men alone. There were seven reasons that a man could provide for easily divorcing his wife. They included her inability to bear children; her immorality; being argumentative with her in-laws, too talkative, dishonest, jealous, or diseased (Condon, 1985). A letter such as the following, sent to the proper authorities, would accomplish divorce: "You are incompatible with the customs in my family. So you are no longer needed and are free to seek happiness elsewhere" (quoted in Condon, 1985:45). A divorced woman was returned to her family.

Women's divorce options were limited to running to a Buddhist temple or nunnery where, if she was admitted, she could stay for a two-year period and then would be declared officially divorced. It was not until the Meiji Civil Code of 1898 that women were given the right to divorce. But even with that legal option, a divorced woman had few economic opportunities for self-support.

The advent of industrialization in Japan occurred in the mid-nineteenth century. As Goode observes, while the Japanese wanted to learn and apply industrial *technology* they did not intend to accept the Western *ideology* of industrialization (1993:224). In regard to the family, rather than let the ideology of individualism and the conjugal family develop, the Japanese sought the intensify the patriarchal family hierarchy and to strengthen the control over the individual. This control extended to the determination of marital partners and the rights of divorce. The immediate consequence was a decline in the divorce rates for the ultimate purpose of strengthening industrial and national power through strengthening the power of the extended family. Statistical data reveals that the Japanese divorce rate has declined since 1890 (Goode, 1963; 1993). Citing his own *World Revolution and Family Patterns*, Goode explains that because the Japanese family system "begins with so high a rate of marital dissolution . . . the long-time trend is *downward* during industrialization, not upward" (1993:225).

Yet, while Japan sought to control the ideology of industrialization, it has not fully succeeded. People's attitudes and behavior began to change and more marriages were based on free choice by the marital couple. The result was that industrialization "reduced divorces from traditional causes (elder-in-laws sending the bride back) but may *increase* the number of divorces due to individual incompatibility between husband and wife" (Goode, 1993:225). Rumblings of change began after World War II, and beginning in the 1960s, the divorce rate did start up again.

After World War II, when most women's rights were gained, there was an appreciable change in the initiation of divorce proceedings. Today, 74 percent of all family court petitions for divorce are initiated by women (Condon, 1985). Similarly, there has been a change in which parent gets custodial rights. In 1950, 49 percent of the fathers got custody compared to 40 percent for the mother. However, by 1981, mothers received custody in 69 percent of the cases and the father in only 24 percent (O'Kelly and Carney, 1986).

In the last fifteen years, the Japanese Health and Welfare Ministry statistics show that the divorce rate has doubled (Condon, 1985). In comparison to the United States (1.5 per 1,000 population compared to 5.3 per 1,000), the divorce rate is still low. In comparison to a world scale, Japan's divorce rate is still one of the lowest. This low rate is attributed to the fact that divorce is still disapproved of and stigmatizes the family name.

Surveys that have found that more than 70 percent of men and women are in disagreement with the view that people should feel free to divorce (cited in O'Kelly and Carney, 1986). Divorce creates scandals. Children of divorce find that their marriage prospects are diminished. The dominant belief is that divorce is bad for children and that couples with children should not divorce. However, since 1963, the divorce rate has risen especially among older couples, reflecting the fact that couples have delayed divorce until after their children have married. Often it is women who initiate these divorces. "Husbands are said sometimes to be taken by surprise when an otherwise dutiful wife declares that she wants a divorce now that they are older and their parental responsibilities have been completed. Husbands who saw nothing wrong in their marriages can be faced with wives who suddenly tell them they have loathed them for years" (O'Kelly and Carney, 1986:210-211).

A major factor accounting for the low divorce rate is the fact there is no provision for alimony in Japanese law. A divorce agreement usually includes only one lump-sum settlement payment that is relatively small. The reason for this stems from the traditional practice of a divorced woman returning to her family. Indeed, as Condon (1985) points out, the Japanese word for "divorcee" (*demodori*) means someone who *de* (goes out) and *modori* (comes back). This is particularly hard on the divorced woman, who is often faced with economic difficulties. Japanese social services and public assistance provide minimum assistance.

Another factor that minimizes the divorce rate is that child support is often minimal or nonexistent. Condon cites figures that indicate that more than 75 percent of divorced men do not keep up the payments. Social services and public-assistance programs provide some help, but often are inadequate. The result is that divorced mothers often find that they cannot make ends meet. The divorced mother's average annual income is less than half the national average for heads of households (Condon, 1985). The lack of social supports, combined with the lack of family supports, often makes divorce a difficult and discouraging option for unhappy wives. The result is that they often stay married. One Japanese lawyer sums up the situation for these women: "More than 50 percent of married women are unhappy, but they tell themselves 'Be patient. Be patient'" (quoted in Condon, 1985:59).

William J. Goode (1993) in his assessment of divorce patterns in Japan reports that 75 percent of the lone mothers surveyed report that they suffered from economic distress. He attributes this distress as a consequence of the fact that women's labor wage incomes are significantly lower than men's and that men, for the most part, do not have the burden of supporting their children after divorce. Further, the wives usually receive little or no monetary awards after divorce.

Goode concludes that the Japanese family has moved toward a conjugal nuclear family pattern in which the young are freer to choose their own mates and set up their own households. While these trends are similar to the Western pattern, in absolute figures the preference for living in an extended family continues. "Consequently, without examining a full list of the alterations in the Japanese family, which do at least move toward 'Western' conjugal patterns, it seems unlikely that the divorce rate of Japan will rise to the level of Western nations over the next few decades" (Goode, 1993:240).

In Iran

Iran is an Islamic country. However, it is not an Arab country. Unlike Arab countries that practice Sunni Islam, Iran is a Shi'ite Islamic country whose people practice a more fundamentalist form of Islam. The story of Iran in the last thirty-five years is the story of the trials and tribulations of modernization processes and its impact on family dynamics. Mohammed Reza Shah Pahlavi was the reigning monarch from 1941 until he was ousted by the Islamic revolutionary forces of the Ayatollah Ruhollah Khomeini in February 1979.

Under the shah, the attempt was to build a country that would approximate European standards and would be one of the advanced nations of the world. Economically supported by its rich oil fields, modernization processes were instituted to accomplish this goal. Urbanization and industrialization occurred, with Teheran becoming the symbol of the new Iran. Under pressure from the United States to liberalize his regime, a series of laws designed for social and land reform were passed during the 1960s and 1970s. However, this program of land reform, parliamentary elections, and improvements in education and social services—grandiloquently dubbed the "White Revolution"—proved to be very inadequate and did not end the underlying social inequality, injustices, and lack of civil rights prevailing in the country. Military expenditures continued to climb, political freedom actually lessened, and land reform did little good.

In the late 1970s, there was a coalescing of forces against the shah; his policies were seen to have resulted in foreign social and cultural domination. There was bitterness over political repression and the wasting of the financial gains from oil sales (Apple, 1979). Popular sentiment called for the shah's overthrow. The Shi'ite faith and its leaders, the ayatollahs (holy men) and mullahs (priests), were seen as the embodiment of Iranian nationalism, integrity, and selflessness that would replace the corruption and hedonism of the shah's regime. The revolution occurred in late 1978 and early 1979 and, after a quick succession of caretaker governments, they were finally replaced by a government controlled by the Shi'ite leaders who installed a Shi'ite Islam state based on fundamentalist Islamic jurisprudence.

The impact of Shi'ism on women's rights in marriage and divorce in Iran is of interest. Under the shah, women gained the right to vote in 1963. The land-reform policies that were implemented during the 1960s had little effect on women since they were prohibited from getting land grants. The Family Protection Law (FPL) was passed in 1967 and amended in 1975. Before the law, in the 1960s, Iran had one of the highest divorce rates, compared to other countries (Aghajanian, 1986). The reason for this is that the common practice allowed husbands to divorce their wives with relative ease and whenever they decided to do so. The only requirement was the presence of two male witnesses to hear the husband say *talagh* (I divorce you).

The 1967 law allowed divorce only through legal procedures. The FPL called for disputes between married persons to be filed in court, and recognized divorce by mutual consent and divorce by judicial decree through annulment or dissolution. It gave women the right to divorce under special circumstances. The impact of the new law was a depressive effect on the rate of divorce that was nearly halved from 1.0 per thousand population in 1965 to 0.6 in both 1970 and 1975. Aghajanian (1986) attributes this decline in part to the slowness of the judicial process and the requirement that Iranian husbands had to produce evidence to justify a divorce.

The Family Protection Court was replaced with a Special Civil Court based on Islamic laws. This court is anchored by the Islamic belief that to protect a family from instability and divorce an Islamic judge first tries to reconcile the divorcing couple. Mutually consenting couples who seek divorce can obtain it by simply registering their divorce before two witnesses at a notary-public office. Aghajanian (1986) observes that the ease of divorce under this new law can be abused in the case of "mutually consenting" couples. The Iranian family is patriarchal, and women may be forced to consent. All sorts of pressures may be used. Coercion may also be used to affect the wife's "consent" to forfeit her property (dowry). "This practice has such a long tradition in the Iranian society that there is a saying that a man may persist in annoying his wife so that she says: 'Get my *Mahr* (dowry) and free my life'" (Aghajanian, 1986:751).

The rate of divorce has been rising in Iran since 1981. Aghajanian (1986) attributes this rise to a number of factors that include the legal and social changes introduced in Iran since the revolution, increasing unemployment and unfavorable economic conditions, and the ongoing war with Iraq. Among the legal changes was the reduction of the minimum age for marriage of females from 18 to 13 (18 for males). In accordance with Shi'ite ideology, there was strong encouragement for early marriage and having children. The number of marriages increased from 184,000 in 1979 to 280,000 only one year later (Aghajanian, 1986). Aghajanian believes that the lack of preparation for family responsibilities of many of these young couples accounts for the rise in divorce. In addition, the increasing number of remarriages of war widows, some into polygynous marriages, may also account for this rise in divorce.

Family instability and resultant divorce is seen by Aghajanian (1986) particularly to affect urban middle-class families. These people have had to make major readjustments to the Islamic value system. Educated women have had to accommodate themselves to the new values and lifestyles of fundamentalist Islam. This is seen as a major source of conflict in urban middle-class families and has contributed to marital tension and divorce. Shahla Haeri (1993), an anthropologist with expertise on Islamic law, reports that in the 1980s the most frequent complaint voiced by women was of their husband's plural marriages or her own unfair divorce. In one case cited, a woman who complained about her husband's multiple wives was told by the Islamic court that polygamy was a man's right: "He can have ten wives if he can support them financially; four permanently and the rest temporarily" (in Haeri, 1993). In general, Aghajanian (1986) sees a deterioration in the psychological and economic conditions of divorced women in Iran. Indeed, the history of the Iranian revolution has had serious negative consequences for women and their civil rights.

In 1985-1986, the Islamic revolutionary regime articulated a new set of directives known as the "conditions at the time of marriage contract." A set of twelve conditions were proposed to be included in the marriage contract that must be read and signed by both the husband and wife to become effective. The first condition was the most controversial. It reads: "In a marriage contract if divorce is requested by the wife, and if in the court's judgment the request for divorce is not due to her ill temper and behavior, then the husband is required to pay her up to half of his income earned during the time they have been married together, or something equivalent to it as deemed appropriate by the court" (quoted in Haeri, 1993:192).

Haeri comments that this condition stipulates that divorce must not come from a wife. In those circumstances when it does, the wife receives no alimony and must even pay something to her husband to secure her release from the marriage. This condition also asserts that the divorce must not be because of her "ill temper and behavior." This of course is always a subjective opinion. In those circumstances where a wife "qualifies" for divorce, she is entitled to receive up to half her husband's income earned during their married life at the court's discretion. At face value, the conditions set forth in this marriage contract are designed to improve the status of women and change aspects of the marital arrangement. However, in practice, the Islamic courts burdened the process with qualifications and conditions and did not fully explain the contractual process. Further, there was no incentive for men to sign the contract, because many women would marry without the contract. This factor, combined with the ambivalence of leading clerics on how the process should be implemented and whether women should have an active role in negotiating on their own behalf has led these directives to fall somewhat into a limbo stage.

Finally, in replacing the shah's FPL, the new directives removed the issue of child custody from negotiation. Based on traditional Shi'ite Islamic law, custody of boys over 2 years of age and of girls over 7 years of age automatically goes to the father. Patrilineal descent is also followed in cases of husband's absence or death; his father assumes legal responsibility over the children. It is only in cases where both the father and paternal grandfather are absent does the wife have custody rights. Haeri concludes: "Fear of separation from their children keeps many women in bad marriages and prohibits them from initiating a divorce" (Haeri, 1993:193).

The aftermath of the Iranian revolution has seen a continuous policy in which women's rights won under the shah's monarchy have been abolished by the Shi'ite government. From the inception of the Khomeini government, an anti-feminist campaign was conducted. In media campaigns just before and after the revolution, attacks were made on women who were active in the overthrow of the shah but who were against Shi'ite fundamentalism. They were accused of immorality, of weakening family ties, and of sexual misconduct. Pictures of women in bathing suits were used to support charges of prostitution against women working in the government bureaucracy. The goal was to belittle and discredit women leaders (Afkami, 1984).

Since the 1979 revolution, a massive purge of female workers has been implemented. Women's participation in agriculture, engineering, metallurgy, chemistry, computer programming, accounting, and commerce were curtailed. Their services were terminated with either some financial compensation or a simple dismissal. The Iran-Iraq War and its consequent male-labor shortage, however, allowed many women to return temporally to the labor market. However, the underlying belief of the Islamic fundamentalist is "to define woman's role and function in terms of the 'rights' and privileges of men; accordingly, the clerics-turned-bureaucrats who administer goods and services evaluate women's capacities for participating in the job market in relation to their responsibilities towards their husbands and children, their traditional household duties, and their influence on men" (Haeri, 1993:194).

In March 1979, more than 8,000 women marched in protest—under the slogan "In the dawn of freedom, there is no freedom"—of the Khomeini's fundamentalist policies (Morgan, 1984b). Similar demonstrations occurred in other major Iranian cities. However, Shi'ite activists countered by attacking and stoning these marchers. More repressive practices quickly followed. In 1981, women were banned from most sports events. In April 1983, veiling was made compulsory for women. In June 1981, fifty schoolgirls were shot and thousands were arrested for their "counterrevolutionary" or "anti-Islamic" activity. Morgan cites reports that by 1983 more than 20,000 women had been executed, including pregnant and elderly women and young girls.

In December 1984, John Kifner (1984), chief of the *New York Times* bureau in Beirut, Lebanon, visited Iran. He gave us a rare glimpse of life under the Khomeini government. The following passage is indicative of some of these changes in everyday life:

> Islamic virtue reigns in every aspect of public life. Alcohol is strictly forbidden, of course, and every woman on the street wears either the traditional black *chador*, a cloth wrapping that must be grasped with hands and teeth to keep it in place, or the more practical *hijab*, a dark scarf pulled over the forehead, a baggy, dark smock and loose trousers. Indeed, the Government seems obsessed by sex. *Time, Newsweek* and other Western publications are regularly available, but a Government functionary goes through them first, carefully inking over with felt pen all but the face in any woman's picture, particularly in the cases of the starlets in the newsmaker sections . . . An Islamic skiing garment has been designed, at some cost in wind resistance, for women who want to try the snow at the ski resorts in the Elburz mountains—separate slopes, of course—and a solid fence is being constructed down the middle of the beach along the Caspian Sea for segregated bathing . . .
>
> . . . there are patrols of Islamic enforcers in white Nissan jeeps who can grab a woman off the streets if they do not like her garb—perhaps her scarf is set too far back, showing a fringe of hair—and carry her off to Evin prison, where she is treated as a prostitute.
>
> Of the untidy alliance that opposed the Shah—Westernized intellectuals, leftist students educated abroad, disaffected government officials and technocrats, traditionalist merchants of the powerful bazaar, slum dwellers of south Teheran and the militant fundamentalist mullahs—it is the clergy who have survived and triumphed. (Kifner, 1984:47, 48, 52)

In the United States

Paul H. Jacobsen (1959), in his much cited work on American divorce patterns from 1860 to 1956, reports that at about the time of the Civil War (1860-1864), the divorce rate per 1,000 of existing marriages was 1.2. By the turn of the century (1900-1904), the rate had risen to 4.2, and twenty-five years later (1925-1929), the rate climbed to 7.6. Through the Depression years of the 1930s, the rate stayed relatively stable; but, near the end of World War II and the postwar 1940s, the rate hit a high of 13.7, which was not reached again until the 1970s. The high rates reached during the 1940s can be seen as an aftermath of a stressful period when many marriages deteriorated. The divorce rate declined steadily through the 1950s until the end of that decade, at which time the rate (9.4) reached approximately the same level as that for 1940. However, between 1960 and a peak in 1979 the divorce rate had dramatically risen (U.S. National Center for Health Statistics, 1990). It more than doubled in that twenty-year span from 9.2 divorces per 1,000 married women age 15 and older in 1960 to 22.8 divorces by the end of the 1979. The renowned demographer Paul C. Glick (1990) observes that about one-half of the marriages of persons now in their thirties are likely to end in divorce, or already have done so.

The annual divorce rate published by the National Center of Health Statistics (NCHS) indicates that the divorce rate has leveled off after showing a steep rise between 1966 and 1976 (Saluter, 1983). Paul C. Glick and Sung-Ling Lin (1986) corroborate this finding in their own analysis of vital statistics by NCHS, the Census Bureau's data and Current Population Surveys. Their study, in fact, indicates that the level during the early 1980s was slightly below the peaks reached in 1979 and 1981. By the end of 1980s the divorce rate dropped to 20.7, lower than it had been since 1975. Glick and Lin share the belief of Theodore Kemper (1983) that the leveling, and possible slight decline in the number of divorces, may reflect the trend toward lower remarriage rates, which would lower the pool of eligibles for redivorce. Also, the rising age at marriage and the presumed maturity of young adults in their choice of marriage partners and a growing concern or fear with the consequences of divorce are all seen as possible indicators for the stability of divorce rates, albeit high rates, for the immediate future. The following discussion examines why the divorce rate is so much higher today than it was in the past.

The rise in the divorce rate in the United States can best be seen by relating it to other family and social changes. Probably the most important change is the relation of the family to the economic process. In earlier times, the family had greater economic self-sufficiency. Both men and women were involved in the economic process. Men worked in an agricultural and hunting setting to produce food, clothing materials, and other economic necessities. Women's work was interdependent with that of the men. In addition to domestic household and child-rearing activities, women processed the food, made the clothing, and assisted the men whenever needed. In situations where domestic industry prevailed, the home served as a production unit, with all family members involved in labor participation. The result was an economic interdependence that often translated into an emotional interdependence as well.

With technological development, all this has changed. Domestic activities, once exclusively the province of women, were taken over by outside institutions. The manufacturing of clothing and many aspects of food processing and production moved outside the home to commercial establishments. The husband became a wage earner, and work became separated from domestic activities. The family became more a center of consumption than of production.

A second major change that has affected marital relationships has been the urbanization and increased geographical mobility of the American population. This has effectively diminished the controls and sanctions of the community and religious institutions over family members and their treatment of each other. As previously observed, the family was once integrally tied to the community. The community exerted pressure and control over family members. The family's openness to community scrutiny assured the conformity of the family to community standards. Community influence was enhanced by religious institutions that through church religious and secular activities for all members of the family tied the family even more tightly to the community. The church served as a reinforcer of the parental-authority structure and imposed prescribed attitude and role patterns to govern the relationship between husband and wife and between parents and children. Collective religious ritual and family religious and secular devotions and rituals reinforced the ideology on the sanctity of marriage and the abhorrence of divorce. In essence, then, there may be some truth to the adage that "the family that prays together, stays together."

These changes interacted with the changes occurring in family ideology—that is the new emphasis on the independence and the privatization of the nuclear family. New marital orientations and expectations developed that sought maximum and almost exclusive personal and emotional involvements within the nuclear family. The husband and the wife became dependent on each other for their emotional gratification and allowed few external sources of additional support—unlike the earlier period when marital solidarity and interdependence were tied to an interdependent familial economy. However, the new economic system does not foster such interdependence. The development of specialized services in an industrialized economy permits one to purchase many domestic goods and services, such as clothing, laundry services, prepared foods, and housing. The wife finds increased opportunities to enter the labor force and thus has obtained self-supporting economic options.

The increasing economic independence of women allows them greater opportunity to dissolve unsatisfactory marriages. Ross and Sawhill in 1975 and later Greenstein in 1990 observed that as the wife's earnings increased, so did the likelihood that her marriage would end in divorce. One may interpret this finding to mean that occupational involvement takes too much time away from a woman's domestic and marital life or that the woman sought employment in preparation for divorce. A more likely and plausible explanation, however, is that financial security gives her the options to pursue more satisfactory possibilities than remaining in an unhappy marriage. I would argue, then, that part of the explanation for the lower divorce rates of several decades ago was that the great majority of women were financially dependent on their husbands and thus did not have the financial independence to leave them. Their increased involvement in the labor force has led to the removal of this economic barrier to divorce.

Taken together, all the above-mentioned factors lead to a highly unstable situation. Unrealistic or hard-to-satisfy expectations are placed on the marital relationship. Marriage is expected to lead to the exclusive attainment and fulfillment of an individual's affectional, personal, and communal needs. When it proves incapable of meeting those needs, marital unhappiness and often divorce occur. The increased independence of men and women combined with the lessened stigma attached to divorce and the possibilities of remarriage help account for the rise in the divorce rate. In sum, the rising divorce rate is an indication that, for an increasing number of people, divorce with all its future unknown uncertainties is a preferable option to continuing in a marriage relationship that has proved debilitating and unsatisfactory.

A more detailed examination of the implications of marital, family, and social changes on American divorce and remarriage structures and processes follows. It begins by looking at how these changes are reflected in American divorce laws. Attention centers on an analysis of no-fault divorce laws and the adjudication of child custody. Then there is an examination of the single-parent household and the effects of divorce on children follows. A discussion of remarriage concludes the chapter.

Legal Aspects of American Divorce

No-Fault.   Laws governing divorce reflect the society's definition of marriage, provide the parameters for appropriate marriage behavior, and point out the reciprocal rights and obligations of marriage partners (Weitzman and Dixon, 1980). Further, divorce laws also define the continued obligations that the formerly married couple have to each other after divorce: "One can generally examine the way a society defines marriage by examining its provisions for divorce, for it is at the point of divorce that a society has the opportunity to reward the marital behavior it approves of, and to punish spouses who have violated its norms" (Weitzman and Dixon, 1980:355). A study of changing divorce laws will reflect social changes in family patterns. For this reason, in this section I will examine no-fault divorce laws to demonstrate how "this new legislation seeks to alter the definition of marriage, the relationship between husbands and wives, and the economic and social obligations of former spouses to each other and to their children after divorce" (1980:354).

Prior to no-fault divorce in America, divorce laws followed Anglo-American legal tradition. Divorce was cast in the traditional common-law model of an adversary procedure. The plaintiff's success depended on proving defendant's fault. Both parties were assumed to be antagonists and were expected to be at odds and were expected to bring forth all the relevant facts to be assessed by the judge in reaching his or her verdict.

No-fault divorce laws are based on a new concept of marital dissolution. The first such law in the United States, the Family Law Act, was passed in 1970 by the California legislature. The suggested procedure begins with a neutral petition—"In re the marriage of John and Jane Doe" rather than "*Doe vs. Doe*" requesting the family court to inquire into the continuance of the marriage.

The California law abolished completely any requirement of fault as the basis to dissolve the marriage. One spouse is not required to bring charges against the other nor is evidence needed of misconduct. Under traditional divorce laws, the division of property and the allocation of alimony payments are determined under the concept of fault. Property and support are given to the judged "innocent party" as a reward extracted from the "guilty party" as punishment. The no-fault law gives legal recognition to "marital breakdown" as a sufficient justification for divorce. Indeed, the Californian legislation eliminated the term *divorce* replacing it with the phrase, *dissolution of marriage*. The dissolution is granted on the basis of *irreconcilable differences* that have caused the irremediable breakdown of the marriage. Under the no-fault law, property is substantially divided equally, and alimony is based on the duration of the marriage, the needs of each party, and their respective earning ability.

By 1977, provisions for no-fault divorce existed in all but three states. Its popularity reflects the increased recognition that the cause for the marital dissolution is usually a result of a number of factors and is shared by both partners. Carter and Glick pointed out the positive aspects of no-fault divorce laws: "No-fault divorce procedures avoid exploring and assessing blame and concentrate on dissolving the marriage and tidying up the inevitable problems—responsibility for the care of the children (there still are children involved in the majority of divorce cases despite the decline in the birth rate), financial support of children, division of jointly owned property, and spousal support (alimony) if this seems indicated" (1976:458). The question of blame is now considered irrelevant and the hope is that the bitterness of the divorce proceedings will be lessened.

In one of the early studies of no-fault divorce, Weitzman and Dixon (1980) argued that no-fault divorce reflects changes in the traditional view of legal marriage. By eliminating the fault-based grounds for divorce and the adversary process, the then new law recognized the more contemporary view that frequently both parties are responsible for the breakdown of the marriage. Further, the law recognized that the divorce procedure often aggravated the situation by forcing the potentially amicable individuals to become antagonists.

No-fault divorce laws advocate that the financial aspects of marital dissolution are to be based on equity, equality, and economic need rather than on fault- or gender-based role assignments. Alimony is also to be based on the respective spouses economic circumstances and on the principle of social equality, not on the basis of guilt or innocence. No longer can alimony be awarded to the "injured party," regardless of that person's financial needs. No-fault sought to reflect the changing circumstances of women and their increased participation in the labor force. By so doing, it encouraged women to become self-supporting and removed the expectation that husbands have to continue support of wives throughout their lives. Although it considered custodial care for children, the thrust of the law was on financial criteria. California judges were directed to consider the following in setting alimony: "the circumstances of the respective parties, including the duration of the marriage, and the ability of the supported spouse to engage in gainful employment without interfering with the interests of the children of the parties in the custody of each spouse" (California Civil Code 4801, cited in Weitzman and Dixon, 1980:363).

Weitzman and Dixon (1980) saw the overall impact of no-fault legislation was its redefinition of the traditional marital responsibilities of men and women by instituting a new norm of equality between the sexes. No longer were husbands to be designated as the head of the household and solely responsible for support, nor were wives alone obligated to domestic household activities and child rearing. Gender-neutral obligations, which fell equally on husband and wife, were institutionalized. These changes were reflected in the new considerations for alimony allocation. In addition, the division of property was to be done on an equal basis. Finally, child-support expectations and the standards for child custody reflected the new equality criteria of no-fault divorce legislation. Both father and mother were equally responsible for financial support of their children after divorce. Mothers were no longer automatically given custody of the child; rather, a sex-neutral standard instructed judges to award custody in the "best interests of the child."

In conclusion, Weitzman and Dixon (1980), while praising the changes in divorce legislation, raised one important caveat. They saw the law as reflecting idealized gains for women in social, occupation, and economic areas; gains toward equality that may, in fact, not reflect women's actual conditions and circumstances. This could have extremely detrimental effects on women's ability for self-sufficiency after divorce.

And, as we shall see in the next section, this negative effect has occurred. No-fault divorce has been a major factor in the "feminization of poverty" and the downward mobility of divorced women and children.

No-Fault Divorce, Downward Mobility, and the Feminization of Poverty: Unexpected Consequences

By 1985, the new no-fault divorce laws had been adopted in some form by every state except Illinois and South Dakota. The new laws were designed to reduce accusation, acrimony, and manufactured marital misconduct as the necessary grounds for divorce. They sought to base monetary awards on need and ability to pay rather than treating them as rewards on punishments for alleged sins. They were intended to correct an outmoded legal code that was seen as degrading and humiliating to all parties involved in the divorce process and often unfair in the outcome. However, an unintended consequence is that they may help undermine the very conceptualization of marriage, and husbands' and wives' roles in marriage. This is the provocative view Lenore J. Weitzman (1985), one of this country's leading divorce researchers, reached in her provocative book, *The Divorce Revolution.*

Weitzman (1985)—after studying the results of these laws and focusing her attention mostly on California, which initiated the first no-fault, no-consent statute fifteen years earlier—finds "unexpected," "unfortunate," and "unintended" social and economic consequences for women and children in America. Her research is based largely on an analysis of 2,500 California court cases, supplemented by interviews of hundreds of recently divorced men and women as well as lawyers and judges in Los Angeles and San Francisco.

Weitzman's major finding is that under no-fault divorce, divorced women and their children are becoming a new underclass. Divorced women are often impoverished by no-fault because courts, in dividing property, interpret "equality" at divorce by disregarding the economic inequalities created during marriage. Further, the equal division of property often forces women to sell their homes to divide what usually constitutes the couple's only real property. Less tangible, and often more valuable, the husband's property and assets such as education, professional licenses, career advancements, pensions, and health insurance are often not taken into account in court decisions. As a consequence, rather than alleviating the injustice, no-fault exacerbates it.

Divorce settlements also assume self-sufficiency for both husband and wife as soon as possible (usually in about two years). While this is a laudable goal, Weitzman points out that as our society is currently structured, it is naive, to say the least, to assume that women who may have been out of work for many years devoting full attention to child rearing can become self-sufficient that quickly.

The problem is compounded by a child-support system that is often inadequate, unpaid, and uncollectible. Weitzman reports that 60 to 80 percent of all fathers, regardless of social class, do not comply with court orders. Adding to the problems is that no-fault divorce continues to follow the old-law divorce patterns with 90 percent of custodial parents being women. But some gender-neutral provisions now force women to fight for what used to be their custodial right. The result of these provisions is that to win custodial rights, women often are forced to bargain away support.

Terry Arendell (1986), in a powerful ethnography, documents the resultant downward mobility in her study of sixty divorced women and their children. These women often experienced inadequate levels of personal and child support from divorced husbands, social assistance, and other governmental programs. The vast majority of women spoke of recurring struggles with depression and despair. Nearly half of them contemplated suicide; but it was their concern for their children that gave these women the strongest incentive to continue the struggle. The worst pain came from observing the effects of sudden economic hardship on their children. Most expressed feelings of entrapment and had little hope for a better future.

Weitzman argues that no-fault divorce laws reflect the larger cultural themes of individualism, personal fulfillment, and self-sufficiency. These new norms imply that neither spouse should invest too much in marriage or place marriage above self-interest. She alludes to Lawrence Stone's term *affective individualism,* which historically gave rise to the emotional closeness between nuclear-family members as well as to a greater appreciation for the individuality of each member. At the same time, this norm helped develop and strengthen the husband-wife bond at the expense of extended-kinship contacts and involvements. Now, the strength of the husband-wife unit, the conjugal family, is declining as values of "pure" individualism are emerging. The rise in divorce rates and the new no-fault divorce laws reflect this evolution of individualism and the importance of personal primacy.

This contemporary version of individualistic norms implies a new view of marriage that sees marriage as a means of serving individual needs. It replaces the traditional dictum that individuals should submerge their personal desires whenever they conflict with the "good of the family." Norms of reciprocity and mutual dependency are challenged: "If men are no longer solely responsible for support, and if women are no longer responsible for homemaking and child care, then neither sex can count as much on the other for support or services" (Weitzman, 1985:375). The implications of Weitzman's important study are clear. For women who wish to devote themselves to homemaking and child rearing, they may be pursuing a perilous and foolhardy course. They may find themselves impoverished and abandoned by a society that no longer shares their priorities or values their skills. Indeed, this is the implication of the new divorce laws.

The far-reaching consequence of the new divorce laws is that marriage is likely to become increasingly less central to the lives of individual men and women. Weitzman believes that traditional family law gave privileged status to marriage. It placed protections and restrictions on its inception and dissolution. These laws reinforced the importance of marriage, and encouraged husbands and wives to invest in and to make marriage the center of their lives. In contrast, the new laws are based on belief in absolute individualism and reflect the values of the "Me Decade." They discourage the conceptualization of marriage as a shared partnership investment and encourage both husbands and wives to pursue individual self-fulfillment. The result, in Weitzman's view is that "As more men and women follow the apparent mandate of the new laws, it seems reasonable to predict that marriage itself will lose further ground" (1985:376).

Child Custody

It is most interesting to note that cross-culturally where patrilineal descent is the prevalent form of kinship descent systems, children remain in the father's family when a marriage dissolves. However, as William Goode observes, child custody is not the equivalent of child care:

> . . . East or West, men have never been willing to take on the daily tasks of child-care. They wanted—and perhaps still want—to have custody as long as they did not have to take care of the children. They were willing to demand formal custody only as long as the women in their extended kin (aunts, sisters, mothers, sisters-in-law, and so on) would accept the burden. Moreover, since the importance of the *lineage* continues to decline, even the ideological value of custody decreases. (1993:278)

A father waits with his twin daughters just an hour before a probate judge will take the girls away from their divorced parents and place them in the custody of the Massachusetts Department of Social Services.

In this section I will investigate another legal change regarding divorce in the United States. It involves decisions of which parent should be given custody of children. Robert S. Weiss (1979b) reported that in the 1970s mothers were awarded legal custody of children in about 90 percent of American divorce cases. However, in recent years there has been an increased recognition of fathers' rights regarding custody. It reflects a recognition of the changing role of American fathers. This change has been popularized in the 1980 Oscar-winning motion picture *Kramer vs. Kramer.* Furstenberg and Cherlin (1991) citing governmental statistics report that there has been an increase in the number of children who were in custody of their fathers from 8.8 percent to 11.4 from 1981 to 1986. In addition, increasingly courts were beginning to view joint custody as another legal option. By 1988, thirty-three states had joint custody laws (Freed and Walker, 1988). To understand the basis for custody adjudication decisions, a brief review of the historical changes in parental roles and their relationship to the judicial principle of "best interest" is necessary.

Weiss (1979b) points out that courts have historically been governed by the "best interests" principle in awarding custody of children. Judges are supposed to treat as irrelevant the issue of which parent was at "fault" in the divorce; rather, their sole concern is to ascertain which parent would best serve to maximize the children's future well-being and welfare. Prior to the mid-nineteenth century, fathers were judged as the parent who could best take care of and educate the child. Women were thought to be too dependent on men, whether it was their fathers, husbands, or related kin. Since they too needed the protection of men, the courts judged them as not being the parent best able to provide for the children.

Beginning in the mid-nineteenth century, there was a change in judicial decisions in custody awards, which became almost standard by the end of the century. Mothers came to be seen as better able to serve the child's "best interests." This change reflected the changing popular belief about the aims of the family and the raising of children. With increased industrialization, fathers withdrew from taking an active role in domestic matters, including child care, and they devoted more of their attention to earning a living outside the home. This movement away from domestic-oriented economic involvements to commerce and factories also affected children. They were gradually removed from the workforce and were no longer economic assets. The family household began to be viewed in Christopher Lasch's eloquence as a "haven in a heartless world" (1977a). The home was designed to protect the child from the incursions of a changing and threatening outside world. The family was viewed as a place where children should be nurtured and protected, and, increasingly, it was the mother who was considered the preferred parent to do this.

In the twentieth century, this pattern continued. It reached its culmination in the post-World War II period of the 1950s and 1960s. The affluence and materialism of this era, embodied in the development of middle-class suburbia, heightened the division between husband-father and wife-mother. The feminine mystique and the motherhood myth dominated—only the mother was deemed as the appropriate parent and was thus given almost complete responsibility for child rearing. The total responsibility for child care carries over to divorce. The legal assumption regarding the mother's natural superiority in parenting is reflected in custodial dispositions. As mentioned earlier, women are awarded custody in over 90 percent of divorce cases.

Lenore Weitzman (1977) has made some interesting observations on the implications of courts' automatically granting custody to the mother. Although it is true that most divorcing women want custody of their children, this practice also tends to reinforce the women's social role as housewife and mother. It also frequently reinforces women's dependency on their husbands for support. Further, this judicial preference may coerce women to accept custody even if they do not wish to do so. They may bow to social pressures and be subject to feelings of deviance and guilt.

Fathers are also subjected to discrimination by this practice. They are often legally advised of the futility of contesting custody, particularly in the case of young children. The burden of proof is on them, either to document the unfitness of the mother or to show that they could do a qualitatively better job of parenting. In those cases where the father could be the better parent, both his interests and the "best interests" of the child are denied.

In recent years, the increased recognition of the changing role of fathers has begun to influence the judicial decision-making process of custodial award. In addition, inherent contradictions in the principle of "best interests" has also led to a reevaluation of the practice of automatically giving mothers custody of the children. Let us look at each of these changes in turn.

With the end of the period of prosperity of the 1950s and 1960s, there was a growing disenchantment with family-role segregation, which extended from the end of the 1960s on through the 1970s. The feminist movement began to articulate fully women's dissatisfaction with their confinement to the home and exclusive parenthood. In addition, fathers were reevaluating their role involvements. An increasing number of them began to express doubts about lives characterized by an almost total involvement in occupational careers and almost complete withdrawal from family matters, including the raising of children. Kelin E. Gersick (1979) expressed these changes this way:

> In recent years the role of the American father has been enjoying a resurgence. Several factors may be involved: a decrease in the average man's working hours and resulting increase in leisure time; the woman's dissatisfaction with her role limitations and movement toward greater economic and social flexibility; and the spreading disenchantment with material acquisition as the exclusive measure of the good life, along with the espousal of close relationships as a principal measure of happiness. Whatever the reasons, there appears to be a recent upswing in father's involvement in their families. (Gersick, 1979:307)

Additional factors that became particularly apparent in the 1980s included the change in the economic fortunes of Americans during inflation and recession became a way of life. This increased the economic necessity for women to work. The transition of women into the labor force was made smoother as a result of the women's movement, which persuaded most men and women of the legitimacy of women's work. This led to the growth of dual-income families with more and more households composed of working parents. There was some movement to share domestic involvements and child care. These changes have played a contributory role in the reassessment by judicial court systems on the adjudication of custody of children when parents separate.

Robert S. Weiss (1979a) observes that criticism of the legal presumption in favor of the mother began to appear in the 1960s, and by the early 1970s some state statutes that had required mothers be preferred had been repealed. In 1973 the bellwether state of California repealed such a statute and replaced it with the "best interests" principle. The growing sensitivity to sexual discrimination has also played a contributing role in these changes. One way that this has been shown is in the increased debunking of the belief in the natural superiority of women in parenting. It is now argued in several states that a presumption in favor of the mother constitutes unfair discrimination owing to sex and deprives the father of his right to equal protection by the law (Weiss, 1979a:327). Weiss mentions a second element contributing to this change, which ties in with the arguments against job discrimination because of gender. He says that "defenders of fathers' rights pointed out that if men are to have no advantage over women in the competition for jobs, and if most single mothers can be expected to work, then women should not be seen as having more right to the children: 'A man can hire a babysitter as well as a woman'" (Weiss, 1979a:327).

In summary, changes in divorce and custody laws were designed to reduce the traumas associated with divorce. In the previous section I discussed how the implications of no-fault divorce often meant the downward mobility for women. In the next section I will discuss children's adjustment after divorce.

The Effects of Divorce on Children

"'What will happen to me if anything goes wrong, if Mommy dies or Daddy dies, if Daddy leaves Mommy or Mommy leaves Daddy?'" (Mead, 1970a:113). This question has particular meaning to American children since our society stresses the importance of parents in raising children. Father's kin or mother's kin, including the respective grandparents, have no legal responsibility for children as long as the parents are alive. Further, cultural norms emphasize parental independence and freedom from extended-family involvements in child rearing. In contrast, the larger extended family, or clan, which still exists in many societies, has formally defined rights, duties, and obligations over each member of the family grouping, including children. For such children, the question of death, divorce, or separation of their own parents is less problematic than in the American situation. Extensive kinship ties provide sufficient sources of intergenerational involvement so that marital disruption or dissolution has relatively minimal impact on children's psychological well-being. In the contemporary United States, these wider kinship networks are lacking at a time when many families are dissolving because of divorce. This fact is complicated by the lack of sufficient preparation or the development of alternatives for the child's psychological dependence on his or her parents. Margaret Mead addresses herself to this anomaly:

> We have constructed a family system which depends upon fidelity, lifelong monogamy, and the survival of both parents. But we have never made adequate social provision for the security and identity of the children if that marriage is broken, as it so often was in the past by death or desertion, and as it so often is in the present by death or divorce. We have saddled ourselves with a system that won't work. (Mead, 1970a:115)

From 1900 to 1980, the proportion of children affected by marital disruption has been between 25 and 30 percent of the total population of children under the age of 18 (Bane, 1979). There has been a change, however, in the dominant cause of the disruption. At the turn of the century, the ratio of disruption by death was much higher than disruption by divorce and long-term separation. By 1980, the ratio was reversed; divorce affected more children, particularly at an earlier age, than did the death of a parent. The number of children involved in divorces has risen sharply since the 1950s. In 1955, 348,000 children under 18 years of age were involved in divorce cases (National Center for Health Statistics, 1977, 1978). The figure almost doubled by 1965 to 630,000. In 1972, for the first time, more than 1 million children were annually affected by divorce. This figure has remained relatively stable through the 1970s but started to rise again by the end of the decade. In the 1980s the figure began a slight decline, which continues to the present. Yet, today, more than 1 million children under the age of 18 experience the divorce of their parents each year (U.S. Bureau of the Census, 1992b).

Mary Jo Bane (1979) foresaw the negative economic effects of marital disruption that would plague divorced women and their children through the 1980s and 1990s. During the years that children will be living in a single-parent household, financial resources will be limited. This results from the following causes: the greater prevalence of divorce among low-income families; irregular and low levels of alimony, child support, and public assistance; fewer adult wage earners in the family; fewer opportunities for females heading the household to find employment; and the lower wages paid women as compared to men (Bane, 1979:283).

The recitation of statistics and the delineation of the economic difficulties accompanying divorce cannot reveal the potentially negative effects on children's psychological well-being. For the parents involved, divorce often produces anger and a sense of failure. For children it raises issues of conflicting loyalties and it necessitates their readjustment from a two-parent family to a single-parent household. The popular as well as academic impression is that divorce contributes to the development of children's psychological disorganization and has had other ill effects including low academic achievement, juvenile delinquency, and other social and emotional adjustment problems. Others are of the opinion that the divorce may actually benefit the child if it would result in the removal of the everyday experience of an unhappy marriage characterized by conflict, verbal quarrelling, and possible violence. Some of the factors that may help mitigate the impact of divorce on children include the beneficial effects of a good parent-child relationship, a supportive network of friends and relatives, and an ex-husband who continues to be supportive toward his family (Longfellow, 1979).

Psychologist Judith Wallerstein has been in the forefront of the investigation of the psychological consequences of divorce on children. Beginning in 1971, she began a study of sixty middle-class families going through the divorce process. Wallerstein and Blakeslee (1989) report on the longitudinal study of 131 children of these divorced parents in their seminal book *Second Chances*. They found that the effects of divorce were long-lasting and interfered with normal social and emotional development for a significant number of children. Wallerstein and Blakeslee report that divorce had a long-term negative "sleeper" effect; it impacted on the children when they matured into adulthood.

McLanahan and Bumpass (1988) using national survey research data similarly found that evidence among women whose parents had divorced were more likely to marry young, bear children before marriage, and then eventually divorce. In a later study, McLanahan and Sandefur (1994) analyzed four national surveys and found that low income and declines in income are significant contributory factors for these undesirable outcomes. The sociologist Paul R. Amato, in a review of the literature, reports that "children who experience parental divorce, compared with children in continuously intact two-parent families, exhibit more conduct problems, more symptoms of psychological maladjustment, lower economic achievement, more social difficulties and poorer self concepts" (1994:143).

In comparison to European Americans, Amato (1994) found that African American adults were affected less by parental divorce. He reasons that the strength of extended kin relations may result in more support for African American mothers than for their white counterparts. The difference may also be related to the fact that divorce is more common and more accepted among African Americans. Further, African Americans who face major structural barriers as it is, may not experience any additional disadvantage by growing up in a divorced single-parent household.

SINGLE PARENTHOOD

In the end of the 1970s sociologist began to see that single parenthood was becoming more common in our society. Paul C. Glick and Arthur J. Norton (1979), in their review of governmental statistics, report that the proportion of children living with one parent has more than doubled from 1960 to 1978. By 1978, a little more than 5.5 million American families with children were headed by a single adult. This represents 19 percent of the 30 million families with children in the United States. Five years later, in 1983, there were almost 6 million children living with divorced parents in single-parent households. Most of these children lived with divorced mothers (U.S. Bureau of the Census, 1984a: Table D).

The total number of children living with one parent (as a result of death, divorce, separation, or parent never marrying) has more than doubled since 1970. In 1970, 7.4 million children under the age of 18 lived with a single parent. This was 11 percent of all children in that age group. By 1983, the number had risen to 13.7 million, an 85 percent increase. This comprised 22 percent of the population of children (Glick, 1984a). Ten years later, more than a quarter (27 percent) of all American children had experienced a single-parent household. The proportion of children in single-parent situations had shifted, with increased proportions living with a never-married parent than with a divorced parent (Saluter, 1994).

Alvin L. Schorr and Phyllis Moen (1980), citing early 1970s statistics, observe that the popular image of the conventional family—husband, wife, and children—is, in fact, a minority family form in the United States. Single parenthood, couples without children, and reconstituted families (remarrieds with and without children) represent 55 percent of American families; the conventional form accounts for only 45 percent of American families. (It should be noted that the dramatic decrease in the husband/wife/child(ren) form is in part explained by the aging of the population, i.e., more couples are in the empty nest stage as well as in the increases in single parent-hood and reconstituted families.)

In 1979, Mary Jo Bane estimated that nearly 30 percent of the children born around 1970 will experience parental divorce by the time they are 18. An additional 15 to 20 percent may live in a one-parent household because of death, long-term separa-tion, or birth to an unmarried mother. Together, then, 45 to 50 percent of the children born around 1970 will live for a period of time with a single parent. A startling change in the ratio of children living with a single-parent as a result of divorce as opposed to those living with a never-married parent has also occurred. In 1983, a child was twice as likely to live with a divorced parent than a never-married parent. Ten years later, the odds were almost equal (Saluter, 1994). Further, this parent, regardless of circum-stances, was most likely to be the mother. As pointed out earlier, mothers currently become the custodians of children in about 90 percent of all American divorces; and the percentage is roughly the same for mothers who never married.

Single-parent families are more likely to be found among the lower-income, lower-education, and lower-occupational-status population. While a majority of single-parent families are white, there are proportionally more single parents among African American and Latino populations. One common characteristic shared by many female-headed single-parent families is poverty. The mother, in the vast majority of cases, must provide for the child's care as well as be the principal, and—in the case of no employ-able older children—the only, wage earner in the family. Often this proves an impossi-ble task, with an appreciable number of such families falling into poverty. Single-parent families have lower average income than do two-parent families. Bureau of the Census figures report that 38 percent of children in divorced single-parent families live in poverty. The number rises to 66 percent of children in never-married single-parent families (Saluter, 1994). Ross and Sawhill, in their pioneer study of the problems of female-headed households, provide the following explanation of the situation:

> The inadequate incomes of most female-headed families stem from the loss of a male earner, the mother's continuing responsibility for the care of young children, and the inability of most women to earn enough to support a fami-ly. However, the loss of a male earner within the household need not mean the loss of all of the father's income. Alimony and child-support payments as well as more informal gifts of money and other items help to maintain women and children living on their own. But indications are that the flow of those private transfers is somewhat smaller than is commonly believed. They are certainly inadequate to the task of keeping many women and children out of poverty. (Ross and Sawhill, 1975:175)

Female-Headed Single-Parent Families

The female-headed single-parent family can be studied best within the larger context of the "proper" roles of the husband-father and wife-mother and the importance of the intact, or unbroken, family. Social scientists (see Brandwein, Brown, and Fox, 1974; Schorr and Moen, 1980) have pointed out that our society is dominated by the assumption that families headed by a single parent, particularly when that parent is a woman, are deviant and pathological. Such families are characterized as broken, disorganized, or disintegrated, rather than being recognized as a viable alternative family form. Rather than being seen as a solution to circumstances and examined in terms of their strengths, they are viewed negatively with emphasis on their alleged weaknesses and problems.

Similar to the simplifications and distortions of poverty-level families taken by culture-of-poverty advocates, depicting the single-parent family in these terms denies the realities of this family form and misrepresents it. This has led to biased governmental, employment, and social policies that have proved detrimental to single-parent families. Further, many separated and divorced women reacting to their stigmatized status have often incorporated the negative images into their own self-images. This can prove particularly disabling in their attempts to readjust their lives after separation and divorce. Thus taken together, a self-fulfilling prophecy can come into effect and thus limit the capabilities of the single-parent family. Let us see how this operates in more detail.

Our society has believed that men should be primarily involved in outside-the-home matters. Through such activities they dominate the economic resources of the family and are legitimated as the head and brains of the family. This situation forces women to be dependent on husbands, particularly when they are parents and society dictates that their appropriate roles are housewives and mothers. This dependency situation becomes even more problematic and acute if a woman is granted custody of the children after divorce. Far too often she does not have access to resources comparable to her husband's. Janet A. Kohen, Carol A. Brown, and Roslyn Feldberg (1979) make the following observations on this situation:

> If a couple divorces, the woman loses most of her right to the man's resources, but she also loses her personal dependence and obligations of service. She now stands in direct relationship to society as the head of her family. But male-dominated society neither recognizes a divorced woman's right to head a family nor makes available to her, as a woman, the necessary resources. The divorced mother has exchanged direct dependence on one man for general dependence on a male-dominated society. Employers, welfare officials, lawyers, judges, politicians, school authorities, doctors, even male relatives and neighbors, set the parameters of her ability to take on successfully the role of family head. (1979:229)

Economic discrimination particularly affects divorced mothers. The traditional view that the proper role for women is housework and child care has fostered the opinion that women are marginal workers and should be given only marginal jobs, which pay less, have less status, and are less secure than those given to men. The result is that women, regardless of marital status, do not earn the same salaries as men in comparable jobs. They also are found in more dead-end jobs that have little or no possibilities for promotion. The jobs are more likely to be nonmanagerial and nonadministrative. These biases and discrimination make it extremely difficult for women raising their children alone to support a family.

Inadequate, unreliable, and, when available, expensive child-care facilities complicate the divorced mother's situation. The scarcity of child-care facilities reflects society's values—that the only acceptable setting for the care of children is in the home and by the mother. Child-care facilities are viewed negatively; they can only hinder the psychological development of the child and thus they are deemed undesirable and unnecessary. Unfortunately, for single parents the absence of alternative child care prevents their full involvement in the labor force and limits them to marginal, part-time, or seasonal jobs. Such women often suffer severe economic hardships because far too frequently their insufficient earnings are not offset by other forms of child support. The child-support payments from the ex-husband are often inadequate, irregular, or nonexistent, as is welfare and assistance from governmental programs and social agencies. Ironically, then, the parent least able to support the family is often left with the major economic responsibility. The effects of this downward income mobility can be severe.

> Lowered income means not only a drop in consumption within the home, but often a change in housing to poorer accommodations in a poorer neighborhood. . . . Moving is itself a stress . . . in this case often compounded by problems of reduced personal safety, higher delinquency rates, and poorer schools. A rapid change in socioeconomic status is associated with anomie . . . adding to the problems of emotional support . . . Some of the correlation between multi-problem families and divorced parents has been explained in terms of lowered SES and poorer housing. (Brandwein, Brown, and Fox, 1974)

In our society, men are commonly depicted as the household member with the power and authority to command respect within the family and as the one who can act on behalf of the family in dealings with outside social agencies and institutions. The divorced mother may legally be the head of the family, but her family group is considered deviant because she and not a man heads it. Kohen, Brown, and Feldberg, in their study of thirty mothers who were divorced or separated from one to five years, report that intrusions that did not occur when these mothers were married occurred in their new status. These intrusions included "schools and hospitals ignoring their requests for their children, men attempting to break into the house, landlords refusing to rent to them, [and] their own parents interfering in their lives" (Kohen, Brown, and Feldberg, 1979:236). These researchers believe that such incidents provide indications of the lack of social legitimacy to females heading families. Additional evidence is the disproportionate number of divorced mothers who are confronted with discrimination by businesses, credit-granting institutions, and mortgage banks who, in effect, deny these women their head-of-household status.

The divorced mother's authority within the home can also be undermined by these patriarchal ideas. This is a difficult task because of the lack of external social institutions to provide such services. I have already described this factor in the discussion of child-care facilities. The same holds true for other institutions, such as schools and businesses, that in their independent demands on a single-parent mother, often require her to be in two places at the same time.

In addition, the cultural denial of the legitimacy of the female-headed family can affect both the women herself and her children. She is now required to assume both the mother and father roles within the family. Neither she nor her children may be ready to accept this amalgamation. However, research reported by Brandwein, Brown, and Fox (1974) show that women's ability to overcome this difficulty should not be underestimated. Likewise, Kohen, Brown, and Feldberg (1979) point out that their sample of divorced and separated mothers report that they developed increased feelings of mastery over their relationships with their children. They were also able to take on new responsibilities and perform unfamiliar tasks around the household and outside it—tasks that had been exclusively in the province of the husband-father before the separation or divorce. Finally, they developed more positive self-images and stronger self-concepts.

The future for female-headed single-parent families can improve if and when governmental and social policies provide adequate financial supports—either directly or by enforcing spouses' child-support agreements—as well as such services as child care and crisis intervention when needed. Finally, societal attitudes toward women must change to allow them to gain employment opportunities that would provide them with the financial security to take care of themselves and their families.

Teenage Mothers

Much media attention has been given to the rise in teenage pregnancy and parenthood. In a 1985 cover story, "Children Having Children," *Time* reports that four out of five of the more than one million American teenage girls who will become pregnant in the next year will be unmarried. Of this number, 30,000 are under the age of 15. Further, the estimate is that fully 40 percent of today's teenage girls will be pregnant at least once before the age of 20.

By the late 1980s there was a sharp upswing in teenage pregnancy and particularly among younger teens (Ahlburg and DeVita, 1992). The U.S. Bureau of the Census (1994a,b) reports that the births to never-married women increased 70 percent between 1980 and 1991. This was a jump from 20 percent to 30 percent of all births. Of these births, almost one-third are to never-married adolescents (U.S. Bureau of the Census, 1994a,b).

While about two-thirds of the teenage childbearing is to whites, minority teens are at greater risk of early parenthood (Ahlburg and DeVita, 1992). The birthrate for African American teens was 115 per 1,000 births compared to 47 births for white teenagers; nearly two and one-half times higher. For Latino teens the birthrate was 58. More than half (60 percent) of these teenagers did not finish high school.

A good many of them will eventually graduate and some will go on to college. Staples and Johnson (1993) in their assessment of African American teenage mothers reports that a decade later nearly 70 percent of them received a high school diploma, and at least 5 percent went on to college. Research by Frank Furstenberg and his colleagues (Furstenberg, Morgan, Moore, and Peterson, 1987) further refutes the notion that teenagers who become pregnant are simply looking for a welfare handout. In 1967 Furstenberg and his research team from the University of Pennsylvania inter-

A 15-year-old with her 5-month-old son, Seattle, Washington.

viewed a group of about 300 Baltimore black teenage mothers, then reinterviewed them five years later in 1972 and again in 1984. He found that during this seventeen-year period, only one-quarter of them were receiving welfare assistance. Most of them finished high school, got jobs, and improved their circumstances. However, even given these positive assessments of the future of teenage mothers, they still face the prospect of suffering long-term economic consequences because of their lower educational skill levels at the time they dropped out of school.

The patterns of teenage pregnancy found in the United States varies in comparison to the European and Japanese experience. The Alan Guttmacher Institute (a nonprofit research center in New York City), based on a thirty-seven-country study, concludes that the United States leads nearly all other developed nations in its incidence of pregnancy among girls ages 15 through 19 (Jones, et al., 1985). Data analyzed five years later shows that in comparison to Denmark, France, Germany (western), Netherlands, and Japan, the United States rate is five times as great (Ahlburg and DeVita, 1992). The Guttmacher researchers compared in detail five Western countries—Sweden, Holland, France, Canada, and Great Britain—with the United States. They found that, while American adolescents were not more sexually active than their European counterparts, they were more likely to become pregnant. Further, even omitting black teenagers in the United States, who have a higher pregnancy rate than whites, whites alone had nearly double the rate of British and French teenagers and six times the rate of the Dutch. These figures lead Jeannie Rosoff, the

BOX 16-1   The Contemporary American Family

Teen Pregnancy "Epidemic" Is Hyperbole

Rene Denfeld

Teenage pregnancy is a powerful political issue as politicians scramble to swear allegiance to family values.

"To strengthen the family we must do everything we can to keep the rate of teen pregnancy going down," said President Clinton in his State of the Union message on Tuesday. A group of prominent Americans, he added, was forming a grassroots effort to campaign against it.

Yet, despite all we have been told, there is *no* epidemic of teen pregnancy. Heart-rending stories of 14-year-old girls with infants, photos of pregnant 12-year-olds clutching teddy bears, and politicians lamenting a nation of "children raising children" are pure hyperbole.

This is underscored by a report on out-of-wedlock childbearing submitted to Congress last fall by the Centers for Disease Control and Prevention. The report states that while "many Americans picture a teenage girl having a first child" as the typical unmarried parent, this simply isn't the case. Only a minority of out-of-wedlock births are to teens.

And with a few bumps and dips, the teen birth rate has stayed relatively steady for years. It's actually *lower* today than the past. In 1955, for instance, roughly 90 out of every 1,000 women age 15 to 19 gave birth. By 1993 the number was down to 59 per 1,000. This is about half of the birth rate for women ages 25 through 29.

The rate of teen pregnancy was actually higher in 1955.

Most "teen" births occur to women who are already considered adults, or at least close: 18- and 19-year-olds. The incidence of girls under age 15 having babies is actually quite uncommon. The birth rate for girls ages 10 to 14 is about one in a thousand. This number has remained roughly the same for decades.

Many of our mothers and grandmothers gave birth to their first child at age 17 or earlier. Of course, the difference is many of these teen moms were married at the time—though quite a few aren't married anymore. Or at least not to their first husbands.

Although many argue a married teenage mother is substantially better off than an unmarried one, Princeton Professor Sara McLanahan has found that early childbearing has similar consequences for both married and unmarried mothers. One reason is those who marry young have a very high divorce rate, negating any positive effects of marriage.

If teen births are not on the rise—and if they are actually relatively uncommon at younger ages—then why is the public constantly told that we are suffering a scourge of teen pregnancy?

The reason is some politicians confuse (deliberately, it seems) *teen pregnancy* with *out-of-wedlock pregnancy*, which has risen. They are actually dramatically different phenomena. Most women having babies out-of-wedlock are over the age of 25. A substantial portion are divorced, separated, or widowed older mothers. Some are unmarried at the time of the birth but later marry.

And not all are single. Over a quarter of out-of-wedlock births are to parents who are living together but are not legally married. As much as my grandparents would shake their heads at the young "living in sin," the fact of the matter is marriage is now more an option than an institution. The substantial number of committed but unmarried two-parent heterosexual couples gets even less recognition than gay and lesbian couples (who also raise children out of marriage).

The popular picture of unmarried mothers may be 14-year-olds with wide eyes like a Keene painting, but the reality is a divergent cross-section of Americans.

According to the CDC report, the reason why so many births today occur out-of-wedlock is "complicated"—a word [that] gives politicians hives. One factor is there are simply more unmarried people. The median age of marriage has risen, and divorce and separation are more common, even among those who espouse family values.

As the report puts it: "Americans are not having more babies; they're having fewer marriages." Rampant teenage sexuality or MTV can't be blamed.

The report also makes emphatically clear that out-of-wedlock births are *not* the result of a welfare state. Nor did it find much connection between nonmarital births and crime or poverty. Other countries, including Canada, France, Sweden and Denmark, also have high rates of out-of-wedlock childbearing. The economic and social health of these countries suggests that unmarried parenting may be an international trend that proves impervious to simple-minded national policy.

Out-of-wedlock pregnancy is up mostly among older mothers.

That teenage births aren't exploding doesn't mean that those that do occur are positive. Early childbearing is hard on parents and children. In many cases it would be wiser to wait.

But the most surprising—and disheartening—finding of the CDC report hints at why reducing birth rates is difficult. The majority of pregnancies are not planned. Among unmarried mothers, a full 88 percent of births are unintended. Married women are not immune to this problem, with a remarkable 40 percent saying they didn't intend to get pregnant either.

That so many children are not intended is deeply troubling. Even in the most ideal circumstances, an unplanned pregnancy causes tremendous disruption. It would be hard to argue that this path to children is as positive as a planned family.

The real reproductive problem facing this country is not teen pregnancies, or even out-of-wedlock births but unintended pregnancies. The answers are boringly unsexy and politically unpopular. One key is birth control. The CDC found that "parents are unable to obtain, do not choose, or fail to use effective contraception on a regular basis." The other two are job opportunities and education. Adults who feel optimistic about their future are more likely to conscientiously plan families.

Purple stories of pregnant grade schoolers serve little purpose, and some cases may backfire. A false epidemic inspires false solutions.

The political antidotes of the moment—cutting welfare to young mothers, restricting birth control, and preaching chastity via sexual ignorance—could too easily create a contagion. And start a real epidemic.

Rene Denfeld is the author of *The New Victorians*, published last year by Warner Books.

Philadelphia Inquirer, 25 January 1996.
Reprinted with permission by the Philadelphia
Inquirer, 1996.

president of the Alan Guttmacher Institute, to conclude that "It's not a black problem. It's not an East Coast problem. It's a problem for all of us" (quoted in Wallis, 1985:80).

The Guttmacher researchers believe that the lack of openness in American society about birth control constitutes a striking difference between American teenagers and their European peers. The policy in Sweden, to cite another country's handling of this problem, is to educate children from the age of 7 on reproductive biology. By the time Swedish children are 10 or 12, they are knowledgeable about the various types of contraceptives. The goal, as one Swedish educator states, is "The idea is to dedramatize and demystify sex so that familiarity will make the child less likely to fall prey to unwanted pregnancy and venereal disease" (Annika Strandell quoted in Wallis, 1985:82).

Holland has a similar sex-education program that seeks to demystify sex. Contraceptive counseling is available at government-sponsored clinics for a minimal fee. Media attention is also given to the sex education. The result is that birth control is commonly used by Dutch teenagers. In contrast, in the United States public opinion prevails that minimizes public sex education. Faye Wattleton, president of the Planned Parenthood Federation, believes that our puritanical heritage accounts for this orientation. She states: "While European societies have chosen to recognize sexual development as a normal part of human development, we have chosen to repress it. At the same time, we behave as if we're not repressing it" (quoted in Wallis, 1985:82). The birth-control result is a double standard that allows teenagers to have sex as a result of a spontaneous passion. But to plan for sex by taking the pill or using a diaphragm is viewed as something wrong.

The Guttmacher researchers in their cross-cultural data analysis conclude that the result of this practice is that societies that have the least open attitudes toward sex are the ones that have the highest teenage pregnancy rates. They are also the societies with the highest teenage abortion rates. They also report that countries like Holland, Sweden, and France—while providing far more generously for indigent young mothers—still have low pregnancy rates.

Ahlburg and DeVita (1992) in their assessment of the cross-cultural differences in teenage childbearing cite a number of explanations. They include the fact that in the United States a higher proportion of women do not use any contraception. And, those who do, use the least effective forms of contraception. Family-planning clinics are often frowned upon and seen as only something that the poor would use; in Europe they are widely utilized. Information about sexuality and contraception is not as readily available in the United States. Sex education courses and information from the media are also more accessible to teens in European countries. Ahlburg and DeVita conclude by suggesting that these factors may account for the much higher abortion rate in the United States than in Europe: "Teenagers accounted for 26 percent of abortions in the United States in 1988, compared with 17 percent in Denmark, 13 percent in the United Kingdom, and 12 percent in France" (1992:22).

REMARRIAGE AFTER DIVORCE

Even with today's liberalizing attitudes toward divorce, women and men report varying degrees of loneliness, confusion, and depression after divorce (see Bohannan, 1971; Goode, 1956; S. Gordon, 1976; Kitson and Morgan, 1990; Myers, 1989; Vaughan, 1986). Many find that they are not able to confide in their friends and relatives. The failure of the society to provide clear-cut normative standards to guide the divorced individual aggravates the situation. Further, the social ideologies that stress individualism and separation from extended kinship structures often prevent divorced persons from seeking aid or involvement with their families. The individual's ties and interpersonal relationships with married friends are also often shattered by divorce. The somewhat stigmatized identity combined with the necessity to change old relationships often prove difficult to resolve.

Combined, all these factors often result in the desire of the divorced person to remarry. Indeed, a society that provides few alternate emotional resources outside of marriage limits the institutionalized options of the divorced person. The ideology that stresses the marital relationship as the most beneficial institution for the realization of individual emotional gratification and happiness almost mandates that the individual seek a new marital partner. The result is that remarriage is increasingly becoming more predominant. Almost one out of five currently married people was married previously; one out of four marriages is a remarriage for one of the spouses. Furthermore, the divorced are remarrying sooner after their divorce.

William J. Goode (1956), in his seminal study *After Divorce*, argues that high divorce rates do not imply social disorganization. The high remarriage rate provides corroborating evidence. It leads us to reconsider divorce as a temporary state rather than a permanent one for many people committed to marriage:

> Indeed, the divorce system then becomes in effect part of the courtship and marriage system: that is, it is part of the "sifting out" process, analogous to the adolescent dating pattern. Individuals marry, but there is a free market both in getting a first spouse, and in getting a second spouse should the individual not be able to create a harmonious life with the first one. Indeed, to the extent that marriage becomes a personal bond between husband and wife, and they marry after they are formed psychologically, there would seem to be at least some ideological arguments for their being free to shift about in order to find someone who fits better (Goode, 1962/1966:387).

The American Experience

Remarriages have always been common in the United States. During the colonial period and through the nineteenth century, the death of a spouse was almost always followed quickly by remarriage. The harshness of life demanded that a single parent obtain a spouse to help care and provide for children. Although remarriage after the death of a spouse has been an accepted institution, our society rejected the remarriage of divorced individuals. Duberman (1977) states that the American clergy were disinclined to remarry divorced individuals. State laws also existed to discourage this practice.

However, after World War I, the divorce rate in the United States began to rise. This gradually affected the attitudes and rates of remarriage of divorced people. Jacobson (1959) estimates that into the 1920s there were still more remarriages after the death of a spouse than after divorce. But, beginning in the 1930s, this pattern changed. Arthur J. Norton and Paul C. Glick (1976), reporting on remarriage patterns, have observed that by 1975 the overwhelming majority of remarriages occurred as a result of the divorce or one or both of the new partners.

The proportion of remarriage to all marriages occurring is steadily increasing. At the turn of the century, about nine-tenths of all marriages were first marriages; most of the remaining one-tenth involved widows or widowers. Jacobson (1959) calculates that only about 3 percent of all brides were previously married in 1900. The figure increased threefold to 9 percent by 1930. By 1975 about one-fourth (25 percent) of all brides were previously divorced (Carter and Glick, 1976). By 1990, over half of all marriages in the United States are marriages in which at least one spouse has been previously married (Bumpass, Sweet, and Martin, 1990; Ganong and Coleman, 1994).

Concurrent with the rise of divorced persons who remarry is the increasing presence of children found in these remarriages. Andrew Cherlin (1981), citing U.S. Bureau of the Census figures, reports that nearly 9 million children lived in two-parent families where one or both parents had been previously divorced. He conjectures that a significant number of the children were from previous marriages.

In an analysis of long-term trends in remarriage, focusing on changes in recent years, Glick and Lin (1986) report that remarriage rates went up during the 1960s, but then started a steep decline that continued until the late 1970s, after which the decline moderated. Among the significant findings: Remarriage rates are higher for men (84 percent) than for women (77 percent). One finding that is highlighted is the fact that young divorced women with children were becoming more likely than their childless counterparts to remarry and to do so quickly.

The childless divorced women stayed divorced longer than the divorced mothers. The reluctance of young, childless, divorced women to remarry was seen as reflecting an alternative lifestyle. They included cohabitation outside marriage, the experience of costs and benefits of living alone, and an option to deliberate in seeking an acceptable unmarried man to marry. On the other hand, the ability of young divorced mothers to remarry soon after divorce is perceived by Glick and Lin to reflect the increased acceptability of divorce. Early remarriage for divorced mothers reflects a desire to increase the divorcee's financial security. Typically, remarriage means adding not only an additional income but additional support in the running of the household.

Cohabitation instead of remarriage among the formerly married has become an increasingly popular option in recent years (Bumpass, Sweet, and Cherlin, 1991). One pattern that has emerged is for the remarried person to live with someone, usually but not always the person that they will eventually marry, before they remarry (Ganong and Coleman, 1994). Ganong and Coleman (1994) describe cohabitation before remarriage as the primary way of remarriage preparation. Surprisingly, these people do not discuss step-parent adjustment concerns any more than those who did not cohabit.

The large number of people who remarry and the large number of children who are involved in these families of remarried divorced people today necessitate an in-depth examination of the adjustments that these family members have to make after remarriage occurs.

Adjustment of Members of Remarried Families

There is a myth surrounding remarriage that says that the second marriage is more successful than the first. In popular parlance, "love is better the second time around." The explanations given include the belief that remarried individuals are now older, wiser, and more mature. Also, it is assumed that divorced persons who remarry will work harder to assure a more successful second marriage. Yet, the divorce rate for persons who remarry after divorce is higher than for persons who marry for the first time (Cherlin, 1992; Sweet and Bumpass, 1987).

An apparent contradiction is noted by William J. Goode (1956) who, in his landmark study *After Divorce*, cautions against viewing the divorced remarrieds as divorce-prone. Instead of comparing divorce rates, he suggests that one should ask all those who have remarried to compare their second marriages with their first. He reasons:

> Granted that the divorced who remarry are somewhat more prone to divorce than those who marry for the first time; nevertheless, the only comparison that makes sense to those divorced people is between their second marriage and *their own first marriage*. Our divorcees are not, after all, asserting that their second marriages are better than marriages of *others* who are first married. They are only claiming that their second marriages are "happier" than *their own first marriages*. (Goode, 1956:334-335)

Andrew Cherlin (1991), however, argues that the divorce rate is the best indication of the differences in the unity between families of remarriages after divorce that include children from previous marriages and those of first-marriage families. Cherlin contends that there are insufficient institutional supports and guidelines to assure optimal success of these remarriages. He observes that family members of such remarriages face unique problems that do not exist in first-marriage families. He believes that the origins of these problems lie in the complex structure of remarried families and the normative inadequacies to define these familial roles and relationships:

> These families are expanded in the number of social roles and relationships they possess and also are expanded in space over more than one household. The additional social roles included stepparents, stepchildren, stepsiblings, and the new spouses of noncustodial parents, among others. And the links between the households are the children of previous marriages. These children are commonly in the custody of one parent—usually the mother—but they normally visit the noncustodial parent regularly. Thus they promote communication among the divorced parents, the new stepparent, and the noncustodial parent's new spouse. (Cherlin, 1991:769)

Cherlin is of the opinion that our society's overemphasis on first marriages provides little guidance for the handling of the potential problems of remarriages stemming from these complexities. To support this contention, he refers to the study by Paul Bohannan (1971) that calls attention to the inadequacies of our kinship terminology. Bohannan states that the term stepparent originally meant the individual whom the surviving parent married to replace a parent who had died. A stepparent after divorce is an additional parent, not a replacement. Our society has not developed norms on how to handle this situation. We do not have norms to govern our behavior and expectation, nor do we have norms to show the differences between parent and stepparent. The difficulties in what we call these stepparents highlight this problem. If a noncustodial biological parent is still alive and maintains contact with his or her child, does the child also call the stepparent "Mom" or "Dad"? Cherlin points out that the lack of appropriate terms also exists for the new complex of extended relationships, including uncles, aunts, and grandparents. The significance of these absent terms is stated by Cherlin:

> Where no adequate terms exist for an important social role, the institutional support for this role is deficient, and general acceptance of the role as a legitimate pattern of activity is questionable. . . . These linguistic inadequacies correspond to the absence of widely accepted definitions of the form of many of the roles and relationships in families of remarriage. The absence of proper terms is both a symptom and a cause of some of the problems of remarried life. (Cherlin, 1991:770-771)

Legal and social difficulties also confront the families of the persons who remarry after divorce. The social and financial obligations of former spouses who have also remarried as well as the obligation incurred as the result of subsequent divorces and remarriages further complicate matters. Bohannan (1971) indicates that there is a whole series of social groups that emerge with remarriage. He refers to them as quasi-kinship groups as a result of the chain of relationships that are formed among spouses and their ex-spouses. These "divorce chains also result from complications which exist within the household which contains stepparents, stepsiblings, and halfsiblings and by the ways that these household members behave in relation to ex-spouses and their families" (Bohannan, 1971:128-129).

Margaret Mead (1971) has identified the legal regulations regarding incest and consanguineal marriages that become problematic for remarried family members. She argues that incest taboos allow children to develop affection for and identification with other family members without risk of sexual exploitation. But incest prohibitions are drawn to blood or genetic relationships rather than to domestic relationships among household members. This failure in incest taboos can lead to inadequate security and protection of children. In more dramatic situations, it can lead to the sexual abuse and exploitation of individuals by their stepparents or stepsiblings. In ordinary circumstances, it can lead to psychological confusion and inability to develop adult relationships.

> As the number of divorces increases, there are more and more households in which minor children live with stepparents and stepsiblings, but where the inevitable domestic familiarity and intimacy are not counterbalanced by protective, deeply felt taboos. At the very least, this situation produces confusion in the minds of growing children; the stepfather, who is seen daily but is not a taboo object, is contrasted with the biological father, who is seen occasionally and so is endowed with a deeper aura of romance. The multiplication of such situations may be expected to magnify the difficulties young people experience in forming permanent-mating relationships, as well as in forming viable relationships with older people. (Mead, 1971:120)

Indeed, most customs and conventions of family life are not applicable to remarried families after divorce. These include such everyday activities as discipline of children (how much authority should stepparents have), the relationships of individuals with their spouse's ex-spouse, and the relationship among siblings and stepsiblings resulting from the various combinations that could come about when individuals remarry, divorce, and remarry. In all, the everyday nature of family life can be seen as problematic to these remarried family members.

Another concern is the impact of remarriage on grandparents, both natural and stepgrandparents. In a study of remarried couples living in central Pennsylvania, Spanier and Furstenberg (1982) observe that children in these families have at least one extra pair of grandparents. While children get a new set of grandparents, these new grandparents' roles are not clearly delineated. However, the researchers found that grandparents were usually quick to accept their "instant" grandchildren. Most of the remarried persons studied reported that the process of introducing their children to their new partner's families was comfortable and pleasant. Similar findings were found by Cherlin and Furstenberg (1986) who report that only 9 percent of the step-grandparents agreed with the statement, " 'You've had problems accepting your stepgrandchildren as grandchildren' " (1986:160). In addition, in both studies, the contact with stepgrandparents did not diminish the children's involvements with their biological grandparents. Further divorces and remarriages would result in more than three sets of grandparents. Cherlin and Furstenberg (1986), in their examination of this potential situation, feel that the nature of these new, post-divorce relationships is still unknown.

The necessity for a critical examination of remarriage after divorce, especially when children are involved, is vitally apparent. Such empirical research and analysis not only will increase our understanding of these family structures and processes, but can also be of immeasurable aid in understanding the nature of the institutional relationship between the family and society in the transmission of social norms governing individuals.

CONCLUSION

All societies permit divorce or the dissolution of marriage. In this cross-cultural examination of divorce it became apparent that there is no necessary association between divorce rates and societal breakdown or disorganization. Indeed, for many preliterate societies high divorce rates often serve to stabilize extended family systems. In the study of divorce in Japan and Egypt it was observed that their respective rates of divorce have declined in the twentieth century, whereas the rates in the United States have risen. Yet, as William J. Goode (1963) has observed, these changes in the divorce rates, although going in opposite directions, reflect a similar pattern—a growing tendency for both women and men to have equal rights of divorce. The impact of modernization process on Japan and the Islamic revolution on Iran and women's rights and divorce patterns in these two societies was then examined.

Attention then turned to an in-depth examination of divorce in the United States. The steady climb in the American divorce rate was shown to be related to social and familial changes closely associated with the family's relationship to economic processes.

Changes in family ideology reflecting an emphasis on the independence and the privatization of the nuclear family have also played an important role in changes in the divorce rate. Of particular interest is the relationship of working wives and their increased economic independence, and the possibility that their marriages may end in divorce.

Changes in law regarding divorce and child custody were shown not only to reflect changes in familial roles, but also to serve as an impetus for bringing about changes in the definition of marriage and the responsibilities of husbands and wives with each other and with their children. Further, divorce laws and custody decisions also define the continued obligations that the formerly married couple have to each other and to their children after divorce.

What happens to the wives, husbands, and children following a divorce and how familial roles change with the dissolution of the marriage was the next topic of concern. The effects of divorce on children were seen to be associated with the child's conceptualization of the parents' marriage. They were also associated with the child's age. I emphasized the need for more systematic research in this area and cautioned against imputing solely negative consequences of divorce on children. The readjustments, problems, and solutions of single parents' raising children alone was then investigated. In the case of female-headed single-parent households, we saw the interrelated effects of government and social policies regarding financial support—either directly or by enforcing spouse's child-support agreements—social services—such as child care and crisis intervention—and social attitudes toward divorced women, especially in terms of employment opportunities and their ability to cope with circumstances.

The final discussion was on remarriage. Remarriage rates, divorce rates of remarrieds, and the problems confronted by reconstituted families were analyzed. Here again, the necessity for more systematic investigation of remarriage was demonstrated.

REFERENCES

Abernathy, Virginia D. 1993. *Population Politics: The Choices That Shape Our Future*. New York: Insight Books, Plenum.

Adams, Bert N. 1975. *The Family. A Sociological Interpretation*, 2d ed. Chicago: Rand McNally.

Afkhami, Mahnaz. 1984. "Iran: A future in the past—The 'prerevolutionary' women's movement." In Robin Morgan (ed.), *Sisterhood is Global: The International Women's Movement Anthology* (pp. 333–341). Garden City, NY: Anchor Press/Doubleday.

Aghajanian, Akbar. 1986. "Some notes on divorce in Iran." *Journal of Marriage and the Family* 48 (Nov.):749–755.

Ahlburg, Dennis, and Carol J. De Vita. 1992. "New realities of the American Family." *Population Bulletin* 47, 2 (August):1–44. Washington, DC: Population Reference Bureau.

Alba, Richard D. 1976. "Social assimilation among American Catholic national origin groups." *American Sociological Review* 41:1040–1044.

———. 1981. "The twilight of ethnicity among American Catholics of European ancestry." *The Annals* 454:86–97.

———. 1986. "Patterns of interethnic marriage among American Catholics." *Social Forces* 65: 202–223.

———. 1990. *Ethnic Identity: The Transformation of White America*. New Haven, CT: Yale University Press.

Ahuvia, Aaron C., and Mara B. Adelman. 1992. "Formal intermediaries in the marriage market: A typology and review." *Journal of Marriage and the Family* 54(May):452–463.

Aldous, Joan. 1968. "Urbanization, the extended family, and kinship ties in West Africa." In Sylvia Fleis Fava (ed.), *Urbanism in World Perspective: A Reader* (pp. 297–305). New York: Thomas Y. Crowell.

Allon, Natalie, and Diane Fishel. 1981. "Singles bars as examples of urban courting patterns." In Peter J. Stein (ed.), *Single Life: Unmarried Adults in Social Context* (pp. 115–121). New York: St. Martin's Press.

Altman, Lawrence K. 1994. "AIDS cases increase among heterosexuals." *The New York Times* (March 11).

Amato, Paul R. 1994. "Life-span adjustment of children to their parents' divorce." *The Future of Children*. Children and Divorce issue. 4 (1) (Spring): 143–164.

Ames, Katrine, Christopher Sulavik, Nadine Joseph, Lucille Beachy, and Todd Park. 1992. "Domesticated bliss." *Newsweek* (March 23).

Anderson, J.E., L. Kahn, D. Holtzman, S. Arday, B. Truman, and L. Kolbe. 1990. "HIV/AIDS knowledge and sexual behavior among high school students." *Family Planning Perspectives* 22, 6 (November/December):252–255.

Anderson, Michael. 1971. *Family Structure in Nineteenth-Century Lancashire*. Cambridge, England: Cambridge University Press.

———. 1980. *Approaches to the History of the Western Family 1500–1914*. London and Basingstoke: The Macmillan Press Ltd.

Angier, Natalie. 1993. "Bias against gay people: Hatred of a special kind." *The New York Times* (December 26).

Apple, R.W., Jr. 1979. "Iran: Heart of the matter." *The New York Times Magazine* (Mar. 11):19, 101–102, 104–106.

Archdeacon, Thomas J. 1983. *Becoming American: An Ethnic History*. New York: Free Press.

Archer, Dane, and Rosemarie Gartner. 1984. *Violence and Crisis in Cross-National Perspective*. New Haven, CT: Yale University Press.

Arendell, Terry. 1986. *Mothers and Divorce: Legal, Economic and Social Dilemmas*. Berkeley, CA: University of California Press.

Arensberg, Conrad M. 1937. *The Irish Countryman*. Gloucester, MA: Peter Smith. (Reprinted 1959.)

———, and Solon T. Kimball. 1968. *Family and Community in Ireland*, 2d ed. Cambridge, MA: Harvard University Press.

Ariès, Philippe. 1962. *Centuries of Childhood: A Social History of Family Life*, Robert Baldick (trans.). New York: Knopf.

Armstrong, Alice. 1994. "Maintenance in southern Africa: The role of law." In Helen O'Connor (ed.), *Women and the Family* (pp. 58–60). London & New Jersey: Zed Books Ltd.

Arungu-Olende, Rose Adhiambo. 1984. "Not just literacy, but wisdom." In Robin Morgan (ed.), *Sisterhood is Global: The International Women's Movement Anthology* (pp. 394–398). Garden City, NY: Anchor Press/Doubleday.

Associated Press. 1981. "Child marriages in India." *Detroit Free Press* (May 9). Cited under this title in J. Ross Eshleman. 1994. *The Family* (p. 245), 7th ed. Boston: Allyn & Bacon.

Associated Press. 1989. "Cross-cultural/semiarranged courtship in India." *Baltimore Evening Sun* (February 6). Cited under this title in Nijole V. Benokratis, 1993. *Marriages and Families* (p. 197). Englewood Cliffs, NJ: Prentice-Hall.

Associated Press. 1993. "AIDS is top killer among young men." *The New York Times* (October 31).

Axelrod, Morris. 1956. "Urban structure and social participation." *American Sociological Review* 21: 13–18.

Aziz-Ahmed, Shereen. 1967. "Pakistan." In Raphael Patai, *Women in the Modern World* (pp. 42–58). New York: The Free Press.

Baca Zinn, Maxine. 1994. "Adaptation and Continuity in Mexican-Origin Families." In Ronald L. Taylor (ed.), *Minority Families in the United States: A Multicultural Perspective* (pp. 64–81). Englewood Cliffs, NJ: Prentice-Hall.

Bachofen, J.J. 1948. *Das Mutterecht*. Basel: Beno Schwabs. (Originally published, 1861.)

Bakan, David. 1971. *Slaughter of the Innocents*. Boston: Beacon Press.

Baker, Susan Gonzalez. 1994. "Gender, ethnicity, and homelessness: Accounting for demographic diversity on the streets." *American Behavioral Scientist* 37, 4 (February):476–504.

Bane, Mary Jo. 1976. *Here to Stay: American Families in the Twentieth Century*. New York: Basic Books.

———. 1979. "Marital disruption and the lives of children." In George Levinger and Oliver C. Moles (eds.), *Divorce and Separation: Context, Causes, and Consequences* (pp. 276–286). New York: Basic Books.

Baron, Larry, and Murray A. Straus. 1985. "Legitimate violence and rape: A test of the cultural spillover theory." Mimeograph of paper presented at the 1985 meeting of the Eastern Sociological Society.

Barrett, K. 1982. "Date rape: A campus epidemic." *Ms.* (Sept.):48–51, 130.

Bartelt, Pearl W., and Mark Hutter. 1977. "Symbolic interaction perspective on the sexual politics of etiquette books." Paper presented at the meeting of the American Sociological Association, Chicago, IL (Sept.).

Becker, Gary S. 1991. *A Treatise on the Family*. Enlarged edition. Cambridge, MA: Harvard University Press.

Bell, Wendell. 1958. "Social choice, life styles and suburban residence." In William Dobriner (ed.), *The Suburban Community* (pp. 225–247). New York: G.P. Putnam's Sons.

———, and Marion D. Boat. 1957. "Urban neighborhood and informal social behavior." *American Journal of Sociology* 62:391–398.

Bellah, Robert N. 1957. *Tokugawa Religion: The Values of Preindustrial Japan*. New York: Macmillan.

———, et al. 1985. *Habits of the Heart: Individualism and Commitment in American Life*. New York: Harper & Row.

Bendix, Reinhard. 1967. "Tradition and modernity reconsidered." *Comparative Studies in Society and History* 9:292–346.

Benedict, Ruth. 1973. "Continuities and discontinuities in cultural conditioning." In Harry Silverstein (ed.), *The Sociology of Youth: Evolution of Revolution* (pp. 100–108). New York: Macmillan. (Originally published in *Psychiatry* 1:161–167, 1938.)

Bennett, Neil, Ann Klimas Blanc, and David Bloom. 1988. "Commitment and the modern union: Assessing the link between premarital cohabitation and subsequent marital stability." *American Sociological Review* 53 (February): 997–1008.

Benokratis, Nijole. 1983. *Marriages and Families.* Englewood Cliffs, NJ: Prentice-Hall.

Berger, Bennett. 1960. *Working Class Suburb: A Study of Auto Workers in Suburbia.* Berkeley, CA: University of California Press.

Berger, Brigitte. 1971. *Societies in Change.* New York: Basic Books.

———, and Berger, Peter L. 1983. *The War Over the Family: Capturing the Middle Ground.* Garden City, NY: Anchor Press/Doubleday.

Berger, Miriam E. 1971. "Trial marriage: Harnessing the trend constructively." *The Family Coordinator* 20:38–43.

Berger, Peter L., 1963. *Invitation to Sociology: A Humanistic Perspective.* Garden City, NY: Doubleday (Anchor Books).

———, Brigitte Berger, and Hansfried Kellner. 1973. *The Homeless Mind: Modernization and Consciousness.* New York: Random House.

———, and Hansfried Kellner. 1964. "Marriage and the construction of reality." *Diogenes* 46:1–25.

———, and Thomas Luckmann. 1966. *The Social Construction of Reality.* Garden City, NY: Doubleday.

Berkner, Lutz K. 1975. "The use and misuse of census data for the historical analysis of family structure." *Journal of Interdisciplinary History* 4: 721–738.

Berman, Eleanor. 1977. *The Cooperating Family.* Englewood Cliffs, NJ: Prentice-Hall.

———. 1975. *The Future of Motherhood.* New York: Penguin Books.

Bernard, Jesse. 1975. *The Future of Motherhood.* New York: Penguin Books.

———. 1981. "The good provider role: Its rise and fall." *American Psychologist* vol. 36, no. 1 (Jan.): 1–12. Reprinted in Mark Hutter (ed.), 1997. *The Family Experience: A Reader in Cultural Diversity.* 2d ed. Pp. 257–271. Boston, MA: Allyn & Bacon.

Berrol, Selma. 1975. "Turning little aliens into little citizens: Italians and Jews in New York City public schools, 1900–14." In Jean Scarpaci (ed.), *The Interaction of Italians and Jews in Amer-ica* (pp. 32–41). Staten Island, NY: The American Italian Historical Association.

Berry, Brian J.L. 1973. *The Human Consequences of Urbanization: Divergent Paths in the Urban Experience of the Twentieth Century.* New York: St. Martin's Press.

Berry, Mary Frances. 1993. *The Politics of Parenthood: Child Care, Woman's Rights, and the Myth of the Good Mother.* New York: Viking Penguin.

Berube, Allan. 1981. "Marching to a different drummer." *Advocate* (Oct. 15).

Best, Joel. 1990. *Threatened Children: Rhetoric and Concern about Child-Victims.* Chicago, IL: University of Chicago Press.

Billingsley, Andrew. 1968. *Black Families in White America.* Englewood Cliffs, NJ: Prentice-Hall.

———. 1969. "Family functioning in the low income black community." *Social Casework* 50: 563–572.

———. 1992. *Climbing Jacob's Ladder: The Enduring Legacy of African-American Families.* New York: Touchstone.

Bissinger, H.G. 1986. "Residents of a Lima shantytown improve their lot." *The Philadelphia Inquirer* (August 9).

Blake, Judith. 1972. *Coercive Pronatalism and American Population Policy.* (Preliminary paper no. 2 on results of current research in demography). In *International Population and Urban Research* (pp. 17–22). Berkeley: University of California.

Blood, Robert O., Jr. 1967. *Love Match and Arranged Marriage. A Tokyo–Detroit Comparison.* New York: The Free Press.

———. 1972. *The Family.* New York: The Free Press.

———, and Donald M. Wolfe. 1960. *Husbands and Wives.* New York: The Free Press.

Blumberg, Leonard, and Robert R. Bell. 1959. "Urban migration and kinship ties. *Social Problems* 6:328–333.

Blumberg, Rae Lesser. 1979. "A paradigm for predicting the position of women: Policy implications and problems." In Jean Lipman-Blumen and Jessie Bernard (eds.), *Sex Roles and Social Policy* (pp. 113–142). London: Sage Studies in International Sociology.

Blumstein, Philip, and Pepper Schwartz. 1983. *American Couples: Money, Work, Sex.* New York: Morrow.

Bohannan, Paul. 1971. "The six stations of divorce." In Paul Bohannan (ed.), *Divorce and*

After (pp. 33–62). Garden City, NY: Double-day Anchor.

Bolig, R., P. Stein, and P. McKenry. 1984. "The self-advertisement approach to dating: Male-female differences." *Family Relations* 33:587–592.

Boneparth, Ellen. 1986. "In the land of the patriarchs: Public policy on women in Israel." In Lynn B. Iglitzen and Ruth Ross (eds.), *Women in the World, 1975–1985, The Women's Decade*. Santa Barbara, CA: ABC-Clio.

Boserup, Ester. 1970. *Women's Role in Economic Development*. London: Allen & Unwin.

Boswell, John. 1994. *Same-Sex Unions in Premodern Europe*. New York: Villard Books.

Bott, Elizabeth. 1957. *Family and Social Network*. London: Tavistock Publications.

Bowen, Gary Lee. 1983. "The evolution of Soviet family policy: Female liberation versus social cohesion." *Journal of Comparative Family Studies* 14 (Autumn):299–313.

Brandwein, Ruth A., Carol A. Brown, and Elizabeth Maury Fox. 1974. "Women and children last: The social situation of divorced mothers and their families." *Journal of Marriage and the Family* 36:498–514.

Briggs, Kenneth A. 1981. "Reform Jews to seek conversion of non-Jews." *The New York Times* (Dec. 9).

Brody, Elaine M. 1990. *Women in the Middle: Their Parent-Care Years*. New York: Springer.

———, S.J. Litvin, C. Hoffman, and M.H. Kleban. 1992. "Differential effects of daughters' marital status on their parent care experiences." *The Gerontologist* 32, 1:58–67.

Bronson, B.H. 1959. *The Traditional Tunes of the Child Ballads*, vol. I. Princeton, NJ: Princeton University Press.

Broude, Gwen, and Sarah Greene. 1976. "Cross-cultural codes on twenty sexual attitudes and practices." *Ethnology* 15:409–428.

Browett, John. 1982. "The evolution of unequal development within South Africa: An overview." In David M. Smith (ed.), *Living Under Apartheid* (pp. 10–23). London: Allen & Unwin.

Brozan, Nadine. 1983. "Family issues of Jewish couples." *The New York Times* (Nov. 3).

Brydon, Lynne, and Sylvia Chant. 1989. *Women in the Third World: Gender Issues in Rural and Urban Areas*. New Brunswick, NJ: Rutgers University Press.

Bumiller, Elisabeth. 1985. "First comes marriage—Then maybe, love." Washington, DC: *Washington Post*. In James M. Henslin (ed.), *Marriage and Family in a Changing Society* (pp. 120–125), 4th ed. 1992. New York: Free Press.

———. 1990. *May You Be the Mother of a Hundred Sons: A Journey Among the Women of India*. New York: Random House.

Bumpass, Larry L. 1990. "What's happening to the family? Interactions between demographic and institutional change." *Demography* 27 (November):483–498.

———, James Sweet, and Andrew Cherlin. 1991. "The role of cohabitation in declining rates of marriage." *Journal of Marriage and the Family* 53 (6) (November):913–927.

———, James Sweet, and Teresa Castro Martin. 1990. "Changing patterns of remarriage." *Journal of Marriage and the Family* 52(3) (August):747–756.

Burgess, Ernest W., and Harvey J. Locke. 1945. *The Family from Institution to Companionship*. New York: American Book.

Burris, Beverly. 1991. "Employed mothers." *Social Science Quarterly* 72 (March): 5–66.

Business and Professional Women's Foundation. 1992. *You Can't Get There From Here: Working Women and the Glass Ceiling*. A Report (April). Washington, DC: The Business and Professional Women's Foundation.

Campbell, Colin. 1976. "What happens when we get the manchild pill." *Psychology Today* 10 (3) (Aug.):86–91.

Cancian, Francesca. 1987. *Love in America*. Cambridge, MA: Cambridge University Press.

Capellanus, Andreas. 1969. *The Art of Courtly Love*. Translated with introductions and notes by John Jay Parry. New York: Norton.

Carlier, Auguste. 1972. *Marriage in the United States*. New York: Arno Press. (Originally published, 1867).

Carter, Hugh, and Paul C. Glick. 1976. *Marriage and Divorce: A Social and Economic Study*, rev. ed. Cambridge, MA: Harvard University Press.

Cate, Rodney. 1982. "Premarital abuse: A social psychological perspective." *Journal of Family Issues* 3, 1 (Mar.):79–90.

Centers for Disease Control. 1991. "Premarital sexual experience among adolescent women—United States, 1970–1988. *Morbidity and Mor-*

tality Weekly Report 39, 51/52 (January 4): 929–932.

———. 1993. *HIV/AIDS surveillance report. Second quarter edition.* U.S. Department of Health and Human Services, Public Health Service, National Center for Infectious Diseases, Division of HIV/AIDS, Atlanta, Georgia 30333, July, 1–19.

Chase, Naomi Feigelson. 1975. *A Child Is Being Beaten.* New York: McGraw-Hill.

Chen, Victor. 1994. "Crisis of a crowded world: Population and development." *Audubon* (July-August):51–59.

Cherlin, Andrew. 1981. *Marriage, Divorce, Remarriage.* Cambridge, MA: Harvard University Press.

———. 1991. "Remarriage as an incomplete institution." In Mark Hutter (ed.), *The Family Experience: A Reader in Cultural Diversity* (pp. 763–777). New York: Macmillan Publishing Company. (Reprinted from *American Journal of Sociology*, 1978, 84:634–650).

———. 1992. *Marriage, Divorce, Remarriage.* Revised and enlarged edition. Cambridge, MA: Harvard University Press.

———, and Frank F. Furstenberg, Jr. 1986. *The New American Grandparent: A Place in the Family, A Life Apart.* New York: Basic Books.

Chinoy, Ely. 1955. *Automobile Workers and the American Dream.* Garden City, NY: Doubleday.

Chodak, Szymon. 1973. *Societal Development: Five Approaches with Conclusions from Comparative Analysis.* New York: Oxford University Press.

Christensen, Harold T. (ed.). 1964. *Handbook of Marriage and the Family.* Chicago: Rand McNally.

Chudacoff, Howard P. 1989. *How Old Are You?: Age Consciousness in American Culture.* Princeton, NJ: Princeton University Press.

Church, George J., and Richard Lacayo. 1995. "Social *In*Security." *Time* (March 20):24–31.

Cicirelli, Victor G. 1983. "Adult children and their elderly parents." In Timothy H. Brubaker (ed.), *Family Relations in Later Life* (pp. 31–46). Beverly Hills, CA: Sage Publications.

Clark, Alice. 1919. *The Working Life of Women in the Seventeenth Century.* London: G. Routledge & Sons. (Reissued by Frank Cass, 1968.)

Clark, Matt, with Vincent Coppola. 1985. "AIDS: A growing 'pandemic'?" *Newsweek* (Apr. 29): 71.

———, with Mariana Gosnell, Deborah Witherspoon, Mary Hager, and Vincent Coppola. 1985. "AIDS: Once dismissed as the 'gay plague,' the disease has become the no. 1 public-health menace." *Newsweek* (Aug. 12):20–24, 26–27.

Clayton, Richard R. 1979. *The Family, Marriage, and Social Change,* 2d ed. Lexington, MA: D.C. Heath.

Coleman, Marilyn, and Lawrence H. Ganong. 1990. "Remarriage and stepfamily research in the 1980s: Increased interest in an old family form." *Journal of Marriage and the Family* 52 (November):925–940.

Coles, Robert. 1968. "Life in Appalachia—the case of Hugh McCaslin." *Transaction* (June):22–33.

Collier, Jane, and Michelle Rosaldo. 1981. "Politics and gender in simple societies." In Sherry Ortner and Harriet Whitehead (eds.), *Sexual Meanings: The Cultural Construction of Gender and Sexuality* (pp. 275–329). Cambridge, MA: Cambridge University Press.

Collins, Patricia Hill. 1994. "The meaning of motherhood in Black culture." In Robert Staples (ed.), *The Black Family: Essays and Studies* (pp. 165–173). Belmont, CA: Wadsworth Publishing Company.

Collins, Randall. 1971. "A conflict theory of sexual stratification." *Social Problems* 19:3–21.

Condon, Jane. 1985. A *Half Step Behind: Japanese Women of the 1980s.* New York: Dodd, Mead.

Cortes, Carlos E. 1980. "Mexicans." In Stephen Thernstrom (ed.), *Harvard Encyclopedia of American Ethnic Groups* (pp. 697–719). Cambridge, MA: The Belknap Press of Harvard University Press.

Coser, Rose Laub. 1991. *In Defense of Modernity.* Stanford, CA: Stanford University Press.

Cott, Nancy. 1979. "Passionlessness: An interpretation of Victorian sexual ideology, 1790–1850." In Nancy F. Cott and Elizabeth H. Pleck (eds.), *A Heritage of Her Own* (pp. 162–181). New York: Simon and Schuster.

Covello, Leonard. 1967. *The Social Background of the Italo-American School Child.* Leiden, the Netherlands: E.J. Brill.

Cowan, Ruth Schwartz. 1983. *More Work for Mother: The Ironies of Household Technology from the Open Hearth to the Microwave.* New York: Basic Books.

Curtin, Katie. 1975. *Women in China.* New York: Pathfinder Press.

Dahlstrom, Edmund (ed.). 1962. *Kvinnors Liv och Arbete* [The Life and Work of Women]. Stockholm: Studieforbundet Naringsliv & Samhalle.

———. 1971. *The Changing Roles of Men and Women.* Boston: Beacon Press.

Daley, Suzanne. 1995. "Whites evict Black farmers in South Africa Land Conflict." *The New York Times* (October 14).

D'Andrade, Roy G. 1966. "Sex differences and cultural institutions." In E.E. Maccoby (ed.), *The Development of Sex Differences* (pp. 174–204). Stanford, CA: Stanford University Press.

Danes, Sharon M., Olga N. Doudchenko, and Ludmilla V. Yasnaya. 1994. "Work and family life." In James W. Maddox, M. Janice Hogan, Anatolyi I. Antonov, and Mikhail S. Matskovsky (eds.), *Families Before and After Perestroika: Russian and U.S. Perspectives* (pp. 156–185). New York: Guilford Press.

Darling, Carol A., David J. Kallen, and Joyce E. VanDusen. 1984. "Sex in transition, 1900–1980." *Journal of Youth and Adolescence* 13, 5. (Reprinted in Arlene S. Skolnick and Jerome H. Skolnick (eds.) *Family in Transition* [pp. 151–160], 7th Ed. New York: HarperCollins.)

Darwin, Charles. n.d. *Origin of Species.* New York: Random House, Modern Library. (Originally published, 1859).

Davenport, William H. 1977. "Sex in cross-cultural perspective." In Frank A. Beach (ed.), *Human Sexuality in Four Perspectives* (pp. 115–153). Baltimore, MD: The Johns Hopkins University Press.

Davidoff, Leonore. 1975. *The Best Circles: Women and Society in Victorian England.* Totowa, NJ: Rowman & Littlefield.

Davis, Elizabeth Gould. 1971. *The First Sex.* New York: G.P. Putnam's Sons.

Davis, Kingsley. 1955. "Institutional patterns favoring high fertility in underdeveloped areas." *Eugenics Quarterly* 2:33–39.

———. 1976. "Sexual behavior." In Robert K. Merton and Robert Nisbet (eds.), *Contemporary Social Problems* (pp. 219–261), 4th ed. New York: Harcourt Brace Jovanovich.

Day, Charles R., Jr. 1989 "Tear up the tracks." *Industry Week* 239, 5 (March 5):5.

de Beauvoir, Simone. 1973. *The Coming of Age.* New York: Warner Books (Warner Paperback Library).

DeBuono, Barbara A., Stephen H. Zinner, Maxim Daamen, and William H. McCormack. 1990. "Sexual behavior of college women, in 1985, 1986, and 1989." *The New England Journal of Medicine* 322 (March 22):821–825.

Degler, Carl N. 1980. *At Odds: Women and the Family from the Revolution to the Present.* New York: Oxford University Press.

D'Emilio, John. 1983a. "Capitalism and gay identity." In Ann Snitow, Christine Stansell, and Sharon Thompson (eds.), *Powers of Desire: The Politics of Sexuality* (pp. 100–113). New York: Monthly Review Press.

———. 1983b. *Sexual Politics, Sexual Communities.* Chicago: University of Chicago Press.

Demos, John. 1970. *A Little Commonwealth.* New York: Oxford University Press.

———. 1974. "The American family in past time." *American Scholar* 43:422–446.

De Vita, Carol J. 1996. "The United States at Mid-Decade." *Population Bulletin* 50,4, (March): 1–48. Washington, DC: Population Reference Bureau.

DeWitt, P.M. 1992. "All the lonely people." *American Demographics* 14(4): 44–46, 48.

di Leonardo, Micaela. 1992, "The female world of cards and holidays: Women, families, and the work of kinship." In Barrie Thorne (ed.) with Marilyn Yalom, *Rethinking the Family: Some Feminist Questions* (pp. 246–261), rev. ed. Boston, MA: Northeastern University Press. [First published in *Signs: Journal of Women in Culture and Society,* 1987 12(3).]

Dinnerstein, Leonard, and David M. Reamers. 1975. *Ethnic Americans: A History of Immigration and Assimilation.* New York: Dodd, Mead.

Doherty, William J., M. Janice Hogan, Ekaterina V. Foteeva, and Galina A. Zaikina. 1994: "Divorce and its aftermath." In James W. Maddox, M. Janice Hogan, Anatolyi I. Antonov, and Mikhail S. Matskovsky (eds.) *Families Before and After Perestroika: Russian and U.S. Perspectives* (pp. 76–95). New York: Guilford Press.

Donzelet, Jacques. 1979. *The Policing of Families.* New York: Pantheon.

Dore, R.P. 1965. *City Life in Japan: A Study of a Tokyo Ward.* Berkeley/Los Angeles: University of California Press.

Duberman, Lucile. 1977. *Marriage and Other Alternatives,* 2d ed. New York: Praeger.

Dubois, Ellen Carol, and Linda Gordon. 1984. "Seeking ecstasy on the battlefield: Danger and pleasure in nineteenth-century feminist sexual thought." In Carole S. Vance (ed.), *Pleasure and Danger: Exploring Female Sexuality* (pp. 31–49). Boston, MA: Routledge & Kegan Paul.

Durkheim, Emile. 1915. *The Elementary Forms of the Religious Life,* Joseph Ward Swain (trans.). London: Allen & Unwin. (Originally published, 1912.)

———. 1951. *Suicide: A Study in Sociology,* John A. Spaulding and George Simpson (trans.). New York: The Free Press of Glencoe. (Originally published, 1897.)

———. 1964. *The Division of Labor in Society,* George Simpson (trans.). New York: The Free Press. (Originally published, 1893.)

Dworkin, Andrea. 1974. *Women Hating.* New York: E.P. Dutton.

Dyer, Everett D. 1963. "Parenthood as crisis: A restudy." *Marriage and Family Living* 25:196–201.

Ehrhardt, Anke A., Sandra Yingling, and Patricia A. Warne. 1991. Sexual behavior in the era of AIDS: What has changed in the United States?" *Annual Review of Sexual Research* 2:25–27.

Ehrlich, Elizabeth. 1990. "The mommy track." *Business Week* (March 20):126–134.

Eisenstadt, S.N. 1971. *From Generation to Generation.* New York: The Free Press.

Ekong, Sheilah Clarke. 1986. "Industrialization and kinship: A comparative study of some Nigerian ethnic groups." *Journal of Comparative Family Studies* 12 (Summer):197–206.

Elder, Glen H., Jr. 1974. *Children of the Great Depression.* Chicago: University of Chicago Press.

Elliott, Michael, and Christopher Dickey. 1994. "Body politics: Population Wars." *Newsweek* (September 12).

Engels, Friedrich. 1972. *The Origin of the Family, Private Property, and the State.* New York: Pathfinder Press. (Originally published, 1884.)

Eshleman, J. Ross. 1994. *The Family: An Introduction.* 7th ed. Boston: Allyn & Bacon.

Espanshade, Thomas J. 1985. "Marriage trends in America: Estimates, implications and underlying causes." *Population and Development Review* 11,2 (June):193–243.

Fanon, Frantz. 1965. *The Wretched of the Earth* (Preface by Jean Paul Sartre), Constance Farmington (trans.). New York: Grove Press.

———. 1967. *Black Skin White Masks,* Charles Lam Markmann (trans.). New York: Grove Press.

Farber, Bernard. 1964. *Family: Organization and Interaction.* San Francisco: Chandler.

Farley, Reynolds, and Walter Allen. 1987. *The Color Line and the Quality of Life in America.* New York: Oxford University Press.

Field, Mark G., and Karin I. Flynn. 1970. "Worker, mother housewife: Society woman today." In Georgene H. Seward and Robert C. Williamson (eds.), *Sex Roles in Changing Society* (pp. 257–284). New York: Random House.

Fineman, Mark. 1983. "In India, a judge avenges a social evil." *The Philadelphia Inquirer* (June 27).

———. 1985. "Computer joins ancient rite of matchmaking: Report on arranging marriage in India." *The Philadelphia Inquirer* (June 6).

Finkelhor, David, and Kersti Yllo. 1985. *License to Rape: Sexual Abuse of Wives.* New York: Holt, Rinehart, and Winston.

Firestone, Shulamith. 1970. *The Dialectic of Sex: The Case for Feminist Revolution.* New York: William Morrow.

Fischer, Claude S. 1982a. "The dispersion of kinship ties in modern society: Contemporary data and historical speculation." *Journal of Family History* 7 (Winter):353–375.

———. 1982b. *To Dwell Among Friends: Personal Networks in Town and City.* Chicago: University of Chicago Press.

———. 1992. "Gender and the residential telephone: 1890–1940." In Mark Hutter (ed.), *The Family Experience: A Reader in Cultural Diversity* (pp. 128–147). New York: Macmillan Publishing Company. [First published in *Sociological Forum* 1988, 3(2):211–233.]

Fischer, David Hackett. 1977. *Growing Old in America.* New York: Oxford University Press.

Fitzpatrick, Joseph P. 1971. *Puerto Rican Americans:*

The Meaning of Migration to the Mainland. Englewood Cliffs, NJ: Prentice-Hall.

Flandrin, Jean-Louis. 1979. *Families in Former Times: Kinship, Household, and Sexuality*, Richard Southern (trans). Cambridge, England: Cambridge University Press.

Flaste, Richard. 1979. "Research begins to focus on suicide among the aged." *The New York Times* (Jan. 2):C2.

Fogarty, Michael P., Rhona Rapoport, and Robert N. Rapoport. 1971. *Sex, Career and Family.* Beverly Hills, CA: Sage.

Foner, Ann. 1978. "Age stratification and the changing family." In John Demos and Sarane Spence Boocock (eds.), *Turning Points: Historical and Sociological Essays on the Family. American Journal of Sociology* 89(suppl):pp. S340–S365.

Ford, Clellan S. 1970. "Some primitive societies." In Georgene H. Seward and Robert C. Williamson (eds.), *Sex Roles in Changing Society* (pp. 25–43). New York: Random House.

———, and Frank A. Beach. 1951. *Patterns of Sexual Behavior.* New York: Harper & Row.

Forrest, Jacqueline, and Susheela Singh. 1990. "The sexual and reproductive behavior of American women." *Family Planning Perspectives* 22 (September/October):206–214.

Foucault, Michel. 1978. *The History of Sexuality. Volume 1, An Introduction.* New York: Random House.

Frank, Andre Gunder. 1966/1995. "The development of underdevelopment." In Stephen K. Sanderson (ed.), *Sociological Worlds: Comparative and Historical Readings on Society* (pp. 135–141). Los Angeles: Roxbury Publishing Company.

Franke, L.B. 1982. *The Ambivalence of Abortion.* New York: Random House.

Frazer, Sir James George. 1960. *The Golden Bough: A Study in Magic and Religion.* One volume, abridged ed. New York: The Macmillan Company. (Originally published, 1922.)

Freed, Doris, and Timothy Walker. 1988. "Family law in the fifty states." *Family Law Quarterly* 21:417–573.

Freedman, Ronald. 1963. "Norms for family size in underdeveloped areas." *Proceedings of the Rural Society*, B 159: 220–245. Reprinted in David M. Heer (ed.), 1968, *Readings on Population* (pp.

157–180). Englewood Cliffs, NJ: Prentice-Hall.

Freeman, Linton C. 1974. "Marriage without love: Mate-selection in non-Western societies." In Robert F. Winch and Graham B. Spanier (eds.), *Selected Studies in Marriage and the Family* (pp. 354–366), 4th ed. New York: Holt, Rinehart & Winston.

Freeman, M.D. 1979. *Violence in the Home.* Westmean, England: Saxon House.

Friedan, Betty. 1993. *The Fountain of Age.* New York: Simon and Schuster.

Friis, J.A. 1888. *Jajla: A Tale of Finmark.* London: G.P. Putnam's Sons.

Furstenberg, Frank F., and Andrew J. Cherlin. 1991. *Divided Families: What Happens to Children When Parents Part.* Cambridge, MA: Harvard University Press.

Furstenberg, Frank K., Jr., Philip Morgan, Kristin Moore, and James Peterson. 1987. "Race differences in the timing of adolescent intercourse." *American Sociological Review* 52(4) (August): 511–518.

Gambino, Richard. 1974. *Blood of My Blood: The Dilemma of the Italian-Americans.* New York: Doubleday Books.

Ganong, Lawrence, and Marilyn Coleman. 1994. *Remarried Family Relationships.* Newbury Park, CA: Sage Publications.

Gans, Herbert. 1962a. *The Urban Villagers: Group and Class in the Life of Italian-Americans.* New York: The Free Press.

———. 1962b. "Urbanism and suburbanism as ways of life: A reevaluation of definitions." In Arnold Rose (ed.), *Human Behavior and Social Process* (pp. 624–648). Boston: Houghton-Mifflin.

———. 1967a. "The Negro family: Reflections on the Moynihan report." In Lee Rainwater and William B. Yancey (eds.), *The Moynihan Report and the Politics of Controversy* (pp. 445–457). Cambridge, MA: M.I.T. Press.

———. 1967b. "Culture and class in the study of poverty: An approach to anti-poverty research." In Daniel P. Moynihan (ed.), *On Understanding Poverty* (pp. 201–228). New York: Basic Books.

———. 1967c. *The Levittowners.* New York: Vintage Books.

———. 1982/1979. "Symbolic ethnicity: The future

of ethnic groups and cultures in America." In Norman R. Yetman and C. Hoy Steele (eds.), *Majority and Minority* (pp. 495–508), 3d ed. Boston: Allyn & Bacon. [First published in *Ethnic and Racial Studies* 2, 1 (Jan. 1979)].

Gargan, Edward A. 1993. "For many brides in India, a dowry buys death." *The New York Times* (December 30).

Gee, Emma. 1978. "Japanese picture-brides." In Marjorie P.K. Weiser (ed.), *Ethnic America. The Reference Shelf* (pp. 53–60), Vol. 50, No. 2. New York: H.W. Wilson Company.

Gelles, Richard J. 1974. *The Violent Home*. Beverly Hills, CA: Sage.

———. 1979. Family *Violence*. Beverly Hills, CA: Sage.

———. 1983. "An exchange/social control theory." In David Finkelhor et al. (eds.), *The Dark Side of Families*. Beverly Hills, CA: Sage.

———, and Claire Pedrick-Cornell (eds.). 1983. *International Perspectives on Family Violence*. Lexington, MA: Lexington Books/D.C. Heath.

———, and Eileen F. Hargreaves. 1987. "Maternal employment and violence toward children." In Richard J. Gelles (ed.), *Family Violence* (pp. 108–225). Newbury Park, CA: Sage.

———, and Murray A. Straus. 1988. *Intimate Violence*. New York: Simon and Schuster.

Gelman, David, with Pamela Abramson, George Raine, Peter McAlvey, and Peter McKillop. 1985. "Who's taking care of our parents?" *Newsweek* (May 6):61–68.

Gersick, Kelin E. 1979. "Fathers by choice: Divorced men who receive custody of their children." In George Levinger and Oliver C. Moles (eds.), *Divorce and Separation: Context, Causes, and Consequences* (pp. 307–323). New York: Basic Books.

Ghurayyib, Rose. 1984. "The harem widow." In Robin Morgan (ed.), *Sisterhood is Global: The International Women's Movement Anthology* (pp. 419–423). Garden City, NY: Anchor Press/Doubleday.

Giordano, N.H., and J.A. Giordano. 1984. "Elder abuse: A review of the literature." *Social Work* 29:232–236.

Gist, Noel P., and Sylvia Fleis Fava. 1974. *Urban Society*, 6th ed. New York: Thomas Y. Crowell.

Glendon, Mary Ann. 1989. *The Transformation of Family Law: State, Law and the Family in the U.S. and Western Europe*. Chicago: University of Chicago Press.

Glenn, Norval D. 1982. "Interreligious marriage in the United States: Patterns and recent trends." *Journal of Marriage and the Family* 44 (Aug.): 555–566.

Glick, Paul C. 1975. "A demographer looks at American families." *Journal of Marriage and the Family* 37:15–26.

———. 1984b. "Marriage, divorce and living arrangements: Prospective changes." *Journal of Family Issues* 5:7–26.

———. 1984a. "American household structure in transition." *Family Planning Perspectives* 16:205–211.

———. 1990. "Remarried families, stepfamilies, and stepchildren: A brief demographic analysis." *Family Relations* 38:7–26.

———, and Arthur J. Norton. 1979. "Marrying, divorcing, and living together in the U.S. today." *Population Bulletin* 32, 5. Washington, DC: Population Reference Bureau.

———, and Graham B. Spanier. 1980. "Married and unmarried cohabitation in the United States." *Journal of Marriage and the Family* 42:19–30.

———, and Sung-Ling Lin. 1986. "Recent changes in divorce and remarriage." *Journal of Marriage and the Family* 48 (Nov.):737–747.

Goldscheider, Calvin. 1971. *Population, Modernization and Social Structure*. Boston: Little, Brown.

———, and A.S. Zuckerman. 1984. *The Transformation of the Jews*. Chicago, IL: University of Chicago Press.

Goldscheider, Frances K., and Linda J. Waite. 1991. *New Families, No Families: The Transformation of the American Home*. Berkeley, CA: University of California Press.

Goldsmith, M.F. 1992. " 'Critical moment' at hand in HIV/AIDS pandemic: New global strategy to arrest its spread proposed." *The Journal of the American Medical Association* 268:445–446.

Goldwyn, Edward (writer and producer). 1984. "China's only child." *Nova*. This program was originally broadcast on PBS on February 14, 1984.

Goliber, Thomas J. 1985. "Sub-Saharan Africa:

Population pressures on development." *Population Bulletin* 40, 1 (Feb.).

Gonzales, Phillip B. 1993. "Historical poverty, restructuring effects, and integrative ties: Mexican American neighborhoods in a peripheral sunbelt economy." In Joan Moore and Raquel Pinderhughes (eds.), 1993, *In the Barrios: Latinos and the Underclass Debate* (pp. 149–171). New York: Russell Sage Foundation.

Good Housekeeping. 1982. "Rape: The likeliest time, place, and victim." (July): 195.

Goode, William J. 1956. *After Divorce.* Glencoe, IL: The Free Press.

———. 1959. "The theoretical importance of love." *American Sociological Review* 24:38–47.

———. 1960. "A theory of role strain." *American Sociological Review* 25 (Aug.):483–496.

———. 1962. "Marital satisfaction and instability: A cross-cultural analysis of divorce rates." In Reinhard Bendix and Seymour M. Lipset (eds.), *Class, Status, and Power* (pp. 377–387), 2d ed. New York: The Free Press.

———. 1963. *World Revolution and Family Patterns.* New York: The Free Press.

———. 1964. *The Family.* Englewood Cliffs, NJ: Prentice-Hall.

———. 1971. "Force and violence in the family." *Journal of Marriage and the Family* 33:624–636.

———. 1976. "Family disorganization." In Robert K. Merton and Robert Nisbet (eds.), *Contemporary Social Problems* (pp. 511–554), 4th ed. New York: Harcourt Brace Jovanovich.

———. 1993. *World Changes in Divorce Patterns.* New Haven, CT: Yale University Press.

Goodwin, John. 1973. *The Mating Trade.* Garden City, NY: Doubleday.

Gordon, Michael. 1977. "Review of *The Making of the Modern Family,* by E. Shorter." *Contemporary Sociology,* 6:169–171.

———. 1978. *The American Family: Past, Present, and Future.* New York: Random House.

———. 1981. "Was Waller ever right? The rating and dating complex reconsidered." *Journal of Marriage and the Family* 43:67–76.

Gordon, Milton. 1964. *Assimilation in American Life.* New York: Oxford University Press.

Gordon, Suzanne. 1976. *Lonely in America.* New York: Simon & Schuster (Touchstone Books).

Gough, Kathleen. 1971. "The origin of the family."

Journal of Marriage and the Family 33:760–770.

Gould, Stephen Jay. 1981. *The Mismeasure of Man.* New York: Norton.

Gray, Francine Du Plessix. 1989. *Soviet Women: Walking the Tightrope.* New York: Doubleday.

Gray, L.A., and M. Saracino. 1991. "College students' attitudes, beliefs, and behaviors about AIDS: Implications for family life educators." *Family Relations* 40:258–263.

Greenstein, Theodore N. 1990. "Marital disruption and the employment of married women." *Journal of Marriage and the Family* 52, 3 (August):657–676.

Greer, Scott. 1956. "Urbanism reconsidered: A comparative study of local areas in a metropolis." *American Sociological Review* 21:19–25.

Greven, Philip J., Jr. 1970. *Four Generations: Population, Land, and Fertility in Colonial Andover, Massachusetts.* Ithaca, NY: Cornell University Press.

Gross, Jane. 1994. "Second wave of AIDS feared by officials in San Francisco." *The New York Times* (December 11):1,10.

Grossman, James R. 1989. *Land of Hope: Chicago, Black Southerners, and the Great Migration.* Chicago, IL: University of Chicago Press.

Gusfield, Joseph R. 1967. "Tradition and modernity: Misplaced polarities in the study of social change." *American Journal of Sociology* 72:351–362.

Gutman, Herbert. 1976. *The Black Family in Slavery and Freedom: 1750–1925.* New York. Random House.

Gwartney-Gibbs, Patricia A. 1986. "The institutionalization of premarital cohabitation: Estimates from marriage license applications, 1970 and 1980." *Journal of Marriage and the Family* 48 (May):423–434.

Haas, Linda. 1992. *Equal Parenting and Social Policy: A Study of Parental Leave in Sweden.* Albany: State University of New York Press.

Haeri, Shahla. 1993. "Obedience versus autonomy: Women and fundamentalism in Iran and Pakistan. In Martin E. Marty and R. Scott Appleby (eds.), *Fundamentalisms and Society Reclaiming the Sciences, the Family, and Education* (pp. 181–213). Chicago: University of Chicago Press.

Hagestad, Gunhilde O. 1981. "Problems and promises in the social psychology of intergenerational relations." In Robert W. Fogel et al. (eds.), *Aging: Stability and Change in the Family* (pp. 11–46). New York: Academic Press.

Hall, G. Stanley. 1904. *Adolescence: Its Psychology and Its Relation to Physiology, Anthropology, Sociology, Sex Crime, Religion and Education*. New York: Appleton.

Halperin, Rhoda H. 1990. *The Livelihood of Kin: Making Ends Meet "The Kentucky Way"*. Austin: University of Texas Press.

Hareven, Tamara K. 1971. "The history of the family as an interdisciplinary field." In Theodore K. Rabb and Robert I. Rotberg (eds.), *The Family in History: Interdisciplinary Essays* (pp. 211–226). New York: Harper (Torchbooks).

———. 1975. "Family time and industrial time: Family and work in a planned corporation town, 1900–1924." *Journal of Urban History* 1:365–389.

———. 1976. "The last stage: Historical adulthood and old age." *Daedalus* 105:13–27. (Fall issue titled, "American Civilization: New Perspectives.")

———. 1978. "The dynamics of kin in an industrial community." In J. Demos and S.S. Boocock (eds.), *Turning Points: Historical Points: Historical and Sociological Essays on the Family* (pp. 151–182). Chicago: University of Chicago Press.

———. 1982. *Family Time and Industrial Time*. New York: Cambridge University Press.

———, and John Modell. 1980. "Family patterns." In Stephen Thernstrom (ed.), *Harvard Encyclopedia of American Ethnic Groups* (pp. 345–354). Cambridge, MA, and London, England: The Belknap Press of Harvard University Press.

Harris, Marvin. 1968. *The Rise of Anthropological Theory: A History of Theories of Culture*. New York: Thomas Y. Crowell.

———. 1988. *Culture, People, Nature: An Introduction to General Anthropology*, 5th ed. New York: Harper/Collins.

Hartman, Harriet, and Moshe Hartman. 1993. "How equal is equal? A comparison of gender equality among Israeli and American Jews." *Contemporary Jewry* 14:48–72.

Haub, Carl. 1993. "China's fertility drop lowers world growth rate." *Population Today* 21,6 (June):1–3.

Hedges, Chris. 1994. "Key panel at Cairo talks agrees on population plan." *The New York Times* (September 13).

Helfer, Ray E., and C. Henry Kempe (eds.). 1968. *The Battered Child*. Chicago: University of Chicago Press.

Helgesen, Sally. 1982. "Do your parents ask too much of you?" *Seventeen* (Apr.):176–177.

Henretta, James A. 1971. "The morphology of New England society in the colonial period." In Theodore K. Rabb and Robert I. Rotberg (eds.), *The Family in History. Interdisciplinary Essays* (pp. 191–210). New York: Harper (Torchbooks).

Herman, Sondra R. 1974. "The liberated women of Sweden." *The Center Magazine* 7:76–78.

Hobart, Charles. 1993. "Interest in marriage among Canadian students at the end of the eighties." *Journal of Comparative Family Studies* 24.1: 45–61.

Hobbs, Daniel F. 1965. "Parenthood as crisis: A third study." *Journal of Marriage and the Family* 27:367–372.

———. 1968. "Transition to parenthood: A replication and an extension." *Journal of Marriage and the Family* 30:413–417.

———, and Sue Peck Cole. 1976. "Transition to parenthood: A decade replication." *Journal of Marriage and the Family* 38:723–731.

Hochschild, Arlie Russell. 1976. "Communal life systems for the old." In Cary S. Kart and Barbara B. Manard (eds.), *Aging in America: Readings in Social Gerontology* (pp. 367–384). Port Washington, NY: Alfred Publishing. (Reprinted from *Society* 10, 1973.)

———. 1989a. *The Second Shift: Working Parent and the Revolution at Home*. New York: Viking/Penguin.

———. 1989b. "The economy of gratitude." In David D. Franks and E. Doyle McCarthy (eds.), *The Sociology of Emotions: Original Essays and Research Papers* (pp. 95–113). Greenwich, CT: JAI Press.

Hoem, Britta, and Jan M. Hoem. 1988. "The Swedish family: Aspects of contemporary development." *Journal of Family Issues* 9 (September):397–424.

Hogan, David. 1983. "Ethnicity and education." Paper presented at "Making it in America," a conference sponsored by the Balch Institute for

Ethnic Studies and the American Jewish Committee, Philadelphia, Apr. 21.

Hogan, M. Janice, James W. Maddock, Anatolyi I. Antonov, and Mikhail S. Matskovsky. 1994. "The future of families." In James W. Maddox, M. Janice Hogan, Anatolyi I. Antonov, and Mikhail S. Matskovsky (eds.), *Families Before and After Perestroika: Russian and U.S. Perspectives* (pp. 220–234). New York: Guilford Press.

Holden, W.C. 1871. *The Past and Future of the Kafir Races*. London: Author.

Hollingshead, August de B. 1949. *Elmtown's Youth: The Impact of Social Class on Adolescents*. New York: John Wiley & Sons.

Horowitz, Ruth. 1983. *Honor and the American Dream: Culture and Identity in a Chicano Community*. New Brunswick, NJ: Rutgers University Press.

Hosken, F.P. 1982. *The Hosken Report: Genital and Sexual Mutilation of Females*. Lexington, MA: Women's International Network News.

Howell, Joseph T. 1973. *Hard Living on Clay Street*. Garden City, NY: Doubleday (Anchor Books).

Huber, Joan. 1990. "Macro-micro links in gender stratification." *American Sociological Review* 55:1–10.

———. 1993. "A theory of gender stratification." In Laurel Richardson and Verta Taylor (eds.), *Feminist Frontiers III* (pp. 131–140). New York: McGraw-Hill.

———, and Glenna Spitze. 1988. "Trends in family sociology." In Neil J. Smelser (ed.), *Handbook of Sociology* (pp. 425–448). Newbury Park, CA: Sage Publications.

Hughes, Pennethorne. 1971. *Witchcraft*. Harmondsworth, England: Penguin Books.

Hunt, Janet G., and Larry L. Hunt. 1982. "The dualities of careers and families: New integrations or new polarizations?" *Social Problems* 29 (June):499–510.

Hunt, Morton M. 1959. *The Natural History of Love*. New York: Knopf.

Hutter, Mark. 1970. "Transformation of identity, social mobility and kinship solidarity." *Journal of Marriage and the Family* 32:133–137.

Iaconetti, Joan. 1988. "Coping with the decision not to have children." In J. Gipson Wells (ed.), *Current Issues in Marriage and the Family* (pp. 143–148). New York: Macmillan Publishing Company.

India Abroad. 1988. "Modern classified matrimonial ads in *India Abroad*." In Mark Hutter, *The Changing Family: Comparative Perspectives* (p. 73), 2d ed. New York: Macmillan.

Inkeles, Alex. 1983. *Explaining Individual Modernity*. New York: Columbia University Press.

Internal Medicine World Report 1987. "Roundup, AIDS—The year in review" (Nov.) 2:2–4; 34–35.

Itoli, K., and B. Powell. 1992. "Take a hike, Hiroshi." *Newsweek* (August 10): 38–39.

Jackson, Kenneth T. 1985. *Crabgrass Frontier: The Suburbanization of the United States*. New York: Oxford University Press.

Jacobs, Jerry. 1976. "An ethnographic study of retirement setting." In Cary S. Kart and Barbara B. Manard (eds.), *Aging in America: Readings in Social Gerontology* (pp. 385–394). Port Washington, NY: Alfred Publishing Co. (Reprinted from *Gerontologist* 14:483–487, 1974.)

Jacobson, Paul H. 1959. *American Marriage and Divorce*. New York: Rinehart.

Jacoby, Arthur P. 1969. "Transition to parenthood: A reassessment." *Journal of Marriage and the Family* 31:720–727.

Johnson, John M., and Kathleen J. Ferraro. 1984. "The Victimized Self: The Case of Battered Women." In Joseph A. Kotarba and Andrea Fontana (eds.), *The Existential Self in Society* (pp. 119–130). Chicago, IL: University of Chicago Press. Reprinted in Mark Hutter (ed.), 1997. *The Family Experience: A Reader in Cultural Diversity* (pp. 395–403), 2d ed. Boston, MA: Allyn & Bacon.

Jones, Charles L., Lorne Tepperman, and Susannah J. Wilson. 1995. *The Futures of the Family*. Englewood Cliffs, NJ: Prentice-Hall.

Jones, Elise, et al. 1985. "Teenage pregnancy in developed countries: Determinants and policy implications." *Family Planning Perspectives* 17(2):53–65. Reprinted in Mark Hutter (ed.), 1991. *The Family Experience: A Reader in Cultural Diversity*. New York: Macmillan Publishing Company.

Jones, Maldwyn Allen. 1960. *American Immigration*. Chicago: University of Chicago Press.

Judd, Eleanore Parelman. 1990. "Intermarriage and the maintenance of religio-ethnic identity a case study: The Denver Jewish community." *Journal of Comparative Family Studies* 21 (Summer) 2:251–265.

Juran, S. 1991. "Sexual behavior changes among heterosexual, lesbian and gay bar patrons as assessed by questionnaire over an 18-month period." *Journal of Psychology and Human Sexuality* 4:111–121.

Juviler, Peter H. 1984. "The urban family and the Soviet state: Emerging contours of a demographic policy." In Henry W. Morton and Robert C. Stuart (eds.), *The Contemporary Soviet City* (pp. 84–112). Armonk, NY: M.E. Sharpe.

Kalish, Susan. 1992. "New UN projections include local effects of AIDS." *Population Today*. 20, 10(October):1–2.

Kantrowitz, Barbara. 1989. "Advocating a 'mommy track'." *Newsweek* (March 13):45.

Kaplan, Gisela. 1992. *Contemporary Western European Feminism*. New York: New York University Press.

Kart, Cary S., and Barbara B. Manard (eds.). 1976. *Aging in America: Readings in Social Gerontology*. Port Washington, NY: Alfred Knopf Publishing Co.

Katz, Jonathan Ned. 1995. *The Invention of Heterosexuality*. New York: Dutton.

Keller, Bill. 1993. "Squatters testing limits as apartheid crumbles." *The New York Times* (Nov. 14).

———. 1995. "After apartheid, change lags behind expectations." *The New York Times* (April 27).

Kemper, Theodore D. 1983. "Predicting the divorce rate: Down?" *Journal of Family Issues* 4:507–524.

Keniston, Kenneth. 1965. *The Uncommitted: Alienated Youth in American Society*. New York: Harcourt, Brace and World.

———, and The Carnegie Council on Children. 1977. *All Our Children: The American Family Under Pressure*. New York: Harcourt Brace Jovanovich.

Kenkel, William F. 1977. *The Family in Perspective*, 4th ed. Santa Monica, CA: Goodyear.

Kett, Joseph F. 1977. *Rites of Passage: Adolescence in America 1790 to the Present*. New York: Basic Books.

Key, William H. 1961. "Rural urban differences and the family." *Sociological Quarterly* 2:49–56.

Kifner, John. 1984. "Iran: Obsessed with martyrdom." *The New York Times Magazine* (Dec. 16):36–42, 47, 52, 54, 56.

Kikumura, Akemi, and Harry H.L. Kitano. 1981. "The Japanese American family." In Charles H. Mindel and Robert W. Habenstein (eds.), *Ethnic Families in America: Patterns and Variations* (pp. 43–60), 2d ed. New York: Elsevier.

Kitano, Harry H.L. 1980. "Japanese." In Stephan Thernstrom (ed.). *Harvard Encyclopedia of American Ethnic Groups* (pp. 561–571). Cambridge, MA and London, England: Belknap Press of Harvard University Press.

———. 1988. "The Japanese American Family." In Charles H. Mindel, Robert W. Habenstein, and Roosevelt Wright, Jr. (eds.), *Ethnic Families in America: Patterns and Variations* (pp. 258–275), 3d ed. New York: Elsevier.

Kitson, Gay C., and Leslie A. Morgan. 1990. "The multiple consequences of divorce: A decade review." *Journal of Marriage and the Family* 52(4) (November):913–924.

Klemesrud, Judy. 1976. "Many elderly in the Bronx spend their lives in terror of crime." *The New York Times* (Nov. 22).

Knox, David, and Kenneth Wilson. 1981. "Dating behaviors of university students." *Family Relations* 30:225–258.

Kohen, Janet A., Carol A. Brown, and Roslyn Feldberg. 1979. "Divorced mothers: The cost and benefits of female control." In George Lovinger and Oliver C. Moles (eds.), *Divorce and Separation: Context, Causes, and Consequences* (pp. 228–245). New York: Basic Books.

Kooy, Gerrit A. 1963. "Social system and the problem of aging." In Richard H. Williams, Clark Tibbits, and Wilma Donahue (eds.), *Processes of Aging: Social and Psychological Perspectives* (pp. 45–60), Vol. 2. New York: Atherton Press.

Korman, Sheila. 1983. "Nontraditional dating behavior: Dating initiation and date expense-sharing among feminists and non-feminists." *Family Relations* 32 (October):575–581.

Kosberg, Jordan I. 1988. "Preventing elder abuse: Identification of high-risk factors prior to placement decisions." *Gerontologist* 28:1.

Kosmin, Barry. 1991. *1990 National Jewish Population Survey*. New York: Council of Jewish Federation.

Koss, Mary P. 1988. "Hidden rape: Sexual aggression and victimization in a national sample of students in higher education." In Ann Wolber Burgess (ed.), *Rape and Sexual Assault* (pp. 3–25), Vol. II. New York: Garland.

Kozol, Jonathan. 1988. *Rachel and Her Children: Homeless Families in America*. New York: Crown Publishers.

Lacayo, Richard. 1992. "Abortion: The future is already here." *Time* (May 4).

Lambert, William W., Leigh Mintum Triandis, and Margery Wolf. 1959. "Some correlates of beliefs in the malevolence and benevolence of supernatural beings: A cross-societal study." *Journal of Abnormal and Social Psychology* 58 (Mar.):162–169.

Landor, A.H.S. 1893. *Alone With the Hairy Ainu*. London: J. Murray.

Laner, Mary Reige. 1989. *Dating: Delights, Discontents, and Dilemmas*. Salem, WI: Sheffield.

Lapidus, Gail Warshofsky. 1978. *Women in Soviet Society*. Berkeley, CA: University of California Press.

———. 1982. "Introduction: Women, work, and family: New Soviet perspectives." In Gail Warshofsky Lapidus (ed.), *Women, Work, and Family in the Soviet Union* (pp. ix–xlii). Armonk, NY: M.E. Sharpe.

LaRossa, Ralph. 1983. "The transition to parenthood and the social reality of time." *Journal of Marriage and the Family* 43 (Aug.):579–589.

———, and Maureen M. LaRossa. 1981. *Transition to Parenthood: How Infants Change Families*. Beverly Hills, CA: Sage Publications.

Lasch, Christopher. 1975a. "The emotions of family life." *New York Review of Books* (Nov. 27).

———. 1975b. "The family and history." *New York Review of Books* (Nov. 13).

———. 1975c. "What the doctor ordered." *New York Review of Books* (Dec. 11).

———. 1977a. *Haven in a Heartless World: The Family Besieged*. New York: Basic Books.

———. 1977b. "The siege of the family." *New York Review of Books* (Nov. 24).

———. 1979. *The Culture of Narcissism*. New York: W.W. Norton.

Laslett, Barbara. 1973. "The family as a public and private institution: An historical perspective." *Journal of Marriage and the Family* 35:480–492.

Laslett, Peter. 1965. *The World We Have Lost. England Before the Industrial Revolution*. New York: Charles Scribners Sons.

———, (ed.). 1972. *Household and Family in Past Time*. Cambridge, MA: Cambridge University Press.

Lau, E.E., and J.I. Kosberg. 1979. "Abuse of the elderly by informal care providers." *Aging:* 10–15.

Lelyveld, Joseph. 1986. *Move Your Shadow: South Africa, Black and White*. New York: Penguin Books.

Lemann, Nicholas. 1991. *The Promised Land: The Great Black Migration and How It Changed America*. New York: Alfred A. Knopf.

LeMasters, E.E. 1957. "Parenthood as crisis." *Marriage and Family Living* 19:352–355.

———. 1977. *Parents in Modern America*. Homewood, IL: Dorsey.

Lemon, Anthony. 1982. "Migrant labour and frontier commuters: Reorganizing South Africa's black labour supply." In David M. Smith (ed.), *Living Under Apartheid* (pp. 64–89). London: George Allen & Unwin.

Lenin, V.I. 1966. "The tasks of the working women's movement in the Soviet republic." (Speech delivered at the fourth Moscow City conference of nonparty working women, September 23, 1919.) In *The Emancipation of Women: From the Writings of V.I. Lenin* (Preface by Nadezhda K. Krupskaya) (pp. 66–72). New York: International Publishers.

Lenski, Gerhard, and Jean Lenski 1982. *Human Societies: An Introduction to Macrosociology*, 4th ed. New York: McGraw-Hill.

Le Play, Frederic. 1855. *Les Ouvriers Europiens*. Paris: Imprimerie Royale.

Lerner, Daniel. 1958. *The Passing of Traditional Society: Modernizing the Middle East*. Glencoe, IL: The Free Press of Glencoe.

Lerner, Gerda. 1986. *The Creation of Patriarchy*. New York: Oxford University Press.

Leslie, Gerald R. 1979. *The Family in Social Context*, 4th ed. New York: Oxford University Press.

Levinson, David. 1989. *Family Violence in Cross-Cultural Perspective*. Newbury Park, CA: Sage Publications.

Levi-Strauss, Claude. 1957. "The principle of reciprocity." In Lewis A. Coser and Bernard Rosenberg (eds.), *Sociological Theory: A Book of Readings* (pp. 84–94). New York: Macmillan.

———. 1971. "The family." In H.L. Shapiro (ed.), *Man, Culture and Society* (pp. 333–357). New York: Oxford University Press.

Levy, Marion J., Jr. 1966. *Modernization and the Structure of Societies*. Princeton, NJ: Princeton University Press.

Lewin, Tamar. 1989. "Family or career? Choose, women told." *The New York Times* (March 8).

———. 1995. "Family decay global, study says." *The New York Times* (May 30).

Lewis, Anthony. 1995. "The new South Africa." *The New York Times* (January, 19).

Lewis, Oscar. 1966. *La Vida: A Puerto Rican Family in the Culture of Poverty—San Juan and New York*. New York: Random House.

Liebow, Elliot. 1967. *Tally's Corner: A Study of Negro Street Corner Men*. Boston: Little, Brown.

Liljestrom, Rita. 1970. "The Swedish model." In Georgene H. Seward and Robert C. Williamson (eds.), *Sex Roles in Changing Society* (pp. 200–219). New York: Random House.

———. 1978. "Sweden." In Sheila B. Kamerman and Alfred J. Kahn (eds.), *Family Policy: Government and Families in Fourteen Countries* (pp. 19–48). New York: Columbia University Press.

Linden, Eugene. 1994. "More power to women, fewer mouths to feed." *Time* (September, 26).

Lindsey, Linda. 1994. *Gender Roles: A Sociological Perspective*. 2d ed. Englewood Cliffs, NJ: Prentice-Hall.

Litvin, Sandra J. 1992. "Status transitions and future outlook as determinants of conflict: The caregiver's and care receiver's perspective." *The Gerontologist* 32, 1:68–76.

Litwak, Eugene. 1959–1960. "The use of extended family groups in the achievement of social goals." *Social Problems* 7:177–188.

———. 1960a. "Geographical mobility and extended family cohesion." *American Sociological Review* 25:385–394.

———. 1960b. "Occupational mobility and extended family cohesion." *American Sociological Review* 25:385–394.

London, Kathryn A. 1991. "Cohabitation, marriage, marital dissolution, and remarriage: United States, 1988." *Vital Health Statistics*. Hyattsville, MD: National Center for Health Statistics.

Longfellow, Cynthia. 1979. "Divorce in context: Its impact on children." In George Levinger and Oliver C. Moles (eds.), *Divorce and Separation: Context, Causes, and Consequences* (pp. 287–306). New York: Basic Books.

Luker, Kristin. 1984. *Abortion and the Politics of Motherhood*. Berkeley, CA: University of California Press.

Mace, David, and Vera Mace. 1960. *Marriage: East and West*. Garden City, NY: Doubleday.

Macionis, John J. 1993. *Sociology*. 4th ed. Englewood Cliffs, NJ: Prentice-Hall.

Macklin, Eleanor D. 1972. "Heterosexual cohabitation among unmarried college students." *The Family Coordinator* 21:463–472.

———. 1978. "Nonmarital heterosexual cohabitation." *Marriage and Family Review* 1:1–12.

———. 1981. "Cohabitating college students." In Peter J. Stein (ed.), *Single Life: Unmarried Adults in Social Context* (pp. 210–220). New York: St. Martin's Press.

Maine, Henry Sumner. 1960. *Ancient Law*. London: J.M. Dent & Sons. (Orginally published, 1861.)

Makepeace, James. 1981. "Courtship violence among college students." *Family Relations* 30, 1 (Jan.):97–102.

Mamonova, Tatyana (ed.) 1984. *Woman and Russia: Feminist Writings from the Soviet Union*. Boston: Beacon.

Mangin, William. 1960. "Mental health and migration to cities." *Annals of the New York Academy of Sciences* 84:911–917.

———. 1968. "Tales from the barriadas." *Nickel Review*, September 25-October 8, 1968. Reprinted in William Mangin (ed.), 1970, *Peasants in Cities: Readings in the Anthropology of Urbanization* (pp. 55–61). Boston: Houghton-Mifflin.

——— (ed.). 1970. *Peasants in Cities: Readings in the Anthropology of Urbanization*. Boston: Houghton-Mifflin.

Marris, Peter. 1958. *Widows and Their Families*. London: Routledge & Kegan Paul.

———. 1961. *Family and Social Change in an African City: A Study of Rehousing in Lagos*. Evanston, IL: Northwestern University Press.

Martin, Del. 1976. *Battered Wives*. San Francisco: Glide Publications.

Martin, Teresa Castro, and Larry Bumpass. 1989. "Recent trends in marital disruption." *Demography* 26:37–51.

Martindale, Don. 1960. *The Nature and Types of Sociological Theory*. Cambridge, MA: Houghton-Mifflin.

Matloff, Judith. 1995. "Life in the new South Africa: Racial strife slowly easing." *The Christian Science Monitor* (April 27).

Mbate, Robert Muema. 1969, Nairobi. "Identity." *Bursara* 2, 3:31–34.

McCall, Michal M. 1966. "Courtship as social exchange: Some historical comparison." In Bernard Farber (ed.), *Kinship and Family Organization* (pp. 190–200). New York: John Wiley & Sons.

McKee, Michael, and Ian Robertson. 1975. *Social Problems*. New York: Random House.

McLanahan, Sara S., and Julia Adams. 1989. "The effects of children on adults' psychological well-being." *Social Forces* 68 (September): 79–91.

———, and Larry Bumpass. 1988. "Intergenerational consequences of family disruption." *American Journal of Sociology* 94 (1):130–152.

———, and Gary Sandefur. 1994. *Growing Up with a Single Parent: What Hurts, What Helps*. Cambridge, MA: Harvard University Press.

McNally, J.W., and W.D. Mosher. 1991. "AIDS-related knowledge and behavior among women 15–44 years of age: United States, 1988." *Family Planning Perspectives* 23 (September/October):234–235.

Mead, Margaret. 1928. *Coming of Age in Samoa*. New York: William Morrow.

———. 1949. *Male and Female: A Study of the Sexes in a Changing World*. New York: William Morrow.

———. 1954. "Some theoretical considerations on the problems of mother-child separation." *American Journal of Orthopsychiatry* 24:471–483.

———. 1963. *Sex and Temperament in Three Primitive Societies*. New York: William Morrow. (Originally published, 1935; reprinted in 1950.)

———. 1966. "Marriage in two steps." *Redbook* 127:48–149.

———. 1971. "Anomalies in American postdivorce relationships." In Paul Bohannan (ed.), *Divorce and After* (pp. 107–125). Garden City, NY: Doubleday (Anchor Books).

———. 1970. *Culture and Commitment: A Study of the Generation Gap*. New York: Natural History Press/Doubleday.

———. 1975. *Blackberry Winter: My Earlier Years*. New York: Pocket Books.

Merton, Robert K. 1957. *Social Theory and Social Structure*. New York: Free Press.

Metcalf, Ann. 1979. "Family reunion: Networks and treatment in a Native American community." *Group Psychotherapy, Psychodrama, and Sociometry* 32:179–189.

Metzker, Isaac (ed.). 1971. *A Bintel Brief*. New York: Ballantine Books.

Mill, John Stuart. 1966. *On Liberty, Representative Government, the Subjection of Women. Three Essays*. London: Oxford University Press (The World Classics). (*The Subjection of Women* was originally published in 1869.)

Miller, Dorothy. 1979. "The Native American family: The urban way." In Eunice Corfman (ed.), *Families Today: A Research Sampler on Families and Children* (pp. 441–484). Washington, DC: US Government Printing Office.

Millett, Kate. 1970. *Sexual Politics*. Garden City, NY: Doubleday.

Milne, Leslie. 1924. *The Home of an Eastern Clan*. Oxford: Clarendon Press.

Minturn, Leigh, and William W. Lambert. 1964. *Mothers of Six Cultures: Antecedent of Child Rearing*. New York: John Wiley & Sons.

Mitchell, Juliet. 1984. *Women: The Longest Revolution*. New York: Pantheon.

Moen, Phyllis. 1989. *Working Parents: Transformations in Gender Roles and Public Policies in Sweden*. Madison, WI: University of Wisconsin Press.

Mogey, John. 1964. "Family and community in urban-industrial societies." In Harold T. Christensen (ed.), *Handbook of Marriage and the Family* (pp. 501–534). Chicago: Rand McNally.

Montague, Ashley. 1973. *Man and Aggression*, 2d ed. London: Oxford University Press.

Monter, E. William. 1977. "The pedestal and the stake: Courtly love and witchcraft." In Renate Bridenthal and Claudia Koonz (eds.), *Becoming Visible: Women in European History* (pp. 119–136). Boston: Houghton-Mifflin.

Montero, Darryl. 1981. "The Japanese Americans: Changing patterns of assimilation over three generations." *American Sociological Review* 46 (Dec.):829–839.

Montiel, Miguel. 1970. "The social science myth of the Mexican American family." *El Grito: A Journal of Contemporary Mexican American Thought* 3 (Summer):56–63.

———. 1973. "The Chicano family: A review of research." *Social Work* 18 (March):22–31.

Moore, Henrietta L. 1988. *Feminism and Anthropology*. Minneapolis: University of Minnesota Press.

Moore, Joan, and James Diego Vigil. 1993. "Barrios in transition." In Joan Moore and Raquel Pinderhughes (eds.), 1993. *In the Barrios: Latinos and the Underclass Debate* (pp. 27–49). New York: Russell Sage Foundation.

———, and Raquel Pinderhughes (eds.). 1993. *In the Barrios: Latinos and the Underclass Debate*. New York: Russell Sage Foundation.

Moore, Molly. 1994. "Changing India, wedded to tradition." *Washington Post* (October 8).

Moore, Wilbert E. 1964. "Social aspects of economic development." In Robert E.L. Faris (ed.), *Handbook of Modern Sociology* (pp. 882–911). Chicago: Rand McNally.

Morgan, Lewis Henry. 1963. *Ancient Society*. Edited with an introduction and annotations by Eleanor B. Leacock. New York: World (Meridian Books). (Originally published, 1870.)

Morgan, Robin. 1984a. "India." In Robin Morgan (ed.), *Sisterhood Is Global: The International Women's Movement* (pp. 294–305). Garden City, NY: Anchor Press/Doubleday.

———. 1984b. "Planetary feminism: The politics of the 21st century." In Robin Morgan (ed.), *Sisterhood Is Global: The International Women's Movement* (pp. 1–37). Garden City, NY: Anchor Press/Doubleday.

———. (ed.). 1984c. *Sisterhood Is Global: The International Women's Movement*. Garden City, NY: Anchor Press/Doubleday.

Morris, Desmond. 1970. *The Human Zoo*. New York: McGraw-Hill.

Murdock, George. 1937. "Comparative data on the division of labor by sex." *Social Forces* 15:551–553.

———. 1949. *Social Structure*. New York: Macmillan.

———. 1950. "Family stability in non-European cultures." *Annals of the American Academy of Political and Social Science* 272:195–201.

———. 1957. "World ethnographic sample." *American Anthropologist* 59:664–687.

Murillo, Nathan. 1971. "The Mexican American family." In Nathaniel N. Wagner and Marsha J. Haug (eds.), *Chicanos: Social and Psychological Perspectives* (pp. 99–102). St. Louis: Mosby.

Musgrove, Frank. 1964. *Youth and the Social Order*. Bloomington: Indiana University Press.

Myers, Michael F. 1989. *Men and Divorce*. New York: Guilford Press.

Nam, Charles B. 1994. *Understanding Population Change*. Itasca, IL: F.E. Peacock Publishers.

National Center for Health Statistics. 1977. "Marriage and divorce." *Vital Statistics of the United States 1973*, Vol. III. Washington, DC: U.S. Government Printing Office.

———. 1978. "Births, Marriages, Divorces and Deaths for 1977." *Monthly Vital Statistics Report*, 26, 12. Washington, DC: U.S. Government Printing Office.

National Council for the Prevention of Child Abuse (NCPCA). 1991. *Current Trends in Child Abuse Reporting and Fatalities:* The results of the 1990 annual fifty state survey. Chicago: NCPCA.

Neal, Arthur G., H. Theodore Groat, and Jerry W. Wicks. 1989. "Attitudes about having children: A study of 600 couples in the early years of marriage." *Journal of Marriage and the Family* 51 (May): 313–328.

Neugarten, Bernice, and Karol K. Weinstein. 1964. "The changing American grandparent." *Journal of Marriage and the Family* 26, 2 (May):199–204.

Newsweek. 1990. "Trading Places." (July 16).

Nisbet, Robert A. 1966. *The Sociological Tradition*. New York: Basic Books.

Norton, Arthur J., and Paul C. Glick. 1976. "Marital instability: Past, present, and future." *Journal of Social Issues* 32:5–20.

Nullis, Clare. 1995. "U.N. sees new effort on AIDS." *The Philadelphia Inquirer* (May 30).

O'Brien, John E. 1971. "Violence in divorce-prone families." *Journal of Marriage and the Family* 33:692–698.

O'Connell, Helen. 1994. *Women and the Family*. London, England and Atlantic Heights, NJ: Zed Books Ltd.

O'Hare, William P., Kelvin M. Pollard, Taynia L. Mann, and Mary M. Kent. 1991. "African Americans in the 1990s. *Population Bulletin* 46,1 (July): entire issue.

O'Kelly, Charlotte G., and Larry S. Carney. 1986. *Women and Men in Society: Cross Cultural Perspectives on Gender Stratification*, 2d ed. Belmont, CA: Wadsworth.

O'Reilly, David. 1986. "The meet market." *The Philadelphia Inquirer* (August 5).

O'Reilly, Jane. 1983. "Wife beating: The silent crime." *Time* (Sept. 5).

Oakley, Ann. 1974. *Woman's Work. The Housewife, Past and Present.* New York: Pantheon Books.

Ogburn, William F. 1922. *Social Change.* New York: Viking Press.

———, and Meyer F. Nimkoff. 1955. *Technology and the Changing Family.* Boston: Houghton-Mifflin.

Oke, E. Adewaide. 1986. "Kinship interaction in Nigeria in relation to societal modernization: A pragmatic approach." *Journal of Comparative Family Studies.* 12 (Summer):185–196.

Orthner, Dennis K. 1990. "The Family in Transition." In David Blankenhorn, Steven Bayme, and Jean Bethke Elshtain (eds.), *Rebuilding the Nest: A New Commitment to the American Family* (pp. 93–118). Milwaukee, WI: Family Service America.

Ortner, Sherry. 1974. "Is female to male as nature is to culture?" In Michelle Zimbalist Rosaido and Louise Lamphere (eds.), *Woman, Culture and Society* (pp. 67–87). Stanford, CA: Stanford University Press.

Pace, Eric. 1975. "A changing Iran wonders whether the gain will exceed the loss." *The New York Times* (Jan. 16).

Packard, Vance. 1968. *The Sexual Wilderness.* New York: David McKay.

Padan-Eisenstark, Dorit D. 1973. "Are Israeli women really equal? Trends and patterns of Israeli women's labor force participation: A comparative analysis." *Journal of Marriage and the Family* 35:538–545.

Palen, J. John. 1992. *The Urban World.* New York: McGraw-Hill.

———. 1995. *The Suburbs.* New York: McGraw-Hill.

Palgi, Phyllis. 1973. "Discontinuity in the female role within the traditional family in modern society: A case of infanticide." In E. James Anthony and Cyrille Koupernik (eds.), *The Child in His Family: The Impact of Disease and Death* Vol. 2. New York: John Wiley & Sons.

Parillo, Vincent N. 1985. *Strangers to These Shores: Race and Ethnic Relations in the United States.* New York: John Wiley & Sons.

Park, Robert E., and Herbert A. Miller. 1925. *Old World Traits Transplanted.* Chicago: Society for Social Research, University of Chicago. Copyright 1921, New York: Harper and Bros.

———, Ernest W. Burgess, and Roderick D. McKenzie. 1925. *The City.* Chicago: University of Chicago Press.

Parsons, Talcott. 1942. "Age and sex in the social structure of the United States." *American Sociological Review* 7:604–616.

———. 1943. "The kinship system of the contemporary United States." *American Anthropologist* 45:22–38.

———. 1949. *Essays in Sociological Theory, Pure and Applied.* Glencoe, IL: The Free Press.

———. 1955. "The American family: Its relation to personality and to the social structure." In Talcott Parsons and Robert F. Bales (eds.), *Family, Socialization and Interaction Process* (pp. 3–33). New York: The Free Press.

Patterson, J., and P. Kim. 1991. *The Day Americans Told the Truth: What People Really Believe about Everything That Really Matters.* Englewood Cliffs, NJ: Prentice-Hall.

Pedrick-Cornell, Claire, and Richard J. Gelles. 1982. "Elder abuse: The status of current knowledge." *Family Relations* 31 (July):457–465.

Pinchbeck, Ivy. 1930. *Women Workers and the Industrial Revolution 1750–1850.* London: Routledge & Kegan Paul. (Reissued by Frank Cass, 1969; reissued by Augustus M. Kelley, New York, 1971.)

Piven, Frances Fox, and Richard Cloward. 1971. *Regulating the Poor.* New York: Vintage Books.

Pizzey, Erin. 1974. *Scream Quietly or the Neighbors Will Hear.* London: IF Books.

Platt, Anthony M. 1969. *The Child Savers: The Invention of Delinquency.* Chicago: University of Chicago Press.

Platt, Steve. 1993. "Without walls." *Statesman and Society* 6(April 2):5–7.

Pleck, Joseph H. 1985. *Working Wives/Working Husbands.* Beverly Hills, CA: Sage Publications.

Polman, Dick. 1995. "Western Europe's elderly fear for future." *The Philadelphia Inquirer.* (January 30).

Popenoe, David. 1987. "Beyond the nuclear family: A statistical portrait of the changing family in

Sweden." *Journal of Marriage and the Family* 49 (February):173–183.

———. 1988. *Disturbing the Nest: Family Change and Decline in Modern Societies*. New York: Aldine de Gruyter.

———. 1991. "Family decline in the Swedish welfare state." *The Public Interest* 102 (Winter): 65–77.

Population Reference Bureau. 1976. *World Population Growth and Response*. Washington, DC: Author.

Postman, Neil. 1982. *The Disappearance of Childhood*. New York: Laurel Books.

Power, Eileen. 1975. *Medieval Women*. Cambridge, England: Cambridge University Press.

Queen, Stuart A., Robert W. Habenstein, and Jill S. Quadagno. 1985. *The Family in Various Cultures*, 5th ed. New York: Harper & Row.

Rainwater, Lee. 1966. "Crucible of identity." *Daedalus*. 95:172–216.

———, and William B. Yancey (eds.). 1967. *The Moynihan Report and the Politics of Controversy*. Cambridge, MA: M.I.T. Press.

Rathbone-McCuan, E. 1980. "Elderly victims of family violence and neglect. *Social Casework* 61:296–304.

Redfield, Robert. 1941. *The Folk Culture of Yucatan*. Chicago: University of Chicago Press.

———. 1947. "The folk society." *The American Journal of Sociology* 52:293–308. Reprinted in Richard Sennett, (ed.), 1969, *Classic Essays on the Culture of Cities* (pp. 180–205). New York: Appleton-Century-Crofts.

———. 1953. *The Primitive World and Its Transformations*. Chicago: University of Chicago Press.

———. 1955. *The Little Community*. Chicago: University of Chicago Press.

Red Horse, John G. 1980. "Family structure and value orientation in American Indians." *Social Casework* 61, 8:490–493.

———, G.R. Lewis, M. Feit, and J. Decker. 1978. "Family behavior of urban American Indians." *Social Casework* 59, 2:67–72.

Redmond, Ron. 1986. "China to tighten its population controls." *The Philadelphia Inquirer* (July 31).

Reiss, Ira. 1960. *Premarital Sexual Standards in America*. New York: The Free Press.

Reissman, Leonard. 1972. *Inequality in American Society: Social Stratification*. Glenview, IL: Scott, Foresman.

Renzetti, Claire M., and Daniel J. Curran. 1995. *Women, Men, and Society*. Boston: Allyn & Bacon.

Repetto, Robert et al. 1994. *The 'Second India' Revisited*. Washington, DC: World Resource Institute.

Riis, Jacob A. 1957/1890. *How the Other Half Lives: Studies Among the Tenements of New York*. New York: Hill and Wang.

Rimmer, Robert H. 1966. *The Harrad Experiment*. Los Angeles: Sherbourne Press.

Ritter, Malcolm. 1985. "Fearful hospital staff gives poor care." *Courier-Post* (Sept. 15):15f.

Robinson, Ira, K. Ziss, B. Ganza, and S. Katz. 1991. "Twenty years of the sexual revolution, 1965–1985: An update." *Journal of Marriage and the Family* 53 (October):216–220.

Rodman, Hyman. 1963. "The lower-class value stretch." *Social Forces* 42, 2 (December):205–215.

———. 1965. "Middle-class misconceptions about lower-class families." In Hyman Rodman (ed.), *Marriage, Family, and Society: A Reader* (pp. 219–230). New York: Random House.

———. 1971. *Lower-Class Families: The Culture of Poverty in Negro Trinidad*. New York: Oxford University Press.

Rogers, A.B. 1988. "Does biology constrain culture?" *American Anthropologist* 90 (December):819–831.

Rollin, Betty. 1970. "Motherhood: Who needs it?" *Look* (September 22):15–17. Reprinted in Arlene S. Skolnick and Jerome H. Skolnick (eds.), 1971, *Family in Transition: Rethinking Marriage, Sexuality, Child Rearing, and Family Organization* (pp. 346–356). Boston: Little, Brown.

Roper Organization. 1990. *The 1990 Virginia Slims Opinion Poll: A 20-Year Perspective on Women's Issues*. Storrs: University of Connecticut.

Rosaldo, Michelle Zimbalist. 1974. "Woman, culture and society: A theoretical overview." In Michelle Zimbalist Rosaldo and Louise Lamphere (eds.), *Woman, Culture and Society* (pp. 17–42). Stanford, CA: Stanford University Press.

Roscoe, Bruce, and Nancy Benaske. 1985. "Courtship violence experienced by abused wives: Similarities in patterns of abuse." *Family Relations* 34, 3 (July):419–424.

Rosen, Lawrence. 1973. "I divorce thee." In Helena Z. Lopata (ed.), *Marriage and Families* (pp. 39–43). New York: Van Nostrand.

Rosow, Irving. 1973. "And then we were old." In Helena Z. Lopata (ed.), *Marriages and Families* (pp. 229–234). New York: Van Nostrand.

———. 1976. "Status and role change through the life span." In R.H. Binstock and E. Shanas (eds.), *Handbook of Aging and the Social Sciences* (pp. 457–482). New York: Van Nostrand.

Ross, Heather L., and Isabel V. Sawhill. 1975. *Time of Transition: The Growth of Families Headed by Women.* Washington, DC: The Urban Institute.

Rossi, Alice S. 1968. "Transition to parenthood." *Journal of Marriage and the Family* 30:26–39.

———. 1977. "A biosocial perspective on parenting." *Daedalus* 106:1–31.

Rossi, Peter H. 1989. *Down and Out in America.* Chicago: University of Chicago Press.

———. 1994. "Troubling families: Family homelessness in America." *American Behavioral Scientist* 37 (January) 3:342–395.

Rothman, David J. 1971. "Documents in search of a historian: Toward a history of children and youth in America." In Theodore K. Rabb and Robert I. Rothberg (eds.), *The Family in History: Interdisciplinary Essays* (pp. 179–190). New York: Harper (Torchbooks).

Rothman, Ellen K. 1984. *Hands and Hearts: A History of Courtship in America.* New York: Basic Books.

Rubin, Gayle. 1984. "Thinking sex: Notes for a radical theory of the politics of sexuality." In Carole S. Vance (ed.), *Pleasure and Danger: Exploring Female Sexuality* (pp. 267–319). Boston: Routledge & Kegan Paul.

Rubin, Lillian. 1976. *Worlds of Pain.* New York: Basic Books.

Ruskin, John. n.d. *Sesame and Lilies: Three Lectures.* New York: Chatterton-Peck Company. (Originally published, 1865.)

Russell, Candyse S. 1974. "Transition to parenthood: Problems and gratifications." *Journal of Marriage and the Family* 36 (May):294–302.

Russell, Diana E.H. 1990. *Rape in Marriage*, Rev. ed. Bloomington, IN: Indiana University Press.

Ryan, William. 1971. *Blaming the Victim.* New York: Random House (Vintage Books).

Safir, Marilyn P., and Dafna N. Izraeli. 1991. "Growing up female: A life-span perspective on women in Israel." In Leonore Loeb Adler (ed.), *Women in Cross-Cultural Perspective* (pp. 90–105). New York: Praeger.

Salholz, Eloise, et al. 1986. "Too late for Prince Charming?" *Newsweek* (June 2):54–57, 61.

Saluter, Arlene. 1983. *Current Population Reports.* Washington, DC: U.S. Government Printing Office, Series P-20, No. 380.

———. 1994. "Marital status and living arrangements: March 1993." *Bureau of the Census Current Population Reports.* (Population Characteristics Series P-20 No. 478). Washington, DC: Government Printing Office.

Sanday, Peggy Reeves. 1979. *The Socio-Cultural Context of Rape.* Washington, DC: United States Department of Commerce, National Technical Information Service.

———. 1981. "The socio-cultural context of rape: A cross-cultural study." *Journal of Social Issues* 37:5–27.

Sandler, Jack, Marilyn Myerson, and Bill N. Kinder. 1980. *Human Sexuality: Current Perspectives.* Tampa, FL: Mariner.

Scheper-Hughes, Nancy. 1983. "Deposed kings: The demise of the rural Irish gerontocracy." In J. Sokolovsky (ed.), *Growing Old in Different Cultures* (pp. 130–46). Belmont, CA: Wadsworth.

———. 1992. *Death Without Weeping: The Violence of Everyday Life in Brazil.* Berkeley, CA: University of California Press.

Schoen, Robert. 1992. "First unions and the stability of first marriages." *Journal of Marriage and the Family* 54 (May):281–284.

Schorr, Alvin L., and Phyllis Moen. 1980. "The single parent and public policy." In Arlene S. Skolnick and Jerome H. Skolnick (eds.), *Family in Transition: Rethinking Marriage, Sexuality, Child Rearing, and Family Organization* (pp. 554–566). Boston: Little, Brown.

Schwartz, Felice N. 1989. "Management women and the new facts of life." *Harvard Business Review* 89,1 (January-February):65–76.

Schwartz, Pepper, and Janet Lever. 1976. "Fear and loathing at a college mixer." *Urban Life* 4 (Jan.):413–430.

Scully, Diana. 1985. "'Riding the bull' at Galley's: Convicted rapists describe the rewards of rape." *Social Problems* 32, 3 (Feb.):251–263.

———, and Joseph Marolla. 1985. "Convicted

rapists' vocabulary of motive: Excuses and justifications." *Social Problems* 31, 5 (June):530–544.

Seeley, John R., Alexander Sim, and E.W. Loosley. 1956. *Crestwood Heights: A Study of the Culture of Suburban Life*. Toronto: University of Toronto Press.

Segal, A.T., and W. Zellner. 1992. "Corporate women." *Business Week* (June 8):74–76; 78.

Seligmann, Jean. 1984. "The date who rapes." *Newsweek* (Apr. 9):91–92.

———. 1990. "Variations on a theme." *Newsweek* Special edition (Winter/Spring): 38–46.

Seller, Maxine. 1977. *To Seek America: A History of Ethnic Life in the United States*. Englewood, NJ.: Jerome S. Ozer.

Sennett, Richard. 1973. "The brutality of modern families." In Helena Z. Lopata (ed.), *Marriage and Families* (pp. 81–90). New York: Van Nostrand.

Shanas, Ethel. 1980. "Older people and their families: The new pioneers." *Journal of Marriage and the Family* 42, 1 (Feb.):9–15.

Sharistanian, Janet (ed.). 1987. *Beyond the Public/Domestic Dichotomy: Contemporary Perspectives on Women's Public Lives*. Westport, CT: Greenwood Press.

———. 1987, "Introduction: women's lives in the public and domestic spheres." In Janet Sharistanian (ed.), *Beyond the Public/Domestic Dichotomy: Contemporary Perspectives on Women's Public Lives* (pp. 1–10). Westport, CT: Greenwood Press.

Sharma, Ursula. 1980. *Women, Work and Property in North-West India*. New York: Tavistock.

Shinn, Marybeth, J.R. Knickman, and B.C. Weitzman. 1991. "Social relations and vulnerability to becoming homeless among poor families." *American Psychologist* 46:1180–1187.

———, and Beth C. Weitzman. 1994. "You can't eliminate homelessness without housing." *American Behavioral Scientist* 37 (January) 3:435–442.

Shipler, David K. 1976. "Life for Soviet woman all work, little status." *The New York Times* (Aug. 9).

Shorter, Edward. 1975. *The Making of the Modern Family*. New York: Basic Books.

Shwed, John A., and Murray A. Straus. 1979. "The military environment and child abuse." Mimeographed manuscript.

Simmons, Leo W. 1945. *The Role of the Aged in Primitive Society*. New Haven: Yale University Press.

———. "The aging in preindustrial societies." 1960. In Clark Tibbitts (ed.), *Handbook of Social Gerontology: Societal Aspects of Aging* (pp. 62–91). Chicago/London: University of Chicago Press.

Sipris, Alan. 1994. "Population conference reaches accord." *Philadelphia Inquirer*. (September 13).

Sirjamaki, John. 1964. "The institutional approach." In H.T. Christensen (ed.), *Handbook of Marriage and the Family* (pp. 33–50). Chicago: Rand McNally.

Skolnick, Arlene. 1991. *Embattled Paradise: The American Family in an Age of Uncertainty*. New York: Basic Books.

Smelser, Neil J. 1959. *Social Change in the Industrial Revolution*. Chicago: University of Chicago Press.

———. 1973. "Processes of social change." In Neil J. Smelser (ed.), *Sociology: An Introduction* (pp. 709–761), 2d ed. New York: John Wiley & Sons.

Smith, David M. 1982. "Urbanization and social change under apartheid: Some recent developments." In David M. Smith (ed.), *Living Under Apartheid* (pp. 24–46). London: George Allen & Unwin.

Smith, Joel, William H. Form, and Gregory P. Stone. 1954. "Local intimacy in a middle-sized city." *American Journal of Sociology* 60:276–283.

Snow, David A., and Leon Anderson. 1993. *Down on Their Luck: A Study of Homeless Street People*. Berkeley, CA: University of California Press.

———, Susan G. Baker, Leon Anderson, and Michael Martin. 1986. "The myth of pervasive mental illness among the homeless." *Social Problems* 33(June):407–423.

Solomon, Theodore. 1973. "History and demography of child abuse." *Pediatrics* (Part 2) 51, 4: 773–776.

Sorrentino, Constance. 1990. "The changing family in international perspective." *Monthly Labor Review* 113:41–55.

Sosin, Michael. 1986. *Homelessness in Chicago*. Chicago, IL: School of Social Service Administration, University of Chicago.

Spanier, Graham B. 1983. "Married and unmarried cohabitation in the United States, 1980." *Journal of Marriage and the Family* 45 (May): 277–288.

———, and Frank J. Furstenberg, Jr. 1982. "Remarriage after divorce: A longitudinal analysis of well-being." *Journal of Marriage and the Family* 43 (Aug.):709–720.

Spencer, Herbert. 1897. *The Principles of Sociology* (3 vols.). New York: Appleton.

Stacey, Judith. 1985. *Patriarchy and Socialist Revolution in China.* Berkeley, CA: University of California Press.

———. 1990. *Brave New Families: Stories of Domestic Upheaval in Late Twentieth Century America.* New York: Basic Books.

———. 1991. "Backward toward the postmodern family: Reflections on gender, kinship, and class in the silicon valley." In Alan Wolfe (ed.), *America at Century's End* (pp. 17–34). Berkeley, CA: University of California Press.

Stack, Carol B. 1974. *All Our Kin.* New York: Harper & Row.

Staples, Robert. 1971. "Towards a sociology of the black family: A theoretical and methodological assessment." *Journal of Marriage and the Family* 33:119–138.

———. 1981. *The World of Black Singles: Changing Patterns of Male-Female Relations.* Westport, CT: Greenwood Press.

———. 1994. *The Black Family: Essays and Studies.* Fifth Edition. Belmont, CA: Wadsworth Publishing Company.

———, and Leanor Boulin Johnson. 1993. *Black Families at the Crossroads: Challenges and Prospects.* San Francisco: Josey-Bass.

———, and Alfredo Mirande. 1980. "Racial and cultural variations among American families: A decennial review of the literature on minority families." *Journal of Marriage and the Family* 42 (Nov.):157–173.

Starr, Joyce R., and Donald E. Carns. 1973. "Singles in the city." In Helena Z. Lopata (ed.), *Marriages and Families* (pp. 154–161). New York: Van Nostrand.

Stearn, J. 1993. "What crisis?" *Statesmen and Society* 6 (April 2):7–9.

Steele, Brandt F., and Carl B. Pollock. 1968. "A psychiatric study of parents who abuse infants and small children." In R.E. Helfer and C.H. Kempe (eds.), *The Battered Child* (pp. 103–113). Chicago: University of Chicago Press.

Stein, Maurice. 1964. *The Eclipse of Community.* New York: Harper (Torchbooks).

Stein, Peter J. 1975. "Singlehood: An alternative to marriage." *Journal of Marriage and the Family* 24:489–503.

———. 1976. *Single.* Englewood Cliffs, NJ: Prentice-Hall.

———. 1981a. "The never-married." In Peter J. Stein (ed), *Single Life: Unmarried Adults in Social Context* (pp. 5–8). New York: St. Martin's Press.

———. 1981b. "Understanding single adulthood." In Peter J. Stein (ed.), *Single Life: Unmarried Adults in Social Context* (pp. 21–34). New York: St. Martin's Press.

Steinberg, Stephen. 1981. *The Ethnic Myth.* New York: Atheneum.

Steinfirst, Susan, and Barbara B. Moran. 1989. "The new mating game: Matchmaking via the personal columns in the 1980's." *Journal of Popular Culture* 22, 4:129–140.

Steinmetz, Suzanne K. 1977. *The Cycle of Violence: Assertive, Aggressive and Abusive Family Interaction.* New York: Praeger.

———. 1978. "Battered parents." *Society* 15 (July-August):55–56.

———. 1981. "Elder abuse." *Aging:* 6–10.

———. 1987. "Family violence: Past, present, and future." In Marvin B. Sussman and Suzanne K. Steinmetz (eds.), *Handbook of Marriage and the Family* (pp. 725–765). New York: Plenum Press.

———, and Murray A. Straus (eds.). 1974. *Violence in the Family.* New York: Dodd, Mead.

Stephen, Cookie White, and Walter G. Stephen. 1989. "After intermarriage: Ethnic identity among mixed-heritage Japanese-Americans and Hispanics." *Journal of Marriage and the Family* 51:507–519.

Stephens, William N. 1963. *The Family in Cross-Cultural Perspective.* New York: Holt, Rinehart & Winston.

Sterba, James P. 1979. "Chinese will try to halt growth of population by end of century." *The New York Times* (Aug. 13).

Stevens, William K. 1994. "Green revolution is not enough, study finds." *The New York Times* (September 6).

Stone, Gregory P. 1954. "City shoppers and urban identification: Observations on the social psychology of city life." *American Journal of Sociology* 60:36–45.

Stone, Lawrence. 1977. *The Family, Sex and Marriage: In England 1500–1800*, abridged ed. New York: Harper/Colophon Books.

Strasser, Susan. 1982. *Never Done: A History of American Housework*. New York: Pantheon.

Straus, Murray A. 1977. "Societal morphogenesis and intrafamily violence in cross-cultural perspective." *Annals of the New York Academy of Sciences* 285:719–730. Reprinted in Richard J. Gelles and Claire Pedrick-Cornell (eds.), 1983, *International Perspectives on Family Violence* (pp. 27–43). Lexington, MA: Lexington Books/D.C. Heath.

———, and Richard J. Gelles. 1986. "Societal change and change in family violence from 1975 to 1985 as revealed by two national surveys." *Journal of Marriage and the Family* 48, 3 (Aug.):465–479.

———, Richard J. Gelles, and Suzanne K. Steinmetz. 1980. *Behind Closed Doors: Violence in American Families*. New York: Doubleday.

Streib, Gordon F. 1973. "Old age in Ireland: Demographic and sociological aspects." In Donald O. Cowgill and Lowell D. Holmes (eds.), *Aging and Modernization* (pp. 167–181). New York: Appleton-Century-Crofts.

Strong, Bryan, and Christine DeVault. 1995. *The Marriage and Family Experience*, 6th ed. Minneapolis/St. Paul, MN: West Publishing Company.

Sudarkasa, Niara. 1988. "Interpreting the African heritage in Afro-American family organization." In Harriet P. McAdoo (ed.), *Black Families* (pp. 27–43). Newbury Park, CA: Sage.

Sullerot, Evelyne. 1971. *Women, Society and Change*. New York: World (University Library).

Sumner, William Graham. 1906. *Folkways*. Boston: Ginn.

Surra, Catherine. 1991. "Research and theory on mate selections and premarital relationships in the 1980s." In Alan Booth (ed.), *Contemporary Families: Looking Forward, Looking Back* (pp. 54–75). Minneapolis, MN: National Council on Family Relations.

Sussman, Marvin B. 1953. "The help pattern in the middle class family." *American Sociological Review* 18:22–28.

———. 1959. "The isolated nuclear family 1959: Fact or fiction?" *Social Problems* 6:333–340.

———, and Lee Burchinal. 1962. "Kin family network: Unheralded structure in current conceptualizations of family functioning." *Marriage and Family Living* 24:231–240.

The Swedish Institute. 1982. "Child care programs in Sweden." *Fact Sheets on Sweden* (Oct.). Stockholm: The Swedish Institute.

Sweet, James A., and Larry Bumpass. 1987. *American Families and Households*. New York: Russell Sage Foundation.

Swirski, Barbara, and Marilyn Safir (eds.) 1991. *Calling the Equality Bluff: Women in Israel*. New York: Pergamon Press.

Takagi, Dana Y. 1994. "Japanese American Families." In Ronald L. Taylor (ed.), *Minority Families in the United States* (pp. 146–163). Englewood Cliffs, NJ: Prentice-Hall.

Tallman, Irving. 1969. "Working-class wives in suburbia: Fulfillment or crisis." *Journal of Marriage and the Family* 31:65–72.

———, and Romona Morgner. 1970. "Life style differences among urban and suburban blue collar families." *Social Forces* (March):334–348.

Talmon, Yonina. 1964. "Mate selection in collective settlement." *American Sociological Review* 29:468–508.

———. 1965a. "The family in a revolutionary movement-the case of the kibbutz in Israel." In Meyer Nimkoff (ed.), *Comparative Family Systems* (pp. 259–286). Boston: Houghton-Mifflin.

———. 1965b. "Sex-role differentiation in an equalitarian society." In Thomas F. Lasswell, John H. Burma, and Sidney H. Aronson (eds.), *Life in Society* (pp. 144–155). Chicago: Scott, Foresman.

Taylor, Lesli, and Eli H. Newberger. 1983. "Child abuse in the international year of the child." In Richard J. Gelles and Claire Pedrick-Cornell (eds.), *International Perspectives on Family Violence* (pp. 45–62). Lexington, MA: Lexington Books/D.C. Heath.

Taylor, Robert J., Linda M. Chatters, M. Belinda Tucker, and Edith Lewis. 1990. "Development in research on black families: A decade review." *Journal of Marriage and the Family* 52 (November):993–1014. Reprinted in Alan Booth (ed.), *Contemporary Families: Looking Forward, Looking*

Back (pp. 275–296). Minneapolis, MN: National Council on Family Relations.

Thomson, Elizabeth, and Ugo Colella. 1992. "Cohabitation and marital stability: Quality or commitment?" *Journal of Marriage and the Family* 54 (May):368–378.

Thompson, E.P. 1963. *The Making of the English Working Class.* London: Goilancz.

Thorne, Barrie. 1992. "Feminism and the family: Two decades of thought." In Barrie Thorne with Marilyn Yalom (eds.), *Rethinking the Family: Some Feminist Questions* (pp. 3–30). Rev. ed. Boston: Northeastern University Press.

Thorson, James A. 1995. *Aging in a Changing Society.* Belmont, CA: Wadsworth Publishing Company.

Tiger, Lionel, and Robin Fox. 1971. *The Imperial Animal.* New York: Holt, Rinehart & Winston.

———, and Joseph Shepher. 1975. *Women in the Kibbutz.* New York: Harcourt Brace Jovanovich.

Time. 1977. "Jobs: Challenging the 65 barrier" (Aug. 8):67–68.

———. 1981a. "The battle over abortion." (Apr. 6):20–28.

———. 1981b. "Private lives, public places" (Apr. 6):27.

———. 1985. "AIDS: A Spreading Scourge." Claudia Wallis, reported by Melissa Ludtke and other bureaus. (August 5).

———. 1987. "Stretching their options" (Jan. 26):23.

Tönnies, Ferdinand. 1963. *Community and Society [Gemeinschaft und Gesellschaft],* Charles P. Loomis (trans. and ed.). New York: Harper (Torchbooks). (Originally published, 1887; original translation, 1957.)

Townsend, Peter. 1957. *The Family Life of Old People.* London: Routledge & Kegan Paul.

Troll, Lillian E. 1983. "Grandparents: The family watchdogs." In Timothy H. Brubaker (ed.), *Family Relationships in Later Life* (pp. 63–74). Beverly Hills, CA: Sage.

Trost, Jan. 1975. "Married and unmarried cohabitation: A case of Sweden, with some comparisons." *Journal of Marriage and the Family* 37: 677–682.

———. 1978. "A renewed social institution: Nonmarital cohabitation." *Acta Sociologica* 21:303–315.

———. 1983. "Parental benefits—A study of men's behavior and views." *Current Sweden* (June): 1–7. Stockholm: The Swedish Institute.

———. 1985. "Marriage and nonmarital cohabitation." In John Rogers and Hans Norman (eds.), *The Nordic Family: Perspectives on Family Research.* Uppsala, Sweden: Uppsala University Press.

Turnbull, Colin M. 1962. *The Lonely African.* New York: Simon & Schuster.

———. 1972. *The Mountain People.* New York: Simon & Schuster.

Turner, John F.C. 1969. "Uncontrolled urban settlement: Problems and policies." In Gerald Breese (ed.), *The City in Newly Developing Countries: Readings on Urbanism and Urbanization* (pp. 507–534). Englewood Cliffs, NJ: Prentice-Hall.

———. 1970. "Barriers and channels for housing development in modernizing countries." In William Mangin (ed.), *Peasants in Cities: Readings in the Anthropology of Urbanization* (pp-1–19). Boston: Houghton-Mifflin.

Uhlenberg, Peter. 1980. "Death and the family." *Journal of Family History* 5 (Fall):313–329.

United Nations. 1991. *The World's Women 1970–1990.* New York: United Nations.

U.S. Bureau of the Census. 1983. *Statistical Abstract of the United States 1984,* 104th ed. Washington, DC: U.S. Bureau of the Census.

———. 1984a. *Current Population Reports.* Washington, DC: U.S. Government Printing Office, Series P-25, No. 949.

———. 1984b. *Current Population Reports.* Washington, DC: U.S. Government Printing Office, Series P-20, No. 358.

———. 1991. "Marital status and living arrangements: March 1990." *Current Population Reports.* Series P-20, no. 450. Washington, DC: Government Printing Office.

———. 1992a. *Statistical Abstracts of the United States.* Washington, DC: Government Printing Office.

———. 1992b. "Households, Families, and Children: A 30 Year Perspective." *Current Population Reports.* Series P23-181. Washington, DC: Government Printing Office.

———. 1994a. "Marital status and living arrangements: March 1994." *Current Population Reports.*

Series P-20, no. 478. Washington, DC: Government Printing Office.

———. 1994b. *Statistical Abstracts of the United States*. Washington, DC: Government Printing Office.

U.S. Department of Commerce, Bureau of the Census. 1981. *Marital Status and Living Arrangements: March, 1980. Current Population Reports*, Series P-20, No. 365. Washington, DC: U.S. Government Printing Office.

———. 1983. *Marital Status and Living Arrangements: March 1982. Current Population Reports*, Series P-20, No. 380. Washington, DC: U.S. Government Printing Office.

U.S. Department of Labor. 1965. *The Negro Family: The Case for National Action*. U.S. Department of Labor, Office of Policy Planning and Research. Washington, DC: U.S. Government Printing Office.

U.S. National Center for Health Statistics. 1990. "Advance report of final divorce statistics, 1987." *Monthly Vital Statistics Report* 38(12), Suppl., June 29.

———. "Advance report of final divorce statistics, 1988." *Monthly Vital Statistics Report* 39(12), Suppl., May 21.

Valentine, Charles. 1968. *Culture and Poverty: Critique and Counter-Proposals*. Chicago: University of Chicago Press.

Vamos, M.N. 1992. "The gains are slow, say many women." *Business Week* (June 8):77.

Van Allen, Judith. 1974. "Modernization means more dependency: Women in Africa." *The Center Magazine* 7:60–67.

Vanderstaay, Steven. 1992. *Street Lives: An Oral History of Homeless Americans*. Philadelphia: New Society Publishers.

Vann, Richard T. 1976. "Review of *The Making of the Modern Family*" by E. Shorter." *Journal of Family History* 3:106–117.

Vaughan, Diane. 1986. *Uncoupling: Timing Points in Intimate Relationships*. New York: Oxford University Press.

Velez-Ibanez, Carlos. 1993. "U.S. Mexicans in the borderlands: Being poor without the underclass." In Joan Moore and Raquel Pinderhughes (eds.), 1993, *In the Barrios: Latinos and the Underclass Debate* (pp. 195–220). New York: Russell Sage Foundation.

Vosburgh, Miriam G., and Richard N. Juliani. 1990. "Contrasts in ethnic family patterns: The Irish and the Italian." *Journal of Comparative Family Studies* 21 (Summer) 2:269–286.

Voyandoff, Patricia. 1989. "Work and family: A review and expanded conceptualization." In Elizabeth B. Goldsmith (ed.), *Work and Family* (pp. 1–22). Newbury, CA: Sage.

Vrazo, Fawn. 1995. "Abortion fight here like none in world." *The Philadelphia Inquirer* (February 19, 1995).

Vreeland, Rebecca S. 1972a. "Is it true what they say about Harvard boys?" *Psychology Today* 5:65–68.

———. 1972b. "Sex at Harvard." *Sexual Behavior*: 3–10.

Walkowitz, Judith. 1980. *Prostitution and Victorian Society*. Cambridge, England: Cambridge University Press.

Waller, Willard. 1937. "The rating dating complex." *American Sociological Review* 2:727–734.

———. 1938. *The Family: A Dynamic Interpretation*. New York: Dryden.

Wallerstein, Immanuel. 1974. *The Modern World System*. New York: Academic Press.

Wallerstein, Judith S., and Sandra Blakeslee. 1989. *Second Chances: Men, Women and Children A Decade After Divorce*. New York: Ticknor & Fields.

———, with Melissa Ludtke. 1985. "AIDS: A spreading scourge." *Time* (Aug. 5).

Wallis, Claudia. 1985. "Children having children: Teen pregnancies are corroding America's social fabric." *Time* (Dec. 9):78–82, 84, 87, 89–90.

Warren, R., and J. Passel. 1987. "A count of the uncountable: Estimates of undocumented aliens counted in the above 1980 United States Census." *Demography* 24:375–393.

Webb, Craig. 1987. "New odds: Marriage data disputed." *The Philadelphia Inquirer* (Jan. 13).

Weber, Eugen. 1976. *Peasants into Frenchmen*. Stanford, CA: Stanford University Press.

Weber, Max. 1949. *The Methodology of the Social Sciences*, Edward H. Shils and Henry A. Finch (trans. and eds.). New York: The Free Press.

Weeks, Jeffrey. 1981. *Sex, Politics and Society: The Regulation of Sexuality since 1800*. New York: Longman.

Weeks, John R. 1994. *Population: An Introduction to*

Concepts and Issues. Updated 5th ed. Belmont, CA: Wadsworth Publishing Company.

Weiner, Myron (ed.). 1966. *Modernization: The Dynamics of Growth.* New York: Basic Books.

Weiss, Robert S. 1979a. *Going It Alone: The Family Life and Social Situation of the Single Parent.* New York: Basic Books.

———. 1979b. "Issues in the adjudication of custody when parents separate." In George Levinger and Oliver C. Moles (eds.), *Divorce and Separation: Context, Causes, and Consequences* (pp. 324–336). New York: Basic Books.

Weitzman, Lenore. 1977. "To love, honor and obey." In Arlene S. Skolnick and Jerome H. Skolnick (eds.), *Family in Transition: Rethinking Marriage, Sexuality, Child Rearing, and Family Organization* (pp. 288–313), 2d ed. Boston: Little, Brown.

———. 1985. *The Divorce Revolution: The Unexplored Consequences.* New York: The Free Press.

———, and Ruth B. Dixon. 1980. "The transformation of legal marriage through no-fault divorce." In Arlene S. Skolnick and Jerome H. Skolnick (eds.), *Family in Transition: Rethinking Marriage, Sexuality, Child Rearing, and Family Organization* (pp. 354–367), 3d ed. Boston: Little, Brown.

Welter, Barbara. 1966. "The cult of true womanhood: 1820–1860." *American Quarterly,* 18 (Summer):151–174.

Whiting, Beatrice B., and John W.M. Whiting. 1975. *Children of Six Cultures.* Cambridge, MA: Harvard University Press.

Whyte, Martin King. 1990. *Dating, Mating, and the Marriage.* New York: Aldine de Gruyter.

———. 1992. "Choosing mates—the American way." *Society.* (March-April):71–77.

Willie, Charles V. 1979. *Caste and Class Controversy.* Bayside, NY: General Hall.

———. 1981. *A New Look at Black Families.* Bayside, NY: General Hall.

———. 1988. *A New Look at Black Families,* 3d ed. Bayside, NY: General Hall.

Willmott, Peter, and Michael Young. 1960. *Family and Class in a London Suburb.* London: Routledge & Kegan Paul.

Wilson, Edmund. 1975. *Sociobiology: The New Synthesis.* Cambridge, MA: Belknap and the Harvard University Press.

———. 1978. *On Human Nature.* Cambridge, MA: Harvard University Press.

Wilson, William Julius. 1978. *The Declining Significance of Race.* Chicago: University of Chicago Press.

———. 1987. *The Truly Disadvantaged.* Chicago: University of Chicago Press.

———, and Kathryn J. Neckerman. 1986. "Poverty and family structure: The widening gap between evidence and public policy issues." In Sheldon H. Danziger and Daniel H. Weinberg (eds.), *Fighting Poverty: What Works and What Doesn't* (pp. 232–259). Cambridge, MA: Harvard University Press.

Winn, Marie. 1983. *Children Without Childhood.* New York: Pantheon.

Wirth, Louis. 1938. "Urbanism as a way of life." *American Journal of Sociology* 44:1–24.

Wisensale, Steven K., and Kathryn E. Heckart. 1993. "Domestic partnerships: A concept paper and policy discussion." *Family Relations* 42: 199–204.

Wolf, Margery. 1985a. "Marriage, family, and the state in contemporary China." In Kingsley Davis (ed.), *Contemporary Marriage* (pp. 223–251). New York: Russell Sage Foundation.

———. 1985b. "The People's Republic of China." In Jennie Farley (ed.), *Women Workers in Fifteen Countries* (pp. 33–48). Ithaca, NY: ILR Press, Cornell University Press.

Woll, Stanley B., and P. Chris Cozby. 1987. "Videodating and other alternatives to traditional methods of relationship initiation. In Warren Jones and Daniel Perlman (eds.), *Advances in Personal Relationships* (pp. 69–108), Vol 1. Greenwich, CT: JAI Press.

———, and Peter Young. 1989. "Looking for Mr. or Ms. Right: Self-presentation in videodating." *Journal of Marriage and the Family* 51:483–488.

Woodward, Kenneth L. 1994. "Do you Paul, Take Ralph. . . ." *Newsweek* (June 20):76–77.

Wortis, Rochelle Paul. 1977. "The acceptance of the concept of the moral role by behavioral scientists: Its effects on women." *The American Journal of Orthopsychiatry* 41:733–746. [Reprinted in Arlene S. Skolnick and Jerome H. Skolnick (eds.), *Family in Transition: Rethinking Marriage, Sexuality, Child Rearing, and Family Organization* (pp. 362–378), 2d ed. Boston: Little, Brown.]

WuDunn, Sheryl. 1995. "Many Japanese women are resisting servility." *The New York Times* (July, 9).

Yancey, William L., Eugene P. Ericksen, and Richard N. Juliani. 1976. "Emergent ethnicity: A review and reformulation." *American Sociological Review* 41 (June):391–402.

Yans-McLaughlin, Virginia. 1971. "Patterns of work and family organization." In Theodore K. Rabb and Robert I. Rotberg (eds.), *The Family in History: Interdisciplinary Essays* (pp. 111–126). New York: Harper (Torchbooks).

Ybarra, Lea. 1982. "When wives work: The impact on the Chicano family." *Journal of Marriage and the Family* 44 (Feb.):169–178.

Yorburg, Betty. 1974. *Sexual Identity: Sex Roles and Social Change*. New York: John Wiley & Sons.

Young, Michael, and Peter Willmott. 1957. *Family and Kinship in East London*. Baltimore: Penguin Books. (Rev. ed., 1963.)

———. 1973. *The Symmetrical Family*. New York: Pantheon Books.

Zalba, Serapio R. 1974. "Battered children." In Arlene S. Skolnick and Jerome H. Skolnick (eds.), *Intimacy, Family, and Society* (pp. 407–415). Boston: Little, Brown.

Zelizer, Viviana A. 1985. *Pricing the Priceless Child*. New York: Basic Books.

Zimmerman, Carle C., and Merle E. Frampton. 1966. "Theories of Frederic Le Play." In Bernard Farber (ed.), *Kinship and Family Organization* (pp. 14–23). New York: John Wiley & Sons.

INDEX

Further information about chapter opener photos:

Chapter 1: The bronze sculpture, "Family Group," executed in 1946 by Henry Moore, is a part of the Phillips Collection, Washington, D.C.

Chapter 2: 1886 woodcut from the "London Illustrated News" showing relief of the unemployed in London. Workers at this model soup kitchen are giving out soup tickets.

Chapter 3: At the Kuantan Beach, Malaysia, a Chinese family in swimming gear and Muslim girls in traditional Islamic headdress.

Chapter 4: Father and son enjoying an outing at the Philadelphia Zoo.

Chapter 5: New York City, Lower East Side at Hester and Orchard Streets, circa 1910.

Chapter 6: Eastern Kentucky, young mother of three children doing laundry in front of her home.

Chapter 7: "Nomads of Niger" men in ceremonial dance makeup to accentuate their sexuality.

Chapter 8: College students relaxing at Northeastern University, Boston, Massachusetts.

Chapter 9: Protestant wedding ceremony at the Wayfarer's Chapel, near Los Angeles. This Church of the New Jerusalem (Swedenborgian) was designed by Lloyd Wright, son of Frank Lloyd Wright.

Chapter 10: A proud father shows off his daughters in Soweto, South Africa.

Chapter 11: A business-suited executive mom and her 19-month-old daughter in Newport Beach, California.

Chapter 12: Expectant couples learn relaxation techniques at a California Lamaze birth class.

Chapter 13: A Summer Jobs Program employee at a retail cheese shop in New York City.

Chapter 14: A grandmother and her granddaughter read together.

Chapter 15: Shannon Booker was one the the "Framingham 8," a group of women who killed their batterers and were incarcerated in the Framingham Correctional Facility. This photograph was taken in Roxbury, Massachusetts, where she was participating in a rally against domestic violence.

Chapter 16: A single father spending time with his daughter at a carnival.

Photo Credits:

Henry Moore/The Phillips Collection, p. 3; Judy Gelles/Stock Boston, Inc., p. 14; North Wind Picture Archives, pp. 28, 76, 215; Brown Brothers, p. 43; Abbas/Magnum Photos, Inc., pp. 49, 187; United Artists Corporation/The Everett Collection © 1971, p. 52; Larry Mulvehill/Photo Researchers, Inc., p. 59; Lorraine Hutter, p. 73; Culver Pictures, Inc., pp. 112, 329; Courtesy of the George Eastman House, p. 118 (left); Courtesy of The Balch Institute, p. 118 (center, right); Lawrence Migdale, p. 138; Leonard Freed/Magnum Photos, Inc., p. 144; C. Carrion/Sygma, p. 147; Emilio Mercado/The Picture Cube, Inc., p. 172; Carol Beckwith/Robert Estall Photo Library, p. 181; Will Hart, pp. 198, 427; Barbara Rios/Photo Researchers, Inc., p. 209; Kazuko Gunn/Gunn Photography, p. 245; Reuters/Corbis-Bettmann, p. 251; Michael Krasowitz/FPG International, p. 271; Linda Rosier/Impact Visuals, p. 279; Hilary Marcus/Impact Visuals, p. 312; Spencer Grant/Stock Boston, Inc., p. 318; Cornelius Johnson/National Portrait Gallery, London/SuperStock, p. 321; Spencer Grant/The Picture Cube, Inc., p. 353; Owen Franken/Stock Boston, Inc., p. 365; Robert Harbison, p. 388; Rafael Macia/Photo Researchers, Inc., p. 395; Library of Congress, p. 408; Addison Geary/Stock Boston, Inc., p. 455; Marilyn Humphries/Impact Visuals, p. 465; Grant LeDuc/Stock Boston, Inc., p. 475; Bob Daemmrich Photos, p. 500; Jim Rogash/AP/Wide World, p. 517; Eli Reed/Magnum Photos, p. 527.